W9-AOK-612

PUBLIC RELATIONS

THE PROFESSION AND THE PRACTICE

SECOND EDITION

PUBLIC RELATIONS

THE PROFESSION AND THE PRACTICE

SECOND EDITION

OTIS W. BASKIN
Arizona State University
West Campus

CRAIG E. ARONOFF
Kennesaw State College

wcb
Wm. C. Brown Publishers
Dubuque, Iowa

Book Team

Editor *Stan Stoga*
Designer *K. Wayne Harms*
Production Editor *Kennie Harris*
Photo Research Editor *Shirley Charley*
Visuals Processor *Joseph P. O'Connell*

wcb group

Chairman of the Board *Wm. C. Brown*
President and Chief Executive Officer *Mark C. Falb*

wcb

Wm. C. Brown Publishers, College Division

President *G. Franklin Lewis*
Vice President, Editor-in-Chief *George Wm. Bergquist*
Vice President, Director of Production *Beverly Kolz*
National Sales Manager *Bob McLaughlin*
Director of Marketing *Thomas E. Doran*
Marketing Information Systems Manager *Craig S. Marty*
Marketing Manager *Kathy Law Laube*
Executive Editor *John Woods*
Manager of Visuals and Design *Faye M. Schilling*
Manager of Design *Marilyn A. Phelps*
Production Editorial Manager *Colleen A. Yonda*

Cover art by Kay Fulton

Illustrations by ArtNET

The credits section for this book begins on page 469, and is considered an extension of the copyright page.

Library of Congress Catalog Card Number: 87–71282

ISBN 0-697-01485-1

Printed in the United States of America by Wm. C. Brown Publishers
2460 Kerper Boulevard, Dubuque, IA 52001

10 9 8 7 6 5 4 3 2

To Maryan and Kathy

CONTENTS

▲　▲　▲

PART I

Public Relations: The Profession

3

A Theoretical Basis for Public Relations   49

▲ ▲ ▲

4

Public Relations in Organizational Decision Making   69

▲ ▲ ▲

5

Ethics and Professionalism   84

▲ ▲ ▲

PART II

Public Relations: The Process

6

Research: Understanding Public Opinion   100

▲ ▲ ▲

PART III

Public Relations: The Publics

12

Employee Communication
244

▲ ▲ ▲

11

Community Relations   218

▲ ▲ ▲

13

Consumer Relations   285

▲ ▲ ▲

14

Financial Relations   304

▲ ▲ ▲

PART IV

Public Relations: The Practice

19

The Legal Environment of Public Relations Practice *423*

▲ ▲ ▲

20

Public Relations as a Career *443*

▲ ▲ ▲

MINI-CASES

PREFACE

▲ ▲ ▲

Public relations is a profession in transition. In an environment of rapid social change, every organization must change or die. Public relations practitioners must possess the communications expertise and social sensitivity necessary to help organizations adapt to their changing environments.

In many ways, this is a new role for public relations practitioners. No longer are they mere technicians who shape and transmit messages from organizations to their publics. Rather, public relations has become a critical dimension of management itself. All managers now recognize that they themselves practice public relations. They are also seeing that public relations practitioners should be part of the management mainstream.

To this broadened role, the public relations practitioner must bring all of the traditional skills of the craft. The ability to understand public opinion, to plan public relations programs, to create effective messages in all media for all organizational publics, and to evaluate public relations effectiveness remain crucial areas of talent, skill, and knowledge. But public relations as it is practiced today demands much more. A full understanding of all communication processes and a complete acquaintance with the methods of management are critical to the successful practice of public relations. Thorough knowledge of the environment of the organization in which the practitioner works is a prerequisite to public relations effectiveness.

The first edition of *Public Relations: The Profession and the Practice* was designed to be the first realistic guide to the practice of public relations in the 1980s. It went much further than any previous text in developing a process of public relations and applying it to all aspects of professional practice. We are pleased to note its influence on all major public relations texts since, including advanced editions of what have served as standards in the field. This spirit of innovation has continued in the second edition of our text. The book deals with public relations in the overall context of organizational communications. It stresses the practitioner's role in organizational and societal communication systems. It comes to grips with challenges to the profession from within organizations and from organizations' surrounding environments. It views public relations from the perspective of overall organizational decision making, examining how public relations affects and is affected by decisions that are made.

This second edition benefits from the tremendous feedback we received on our earlier effort. It also benefits from insight gained through the service of one of the authors on the recent Commission of Undergraduate Education in Public Relations, jointly sponsored by the Public Relations Society of America and the Association for Education in Journalism and Mass Communication. Working from this body of information has enabled us to fine-tune this volume in concert with the future needs of public relations education. We learned that certain subjects needed more coverage—thus the addition of chapter 5 on ethics and chapter 19 on law. Many other chapters have been subjected to major revisions with an entirely updated focus. For example, chapters on consumer relations, media relations, and financial relations as well as the chapter on careers have been substantially revised. Still present, however, is our unique segment on getting a job. We sought to improve the applicability of the book by carefully monitoring the reading level for undergraduates, by employing a practical approach, and by using more in-text examples and mini-cases. This new edition contains thirty mini-cases and twenty end-of-chapter case studies. In addition, a single integrating case study has been used in chapters 6–9. This approach will link together the mainstream processes of research, planning, action, and communication in the minds of students in a way no other book has been able to achieve.

Our goals in writing the second edition remained quite ambitious. We feel we have probed the deepest issues of public relations for a profession that has come of age. Part I describes the current state, historical roots, and future issues of *The Profession.* Part II examines the core issues of *The Process* that underlies public relations, and Part III focuses on *The Publics* that are the objects of these efforts. Finally, Part IV summarizes *The Practice* of public relations in its various environments.

We believe that our work here is truly a reflection of the progression of the field of public relations. This book, like the profession it describes, is fundamentally eclectic, drawing its major theories, research, and principles from the fields of journalism, speech communication, and management. This is of course due to the graduate training, research, and teaching experience of the authors in each of these disciplines. But, it also reflects the needs of students who will be practicing public relations in a diverse environment.

We have attempted to give public relations students and practitioners the necessary tools and knowledge they need in ways that reflect the reality of the public relations world. Moreover, we have consistently attempted to provide that information in a direct, interesting, and highly readable form. In short, we have tried to make *Public Relations: The Profession and the Practice* the public relations textbook most able to move along with the profession into the 1990s.

Acknowledgments

Our thanks are due to many people: colleagues with whom we have worked in the public relations field, leading practitioners with whom we have spent hours in rewarding conversation, students and fellow teachers on whom we tested concepts contained in this book. They are too numerous to name, but all have our gratitude.

We owe a particular debt to Alan Scott, our public relations mentor, who helped shape our understanding of the field. Gene Donner and Darrel Alexander gave us our first public relations jobs and perhaps started us on the course that led to this book. Frederick C. Teahan, former vice president–education for the Public Relations Society of America, was especially helpful in our preparation and research.

The following professors reviewed our manuscript and helped us make it as useful as possible to students and teachers:

James Anderson
University of Florida

Bill Brody
Memphis State University

Dennis Corrigan
University of Iowa

Bonita Dostal Neff
Purdue University, Calumet

Patricia Downing
Valparaiso University

Robert Fields
University of Texas at Arlington

Marilyn Kern-Foxworth
University of Tennessee

Guy Meiss
Central Michigan University

David Pincus
California State University at Fullerton

Maureen Rubin
California State University at Northridge

Karyn Rybacki
Northern Michigan University

Charles Salmon
University of Wisconsin at Madison

Nancy Somerick
University of Akron

We are deeply appreciative to those who distilled from their professional and teaching experience the cases which appear after each chapter. Our thanks to:

James Anderson
University of Florida

S. Carlton Caldwell
University of Maryland

Mary Cawley
Kennesaw College

Carolyn Cline
University of Texas at Austin

R. Ferrell Ervin
Southeast Missouri State University

Art Guillermo
University of Northern Iowa

Charlotte Hatfield
Ball State University

Fred Kiesner
Loyola Marymount University

Donald B. McCammond, APR
Public Relations Society of America

Dulcie Murdock
University of North Carolina at Chapel Hill

Walt Seifert
Ohio State University

Melvin Sharpe
Ball State University

Nancy Somerick
University of Akron

Robert Taylor
University of Wisconsin at Madison

Jim VanLeuven
Colorado State University

Our love and thanks go to our wives, Maryan and Kathy, who have suffered with us through this and many collaborations. Our appreciation goes to our universities and departments for support, services, and resources. We are especially grateful to Mary Cawley who collaborated on chapter 19 and to Mary Markell and Maureen Johnson who have been so helpful in the preparation of our manuscript. Finally, we give our sincere thanks to the professionals at William C. Brown Publishers, particularly our editor, Stan Stoga, and our production editor, Kennie Harris, who worked so hard and long with us.

Otis W. Baskin, Ph.D.
Arizona State University–West Campus
Craig E. Aronoff, Ph.D.
Kennesaw College

Public Relations: The Profession

This book deals with the field of public relations—its process, its publics, the kinds of organizations in which it is practiced, and the critical issues that confront it. *Public Relations: The Profession and the Practice* takes a practical approach, drawing on the experiences of many practitioners and executives. It also incorporates the theoretical perspectives of researchers and scholars from various disciplines including communications, business, and psychology. It is intended to provide students with a thorough understanding of public relations and a basis for successful practice today and in the future.

Part I covers fundamentals of public relations practice. Chapter 1 gives a working definition of public relations, reviewing and refining the definitions of previous studies. Chapter 2 describes the history of public relations, providing a useful perspective on the field. Chapter 3 deals with communications and systems theory, while chapter 4 discusses the most important application of public relations—its contribution to organizational decision making. And finally, chapter 5 looks at the ethical and professional responsibilities of public relations practitioners in our society.

▲ ▲ ▲

CHAPTER 1

The Nature of Public Relations
Preview

P ublic relations is a management function that helps define organizational objectives and philosophy.

Public relations practitioners communicate with all relevant internal and external publics in the effort to create consistency between organizational goals and societal expectations.

Public relations practitioners develop, execute, and evaluate organizational programs. Their goal is to promote the exchange of influence and understanding among an organization's constituent parts and publics.

As President Ronald Reagan and Soviet Premier Mikhail Gorbachev approached the Reykjavik Summit in October, 1986, a new strategic weapon was on their minds. Rather than missiles and antimissile satellites, both superpowers were seeking new ways to escalate a different type of offensive firepower: Public relations had become the strategic weapon of choice for a worldwide duel over public opinion. The Soviets had demonstrated at a prior meeting in Geneva that they had learned the American art of influencing public opinion through a free press. Going in, Reagan's staff knew they were facing what one senior official called a team of media-savvy, "blow-dried Bolsheviks." The United States' response was an unparalleled media blitz, with top officials headed by Secretary of State George Schultz making on-the-record comments about the strategy and results of the meeting. With Reykjavik, public relations became recognized as an instrument for international peace and strategic advantage.

What Is Public Relations?

Attempts to define the public relations field are frequently conflicting and generally diverse. Some definitions list the kinds of organizations that utilize public relations (all kinds); some dwell on the media used for public relations communications (all media); and still others focus on the publics, or target audiences, with which public relations communicates (all publics). Many authorities give exhaustive lists of what public relations is not, while a few even claim that "public relations" as such no longer exists, preferring another name for the process. Indeed, in major corporations, the term *corporate communications* has recently replaced public relations as the most common name for departments having that responsibility.[1]

A Working Definition

Public relations is difficult to sum up in a brief statement. The very nature of the profession and its constant adaptation to the needs of society make it at best a moving target for definition.

Public relations is practiced in organizations that range in type from giant, multinational oil companies to small, human service agencies. A public relations manager for a private university may devote most of his or her efforts to fund-raising and student recruitment. On the other hand, the public relations staff of a large corporation may be responsible for the firm's relationships with customers, suppliers, investors, employees, and even foreign governments.

Public relations practitioners are individuals who help others establish and maintain effective relationships with third parties. Their work is usually performed in organizational environments like those already mentioned, even if they are not employees of that organization. Some public relations practitioners are independent counselors, some work for public relations firms, and still others are directly employed by an organization.

For the purposes of this book—and to establish a broad, realistic, and accurate description of the public relations function—we offer the following working definition:

> Public relations is a management function that helps to define organizational objectives and philosophy and facilitate organizational change. Public relations practitioners communicate with all relevant internal and external publics in the effort to create consistency between organizational goals and societal expectations. Public relations practitioners develop, execute, and evaluate organizational programs that promote the exchange of influence and understanding among organizations' constituent parts and publics.

Not all people who say they practice public relations do all that is implied by this definition. Some interpret their jobs even more broadly. But for now and for the foreseeable future, this description captures the essential aspects of public relations practice. Our next chapter demonstrates that this definition is valid for much of the past as well.

An Overview of Public Relations

We have divided the chapters in this book into four parts: the profession, the process, the publics, and the practice. Figure 1.1 illustrates the progression of the book and the relationship between the various sections.

The profession sets the historical foundations of the field in a context that will help explain the origins and reasons for much current practice. Likewise, the theoretical foundations are presented in the context of relevant application. The pivotal role of public relations in organizational decision making further defines its management function along with its ethical and social responsibilities. These elements fit together to describe a professional climate that feeds every aspect of the process.

Figure 1.1 A conceptual schema for studying public relations

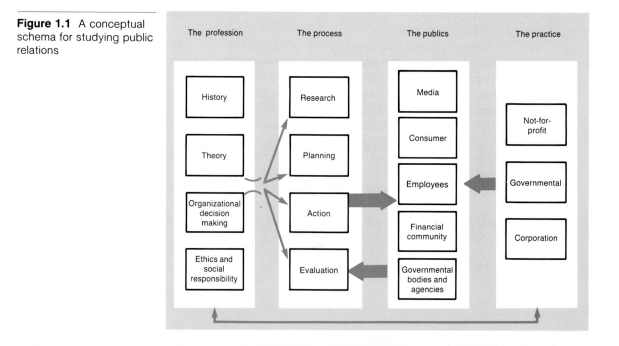

The process begins and ends with research. Although public relations had its beginnings as a reactive force, it has become proactive through its ability to predict trends and respond to needs before they become emergencies. As a management function, public relations gathers information, makes plans, implements action, and evaluates results.

The publics are the targets of public relations action and the source of feedback for evaluation. Any identifiable group can be considered a public; however, most are encompassed by the following: media, consumers, employees, the financial community, and government. These are the target audiences of public relations practice.

The practice of public relations is molded to a great extent by the publics it responds to and the types of organizations it serves. The ever increasing and changing varieties of public relations practice all fall into one of the categories discussed in Part IV.

In this chapter, we will explain some of the ways of defining public relations—as a management function, as communication, and as a means of influencing public opinion. We will also define the specific tasks performed by public relations practitioners. And finally, we will look at the field from a systems view.

Public Relations as a Management Function

It is first necessary to recognize that public relations is a management function. While it may support or facilitate production or sales, public relations is not merely an adjunct of personnel, marketing, or advertising. Ideally, public relations helps an organization establish its objectives and philosophy and adapt to a changing environment.

The managerial responsibilities associated with the public relations function are both general and specific. Some public relations duties are shared by all managers. For example, all managers spend much of their time communicating with various external or internal publics. All managers, indeed virtually all employees, represent their organizations to some public. Public relations also contributes to general management. Recent research into the job responsibilities of senior production managers found that public relations is one of "the most demanding aspects of their jobs. It is the part of their jobs for which they feel least prepared and qualified."[2]

Other public relations functions are the particular responsibility of public relations specialists. Editors of internal publications and managers of government, consumer, media, and financial relations, for example, tend to be public relations professionals trained specifically for their areas of expertise.

Johnson & Johnson
Pulls Together

Mini-Case 1.1

When Johnson & Johnson was suddenly faced with the cruel reality that people in Chicago had died from cyanide poisoning after taking Extra-Strength Tylenol capsules, public relations became the job of virtually every employee. This was especially true in the ranks of top management. Even before it had been determined that the problem was the result of tampering, James E. Burke, Johnson & Johnson's chairman, formed a seven-member strategy group to guide the company's response. This group consisted of Burke; David R. Clare, Johnson & Johnson president; Wayne K. Nelson, company group chairman; Arthur M. Quilty, executive committee member; George S. Frazza, general counsel; David E. Collins, chairman of McNeil Consumer Products Company; and Lawrence G. Foster, corporate vice president, public relations.

Meeting twice a day to make decisions on rapidly developing events and to coordinate company-wide efforts, this group closely monitored public reaction to the crisis. As they directed the Tylenol comeback strategy, everyone's efforts were aimed toward regaining consumer confidence and making sure the company reacted to the tragedy in a socially responsible manner. Thus, public relations was the function of each of these managers in a very real sense.

Source: Interview with Lawrence G. Foster, corporate vice president, public relations, Johnson & Johnson, November 1983.

James E. Burke, CEO of Johnson & Johnson, announcing Tylenol comeback campaign.

Public relations can make important contributions to forming an organization's ideas about what it is, what it should do, and what society wants and expects from it. Charles Steinberg describes this aspect of public relations as the "structuring of company philosophy and carrying out of that philosophy in practice so that what the institution says is not at variance with what it does."[3]

Defining Objectives,
Philosophies,
and Policies

Other public relations authorities make the point that as a profession, public relations is obligated to advise management in the development of sound policies that are in the best interests of the public as well as the company.[4] Of course, public relations practitioners rarely have final authority in setting objectives, policies, or philosophy within their organizations. But in most modern organizational structures, they are important members of policy-making groups. The participation of Larry Foster, vice president of public relations, in Johnson & Johnson's executive strategy group during the Tylenol crisis is but one example.

The role of public relations is critically important, especially in crisis situations, for two reasons. First, because public relations monitors public opinion, practitioners can represent the public interest and predict public reaction to institutional decisions. Second, public relations communicates organizational decisions to the public, thus the commitment and understanding gained from helping make those decisions are tremendous assets.

While all managers are concerned with adapting their organizations to changing environments, public relations managers play a particularly important role in this area. Indeed, facilitating organizational change has become a frequently mentioned part of public relations definitions.

Helping Organizations
Change

Again, public relations managers do not make all the decisions that lead to change within organizations. But because they constantly monitor and interact with the organizational environment, they often possess information that suggests a need for change or indicates the direction change should take. Public relations practitioners can often discover a problem when it is still manageable, thus avoiding unnecessary crises.

Harlow's historical review of public relations definitions indicates that emphasis on change has grown steadily since the 1940s when *PR News* suggested this definition: "Public relations is the activities of a corporation . . . building and maintaining sound and productive relations . . . so as to adapt itself to the environment."[5]

In the 1950s, public relations practitioner Thomas Gonser stressed acceptance of change as a necessary attitude of public relations—"a willingness to make the business what the public wants it to be, rather than trying to convince them that they should like the business for what it is."[6]

The turbulent 1960s brought forth a flood of change-oriented definitions. Charles B. Coates, a leading professional, called public relations "a kind of pilot . . . it knows the rocks, the shoals . . . and it can gauge the probable consequences of the choice of one direction as against the other." Others identified public relations as "an engineer of change," and claimed that it "senses, even anticipates, the changing temper of the times before a problem or crisis stage is reached."[7]

By the 1970s, leaders in the public relations field were describing their profession in terms that reflected the turbulence of that society. David Finn, chairman of Ruder and Finn, Inc., one of the world's leading public relations firms, suggested that public relations try "to prevent the crisis from getting out of hand . . . to help clients conduct their business in a way that is responsive to the new demands made by concerned scientists, environmentalists, consumerists, minority leaders, underprivileged segments of the community, the young generation."[8]

These definitions make an important point about the fundamental nature of public relations—that it reflects the needs of the society in which it is practiced. While the 1980s in some ways have been calmer than the 1960s and the 1970s, public relations continues to help harmonize organizations with their environments and promote positive organizational change. The process of defining goals and facilitating change is further discussed in chapter 4.

Public Relations as Communication

Some definitions emphasize the communication function of public relations. All managers are involved in and responsible for communication, but public relations managers have additional, more specific responsibilities in this regard. *Communication* applies to the definition of the public relations role in at least four specific ways. It refers to *skills* possessed by public relations practitioners, to *tasks* performed, to *systems* established, and to *operations* of established systems.

Logos from three prominent public relations firms—Hill and Knowlton, Ketchum Public Relations, and Manning, Selvage & Lee.

Ketchum
Public Relations.

HILL AND KNOWLTON

Many authors point out that public relations practitioners need to be excellent writers and speakers. Some call for expertise in graphics or audiovisual communication as well. Public relations authority Allen Center, calling public relations practitioners "technicians in communication," adds to the list a "knack for persuasion."[9] Practitioners are certainly more than technicians, they also need to be able to conduct research, formulate plans, and evaluate results. However, the ability to write and speak effectively is a basic prerequisite.

Skills

Many commentators on public relations point out the tasks and goals of communication. John Marston in his book *The Nature of Public Relations* defines the process as "planned, persuasive communication designed to influence significant publics."[10] The early work of public relations scholars Gene Harlan and Alan Scott also stressed a task orientation: "skilled communication of ideas to various publics with the object of producing desired results."[11] Production of a media release, an annual report, or an employee magazine might be among the tasks of public relations practitioners. The creation and management of campaigns to achieve awareness of an issue or change opinions about a subject are others.

Tasks

Rather than stressing individual skills or tasks, some public relations writers have advocated the establishment of systems for ongoing communications. Thus, Frank Jefkins describes "a system of communications to create goodwill,"[12] while Rex Harlow emphasizes "establishment and maintenance of mutual lines of communication."[13] The systematic methods of gathering information, the relationships established with editors and publishers, and the creation of community or consumer groups to provide insights and perspectives are examples of ongoing communication systems.

Systems

Finally, several observers concentrate on how such systems should be used once established. Most who carry the definitions to this extent hold that public relations is responsible for maintaining systematic two-way communication. The nature of communication is treated more extensively in chapter 3, while specific problems in communicating to external and internal audiences are covered in chapters 8 and 10.

Systems Operations

As we have already mentioned, exerting influence on public opinion is often considered a part of the public relations mission. Just how public relations should deal with public opinion, however, is a matter of considerable debate. The opinions of scholars in the field range from simple plans to complex prescriptions for pumping up corporate prestige and establishing mutual understanding between management and its publics.

Public Relations as a Means of Influencing Public Opinion

Perhaps the most basic way that public relations influences public opinion is by enhancing an organization's prestige. Harlow and Jefkins touch on this aspect of public relations. Another simple and widely quoted conception of public relations is "good performance publicly appreciated."[14] Indeed, effective public relations depends upon the effective performance of the organization being represented. Another theme holds that it is the task of public relations to supply accurate information concerning subjects of value to the public. Most news releases seek to achieve this goal. When Dayton-Hudson, the big retailing concern, opens stores in a new city, it makes major contributions to local charities—then issues news releases to let local customers know of the role Dayton-Hudson plays when it comes to town. Beyond dispassionately dispensing information, public relations should be an active process of interpreting the organization to its publics. This interpretation leads directly to a definition of public relations that stresses pursuit of public understanding and acceptance of the organization.

Thus far, our attempts to define how public relations influences public opinion have dealt with informing, promoting, understanding, and interpreting. But affecting public opinion also implies conscious efforts to exert influence. A number of public relations textbook authors describe influence as an important component when defining the field. Howard Stephenson says public relations is "convincing people that they should adopt a certain attitude."[15] *Fortune* magazine writer Irwin Ross calls it the "attempt, by information and persuasion, to engineer public support."[16] Similarly, in the late 1940s, Philip Lesly, chairman of his own public relations firm for over thirty-five years, defined public relations as "all activities and attitudes intended to judge, influence, and control the opinion of any group or groups of persons in the interest of any individual, group, or institution."[17] William Nielander and Raymond Miller, in their 1968 public relations book, are less blunt; they call public relations "the gentle art of letting the other fellow have your way."[18]

Effective influence or persuasion inevitably rests upon an understanding of those to whom the effort is directed. The price of influence is being influenced. Not surprisingly, certain writers suggest that communication must not flow in only one direction. In his 1947 textbook, Verne Burnett stressed that public relations means "trying to understand other people . . . and then trying to influence them."[19] More recently, Edward Stan called it a "planned effort to influence opinion through acceptable performance and two-way communication."[20] Once the recognition of two-way communication has been established, it becomes possible to define public relations in literal terms; that is, in terms of *relations with publics*.

Establishing Relations with Publics

A **public** is a group of people who share a common problem or goal and recognize their common interest. The cumulative experience of public relations practitioners suggests that public opinion is an ornery beast, nearly impossible to push or prod. It will move, however, if you understand its needs and cater to them. Some practitioners believe that rather than seeking to engineer, control, or convince the public, public relations is a means of seeking common ground. It is the linking pin in a relationship that looks past short-term goals and interests toward the kind of long-term success that requires positive public opinion. Author and practitioner Charles S. Steinberg's 1958 definition of public relations exemplifies this viewpoint:

> Public relations is that specific operating philosophy by which management sets up policies designed to serve both in the company's and the public's interest . . . (the) long-range, carefully nurtured effort to develop and maintain a strong, resilient and positive consensus from all of the publics upon whom the activities of the institution impinge.[21]

While certain aggressive organizations like Mobil still seek to create their own public opinion climates, most perceive public opinion as a significant environment which needs constant attention and active response. A primary aim of public relations, rather than attempting to manipulate various publics, is to sensitize the organization to public images and expectations. Public relations staffs effectively link institutions and help organizations harmonize their behavior with the expectations of various external and internal publics.

Many thoughtful observers of the contemporary world maintain that adaptability is an organization's greatest asset. For example, in 1985, when sales of the "new Coke" went flat, the Coca-Cola Company proved itself an effective organization by reacting rapidly to the negative response and bringing back the old formula, newly labeled "Coca-Cola Classic." With regard to public relations, this view suggests that emphasis should be placed on gathering and interpreting information from the organization's relevant publics and disseminating it to management. Thus, the traditional direction of public relations information flow is reversed. This idea is closely related to the general function of facilitating organizational change.

Interpreting Public Opinion

Such an approach to public relations suggests that some of the most important messages communicated by public relations practitioners are aimed neither at the media, nor at customers and the general public, nor even at employees. The most important messages, rather, are developed with management in mind and deal with fundamental aspects of organizational direction, decision making, and coordination. With this perspective, public relations is established as an integral part of organizational management. Although public relations definitions stressing interpretation of public opinion vary, opinion research and management consultation are the most commonly mentioned activities. Alan Scott sums it up best by emphasizing "the sensitive interpretation of the human scene to management . . . evaluating and interpreting public opinion, public issues and the public demands."[22] Further discussion of the nature of public opinion and the public relations issues involved in it can be found in chapter 6.

Exercising Social Responsibility

Whenever the potential for influencing public opinion exists, the issue of social responsibility becomes significant. During the past thirty years, social responsibility has become a major concern in American society. Many thoughtful observers feel that institutions should assume responsibility for the consequences of their actions. Within the context of public relations, according to Donald Wright, this implies that "public relations people . . . should act at all times with the best interests of society in mind."[23]

Rex Harlow makes much of the social responsibility theme, maintaining that the public relations practitioner "defines and emphasizes the responsibility of management to serve the public interest."[24] In addition, he says, the practitioner suggests ways the organization can adjust its behavior to meet social, political, and economic responsibilities and the needs created by shifting human standards and attitudes. Moreover, the practitioner tries to help the organization demonstrate a keen sense of social responsibility along with profit responsibility. The logical extreme of this position, which suggests that public relations be defined as representing the public and attempting to influence management, has been argued. Some even claim public relations gives the public "a voice at policy-making tables."[25]

Although the exercise of social responsibility should not be mistaken for the sum total of the practice, it nonetheless remains vitally important as a public relations ideal. Social responsibility is being increasingly perceived as an integral aspect of the public relations function, as we discuss more extensively in chapter 5.

The Nature of Public Relations Work

One of the best ways to define public relations is to describe what its practitioners do. While none of the following descriptions are brief, they do elaborate and encompass the field better than most definitions. One such description was adopted formally by the Public Relations Society of America (PRSA) in 1982 (see Exhibit 1.1).

PRSA
Official Statement

Exhibit 1.1

Official Statement on Public Relations

Public relations helps our complex, pluralistic society to reach decisions and function more effectively by contributing to mutual understanding among groups and institutions. It serves to bring public and public policies into harmony.

Public relations serves a wide variety of institutions in society such as businesses, trade unions, government agencies, voluntary associations, foundations, hospitals and educational and religious institutions. To achieve their goals, these institutions must develop effective relationships with many different audiences or publics such as employees, members, customers, local communities, shareholders and other institutions, and with society at large.

The managements of institutions need to understand the attitudes and values of their publics in order to achieve institutional goals. The goals themselves are shaped by the external environment. The public relations practitioner acts as a counselor to management, and as a mediator, helping to translate private aims into reasonable, publicly acceptable policy and action.

As a management function, public relations encompasses the following:

- ▲ Anticipating, analyzing and interpreting public opinion, attitudes and issues which might impact, for good or ill, the operations and plans of the organization.

- ▲ Counseling management at all levels in the organization with regard to policy decisions, courses of action and communication, taking into account their public ramifications and the organization's social or citizenship responsibilities.

- ▲ Researching, conducting and evaluating, on a continuing basis, programs of action and communication to achieve informed public understanding necessary to the success of an organization's aims. These may include marketing, financial, fund-raising, employee, community or government relations and other programs.

- ▲ Planning and implementing the organization's efforts to influence or change public policy.

- ▲ Setting objectives, planning, budgeting, recruiting and training staff, developing facilities—in short, *managing* the resources needed to perform all of the above.

- ▲ Examples of the knowledge that may be required in the professional practice of public relations include communication arts, psychology, social psychology, sociology, political science, economics and the principles of management and ethics. Technical knowledge and skills are required for opinion research, public issues analysis, media relations, direct mail, institutional advertising, publications, film/video productions, special events, speeches and presentations.

In helping to define and implement policy, the public relations practitioner utilizes a variety of professional communication skills and plays an integrative role both within the organization and between the organization and the external environment.

Source: *Formally adopted by PRSA Assembly, November 6, 1982.*

Practitioners of public relations apply their skills and knowledge in many different ways. The *Occupational Outlook Handbook* suggests that public relations specialists are responsible for maintaining positive relationships with the press, employees, community, consumers, investors, regulatory agencies, contributors, constituents, and a number of other publics. They must be involved in activities as diverse as sales promotion, political campaigning, interest group representation, fund-raising, and employee recruitment.[26]

The Duties of
the Profession

Public relations practitioners are basically responsible for assimilating and communicating information between an organization and its environment. Public relations employees span the boundaries of an organization. They attempt to relate to the needs and interests of its publics, informing them about the organization's impact on their lives and thus building positive relationships.

As they perform these services, public relations practitioners must maintain effective relationships with the media representatives who publish or broadcast information about the organization and its publics. Public relations departments are frequently the source of information for special reports and news and feature articles for television, radio, newspapers, and magazines.

Public relations messages do not always advertise the organization or its services and products directly. Instead, releases may be designed to aid consumers or some other public, and only indirectly contribute to a positive image for the organization. Information about health, nutrition, energy, and the environment may be researched and communicated because the organization recognizes an obligation to respond to its publics in a socially responsible way.

Public relations duties may also include arranging for company representatives to have direct contact with various publics. Speakers' bureaus, which arrange for members of the organization to speak to civic and social groups on topics of current interest, frequently come under the umbrella of public relations. In addition to arranging such events, public relations specialists may write speeches for members of the organization or even serve as representatives themselves. Other common public relations activities include editing in-house publications, producing and distributing films, slides, and other audiovisual programs, and managing fund-raising campaigns and community activities.

Organizational
Departments and
Counseling Firms

More than half of practitioners work in departments with four or fewer public relations professionals, a 1986 survey indicated.[27] But even in organizations with exceptionally large public relations staffs, it may be useful to contract for the services of a **counseling firm.** Chester Burger has provided six reasons for hiring outside consultants:

1. Management has not previously conducted a formal public relations program and lacks experience in organizing one.
2. Headquarters may be located away from New York City, the communications and financial center of the nation.
3. A wide range of up-to-date contracts is maintained by an agency.
4. An outside agency can provide services of experienced executives who would be unwilling to move to other cities or whose salaries could not be afforded by a single firm.
5. An organization with its own PR department may be in need of highly specialized services that it cannot afford on a permanent basis.
6. Crucial matters of overall outside policy dictate a need for the independent judgment of an outsider.[28]

Basically, an organization may decide to retain the services of a counseling firm because of special needs that it cannot meet internally. In addition to supplementing their own talent, organizations frequently employ outside public relations consultants to provide a third-party opinion. "We tell our clients not only how to say things but what to say," notes Michael Rowan, vice president for survey research at Hill and Knowlton.[29] Burson-Marsteller president James Dowling goes further. In the 1950s, he says, consulting firms were asked, "How do I say this?" In the 1960s and 1970s, faced with various confrontations, corporations asked, "What do I say?" But, Dowling notes, "In the 80s, the question has become 'What do I do?' "[30]

The principal advantages of an in-house public relations staff—familiarity with issues, loyalty, team membership—may also be important drawbacks in some decision-making situations. Like all managers, public relations executives may be too close to a situation to maintain an objective point of view. Public relations consultants can often bring a startlingly fresh approach to the problems and programs of an organization. They are called on to assess the effectiveness of various programs and to help plan public relations strategies. Firms are now offering other services as well—rehearsals for hostile news conferences, advice on lobbying, strategic counsel on new product marketing and takeover defenses, and arrangement of corporate sales meetings.

Although the use of public relations counseling firms is expected to continue, organizations appear to be enlarging their own public relations staffs and relying more on them for the majority of the services they need. This trend is due in large part to the greater need for public relations services, which has made it more economical to employ full-time specialists in a variety of areas. Also, the increased need for public relations expertise in all levels of management has necessitated the internalization of many functions that were once contracted.

Public relations jobs both in organizational departments and counseling firms still tend to be concentrated in the larger cities because of access to government, media, corporate, union, and trade association headquarters, although these jobs are available throughout the country. For example, more than half of the approximately two thousand public relations counseling firms are located in New York, Los Angeles, Chicago, and Washington, D.C.

Public relations departments range in size from more than two hundred members in large corporations to one or two individuals in small organizations. Large corporations frequently have an officer at the vice presidential level who is in charge of the public relations function and helps develop overall policy as a member of top management. In addition, large organizations typically include various other public relations managers at both corporate and division levels. They may also employ a number of public relations specialists such as writers, researchers, and representatives to the media. On the other hand, in a small organization, one individual may handle all these responsibilities. Public relations counseling firms may contain specialists in a particular area, such as merger or takeover campaigns, or generalists who advise management on a wide range of matters.

Public Relations Professionals at Work

This great diversity in the duties of public relations practitioners is illustrated by the list of public relations functions published by PRSA in a booklet entitled *Careers in Public Relations*.

1. *Programming* This involves analyzing problems and opportunities, defining goals and publics (or groups of people whose support or understanding is needed), and recommending and planning activities. It may include budgeting and assigning responsibilities to the appropriate people, including non–public relations personnel. For example, an organization's president or executive director is often a key figure in public relations activities.

2. *Forming relationships* Successful public relations people develop skill in personally gathering information from management, from organizational colleagues, and from external sources. Continually evaluating what they learn, they formulate recommendations and gain approval for them from their managements.

   Many public relations activities require working with and sometimes through other functions, including personnel, legal, and marketing staffs. The practitioner who learns to be persuasive with others will be most effective.

   Public relations people also represent their organizations. Sometimes this is formal, such as when an individual is designated a firm's official representative to a trade or professional association. But actually, public relations practitioners are "at work" on behalf of their organizations in their relationships with all others—including people in industry groups, regulatory agencies and government, educational institutions, and the general public.

3. *Writing and editing* Since the public relations worker is often trying to reach large groups of people, the printed word is a common tool. Examples of its use are reports, news releases, booklets, speeches, film scripts, trade magazine articles, product information and technical material, employee publications, newsletters, shareholder reports, and other management communications directed to both organization personnel and external groups. A sound, clear writing style that communicates effectively is essential for public relations work.

4. *Working with media* Setting up channels for disseminating information to appropriate newspaper, broadcast, general, and trade publication editors, and enlisting their interest in publishing an organization's news and features are normal public relations activities. This requires knowing how newspapers and other media operate, the specialization areas of various publications, and the interests of individual editors. Competition is keen for the attention of editors

and broadcasters who have a limited amount of space and time at their disposal. As one public relations practitioner puts it, "You have to get to the right editor of the right publication with the right story at the right time." Although ideas are accepted on the basis of newsworthiness and other readership values, developing relationships of mutual respect and cooperation can be useful to both the practitioner and the newsperson.

Several corporations join in sponsoring the StrideBoston walk to benefit the Museum of Science in that city.

5. *Producing materials* Brochures, special reports, films, and multi-media programs are important ways of communicating. The public relations practitioner need not be an expert in art, layout, typography, and photography, but background knowledge of those techniques is needed for intelligent planning and supervision of their use.

6. *Planning special events* News conferences, convention exhibits and special showings, new facility and anniversary celebrations, contest and award programs, tours, and special meetings make up a partial list of special events staged for publicity purposes. They involve careful planning, coordination, and attention to detail. Often special booklets, publicity, and reports must be prepared for them as well.

Table 1.1 Public Relations Activities Reported	
Activity	**Percent***
Media relations	64.0
PR management or administration	60.4
Publicity	60.0
Community relations	45.8
PR counseling	40.9
Editor of publications	33.9
Employee relations	27.8
Government relations	24.3
Investor relations	16.3
Consumer affairs	14.2
PR teaching	7.9
Advertising/sales promotion	4.4
*Multiple responses were invited on this question.	

Source: James A. Morrissey, "Will the Real Public Relations Professional Please Stand Up," *Public Relations Journal* (December 1978): 25. Copyright 1978 by the Public Relations Society of America. Reprinted by permission.

7. *Speaking* Public relations work frequently requires skill in face-to-face communication—finding appropriate platforms, preparing speeches for others, and even delivering speeches. The person who can effectively address individuals and groups will enjoy an advantage over one whose facility of expression is limited to writing.

8. *Conducting research and evaluating results* Gathering facts is the first activity undertaken by a public relations practitioner. Data may come from interviews, library materials, or informal conversations. Practitioners can also use formal survey techniques or employ firms that specialize in designing and conducting opinion research. After a program is completed, the public relations practitioner should study the results and make an evaluation about its implementation and effectiveness. More and more managements expect research and evaluation from their public relations advisers.[31]

The Changing Nature of the Profession

The changing nature of public relations work can be seen from a PRSA survey (Table 1.1) which lists the percentage of practitioners who identified various activities as part of their jobs. The first three activities—media relations, public relations management, and publicity—were reported far more frequently than the remaining nine. It should be noted that media relations and public relations management are both managerial functions. They do not depend only upon hands-on skills that enable an individual to complete a piece of work from start to finish. Instead, they emphasize the ability of the practitioner to accomplish his or her job through the cooperation of other people. Philip Lesly has identified "the trend . . . toward putting non–public relations people into the top public relations positions . . . as cause for concern in the decade of

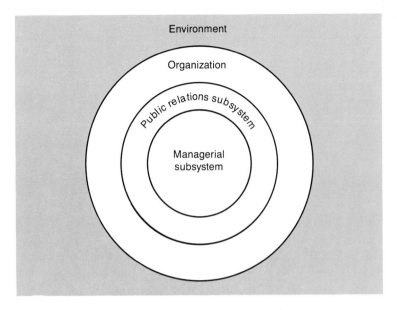

Environment

Organization

Public relations subsystem

Managerial
subsystem

Figure 1.2 Public relations as an organizational subsystem

the '80s."[32] This development suggests that public relations practitioners have not been as competent in the managerial functions of their profession as they have been in the more traditional activities.

We began this discussion by defining public relations as a management function. Since then, we have discussed various other definitions, each dealing with a particular aspect of the practice of public relations and helping us to better understand this rapidly expanding, multifaceted field. In preparing to read the remainder of this book, think back to where this discussion began—management. The managerial context is required to understand public relations most completely.

One of the most widely accepted views of management can be found within the concept of systems theory. This view describes organizations in our society as systems with permeable boundaries. Two-way communication flows between organizations and their environments. Systems of this type are called open systems; you will read about them further in chapter 9. Open systems are composed of various subsystems that give them their identity and purpose, such as the production of goods or a service. The management subsystem is at the center of each organizational system.

Open systems with their permeable boundaries must constantly respond to and interact with their environment. This interaction makes public relations a part of every manager's job, as Figure 1.2 shows. The earlier example of the Johnson & Johnson executive strategy group formed during the Tylenol crisis also illustrates this point. Therefore, *public relations becomes the central subsystem through which management responds to and attempts to influence an organization's environment.*

A Systems View
of Public Relations

Figure 1.3 The public
relations system

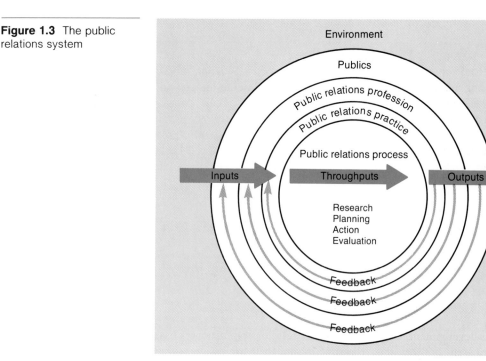

Environment

Publics

Public relations profession

Public relations practice

Public relations process

Inputs Throughputs Outputs

Research
Planning
Action
Evaluation

Feedback

Feedback

Feedback

Systems theory also provides an excellent vehicle to describe public relations itself. Figure 1.3 presents public relations as a system within society, bounded by the environment to which it must respond. At the center of this system is a four-step process that is its core: research, planning, action, and evaluation. Surrounding this core are successive rings of permeable boundaries. Inputs from the environment penetrate through these boundaries and become throughputs when the process of public relations occurs. After the public relations process has responded, outputs are directed back through the boundaries to the environment.

Therefore, when the Houston Independent School District was faced with an outside group's discovery that lead-based paint had been used to refinish student desks (input), officials checked the facts and formulated a response strategy (throughput). Once the strategy of repainting the desks over the Thanksgiving and Christmas holidays was set, it was announced to the news media and parents (output).

This system illustrates that public relations responds to certain elements of the general environment we have previously defined as publics. While these are most frequently the media, consumers, employees, the financial community, and governmental bodies, any definable group can be classified as a public. These publics are serviced by a profession that has a distinct history, an expanding body of knowledge, and a governing code of ethics.

Although many useful definitions of public relations are available from a variety of sources, the concept of public relations as a management function encompasses most aspects. The duties of public relations practitioners go far beyond the skills of communicating because effective communication requires planning and implementing organizational objectives. The public relations practitioner, like his or her counterparts in other functional areas of the organization, must be adept at influencing policy decisions and developing strategies to implement them. Therefore, the perspective of this book is broad enough to consider all aspects of public relations practice—from the fundamental skills necessary to obtain a first job to the decision-making ability needed to direct the public relations actions of a large corporation.

Summary

▲ ▲ ▲

Case Study

You have applied for a public relations position with a $10.2 million savings and loan association, a conservative financial institution that has been in existence for over fifty years. The organization has never employed a public relations person before. Now that its assets have risen above $10 million, however, the president of the institution feels it is time to hire someone to "do the PR."

During an interview, the president admits he is not sure what public relations is, but he is fairly sure he wants the person he hires to plan promotions and stage events that will attract new customers; write stories that will get free space and time in the local media; and start an employee publication. The president also states that he is open to suggestions about the position and asks you to explain how you would establish a professional, effective public relations program if you were hired.

Questions

1. Do the responsibilities outlined by the president indicate that he understands how the public relations function can be utilized most effectively?
2. What would you tell the president about your plans for establishing an effective public relations program for the financial institution?

"Doing" Public Relations

By Nancy M. Somerick
Department of Mass Media-Communication University of Akron Akron, Ohio

Notes

1. "Corporate Communication Most Popular Name Used," *Communication World* (September 1983):2.
2. Howard Feldman, unpublished dissertation, 6.22–6.25.
3. Charles S. Steinberg, *The Creation of Consent: Public Relations in Practice* (New York: Hastings House, 1975), 19.
4. Richard W. Darrow, Dan J. Forrestal, and Aubrey Cookman, *The Cantrell Public Relations Handbook* (Chicago: Dartnell, 1967), 30.
5. Rex F. Harlow, "Public Relations Definitions Through the Years," *Public Relations Review* (Spring 1977):56.
6. Ibid., 56.
7. Ibid., 58.
8. Ibid., 61.
9. Allen H. Center, "What About the State of the Art?" *Public Relations Journal* (January 1976): 30–31.
10. John Marston, *The Nature of Public Relations* (New York: McGraw-Hill, 1963).
11. Gene Harlan and Alan Scott, *Contemporary Public Relations: Principles and Cases* (New York: Prentice-Hall, 1955), 3.
12. Frank Jefkins, *Public Relations in World Marketing* (London: Crosby, Lockwood and Son, 1966), 4.
13. Harlow, "Public Relations Definitions," 56.
14. See Harlow, "Public Relations Definitions," 56; Irwin Ross, *The Image Merchants* (New York: Doubleday, 1958), 16; and Raymond Simon, *Perspectives in Public Relations* (Norman, OK: University of Oklahoma Press, 1966), 63.
15. Howard Stephenson, *Handbook of Public Relations* (New York: McGraw-Hill, 1960), 9.
16. Ross, *Image Merchants,* 5.
17. Philip Lesly, *Public Relations in Action* (Chicago: Ziff-Davis, 1947), 4.
18. William A. Nielander and Raymond W. Miller, *Public Relations* (New York: The Ronald Press, 1951), 5.
19. Verne Burnett, *You and Your Public* (New York: Harper, 1947), 4.
20. Edward Stan, *What You Should Know About Public Relations* (New York: Oceana Publications, 1968), 1.
21. Charles S. Steinberg, *The Mass Communicators: Public Relations, Public Opinion and Mass Media* (New York: Harper, 1958), 16, 198.
22. Alan W. Scott, "Does PR Need Redefinition?" *Public Relations Journal* (July 1970): 23–24.
23. Donald K. Wright, "Professionalism and Social Responsibility in Public Relations," *Public Relations Review* (Fall, 1979): 23.
24. Harlow, "Building a Definition," 36.
25. Ibid., 35.
26. U.S. Department of Labor, Bureau of Labor Statistics, Bulletin 1978, *Occupational Outlook Handbook,* 1980 ed., 476–478.
27. Christopher Beyer, "Salary Survey," *Public Relations Journal* (June 1986): 28.
28. Chester Burger, *Primer of Public Relations Counseling* (Counselors Section of the Public Relations Society of America, 1972), 81.
29. Alyse Lynn Booth,"Who Are We?" *Public Relations Journal* (June 1985): 15.
30. Alex S. Jones, "New No. 1 in Public Relations," *The New York Times* (February 17, 1985).
31. *Careers in Public Relations,* Public Relations Society of America, 1979.
32. Philip Lesly, "New Dimensions," *Public Relations Journal* (December 1979): 25.

▲ ▲ ▲

CHAPTER 2

The History of Public Relations

Preview

P ublic relations is an outgrowth of three factors: the recognition of the power of public opinion, continuous competition among institutions for public support, and the development of media through which the public could readily be reached.

Historically, public relations has gone through three stages:

manipulation, information, and mutual influence and understanding. While their development was sequential, all three continue to exist.

Public relations has generally moved from a role of using any available means to achieve desired public opinion toward one of informing the public and

providing information and counsel to management.

The future of public relations can be better predicted and prepared for if trends in its history are identified and understood.

▲ ▲ ▲

Vox populi, vox Dei. (The voice of the people is the voice of God.)
—Ancient Roman proverb

Public opinion has always been a force in human events. Leaders have courted the sentiments of the people to sustain their power and gain support for their actions. Only those rulers who were believed to be gods, or chosen by gods, could afford to ignore public attitudes—and even they usually took pains to assure their subjects that their faith was well placed. Many despots, believing they held absolute power and were thus immune to public opinion, later lost their heads.

Public opinion is a force that has been reckoned with in all civilizations. Artifacts of what can be construed as public relations materials survive from ancient India, Mesopotamia, Greece, and Rome. The Crusades, the exploits of Lady Godiva, the actions of Martin Luther, and the adventures of the Conquistadores seeking El Dorado have all been explained as examples of ancient public relations activities. The creation in the seventeenth century of the Congregatio de Propaganda (the congregation for propagating the faith) by the Roman Catholic Church is often pointed to as a keystone in the development of public relations. The action brought us the term "propaganda" but was not a significant development in a church that exists to propagate the faith.

Because public opinion has been a powerful and important factor throughout human history, it is easy to claim that public relations has similarly ancient antecedents. However attractive such a pedigree might be to the public relations historian, it would be erroneous. Sporadic examples of what might be considered public relations can be traced to earliest recorded history. Nonetheless, the widespread practice of public relations as a necessary and respected organizational function is a fairly recent development.

Modern-day public relations is a product of the recognition of the power of public opinion combined with competition among institutions for public support. It prospers if media exist through which the public can be reached and covered. The United States was and is the perfect crucible in which to mold public relations. With its republican government, its democratic sensibilities, its free markets, its various systems of checks and balances, and its independent population forever voting with ballots and dollars while increasing their levels of affluence and education, public relations was in truth "made in America."

American Antecedents to Public Relations

Occasional examples of public relations-like activities were identifiable in the early days of the American colonies. For example, the first systematic U.S. fund-raising campaign was initiated by Harvard College in 1641. The campaign was supported by the first fund-raising brochure, entitled *New England's First Fruits*. In 1758, King's College (now Columbia University) issued the first press release—to announce graduation exercises.

It has been said that public relations prospers under adverse circumstances—when power is threatened or when public support is needed. Public relations has prospered most in times of extreme pressure or crisis. Such were the circumstances preceding the American Revolutionary War, when Samuel Adams initiated what can be called a public relations campaign. Adams was to the communication dimension of the Revolutionary War what George Washington was to the military dimension. He recognized the value of using symbols that were easily identifiable and aroused the emotions.

Adams used slogans remembered to this day, for example, "Taxation without representation is tyranny." Because he got his side of the story to the public first, shots fired into a group of rowdies became known as "the Boston Massacre." Adams directed a sustained-saturation public relations campaign using all available media. He staged the Boston Tea Party to influence public opinion. In the Sons of Liberty and Committees of Correspondence, he maintained mechanisms to implement the actions made possible by his public relations campaign.[1]

In the infancy of the United States, public relations was practiced primarily in the political sphere. The publication and dissemination of the Federalist Papers, leading to the ratification of the U.S. Constitution, has been called "history's finest public relations job."[2]

The Boston Tea Party was staged by Adams in 1773 to influence public opinion.

Public Relations in a Young Nation

Propaganda almanac for
the Temperance Crusade
of 1875

During the 1820s and 1830s, the vote was granted to a larger portion of
the population. Expanding public education increased literacy. The mass medium of the penny press was developing. The campaign that brought Andrew
Jackson to the White House was the first to appeal directly to the public rather
than to the land-owning elite. Amos Kendall, a member of the famous "kitchen
cabinet," served as the candidate's pollster, counselor, ghostwriter, and publicist. Although he did not hold the title, Kendall effectively served as the first
presidential press secretary and congressional liaison. Jackson, who did not
express himself terribly well, used Kendall as a specialist to convey his ideas
to Congress and the American people.

Jackson's foes were forced to adopt similar tactics in the effort to gain
public favor. In March 1831, the Bank of the United States, locked in a life-
or-death struggle with President Jackson, decided "to cause to be prepared
and circulated such documents and papers as may communicate to the people
information in regard to the nature and operations of the bank."[3] Jackson and
Kendall, however, prevailed.

With the majority of Americans living on farms or in small communities, communication was primarily person-to-person and face-to-face during
the nineteenth century. There was limited need for public relations intermediaries. Still, the various potentials and applications of public relations began
to be explored.

"Manifest Destiny" and America's settlement of her western frontier
were driven by publicity. From Daniel Boone to Davy Crockett to Buffalo Bill,
skillful and sometimes exaggerated promotion was the way to move easterners
to the West. Even Jesse James got in on the act when he issued a news release
about one of his particularly daring train robberies.

Business became aware of publicity's virtues. When Burlington Railroad initiated its 1858 publicity campaign, Charles Russell Lowell stated, "We
must blow as loud a trumpet as the merits of our position warrants."[4] Political
agents gained increasing sophistication as Tammany Hall, New York City's
famous political machine, used interviewing to obtain information in the late
1850s.

More dramatic were campaigns related to the issues of the day—movements for the abolition of slavery, women's rights, and prohibition. Dramatic
demonstrations and endorsements by public figures and the press were used
to promote these and other causes.

Still, through the better part of the nineteenth century, public relations
remained a rudimentary adjunct to political activities. The vigorous expansion
of American business was tremendously popular and faced few challenges. In
its early days, big business played its cards close to the vest—the less the public
knew, the better. By the latter part of the century, however, business had
overplayed its hand.

The 1880s saw government's first major steps into the marketplace. Markets were growing rapidly, as was the size of business organizations. Simultaneously, dramatic shifts occurred in public attitudes toward business and in the roles played by several institutions. Workers were beginning to organize themselves into unions, and they perceived their interests in many cases as directly opposed to those of business owners. Business was at once highly successful and increasingly besieged.

By this era, big institutions removed from people's day-to-day interactions were emerging. In an increasingly diverse society, consensus was breaking down, with a rise in the incidence of conflict and confrontation.

Not surprisingly, the term *public relations* came into use at this time; its earliest appearance was probably in Dorman B. Eaton's 1882 address to the graduating class of the Yale Law School. The concept, as noted, was not new, but the coining of the term suggests a new level of importance and consciousness. As historian Marc Bloch has commented, "The advent of a name is a great event even when the object named is not new, for the act of naming signifies conscious awareness."[5]

Institutions in Conflict

The Industrial Revolution hit America with full force during the last quarter of the nineteenth century. The nation's population doubled as immigrants rushed to the land of opportunity. New products and new patterns of life rapidly emerged. The enforced rhythm of the factory, the stress of urban life, and the vast distinction between the bosses and the workers were new and not always pleasant realities of American life.

According to historian Marie Curtl:

> Corporations gradually began to realize the importance of combating hostility and courting public favor. The expert in the field of public relations was an inevitable phenomenon in view of the need for the services he could provide.[6]

The Industrial Revolution

By 1883, American Telephone and Telegraph (AT&T) leader Theodore Vail expressed concern about the company's relationship with the public and the public's conflicts with the company. In 1888, the Mutual Life Insurance Company employed Charles J. Smith to manage a "species of literary bureau" in response to similar concerns.

In 1889, George Westinghouse, founder of the industrial giant that still bears his name, saw the light. He established the first corporate public relations department and hired E. H. Heinrichs, a Pittsburgh newspaperman, to run it. Heinrich's immediate task was to direct a fierce struggle with Thomas Alva Edison over whether the nation would be wired for alternating or direct electric current.

Edison was a formidable adversary. Forest McDonald describes the battle this way:

Edison General Electric attempted to prevent the development of alternating current by unscrupulous political action and by even less savory promotional tactics. . . . The promotional activity was a series of spectacular stunts aimed at dramatizing the deadliness of high voltage alternating current, the most sensational being the development and promotion of the electric chair.[7]

Ultimately, Westinghouse won. Consequently, we use alternating current today. Seeing his success, other businesses followed Westinghouse's example.

Just as the era brought changes to business, politics was forced to adapt to new realities. The hard-fought 1896 Bryan-McKinley presidential race was the first to use modern methods of political campaigning.

The massive social and economic changes of the late nineteenth century and the resulting pressures upon business forced the most dramatic change in the attitudes of businessmen. A philosophy of pure competition gave way to different concerns. Social as well as economic benefits had to be taken into consideration when weighing alternative reasons. As the twentieth century began, public relations practitioners concentrated increasingly on this aspect of corporate legitimacy.

Public Relations: Three Stages of Development

The development of public relations in the United States can be divided into three stages. To some degree, their progression was sequential, but all have existed simultaneously, and indeed, do so today. Moreover, while the intellectual and theoretical bases of all three stages evolved rapidly during the first quarter of this century, in practice, the most advanced stage has only recently gone beyond the point of novelty. The three stages are:

1. *Manipulation*   Public relations is assumed to use whatever means are available to achieve desired public opinion and action. Traditionally, practitioners of this type of public relations have been called **press agents.**

2. *Information*   Public relations is regarded as a conduit for information flowing from organizations to the public so that the public will understand, sympathize with, and patronize the organization. Practitioners of this form of public relations are called **publicity agents.**

3. *Mutual influence and understanding*   In this most recent stage, public relations continues to accept the responsibilities of Stage 2, but in addition, sees its role as providing information and counsel to management on the nature and realities of public opinion and methods by which the organization can establish policy, make decisions, and take action in light of public opinion. Practitioners who follow this approach are called **public relations counselors.** Not everyone who assumes this title, however, deserves it.

Manipulation was the technique of nineteenth-century press agents who served
political campaigns and carnival shows more than mainstream business. The
frequently quoted remark, "There's a sucker born every minute," exemplifies
the manipulative approach.

In their efforts to promote land sales in the American West or attract
attention for politicians, early publicists did not hesitate to embellish the truth.
Press agents made exaggeration into a high art. The myth of Davy Crockett
was a creation of the political enemies of Andrew Jackson. Matthew St. Clair
Clarke, Crockett's press agent, was attempting to lure the frontier vote away
from Jackson.[8]

Old-time press agents played upon the credulity of the public. Exaggeration, distortion, and deception were their stock-in-trade. They became
masters of the publicity stunt or what later came to be known as the "pseudo
event," a planned happening that occurs for the purpose of being reported.

P. T. Barnum   Phineas T. Barnum has always been considered the master of
press agentry—a promoter with endless imagination in a calling in which
imagination is the main ingredient. Barnum promoted the midget General
Tom Thumb; Jenny Lind, the "Swedish Nightingale"; Jumbo the elephant;
Joice Heath, a 161-year-old woman (it was claimed); and a "mermaid" possessing the body of a fish and the head and hands of a monkey. Barnum used
publicity to make money, pure and simple.

Indeed, nearly a century after his death, the Ringling Brothers, Barnum
and Bailey Circus still uses Barnum's technique with virtually no alteration.
In 1985–86, the circus claimed to exhibit a living example of the mythical
unicorn. Informed opinion said that the horn had been grafted to the head of
a young goat. The Society for the Prevention of Cruelty to Animals protested
and picketed, but people bought tickets to see the creature—and the circus.
Barnum's spirit must have smiled from that three-ring circus in the sky.

When P. T. Barnum died, the *London Times* fondly called him a "harmless deceiver." As long as press agentry was used to promote circuses, entertainment, and professional sports, its negative potential was limited. Its use
in business and politics, however, was more threatening.

In the quest to gain media and public attention, press agentry tends to
become increasingly outrageous, exploitive, and manipulative. Moreover, the
manipulative attempt to gain the attention of the public through the media
has an even darker side.

The Downside of Press Agentry   In 1878, French socialist Paul Brousse described what he called "the Propaganda of the Deed." The term refers to a
provocative act committed to draw attention toward an idea or grievance in
order to get publicity.

In the hands of European anarchists in the late nineteenth and early
twentieth centuries, propaganda of the deed meant bombings, murder, and
assassination. During those days, fear gripped the people of Paris as they knew
they might be victims of a bomb exploded in the effort to gain attention. While
these techniques were used less often after the start of World War I, they have

been revived since the 1960s and have been used quite broadly throughout the world during the 1980s. Violent forms of **propaganda of the deed** today are known as terrorism.

Violent efforts to attract attention must be differentiated from illegal but nonviolent efforts. Exemplified by the philosophies and activities of Gandhi and Martin Luther King, Jr., these acts also are akin to the tactics of press agentry.

The tools of press agentry, indeed any of the means and methods of public relations, are available to all—true or false, right or wrong, evil or good. The success of press agents in attracting attention and public response, coupled with their blatantly manipulative aims, inevitably aroused hostility from the press and the public. Press agentry gave public relations an odor that persists to this day.

Stage 2: Information

By the early 1900s, business was forced to submit to more and more governmental regulations and encountered increasingly hostile criticism from the press. Because of the social forces that gathered against business at the turn of the twentieth century, public relations became a specialized function broadly accepted in major corporations. Furthermore, it was rapidly recognized that deception, manipulation, and self-serving half-truths were inappropriate responses to challenges raised by media and government. Edward L. Bernays, public relations pioneer, first teacher of public relations at the college level, and author of the first book on the subject, explained the emergence of the public relations function in this way:

> The first recognition of distinct functions of the public relations counsel arose, perhaps, in the early years of the present century as a result of the insurance scandals coincident with the muckraking of corporate finance in the popular magazines. The interests thus attacked suddenly realized that they were completely out of touch with the public they were professing to serve, and required expert advice to show them how they could understand the public and interpret themselves to it.[9]

Former journalists began to find it possible to make a living in the public relations business. In 1900, George V. S. Michaelis established the Publicity Bureau in Boston. His job, as he saw it, was to gather factual information about his clients for distribution to newspapers. By 1906, his major clients were the nation's railroads. The railroads engaged the Publicity Bureau to head off adverse regulations being promoted by Theodore Roosevelt. The agency used fact-finding publicity and personal contact to push its clients' position, but kept secret its connection with the railroad. Publicity Bureau staff increased dramatically, with offices set up in New York, Chicago, Washington, D.C., St. Louis, and Topeka and with agents in California, South Dakota, and elsewhere.

President Roosevelt, who saw the presidency as "a bully pulpit," proved to be more than a match for the Publicity Bureau. The first president to make extensive use of press conferences and interviews, Roosevelt was said to rule

Edward L. Bernays, a
pioneer in public relations
education.

the country from the newspapers' front pages. The passage of the Hepburn
Act extended government control over the railroad industry and represented
a clear victory for the Roosevelt Administration.

Other early publicity offices were established by William Wolf Smith in
Washington, D.C. in 1902; Hamilton Wright, San Francisco, 1908; Pendleton
Dudley, New York's Wall Street district, 1909; Rex Harlow, Oklahoma City,
1912; and Fred Lewis and William Seabrook, Atlanta, 1912.

Ivy Lee   The father of public relations, however, and the man who nurtured
the fledgling profession, was Ivy Ledbetter Lee, son of a Georgia preacher.
Lee was a reporter who saw better prospects in the publicity arena. After
working in New York's 1903 mayoral campaign and for the Democratic National Committee, Lee joined George Parker, another newspaper veteran, to
form the nation's third publicity agency in 1904.

Two years later, coal operators George F. Baer and Associates hired the
partnership to represent their interests during a strike in the anthracite mines.
John Mitchell, leader of the labor forces, was quite open and conversant with
the press, which treated him and his cause with considerable sympathy. The
tight-lipped Baer would not even talk to the president of the United States.

Lee took the assignment and persuaded Baer to open up. Then he
promptly issued a Declaration of Principles to all newspaper city editors. The
sentiments expressed in this document clearly indicated that public relations
had entered its second stage.

As Eric Goldman observes, "The public was no longer to be ignored, in the traditional manner of business, nor fooled, in the continuing manner of the press agent."[10] Lee declared that the public was to be informed. The declaration read:

> This is not a secret press bureau. All our work is done in the open. We aim to supply news. This is not an advertising agency; if you think any of our matter ought properly to go to your business office, do not use it. Our matter is accurate. Further details on any subject treated will be supplied promptly, and any editor will be assisted most cheerfully in verifying directly any statement of fact. . . . In brief, our plan is, frankly and openly, on behalf of business concerns and public institutions, to supply to the press and public of the United States prompt and accurate information concerning subjects which it is of value and interest to the public to know about.[11]

From his actions and effectiveness in dealing with the coal strike, Lee clearly was not just a press agent coveting publicity. Indeed, he had a sophisticated grasp of the fundamental nature, problems, and opportunities of conflict.

Lee realized that a corporation could not hope to influence the public unless its publicity was supported by good works. Performance determines publicity. To achieve necessary and positive consistency between words and actions, Lee urged his clients in business and industry to align their senses and their policies with the public interest.

Railroads   As previously indicated, railroads were among the early users of public relations consultants. In 1906, the Pennsylvania Railroad retained Lee as publicity counselor. Beginning in 1897, the term "public relations" was frequently used in railroad trade publications. Indeed, publications of the day maintained that as early as 1893, railroads had begun "to research and study the social condition of its public."[12] Lee's activities for the Pennsylvania included publicizing employee benefits and railroad safety. He also emphasized the large numbers of people who owned the railroad's stock (not mentioning that a very few people held the vast majority of stock). He urged executives to accept public exposure and to cooperate fully with community projects. Most controversially, Lee released complete, factual information about accidents. Traditionally, such news had been suppressed.

The railroad industry was convinced of the value of public relations. By 1909, an industry leader called on all major companies to create a:

> Vice President in charge of public relations, a man . . . of mature years and judgment, skilled in railway affairs and human affairs as well, and carrying enough weight in the councils of his company so that his suggestions would be apt to be carried out.[13]

Such an adviser, it was held, could reveal and eliminate the unpopularity of the railroad industry by evaluating and improving customer service.

In a similar vein, a 1912 article stressed that "real publicity" goes beyond appointment of a special agent to court journalists. "It should be inground [sic] in the entire staff from top to bottom. . . ."[14] An early textbook entitled *Railroad Administration* included a chapter devoted to "Public Relations of a Railroad."[15] J. Hampton Baumgartner was hired in 1910 to handle publicity for the Baltimore and Ohio Railroad. In 1913, he told the Virginia Press Association that railroads had endeavored to establish closer relations with the public, chiefly through the press and with its cooperation.

Despite their early adoption of public relations techniques, the railroads were notably unsuccessful in lobbying their cause before government bodies. Over two thousand laws affecting railroads were passed by Congress and the various state legislatures in the period between 1908 and 1913.

Not-for-Profit Organizations   Not-for-profit organizations including colleges, churches, charitable causes, and health and welfare agencies began to use publicity extensively during this era. In 1899, Anson Phelps Stokes converted Yale University's Office of Secretary into an effective alumni and public relations office. Harvard President Charles W. Eliot, who spoke as early as 1869 on the need to influence public opinion toward advancement of learning, was among the Publicity Bureau's first clients in 1900. The University of Pennsylvania and the University of Wisconsin set up publicity bureaus in 1904. By 1917, the Association of American College News Bureaus was formed.

In 1905, the Washington, D.C., YMCA sought $350,000 for a new building. For the first time, a full-time publicist was engaged in a fund-raising drive. By 1908, the Red Cross and the National Tuberculosis Association were making extensive use of publicity agents. The New York Orphan Asylum was paying a publicity man $75 per month.

Churches and church groups were quick to recognize the value of an organized publicity effort. New York City's Trinity Episcopal Church was one of Pendleton Dudley's first clients in 1909. The Seventh-Day Adventist Church established its publicity office in 1912. George Parker, Ivy Lee's old partner, was appointed to handle publicity for the Protestant Episcopal Church in 1913.

Business   Publicity and public relations were making their greatest strides in business. In 1907, AT&T's Theodore N. Vail hired James Drummond Ellsworth for that corporation's public relations. Ellsworth promoted efficient operation and consideration of customers' needs, a systematic method for answering complaints, and acceptance of governmental regulation as the price for operating a privately-owned natural monopoly.

Samuel Insull, an associate of George Westinghouse, rose to head the Chicago Edison Company, an electric utility. In 1903, he began to publish *The Electric City,* a periodical magazine aimed at gaining the understanding and goodwill of the community. He pioneered films for public relations purposes in 1909. In 1912, he introduced bill stuffers, messages to customers in their monthly statements.

Among the greatest of industrial publicity users was Henry Ford. One commentator suggests, "He may have been an even greater publicist than mechanic." The Ford Company pioneered use of several public relations tools.

World War I U.S. Liberty
Bond poster encouraging
support for the war effort

The employee periodical *Ford Times* was begun in 1908 and continues today. In 1914, a corporate film department was established. Ford surveyed one thousand customers to gain insights into their attitudes and concerns.

The company set up demonstrations for the media, including car races and speed records. Ford sought publicity at every opportunity. Presenting himself as the price-reducing champion of the common man, he was totally accessible to the press and quotable on any subject. "Ford" became a household word.

Most importantly, however, business leaders had been convinced of the legitimacy and importance of publicity and public relations. In the 1911 AT&T annual report, corporation president Theodore Vail advocated a policy of absolute truthfulness, even in treating unfavorable information:

> In all times, in all lands, public opinion has had control at the last word— public opinion is but the concert of individual opinion, and is as much subject to change or to education.

Another business leader who spoke out on public relations was U.S. Steel Board Chairman Elbert H. Gary. In 1909, he maintained, "I believe thoroughly in publicity. . . . The surest and wisest of all regulations is public opinion."[16]

World War I   The greatest public relations effort in history, up to its time, was the one mounted in support of the United States effort in World War I. The military had utilized publicity for several years; the Marine Corps established a publicity bureau in Chicago in 1907. Never before had such a massive, multifaceted, coordinated program been mounted. Moreover, though often used by big business in a defensive fashion, public relations took the offensive when it came to war.

Woodrow Wilson set up a Committee on Public Information in 1917. Newspaperman George Creel was asked to run it. With a staff of journalists, scholars, artists, and others skilled at manipulating words and symbols, Creel mobilized the home front. Before the war, the Red Cross had 486,194 members in 372 chapters and $200,000 in funds. At the war's end, the organization's numbers were twenty million members in 3,864 chapters and $400 million raised. On May 1, 1917, there were 350,000 holders of U.S. Bonds. Six months later ten million held bonds.

Creel did not just work out of a central office; he decentralized the organization and the effort. Every industry had a special group of publicity workers tending to their particular contributions to the war effort. Political scientist Harold D. Lasswell was involved in the Creel organization. Looking back to assess the situation, Lasswell concluded, "Propaganda is one of the most powerful instrumentalities in the modern world."[17]

Many of the publicists trained in the war effort set out to make careers for themselves when the war ended. Impressed with their results, many organizations were eager to put their services to work. In 1919, the Knights of Columbus, a Catholic organization, set up a publicity bureau. Two years later, the American Association of Engineers held its first national conference on public information and published its proceedings as a book called *Publicity Methods for Engineers*. Also in 1921, Sears Roebuck and Company retained Hayes, Loeb and Company to counter a movement by thousands of local merchants fighting mail-order competition. In 1922, a National Publicity Council for Welfare Services was set up.

Public relations was becoming more sophisticated. Edward Bernays used market research, social surveys, and public opinion polls in efforts to, as he called it, "engineer public consent."

Still, the ends to be served by public relations and its practitioners were not always noble by any means. Between 1920 and 1923, for example, Edward Y. Clark and Bessie Tyler increased the membership of the Ku Klux Klan, a group that thrives on notions of bigotry and white supremacy, from a few thousand to some three million members.

Stage 3: Mutual Influence and Understanding

To dedicated and thoughtful public relations professionals in the decade following 1910, it became increasingly obvious that organizations communicate with the public not only by words released through the press, but also by their policies and actions. Consequently, they sought to advise business executives in such matters, attempting to gain a place in the heart of business organization—the decision-making and operational aspects. Ivy Lee was again in the vanguard, recognizing that good words had to be supported by good deeds. Lee sought to elevate his own status to that of "brain trust" for his clients.

N. W. Ayer & Son published a booklet in 1912 recommending that businessmen discuss with their advertising agents ". . . if conditions in the business are in harmony with an advertising program." Like Lee, Ayer wanted businessmen to understand that a successful publicity campaign involved their companies' basic policies as much as their procedures for telling the public about goods or services.[18] These basic policies included not only external, but internal concerns. Following this theme, it was perhaps not so surprising that George Michaelis, who had founded the Publicity Bureau in Boston, advised Westinghouse in 1914 to pay more attention to internal "human relations."[19]

A protracted and violent strike against Colorado Fuel and Iron Company gave Ivy Lee the opportunity to become a consultant on the internal workings of a business. John D. Rockefeller, Jr., the company's principal stockholder, employed Lee in 1914 after savage criticism for his handling of the strike. Lee publicized management's position in the strike (without revealing himself as the source of the information). He also persuaded Rockefeller to visit the stricken area. The man who was perceived as a reclusive tycoon talked with the miners, ate in their dining halls, and danced with their wives. Beyond these traditional actions, however, Lee strongly recommended to management that they improve their communication with workers and establish mechanisms to redress workers' grievances.[20] Thus, Lee became an adviser to Rockefeller not only in relation to dealings with the press and the public, but also in relation to the actual operation of the business. Lee served Rockefeller until his own death in 1934.

Inward Focus   In addition to its outward focus, then, public relations was gaining an inward focus. This had several results. Employees came to be recognized as a significant public and an appropriately important audience for public relations efforts. In this regard, Lee persuaded client American Tobacco Company to introduce profit-sharing for its employees.

By 1925, more than half of all major manufacturing companies were publishing employee magazines.[21] Textbooks of the day stressed the integration of public relations with general business activities. Samuel Kennedy maintained that from the viewpoint of companies, which person had immediate responsibility for directing publicity and giving out news was of little importance. What mattered was that the policies of the organization be guided by executives aware of political considerations.[22]

By the 1920s, the vanguard of public relations practitioners considered themselves responsible not only for informing the press and the public, but also for educating management about public opinion. They saw themselves as advising managerial decisions and actions in terms of public response. Only rarely, however, were public relations persons actually allowed to play such roles.

A new understanding of publicity was developing, based on recognition of its tremendous potentials as well as its very real limitations. Bernard J. Mullaney, who served Samuel Insull's efforts to establish utilites as privately-owned natural monopolies, concluded in 1924: "Honest and intelligent publicity efforts are a most important part of a public relations program . . . but not the whole program; and not even a part of it, as 'publicity' is commonly understood. . . . Publicity that seeks to 'put over' something is unsound; in the long run it defeats itself."

Arthur W. Page   The third stage in the development of public relations became established at American Telephone & Telegraph during the career of Arthur W. Page. A successful businessman, public servant, writer, and editor, Page was approached with an offer to become vice president of AT&T, succeeding the pioneer public relations specialist James D. Ellsworth. Page agreed to accept the position only on the condition that he would not be restricted to publicity in the traditional sense. He demanded and received a voice in company policy and insisted that the company's performance be the determinant of its public reputation. Page practiced the Stage 2 informative approach to public relations. He maintained:

> All business in a democratic country begins with public permission and exists by public approval. If that be true, it follows that business should be cheerfully willing to tell the public what its policies are, what it is doing, and what it hopes to do. This seems practically a duty.[23]

Under Page's leadership, however, the company recognized that winning public confidence required not merely ad hoc attempts to answer criticism. Rather, a continuous and planned program of positive public relations was needed, using institutional advertising, the usual stream of information flowing

Arthur Wilson Page,
AT&T's public relations
pioneer

through press releases, and other methods. Bypassing the conventional print media, the company went directly to the public, establishing, for instance, a film program to be shown to schools and civic groups.

AT&T sought to maintain direct contact with as many of its clients as possible. The company made a total commitment to customer service. Moreover, deposits were broadly distributed among banks; legal business was given to attorneys throughout the country; and contracts for supplies and insurance were made with many local agencies. AT&T paid fees for employees to join outside organizations, knowing that through their presence the company would be constantly represented in many forums. Finally, the company sought to have as many people as possible own its stock. Today, AT&T and the successor companies which were created by divestiture in 1984 are the most widely held of all securities.

What truly set Page apart and established him as a pioneer, however, was his insistence that the publicity department should act as an interpreter of the public to the company, drawing on a systematic and accurate diagnosis of public opinion. Page wanted data, not hunches. Under his direction, the AT&T publicity department (as it was still called) kept close check on company policies, assessing their impact on the public. Thus, Page caused the company "to act all the time from the public point of view, even when that seems in conflict with the operating point of view."[24]

In 1931, General Motors followed AT&T's lead. The automobile giant set up an internal department under Paul Garrett to ascertain public attitudes and execute a program to bring the company fully into public approval. Garrett was told to put the interests of the public first.

Public Relations
Pioneers

Exhibit 2.1

Samuel Adams   Most active prior to and during the Revolutionary War, Adams organized the Sons of Liberty, used the liberty tree symbol, minted slogans like "Taxation Without Representation Is Tyranny," staged the Boston Tea Party, named the Boston Massacre, and mounted a sustained propaganda campaign.

Amos Kendall   During the 1820s and 1830s, Kendall served candidate and President Andrew Jackson as public relations counselor, pollster, and speechwriter. He spearheaded the successful campaign against the Bank of the United States.

Matthew St. Clair Clarke   As publicist for the Bank of the United States in the 1830s, Clarke saturated the press with releases, reports, and pamphlets in the most extensive, albeit unsuccessful, public relations campaign to that date. In an effort to develop a politician to oppose Andrew Jackson, he created the myths surrounding the historical figure Davy Crockett.

P. T. Barnum   A consummate showman during the middle and late 1800s, Barnum originated many methods for attracting public attention.

E. H. Heinrichs   As press secretary to George Westinghouse from the late 1880s through 1914, Heinrichs prevailed over Thomas Edison's forces and established for Westinghouse the use of alternating electric current.

George Michaelis   Organizer of the nation's first publicity firm, the Publicity Bureau of Boston in 1900, Michaelis used fact-finding publicity and personal contact to saturate the nation's press.

Ivy Lee   Often called the father of modern public relations, Lee believed that the public should be informed. He recognized that good words had to be supported by positive actions on the part of individuals and organizations. His career spanned thirty-one years from its beginning in 1903.

James D. Ellsworth   Working with Theodore N. Vail in the early 1900s, Ellsworth established the public relations program of the American Telephone and Telegraph Company. His activities led to public support for the regulated private monopoly concept that has resulted in the world's best communications system.

George Creel   As head of the Committee on Public Information during World War I, Creel used public relations techniques to sell Liberty Bonds, build the Red Cross, and promote food conservation and other war-related activities. In so doing, he proved the power of public relations and trained a host of the twentieth century's most influential practitioners.

Edward Bernays   An intellectual leader in the field, Bernays coined the phrase "public relations counsel," wrote *Crystallizing Public Opinion* (the first book on public relations), and taught the first college-level public relations course at New York University in 1923.

Arthur Page   When offered a vice presidency at AT&T, Page insisted that he have a voice in shaping corporate policy. He maintained that business in a democratic country depends on public permission and approval.

Two major forces influenced the development of public relations in the United States during the 1930s: (1) the depression and (2) the threatening military situation in Europe.

The 1930s to the Present

The impact of the depression on public relations was twofold. First, the economic conditions of the day were viewed widely as a failure by business to maintain prosperity due to speculative excess. Rocked by the criticism and legislative reforms of the New Deal, public relations changed from occasional defensive efforts to positive continuous programs. Stage 3 public relations was reinforced because depressed economic circumstances called for compassionate and responsive business actions and policies. Persuasion and publicity could be effective only to the extent that they were coupled with responsible performance.

The Depression

The nation's diminished economic capacities created increased societal needs with reduced societal means. The need for active and informed constituencies became very clear when welfare, education, defense, other governmental goals, business, and labor fought for limited resources and the support of an awakened public.

The deteriorating military and political situation in Europe caused the military to move massively into public relations in the 1930s. In 1935, Chief of Staff General Douglas MacArthur appointed Major Alexander Surles to head a public relations branch. His orders: "The dual job of getting before the public the War Department's anxiety over things to come in Europe and helping newsmen pry stories out of the War Department."[25]

World War II

Each branch of the service built its own public relations apparatus. The Army Air Corps, under former information officer General H. H. "Hap" Arnold, promoted air power. The Army's efforts employed three thousand military and civilian personnel.

The greatest application of public relations techniques in the 1930s occurred not in the United States, however, but in Germany. In the hands of the Nazis, propaganda demonstrated its effectiveness, but became a dirty word.

In June 1942, with America fully engaged in worldwide struggle, the Office of War Information (OWI) was established. Similar to Creel's effort in World War I, a massive public relations effort was mounted to rally the home front. Elmer Davis directed the program. The goals of the Office of War

Information included selling war bonds, rationing food, clothing, and gasoline, planting victory gardens, and recruiting military personnel. Other issues promoted were factory productivity and efficiency.

Several important communication agencies still active today trace their beginnings to OWI. These include the United States Information Agency (USIA), the Voice of America, and the Advertising Council.

Post-War Era

Following the war, public relations gained increased respectability, acceptance, and professionalism. In 1947, Boston University established the first school of public relations. Two years later, one hundred colleges and universities offered classes in the subject.

Earl Newsom was perhaps the model public relations professional of the immediate post-World War II era. Hired by Standard Oil in 1945, Newsom was best known for helping young Henry Ford II become a public figure known for responsible business management. Newsom was a public relations counselor in the purest sense. He wrote no news releases. He held no press conferences. He simply advised business leaders at the highest levels.

In 1954, the Public Relations Society of America developed the first code of ethics for the profession. The society set up a grievance board for code enforcement in 1962 and a program of voluntary accreditation in 1964.

In the late 1960s and the 1970s, public relations seemed to be enjoying a renaissance of sorts. Corporations again felt themselves beset by adverse circumstances. Some have compared the 1970s with the muckraking era and maintain that public relations was more concerned with helping corporations avoid destructive attacks than with attempting to gain positive attention. "The public relations man now is far less of an ingenious producer of marvelous editorial gifts for his clients," said David Finn in 1977, "and far more of an experienced counselor in relating to potential or actual media attacks."[26]

During this period, new emphasis was placed on public relations functions other than marketing. Business/government relations became increasingly important as the federal government entered a new era of regulation. Environmentalism, consumerism, equal opportunity, urban problems, and nuclear power became issues confronting many organizations and demanding managed responses. The Vietnam War created special problems at home and abroad. Dow Chemical was picketed on college campuses, while overseas, branches of the Bank of America were frequently bombed. Sit-ins and marches were nonviolent events staged to influence public discussion and discourse. But radical young people in the United States and elsewhere also used riots and bombings as "propaganda of the deed."

Public relations had to increase its sophistication in a hurry. New tools and processes were developed. These included issues management, audience analysis, environmental scanning, and strategic planning. Indeed, with the importance of business's traditional technological and economic criteria increasingly challenged on social and political grounds, corporations expanded public relations staffs, budgets, and programs and elevated the function to a higher status in the organizational hierarchy.[27]

All managers and virtually all employees developed a strong public relations dimension in their work. Chief executives assumed more and more public relations responsibility. At companies like McGraw-Edison (where public relations convinced top management to abandon the use of the chemical PCB in electrical capacitors) public relations has now reached the third stage of development. But in return, the results-oriented approach of top management demands from public relations demonstrable achievements similar to those expected of all other corporate functions.

The Present

From the 1930s on, the theory and practice of public relations has centered around variations on the three themes or stages previously discussed. More and more, public relations has become continuous rather than episodic, positive rather than defensive. It is now accepted as a legitimate function within virtually all institutions and organizations.

Other trends are less clear. The argument over the professionalism of public relations practitioners continues. While the practice of public relations often calls for sophisticated technical skills and capabilities, public relations within organizations is frequently practiced, if not directed, by managers with training in other fields. Public relations practitioners as a group are probably more professionally ethical today than in the early years when the residue of press agentry still tainted the practice. But instances of laundering press releases through subsidized agencies, manipulating statistics, doing selective reporting, staging events, and even trying to use advertising clout to influence editorial content are uncomfortably common. Perhaps for this reason, the term public relations still has an unsavory connotation in some circles.

William A. Durbin, former chairman of Hill and Knowlton Public Relations, stated in 1979:

> The PR function is about to cross the threshold from a primarily communications function to a management function participating systematically in the formation of policy and the decision-making process itself.[28]

Durbin sees the profession at the same threshold seen by Michaelis, Lee, and Bernays—the threshold that was crossed more than half a century ago by Arthur W. Page. His perception illustrates how things change and remain the same.

By the 1980s, over 60 percent of the work force were information workers. The precise role public relations will play in post-industrial America is impossible to predict. Societal complexity and interdependence are greater than ever before. Ever more information and voices compete for attention, acceptance, approval, and support.

Society, however, exists through consensus, which seems ever harder to find. Public relations must not only assist those seeking attention, but also help nurture consensus and promote adaptation to changing environments. That public relations in all its stages will prosper for some years to come is a safe bet.

The Future of
Public Relations

While the future is always difficult to gauge, by identifying and describing historical trends, one can make good guesses. We will summarize public relations history and try to fathom its future by identifying and describing nine trends that appear to be influencing the direction of the practice today. Public relations is moving:

From	To
Manipulation	Adaptation
External counselor	Internal team member
Marketing	Management
Program	Process
Craftsperson	Manager
Items	Issues
Output	Input
Firefighter	Fire Preventer
Illegitimacy	Legitimacy

Let's look at each of these trends.

*From Manipulation
to Adaptation*

We begin with the consideration of this trend because it encompasses the entire past century of public relations evolution and because changes in this area are prerequisites for the development of other trends we will discuss. Public relations was born as a manipulative art. Its intent was to achieve specific results in terms of customer response, election outcomes, media coverage, or public attitudes. The job of public relations was to communicate in such ways as to assure the compliance of relevant publics' behavior and attitudes with an individual or organization's plans. The means, methods, and media of communication were determined by what it took to get the job done and little else. Stunts, sensationalism, and embellished and highly selective truth were hallmarks of the trade.

The blatantly manipulative aims of public relations in the past aroused the hostility of press and public. Residual effects of that early hostility still linger. Moreover, in a more subtle and serious way, mistrust of manipulative techniques caused those who employed public relations practitioners to consciously limit their internal influence. Until public relations practitioners moved beyond manipulation, their practice was restricted to specific tasks. They were the errand boys (and sometimes prostitutes) their journalistic colleagues accused them of being. As practitioners began to establish trust and credibility, the manipulative phase became history. Only then could public relations begin to make gains in stature and responsibility within organizations.

As the twentieth century progressed, it became apparent that organizations achieved success not by seeking compliance to their plans from outside entities, but by responding and adapting effectively to environmental demands, constraints, and opportunities. Public relations practitioners found that they could greatly facilitate this adaptive process if they could become trusted, two-way communicators seeking to establish rapport and mutual understanding between groups.

The field of public relations was established as a legitimate occupation and worthwhile field of study by a handful of ex-newspapermen and press agents in the early decades of the twentieth century. These pioneers, for the most part, set up their own firms and frequently succeeded in building larger-than-life reputations for themselves as well as their clients. This external, independent counselor model of public relations practice quickly became the ideal that has been taught in our textbooks and university classrooms ever since.

From External Counselor to Internal Team Member

However, the actual practice of public relations has evolved far beyond this original model. Although counseling firms have continued to flourish, a new breed of practitioner has emerged, primarily within the structures of large complex organizations. Public relations staffs now work for amorphous organizational entities with vast managerial hierarchies that can seldom produce a personality like J. D. Rockefeller. They must be concerned with internal communication as well as external publicity and must provide managerial leadership as well as communication expertise. They are essential members of the management team. Moreover, these new organizational practitioners are achieving, through their anonymous managerial accomplishments, the kind of influence that the pioneers only dreamed about.

Public relations specialists in organizations must be capable of understanding the concerns and attitudes of customers, employees, investors, managers, special interest groups, and a vast array of other publics. The job cannot stop with an understanding of these complex issues, however; public relations practitioners must be able to integrate this information into the organization's managerial decision-making process. Public relations practitioners of today and tomorrow must continue to exhibit high-quality communication skills to do the jobs for which they are hired. In addition, they must understand both their role as managers in affecting the actions of an organization and the importance of public relations input into that process.

Not very long ago, the primary justification for public relations was its effort to sell products. Public relations was seen as an adjunct to the sales effort, concerned primarily with product publicity and getting free advertising.

From Marketing to Management

The trend which has seen public relations move from a marketing adjunct to the management mainstream is a by-product of the changes in both areas. The development of the marketing concept which stresses organizational responsiveness to markets rather than sales efforts has changed the direction of information flow related to the development and sale of products. Management's task has also changed dramatically. Once, the job of management was to keep an established production organization smoothly functioning. Now, management seeks constantly to adapt a flexible organism to dynamic and complex environments.

Naturally, public relations has changed in conjunction with these changes in marketing and management. While still contributing to the marketing effort, the prime responsibility of public relations has become providing the information and environment in which management can function most effectively.

*From Program
to Process*

Traditionally, public relations has placed tremendous emphasis on programs and products, specific tangible outputs of public relations efforts. The job of the public relations practitioner has consisted of a progression of discrete tasks—media releases, publications, public service announcements, publicity campaigns, and the like. Such products and programs continue to be a time-consuming responsibility of public relations departments. However, one of the clearest observable trends in public relations is the growing view that organizational communication is a continuous process, not just a succession of programs.

While public relations practitioners will not be relieved of the duty to develop and deliver specific products and programs, they will be increasingly involved in broader, less discrete responsibilities. They will spend more time and effort developing communication objectives that are consistent with an organization's overall objectives. They will act as counselors to management and serve on teams with managers and other organizational specialists, working closely and cogently on a broad array of organizational programs. They will adopt a long-term, general perspective instead of a short-term, specific perspective.

*From Craftsperson
to Manager*

In conjunction with the traditional emphasis on producing specific products and programs, public relations practitioners have been viewed as possessing a specific set of skills. Writing ability has always led the list, followed by speaking, interpersonal skills, and a potpourri of other abilities, including photography, graphic design, and the like. These skills remain important. But stressing them exclusively leaves the fledgling public relations person in danger of becoming a narrowly specialized craftsperson or technician at a time when trends demand a broadly experienced communication manager.

A young public relations practitioner with less than ten years of experience put it this way: "We're yearning to learn all we can about financial statements and effective management techniques. While many of us still write, edit, layout and design, we have also moved up to greater responsibilities demanding a broad knowledge of business, international affairs, and the issues affecting the industries in which we work." She learned about writing, editing, layout, and design in school, but not the rest.

From Items to Issues

In times past, public relations practitioners sought to place "items" in the media and measured their effectiveness by their success in doing so. The current trend has carried public relations away from that stage, through defending against negative publicity, and toward what has been entitled issues management.

Issues management is the identification of key issues confronting organizations and the management of organizational responses to them. This process involves early identification of potential controversies, development of organizational policy related to these issues, creation of programs to carry out policies, implementation of these programs, communication with appropriate publics about these policies and programs, and evaluation of the results.

The issues management process is an area in which public relations has its greatest potential in terms of contributions to managerial decision making (see chapter 4). Organizations understand that they can avoid negative publicity and gain positive public notice by adapting in advance to environmental demands. In this way, they are able to reap benefits by being perceived as responsible leaders. Public relations practitioners must be prepared to identify and deal with the issues that confront their organizations.

The traditional emphasis of public relations has been on output—the creation of messages for external publics. Increasingly, however, public relations practitioners are realizing that their most important messages constitute input—messages to internal publics from external and internal publics. The trend line indicates the rising importance of employee and managerial audiences for public relations messages.

From Output to Input

Ultimately, public relations enters into the very core of organizations, bearing the information and perspectives which influence fundamental decisions of policy and strategy. Public relations practitioners increasingly provide input and participate in such decisions. Thus, it is necessary too for them to understand the managerial perspective, while maintaining an independent viewpoint that considers social as well as economic variables.

Among the most fully established trends affecting public relations practitioners is the evolution of their role from being "firefighters" to "fire preventers." Effective public relations does not exist merely to clean up messes once they are made, but seeks to avoid such dilemmas to begin with. Preventive public relations is a widely held ideal among practitioners.

From Firefighters to Fire Preventers

The confluence of many of the trends just described makes preventive public relations possible. Public relations practitioners are moving into positions which now allow them to more fully recognize areas of potential danger, to be equipped to deal with those dangers, and to possess sufficient power and influence to effect needed changes before potentials become realities. Once again, managerial skills take precedence over media skills.

Continuing debates about professionalism notwithstanding, and despite the efforts of PRSA and others, public relations has always had an air of illegitimacy about it. Public relations has been a bastard child, a waif that was not really wanted even by those who temporarily took it in. Journalists often treat public relations professionals like cousins who have fallen from grace. Thus, as long as public relations practitioners seek their legitimacy from the working press, they will remain unfulfilled.

From Illegitimacy to Legitimacy

Public relations, however, to the extent that it is no longer a front or a manipulator, has rapidly gained legitimacy in the eyes of organizational managers and executives. The trend of legitimacy has developed because of all the other trends discussed. Members of the profession who help organizations adapt and respond to the demands and opportunities present in society, who provide working linkages between organizations, and who play a critical role in the effective management of our crucial problem-solving organizational systems are not only legitimate, but deserving of honor and esteem.

Summary

While persuasion and public opinion are forces that have always played a role in human events, widespread practice of public relations as a necessary and respected organizational function is largely an American product of this century. Ever evolving and in transition, public relations practice has experienced three distinct stages: manipulation, information, and mutual influence and understanding.

The future of public relations can be understood in terms of nine trends which emphasize the practice's ongoing management role in helping to shape organizations' responses to their environments.

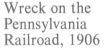

Wreck on the Pennsylvania Railroad, 1906

By Craig E. Aronoff
Kennesaw College
Marietta, Georgia

Case Study

In the first years of this century, business executives had an acute understanding of the phrase: "None of Your Business." While they preferred favorable treatment in the press, to outsiders who sought to know and understand the inner workings of the day's great enterprises, the answer was firm and clear.

The great railroads of the day subscribed to the same philosophy. While rail executives might attempt to buy a reporter's goodwill with a free ticket, access to information on railroad operations and events was strictly limited.

Severe railroad regulations passed in 1903 and 1906 caused Alexander J. Cassatt, president of the Pennsylvania Railroad, to seek the counsel of Ivy Ledbetter Lee concerning how to deal better with the press and the public.

Lee went right to work. He believed in absolute frankness with the press. Veteran railroad men were distressed at Lee's behavior. They were convinced that revealing facts about accidents would frighten customers.

A golden opportunity for Lee to put his ideas into practice soon arose. A train wrecked on the Pennsylvania Railroad main line near the town of Gap, Pennsylvania. As was its time-honored practice, the company sought to suppress all news of the accident.

When Ivy Lee learned of the situation, he took control. He contacted reporters, inviting them to come to the accident scene at company expense. He provided facilities to help them in their work. He gave out information for which the journalists had not considered asking.

The railroad's executives were appalled at Lee's actions. His policies were seen as unnecessary and destructive. How could the propagation of such bad news do anything but harm the railroad's freight and passenger business?

At about the time of the wreck on the Pennsylvania, another train accident struck the rival New York Central. Sticking with its traditional policy, the Central sought to avoid the press and restrict information flow concerning the situation.

Confronted with the Central's behavior, and having tasted Lee's approach to public relations, the press was furious with the New York line. Columns and editorials poured forth chastising the Central and praising the Pennsylvania. Lee's efforts resulted in positive publicity, increased credibility, comparative advantages over the Central, and good, constructive press coverage and relations. Lee critics were silenced.

Earl Newsom, himself a public relations giant, looked back at this accident nearly sixty years later and said:

> This whole activity of which you and I are a part can probably be said to have its beginning when Ivy Lee persuaded the directors of the Pennsylvania Railroad that the press should be given all the facts on all railway accidents—even though the facts might place the blame on the railroad itself.*

When Ivy Lee died in 1934, among the many dignitaries at his funeral were the presidents of both the Pennsylvania and the New York Central railroads.

Questions

1. Were Lee's actions in response to the railroad accident consistent with Stage 1, Stage 2, or Stage 3 of public relations development? Explain your answer.
2. Had the New York Central accident not occurred, what do you think would have happened to Ivy Lee and his relationship with the Pennsylvania Railroad? Do you think the course of public relations development would have been affected?
3. In certain totalitarian states, news of accidents and disasters is often largely suppressed. What do you consider their reasons to be for retaining a posture given up by American public relations practice more than eighty years ago?

*Earl Newsom, "Business Does Not Function by Divine Right," *Public Relations Journal* (January 1963), 4.

Source: Material for this case was gathered from Ray Hiebert's *Courtier to the Crowd* (Ames, IA: Iowa State University Press, 1966), 55–61, and Eric Goldman's *Two-Way Street* (Boston: Bellman Publishing Co., 1948), 8.

Notes

1. Philip Davidson, *Propaganda and the American Revolution, 1763–1783* (Chapel Hill, NC: University of North Carolina Press, 1941), 3.
2. Allan Nevins, *The Constitution Makers and the Public, 1785–1790* (New York: Foundation for Public Relations Research and Education, 1962), 10.
3. Quoted in James L. Crouthamel, "Did the Second Bank of the United States Bribe the Press?" *Journalism Quarterly* 36 (Winter 1959): 372.
4. Richard Overton, *Burlington West* (Cambridge, MA.: Harvard University Press, 1941), 158–159.
5. Marc Bloch, *The Historian's Craft* (New York: Knopf, 1953), 168.

6. Marie Curtl, *The Growth of American Thought,* 3rd ed. (New York: Harper & Row, 1964), 634.

7. Forest McDonald, *Insull* (Chicago: University of Chicago Press, 1962), 44–45.

8. Marshall Fishwick, *American Heroes: Myths and Realities* (Washington, D.C., 1954), 70–71.

9. Edward L. Bernays, *Propaganda* (New York: Horace Liveright, 1928), 41.

10. Eric F. Goldman, *Two-Way Street* (Boston: Bellman Publishing Co., 1948), 21.

11. Quoted in Sherman Morse, "An Awakening on Wall Street," *American Magazine* 62 (September 1906): 460.

12. Theodore Dreiser, "The Railroads and the People," *Harper's Monthly* 100 (February 1900): 479–480.

13. Ray Morris, "Wanted A Diplomatic Corps," *Railroad Age Gazette* (27 January 1909): 196.

14. James H. McGraw, "Publicity," *Electric Railway Journal* 39 (27 January 1912): 154.

15. Ray Morris, *Railroad Administration* (New York: Appleton & Company, 1910).

16. N. S. B. Gras, "Shifts in Public Relations," *Bulletin of the Business Historical Society* 19, no. 4 (October 1945): 120.

17. Harold D. Lasswell, *Propaganda Techniques in the World War* (New York: Knopf, 1927), 220.

18. Allan R. Raucher, *Public Relations and Business,* 1900–1929 (Baltimore: The Johns Hopkins Press, 1968), 4–5.

19. George V. S. Michaelis, "The Westinghouse Strike," *Survey* 32 (1 August 1914): 463–465.

20. Ray E. Hiebert, *Courtier to the Crowd: The Story of Ivy Lee and the Development of Public Relations* (Ames: Iowa State University Press, 1966).

21. National Industrial Conference Board, *Employee Magazines in the United States* (New York: National Industrial Conference Board, Inc., 1925).

22. Samuel M. Kennedy, *Winning the Public* (New York: McGraw-Hill, 1920).

23. George Griswold, Jr., "How AT&T Public Relations Policies Developed," *Public Relations Quarterly* 12 (Fall 1967): 13.

24. Raucher, *Public Relations and Business,* 80–81.

25. Sidney A. Knutson, "History of Public Relations Programs of the U.S. Army" (Unpublished Masters Thesis, University of Wisconsin, 1953).

26. David Finn, "The Media as Monitor of Corporate Behavior," in *Business and the Media,* Craig E. Aronoff, ed. (Santa Monica: Goodyear Publishing Company, 1979), 117–121.

27. The Corporate Image: PR to the Rescue," *Business Week* (22 January 1979): 47.

28. Ibid., 60.

CHAPTER 3

A Theoretical Basis for Public Relations

Preview

Communication problems are as often a symptom as they are a disease. Because public relations practitioners are asked to deal with what are perceived to be communication problems, they must have a thorough understanding of all aspects of communication processes.

Most of us have developed "common sense theories" of communication. But while of some value, these theories lack scientific objectivity.

The "systems approach" provides a meaningful theoretical perspective for understanding communication and public relations.

Public relations professionals deal with communication on many levels, most importantly in terms of individual communicators, interpersonal communication, communication within and between organizations, and public communication.

Public relations personnel play at least four specific communication roles for their organizations: gatekeeper, liaison, opinion leader, and external boundary spanner.

Breakdowns in communication can cause conflict. A USX employee protests during the first day of a lockout from MINNTAC iron ore mine in Mountain Iron, MN.

What we have here is a problem of communications.

This may be the single most widely used sentence in the world today. Inefficiency, waste, conflict, laziness, and many other problems are seen as the result of communication failures, blockages, and breakdowns.

Lack of communication is an easy explanation when things go wrong. And since communication is involved in all human interaction, it is always around to take the blame. But in fact, communication sometimes gets a bum rap. Poor communication is as often a result of a problem as it is the problem's cause; it is as often a symptom as it is the actual disease.

Public relations practitioners are frequently called upon to deal with communication problems. Sometimes they are blamed for the problem or for not solving it. When the citizens of a community are enraged about smells from a factory, when customers are incensed because prices have doubled, when voters turn incumbents out of office because they have failed to serve, when employees strike, when investors sell, when the media expose questionable practices—all of these instances may be labeled problems of communication, and public relations professionals may be asked to help find solutions. It is essential, then, that public relations people thoroughly understand the communication process as it relates to individuals, groups, organizations, and the public, both in theory and in practice. This chapter explains some communication theories and models in an effort to broaden and deepen your understanding of communication and provide a theoretical underpinning for the practical discussion of public relations.

A **theory** is an explanation or belief about how something works. A **model** is a way of looking at something. Models are often simplified abstractions designed to make complex systems, processes, or structures more easily understood. Theories and models may be developed and tested through rigorous scientific methods. They may also be formulated rather casually by people who generalize from their own experiences; such theories and models are sometimes described as "common sense." Other theories and models may be passed from generation to generation or shared through socialization or enculturation.

Once our theories or models are formulated or adopted, they can be very powerful. Without even realizing it, we rely on them for our views of the world and the relationships within it. Our theories and models of public relations and communication shape the way we understand and participate in those processes.

Because we are all experienced communicators (and often miscommunicators), most of us have developed communication theories of our own. Public relations authorities give theoretical advice to youngsters just entering the field, some of it similar to the theories listed below. These ideas are quite common outside the profession as well, and when challenged, are defended on the grounds of "common sense."

Some Common Sense Theories of Communication

According to the Decibel Theory, the best way to get your message across is to state it frequently and loudly. Public relations practitioners subscribing to this theory exaggerate the importance of events, flood the media with news releases, and generally seek to attract attention by making lots of noise. While repetition can be very important to assure message penetration, advocates of the Decibel Theory should be told that shouting only makes poor communication louder.

Decibel Theory

The Sell Theory assumes that one person sells information and the other person buys. Communication is seen as a one-way street. The goal of such communication is to manipulate an audience to accept the message. Public relations people who operate according to this theory are always trying to sell ideas to the media or to the public. While an occasional "sale" might be made, fundamental relationships are often injured by the approach. Communication based on the Sell Theory increases distrust and raises barriers between groups. Consequently, the chances of achieving mutual understanding are reduced.

Sell Theory

The Minimal Information Theory stresses secrecy, keeping a low profile, and playing it close to the vest. Public relations practitioners rarely subscribe to this communication theory, but the organizations they work for sometimes do. When public meetings go behind closed doors, when questions are consistently answered with "No comment," when cover-ups are normal operating procedure, the Minimal Information Theory is at work. Operating on the notion that "What they don't know can't hurt us," proponents of minimal information fail to recognize the harm done by a lack of trust, commitment, and openness.

Minimal Information Theory

"If I Were Them"
Theory

The "If I Were Them" Theory assumes that communication will be successful if the senders of information can place themselves in the position of the receivers of information and then communicate appropriately. Actually, this is one of the better informal communication theories, growing as it does from the Golden Rule: "Do unto others as you would have them do unto you." George Bernard Shaw, however, found it necessary to rewrite the Golden Rule: "Don't do unto others as you would have them do unto you because their tastes may be different." Shaw's revision lends insight into the major problem with the "If I Were Them" Theory. While it is often helpful to imagine oneself in another's place, this theory overlooks the fact that different people respond in different ways to the same information.

Many other common sense communication theories exist, and most are similarly flawed. To better understand communication, let us look at some theories and models developed by those who deal with communication from a more scientific perspective. Researchers have developed a variety of theories and models that attempt to clarify the communication process. The most broadly accepted theoretical framework for understanding communication behavior (indeed, all behavior) is known as systems theory, or the systems approach.

The Systems Approach

Communication researchers now seem to agree that communication is a process, not a thing, not a tool. It is not something one person does to another. It is dynamic, not static. It has no discernible beginning or end. To say that communication is a process is also to say that it operates in the form of systems; therefore, to understand how communication operates, we must first understand how systems work. Figure 3.1 illustrates this concept.

Figure 3.1 The process of communication

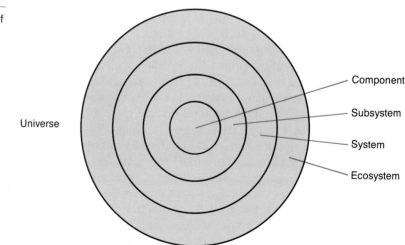

A **system** is a set of objects or events grouped together by sets of relationships. A system exists in and interacts with its environment. For example, if two people are talking face-to-face, that two-person conversation could be regarded as a system existing in a particular physical, social, and cultural environment. Each of the individuals in the conversation could be considered a **subsystem** of a two-person communication system.

One larger system may serve as the environment for several smaller systems. That is, the two-person system may, in turn, be seen as a component, part, or subsystem of still larger systems called **ecosystems.** Let us say in this case that the ecosystem is made up of a large number of face-to-face interactions.

Actually, what is considered a component, a subsystem, a system, or an ecosystem depends mainly on what you are looking for when you examine the situation. What you are looking for is called your **level of analysis.** Almost any possible component could be examined in detail as a system of still smaller components. Almost any ecosystem could be examined as one component of some larger ecosystem. Generally, the smallest unit you care to look at in any analysis is, for convenience, called a component. A component exists in the environment of a subsystem, the environment of which is a system, the environment of which is an ecosystem, the environment of which is a **universe.** From the most inclusive on down, then, we have universe, ecosystem, system, subsystem, and component. The reason for looking at communication this way is to develop a perspective for viewing relationships between entities, parts, and sets of interacting factors. It also helps account for a large bunch of simultaneous events that affect each other.

A business organization is a good example of an operating system. Various departments are its subsystems. Its industry or its community are among its ecosystems.

To understand systems theory, we must understand four propositions that underlie it: hierarchy, interdependence, synergy, and regulation. The subsystem–system–ecosystem vantage point suggests the first proposition of systems theory—that *behavior is structured hierarchically.* Let us examine the proposition of **hierarchy** more closely.

Behavior connotes action, motion. Systems move. They are always evolving, changing, growing, decaying. Of course, some systems move more quickly or obviously than others. A language is a communication system made up of sounds and the relationships between sounds. Over generations and centuries, it evolves, changes, and grows. Individuals using language are part of language systems. People as well as sounds are subsystems of language, while language exists in the ecosystem of society, a culture, or the human species. A table is a system. So is a building, a forest, or a dog. All contain elements that relate to each other and act upon each other, even if we cannot see the action.

Hierarchy

Structured connotes that these actions occur in relatively consistent and predictable ways. Rules govern behavior. Again, some systems are more rigidly structured than others. The right combination of oxygen, hydrogen, and heat will always produce water. But a smile and a friendly hello will not always get the same response. Nonetheless, to understand behavior, especially communication behavior, systems theory suggests that we first understand the rules governing it. The rules themselves vary in terms of their explicitness and flexibility; they may be called norms, rules, values, expectations, boundaries, agendas, laws, policies, procedures, or the like.

Hierarchically suggests, as we have mentioned, the organization of behavior into successive subsystems, systems, and ecosystems. To understand a system of behavior fully, one must examine the subsystems and ecosystems of which it is a part, as well as the behavior itself.

The second proposition of systems theory says that *all elements of a system are interdependent.* **Interdependence** is the opposite of independence. In this context, the word suggests that elements of a system cannot act alone. They cannot behave unilaterally. Thus, whatever affects any element of a system in some way—however small—affects every element of that system. The action of any system element must be seen as an outcome of the whole system rather than as an outcome of the element itself, or of some other isolated element or elements.

In practical terms, the principle of interdependency says a great deal about how we understand, predict, and control behavior. When somebody does something that strikes us as out of the ordinary, we wonder why. We try to identify a particular external cause for that behavior. If unable to do so, we attribute it to the individual's internal state.

Both of these explanatory procedures assume simple linear cause-and-effect frameworks. They frequently restrict our understanding of behavior. Interdependency suggests that we move beyond notions of cause and effect or credit and blame. We must recognize that the responsibility for behavior is not simply assigned. Rather, while it may appear that an individual is doing the behavior, the behavior is actually the product of the interaction of the many systems to which the individual or the behavior belongs.

A simple example of the difference between linear and systems perspectives can be found in the way some managers explain their employees' work behavior. Confronted with workers who are lax producers and generally unmotivated, one manager may assume that each of these people and, in fact, workers as a group, are lazy by nature. Another manager, however, realizing that workers in other situations are quite energetic and productive, may realize that elements of the particular situation in which these people are working create conditions that reinforce unproductive behavior.

The first manager may try to effect a change in behavior by using threats, rewards, firings, or tearing out hair. The second manager will probably look at the structure of the work environment, the interaction norms of the people in the environment, and other behavioral factors in an effort to change the system that resulted in unproductive behavior. While the first manager may make temporary improvements, the second manager is more likely to achieve long-term success.

The principle of **synergy** is the third proposition of systems theory. Synergy is most simply defined as *the whole is greater than the sum of its parts*. If a system were broken down into all its components, and the behavior of each component were explained, the behavior of the system as a whole would still not be explained. The relationships between the elements of a system, a very real and important aspect of systems, are lost when the system is broken up. As the Eastern philosopher Jiddu Krishnamurti expressed it, "One cannot take one problem separately and try to solve it by itself; each problem contains all the other problems. . . ."

Synergy

Synergy suggests a perspective, the necessity of understanding the big picture. Of course, it is difficult to examine a system whole. But at the very least, as one examines a system's parts, one should bear in mind that the purpose of examination is to understand how each part behaves in relation to the others.

The fourth systems proposition is **regulation.** The behavior of any system is a function not only of the interaction of its elements, but also of the interaction of the entire system with other systems. Thus, *the behavior of any system is constrained or regulated*. Behavior occurs within acceptable limits. If behavior exceeds those limits, compensatory behavior will occur.

Regulation

The clearest example of regulation occurs in economic systems. Producers of goods and services must behave within limits if they are to survive as businesses. One limit is set by the necessity of profit. Another is set by the necessity of providing goods and services at levels of price and quality acceptable to customers. When a business fails to perform within these limits, regulatory behavior called bankruptcy occurs.

Everyday human behavior is similarly regulated. If you walk what has been appropriately called the straight and narrow, you have no problems. But if you increasingly deviate from the norm, you meet compensatory regulatory activities of increasing severity. Friendly ribbing becomes criticism; criticism becomes scorn, which becomes ostracism, which can lead to incarceration (in prison or a mental hospital), exile, or even death. This is not to say that you must always walk the straight and narrow, but that you should have a good idea of acceptable ranges of behavior in various situations and realize that you venture near or beyond accepted limits at your own risk.

Regulation offers another means for understanding human behavior from a systems perspective. It encourages us to ask not only why something happens, but also why alternatives do *not* happen.

Systems theory is not a communication theory per se. It does apply, however, to all forms of behavior. Because communication is a form of behavior and all behavior is at least potentially communicative, systems theory applies directly and appropriately to communication.

Applying Systems Theory to Communication

Most importantly, transfer of information is what allows human systems (and the systems that humans invent) to work. Systems interact with their environments by gathering information about the environment and then interpreting that information. On the basis of that interpretation, appropriate responses are formulated. The appropriateness of the system's behavior can be ascertained by the feedback received from the environment.

The study of the ways systems use communication for direction and control is called **cybernetics.** The word is derived from a Greek word denoting the pilot of a ship who scans the sea for information and takes corrective action to keep the ship on course.

Analyzing Communication Systems   Professor Robert Hopper in his book *Human Message Systems*[1] suggests six questions to ask in analyzing almost any system:

1. What system is being examined?
2. What are its goals?
3. What are its components?
4. What is its environment?
5. How well is the system working?
6. How could the system be changed to work better?

Let us say that we are interested in analyzing the communication behavior of an organization's public relations person in relation to its president. What system is being examined (question 1)? Are we observing a two-person relationship? Do we consider these people in terms of group communication? Or do we analyze organizational structure—rules, norms, attitudes, climate? What about the backgrounds of the public relations person and the executive? Do we restrict ourselves to semantics, the words used in the situation? How we define the system of communication in which we are interested will largely determine the nature, validity, and usefulness of our analysis.

In the case we are considering, the system's goals (question 2) refer to the purposes of communication between supervisor and subordinates. Some possible purposes might be to inform, control, motivate, direct, persuade, build relationships, seek information and ideas, or introduce change. In analyzing the system, we want to know both the extent to which the system's goals are appropriate and the extent to which they are being accomplished.

As mentioned, all systems have subsystems. Once a system has been defined and its major functions described, the system's operation can be broken down into its component parts (question 3). Each part, in turn, should be described in terms of its own operation and its contributions to the system as a whole. In our example, each individual in the system could be described as a subsystem, with particular attention paid to personality, attitudes, communication tactics, personal goals, and relationships. Other subsystems that would require analysis are communication rules, norms, and roles present in the system, as well as the organizational units each person represents.

All systems exist within ecosystems. Thus, the system's environment (question 4) is important to its operation. A system's environment includes the things that are important to the system's goals and cannot be changed from within the system. Relevant environmental considerations in our case may include organizational expectations, norms and rules imposed from outside the system, networks of external relationships, and more.

To determine how well the system is working (question 5), we evaluate (using questions 3 and 4) whether the system (question 1) is achieving its objectives (question 2).

The sixth and final question is, "How can the system be changed so that it works better?" Proceed with caution. System changes frequently result in unintended and sometimes negative consequences. In the case of the public relations staffer and the president, needed changes could range from a mild suggestion that the president be more open with the media, to putting everyone through intensive communication training, restructuring relationships by altering rules, norms, and roles, or even transferring or firing personnel. Of course, once a change is made, the system has been changed, and analysis must begin anew.

As we seek to understand public relations from the perspective of the systems approach, we must examine the ecosystems and subsystems of public relations. The environment of public relations has political, cultural, social, and economic dimensions, but is generally known as **public opinion.** The components of public relations include individual communicators, their interpersonal communications, the organizations for which public relations is practiced, and the interactions between the organizations that public relations strives to influence.

Public opinion is the socio-psychological and political environment in which organizations succeed or fail. A very complex phenomenon, public opinion can perhaps be best understood by looking at *publics* and *opinion* each in turn. The concept of publics will be discussed more thoroughly in chapter 6. At this point, we will merely point out that there is no single public—that the public actually consists of many publics, groups of individuals tied by a sense of common characteristics or responses. Opinions are outward expressions of inwardly held attitudes. Public opinion, thus, is the outward expression of group consensus that emerges over time.

The environment of public opinion surrounds the efforts of public relations. Public relations practitioners may attempt to create opinion, change or neutralize hostile opinion, surface latent opinion, reinforce or activate favorable opinion, or help their organizations adapt to the reality of public opinion.

Applying Systems Theory to Public Relations

People, groups, organizations, and the relationships between them are the basic components of public relations systems. Thus, to understand a public relations system, we must first examine its subsystems.

Subsystems of Public Relations Communication

Figure 3.2 The individual communicator

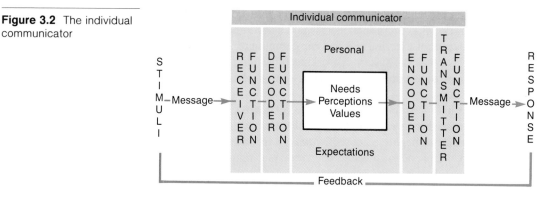

Figure 3.2 The individual communicator

Individual Communicators Communication flows through individuals. You cannot communicate with a newspaper; you must deal with reporters or editors. You cannot talk with a government; you must deal with a mayor, commissioner, alderman, or representative. You cannot correspond with a business; an individual is answering the mail (or has programmed a computer to respond). To understand communication processes, it is necessary to understand how individuals communicate.

Individuals simultaneously send and receive messages which are filtered through **perceptual screens** comprised of their needs, values, attitudes, expectations, and experiences. Figure 3.2 shows that stimuli (or messages) are received and interpreted in terms of people's needs, perceptions, and values.

No matter what role an individual is playing at a given time, the process remains the same. Employees, stockholders, editors, voters, customers, taxpayers, neighbors, contributors, regulators, and all others comprehend and send messages according to the psychological factors mentioned above. The ability to understand these factors in oneself or others enhances one's ability to predict behavior. However, because meaning is derived from messages only through perceptual screens, communicators cannot control the way their messages will be understood.

For the public relations practitioner, perhaps the most crucial variable related to individual communication is **perception.** Perception is the process of making sense of incoming stimuli. Its importance is well illustrated by a discussion that took place among three baseball umpires. "Some's balls and some's strikes and I calls 'em as they is," claimed the first umpire. The second umpire made a subtle but important distinction: "Some's balls and some's strikes and I calls 'em as I sees 'em." The third umpire disagreed with both his colleagues: "Some's balls and some's strikes," he maintained, "but they ain't nothing till I calls 'em."

Like umpire number three, it is the receiver of the message who determines its meaning. The editor who receives the news release decides whether it is actually news or not. The stockholder who receives an annual report decides whether the information contained therein bodes good or ill. The announcement of cutbacks in government programs will be seen as positive or negative depending on the needs, experiences, and attitudes of those who hear the announcement.

Since communicators cannot assume that messages will be understood as intended, effective communication requires a knowledge of one's audience, a means of receiving **feedback** from that audience, consistency of messages provided by words and deeds, and mutual responsiveness, understanding, and trust between communicators and those with whom they share messages.

Interpersonal Communication As individual communicators exchange messages, they also share their needs, perceptions, and values. This sharing leads to the development of mutual meanings and **mutual expectations.** Figure 3.3 shows such a communication situation between two individuals. The source of messages (encoder) and their destination (decoder) are able to communicate about a given subject to the extent that their experiences with it overlap and result in mutual understanding (shared image).

As individuals exchange more messages, they build upon their mutual understanding and expand their range of constructive interaction. When similar stimuli evoke markedly different images, however, the opportunity to develop constructive action is restricted severely. If an organization thinks of itself as a friendly giant while its public considers it a fierce dragon, communication problems inevitably result.

What is most striking about interpersonal communication is the extent to which the process is structured by rules or expectations. All interpersonal relationships operate within certain stated or implied rules of behavior that are acknowledged by the participants and serve as boundaries for the interaction. These boundaries reduce uncertainty in relationships and indicate ranges of acceptable behavior.

Certain rules governing interpersonal communication are found in the culture to which the participants belong. For example, conflicts in most work organizations are not settled by physical violence because such behavior breaks our cultural rules. Other sources of rules are found within the organization and work group. Although many formal and informal rules are imposed on interpersonal interactions, people need to develop their own rules for communicating with each other.

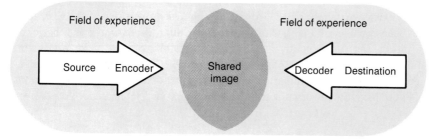

Figure 3.3 An interpersonal model of communication

A lack of understanding about **communication rules** governing particular relationships can cause the most serious communication breakdowns. As communication scholar Bonnie Johnson explains: "A disagreement on (rules) is more serious . . . than a disagreement about attitudes because (rules) are the basis of coordination."[2] Without agreement on rules governing interpersonal communication behavior, organized activity is not possible.

This understanding of how interpersonal communication works suggests that public relations practitioners must be concerned with more than attitudes and opinions; they must deal with the rules by which people interact. In many cases, the public relations task is to gain mutual understanding and acceptance of rules. Oftentimes, the task is to substitute positive and productive rules (like trust) for those which are harmful or counterproductive (distrust).

Organizational Communication   Most public relations texts, taking their cue from the importance of the mass media to public relations practice, use public communication as a model for understanding the communication process. While not denying the necessity of addressing mass communication, we feel that new understandings point to the even greater importance of communication processes within and between organizations.

Gerald Goldhaber, a leading organizational communication scholar, identifies three propositions common to most organizational communication studies:

1. Organizational communication occurs within a complex open system which is influenced by and influences its environment.
2. Organizational communication involves messages, their flow, purpose, direction and media.
3. Organizational communication involves people, their attitudes, feelings, relationships and skills.[3]

Communication within the organization is influenced by information and messages that originate in the organization's environment. Within the organization, communication flows in the form of messages within networks of interdependent relationships. People are the linking pins of the organizational communication process, thus their attitudes, feelings, needs, perceptions, and values have an effect on message flows. This process is represented in Figure 3.4.

An organization can be defined as a network of interdependent relationships. Communication, then, is among the control processes of organizational existence. Chester Barnard, whose book *The Functions of the Executive* has been considered a classic of management literature for nearly fifty years, maintains that the executive's primary responsibility is to develop and maintain an organizational system of communication. The nature of an organization's system of communication can have tremendous impact on its decisions and actions. How the organization's communication system is developed often

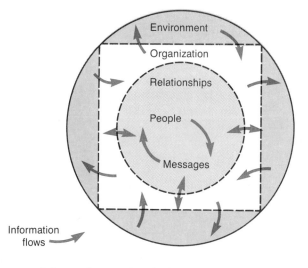

Figure 3.4 A model of organizational communication

determines whether necessary information reaches decision makers, the quality of information sent and received, and the kinds of information sought and considered important. A critical factor is the extent to which communication channels are standardized and centralized.

When communication within an organization is highly standardized, information and decisions are forced into molds. People feel less free to express their ideas. Creativity is not stimulated; open communication is not encouraged. Ambiguity is not tolerated; change is feared.

Similarly, centralizing communication makes information overload more likely, lowers organization members' satisfaction, and reduces efficiency in solving complex problems. Information used in decision making is often distorted, while participation and responsibility are discouraged.

All of these factors can have great influence on the role and practice of public relations within a given organization. Practitioners often find that the hardest part of their jobs is getting information from their own organizations. They must be sensitive to the nature and flow of the organization's communication. Moreover, one of their primary jobs should be to counsel management as it creates and maintains the organization's communication system. (This topic will be discussed more fully in chapters 4 and 12.)

Interorganizational Communication   While the importance of an organization's environments is made clear in our discussion of communication within organizations, we must now recognize that environments also encompass other organizations. Organizations, of course, communicate with each other. Corporations, for example, communicate with government, media, labor, consumer, community, and educational groups, as well as with other businesses.

Like communication within organizations, communication among organizations is structured. Employees within organizations are assigned the responsibility of receiving information from and sending it to other organizations.

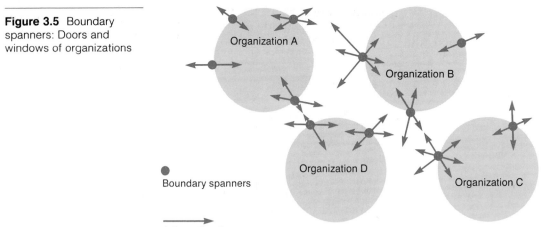

Figure 3.5 Boundary spanners: Doors and windows of organizations

Organization A

Organization B

Boundary spanners

Organization D

Organization C

Information flows

Individuals occupying such positions have been termed **boundary spanners** or liaisons.[4] These individuals act as the doors and windows of organizations (Figure 3.5). Through them, organizational communication systems link the organization with its environments.

Those who function as external boundary spanners pay a substantial price for their efforts. Social psychologist David Kahn and his associates found in studies of individuals occupying boundary positions that:

> As a person's job-required contacts outside his company increase, there is a corresponding increase in the extent to which he feels caught between the demands of the outsiders and the requirements of his own management.[5]

Public relations practitioners working with media are a perfect example of boundary spanners caught between the demands of editors and reporters on one hand and their own management on the other. While management may wish to make a statement in a particular way or release only selected bits of information, public relations practitioners, knowing the demands of media personnel, will be forced to argue the position of reporters or editors against their own bosses. Bosses well may inquire, "Which side are you on?" Then, when practitioners present the information to reporters or editors, the response may well be, "This stuff is self-serving—whose side are you on?" Public relations practitioners in this situation must seek harmony between the needs and values of their constituents. Their paychecks may depend on it.

Public Communication   The process of public or mass communication is closely related to interpersonal and organizational communication. As Paul Lazarfeld points out, "The closer one observes the working of the mass media, the more it turns out that their effects depend on a complex network of specialized personal and social influences."[6] Research on public communication has been carried on for about fifty years. In the early period, it was assumed that mass media acted like hypodermic needles, injecting messages into members of the public who would then respond in particular ways. We now know that mass communication is a far more complicated process. Since 1930, many models of mass communication have been developed, only to be proven inaccurate or overly simplistic. It is clear, however, that public communication is a multi-step, multi-directional process. We know that messages move through complex networks of active transmitters who select, distort, amplify, or otherwise affect messages in passing them on. We also know that the meanings ascribed to messages by members of the public (and indeed whether these messages will be perceived at all) depend upon those who receive them.

It should be clear by now that the communication process can be viewed from several perspectives. To fully appreciate the process, it must be considered from individual, interpersonal, organizational, interorganizational, and public viewpoints. Like Jerry Koehler and his colleagues, we come to see communication as:

Putting It All Together

> The internal and external processes by which all of the organization's informing, adjusting, and coordinating activities take place in a dense network of signals and responses, actions, and reactions, effects and countereffects . . . (embracing) the ongoing exchange of information, opinion and attitude by which adjustments are made as required in order to coordinate activities within the organization and interface effectively with the exterior environment.[7]

Through individual and organizational interaction, communication builds upon itself in a continuous stream. Senders and receivers are transmission stations; messages and meanings are the currency of the ongoing system of coadaption by which society and its organizations are sustained.

An organization's image is a composite of people's attitudes and beliefs about the organization. Images cannot be communicated directly. They are built over time, developed through the cumulative effect of many messages. Such messages, which take many forms, are frequently not transmitted intentionally. The image of an organization is formed in the minds of customers, citizens, employees, volunteers, investors, or regulators, not simply through the official statements of the organization, but through all of its activities.

Communicating Images

Of course, all formal organizations attempt to document their public images for people inside and outside their boundaries. Budgets, media releases, advertising, even corporate architecture and interior decor are planned and executed with the organizational image in mind. But as public relations veteran Robert Ross points out:

> The quality of performance communicates eloquently . . . interest or lack of interest in the quality of work and in the customer. . . . Good management or poor management and a host of other things (communicate) more eloquently than words can.[8]

In many cases, it is not what a person hears or reads but what she or he actually experiences that determines a particular image. The image of oil companies as price-gouging profitmongers in the second half of 1979 was not a function of ranting politicians or raving mass media. *Time* magazine and other media went to great lengths to explain why oil industry actions and profits were justified. Noted economists made substantially the same point in national television, as did oil industry executives on televised news clips of congressional hearings. But many people said, in effect: "Don't confuse me with the facts." Their minds were made up by their experiences at the gasoline station, where the cost of filling the tank had doubled. William Weston makes the point very well:

> When institutions encounter hostile attitudes or find support melting away, it is not necessarily because their constituents and others don't understand what they are hearing. It is also possible that they don't like what they are experiencing. The way people experience an institution has its origins in the institution's policies, which are in turn grounded in purpose.[9]

All actions, all products, all pronouncements by an organization generate messages that contribute to people's perceptions of it. These, in turn, are products of organizational policy based on organizational purpose. With so many variables involved, how can organizations hope to manage the process of communication?

Managing Communication

Managing information and communication is a responsibility of executives or supervisors at every level of an organization. As David K. Berlo suggests, "Management of information systems has become one of the central competencies needed in modern society."[10]

Organizational communication researchers R. V. Farace, P. R. Monge, and H. M. Russell propose creating the specialized position of communication manager within organizations. They describe the position as follows:

> In general, the communication manager should be located at the center of the message flow in the organization. This means that the manager has knowledge of all important types of message flow. . . . By operating in or near the center of the organization's message flow, the manager is able to serve as a bridge or liaison to the other units in the organization.[11]

As management generalist or communication specialist, a communication manager assumes at least four specific roles: gatekeeper, liaison, opinion leader, and external boundary spanner.[12]

Gatekeepers are people who are positioned within a communication network so as to control the messages flowing through channels. They can filter, screen, block, or modify messages and determine the overall volume of message flow. Public relations practitioners function as gatekeepers when they determine what and how much information will be transmitted to various external or internal publics, including management itself.

Liaisons are linking pins that connect two or more groups within the organizational communication network. In this role, communication managers integrate the various parts of the overall system. They help different groups develop shared expectations. Public relations practitioners consistently play this role within organizations, bringing together, for example, the functions of advertising or consumer affairs with those of marketing and production.

Opinion leaders are those who often, formally or informally, influence other people's attitudes or actions. Public relations professionals not only seek to influence opinion leaders, but may act as opinion leaders themselves within an organization. In fulfilling this role, communication managers facilitate decision making. They may exert some control in selecting actions consistent with the goals of the organization. Public relations practitioners frequently take this role on issues related to social responsibility or organizational responses to public opinion.

The external boundary spanner, as we discussed previously in this chapter, relates the organizational system to its environment. Thus, the communication manager assesses the behavior of the organization in relation to its environment, assesses the environment to provide direction for the organization, and generally provides the means by which an organization can adapt to meet public expectations.

Public Relations and Organizational Communication

As we seek to understand the responsibility of public relations for organizational communication, we must regard it in terms of all the roles discussed above. As gatekeepers, public relations managers must evaluate and anticipate the effect of every proposed policy or plan and implement action in relation to each organizational public. They can do this because of their experience as external boundary spanners. As liaisons, public relations people help various groups produce coordinated, purposeful action. As opinion leaders, they influence the creation of organizational policy and strategy.

A Conference Board survey of major corporations showed that these functions are served in practice as well as in theory. Phyllis McGrath, who produced the survey report, suggested the following categories:

1. *Advice and counsel* Internal consulting to operating and functional units and the chief executive.
2. *Service* Conceiving, conducting, and carrying out programs relating to various corporate publics.
3. *Control* Involvement in formulation of policy and guidelines that determine the corporation's relations with its various publics, as well as monitoring the implementation of such policy and guidelines.[13]

Figure 3.6
Interdepartmental
coordination—Panhandle
Eastern Pipeline Company

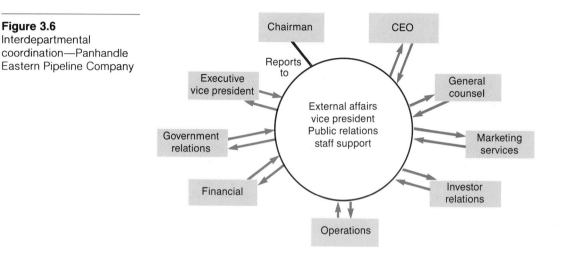

The reality of these functions is also demonstrated by corporate descriptions of the role of public relations manager. Figure 3.6 shows how Panhandle Eastern Pipeline Company conceives the role of its chief communications officer. Centrality, interaction, and influence on all organizational functions is the clear message of this diagram.

The following is a job description for General Telephone and Electric's (GTE) chief communications officer, the vice president–public affairs.[14] It also stresses the functions of evaluating environments, counseling management, developing and communicating policy, and assuring effectiveness.

Job description for GTE Vice President–Public Affairs

1. Identifying and evaluating current situations and future trends having major public affairs implications for the overall organization.
2. Advising and counseling management on methods for acting upon these situations and trends.
3. Developing formal statements of policy on various public affairs matters, and assuring adequate communication of the approved policies throughout the organization.
4. Developing specific programs and procedures to implement these policies.
5. Auditing and reviewing the effectiveness of these activities to assure their maximum possible and practicable effectiveness.

The attitudes and ideas held toward an organization by those who interact with it in any capacity are the result of all the complex interactions between the organization and its environment. This is the arena where public relations is practiced, where its activities are defined, and where its contributions are counted.

Communication is as natural to humans as breathing. But although we breathe alone, we communicate together—complicating the process.

To understand the communications process and to communicate better, we put aside certain common sense notions and adopt a systems approach. This helps us, as individuals and as public relations practitioners, to analyze communication systems and effectively manage them.

Public relations practitioners deal with communication on all levels—individual, interpersonal, organizational, interorganizational, and public—to transmit information and images. They serve in various capacities toward these ends, including as gatekeepers, liaisons, opinion leaders, and boundary spanners. As such, public relations professionals provide advice and counsel, conceive and conduct programs relating to an organization's publics, and help develop policy and guidelines for dealing with various publics.

Summary

▲ ▲ ▲

Case Study

The Difference between Public Relations and Journalism

By Melvin L. Sharpe
Ball State University
Muncie, Indiana

Public relations practitioners must understand the basic messages an organization is seeking to project, and develop corresponding news-information programs designed to maintain and contribute to an organization's image. The importance of this to successful media relations is all too frequently overlooked.

Communication management can maintain sound media relations through well-planned programs. Such programs provide access by the media to information and information sources within the organization. They identify and define goals and objectives clearly understood by top management as well as the media relations staff. Finally, these programs establish a schedule for media releases so that practitioners' time can be best used and media acceptance (and public awareness) can increase.

Achievement of the goals and objectives in a sound communications management program is not measured in terms of news space, but in terms of increased public awareness and understanding of the organization.

The importance of the mutual understanding of communication goals and objectives by an organization's top management and its media relations staff became clear when a major southeastern state university found itself under increasing criticism by black students for what they viewed as inadequate efforts for recruitment of black students and faculty. University administrators readily agreed that more needed to be done, but they were also aware that much had been done, that the faculty and the administration shared a commitment to progress in that area, and that progress had been made in spite of funding limitations. Therefore, the university's information officer was instructed to develop a series of feature articles designed to inform the public as to the steps the university had taken and was taking to improve recruitment efforts. Although the information officer was a competent journalist, he failed to understand or explain to the staff member to whom the task was assigned that the objective of the articles was to show the "progress" the university had made in its minority recruitment. Instead, the articles approached the subject from the students' point of view as well as that of the university. The coverage was defended as an attempt to present both sides of the issue.

Although balancing news is a major responsibility of the press, the university's objectives should have been to educate the public about the progress achieved. The media would have been responsible for including the opposing view. The articles were never used, the information officer was replaced because of his inability to attune his media relations program to the organization's goal and image objectives, and black student unrest increased. Accurate information might have helped to create a climate for positive progress and dialogue without disruption.

Questions

1. How do the responsibilities of media reporters differ from those of the media relations staff of an organization?

2. In a period of economic recession, "stability" could be an important message to project to employees, stockholders, the business community, and the public. Make a list of the types of news and feature stories that a media relations program might include in order to project an image of stability, provided, of course, that the facts exist to support the image projection.

3. Using simple one- or two-word descriptions such as "stability," "progress," and "achievement," develop a list of other messages an organization may need and want to project. Agreement on the part of management and an understanding on the part of the media relations staff as to the emphasis and importance to be given each message projection during a given year will result in the focus needed for the development or maintenance of a sound media relations program.

Notes

1. Robert Hopper, *Human Message Systems* (New York: Harper & Row, 1976), 25–30.
2. Bonnie Johnson, *Communication: The Process of Organizing* (Boston: Allyn & Bacon, 1977), 227.
3. Gerald H. Goldhaber, *Organizational Communication* (Dubuque, IA: Wm. C. Brown Publishers, 1986), 11.
4. D. Katz and R. Kahn, *The Social Psychology of Organizations* (New York: John Wiley and Sons, 1978).
5. D. Kahn et al., *Organizational Stress* (New York: John Wiley, 1964), 103.
6. P. Lazarfeld and H. Menzel, "Mass Media and Personal Influence," in *Science of Human Communication*, Wilbur Schramm, ed. (New York: Basic Books, 1963), 95.
7. J. W. Koehler, K. W. E. Anatol, and R. L. Applbaum, *Organizational Communication* (New York: Holt, Rinehart and Winston, 1981), 6–7.
8. R. D. Ross, *The Management of Public Relations,* (New York: John Wiley and Sons, 1977), 111.
9. W. W. Weston, "Public Relations: Trustee of a Free Society," *Public Relations Review* (Fall 1975): 12.
10. David K. Berlo, "The Context for Communication" in *Communication and Behavior,* J. Hanneman and W. J. McEwen, eds. (Reading, MA: Addison-Wesley, 1975), 10.
11. R. V. Farace, P. R. Monge, and H. M. Russell, *Communicating and Organizing* (Reading, MA: Addison-Wesley, 1977): 252.
12. S. Rogers and R. Agrwala-Rogers, *Communication in Organizations* (New York: The Free Press, 1976): 132–133.
13. Phyllis S. McGrath, *Managing Corporate External Relations: Changing Perspectives and Responses,* (New York: The Conference Board, 1976), 54–55.
14. Ibid., 56–57.

▲ ▲ ▲

CHAPTER 4

Public Relations in Organizational Decision Making

Preview

To play a serious role in organizational decision making, public relations practitioners must: gain management support and understanding; be more than technicians by broadening their knowledge, interests, and perspectives; learn to think like managers while retaining an independent perspective; and become issue-oriented.

Issues management is a process by which organizations can have a voice in influencing public policy. It is also a way by which public relations staffers can play a more effective role in their organizations' decisions.

▲ ▲ ▲

Throughout this book, we stress that the contribution of public relations to organizational decision making is among its most important functions. We do not claim that public relations practitioners actually make the decisions that determine organizational purpose, direction, coordination, and control. We do maintain, however, that all managers can and should take public relations considerations into account when making decisions, and that public relations practitioners can and should make direct contributions to fundamental organizational decisions. As Donald M. Wilson, corporate vice president of public affairs at Time, Inc., puts it: "More attention is being paid to public relations by the boardrooms and top executive suites . . . I think the profession will slowly, steadily influence more policy decisions as years go by."[1]

In chapter 3, we discussed the public relations roles of gatekeeper, liaison, and external boundary spanner. All of these provide the organization with information and insight essential to its decision making. We noted that the public relations specialist as an opinion leader directly facilitates decision making within organizational systems and helps provide organizational direction. We also described how public relations practitioners represent the public interest and predict public reaction to organizational decisions. By active participation in managerial decision making, public relations people can gain the commitment and understanding necessary for effective communication.

In future chapters, we will discuss how the contributions of public relations to organizational decision making affect employee relations, local community opinion, financial activities, and dealings with the government.

In a sense, then, this chapter is a pivotal one in the book. It deals with decision making, which is the essence of the managerial process, and with the position of public relations in that process. The chapter explains the role and function of public relations in organizational decision making. It discusses the nature of public relations inputs and the constraints on those inputs. It tells how public relations can be most influential in organizational decision making.

Staff and Line: Where Public Relations Fits in Decision Making

The most common type of organizational structure is called **line organization.** In its most basic form, it can be thought of as a sequence of ascending levels of responsibility connected by direct vertical links. All functions and activities are directly involved in producing goods or services. Line structures can be found in churches, charities, museums, and not-for-profit clinics, as well as business organizations.

As line organizations grow in size, however, various specialists are added, creating a line and staff organization. These **staff** functions provide advice and support to line management and are designed to contribute to the efficiency and maintenance of the organization. Staff functions might include research and development, personnel management and training, accounting, legal services, and public relations.

As a staff function, public relations must be supportive of management. The entire reason for the existence of public relations is to help create an environment of public opinion in which management can function. It provides counsel which management may ignore or consider, follow or reject. Part of being an effective adviser, however, is taking actions to assure that your advice is heard, heeded, and frequently acted upon. In this way, public relations makes its contribution to organizational objectives and prosperity and earns management's support. Bob Thompson, public relations director of Spring Mills, Inc., points to the bottom line: "In the end, public relations in an organization is what top management says it is."[2]

The current need for public relations to become more thoroughly integrated into the organizational decision-making process cannot be questioned. Government agencies at all levels retrench in the face of new fiscal limitations. Hospitals struggle with regulations, rising costs, new technologies, and changing customer demands. Arts organizations seek new sources of funds. Businesses deal with global competition, economic conditions, and a skeptical public. Successful managers in today's environments are those who maintain "a high batting average in accurately assessing the forces that determine the most appropriate behavior at any given time . . . and in actually being able to behave accordingly."[3] The contributions of a public relations specialist often enable managers to assess such forces accurately.

The Importance of Public Relations in Organizational Decision Making

Even the initiation of organizational decision making can depend on public relations input. "The organizational decision-making process is activated when information is received indicating changes in an organization's internal or external environment calling for an organizational response."[4] Information gathered by the public relations staff can promote the organization's ability to adapt to changing political, social, economic, and cultural conditions. "Public relations should occupy one of the most strategic positions in the organizational structure," James N. Sites explains, "if for no other reason than that it sits squarely astride the communication channels that are absolutely vital to the effective operation of an organization."[5]

Chief executive officers of major corporations are well aware that public relations contributes to decision making. Consider their statements:

> *Walter Wriston, Citibank former chairman* "The principal mission of the public affairs departments . . . is to make sure that when senior officers make important business decisions they do so with a clear understanding of how their action or inaction is likely to be perceived by the public. . . . Our director of public affairs . . . attends all meetings of our senior management policy committee."
>
> *Thomas Murphy, General Motors former chairman* "The public relations staff is charged with two-way responsibility at GM: determining and explaining public demands on the corporation to management; and the more usual job of communicating corporate policy and positions to the public."

James F. Bere, Borg-Warner chief executive officer "Traditionally, the emphasis of (public relations) has been on image, on public esteem, using one-directional media-based techniques. Now it has to shift to being a key function of managing in order to improve the direct returns of the business."

William E. Wall, Kansas Power and Light president "The best public relations person is impotent and wasted unless used and supported by the company. The way to do this is to bring public relations to the heights of management, where public relations advice can be regularly and easily inserted into the development and evolution of the company's policies and practices. The public relations executive can't explain, interpret or defend company policy unless he has seen it at its conception and birth, and participated in both."

To blend public relations goals with organizational goals, public relations information must be part-and-parcel of the organizational decision-making process, and must include intelligence regarding likely reaction and response by relevant publics. Moreover, the commitment and understanding that come through participating in organizational decision making are invaluable assets when communicating decisions to the organization's publics. Perhaps the most important task of public relations is to ensure the public relations-mindedness of management officials so that public relations considerations are in the mainstream of managerial decision making.

Entering the Management Mainstream

Acknowledging the importance of public relations in organizational decision making is one thing. Ensuring that public relations is part of the management mainstream is quite another.[6] To make public relations an effective part of an organization's decision-making process and to be taken seriously in a decision-making role, the public relations practitioner must observe five interrelated steps:

1. Gain management support and understanding.
2. Be more than a technician.
3. Broaden personal knowledge, interests, and perspectives.
4. Learn to think like a manager while retaining an independent perspective.
5. Become issue-oriented.

Gaining Management Support

"Early in his career every public relations practitioner finds to his surprise—and often distress—that he must . . . communicate . . . with those key centers of influence and power within his own organization."[7] Management is one of the key publics for public relations. Like that of any other public, the support of management must be earned. Like those of any other audience, management's needs, wants, attitudes, values, and perceptions must be considered.

The public relations function cannot be taken as a given by those who practice it, for management generally does not view the communications function in that light. Traditionally, public relations has been first on the budgetary chopping block, precisely because management has not perceived it as essential to long-term organizational health. Only in the recession in the early 1980s did this tendency begin to fade. Tom Ruddell, former president of the International Association of Business Communicators (IABC), explained in 1982: "In past recessions public relations and communication departments were too often the first to suffer from staff and budget cuts. This time management seems to be getting the message that communication is a necessity, not a luxury."[8]

Like all other staff specialists within organizations, public relations practitioners must be prepared to explain and justify their existence to managers, and to convince them that public relations "is an investment in the privilege to operate . . . perhaps more an investment in the future than an operating expenditure for the present."[9] Most importantly, public relations can influence organizational action by demonstrating the ability to produce results in accordance with the organization's goals. An example of this ability is shown in Mini-Case 4.1.

Mini-Case 4.1

Communication Improves Silicon Wafer Quality at Monsanto

Monsanto Company's electronics division held a comfortable leadership role in the production of silicon wafers for many years. Suddenly, the company was being challenged by aggressive Japanese and German manufacturers who said their products offered superior quality.

Silicon wafers are used by producers of electronic chips for computers, videogames, and digital watches. The manufacturing process is very labor-intensive, and quality control is critical. The product can be rejected for as little as a stray fingerprint or a speck of dust.

The problem was defined: How can Monsanto Electronics achieve and maintain the highest possible quality level? The answer: Develop in the employees, who are scattered in widely separated geographic areas, a single-minded dedication to a consistently high level of quality.

The challenge of achieving that goal was turned over to John Mason, Monsanto's corporate communications director. Mason explains:

Our department at Monsanto tries to avoid concentrating on the traditional aspects of communications—such as the production of magazines, newsletters and videotapes. We use them but don't stress them. Instead, we offer ourselves to various divisions and departments as internal corporate communications consultants. The traditional approach is to say communications can increase employee involvement, thus leading to productivity gains. We say communications can help produce a product superior to that of the competition.

In response to the need for quality improvement in silicon wafer production, Monsanto's corporate communications department developed a communications program to be used with groups and one-on-one. Video, print, feedback, and recognition methods were employed. Mason insisted on two provisions: that the communications department be held accountable for measurable results and that once started, the program be turned over to the electronics division, freeing communications for new projects.

After its first year, the silicon wafer communications project reduced late shipments from 3 percent to 2½ percent. Moreover, $200,000 was saved in reworks and penalties.

Mason concludes: "I am convinced that we can use communications to produce business results. However, you must look for opportunities to inject yourself into a business decision—don't wait around to be asked."

Source: Based on "Communicating for Bottom Line Results," a talk delivered by John Mason, Monsanto's corporate communications director, at the International Association of Business Communicator's International Conference, Atlanta, Georgia, May 4, 1983.

Assembly line for computer fans. Each step of the process must be carefully coordinated. Only effective communication can achieve this type of organization.

Many communicators conceive of themselves as communicators first, last, and always. They think of their relationship to management in terms of, "Tell me what you want to say and I'll tell you how to say it." Communication skills are essential to effective public relations. But an attitude like that just described simply encourages management to think of public relations as a tool with which to implement policy rather than as a crucial part of the policy-making process.

Whether holding the title "staff writer," "editor," "speechwriter," or "audiovisual specialist," a public relations practitioner must learn to think of the role as more than a technician and the job as more than a communication medium. A writer writes, but a public relations practitioner helps solve problems. An editor reacts to management requests, but a public relations practitioner helps diagnose problems and opportunities while planning solutions and strategies. Writers and editors are typically concerned with the content and techniques of communication; public relations practitioners are concerned with the results. As one public relations professional put it, "Be an architect, not a bricklayer."

The two differing perspectives will lead individuals working in public relations jobs to ask different questions in the performance of their duties, to seek different insights, and ultimately, to offer different kinds of programs and solutions. One reacts, the other anticipates. One responds to decisions after they are made, the other is an essential part of decision making.

Communication consultant Ron Weiser tells of an incident that illustrates this distinction. Early in his career, when he was an editor at a factory in Pennsylvania, Weiser was told to communicate a change in safety policy to plant employees. Everyone in the plant would have to wear safety glasses at all times and in all locations. Instead of simply writing a memo to announce the change, Weiser started asking questions. Why everyone? Why everywhere? How was the policy decided? What prompted the change? What was management's objective? The answers he received demonstrated clearly that management had not really thought the policy through—that the main consideration was ease in administering the rule.

Management then decided to rethink the policy and invited Weiser to help out. The newly formulated policy required safety glasses in areas of the plant where specific hazards justified the requirement. Instead of a memo, a six-week, multimedia program introduced the change. The policy was implemented smoothly, and Weiser gained the respect of management and was allowed to take part in future decisions.

Being more than a technician earns the public relations practitioner management's respect. According to management consultant R. Edward Freeman, the communicator who sticks with traditional tools is in potential jeopardy. "Armed with the traditional weapons of the vitriolic press release, the annual report, a slick videotape, corporate philanthropy, etc., today's PR manager is a sacrificial lamb. . . ."[10]

Being More than a Technician

Public relations practitioner
presenting problem/
opportunity alternatives to
organization members.

Broadening
Knowledge

To be valuable to management in a decision-making role, the public relations practitioner must have the appropriate knowledge, background, interests, and perspectives. Public relations practitioners, no matter what their training or background, must learn everything they can about business and government in general; the specific industry (or areas) in which their corporation (or agency) operates; and the organization itself. To be successful, public relations practitioners should know the functions, viewpoints, and problems of all parts of the organization. They should know its products, markets, internal structures, and external social, economic, and political pressures.

More than any other executives except the chief executive officer, public relations people must understand what is going on inside the organization and how all activities and functions interrelate. They must do their homework and know the why, who, what, where, when, and how of whatever comes up for managerial consideration. They should also be prepared to present and evaluate a variety of alternatives and contingencies related to organizational problems and opportunities.

Increasingly, practitioners must learn about fields that would have seemed unrelated to public relations a few years ago. Required reading may include anything from archaeology to zoology. Drawing on such knowledge, the public relations practitioner is in a position to contribute creative ideas and sound judgment in clarifying and accomplishing organizational objectives.

In order to influence management, public relations practitioners must learn to understand the managerial point of view, realizing at the same time that the greatest asset for public relations in decision making is its access to viewpoints not traditionally included in managerial deliberations. In other words, the public relations practitioner must think in terms of results, accountability, and accomplishments necessary to achieve organizational objectives while retaining a broader perspective that considers social as well as economic variables.

Thinking Like a Manager

Former *Fortune* editor Max Ways points to what he calls the "danger inherent in any kind of concentrated framework of decision." He explains:

> "The public" cannot decide . . . where to put a paper mill. For that decision special competence in pursuit of narrowly defined goals is necessary. Yet if this power is not somehow related to interests outside the framework of competent action, the results will reflect a larger incompetence.[11]

To use Ways' example, the public relations practitioner involved in deciding where to locate a paper mill must understand the economic and geographic considerations of such a decision. But he or she must also understand social considerations, such as displacement of existing houses and pollution of waterways. Moreover, the practitioner must effectively communicate those concerns to other decision makers. If such issues are not resolved early in the process, a mill could be built on a site judged appropriate by economic criteria, only to be prevented from operating by community protests.

Similarly, when planning communication strategy, managers are often faced with the question of how truthful and open they wish to be about a given matter. In such circumstances, the public relations practitioner who does not think like a manager typically will counsel openness, honesty, and the people's right to know. In short order, such individuals are labeled "Johnny-one-notes" who really do not understand the big picture. Their advice and counsel are rejected as impractical or preachy.

The public relations practitioner who thinks like a manager seeks the same goals of openness and honesty, but takes a different approach. Instead of preaching, he or she helps management weigh the pragmatic risks of communicating or not communicating. By pointing out the costs and benefits that could result, this practitioner is much more likely to provide constructive and acceptable advice, to retain credibility in a decision-making role, and to steer the organization toward the course of openness and honesty.

William W. Weston, public relations director of Sun Company, has observed, "How well the public relations practitioner succeeds in retaining some distance and objectivity, resisting the almost irresistible pull toward total absorption into the view of the world held by the leadership of his institution, will critically affect his ability to be truly useful."[12]

All of this suggests that effective public relations practitioners who take part in organizational decision making must frequently tell their executives what they do not want to hear. They must ask hard, probing questions and raise points that may not have been considered. To do so takes a certain amount of assertiveness and guts. It is a role that, while essential, may certainly lead to alienation and ineffectiveness if it is not tempered by understanding of managerial thinking and commitment to organizational goals.

Becoming
Issue-Oriented

Developing a broadened base of knowledge and perspective helps elevate public relations to a central role in identifying and managing the key issues that confront an organization. Issues management is an important means of integrating public relations into organizational planning and operations. The management of issues involves identifying controversies early, ranking issues in terms of importance to the organization, developing policy related to issues, developing programs to carry out policies, implementing programs, communicating with appropriate publics about organizational policies and programs, and evaluating the results of such efforts.[13] Issues may range from ethical standards for organizational behavior to energy conservation, from solid waste disposal to immigration policy.

Spring Mills board chairman H. W. Close explains:

> Meeting issues head-on is perhaps the biggest challenge facing management today. . . . If misunderstandings about the motives for business damage our freedom to run our businesses in the best interests of everyone concerned, then we won't be in business long and everyone loses. That's why this area of issue identification and response is so important. And it's why top management is looking to public relations pros for assistance.[14]

Public relations practitioners must develop the formal and informal research skills necessary to survey their organizations' internal and external environments. Such surveys help determine what issues their organizations must confront and how those issues can be successfully dealt with. Each organization must determine for itself which issues are most crucial at any given time. The issues management process, however, is an area in which public relations can make one of its greatest contributions to managerial decision making.

W. Howard Chase is given credit for coining the term issues management. One of the nation's leading public relations practitioners, he sees issues management as "the highway by which public relations professionals can move even more significantly into full participation in management decision making."[15]

Issues management grows out of the same reality and recognition that lead organizations to practice public relations in the first place. Organizations have been blind-sided for too long by protest groups who gain public support by striking public chords through protests or other tactics. To avoid unpleasant surprises, organizations should scan, monitor, and track external forces. These forces must be analyzed in terms of their effects on an organization's image, profit, and ability to act. Based on that analysis, an organization's policy must be developed, strategy planned, and action implemented.

The issues management process initially serves as an early warning system. Much like the rangers who man spotter stations in our nation's forests, the idea is to locate the "smoke" and take action before a major "fire" develops. In this way, the organization has a better opportuinity to shape, rather than react to public discourse and decision making.

The term issues management can be slightly misleading. No one can manage issues in a free society. Organizations, however, can manage their own actions and statements in relation to public issues. They can determine which issues to become involved in, and when and how to make statements or take action. Like marketing, issues management is an effort to manage an organization so that it can effectively interact with its changing external environment. In short, it is the systematic coordination of an institution's efforts to participate in the public policy process.

In 1970, General Motors established a Public Policy Committee to produce reports on matters of public concern. This pioneering effort in issues management was followed by others including AT&T's Emerging Issues Group (1977) and Aetna Life and Casualty Company's Public Policy Issues Analysis Department (1978). In 1982, the Issues Management Association was formed, and in the last few years, it has acquired more than four hundred members.

What are issues? An issue is a problem, question, or choice being faced. A *public issue* is a problem, question, or choice being faced by society or some segment of society which involves actual or potential governmental action. When public issues impact on an organization's investments, operations, or ability to act, that organization needs to become actively involved with those issues.

Public issues may involve a particular company, as when Minute Maid was accused of taking advantage of migrant labor. More often, issues affect specific industrial categories, such as the chemical industry. An example of one company's response to such an issue is illustrated in Mini-Case 4.2. Perhaps most common, however, are issues of general concern affecting organizations across the spectrum. Such issues include environmentalism, consumerism, unionism, feminism, energy, health and safety, human resources, productivity, and the list goes on.

Issues Management

Pillsbury Keeps Its
Products Healthy

Mini-Case 4.2

In early 1984, a chemical called ethylene dibromide (EDB) was identified as a potential carcinogen. Used as a pesticide in grain fields, traces of EDB were discovered in several grain-based products.

Pillsbury Company was surprised by how quickly and strongly the public reacted to EDB. Industry-wide, over one hundred grain-based products were withdrawn from grocery stores or called into question by health officials. Pillsbury pulled six batches of its products off the shelves. Moreover, EDB cost the company literally thousands of staff hours in management energy and worry. Twelve Pillsbury researchers normally assigned to product development worked six days a week to test the EDB level in company products and raw materials.

Warned by the EDB scare, Pillsbury geared up to ensure that it would not be caught flat-footed again. "We fully expect that behind EDB there will be other chemicals that will get serious public attention," said Gerald Olson, vice president for government relations. In response, the company has now established a task force to catalog and study all pesticides, cleansers, and other chemicals used in its facilities. The idea is to spot the next EDB before it becomes a public issue.

Pillsbury's concerns are well-founded. The government approved the use of EDB thirty years ago, when scientists using instruments that measured parts-per-million could not find any of the substance in food. However, today's instruments, measuring in parts-per-billion, did find traces of the potential cancer causer. The Pillsbury company has since decided not to rely on federal approval of chemicals, but to make its own judgments.

"The worst thing that can happen in this industry is to have someone question the safety of your products," said Rebecca K. Roloff, head of the group coordinating Pillsbury's EDB response. If the company's task force is successful, Pillsbury will not have to respond again—or if it must, it will be prepared to do so.

Source: Based on Betsy Morris, "Pillsbury Co. Tries to Spot the Next EDB," *Wall Street Journal* (23 March 1984):1.

Trenton (NJ) demonstrators protesting nuclear power. Public issues can frequently override organizational and governmental policy.

The issues management process consists of five steps: identification, analysis, strategy, action, and evaluation.

Identification   When identifying issues, organizations use various methods to scan the external environment for potential areas of threat or opportunity. An issue should be identified in the earliest stages of its life cycle—while still unnoticed or of only awakening interest to others. If an issue is not dealt with until it has reached the crisis stage, efforts to influence society's resolution of the problem often prove futile.

The initial identification effort usually points out in excess of one hundred issues that might have impact on a given organization. Issues can be generated in a number of ways, including media scanning, polling of the public or special publics, or use of consultants. Alcoa, for example, explores issues considered important by governmental, academic, and activist organizations. John Naisbett, author of *MegaTrends,* gained his fortune by helping organizations identify and track important trends.

Analysis   Issue analysis is the second step of the issues management process. In this phase, priorities are set by determining an issue's potential and publics. Obviously, organizations cannot effectively manage hundreds of issues at one time. The list must be narrowed to five or ten of the most important. The importance of an issue is determined by its timing and impact. To establish priorities, six questions must be asked:

1. How quickly will this issue unfold?
2. How will it impact our products and operations?
3. How likely is it that this issue will come to fruition?
4. How would our stakeholders expect us to act in relation to this issue?
5. What is our ability to have an impact on this issue?
6. What are the costs of not dealing with the issue?

Ultimately, the organization seeks to determine whether a given issue potentially impacts its success or survival. Those issues with the greatest bottom line impact should be given the most attention.

Different organizations view and prioritize different issues in different ways. Environmental issues may threaten midwestern coal-burning electric utility plants, but present opportunities to companies in scientific waste disposal. The debate over the effects of cigarette smoke on nonsmokers may affect work practices in a bank, but impact the ability of a tobacco company to sell its product.

Strategy   The third step in issues management, developing strategy, is usually accomplished by a committee that includes top management and others in areas affected by the issue. Based on input by those affected and those who would be involved in implementing the organization's response, position papers and plans are developed by staff subject to the approval of senior executives.

Action   An organization's action program is an orchestrated, integrated response to the issue of concern. A campaign is developed and implemented which coordinates the efforts of lobbyists, media relations, general management, advertising, employee communications, and whatever other organizational units need to be included. While some efforts are of relatively short duration, many represent substantial commitments of energy and resources over time.

Evaluation   Evaluation, the final step in the issues management process, seeks to determine the effectiveness and impact of the program. Evaluation may help establish how long the program should continue or whether changes need to be made.

Summary

In this chapter, we have looked at how public relations specialists fit into the organizational decision-making process. We have pointed out that they are playing an increasingly important role in all areas of organizational decision making, particularly through the issues management process.

As we continue through this book, we will consider the public relations practitioner as someone who does much more than write media releases or plan publicity stunts. The expanded role now includes harmonizing an organization with its environments by analyzing those environments, advising management and participating in decisions affecting all areas of organizational activity, as well as communicating with various corporate publics concerning policy, programs, activities, ideas, and images. In the fullest sense, public relations practitioners are not merely communication technicians. They are an integral part of the management team possessed with special skills, training, and sensitivities in the area of communication.

▲ ▲ ▲

Neighbors

By Dulcie Murdock
University of North Carolina
Chapel Hill, North Carolina

Case Study

You are public information director for a city mental health and mental retardation department. Your department plans to open a group home for eight mentally retarded adults. Group homes, in which a small number of clients live together with counselors, are designed to serve as an alternative to institutional living for some mentally retarded people. A house located in a middle-class subdivision was privately donated to the city for use as a group home. This is to be the first group home in your state; other states have been using the group home system for years, while still others have not begun community care programs.

The mentally retarded people (four men and four women) will live in the group home with a married couple who are trained counselors. All eight residents have full-time jobs in the city at places such as McDonald's. The money they earn working will go towards food bills, their clothing, and pocket money.

A few months ago, some general stories about the concept of group home care for mentally retarded people appeared in the local newspaper. One story contained a statement by the city director (your boss) that said a group home was planned in the city "at a future date." After this article appeared in the paper, the director received a few letters from citizens objecting to the idea of mentally retarded persons living in group homes. One concern was that property values would be lowered in neighborhoods where group homes were located.

The director, fearing negative reactions from residents in the neighborhood where the group home is to be located, tells you he wants to keep a low profile about the opening of the group home. In a memo, he tells you not to generate any publicity about the group home's opening. When the counselors and residents arrive at the group home a few days later to move in, they find hand-lettered signs posted on the trees in the yard, saying that they are not welcome in the neighborhood.

The counselors call the director, who calls you to say that something has to be done before the situation gets out of hand. He asks for your advice.

Questions

1. Do you think the city director made the right decision in deciding not to generate any publicity about the group home? What would you, as public information director, suggest be done now?
2. How would the situation have been different had the public information director been involved in the original decision rather than being brought in after the fact?

Notes

1. Quoted in Bill Hunter, "PR'84: Fourteen Experts Tell What's Ahead," *Communication World* (January 1984): 14.
2. H. W. Close, "Public Relations As a Management Function," *Public Relations Journal* (March 1980): 12.
3. R. Tannenbaum and W. H. Schmidt, "How to Choose a Leadership Pattern," *Harvard Business Review* (May–June 1973): 162–180.
4. O. W. Baskin and C. E. Aronoff, *Interpersonal Communication in Organizations* (Santa Monica, CA: Goodyear Publishing Co., 1980): 118.
5. James N. Sites, "Solving Problems That Keep Your Boss Awake at Night," *Public Relations Journal* (August 1974): 6.
6. The authors are indebted to Ron Weiser of the consulting firm Meidinger, Inc. for the phrase "management mainstream" and for some of the ideas contained in this section.
7. Sites, "Solving Problems," 5.
8. Quoted in "Communicators Outline Recession Strategies," *Communication World* (November 1982): 1.
9. Robert D. Ross, *The Management of Public Relations* (New York: John Wiley and Sons, 1977): 10.
10. R. Edward Freeman, *Strategic Management: A Stakeholder Approach* (Boston: Pitman, 1984): 221.
11. Hill and Knowlton Executives, "Critical Issues," *Public Relations* (Englewood Cliffs, NJ: Prentice-Hall, Inc., 1975): xxv.
12. William W. Weston, "Public Relations: Trustee of a Free Society," *Public Relations Review* (Fall 1975): 13.
13. R. P. Ewing, "Issues," *Public Relations Journal* (June 1980): 14–16.
14. Close, "Public Relations as a Management Function," 13.
15. W. H. Chase, "Adjusting to a Different Business/Social Climate," *Public Relations Quarterly* (Spring 1980): 24–26.

▲ ▲ ▲

CHAPTER 5

Ethics and Professionalism
Preview

Legal and ethical issues are closely related in public relations practice; however, they are not identical. Even when no violation of law can be proven, a practitioner can be sanctioned for unethical conduct under the code of the Public Relations Society of America (PRSA).

The history of public relations is filled with allegations and confirmations of unethical behavior. While this may be no different from any other profession, public relations practitioners are especially sensitive to any suggestion of misconduct. This sensitivity may stem from the fact that public relations is frequently called upon to be the source of ethical statements and policies for an organization.

To help provide guidance in ethical decisions, both PRSA and the International Association of Business Communicators (IABC) have established codes for ethical behavior. While both encourage professionals to demonstrate a commitment to ethical behavior, only PRSA has an enforcement procedure.

Ethical questions often arise in professional relationships with clients, news media, financial analysts, and others.

Increased professionalization is one possible answer to questions raised regarding ethical practice. However, even with the legislative force of licensure, ethical practice is still a function of individual behavior.

Unless you are willing to resign an account or a job over a matter of principle, it is no use to call yourself a member of the world's newest profession—for you are already a member of the world's oldest.

—Tommy Ross

Ethics is an area of particular concern for public relations for three reasons: (1) practitioners are aware that to some, public relations has a reputation for unethical behavior; (2) public relations is often the source of ethical statements from an organization and the repository of ethical and social policies; (3) practitioners have struggled to create a suitable **code of ethics** for themselves. As we shall discuss in this chapter, public relations practice is based on a foundation of trust. Members of the profession who violate that trust harm their colleagues as much as themselves.

The Challenge of
Ethical Practice

Public relations practitioners are very sensitive, even defensive, about allegations of unethical behavior. The term public relations is sometimes used, even today, as a synonym for lying, distortion, selective disclosure, or cover-ups. A *Wall Street Journal* article points to the ethical shortcomings of public relations, quoting the former public relations vice president for United Brands. "The more I thought about it, and the more I looked at events around me, the more certain I became that PR was helping to screw up the world," he said. "I could see the hand of the PR man pulling the strings, making things happen, covering things up. . . . Everywhere I looked it seemed as if image and style had taken the place of substance."[1]

Amelia Lobsenz, then co-chair of the Public Relations Society of America's National Task Force on Public Relations, responded to those comments in an article in the *Public Relations Journal*. She claimed that the article was one-sided, concentrating on the unethical practices of a handful of public relations persons who bowed to managerial pressure. To refute the charges, she cited a list of ethical corporate actions taken by organizations with the assistance of public relations practitioners.

Like any other group or profession, public relations has ethical as well as unethical practitioners. However, since public relations as a profession attempts to represent the public as well as the organization in business decision making, its practitioners are frequently held to a higher standard. The media and various publics will quickly point out deception in what might be considered normal behavior for members of other competitive businesses.

At the heart of any discussion of ethics in public relations are some deeply troubling questions for the individual practitioner. Some examples include: Will he or she—

Individual Ethics

1. Lie for a client or employer?
2. Engage in deception to collect information about another practitioner's clients?
3. Help conceal a hazardous condition or illegal act?

4. Provide information that presents only part of the truth?
5. Offer something (gift, travel, or information) to reporters or legislators that may compromise them?
6. Present true but misleading information in an interview or news conference that will mask some unpleasant fact?

Many public relations practitioners find themselves forced to respond to questions like these. Even though most report that they are seldom pressed to compromise their values, the questions are still asked. By conscientiously considering their ethical standards, practitioners can avoid difficult and embarrassing situations. Maintaining ethical standards is the key to establishing trust relationships with employees, employers, clients, media contacts, and others. Because of the importance of ethical behavior to the general practice of public relations, attempts have been made to impose **sanctions** against individuals who violate professional standards.

Practitioners believe it is generally unethical to criticize each others' actions publicly. When some public relations professionals spoke out against the Firestone Tire Company's stonewalling of accurate information about defective radial tires and others denounced conflicting statements that were released to the press during the Three Mile Island nuclear accident, they themselves were criticized. For example, both the *PR News* and the *Public Relations Journal* labeled Firestone's critics unprofessional.

The Public Relations Society of America has established a Code of Professional Standards for the Practice of Public Relations (see Exhibit 5.1). In general, this voluntary code calls for truth, accuracy, good taste, fairness, and responsibility to the public. The question of personal ethics, however, is less controversial than the general issue of business ethics. It is relatively easy to agree in abstract terms that individual professionals have a duty to behave ethically. Unfortunately, translating these abstract concepts into rules governing business practice in a competitive environment has not been so easy.

PRSA Code of Professional Standards for the Practice of Public Relations

Exhibit 5.1

Declaration of Principles

Members of the Public Relations Society of America base their professional principles on the fundamental value and dignity of the individual, holding that the free exercise of human rights, especially freedom of speech, freedom of assembly and freedom of the press, is essential to the practice of public relations.

In serving the interests of clients and employers, we dedicate ourselves to the goals of better communication, understanding and cooperation among the diverse individuals, groups and institutions of society, and of equal opportunity of employment in the public relations profession.

We pledge:

To conduct ourselves professionally, with truth, accuracy, fairness and responsibility to the public;

To improve our individual competence and advance the knowledge and proficiency of the profession through continuing research and education;

And to adhere to the articles of the Code of Professional Standards for the Practice of Public Relations as adopted by the governing Assembly of the Society.

Articles of the Code

These articles have been adopted by the Public Relations Society of America to promote and maintain high standards of public service and ethical conduct among its members.

1. A member shall deal fairly with clients or employers, past and present, or potential, with fellow practitioners and the general public.
2. A member shall conduct his or her professional life in accord with the public interest.
3. A member shall adhere to truth and accuracy and to generally accepted standards of good taste.
4. A member shall not represent conflicting or competing interests without the express consent of those involved, given after a full disclosure of the facts; nor place himself or herself in a position where the member's interest is or may be in conflict with a duty to a client, or others, without a full disclosure of such interests to all involved.
5. A member shall safeguard the confidences of present and former clients, as well as of those persons or entities who have disclosed confidences to a member in the context of communications relating to an anticipated professional relationship with such member, and shall not accept retainers or employment that may involve disclosing, using or offering to use such confidences to the disadvantage or prejudice of such present, former or potential clients or employers.
6. A member shall not engage in any practice which tends to corrupt the integrity of channels of communication or the processes of government.
7. A member shall not intentionally communicate false or misleading information and is obliged to use care to avoid communication of false or misleading information.
8. A member shall be prepared to identify publicly the name of the client or employer on whose behalf any public communication is made.
9. A member shall not make use of any individual or organization purporting to serve or represent an announced cause, or purporting to be independent or unbiased, but actually serving an undisclosed special or private interest of a member, client or employer.
10. A member shall not intentionally injure the professional reputation or practice of another practitioner. However, if a member has evidence that another member has been guilty of unethical, illegal or unfair practices, including those in violation of this Code, the member shall present the information promptly to the proper authorities of the Society for action in accordance with the procedure set forth in Article XII of the Bylaws.
11. A member called as a witness in a proceeding for the enforcement of this Code shall be bound to appear, unless excused for sufficient reason by the judicial panel.

12. A member, in performing services for a client or employer, shall not accept fees, commissions or any other valuable consideration from anyone other than the client or employer in connection with those services without the express consent of the client or employer, given after a full disclosure of the facts.
13. A member shall not guarantee the achievement of specified results beyond the member's direct control.
14. A member shall, as soon as possible, sever relations with any organization or individual if such relationship requires conduct contrary to the articles of this Code.

Business Ethics

Some practitioners have been arbitrarily fired for refusing to write news releases that they felt would be false and misleading. One practitioner worked for a company that wanted him to prepare and distribute a release listing company clients before the companies had signed a contract for services. The practitioner refused, believing that to comply would violate the PRSA code. He was fired, and he subsequently sued the company for unlawful dismissal, receiving almost $100,000 in an out-of-court settlement.

The question of **whistle-blowing** has become significant in recent years. What is the correct response for an ethical practitioner when an employer or client refuses to exercise public responsibility? The PRSA Code of Ethics says he or she should quit. Some practitioners, however, believe more good can be accomplished by staying on to argue for more responsible action. Realistically, few practitioners can afford to quit, and therefore, choose to stay in the face of questionable activities. Out of frustration, they become whistle-blowers. That is, they secretly inform the media about an irresponsible action in order to bring public pressure on the organization. Although whistle-blowing can stop the unethical practice, it usually costs the person involved his or her job in the long run. Thus, the decision to quit is a more direct means to the same end.

Another public relations professional resigned after initially participating in several ethically questionable practices with a multinational fruit conglomerate. He charged the company with the manipulation of press coverage as well as with political and military action involving a Latin American country where it was operating. The increased attention that many corporations are paying to the ethical dimensions of their businesses can be traced back to Watergate and Koreagate. These major national scandals were followed in 1975 by an investigation that revealed dozens of United States companies had made payments to government officials in foreign countries in order to gain lucrative contracts. The Lockheed Aircraft Corporation was the most publicized among more than four hundred firms eventually admitting such practices. Opinion polls soon after the scandal revealed that Americans felt only about 20 percent of business executives had high ethical standards. Most observers believe that these revelations were significantly related to the erosion of public confidence in American business and its leaders.

A 1986 study conducted by one of the authors requested copies of the ethics policies of each of the Fortune 500 companies. Four hundred twenty-one organizations responded with ethics procedures ranging from one to forty-seven pages in length. Most not only affirmed the corporation's intent to do business in an ethical manner but also provided for dismissal of employees who violated the policy. However, closer examination of these documents revealed a tendency to rely on legal rather than ethical standards. Some Fortune 500 companies and other firms are providing ethics training for their managers and other employees. Companies increasingly are using outside consultants or panels to systematically examine the social and ethical implications of impending decisions. Some also use an internal expert or ethics committee to review major decisions.

According to David Finn, public relations may perform the role of keeping management in line. "When functioning well, (public relations) acts as the anvil against which management's moral problems can be hammered. When executives are establishing a public relations policy for their organization," Finn maintains, "they are really concerned with significant ethical questions."[2]

When public relations practitioners participate in organizational decisions, they carry a heavy ethical responsibility. Their responsibilities are not only to themselves and their organizations, but to their profession and the public as well. All these considerations must be weighed when helping make organizational decisions and communicating decisions once they are made.

The examples cited here illustrate the fact that ethical behavior is ultimately an individual decision. Professional codes, corporate policy, and even law are unable to ensure the ethical practice of any profession. Only the application of sound personal values can guarantee ethical behavior. However, professional codes, sound business policies, and appropriate legislation can serve as valuable guidelines for public relations practitioners who desire to maintain a high ethical standard.

Perhaps the most critical relationships to be managed by public relations practitioners are those with the news media. Here, anything less than total honesty will destroy credibility and with it, the practitioner's usefulness to an employer or client. All news media depend upon public relations sources for much of the information they convey to viewers, readers, and listeners (see chapter 10). Although public relations releases are sometimes used simply as leads from which to develop stories, at other times, reporters and editors rely upon the accuracy and thoroughness of public relations copy and use it with little change.

Trust is the foundation of all public relations practice and can be achieved only through ethical performance. Therefore, providing junkets for the press that have doubtful news value, throwing extravagant parties, giving expensive

Ethical Dealings with News Media

gifts, and doing personal favors will ultimately destroy a practitioner's effectiveness. Even if journalists ask for favors, the ethical public relations professional must find a way to tactfully decline. In the long run, establishing a reputation for honesty and integrity will yield dividends in media relations.

Some practitioners are tempted to regard themselves as mere employees or contractors hired to do a job. This technician mentality cannot be used to excuse unethical behavior like that reported in the *Wall Street Journal* on September 13, 1984. The story described how a well known public relations firm distributed a press packet to the media on behalf of Jartran, Inc. Included in the packet was a letter offering information about wheels falling off trucks owned by a rival company. A reporter questioned the ethics of this technique and was told by an account executive for the firm, "It was their idea. We're merely the PR firm that represents them." Such short-sighted and misguided practices harm the credibility of the entire profession.

Although several studies have consistently shown that public relations practitioners and journalists have similar professional values and make similar news judgments, the same studies show that journalists strongly believe public relations practitioners do not have professional values. The unwillingness of a few practitioners to uphold ethical standards could be the reason these misconceptions persist.

Ethics and Laws

While ethical and legal issues frequently evolve from similar circumstances, the public relations professional must understand the difference. Keeping to the letter of the law does not guarantee ethical action. Many unethical claims and promotions have been structured to stay within the legal limits, even though their intent was to trick or deceive someone. While an understanding of the law is important, a professional must rely on a higher standard for decision making.

Public relations practitioners working for publicly held companies have both an ethical and a legal obligation to promptly release news about dividends, earnings, new products, mergers, and other developments that might affect the value of securities. A delay in releasing such news could allow insiders to derive unfair financial benefits. The Securities and Exchange Commission and the individual stock exchanges strictly enforce these regulations.

Corporations are also prohibited from using public relations techniques in connection with the sale of new issues of securities (see chapter 14). Public relations personnel must be thoroughly aware of Federal Trade Commission and Food and Drug Administration regulations regarding the promotion of a product or service. Such practices as unsubstantiated claims, fraudulent testimonials, deceptive pricing, so-called independent surveys, and rigged contests are regulated through these agencies.

James Grunig and Todd Hunt list five characteristics of a professional group.[3] As a relatively young profession, public relations has made remarkable progress in each area. However, there is still a need to do more and to encourage others to accept these norms:

Establishing Standards for a Developing Profession

1. *A set of professional values* In particular, professionals believe that serving others is more important than their own economic gain. Professionals also strongly value autonomy.

2. *Membership in strong professional organizations* Professional organizations provide professionals with the contact with other professionals that they need to maintain an allegiance to the profession.

3. *Adherence to professional norms* True professions have a code of ethics and a procedure for enforcing it.

4. *An intellectual tradition and an established body of knowledge* A profession must have a unique and well-established body of knowledge.

5. *Technical skills acquired through professional training* Professionals should have the technical skills needed to provide a unique and essential service.

As Grunig and Hunt indicate, true professions have strong professional organizations with codes of ethics and the ability to prohibit those who violate the code from practicing the profession. Public relations has several professional organizations, and most have codes of ethics. However, no one central organization can control access to the practice. Therefore, enforcement of these codes has been difficult and the effects of sanctions that can be imposed are questionable.

Ethical Codes

The IABC Code   The International Association of Business Communicators (IABC) has a code that is quite brief and basically states that the professional should be committed to ethical behavior:

> As a communicator concerned with maintaining the highest ideals of ethical performance among the members of IABC and others in this field, I agree to practice and promote the following professional objectives:
>
> To achieve maximum credibility by communicating honestly—conveying information candidly.
>
> To respect the individual's rights to privacy as well as protect confidential information and its sources.
>
> By the practice and promotion of these basic objectives, I hope to foster improved ethical awareness and importance to business and other organizational communication.

The PRSA Code   The code of the Public Relations Society of America is the most detailed and comprehensive in the field. When PRSA was founded in 1948, one of its first actions was to develop a code of ethics so that members would have some common behavioral guidelines and managers would have a clear understanding of their standards. This code became the tool used to distinguish professionals in public relations from shady promoters and publicists who had been quick to appropriate the term public relations to describe their activities.

The PRSA Code was adopted in 1954 and revised in 1959, 1963, 1977, and 1983.

It is most explicit in defining proper relations with news media and government bodies by requiring practitioners to:

1. Present truthful information and divulge their clients.
2. Maintain proper competitive relationships with other practitioners seeking the same accounts or working for competing organizations.
3. Refrain from guaranteeing specific results, such as the placement of an article that is beyond the practitioner's direct control.

Because the PRSA Code seeks to establish specific standards for the practice, it must be changed periodically to address new problems. In 1963, revisions were designed to toughen the standards for financial public relations after an investigation by the Securities and Exchange Commission resulted in a public revelation of the corrupt actions of some practitioners. In 1977, under the threat of antitrust litigation by the Federal Trade Commission, certain provisions of the code barring contingency fees and banning one member's encroaching upon another member's clients were changed. This revision of the code also removed sexist concepts and language from the document.

In 1983, Articles 1 and 5 of the code were revised to cover potential as well as past and present clients. This was the result of a grievance board hearing about a practitioner's disclosure of a potential client's plans to a competitor.

As the result of a scandal involving the newly elected president of the society who was charged with insider trading and violations of a client's confidence, the code was revised again in 1986. This revision gives the ethics board more freedom to communicate its actions and those of members who resign before their cases can be considered. The need for this change was made apparent when a front-page story in the September 26, 1986, issue of the *Wall Street Journal* revealed to many PRSA members for the first time the resignation under fire of their president.[4]

Enforcing the PRSA Code   Complaints against PRSA members can be filed with the National Grievance Board or with a judicial panel in one of PRSA's nine national districts. If evidence of violations is found, charges are filed with one of the district judicial panels and a hearing is held.

The board of directors reviews the district panel's findings and makes the final decision to **censure,** suspend, or expel a member. However, it would be illegal for the society to attempt to punish a member through publicity or to condemn nonmembers for unethical practice. Exhibit 5.2 summarizes the judicial process of PRSA.

The articles of the PRSA Code most often cited according to a 1987 study funded by the Foundation for Public Relations Research and Education are (in order of frequency):[5]

Article 1 A member shall deal fairly with clients or employers, past, present and potential, with fellow practitioners and the general public.

Article 3 A member shall adhere to truth and accuracy and to generally accepted standards of good taste.

Article 2 A member shall conduct his or her professional life in accord with the public interest.

Article 7 A member shall not intentionally communicate false or misleading information, and is obligated to use care to avoid communication of false or misleading information.

Article 6 A member shall not engage in any practice that tends to corrupt the integrity of the channels of communication or the processes of government.

Exhibit 5.2

Summary of PRSA's
Judicial Process

Filing a Complaint with the Ethics Board

A complaint can be brought to the attention of the Board of Ethics and Professional Standards by a nonmember as well as a member. In addition, the Board of Ethics may also act upon a possible violation by a member disclosed in the media or through other public sources.

How the Ethics Board Functions

The Board of Ethics acts somewhat as a Grand Jury by investigating the matter and deciding whether or not to file charges against a member. If the Board of Ethics decides not to bring charges, it may warn the member that his conduct is not appropriate and ask the member to immediately desist. For minor violations, the Board of Ethics may decide that the matter does not warrant the expenditure of time and money required to conduct a complete investigation. In such cases, the member is notified in writing to cease the violation and is requested to confirm to the Board within 30 days that the violation has ceased.

How a Judicial Panel Functions

The Board of Ethics files charges with the Judicial Panel where the member holds his principal chapter membership. But the respondent may request a change of venue. The Judicial Panel holds a hearing, with the complainant being the Board of Ethics. The respondent (accused member) presents his defense at the hearing. The Judicial Panel makes a recommendation to the Board of Directors on one of the following courses of action: dismissal, warning, admonishment, reprimand, censure, suspension, expulsion.

A complaint can be brought directly to the attention of a Judicial Panel by a member or nonmember. If the complainant requests it and the Judicial Panel agrees, the Board of Ethics will be substituted as the complainant. If not, the Board of Ethics may still participate in the proceedings.

The Case Goes to the Board of Directors

The Board of Directors determines whether or not to accept the recommendation of the Judicial Panel after considering written statements by the complainant and respondent supporting or contesting the Judicial Panel's determination. The respondent may ask the Board of Directors for a hearing. The Board may remand the case to the Judicial Panel for additional evidence.

The Board is obligated to give notice to members and may make public an action of censure, suspension, or expulsion. It may or may not make public a warning, admonishment, or reprimand.

The Board of Directors is authorized to make public the resignation of a member under investigation by the Board of Ethics or a Judicial Panel.

If a member is convicted of a felony or misdemeanor in a criminal court, the matter may be referred directly to the Board of Directors without Judicial Panel action.

The Board of Directors, on the recommendation of the Ethics Board, has approved a proposed Bylaws amendment giving the Board of Directors the authority to immediately suspend any member convicted in a criminal court. Under the proposed Bylaws change, the member so suspended may ask for an immediate hearing before the Board of Directors.

According to PRSA's bylaws, all proceedings of the panel, the Board of Ethics and Professional Standards, and of the Board of Directors shall be confidential and in closed sessions.

The same study shows that since 1952, some of the most frequent issues brought before the grievance board and judicial panels, in order of their frequency, include:

1. Indictments in court/Investigations by government agencies for conspiracy, suppressing information, failing to register as a foreign agent (12)
2. Misleading press releases (10)
3. Soliciting another member's client (9)
4. Setting up front organizations to release information (7)
5. Making derogatory remarks against a public relations professional, agency, or profession in general (5)
6. Setting up a front organization (4)
7. Improper use of the APR trademark (3)
8. Issuing false statements about stock (3)
9. Income tax evasion (3)
10. Guaranteeing specific results (2)

By 1987, the society had reprimanded three members, censured three, suspended two, and expelled two. Six others, including a newly elected national president, resigned their memberships before action could be taken. In seventeen other cases, the charges were dropped because of insufficient evidence or other circumstances that made it impossible to pursue the inquiry.

Because professional organizations do not have the force of law behind their codes of practice, enforcement becomes a difficult problem. The investigation of charges independent of those who make them is an expensive process most organizations cannot afford. Moreover, the legal and ethical responsibility to avoid damage to someone's reputation and livelihood without cause requires that any group proceed cautiously in the enforcement of a code of practice. The American Society of Newspaper Editors encountered so many legal problems and other difficulties in its attempts to censure members that it suspended further enforcement attempts soon after its code of ethics was adopted in 1923.

Guidelines for Ethical Practice

As we said earlier in this chapter, codes, policies, and even laws are not the answer to achieving ethical practice in public relations. Only the individual professional can ensure his or her ethical behavior. Those who exemplify the best of any profession develop a personal philosophy that allows them to deal with individual cases as they occur.

Chester Burger, president of a New York-based management consulting firm, revealed his own philosophy in a *Public Relations Journal* article concerning ethics in public relations. The statements below are a capsule of what he learned during a newspaper reporting and public relations career spanning more than four decades:

Lesson 1 Communicators must trust the common sense of their audience. More often than not, the public will justify our trust by seeing accurately the issues and the contenders and the motivations. Communicators should not use clever headlines, gimmicks, distortions, or lies to communicate effectively. Don't underestimate the public's perceptiveness.

Lesson 2 People generally will know or care very little about the issues that concern you. You've got to inform, to clarify, to simplify issues in a truthful manner, and in ways that will relate to the self interest of your audience.

Lesson 3 Don't compromise your own ethical standards for anyone. Don't take the easy way out. Don't say what you don't really believe, and don't do for the sake of expediency what you think is wrong. It ain't worth it. Ask yourself how your action would look if it were reported tomorrow on the front page of your local newspaper. Who would absolve you from the responsibility if you said you wrote it or said it because your boss told you to?

Lesson 4 Choices for communicators between right and wrong are rarely black or white, yes or no. Questions of ethics involve degrees, nuances, differing viewpoints. Too many times in my life have I been wrong to feel sure that I know the right answer. A bit of uncertainty and humility sometimes is appropriate in considering ethical questions.[6]

*The Question
of Licensure*

Some believe codes of behavior will lack wholly effective means of enforcement until practitioners become legally certified. Controlled access has become the hallmark of a recognized profession. Therefore, controlled access, through **licensure,** to the title of "certified public relations counselor" is viewed as the only way to separate the frauds and flacks from legitimate practitioners.

Proposals that public relations be licensed were discussed before PRSA was founded. Proponents such as Edward L. Bernays, who was instrumental in formulating the modern concept of public relations (see chapter 2), believe that licensing can protect the profession and the public from incompetent practitioners.

Those who argue for licensure believe it is the only effective method of enforcing professional standards, but efforts to impose such standards have been highly controversial. The Public Relations Society of America has commissioned several studies on the subject of licensure but has never endorsed it. Even if licensure were to be implemented, many practitioners would probably not be affected because they work in corporate departments. In the legal and accounting professions, many trained practitioners never sit for their bar or CPA examinations because they do not have to represent their firms in official capacities. Thus, licensing standards would probably not result in significant change.

Both PRSA and IABC have accreditation programs for experienced practitioners who pass a comprehensive examination. These programs are the closest anyone has come to licensing procedures. Less than one-half the memberships of both associations are accredited.

The issue of ethical practice in public relations is closely tied to efforts toward accreditation and licensure. While no amount of testing or education can guarantee ethical behavior by an individual, the potential removal of accreditation or a license can give professional codes of practice more leverage. By promoting professional responsibility and recognition, public relations organizations can encourage ethical behavior and awareness by their members.

Summary

Ethical questions arise frequently for public relations professionals during the course of their daily business with clients, the media, and others. In addition, practitioners are often called upon to be the source of ethical statements on behalf of the organizations they represent. Thus, public relations professionals are especially sensitive to any suggestion of misconduct.

To encourage commitment to ethical standards, both PRSA and IABC have established codes for ethical behavior, and PRSA has set up an enforcement procedure as well. Some believe that practitioners would be further influenced to abide by ethical standards if they were required to become legally certified, but licensure is still a controversial issue and has not been implemented. Codes, policies, and laws alone cannot achieve ethical standards; the ultimate responsibility lies with each individual practitioner.

▲ ▲ ▲

Case Study

Sometimes, in everyday practice, situations arise where the proper thing, the ethical thing, even the legal thing to do is not always immediately clear. Following are several such situations.

1. A well-known athlete is charged with selling drugs and planning and carrying out, with others, the death of a young married couple. His attorney calls you, a close friend, to advise and assist him in handling the intense media interest in the case. During the period before trial, you learn that the athlete was, in fact, a drug dealer and did participate in the murder. The lawyer tells you that the information is privileged. You decide to await the outcome of the trial. The lawyer is able to get his client acquitted. What should you do?

2. Your firm is one of six under consideration by a manufacturer planning to introduce a new service into your area. You are given confidential information as to the service and the plans of the company. You are aware that the company will face severe opposition from certain groups and politicians, and that the job will entail overcoming this resistance. Your firm is turned down by the company and the assignment is given to a competitor. Can you disclose the information you have learned to the manufacturer's opposition in your area?

3. Your public relations firm publishes a newsletter directed to brokerage houses. A corporate executive asks your help in making his company better known among the brokerage community. A subsequent issue of the newsletter carries a highly optimistic forecast of the company but omits some information. Nothing in the story indicates any relationship between you and the company. Were you under any obligation to disclose this relationship, and should you print a retraction?

4. You are a corporate public relations director. Your employer tells you to set up a supposedly independent organization to introduce and promote the use of a new product made by your company. This new organization is to be financed secretly by your company and some of its suppliers. Is there anything wrong with establishing this organization?

5. A distributor of medicinal products arranges with your firm to put on a press conference for an independent British scientist who has tested the products and written favorably about them. You also arrange speaking engagements for the visiting scientist. After the press conference, you learn that the scientist was actually an employee of the research arm of the manufacturer of the products. What actions should you take?

6. A client asks you for help in a financial merger situation. You decline because the matter is outside your expertise, and refer the company to a fellow practitioner who is knowledgeable in financial affairs. The fellow practitioner is so appreciative he sends you a check for $500. Can you accept the money without telling the client?

Critical Incidents: The Practical Side of Ethics

By Donald B. McCammond, APR
Chairman, Board of Ethics
Public Relations Society of America

7. One of your clients calls you to assist in a takeover situation. You tell a friend who had originally helped you get the client. Several days later, your friend buys 5,000 shares in one of the companies involved in the takeover. You do not buy any yourself. The day after the merger announcement, your friend sells the shares, at a profit of $15 a share and a total profit of $75,000. Are you guilty of insider trading, even if you made no profit?

8. Your employer asks you to give a series of talks in communities served by your company regarding its new plant and the service it will provide. On a visit to the plant to acquaint yourself with its operation, you get clear evidence that it cannot fulfill the expectations outlined in the talk prepared by your company. Can you give the talks as originally prepared?

Questions

1. Which articles of the PRSA Code (Exhibit 5.1) apply to each incident description?
2. List the ethical questions involved in each.
3. Describe any legal questions raised by these incidents.

Source: *Public Relations Journal* (January 1987): 7.

Notes

1. J. Montgomery, "The Image Makers," *The Wall Street Journal* (August 1, 1978): 1.
2. David Finn, "Struggle for Ethics in Public," *Harvard Business Review* (January–February 1959): 9–11.
3. James E. Grunig and Todd Hunt, *Managing Public Relations* (New York: Holt, Rinehart and Winston, 1984), 66.
4. Joanne Lipman, "PR Society Receives Some Bad PR from Ex-Chief Anthony Franco," *The Wall Street Journal* (September 26, 1986): 1.
5. Donald McCammond, "Ethics and Standards Study," an unpublished report prepared for the Foundation for Public Relations Research and Education, 1987.
6. Chester Burger, *Public Relations Journal* (December 1982).

▲ ▲ ▲

PART II

Public Relations: The Process

It isn't enough just to know what public relations is and what purposes it serves. To practice public relations, one must understand the process by which it operates. As we have already discussed, public relations goes far beyond the task of producing messages. An effective public relations effort is the result of mutual understanding between an organization and its publics. The development of this understanding can be regarded as a four-step process:

1. *Research* An initial fact-finding stage defines the problem areas and differentiates between publics.
2. *Planning* Once the facts have been gathered from the various publics, decisions must be made regarding their importance and potential impact on the organization. Then, strategies must be developed to enable the organization to achieve its goals.
3. *Action and Communication* Strategies are implemented in the form of new organizational policies and/or projects. Messages are then constructed to reach target publics.
4. *Evaluation* Once a public relations campaign has been developed and implemented, it should be followed by an evaluation of its effectiveness in meeting the criteria that were set. The results of the evaluation are used both to assess the effectiveness of the effort and to plan future action. For open system responses, evaluation information becomes a self-correction mechanism; feedback of this type allows plans to be fine-tuned as they are being carried out. The results of closed system evaluations should be stored for use in similar projects in the future.

These four steps are essential to any effective public relations campaign. They are not, however, four independent functions. Each step overlaps the others; if any one of them is neglected, the entire process will be affected. The next four chapters will discuss each of these steps in detail. To help you keep in mind the interdependence of the steps, an integrating case study will open each chapter. The case of Cedar Springs Community Hospital will illustrate a complete public relations project as it progresses through each stage, from research through evaluation. You may find it useful to turn back and review the previous case segments as you read through the next four chapters.

▲ ▲ ▲

Research: Understanding Public Opinion

Preview

R esearch is an important part of the public relations process. Information gained through careful research can be used to guide planning, pretest messages, evaluate results, and guide follow-up efforts.

Effective research techniques for public relations practice include both formal and informal methods.

The use of research data to evaluate current practice and forecast future events is well accepted in most organizations today. Public relations practitioners must be able to evaluate their efforts and demonstrate effectiveness.

Good public opinion research must be sensitive enough to identify publics as definable groups rather than as unrelated masses.

Public relations audits, social audits, communication audits, and environmental monitoring are effective research methods for public relations planning and evaluation.

Research is a vitally important function in the process of public relations. It provides the initial information necessary to plan public relations action and perform the important role of evaluating its effectiveness. No longer can public relations practitioners rely on their hunches and past experience to tell them what communication messages and strategies will be most effective. Management demands hard facts, not intuition or guesswork. Public relations practitioners, like their colleagues in every area of management, must be able to demonstrate convincingly their contribution to organizational goals and objectives. The economic realities of modern organizations have made it necessary for public relations to incorporate data gathering techniques into every phase of the process. The Cedar Springs Hospital case study which follows shows how a public relations effort can utilize research in identifying and dealing with an organizational problem.

The Need for
Research in Public
Relations

Integrating Case Study

Cedar Springs
Community Hospital

Segment 1

Problem Identification

The Cedar Springs Community Hospital, Inc. was formed by the merger of two formerly competing hospitals. Two years later, a new management team was brought in to help resolve concerns about the ability of the newly formed hospital to serve the needs of its patients. Soon after the new administrator and his seven assistants had assumed their duties, they began to hear reports of low employee morale and declining quality in patient care. Much of this input came from physicians who felt that the changes since the merger had produced an environment that was more routine and less personal. Many doctors felt that their relationships with other hospital employees had been undermined by the new organization's attempts to eliminate duplication and build a more efficient structure. In general, the growing consensus among the physicians was that the quality of patient care had significantly declined since the merger.

Informal and Secondary Research

Because physicians are a significant public for any hospital, their concerns received immediate attention from management. The physicians had suggested mounting a campaign to make employees more aware of their responsibility for providing quality patient care. However, the public relations director felt that more information was needed in the form of **secondary research** before an effective communication campaign could be planned. Therefore, he began to look into the background of the merger and the relationships between hospital employees and the medical staff.

A careful review of hospital records and local newspaper files, plus conversations with several long-time employees, revealed the complexity of the situation. Not only had the hospitals formerly been competitors, but they had also originally been founded by two very different religious groups and thus had developed two distinct constituencies. Although the religious affiliations of both hospitals had been discontinued long before the merger, an atmosphere of rivalry remained. This rivalry had been most obvious during a period when the hospitals had attempted to outdo one another in terms of benefits for physicians.

Primary Research

One important public, physicians, clearly believed the quality of patient care was not acceptable. However, employees' and patients' views were not as easily defined. The public relations department devised a **primary research** plan to measure the opinions of each group. A random sample of hospital employees was asked to fill out a questionnaire about various aspects of patient care. Simultaneously, a telephone survey was conducted among recently released patients to gauge their opinions on the same issues. The results were surprising.

On a scale ranging from 1 (poor) to 10 (excellent), employees rated the hospital's performance a disappointing 6.6 overall. However, the survey of former patients produced an overall rating of 8.5. Other questions related to the quality of patient care also received significantly lower marks from the employees than from the patients.

Qualitative Research

In an effort to understand the reasons for the low ratings given by employees, a focus group was assembled to respond to the survey findings. This five-member panel was composed of three representatives from nursing services and one each from ancillary, support, and business services. They were interviewed as a group concerning their responses to the questionnaire. The interview revealed that while employees believed that the hospital in general delivered mediocre patient care, they felt that the care in their specific areas was significantly better than in the rest of the hospital and that they, personally, were slightly above average within their departments. These employees also indicated that their coworkers sensed something was wrong in the organization, but were not sure what. This led to feelings of individual helplessness and produced a high level of stress and frustration.

In the Cedar Springs case, what originally seemed like a rather straightforward employee communication problem was found to be a complex situation involving three important publics. Research showed the physicians' concerns to be overblown. Had the Cedar Springs management acted on the physicians' original recommendation without doing further research, the situation would have just gotten worse, increasing employee frustration and stress.

As you read about the different types of research methods public relations practitioners employ, refer back to this segment and notice how several of the techniques were applied. A quick comparison of the Cedar Springs case

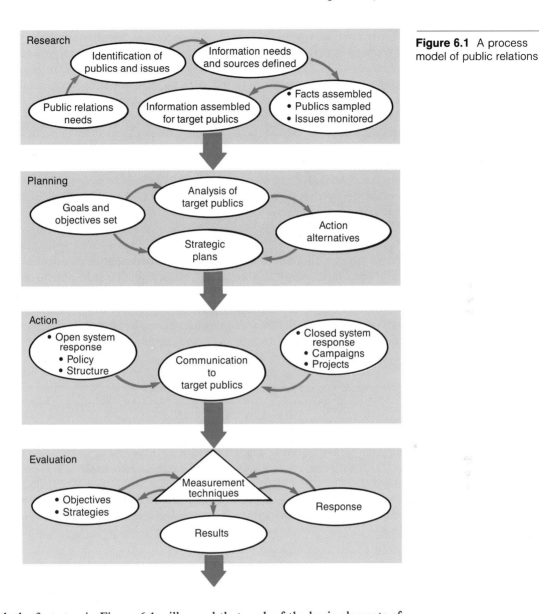

Figure 6.1 A process model of public relations

with the first step in Figure 6.1 will reveal that each of the basic elements of research is present in this example. The surprising nature of the findings in this case illustrates the need for research in public relations.

Because public relations professionals have traditionally been doers rather than researchers, they often assume that others see the value of their function. That assumption places public relations necks squarely on budgetary chopping blocks. Even when economic conditions are not critical, public relations may

Proving the Worth of Public Relations

be perceived as window dressing. Media, regulatory agencies, consumer groups, and many managers doubt that public relations has a useful purpose in American business. Typically, public relations professionals have responded by claiming that they contribute to better understanding between publics and organizations. But they do not present tangible evidence of this contribution. When the Cobb County (GA) Chamber of Commerce went to the city council with a request for $100,000 to promote tourism, they took the council members out to dinner and made an appeal based on generalities. The council agreed to provide $10,000. While the chamber was disappointed, communication chairman Dave Kaplan was circumspect. "We'll have to spend that $10,000 on something that gives us measurable results," he said. "Then we'll come back next year and show them what we can accomplish."

Public relations practitioners must be able to speak with authority when asked to prove their value to business and society. This authority can only come through an ability to conduct research and apply the results to public relations campaigns. Public relations professionals must be able to maintain good media relations, produce employee publications, release financial information, and conduct community relations programs. But, in addition, those who succeed must also be able to measure the effects of their programs, provide sound forecasts of future needs, and account for the resources they consume.

An independent public relations counselor was seeking a new client. "What can you do for me?" asked the client.

"I can get you exposure," explained the public relations person. "I can get you speaking dates and get you in the newspaper."

"*I* can do that," said the person (who was rapidly becoming a less likely client). "What I need is someone to help me make money."

"That's marketing," said the public relations counselor. "I do public relations."

"You do nothing if you don't contribute to my bottom line," was the response. "All my expenditures make me money or they don't get made. No sale."

Informal Research Techniques

Research means gathering information. It can range from looking up the names of editors of weekly newspapers in Nebraska to polling those people to discover their opinions about farm export policy. Research is not always elaborate or highly structured. We want to begin this section by considering a few informal research methods and sources that practitioners use.

Record Keeping

One of the most important skills necessary to the successful practice of public relations is the ability to keep comprehensive and accurate records. Practitioners are frequently asked to produce critical information at a moment's notice for use inside and outside their organizations. Thus, when an editor or manager calls for information, the public relations practitioner must be able to produce the needed data within a relatively short time or suffer loss of credibility. By earning a reputation as a source of valuable information, the public relations practitioner can develop a network of internal and external information contacts.

Key Contacts

Frequently, individuals who are opinion leaders in the community, industry, or organization may act as **key contacts** for the public relations practitioner. Other people who possess special knowledge or who communicate frequently with significant publics are also good sources. For a community college, for example, key contacts would be significant business, political, student, and community leaders. While these individuals can provide valuable information, they may not represent the majority opinion. Because they are leaders or individuals with special knowledge, they must be regarded as nontypical of others in their group. Their special insight may give them a greater sensitivity to an issue than most people would have. Therefore, the practitioner must be careful not to overreact to feedback from these sources or plan major responses based solely upon such information. Key contacts are best used to provide early warning about issues that may become significant.

Special Committees

To help obtain necessary information, many public relations practitioners organize special committees. Internal and external committees of key communicators, decision makers, and opinion leaders can help identify issues before they become problems and suggest alternative courses of action. These advisory groups can be formed for a specified length of time, such as the duration of a campaign, or be permanent boards that replace members periodically.

Focus Groups

Qualitative research is an informal method of gaining an in-depth understanding of an audience without the rigor of more formal research methods. The most widely used technique for qualitative research is the **focus group.** As we saw in the Cedar Springs case, a focus group is a small number of people who are alike in terms of some demographic characteristic. Group members are interviewed, using open-ended questions to encourage interaction and probe the nature of their beliefs. Focus groups are generally assembled only once, and their responses are recorded on videotape or observed from behind a one-way mirror. This enables researchers to take into account not only what is said, but gestures, facial expressions, and other forms of nonverbal communication that may reveal depth of meaning.

Although ethical and legal considerations require researchers to inform focus groups that they are being recorded or observed, experience shows that participants are seldom reluctant to discuss their feelings. Frequently, people selected for focus groups are glad someone is willing to listen to them. Sometimes the process of asking can be just as valuable as the information gained because the organization is then perceived as being responsive to its publics.

Special committee formed
to focus on patient care
issue in a hospital.

Recently, Syracuse University used several focus groups composed of alumni to help plan a major fund-raising drive. The centerpiece for the campaign was to have been a promotional film stressing the scientific and research emphasis at the university. However, feedback from focus group participants revealed that such presentations turned them off. This realization prevented Syracuse from making a costly error in communication.

Casual Monitoring

Many practitioners find it helpful to systematically screen material that regularly comes through their offices. Monitoring news reports in both print and broadcast media should be done in a way that will allow consideration of the quality as well as quantity of coverage. Carefully tracking incoming mail, telephone calls, and sales reports can also provide valuable information. Like all information collected through informal research methods, however, these techniques have built-in biases because the data are not collected from representative samples of the target publics.

Formal Research Techniques

Library and Data Bank Sources

Public and private libraries can be sources of data that would be impossible for the practitioner to collect personally. Reference librarians can be helpful in finding information, and many libraries now subscribe to computerized data retrieval networks that can obtain information from anywhere in the world. Census data and other types of public information are available at libraries that have been designated as government depositories. In addition, a number of independent research organizations, such as the Survey Research Center at the University of Michigan, publish information that may be valuable to the public relations practitioner.

Media guides, trade and professional journals, and other reference books may prove useful in a public relations practitioner's personal library. Further sources that should be noted and can be valuable in researching a future employer or competing organization are:

Dun and Bradstreet Million Dollar Directory
Dun and Bradstreet Middle Market Directory
Standard and Poors' Register of Corporations, Directors, and
  Executives
Thomas' Register of American Manufacturers
Fortune Magazine's "Directory of Largest Corporations"
Fortune Magazine's "Annual Directory Issues"
Black Enterprise Magazine's "The Top 100"

As you read the next section, keep in mind that secondary sources such as those discussed here should be exhausted before a primary research effort is planned. Researchers should review the information available to make certain the questions to be asked have not already been answered by others.

Content analysis is a research method that allows the researcher to systematically code and thereby quantify the verbal content of written or transcribed messages. This technique provides a method of systematic observation for informal research efforts, such as the analysis of transcripts from focus groups. News clippings can be analyzed for quantity and quality of coverage. Many organizations analyze the contents of the annual reports and other publications of their competitors in order to discover strategic plans.

Content Analysis

While the practice of public relations in one way or another employs all types of research processes, the survey method is the most common. Cedar Springs Hospital used survey research to answer some critical questions. Laboratory and field experiments, as well as various types of simulations, can have a place (such as pretesting a message) in a public relations research effort. However, surveys are the most effective way to assess the characteristics of publics in a form that will allow the data to be used in planning and evaluating public relations efforts. Surveys should provide a means of separating publics rather than lumping them all together into one amorphous mass.

Survey Research

The term *survey,* as it is applied in public relations research, refers to careful, detailed examinations of the perception, attitudes, and opinions of members of various publics. The general purpose of a survey is to obtain a better understanding of the reactions and preferences of a specific public or publics. For public relations efforts, we divide survey data into two types: *demographic* and *opinion.* Demographic data are those characteristics (age, sex, occupation, etc.) of the people responding to the survey that help a practitioner classify them into one or more publics. Opinion data are responses to those questions a practitioner raises concerning the attitudes and perceptions of certain publics about critical issues.

*Experimental
Research*

Experimental research is generally divided into two categories: *laboratory* and *field experiments*. Laboratory experiments take place in carefully controlled environments designed to minimize outside effects. Field experiments take place in real-world settings. The trade-off between field and laboratory experiments is essentially one of authenticity versus purity.

In a field experiment, the researcher sacrifices a great deal of control over the setting in order to obtain reactions in a real environment. In a laboratory setting, however, the researcher can control many outside stimuli that might contaminate the results of the study. For example, a public relations practitioner might decide to pretest a particular message by inviting people into a room to view the message in several forms and then measuring their reactions. This method was used when a church foundation attempting to raise funds for a chaplain in a local cancer hospital tested the graphics and photographs in its brochure to avoid negative effects before publication. The laboratory setting ensured that the responses of the subjects were based on the message being studied and not on other stimuli that might be present in a normal environment. On the other hand, to test the effects of a message in a more authentic setting, a field experiment such as a test-market study could be arranged, using a specific group of people in their normal environment.

Collecting Formal Research Data

We have described several methods of research. Now we will look at ways to actually collect information.

*Descriptive and
Inferential Methods*

Formal research information can be obtained in a variety of ways which may be classified as either descriptive or inferential. **Descriptive data** are used to describe something, such as a particular group of people (a public). If the public relations practitioner in an organization asks the personnel department to prepare a demographic profile of its employees (average age, sex breakdown, years of education, experience level, etc.), he or she is requesting descriptive data. Such studies use averages, percentages, actual numbers, or other descriptive statistics to summarize the characteristics of a group or public.

Inferential data do more than describe the particular public from which they were collected. Inferential data describe (infer) the characteristics of people not included in the group from which the information was obtained. Through the process of sampling, which we will discuss later in this section, it is possible to select a relatively small number who represent a larger population. Using inferential statistics, a public relations practitioner can infer the characteristics of a very large public, such as a consumer group, from a relatively small but representative sample of that population.

*Methods for Obtaining
Information*

Whether the research is classified as descriptive or inferential, survey or experimental, and regardless of the sampling technique employed, the three basic means for collecting research data are *observations, interviews,* and *questionnaires.*

Lab-like pretest setting

Observational techniques are easily misused in public relations research because of the informal nature of many observations about publics. The personal observations of a practitioner are severely limited by his or her own perceptions, experiences and sensitivity. These problems can lead to decisions based more on gut feeling than on reliable information. Personal observations can be made more reliable through the use of structural techniques, as observers are trained within established rules to systematically observe and record data. However, this is normally an expensive and complex process.

Interviews can be a successful way to get information from a public. Skilled interviewers can elicit information that subjects might not otherwise volunteer. Interviews may occur in person as well as over the telephone, and are generally classified as structured or unstructured. Structured interviews use a schedule of questions with specific response choices ranging from yes/no to multiple choice; unstructured interviews allow subjects to respond to open-ended questions however they wish. Although interviews are frequently employed, they have disadvantages. For example, the personality, dress, and nonverbal cues of the interviewer may bias the response. To minimize such problems, it is necessary to use expertly trained interviewers, the cost of which can be prohibitive.

Questionnaires are the most common form of data collection because they are stable in presentation and inexpensive to use. Once a questionnaire has been printed, each subject will be asked the same questions in exactly the same way. Questionnaires are generally designed to measure one or more of the following: attitudes, opinions, and demographic characteristics of the

Many polls are taken in person by skilled interviewers.

sample. Figure 6.2 is an example of a questionnaire used to measure the effects of certain messages on the public images of political candidates. Note that it seeks information in all three categories.

The decision about whether to use a questionnaire or an interview in gathering data for public relations research must take into account the study's budget, purpose, subjects, and a variety of other considerations. Questionnaires can be sent in the mail and may be administered to either individuals or groups. They provide anonymity, and present a uniform stimulus to all subjects. On the other hand, interviews are more flexible, get a higher percentage of responses in some situations, and can be used with relatively uneducated publics.

Sampling Methods

A sample is a subset of a population or public. Public relations researchers use samples because in most instances, it is impractical to collect information from every person in the target public. There are numerous sampling techniques, but the best methods rely on the theory of probability to provide a miniature version of the target public. While the theory of probability is too complex to discuss here, it is the basis of all inferential statistics. The following sampling methods rely on the theory of probability to assure a sample that is representative of the public from which it is drawn.

Simple random sampling is a technique that allows each member of a public an equal chance of being selected. As long as the sample is large enough (some experts say at least thirty to sixty people) and is selected totally at random, it will accurately reflect the characteristics of its public. Probably the most common example of simple random sampling is drawing a name from a hat. If the slips of paper have been mixed up adequately, each slip has an equal chance of being selected at the time of the drawing.

Figure 6.2 Sample questionnaire used to measure effects of political advertisements on candidate images

INSTRUCTIONS—Please Read Carefully

We would like to know how you feel about the political candidates whose T.V. advertisements you are about to view. Please judge the candidates in terms of what the descriptive scales mean to you. There are, of course, no "right" or "wrong" answers and we urge you to be as accurate as possible in your ratings. Try to imagine yourself as a potential voter for each of the candidates when viewing the advertisements and checking the scales.

For purposes of illustration, suppose you were asked to evaluate John Doe using the "attractive-ugly" scale. If you judged him to be extremely "ugly" you would check the scale as follows:

___3___   Ugly ✓__:__:__:__:__:__ Attractive

If you judged him to be substantially "ethical," you would check the scale as follows: ___1___ Unethical __:__:__:__:✓__ Ethical

If you judged him to be moderately "harmful," you would check the scale as follows: ___2___ Beneficial __:__:__:✓__:__ Harmful

In the far left column please rank in order the three scales which mean the most to you in describing each candidate.

In summary.....

1. Be sure you mark every adjective-pair for all candidates. Never fill in more than one box on a single scale.

2. Make each item a separate and independent judgment.

3. Work at a fairly high speed through this survey; we want your first impressions—the way you actually feel at the present time toward the candidates.

(Do not write in spaces on right margin.)

___ ___ ___ ___
 1   2   3   4
       Sequence ID

Your response to *every* item is important to the success of this research.

Please check each of the items below:

Sex: _____ Male _____ Female   ___
                                                  5
Age (check one):

_____ 18-20 _____ 21-25 _____ 26-35 _____ over 35   ___
                                                      6
Are you a registered voter? _____ Yes _____ No   ___
                                                      7
How many local, state or national elections have you voted in since becoming eligible to vote?

_____ 1-2 _____ 3-5 _____ 6-10 _____ over 10   ___
                                                      8
Please indicate your political party preference:

_____ Democrat _____ Republican _____ Other   ___
                                                      9
Please indicate your parents' political party preference:

_____ Democrat _____ Republican _____ Other   ___
                                                     10
How strongly do you feel about the political party you prefer?

   Very   Not Very
Strongly __:__:__:__:__:__ Strongly   ___
                                                     11

___ ___ ___ ___
 1   2   3   4
___ ___ ___ ___ ___ ___ ___
 5   6   7   8   9   10   11

Rank Top 3 Here	John Olson-Republican		Do not write in this column
___ 26	Direct __:__:__:__:__:__	Evasive	___ 12
___ 27	Uninspiring __:__:__:__:__:__	Inspiring	___ 13
___ 28	Frightening __:__:__:__:__:__	Reassuring	___ 14
___ 29	Qualified for Political Office __:__:__:__:__:__	Not Qualified for Political Office	___ 15
___ 30	Ugly __:__:__:__:__:__	Attractive	___ 16
___ 31	Knowledgeable __:__:__:__:__:__	Ignorant	___ 17
___ 32	Beneficial __:__:__:__:__:__	Harmful	___ 18
___ 33	Ethical __:__:__:__:__:__	Unethical	___ 19
___ 34	Powerless __:__:__:__:__:__	Powerful	___ 20
___ 35	Genuine Image __:__:__:__:__:__	Artificial Image	___ 21
___ 36	Wrong Political Party __:__:__:__:__:__	Right Political Party	___ 22
___ 37	Our Kind of Man __:__:__:__:__:__	Not Our Kind of Man	___ 23
___ 38	Competent __:__:__:__:__:__	Incompetent	___ 24
___ 39	Represents the Interests of the Few __:__:__:__:__:__	Represents the Interests of the Many	___ 25
___ 40 ___ 41			

Systematic sampling uses a list, such as a telephone directory or mailing list, to select a sample at random. Generally, a table of random numbers is used to find a starting point on the list along with a selection interval. For example, a researcher might pick at random the number 293006 from a table of random numbers. Using the first three digits, the researcher could start on page 293 of the telephone directory; then, using the last three digits, he or she could select every sixth name for the sample. This method is more practical than simple random sampling in most public relations research.

Stratified random sampling is a two-stage process which first divides the public into two or more mutually exclusive categories (such as males and females) and then randomly selects samples from each stratum. This method is used to ensure that each subgroup of a particular public is adequately represented in the sample. For example, if a practitioner wanted information about all ethnic groups in a particular geographical area, it would be necessary to first divide the population into ethnic categories to make certain representatives from each group were included in the sample.

Cluster sampling involves the random selection of groups rather than individuals for a sample. For example, if we wanted to measure the attitudes of United Auto Workers members, we could randomly select local unions to include in our study rather than individual U.A.W. members.

Quota sampling randomly selects a fixed number of people from each of several distinguishable subsets of a public. For example, a researcher may decide to select fifty subjects from each of the following groups by sex and age, regardless of what proportion of the actual public they account for: males 18–25, males 26–40, males over 40, females 18–25, females 26–40, and females over 40. This would allow accurate assessments of the opinions of each subgroup.

Measuring Public Opinion

Most organizational goals and objectives dealing with public relations depend to some extent upon the concept of **public opinion.** Therefore, the first step in public relations research is to sample public opinion. It is important to understand at the outset that an organization does not have a single indistinguishable public. The public relations practitioner who relies on so-called public opinion polls to provide insight into the characteristics of his or her potential audience may be operating with erroneous data. Most polls of this type are not very useful from a public relations point of view, because they actually measure **mass opinion** rather than public opinion. Before using a survey, the practitioner should be aware of the difference between measuring mass opinion and measuring public opinion.

Mass Opinion

Mass opinion represents an average taken from a group with many different opinions. However, averages tend to blur the strength of some attitudes. When opinions that are substantially different are averaged together, the result may be very different from the original opinions stated. For example, if we conduct a poll asking people about the image of a particular organization, we might

The diversity of individuals in our society presents a unique challenge for the selection of target audience groups.

find that 60 percent of our sample give it very high marks while 40 percent feel very negative. Looking at the average of these responses, we might deduce that the organization in question has a moderately positive image; however, this would hide the substantial amount of negative feelings that exist.

Our hypothetical survey has actually uncovered two publics—one that has a very positive image of the organization and another that has a very negative image. In fact, no one in our sample holds the moderately positive view the average implies. To respond properly, we should construct communication strategies for two groups of people with very strong, but opposite opinions. Public relations must be concerned with the strength as well as the direction of public attitudes.

Many mass opinion polls are useful for little more than predicting political elections. They do not shed much light on the complexities of public opinion that an effective public relations program must address.

Public Opinion

Public opinion polls involve carefully targeted populations. The public relations professional must break the audience down into meaningful subgroups and design a specific communication campaign for each segment. Public opinion sampling is not useful unless it reflects accurately the feelings of each significant audience group and provides some insight into why these opinions are held.

Identifying Publics   John Dewey, in his 1927 book *The Public and its Problems,* defines a public as a group of people who:

1. Face a similar indeterminate situation.
2. Recognize what is indeterminate in that situation.
3. Organize to do something about the problem.[1]

A public, then, is a group of people who share a common problem or goal and recognize their common interest. In the remainder of this chapter, we will discuss specific methods for measuring public opinion and applying it effectively in public relations work.

Traditional public opinion polling methods typically break down their results into demographic categories that seldom identify groups of people with common interests. Because of this inadequacy, James Grunig has proposed and tested three categories for the identification of publics based on Dewey's definition:

> *Latent public* A group faces an indeterminate situation but does not recognize it as a problem.
> *Aware public* The group recognizes a problem—what is missing in the situation—and becomes aware.
> *Active public* The group organizes to discuss and do something about the problem.[2]

Such categories group together people who are likely to behave in similar ways. This makes it possible for public relations practitioners to communicate with each group regarding their needs and concerns rather than attempting to communicate with a mythical "average" public. Researching public opinion in appropriate categories can help direct the public relations process. For example, it may be possible to classify the primary audience for a public relations campaign in one of the three categories listed above and develop specific messages for them. In the Cedar Springs case, physicians were an active public. However, if management had not taken care to determine the view of a latent public, the patients, costly errors could have been made.

Uses of Research in Public Relations

A recent study of twenty-eight public and private organizations, funded by the Foundation for Public Relations Research and Education, concluded that "the use of public relations research by corporations is on the rise and its function and contribution are becoming better defined and recognized."[3] The study points out that the term *public relations research* no longer describes specific types of research methodology such as content analysis, public opinion polls, or readership surveys. Instead, the term as it is now employed refers to any type of research that yields data for use in planning and evaluating communication efforts.

The same survey revealed that four basic categories of public relations research activities are most common: environmental monitoring, public relations audits, communication audits, and social audits. These activities may incorporate any or all of the techniques already mentioned, furnishing public relations practitioners with information that is useful in every phase of their task. Table 6.1 illustrates how these categories of research provide useful information in the various areas of public relations practice.

Table 6.1 Categories of Public Relations Research Activities

External Environment	Organization	Publics	Message	Media	Effects
I. Environmental monitoring					
	II. Public relations audit				
	A. Audience identification				
	B. Corporate images				
	III. Communications audit				
			1. Readership survey		
				2. Content analysis	
				3. Readability survey	
IV. Social audits					

Source: Otto Lerbinger, "Corporate Use of Public Relations Research," *Public Relations Review* 3 (Winter 1977): 13.

Environmental Monitoring

Results of the survey by the Foundation for Public Relations Research and Education revealed that **environmental monitoring** is the fastest growing category of public relations research.[4] Because organizations today recognize themselves as dynamic, open systems that must react to changes in the environment, keeping track of those changes is important.

Formal systems for observing trends and changes in public opinion and other areas of the environment can be used to guide many phases of organizational planning, including public relations. Issues management, discussed in chapter 4, is one application of environmental monitoring. Another technique is known as scanning.

Scanning Liam Fahey and W. W. King have described three basic scanning models that various organizations employ to keep track of environmental changes. Table 6.2 lists some of the characteristics of each of the three models.[5]

Irregular model This form of environmental study is an ad hoc approach. Generally, it is precipitated by a crisis situation such as an oil embargo or the introduction of a significant new product by a competitor. Once the unanticipated event occurs, the scanning process begins, focusing on past events that may help explain what has happened. The model is useful for identifying immediate reactions to problem situations and can provide input for short-range planning. However, it does not help identify crises before they occur or form long-range plans for future occurrences.

Regular model More comprehensive and systematic than the first model, the regular model generally employs an annual appraisal of environmental situations. Typically, the focus is on specific issues or decisions facing the organization. Automobile companies use this model when they conduct

Table 6.2 Scanning Model Framework			
	Scanning Models		
	Irregular	*Regular*	*Continuous*
Media for scanning activity	Ad hoc studies	Periodically updated studies	Structured data collection and processing systems
Scope of scanning	Specific events	Selected events	Broad range of environmental systems
Motivation for activity	Crisis initiated	Decision and issue oriented	Planning process oriented
Temporal nature of activity	Reactive	Proactive	Proactive
Time frame for data	Retrospective	Primarily current and retrospective	Prospective
Time frame for decision impact	Current and near-term future	Near-term	Long-term
Organizational makeup	Various staff agencies	Various staff agencies	Environmental scanning unit

Source: Liam Fahey and William R. King, "Environmental Scanning for Corporate Planning," *Business Horizons* 20 (August 1977): 63, Table 1. © 1977 by the Foundation for the School of Business at Indiana University. Reprinted by permission.

annual research on consumer attitudes to help them develop advertising appeals for the automobiles they have already designed. Obviously, the regular model is still directed toward the recent past and the current situation and can only develop limited plans for the next future. However, it is an improvement over the irregular model in that current issues and decisions are examined in reference to the environment, and predictions are made about future impacts on those issues and decisions. Basically, the difference between the regular and irregular model is a matter of degree and regularity.

Continuous model   This third model emphasizes the continuous monitoring of a variety of environmental elements rather than being limited to specific issues and decisions. Any number of environmental segments may have input into this model, including political, regulatory, and competitive systems. Auto companies that conduct consumer research to analyze preference trends are using continuous environmental scanning when the data collected becomes input for future automotive designs. The nature of continuous scanning requires that the system be designed into the organization. Irregular (and to some extent regular) scanning methods can be managed by the particular division or department involved. However, an agency such as the public relations department or another subunit must function as a clearinghouse for environmental data that is appropriate for several areas of the organization. In addition, computerized management information systems (MIS) are generally needed to store, evaluate, and integrate the vast amounts of information generated.

The continuous scanning model supports the strategic planning effort of organizations. Other models support specific issues or decisions, but the continuous model gives data to support a variety of issues and decisions that an organization may face. For example, the American Council of Life Insurance has developed a Trend Analysis Program (TAP). TAP "seeks to identify the direction of major social and economic trends so that companies may plan for the years ahead with greater confidence."[6] The program operates as a cooperative effort, with over one hundred life insurance executives monitoring the specialty press and other publications where emerging social and economic trends may first appear. Reports are issued whenever the data in a particular area is sufficient. For example, one report issued by TAP provided an in-depth survey of possible changes in American culture for the coming years.

The most frequently used type of public relations research is the **audit.** The public relations audit is essentially a broad-scale study that examines the internal and external public relations of an organization. Many of the research techniques we have already discussed are used in public relations audits. The purpose of public relations audits is to provide information for planning future public relations efforts. Carl Byoir and Associates, one of the pioneers of public relations auditing, describes it as follows: "The Public Relations Audit, as the name implies, involves a comprehensive study of the public relations position of an organization: how it stands in the opinion of its various 'publics'. . . ."[7] We can identify four general categories of audits in relation to organizations and their publics.

The Public Relations Audit

Relevant Publics   A list of the organization's relevant publics is made, describing each according to its function—stockholders, employees, customers, suppliers, and the like. Also included may be publics that have no direct functional relationship but are nevertheless in a position to affect the organization, for example, consumer, environmental, community, and other social action groups. The procedure is basically one of audience identification to aid in planning public relations messages. Some audits stop at this step.

The Organization's Standing with Publics   Each public's view of the organization is determined through various research methods, most commonly, image studies and content analysis of newspapers, magazines, and other print media. Both of these research methods are discussed earlier in this chapter.

Issues of Concern to Publics   Environmental monitoring techniques such as those already mentioned are used to construct an issues agenda for each of the organization's relevant publics. These data identify publics according to issues of interest and their stands on those issues. The findings are then compared to the organization's own policies. This has become a vital step in planning public relations campaigns for various audiences.

Power of Publics   Publics are rated according to the amount of economic and political (and therefore regulatory) influence they have. Interest groups and other activist organizations are evaluated according to the size of their membership, size of their constituency, budget size and source of income, staff size, and number of qualified specialists (lobbyists, attorneys, public relations professionals, etc.).

Public relations audits are becoming regular components of many public relations programs. They provide input data for planning future public relations programs and help evaluate the effectiveness of previous efforts. Several public relations counseling firms offer audit services to their clients. Joyce F. Jones of the Ruder Finn Rotman Agency describes the audit process in four steps:[8]

1. *Finding out what "we" think*   Interviews with key management at the top and middle strata of an organization to determine: company strengths and weaknesses, relevant publics, issues and topics to be explored.

2. *Finding out what "they" think*   Researching key publics to determine how closely their views match those of company management.

3. *Evaluating the disparity*   A public relations balance sheet of assets, liabilities, strengths, weaknesses, etc., is prepared based on an analysis of the differences found between steps 1 and 2.

4. *Recommending*   A comprehensive public relations program is planned to fill in the gap between steps 1 and 2, and to correct deficits of the balance sheet prepared in step 3.

Organizational Image Surveys   Attitude surveys that determine a public's perceptions of an organization help public relations managers obtain an overall view of the organization's image. Generally, such research seeks to measure: (1) how familiar the public is with the organization, its officers, products, policies, and other facets; (2) degrees of positive and negative perceptions; and (3) the characteristics various publics attribute to the organization. Frequently, organizations use such surveys as planning tools to compare existing images with desired images. Once the differences are assessed, image goals can be set and strategic plans can be made to overcome the problems that have been identified. Cities seeking to attract convention and tourist business periodically check their images as perceived by key groups, then use this data to evaluate their attraction techniques.

Although several organizations conduct their own image studies, many employ outside consultants or research organizations to supply them with data. Some major organizations that provide this type of data are Opinion Research Center, Inc., Louis Harris and Associates, and Yankolovich, Skelly and White.[9]

The communication audit, like the public relations audit, is applied in many different ways. Generally, it attempts to monitor and evaluate the channels, messages, and communication climate of an organization. Sometimes audits are applied only to internal organizational communication systems; the same technique, however, can be used to evaluate external systems as well. Frequently, results of a communication audit reveal problems of distortion or lack of information.

Communication Audits

Communication audits are ways of packaging several research methods for specific applications. The following research methods are used in appropriate combinations to audit organizational communication and investigate specific problem areas:

1. *Communication climate surveys*   These attitudinal measurements are designed to reveal how open and adequate publics perceive communication channels to be.

2. *Network analysis*   Generally done with the aid of a computer, this research method observes the frequency and importance of an interaction network, based on the most frequent linkages. These patterns can be compared to official organizational charts and communication policies to determine disparities between theory and practice.

3. *Readership surveys*   These identify which articles or sections of publications are read most frequently. While this method is strictly quantitative, it is an excellent way to determine the reading patterns of various publics.

4. *Content analysis*   This quantitative tool, discussed earlier, can analyze the content of all types of messages. It is frequently used to describe the amount of favorable and unfavorable news coverage an organization receives.

5. *Readability studies*   Several methods may be employed to assess how readily written messages can be understood. Most of these methods are based on the number of syllables in the words and the length of the sentences used. These formulas will be discussed in more detail in chapter 9 when we discuss evaluation techniques. For now, we shall only note that they help determine the clarity of a written message and its appropriateness to the educational level of an audience.

The concept of social auditing had its beginning in the early 1960s when businesses and other organizations were challenged to recognize their obligations to society. Social audits are generally attitude and opinion surveys that measure the perceptions of various publics about an organization's social responsiveness. This technique attempts to quantify the impact an organization has upon its public in much the same way that a public relations audit does. However, social audits are generally confined only to issues of social responsibility.

Social Audits

The practice of social auditing was more common in the mid to late 1970s. In recent years, social issues have been included in other types of research such as environmental scanning and public relations and communication audits. One of the best and most complete examples of a social audit was conducted for a city government and published in 1975 by Professor Robert D. Hay.[10]

Summary

Research is an important part of any public relations effort. It supplies the initial inputs to guide strategy and message development and provides a method for predicting effectiveness and assessing results. Public relations professionals must be able to measure the effects of their work and make reasonable predictions about future success if they wish to influence managerial decisions in most organizations today.

Many public opinion surveys are not useful in public relations planning and evaluation because they tend to average responses to the point that the relative strengths of attitudes are disguised. Good public opinion research must be sensitive enough to segment publics according to the strengths of their opinions. Four basic categories of research in public relations appear to be sufficiently sensitive: environmental monitoring, public relations audits, communications audits, and social audits.

▲ ▲ ▲

Designing the Student Union

By Jim VanLeuven
*Associate Professor
of Communications
Colorado State University
Fort Collins, Colorado*

Case Study

Before hiring an architect to design a new student union building, University of Idaho student leaders commissioned an attitude study of student leisure interests. The student leaders wanted to know which kinds of students used which kinds of facilities. Study the following data and then answer the questions.

SAMPLING METHODOLOGY

Three hundred eighty-four students were selected from a student body of 7,000 by taking every seventeenth name in the student directory. Each respondent was asked to complete a four-page mail questionnaire that utilized several question formats. Some 225 students, or roughly 60 percent, completed the procedure.

	Respondents	*Actual Student Body*
Year in school:		
Freshman	21.9	21.3
Sophomore	18.3	19.0
Junior	21.0	20.2
Senior	17.9	18.6
Graduate/Law	20.9	20.9

	Respondents	Actual Student Body
Residence:		
Fraternity	12.1	12.0
Men's hall	22.9	20.6
Sorority	4.0	5.2
Women's hall	5.4	8.2
UI married housing	1.3	1.4
Off-campus	54.3	52.6
Sex:		
Male	68.4	59.2
Female	31.6	40.8

Participation in Activities	Involved: 4/more hrs/wk	Slightly Involved: Up to 4 hrs/wk	Not Involved: No time	Groups Most Involved
ASUI committees	0.9	1.4	97.7	f,s,m,2,3
ASUI senate	0.0	0.9	99.1	f,m,s,3,4
ASUI communications (Arg, KUOI, etc.)	2.3	3.7	94.0	m,w,2,3,4
Other ASUI activity	1.5	2.0	96.5	f,s 2,3
Living group officer	6.9	7.8	85.3	f,s,. .v,3
Living group social activity	17.9	25.5	56.5	f,s,w,1,2,3
Living group recreation activity	11.8	28.4	59.7	f,s,w,m,1,2
Visiting with members of living group	31.4	17.6	51.0	f,s,1,2,3,4
Live off-campus, still take part living group	3.3	10.6	86.1	f,1,2,3,4,5
Campus religious organization	5.2	10.0	84.8	s,w,m,1,2
Religious study group	5.7	12.7	87.3	s,w,m,1,2,3
Campus/community craft groups	0.5	3.8	95.8	o,4,5
Music performance group	3.8	2.3	93.9	m,w,1,2,3
International student organization	0.0	2.5	97.5	m,3,4,5
Other cultural group	11.4	8.9	79.7	m,w,o,3,4
Hunting and fishing	23.0	35.7	41.3	m,f,0,3,4,5
Camping and backpacking	19.3	41.5	39.2	m,o,3,4,5
Campus intramural sports	16.2	25.0	58.8	f,m,s,w,1,2
Swimming and water sports	7.3	38.0	54.6	w,o,3,4,5
Golf and tennis	8.7	33.0	58.3	f,0,2,3,4,5
Handball and gym sports	13.6	28.8	57.6	m,o,4,5
Bowling	4.1	19.8	76.1	m,w,1,2
Skiing	19.5	30.2	50.3	f,s,o,1,2,3
Other sports	31.5	24.3	44.1	

Participation key: 1 = freshman   4 = senior   m = men's hall   u = UI married student
                    2 = sophomore 5 = graduate law   s = sorority   housing
                    3 = junior   f = fraternity   w = women's hall   o = off-campus

Participation in Activities	Involved: 4/more hrs/wk	Slightly Involved: Up to 4 hrs/wk	Not Involved: No time	Groups Most Involved
Television viewing	30.7	42.7	26.6	u,m,w,o,1,2,3,4
Movies and films	8.9	59.8	31.3	u,f,m,s,w,o,1,2,3
Bowling and billiards	8.1	29.9	62.0	m,1
Visiting over coffee or soft drinks	37.7	47.0	15.3	f,s,w,1,2,3
Service clubs and organizations	3.5	12.4	84.2	f,s,o,2,3,4
Honoraries, clubs in my major	7.2	22.5	70.3	u,o,4,5
Political organizations	0.0	8.0	92.0	f,m,w,1,2,3
Other organizations	21.4	14.3	64.3	m,o,3,4

Participation key: 1 = freshman 4 = senior m = men's hall u = UI married student housing
2 = sophomore 5 = graduate law s = sorority o = off-campus
3 = junior f = fraternity w = women's hall

Questions

1. In which eight activities are nearly half or more than half of the respondents involved?
2. How representative of the total campus population are the respondents?
3. If this were your survey, would you feel comfortable suggesting to the management that they act on these findings?
4. In general, what is the relationship between a student's year in school, his or her living arrangements, and participation in student activities?

Notes

1. John Dewey, *The Public and Its Problems* (Chicago: Swallow, 1927).
2. James E. Grunig, "A New Measure of Public Opinions on Corporate Social Responsibility," *Academy of Management Journal* 22 (December 1979): 740–41.
3. Otto Lerbinger, "Corporate Use of Research in Public Relations," *Public Relations Review* 3 (Winter 1977): 11.
4. Ibid., 12.
5. Liam Fahey and William R. King, "Environmental Scanning for Corporate Planning," *Business Horizons* 20 (August 1977).
6. Lerbinger, "Corporate Use of Research," 15.
7. Ibid., 16.
8. Joyce F. Jones, "The Public Relations Audit: Its Purpose and Uses, *R&F Papers,* Number 3 (New York: Ruder Finn Rotman Inc., 1975). Reprinted in *Public Relations Journal* 31 (July 1975): 6–8.
9. Lerbinger, "Corporate Use of Research," 12.
10. Robert D. Hay, "Social Auditing: An Experimental Approach," *Academy of Management Journal* (December 1975): 872.

▲ ▲ ▲

Planning for Public Relations Effectiveness

Preview

P ublic relations effectiveness depends on planning. Good planning is the best way to practice preventive rather than remedial public relations.

Tactical and strategic plans help public relations coordinate its efforts with those of other areas of the organization.

Public relations units in organizations are generally considered expense centers when budgets are prepared because only the inputs or expenditures can be adequately measured. Therefore, to secure an appropriate share of the organization's resources, the public relations unit must do a good job of "selling" its activities to managerial decision makers.

Public relations practitioners can apply the basic four-step planning model discussed in this chapter to increase their effectiveness in organizational settings.

From now on, we will demand the same strategic plans from you that we expect from production and marketing and research—plans based on where the company wants to be . . . , what it needs to get there, and what the communications function can do to help.

—James Bere, Chairman and CEO
Borg-Warner Corporation

Public relations practitioners, like most other managers, tend to be action-oriented. The constant changes that take place both inside and outside any organization produce an endless procession of public relations problems. Too often, because of the number of pressing problems, managers find themselves responding only to exceptional situations. Such situations are usually negative in that they require the practitioner to intervene after a problem has already gotten out of control. Former media relations manager for the New York Yankees Iru Kase summed up his job as follows: "I have to come up with certain statements after the fact (and fend off nastiness in the press)." Thus, public relations managers frequently find themselves so busy putting out fires that they do not have time to prevent them from starting.

While putting out fires is certainly part of the public relations function, it cannot be allowed to dominate all actions. If it does, the practitioner becomes a victim of circumstances, only able to react to the situation at hand. Perhaps the most frequent complaint of public relations practitioners is that other managers ask for their services only after the problem has become unmanageable. When damage to the organization's image has already been done, the public relations manager is often directed to "fix it." This may prove to be a no-win situation both for the organization and for the practitioner who must engage in usually fruitless remedial public relations.

For a long time, public relations practitioners have been advocating preventive public relations to avoid such problems. Part of this approach involves the type of fact-finding research we have already discussed in chapter 6. If practitioners detect potential problems before they erupt into damaging situations, they can give management early warning and advice. Sometimes even early detection cannot forestall some negative impact. When advanced warning is coupled with adequate planning, however, negative effects can be minimized and public relations management can provide well-designed, positive actions rather than hastily conceived reactions. As we continue our integrating case study begun in chapter 6, notice how the pitfalls of hasty reaction were avoided.

▲ ▲ ▲

Integrating Case Study

Y ou may remember that the physicians at Cedar Springs Hospital (chapter 6) were calling for immediate action to correct what they saw as a potentially life-threatening situation in patient care. Reaction to the problem as it appeared at the time would have generated a campaign to make employees more aware of the need for quality patient care and emphasize their responsibility for providing the best care possible. However, before taking action, the public relations director conducted some research to help him better understand the problem. The results were surprising and showed that the first action contemplated would have only made things worse. Employees already believed that the quality of patient care in the hospital was sub-par, and were frustrated because they felt they personally were doing a good job.

In addition, research revealed that recently released patients rated the quality of care significantly better than the employees did.

The sizeable difference between the ratings of employees and patients pointed to a different problem than was originally suspected. The planning process based upon this research redefined the issue from one of actual care to one of perceptions about care.

Objective: The objective which grew out of the research findings was to improve employee and physician views of overall hospital performance. Obviously, since both doctors and individual employees felt they were personally providing the best care they could and patients rated their performance high, the actual quality of care was good. However, their perception of poor performance was creating a morale problem for both doctors and employees.

Planning: Two basic strategies were devised to be implemented in a year-long campaign. The first strategy was to continually reinforce employees' feelings of worth as members of the hospital's medical team through positive feedback from management. The second strategy was to help both physicians and employees more accurately judge the overall quality of care through increased feedback from patients.

A budget of $6,000 was developed to conduct additional surveys of recent patients and communicate the message of quality care through a variety of media. Communication channels would be selected to allow both internal and external audiences to get the message that hospital employees were a quality team. Policies were changed to allow any letters with positive comments from patients to be routed first to the departments involved before being filed.

In the Cedar Springs case, research and careful planning prevented the loss of time and employee confidence that would have resulted from reacting too quickly to the first symptoms of the problem. Only through continuous advance planning can public relations practitioners avoid the burden of having

The Importance
of Planning

to react after the damage has been done. Even though many public relations managers feel they have no time to plan, the opposite is more accurate. The more time managers devote to planning based on adequate research, the less time they will need to spend putting out fires.

Planning actually creates the time needed to plan. It permits the development of integrated public relations efforts that support an organization's goals in a positive rather than a defensive manner. Planning provides the opportunity to involve management from other areas of the organization and to ensure their cooperation and support. One important cause of ineffective public relations efforts is the lack of planning. Through careful, detailed planning, public relations departments can make more efficient use of the funds and personnel allocated to them.

Communicating with Management

Public relations efforts often fail because of communication breakdowns between practitioners and other managers within the organization. The cause of these breakdowns is frequently an imperfect alignment between the public relations planning process and planning done elsewhere in the organization. Misunderstandings can usually be prevented if public relations practitioners analyze the organizational management as carefully as they analyze any other audience.

Public relations departments must prepare messages that communicate their needs and potential contributions to other segments of the organization. Therefore, when planning, they must learn the terms and methods common to organizational management.

The Fundamentals of Managerial Planning

Managerial planning is generally classified into two broad categories: strategic and tactical. **Strategic plans** are long-range plans, usually made by higher levels of management. This type of planning involves decisions concerning the major goals of an organization and policies for their implementation. **Tactical plans** are specific decisions about what will be done at every level of the organization to accomplish the strategic plans. Strategic planners typically deal with future events and must therefore rely on relatively uncertain data. The use of forecasting techniques to predict what effects economic and technical changes will have on an organization in the next five years is an example of strategic planning. Tactical planners, on the other hand, are more concerned with the day-to-day operation of an organization and its immediate future.

Public relations plans may be both strategic and tactical. Decisions concerning the long-range future of an organization often take public relations into consideration. Of course, public relations develops tactical plans in support of strategic plans.

Strategic plans and tactical plans combined produce either **single-use** or **standing plans.** This hierarchy of plans is illustrated in Figure 7.1. *Goals* refer to the basic direction in which an organization is heading. The purpose, mission, objectives, and strategies of an organization are all component parts of

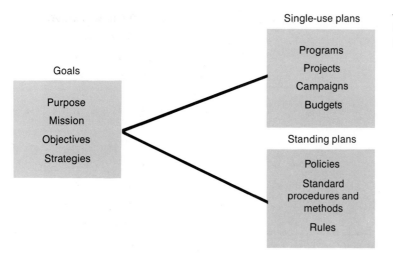

Goals

Purpose
Mission
Objectives
Strategies

Single-use plans

Programs
Projects
Campaigns
Budgets

Standing plans

Policies
Standard
procedures and
methods
Rules

Figure 7.1 Hierarchy of plans

its goals. These terms are frequently used interchangeably; however, they may also be used in various combinations to indicate sublevels of planning. Since there are no universally accepted definitions for these terms, most organizations adopt their own very specific applications.[1]

In this section, we will discuss a four-step process that is characteristic of managerial planning. Understanding this process, along with the specifics of planning, should help public relations practitioners adapt their planning messages to other managers. The elements of the process are: (1) establishing goals, (2) determining the present situation, (3) determining aids and barriers to goals, and (4) forecasting.

Establishing Goals

In the Cedar Springs case, patient care became the goal which unified physicians, administrators, and employees. Agreeing upon a goal or a set of goals must be the first step in deciding what a public relations effort will need. Frequently, from a list of possible goals, it is discovered that two or more are mutually exclusive. When possible goals conflict, each must be evaluated to determine the long- and short-range effects of acceptance or rejection.

Resources often dictate the selection of goals. An organization may not be able (or willing) to devote the time, personnel, and capital necessary to accomplish some goals. Goals that are selected for the public relations function, however, must always relate to organizational purpose. When seeking approval for public relations goals, a manager will be more successful if he or she is able to relate them to the goals and objectives of the entire organization.

Determining the Present Situation

In reality, it is impossible to separate planning from research because they occur almost simultaneously. As a goal is considered, current data about the organization's environment must be collected and used to evaluate the likelihood that the goal can be reached. Information provided by the kind of fact-finding research discussed in chapter 6 is crucial at this point.

Computers have become the primary tool for tracking current data trends and developments.

Again, the Cedar Springs example demonstrates the importance of taking appropriate steps to get accurate information before a plan is begun. It is useless to set unrealistic goals or goals that have already been accomplished. Even after the goal has been firmly set, data about the current situation need to be monitored. If the situation changes, it may be necessary to alter the goal or goals. Goals must be set with a good understanding of the current situation, the available resources, and what limitations must be placed on those goals.

Determining Aids and Barriers to Goals

After determining reasonable goals, a more careful investigation of the environment must take place in order to identify aids and barriers. The resources of an organization in terms of people, money, and equipment are important aids for achieving any goal. Likewise, a shortage of any of these elements represents a barrier that must be overcome. Although money is frequently the first barrier to be considered, it is seldom severe enough to prevent the accomplishment of objectives. Many plans, like the one at Cedar Springs Hospital, can be carried out with relatively small budgets. Key questions to ask in defining aids and barriers include: Do we have the *right individuals?* (rather than enough people) and Do we have *enough* money? (rather than how much money).

The structure and policies of an organization can also be either aids or barriers to reaching goals. For example, the goal of creating a sense of unity between labor and management could be severely hindered by policies that prohibit informal communication between the company and its union. Many other barriers and some aids will be found outside the organization from government, competitors, consumer groups, and other special interest groups.

Planning always involves the future. Predicting aids and barriers that will exist in the future is a much more difficult job than evaluating the existing situation, yet such predictions are necessary to determine the effects of future conditions on the programs being planned. Such variables as unemployment, economic situations, and inflation can reasonably be predicted a year or more in advance through the use of quantitative techniques.

Forecasting

Econometric models and other statistical tools are widely used in most large organizations to predict future events. Public opinion surveys forecast reaction to initiative or actions contemplated by politicians, government officials, and managers. In the early part of his administration, various versions of President Reagan's tax reform plan were given public airing so that reaction could be measured prior to final congressional action. Public relations management must become familiar with these methods and use them to evaluate future effects on publics (see chapter 6).

Predictions should also be made concerning the effects of planned public relations activities on various publics and the corresponding effects public reaction will have on the programs being planned. Often these judgments must be made by qualitative rather than quantitative means. Juries of executive opinion, sales force composites, and customer expectations are frequently employed. The following other forecasting methods may be used as well:

The **Delphi Model** is a method developed by the Rand Corporation as a systematic procedure for arriving at a consensus among a group of experts. The panel of experts is usually separated by great geographical distances and never meets to interact about the topic. A series of detailed questionnaires is mailed to every panelist. Their responses are used to construct subsequent sets of questionnaires that are sent to the same panelists. The process continues until a consensus is apparent.

Brainstorming is a group discussion technique used to generate large numbers of creative alternatives or new ideas. It has been used for some time by advertising agencies, public relations firms, and others who need to generate creative ideas. An example of brainstorming occurred recently when the Atlanta Chamber of Commerce held a breakfast for several top practitioners in the city and asked their ideas on ways to revive the failing Peach Bowl game. Ideas were generated while the game's planning committee listened and took notes for later consideration.

The basic rule of brainstorming is that no one is permitted to interject negative feedback or criticism into the discussion. As the group proceeds to generate ideas, all are carefully recorded, to be critiqued later. No comment is considered too absurd or too simple because it could produce the spark necessary for a truly creative idea. Brainstorming can be effective with a group that is comfortable functioning in a freewheeling atmosphere.

Scenario construction has been used by "think tanks" like the Rand Corporation to create very long-range forecasts. A logical, hypothetical description of future events (scenario) is constructed in order to explore the dynamics of various alternatives. For example, if a large auto company wanted to choose one of several manufacturing plants to close, a scenario could be constructed for each case to detail possible effects on the environment, economic future of the community, availability of replacement jobs, and other positive and negative results.

Developing a Plan for Reaching the Goal

If the current situation has been described, aids and barriers considered, and forecasts completed, listing alternative courses of action should be relatively automatic. After listing as many alternatives as possible, the process of evaluating them should begin. Alternatives should be compared in terms of costs and benefits. In the following discussion, we will describe some management techniques that can be applied in public relations planning.

Management-by-Objectives

Professor Walter W. Seifert of Ohio State University recommends the **management-by-objectives (MBO)** approach to planning that is detailed in Exhibit 7.1. Remember that the public relations plan is a message that must be communicated to an organization's executives. Whether or not that message is accepted depends not only on the effective execution of the planning process, but also on how the plan is communicated to the decision makers who must understand and approve it.

MBO is a widely used administrative planning process characterized by setting both long- and short-range objectives and then developing plans to accomplish those goals. Frequently, the process spreads to every level of an organization. Managers and their subordinates may begin the process by developing separate objectives and plans, then review each other's work and prepare a joint document as a final plan. This can occur at every level up the organization chart. Sometimes this flexible planning technique is called by other names. As we shall discuss in chapter 9, setting prior objectives is critical to the ability to demonstrate effectiveness in public relations efforts.

Public Relations by Objectives

Exhibit 7.1

Public relations often fails because managers do not understand what public relations people are saying and doing. This can be prevented if we talk in management's terms rather than trying to educate them in ours.

Management by Objectives (MBO) is widely practiced in the business world today. Many perceptive public relations people cast their programs in this form.

The Advantages of MBO

1. Communicates the way business people think in terms of business problems and objectives.
2. Raises the importance of public relations in the corporate structure.
3. Presents a structure for implementing effective communications programs.
4. Helps keep the public relations practitioner on target in solving public relations problems.
5. Contributes to the public relations body of knowledge.

The Process

1. Get a fix on the business problem: Analyze the business problem using all available research techniques. Then develop a clear, concise statement of what the problem is.
2. Translate the business problem into public relations objectives: This is the most difficult part of the process. The objectives should be stated in measurable terms.
3. Determine the audience(s): Identify who your message will be directed to. There may be several audiences. Examples: print and broadcast media, company employees, customers, government officials.
4. Determine program elements: Exactly what vehicles will be used to effect the program. Examples: TV, news clips, news releases, institutional ads, speeches, and publicity events.
5. Determine budget: The ideal situation is to fit the budget to the need, using an objective and task approach.
6. Evaluate the program: Utilize appropriate measuring instruments and techniques.

Program evaluation and review technique (PERT) develops a network to depict a plan by showing the sequence, timing, and costs of tasks needed to complete a project. PERT can be used in public relations for planning and controlling anything from single projects to entire campaigns. This technique is most appropriate when the effort being planned has definite start and completion points. After the planning phase is completed and action has begun, PERT can provide information about the status of the task and the alternatives available if the schedule or budget is not being met.[2]

PERT Network Analysis

PERT consists of four basic steps:

1. List all major tasks in a project.
2. Determine the required order of the tasks.
3. Estimate expected completion time for the tasks.
4. Draw a PERT network.

The application of PERT to public relations planning can be illustrated through a hypothetical case. Beverly James, a staff member in the public relations department of Alpha Corporation, was asked to produce a new brochure for an employee community volunteer program.

Bev's first step was to develop a list of the major tasks required to produce a brochure. These tasks are usually called *activities* in PERT analysis. Exhibit 7.2 contains the list of activities Bev developed for her assignment. By simply listing the tasks in the order in which they must be accomplished, Bev had performed step 2, sequencing the activities.

Exhibit 7.2

Activities Required to Develop a Brochure on the Employee Volunteer Program at Alpha Corporation

1. Begin the project.
2. Interview several employees who participate in the program to get details and personal interests.
3. Write copy for the brochure.
4. Obtain photos of employees serving the community through the program.
5. Integrate photos into copy.
6. Review similar publications from other organizations for ideas.
7. Prepare layout and finalize copy.
8. Prepare budget for project including printing.
9. Get final approval of copy, photos, layout, and budget.
10. Make any necessary changes and prepare brochure for submission to print shop.

PERT Network Analysis for Brochure Project

$$t_e = \frac{a + 4m + b}{6}$$

where t_e = expected time to complete an activity
a = optimistic time to complete an activity
m = most likely time to complete an activity (m is multiplied by 4 in the formula to give the highest weight to the most likely time)
b = pessimistic time to complete an activity

Bev noted that some of the activities could be performed simultaneously. For example, she could meet with employees who were participating in the program (activity 2) while the staff photographer took photographs of employees at work in the community (activity 4). The PERT network in Figure 7.2 shows some activities being performed at the same time.

PERT is especially useful in determining the time required to complete each activity. Note on the PERT diagram that each activity is preceded by a time line indicating the amount of time it is expected to take. When the task is fairly simple, experienced guesses can suffice. For complex projects, however, PERT offers a formula for computing expected times based upon three estimates: an optimistic time (a), a pessimistic time (b), and the most likely time of completion (m).

For example, Bev estimated that activity 2 (interviewing employees) could be completed optimistically in three days, pessimistically in ten days, and most likely in five days. Using the formula illustrated in Exhibit 7.2, Bev arrived at an expected time of 5.5 days to complete her interviews. She was able to calculate the time for the other activities in the same way.

PERT allows the planner to identify the *critical path* for completion of the project by discovering the longest sequence of events. The critical path for Bev's project is [1]—[4]—[5]—[7]—[8]—[9]—[10], showing that it should

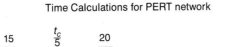

Time Calculations for PERT network

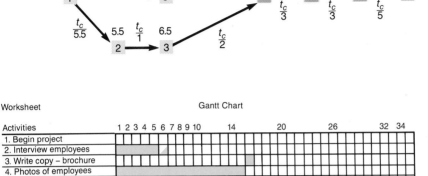

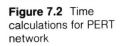

Figure 7.2 Time calculations for PERT network

Worksheet   Gantt Chart

Activities	1 2 3 4 5 6 7 8 9 10	14	20	26	32 34
1. Begin project					
2. Interview employees					
3. Write copy – brochure					
4. Photos of employees					
5. Integrate photos					
6. Review publications					
7. Prepare layout					
8. Prepare budget					
9. Final approvals					
10. Changes – Print brochure					

NOTE: A calendar can be easily integrated into a Gantt Chart with non-work days such as weekends collapsed into a single cell per week.

Figure 7.3 Gantt chart plan to develop a brochure on the employee volunteer program at Alpha Corporation

take a total of thirty-four days to complete the brochure. This tells Bev that if unexpected delays occur along the critical path, she must revise her estimated completion date; however, delays along the other paths probably will not affect the overall schedule. Such information could be very important to the printing department that is scheduling Bev's job; an unexpected delay might necessitate starting another job ahead of hers.

Another tool for planning projects and campaigns is the **Gantt chart.** This method is widely used to plan any activity in which time is the critical variable. Unlike the PERT network, the Gantt chart does not use formulas for more sophisticated control and does not identify a critical path. It simply lists the separate activities or steps in the plan in the order in which they are to be performed and indicates the time allotted to each task. A Gantt chart is a graph, with the activities listed along the vertical axis and the time listed along the horizontal axis. Time can be expressed in minutes, hours, days, or months, depending on the project. Figure 7.3 illustrates the use of a Gantt chart to plan the same brochure we discussed under PERT networks.

Gantt Chart Time Analysis

Table 7.1 Budget for Alpha Corporation Brochure

Resources	Quantities	Costs
1. Bev's time (Interview, write, integrate photos into copy, administer project)	7 days	$ 700. (Based upon $26,000 yearly)
2. Photographer's time (Free-lance)	10 hours	$ 500. (at $50. per hr.)
3. Layout (Graphics dept.)	8 pages	$ 200. (Estimate, graphics dept.)
4. Printing (Outside contractor)	1,000 copies, 2 colors, with halftone	$ 575. (Estimate, printer)
5. Distribution costs (Mailing and handling)	Postage for 1,000 copies Mailing lists of 500 names	$ 270 (Bulk mail at $.12 and cost of list) $2,245.
	10% contingency	$ 225.
	Total budgeted for brochures	$2,470.00

Types of Plans

The three major types of plans used by public relations practitioners are budgets, campaigns, and standing plans.

Budgets

Budgets are perhaps the most common type of plan in any organization. Generally, they are short-range plans designed to project costs through the duration of a campaign or other period of time.

Campaign or *project budgets* are components of plans to accomplish specific public relations activities. They provide structure and discipline in terms of time and money costs. Budgeting for specific activities is a rather straightforward process. Public relations managers budget using a simple, three-step model. First, required resources such as people, time, material, and equipment must be listed. Next, the extent to which these resources will be used is estimated. Finally, the costs of the resources are determined.

When Bev of Alpha Corporation set about producing her employee volunteer program brochure, she first had to develop a budget for the project. Table 7.1 shows her results. The left-hand column lists resources (step 1); the center column shows estimated quantities (step 2); and the right-hand column shows costs and how they are derived (step 3).

Project and campaign budgets are the building blocks for annual public relations departmental budgets as well as the basis for bids submitted by independent public relations counselors. In either case, budgets become instruments in the competition for organizational resources.

Competition for Resources   Because the annual budget represents the life-blood of each subunit of an organization, there is inevitably competition for limited resources. One of the public relations manager's most important jobs, therefore, is to make certain the public relations function gets its fair share. This means that *the public relations professional must be able to understand balance sheets as well as galley proofs.*

In most organizations, the budgeting process is decentralized. Budgets are initially planned by those who must implement them. Supervisors submit their budget proposals to department heads, who in turn prepare department budgets to submit to their supervisors for approval. This process continues in an upward flow until the controller or budget director for the organization assembles all the budgets into one integrated package and submits it to the president or the budget committee. Finally, the master budget goes to the board of directors for approval. At each step of this process, negotiation and alteration occur.

The best writers, designers, and media relations experts cannot do their jobs without the necessary funding. As was indicated in chapter 4, public relations staffs must continually fight to maintain a position of influence within the organizational structure. Their skill in preparing budgetary proposals and getting them funded is often an important measure of their influence throughout the organization.

While there is no substitute for a basic knowledge of financial planning and accounting procedures in understanding the budgeting process, other factors enter in as well. Competition among subunits for funds involves certain vital aspects of organizational politics. It is most important to remember that public relations must constantly "sell" the value of its services to the organization. Unfortunately, too many public relations departments fail to understand the needs of their own internal publics and do not communicate with them as they should. Public relations practitioners in an organizational environment must maintain a professional image as members of the management team.

Practitioners should identify the people in their organization who have both formal and informal power to influence budget allocations. They should then communicate with these individuals on a regular basis, emphasizing the effective and professional way in which the public relations function is being carried out. Some ways to demonstrate and communicate effectiveness are discussed in chapter 9. If these people are ignored until just before the budget request is submitted, they cannot be expected to understand fully the needs of the public relations unit.

Preparing Budget Requests   Budget requests should consider and reflect continuing programs, new programs, and contingencies. Continuing programs are those that have been carried over from the previous budget period for completion. Such carryover must be justified. Was the duration of the program expected from the start? Was it included in the original plans? If so, this fact must be made explicit to avoid criticism for not finishing the job within the previous budget. If the carryover was an unforeseen circumstance, however, an explanation of the extension is in order. Many activities are by nature continuous, but still, an understanding of this should not be assumed. Those who make budgetary decisions must be reminded on a regular basis, and especially at budget time, of the value of these continuous activities.

Requests for new programs must be well-documented, particularly in slow economic periods. The need for each new program should be specified in terms that relate to the most basic functions of the organization. Projections concerning the potential effects of a program should be secured from other departments as well as from the public relations staff.

Unexpected occurrences (contingencies) must also be included in the budget request. Some organizations have a standard percentage that is acceptable for contingency funds; others do not permit such items in a budget. If an organization does not permit the direct budgeting of contingency funds, they are generally included as part of other budget items from which funds can be diverted if necessary. Many organizations also build an inflation factor into their budgets. Economic forecasts are used to establish a percentage figure that will minimize budget erosion due to inflation.

Budget padding is a common practice in many organizations. It usually occurs when the people who propose budget requests know that top management will routinely cut every budget by a certain percentage. Budget requests are then increased enough to allow for cuts and still contain enough money to accomplish department objectives. Such political maneuvering is generally dysfunctional and should be discouraged by top management. Managers who do not understand how the "game" is played, however, may be left without sufficient resources to accomplish their assigned functions.

Types of Budgets   Organizations usually divide the budget planning process into two parts: operating budgets and financial budgets. **Operating budgets** forecast the goods and services the organization expects to consume both in terms of costs and physical quantities (e.g., reams of paper). **Financial budgets** give detailed estimates of how much money an organization expects to spend during the budget period and where the funds will come from (i.e., cash or financing). Figure 7.4 illustrates the components of these types of budgets. *Although public relations managers are typically responsible only for preparing their own operating budgets, an understanding of the entire process will make them more effective in defending their requests.*

Organizations are typically divided into four responsibility centers for purposes of budgetary control.[3]

1. *Revenue centers* Organizational subunits in which outputs are measured in monetary terms, such as sales, but are not compared to costs of input because they have little influence over factors such as product cost and design.

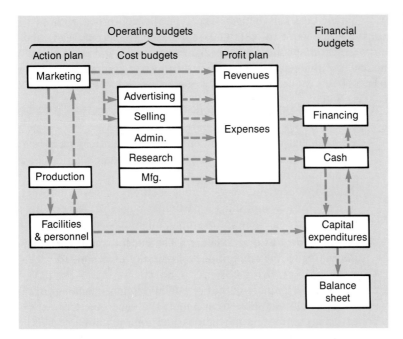

Figure 7.4 Budget components

2. *Expense centers*   Budgets reflect only expenses for these subunits because only inputs (expenses) can be measured in monetary terms. These subunits (such as public relations departments) do not directly generate any revenues for the organization.

3. *Profit centers*   Any organizational subunit that is charged with earning a profit will have its performance measured as the numerical difference between outputs (revenues) and inputs (expenditures).

4. *Investment centers*   In addition to measuring monetarily the inputs and outputs of these subunits, depreciation and costs of capital investments are subtracted before profit is determined.

Public Relations Budgets   Public relations units are generally considered *expense centers* because their budgets reflect only expenditures. The two types of expense centers are: engineered and discretionary. Engineered cost budgets are most often used for manufacturing operations, while discretionary cost budgets are used for public relations and many other administrative functions.

Because output cannot be accurately measured, expense center budgets are concerned only with inputs. At intervals during the budget period, comparisons are made between actual and budgeted expenses. Discretionary cost budgets cannot assess efficiency, however, because of the difficulty in setting performance standards for these functions. This often makes it difficult for the public relations manager to justify a budget request because normal control procedures cannot be used to evaluate performance. In chapter 9, we will discuss some alternative comparisons to help justify public relations expenses to top management.

Public relations budgets are typically concerned with two basic expenses: administrative costs (salaries, benefits, and overhead) and program costs (research, publications, special events, films, and other program-related activities).[4] Budgets are usually justified by one or more of the following factors:[5]

1. *Total funds available*   Public relations is allocated a percentage of available revenue.
2. *Competitive necessity*   Sometimes public relations receives a budget allocation designed to match or equal the public relations budget of a competing organization.
3. *Task to be accomplished*   Public relations shares in an overall budget allotted for accomplishing a particular objective. Advertising and marketing promotion, for example, might also share in these funds.
4. *Profit or surplus over expense*   The budget can fluctuate up or down depending on the amount of profit or surplus generated.

Campaigns

Campaigns are a frequent output of public relations planning. Because campaigns are usually designed to accomplish unique objectives, they must be planned using nonroutine procedures and unprogrammable decisions. Preparing a plan for a public relations campaign is a matter of following the process outline in Figure 7.1. However, some generally accepted guidelines for writing the campaign planning document include:

Problem statement   This statement should reflect the research that has been done to narrow the task to a manageable size. It should define the scope of the effort and recognize any special requirements of the organization, target audiences, and media.

Purpose statement   This statement should present a realistic view of what the campaign is designed to accomplish. Clear objectives should be developed that can be measured against results to determine the effectiveness of the effort.

Audience analysis   Based upon preliminary research, the planning document should describe the primary target audience; identify appeals and points of interest that will attract attention; define audience life-styles; and determine the relative strength of each possible appeal.

Actions recommended   The planning document should tell how the purpose will be accomplished for the audience that has been identified. It should discuss specific tactics and alternatives; define expected outcomes; and specify communication media, activities, and channels to be used.

Time frame   A schedule of activities should be developed. Any of the tools discussed earlier in this chapter (PERT, Gantt chart) can be applied to define the schedule of events.

Projected costs   Plans cannot be evaluated unless they contain a realistic budget. Enough documentation should be included to demonstrate that the projected expenses and fees are realistic.

Evaluation design   A method should be set up in advance to determine the extent to which the objectives of the campaign have been reached. All objectives should lend themselves to an evaluation process that will have credibility with decision makers.

Standing Plans

Within all organizations, certain *programmable decisions* call for a standardized, consistent response. Standing plans provide routine responses to recurring situations. Once set, standing plans allow managers to make more efficient use of their planning time by not having to formulate a new plan for every similar situation. Before going further in our discussion, let us provide one note of caution: overuse of standing plans may limit an organization's responsiveness to its environment, a critical issue for public relations. Nevertheless, standing plans do have a place in the public relations function. We shall discuss three types of standing plans: policies, procedures, and rules.

Policies   Policies are generally established by an organization's top management as guidelines for decision making. Those who make policy usually seek to guide decision-making activities in ways consistent with organizational objectives. Other purposes include improving effectiveness or imposing the values of top management.

Sometimes policies originate informally at lower organizational levels as a pattern of decision making occurs over a long period of time. In such cases, top management merely formalizes what is already happening. In other situations, policy may be established either as a result of recommendations from lower-level managers or directly as a result of top management's observation that a problem exists.

Outside organizations, such as governmental agencies, also set policies or at least influence them. Health and safety policies in most large organizations have changed considerably in recent years as a direct result of actions by government agencies.

Public relations departments, like all other subunits of an organization, must plan their daily operations to avoid conflict with policy. More importantly, public relations practitioners should be included in the strata of policy makers for any organization to ensure sensitivity to the interests of its publics. For example, policies that direct all contact with the press through the public relations department for approval and advice should be reviewed by the public relations staff.

Procedures   Detailed guidelines for implementing policy decisions are called *standard procedures*. Standard procedures, or standard operating procedures, provide detailed instructions for performing a sequence of actions that occur regularly. Most public relations departments have standard procedures for news releases, internal publications, site tours, media interviews, and many other activities that are carried on from year to year. In addition, every organization needs a standard procedure for emergencies.

Emergencies, although infrequent, should be handled through set procedures because of the need to respond quickly and effectively. When a disaster happens, it is too late to begin a deliberate planning process that will consider every alternative before responding. Nevertheless, coordinated, deliberate, and effective response is vitally important. When an emergency situation exists, time becomes the key element in communication; plans must be made in advance so that reaction can be immediate. Exhibit 7.3 shows the set of disaster response procedures that was established by a major metropolitan hospital.

A Disaster
Response Plan

Exhibit 7.3

St. Luke's Episcopal Hospital–Houston, Texas

General Policy/Procedure

Subject/Title:	Staged Preparations for Anticipated Natural Disasters
Effective Date:	November 1, 1986
Review Date:	November 1, 1987
Developed by:	Mary D. Brandt, Vice President
Reviewed by:	Policy Committee/Management Council
Management Central Approval:	Management Council
	Page 1 of 3

This policy/procedure rescinds all other policies/procedures and memoranda issued prior to November 1, 1986.

Purpose

To outline stages of preparation for anticipated natural disasters to assure adequate levels of preparation by all departments.

Statement of Policy

It is the policy of St. Luke's Episcopal Hospital to establish written policies and procedures for response to disaster situations to assure adequate preparations and communications before, during, and after disaster situations.

1.00 Phase 1—General Preparations

1.01 Management Central shall:

Monitor weather broadcasts

Establish a Communications Post from which department managers may obtain current weather information

Assess current inpatient population to determine those that could be discharged in advance of severe weather

Assess preparation of physical plant, including:
    Placement of storm shutters
    Availability of flood stop logs
    Securing of loose items on exterior of building

Notify all department managers to begin making general preparations

1.02 Department Managers shall:

Assess the current status of all essential supplies and make arrangements to restock as necessary

Determine, in consultation with the responsible administrator, which employees are essential to the operation of the department and which employees could be directed to leave early or not report to work, based on weather conditions

Make any special preparations needed to meet their department's responsibility for disaster response

Assure that the department call list is accurate and up-to-date, to facilitate the calling of staff for coverage, should it be necessary

Discuss compensation, staffing, and other severe weather policies with employees. Obtain administrative clarification, as needed.

2.00 Phase II—Implementation of Disaster Response Plan

2.01 Management Central shall:

Direct Nursing to begin census reduction by discharging patients whom the medical staff agrees may go home and consolidate remaining patients to free beds

Notify Admitting to accept only emergency admissions

Establish a central Command Post

Notify Communications to begin paging "CARLA ALERT" or "CARLA," as applicable

Notify department managers to implement their disaster response plans, including arrangements for essential staff

Evacuate underground parking areas, order placement of flood stop logs, and notify the Emergency Center and Admitting of need to move emergency receiving site to Bates Street Lobby

2.02 Department Managers shall:

Implement their department response plans, including calling in or holding over essential staff

Direct non-essential staff members to leave for home even though their shifts may not be over

Contact outpatients scheduled for visits or tests and cancel/reschedule appointments

Report the above information to the Command Post

3.00 Phase III—Operation During Disaster

3.01 Management Central shall:

> Continue Command Post operations
>
> Evaluate need to move patients and staff from threatened areas (such as upper tower floors)
>
> Notify Communications to page physicians to Emergency Center, if needed to handle incoming casualties
>
> Notify departments to curtail use of essential resources, if necessary
>
> Establish Family Holding and Press Center, as appropriate

3.02 Department Managers shall:

> Maintain necessary department operations
>
> Report any problems to the Command Post

Departmental Interface: All departments

Source: Reprinted by permission of St. Luke's Episcopal, Texas Children's Hospital, Texas Heart Institute.

Figure 7.5 shows how the same hospital implemented its disaster response plan in a simulated emergency.

Four areas of emergency planning should be specifically designed in advance.[6]

1. *Notification* Plan ahead of time exactly who should be notified and in what order. Generally, this is handled on a "need to know" basis. For example, an accident within a particular department will generally be reported, as soon as it occurs, directly to the department head and then to specified individuals in management, including the appropriate public relations manager.

2. *Spokesperson* The best strategy to avoid conflicting reports and any appearance of attempting to conceal facts is to direct all inquiries, particularly those from the press, to one person or task force. Generally, this function is handled within the public relations department, which may also need to arrange for statements from others within the organization.

3. *News media* First, notify all media representatives listed in the emergency procedures file, and immediately issue all available facts to press representatives who request them. Never attempt to manipulate, delay, or conceal information. Anything less than full disclosure at such times runs the risk of being interpreted as a cover-up. Mini-Case 7.1 helps illustrate this point.

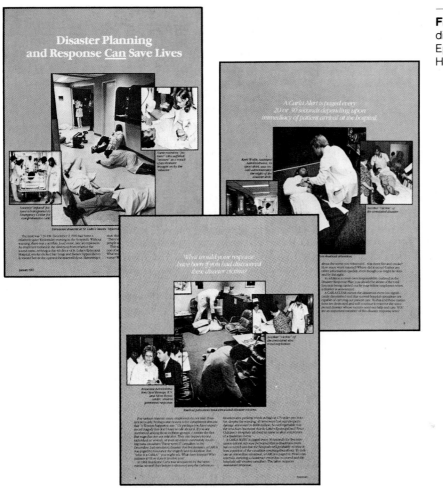

Figure 7.5 Simulated disaster at St. Luke's Episcopal Hospital, Houston, Texas

Remember that reporters want to know all the information as soon as possible. If the public relations staff can facilitate this process, the organization will benefit by receiving objective coverage. If the organization's representatives appear to be holding back information, however, the press will react with suspicion. Help reporters get the kind of information they want within the limits of legal liabilities. Provide them with human interest material about the people involved and as much information as possible about the rest of the circumstances. While it is important to work closely with the organization's legal counsel in such situations, remember that legal staff personnel may not be sensitive to the issues of public and media relations. They may react too conservatively and cause unnecessary problems if allowed to control the situation. Always be sure that public relations has a direct line to top management in emergency situations.

Mini-Case 7.1

There were no reporters or correspondents from any media on hand at Cape Kennedy when the fire broke out. . . . The question of informing the public . . . was thus left entirely to the institutional machinations of NASA. The agency reacted predictably. It not only shut down all lines of communication, but, by either accident or design, issued statements that proved to be erroneous.

Although NASA knew within five minutes after the accident that all three astronauts were dead, the information was not released until two hours later. It was nearly midnight before UPI and AP received a NASA picture of two of the astronauts entering the capsule for the last time.

NASA claimed that the withholding of facts and its issuance of misleading and wrong statements resulted from the lack of a plan for handling information in emergencies. As hard to believe as this may be, coming as it does from an agency with a public information staff of 300, there is undoubtedly some validity to the claim.

NASA's information office has since maintained that an emergency plan was in effect and followed at the time of the Apollo 204 fire. NASA states that it has contingency plans for each mission.*

Early in 1986, tragedy struck the nation's space program again when millions of Americans and people all over the world witnessed live on television the explosion of the space shuttle Challenger. Many professional observers and news reporters in their critiques of NASA's handling of the disaster commented that little seemed to have been learned from the experience of Apollo 204. Although flight controllers knew the fate of the Challenger crew almost instantly, speculation about their ability to survive the accident was allowed to continue for about an hour while technicians "gathered data."

*Source: James Skardon, "The Apollo Story: What the Watchdogs Missed," *Columbia Journalism Review* 6 (Fall 1967): 13–14. Reprinted by permission.

4. *Notification of families* If the emergency has resulted in injury or death, inform the families involved before releasing any names to the news media. Handle such notifications with tact and concern, but because of legal questions regarding liability, take care when speaking to the families. Any acceptance of responsibility or indication of fault should first be cleared through the legal department.

Rules While policies and standard procedures serve as guidelines for decision making, rules substitute for decisions. They are statements which specify the action to be taken in a particular situation. No latitude for application is provided other than the decision either to follow or not follow the rule. Rules may be necessary when certain procedures are crucial. For example, it is often wise to have a rule requiring that signed releases be obtained before photographs or other personal information are used in publicity releases.

Good public relations practice demands good planning. As exciting as they may sound, public relations actions that arise from spur-of-the-moment decisions usually produce short-term gains and long-term losses. Even emergency situations which cannot be predicted must have planned response systems. The process of planning is slow, complex, and frequently boring. However, in public relations, as in other managerial functions, careful planning increases the effectiveness and decreases the frequency of future actions. Adequate planning also establishes a system of goals that can be used to measure public relations success. This aspect of planning will be expanded in chapter 9.

Summary

▲ ▲ ▲

Case Study

Lions Club
Book Sale

By Artemio R. Guillermo
*Assistant Professor of
Speech
University of Northern
Iowa
Cedar Falls, Iowa*

E ach spring the Waterloo (IA) Lions Club holds a used-book sale. The books, which are sold for as little as 10 cents, are donations from the public. Proceeds go to various sightsaving projects including the cornea eye bank in Iowa City.

Since the Lions started the book sales, there has been only limited participation by its members. Three thousand dollars has been the most ever raised in one year. Still, the 1981 goal was set at $4,000. While the goal was raised, no changes were planned for promotion of the event. The Lions would use the same public-service announcements, posters, and press releases that had not done the job before.

Fortunately, however, a group of senior public relations students decided to help the Lions. After analyzing the promotional efforts in the past year and determining target audiences, the team created a public relations plan using the communication tools used before and adding advertising and staged events. The target area was expanded to include Waterloo, Cedar Falls, and the surrounding communities within a fifty-mile radius. The club provided $150 to the team for publicity expenses.

All promotional efforts centered on the slogan "Buy a Book and Help Someone See!" Simple television announcements using two-color posters were placed in strategic places in shopping malls, dining centers at the university, and restaurants and other local businesses. Two students donned lion costumes and paraded in the shopping mall during the book sale week.

Local media supported the promotional effort by donating space and time. Expenses, including classified ads in the student newspaper, display ads in the local papers, rental of the lion costumes, and printing of posters, were carefully budgeted.

The five-day book sale was held in Waterloo's biggest shopping mall after saturating target audiences for four weeks. The receipts were counted. The Lions grossed $5,137—28 percent above their ambitious goal.

Questions

1. What made the difference between the 1981 book sale and those that preceded it?
2. How was public relations planning used to promote the sale?
3. Plan a similar campaign for a not-for-profit group.
4. What was missing from the public relations campaign described in this case?

Notes

1. L. J. Garrett and M. Silver, *Production Management Analysis* (New York: Harcourt Brace Jovanovich, 1966), 364–365.
2. James A. F. Stoner, *Management* (Englewood Cliffs, NJ: Prentice-Hall, 1978), 99–139.
3. Ibid., 594–596.
4. Raymond Simon, *Public Relations: Concepts and Practice* (Columbus, OH: Grid, Inc., 1976), 95.
5. Scott M. Cutlip and Allen H. Center, *Effective Public Relations* (Englewood Cliffs, NJ: Prentice-Hall, 1978), 175.
6. Lawrence W. Nolte, *Fundamentals of Public Relations* (New York: Pergamon Press, 1974), 317–318.

▲ ▲ ▲

Action and Communication

Preview

The public relations actions required in modern organizations have expanded to include managerial decision making in virtually every aspect of operation. Nevertheless, most public relations actions can be described as attempts to spread information within a target audience.

Public relations practitioners can benefit by applying several basic steps in the process of diffusing information. It is also possible to identify certain critical paths that facilitate the adoption of new ideas by target publics. These critical paths lead an idea through five basic steps: awareness, interest, evaluation, trials, and adoption.

Both primary and secondary critical paths are more sensitive to certain channels of influence or to certain media at each step in the adoption process. When a public relations plan is developed, it must consider all five stages of implementation in order to have the most impact.

The process of diffusion must be planned and executed for each target public separately. Therefore, a method such as stakeholder analysis should be used to plan actions appropriate to the needs and interests of each public. Publics can generally be categorized as primary, intervening, or moderating. After channels of influence have been identified for each public, appropriate messages can be prepared within the basic functional areas of public relations.

Most public relations actions involve communication. Writing is the primary tool for constructing messages and is therefore a critical skill for practitioners. By applying the principles of effective writing, public relations messages can be developed for all audiences and media.

Public relations action can be organized around three basic areas of planning: target audiences, channels of influence, and messages. These areas interact to provide a unique plan of action for every audience in every situation. Segment 3 of the integrating case study illustrates **action implementation** in the Cedar Springs Hospital case.

▲ ▲ ▲

Cedar Springs
Community Hospital

Segment 3

Integrating Case Study

Action Implementation

I n chapter 7, goals, objectives, and basic strategies were developed for solving the hospital's problem. Next, the public relations staff turned its attention to the execution of those plans. It was clear from the patient surveys that the hospital's primary goal of quality patient care was already being achieved. Therefore, strategies were developed to try to improve employee and physician perceptions of the hospital's performance.

The two basic strategies for which action steps needed to be developed were (1) reinforcement of employee feelings of worth as members of the medical team and (2) increase in feedback from patients. Several tactics were implemented to address these needs.

Employee Team

A theme was developed to increase all employees' awareness of their value as members of the medical team at Cedar Springs Hospital. The theme "Quality People, Quality Care" was communicated to employees, physicians, and other publics through five media:

1. Signs were painted over the entrances to all three main buildings.
2. Mailing panels were printed for all publications.
3. Birthday cards for employees were redesigned.
4. Special employee name badges were designed for those employees who had passed the ninety-day probationary period, designating them as "Quality Providers."
5. Tee shirts were printed with the theme and used as gifts for participating in the personnel department's annual Benefits Fair.

In addition to the theme, hospital management wanted to make a very public statement about the quality of the employees and their work. Thus, an existing program, "Employee-of-the-Month," was revitalized. To give the recognition more visibility among patients, physicians, and the general public, a twenty-four-inch display ad appeared in the local newspaper every month, featuring the honored employee and the "Quality People, Quality Care" theme.

Patient Feedback

Three primary methods were used to increase feedback from patients to the hospital staff. First, the survey of recently released patients was repeated quarterly. Survey results were disseminated in various ways, such as using the hospital newsletter and table tents in the staff cafeteria. In addition, a contest was begun in which employees tried to guess the survey results before they were published.

Second, positive letters from former patients were disseminated among the hospital employees. Third, a regular feature called "Worth Sharing" was begun in the monthly newsletter to highlight a patient success story.

Public Relations in Action

Traditionally, public relations action has been understood to be communication in some form, often a publicity release for print media. However, the world has changed and so has the practice of public relations. Technology has changed the media with which practitioners must work and is causing organizations to require an increasingly wider range of possible action alternatives from their public relations staffs. When Johnson & Johnson was ready to announce the return of Tylenol capsules to the market after the first wave of poisonings in 1982, satellite technology helped deliver the message.

However, large organizations with access to space-age technology are not the only ones that require a variety of response mechanisms. Cedar Springs Community Hospital took several action steps, none of them press releases. While much of that action involved written communication, several important steps centered on managerial decision making.

Influencing Management Decisions

When it was first proposed that the theme be placed over the entrances to the main buildings, many employees were negative, feeling that "advertising" was too commercial for a medical facility. As a result, an ad hoc committee of department managers investigated the complaints and made recommendations regarding the use of the theme. The committee eventually recommended placing it above the entrances and sold the employees on the integrity of the idea. This group also suggested using the theme only on the name tags of employees who had passed the ninety-day review period.

Management decision making was again the principal action leading to the wider distribution of letters of appreciation from patients. This relatively simple action required a change in organizational policy that could have been politically explosive. Such letters normally had been routed to the personnel department and then on to the manager of the department involved. This meant that for a department to get any recognition, it would have to appear to "blow its own horn." Therefore, most letters of appreciation had been handled internally, without the knowledge of the rest of the organization. The private nature of this process worked against the new objective of improving employee perceptions by sharing patient feedback. Thus, the policy was changed so that the original letter was routed first to public relations where copies were made for the appropriate department manager and for personnel.

A policy change of this type could have alienated both the personnel manager and the department managers if not handled carefully. The public relations manager needed a good understanding of both communication and organizational dynamics to accomplish this objective.

Diffusing Information

Although managerial decision making was one of the public relations actions used in the Cedar Springs case, the primary action process can be described as the **diffusion of information.** More often than not, the action implemented to accomplish a public relations plan can be explained as an attempt to spread information within a **target audience.**

Selecting a Target Audience   The action process begins and ends with the target audiences. Once each public has been identified, its characteristics can be studied, and a *critical path* of influence can be planned for the issue in question.

When considering the individual characteristics of each target audience, it is helpful to categorize them as (1) primary, intervening, or moderating and (2) latent, aware, or active. A **primary public** is the group to which the action is ultimately directed. However, as we have shown, the critical path to this group frequently requires that other audiences be addressed. Individuals in **intervening publics** have direct contact with the primary audience and can pass messages along to them. All of the channels of influence listed in Figure 8.1, except personal experience, may be intervening publics. **Moderating publics** are groups that share a common goal or guiding philosophy and can make an impact on the primary public. These groups usually have high credibility with the primary public in specific topic areas.[1] In Figure 8.1, only mass media and personal experience do not have the potential to be moderating publics.

As you will recall from our discussion in chapter 6, a **latent public** is not aware of a need to change or act. An **aware public** recognizes a need but is not prone to any action, such as accepting a new idea. However, an **active public** is already aware and ready to do something.

The classification system just described helps determine the extent to which a given public is ready and able to respond to any planned action. The relationship between these classifications is diagrammed in Figure 8.2.

The Diffusion Process   Diffusion is a term used to describe *the way in which new ideas are adopted in a society.* Sociologists and communication researchers have long been fascinated by the paths that innovations follow as they make their way through a social system. Publics or target audiences are social systems that public relations practitioners seek to influence. Therefore, it is important that what we know about the diffusion of information be applied to the public relations process.

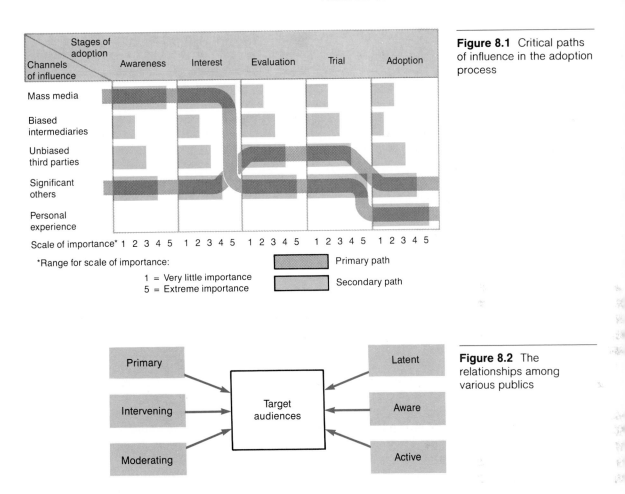

Figure 8.1 Critical paths of influence in the adoption process

Figure 8.2 The relationships among various publics

Critical Paths   Figure 8.1 illustrates some of the critical paths that research has discovered for the adoption of innovations. Those who study the processes through which new products, ideas, and technologies spread have identified five steps that seem to describe how people are influenced to change:[2]

1. *Awareness*   People are aware of the idea or practice, although their knowledge is limited.
2. *Interest*   People begin to develop an interest in the idea, etc., and seek more information about it.

3. *Evaluation*   People begin to mentally apply the idea, etc., to their individual situations. Simultaneously, they obtain more information and make a decision to try the new idea.

4. *Trials*   At this point, actual application begins, usually on a small scale. Potential adopters are primarily interested in the practice, techniques, and conditions necessary for application.

5. *Adoption*   Once the idea, etc., has proven itself worthwhile, it is adopted.

Channels of Influence   Researchers have tracked innovations through the adoption process and concluded that they use five basic channels of influence:

1. *Mass media*   Electronic and print media such as radio, television, newspapers, and magazines.

2. *Biased intermediaries*   Individuals or groups that stand to benefit from another's adoption (such as salespersons).

3. *Unbiased third parties*   Consumer groups, government agencies, and other groups or individuals that have credibility.

4. *Significant others*   Friends, relatives, and others who are admired by potential adopters.

5. *Personal experience*   Actual use of the innovation.

Primary and secondary paths of influence have been traced in Figure 8.1, following the most important and second most important channels at each stage of adoption. In the early stages of awareness and interest, mass media are most effective. However, in the critical stages of evaluation and trial, emphasis shifts to significant others. Finally, at the point of adoption itself, personal experience becomes the primary channel. The secondary or support path begins with significant others, moving to unbiased third parties at the evaluation and trial stages and then back again to significant others at adoption.

Facilitating the Adoption Process

The public relations practitioner can apply the critical path approach by attempting to create awareness and interest through press releases and other media coverage. From the start of the campaign, the practitioner should plan to communicate with other publics that are significant to the target audience. When the initial goals of awareness and interest have been reached, public relations actions should move away from the obvious to more subtle forms of communication through significant others and unbiased third parties. After the evaluation and trial stages have been passed, success can be measured by the extent to which the target public accepts the new idea.

When Mountain Bell decided to introduce Local Measured Service in the Phoenix area, the media devoted a great deal of coverage toward describing the advantages of the new system.[3] Because of the favorable publicity, the telephone company felt confident when the issue came up for approval by

Mothers Against Drunk Drivers (MADD) hold a rally at the state capitol in St. Paul, MN. A relatively small, but well-organized special interest group can sometimes influence decisions that affect the majority.

the Arizona Corporate Commission. However, when Mountain Bell representatives arrived at the hearing, they found senior citizens jamming the chambers and others picketing outside to protest the innovation. Obviously, one important public in the Phoenix area, senior citizens, had not adopted the idea. After its first request was turned down, the phone company began to work with senior citizen groups to win support from significant others and unbiased third parties. The proposal was approved without protest the next time it came before the commission. To secure the cooperation of various publics, Mountain Bell used an action strategy known as **stakeholder analysis.**

Pressure and Special Interest Groups   Traditionally, a great deal of public relations practice has been based upon a generally accepted *two-step flow of information* theory. This theory is built on the premise that certain people in our society are opinion leaders. Therefore, if those opinion leaders can be convinced to support a certain matter, they will influence others to support it also.

While the two-step flow theory contains a great deal of truth, both research and practice have shown that it is too simplistic. The theory allows for only two levels (leaders and followers) in any influence attempt. Further, it presumes a linear flow of information through a social system. From our discussion of systems theory in chapter 3 and the diffusion process in this chapter, it should be apparent that society is much more complex than that.

The proliferation of pressure groups has demonstrated the flaws in the two-step flow theory. As more special interest groups have appeared on the scene, it has become obvious that large masses are not always influenced by a few opinion leaders. Instead, issues may be fragmented by relatively small special interest groups, each with its own agenda. These groups have demonstrated an ability to pressure decision makers far more than the size of their constituencies would justify. Thus, a well organized minority can (and frequently does) influence decisions that affect the majority.

Stakeholder Analysis   The concept of stakeholder management provides a more realistic framework for an organization to visualize its environment. Stakeholder analysis is a method for differentiating among publics. *Stakeholders are those individuals who perceive themselves to have an interest in the actions of an organization.* They may be customers, shareholders, employees, or just members of society. They generally express themselves through groups that share a common purpose, such as environmental or consumer causes.

Applying the stakeholder management approach to public relations practice allows actions to be organized around an entire system of stakeholder groups. The goal is maximum overall cooperation between the stakeholders and the organization's objectives. To accomplish this, strategies are designed to deal simultaneously with issues affecting multiple groups.

The stakeholder process does not fundamentally change public relations communication or other action processes. Instead, it organizes them for more efficient use. Stakeholder management can determine *who* should be the object of an action step, *what* that action should be, *what results* should be sought, and *how* each element will fit into the overall plan.

Traditionally, many public relations activities were managed through delivery systems such as news bureaus, speakers bureaus, and complaint departments. Because these focus on a single action, they have difficulty recognizing the differences between publics. In a stakeholder management system, however, action for each public is planned *separately*. The needs and interests of a given stakeholder group determine what actions are appropriate and how they should be implemented.

When Mountain Bell managers first attempted to begin Local Measured Service, they were trying to reach all consumers through the same action strategies. Their initial view of the problem is illustrated in Figure 8.3. Further analysis led them to realize that the task required a more complex view of their publics (Figure 8.4). Stakeholders who needed to be considered in the Local Measured Service issue included:

1. *Internal stakeholders*   Employees and shareholders.
2. *Residence stakeholders*   Consumer advocates, the handicapped, minorities, low income segments, senior citizens, volunteer and service groups, educational organizations.
3. *Business stakeholders*   Those dependent on telemarketing, small businesses, large businesses.
4. *Other stakeholders*   Media, government, the Arizona Corporate Commission.[4]

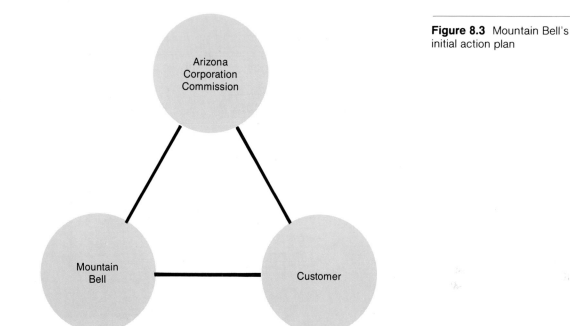

Figure 8.3 Mountain Bell's initial action plan

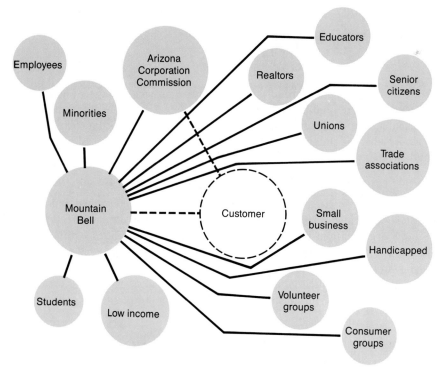

Figure 8.4 Mountain Bell's revised view of its publics

Stakeholders being
addressed by a Mountain
Bell representative.

Each stakeholder group was assigned to a project manager. These practitioners became familiar with the needs and interests of the groups assigned to them and worked with functional departments such as media relations, the speaker's bureau, internal publications, and others to target messages to their audiences.

Designing the Public Relations Matrix

After the appropriate channels of influence have been determined and target audiences selected, messages are prepared within basic action categories. In a large organization, these functional areas or subspecialities within public relations are sometimes performed by different departments. However, even if they are handled by one person, each action category must produce a distinct message. Frequently, different media are used as well. This creates a series of crossover or matrix relationships between target audiences and messages.

Table 8.1 Public Relations Matrix for Mountain Bell

Action Categories	**Target Audience**				
	Media	Residential Consumers	Employees	Business Consumers	Government
Press Releases	Intervening	Primary	Moderating	Primary	Moderating
Speakers Bureaus	Intervening	Primary	Moderating	Primary	Moderating
Internal Publications			Primary		Moderating
External Publications	Primary	Primary	Moderating	Primary	Primary
Advocacy Advertising		Primary	Moderating	Primary	Moderating

Table 8.1 illustrates the relationships between some of Mountain Bell's target audiences (stakeholders) and the action categories used to respond to the situation. In the case of Mountain Bell's response to the Local Measured Service protest, each target audience was assigned to a practitioner, while each action category was the responsibility of a functional department. For any message, at least two members of the public relations staff would be responsible for its design and implementation.

For example, a news release prepared by the press relations group could have been initiated by the residential or business consumer manager and closely reviewed by other managers for potential impact on media, employee, and government stakeholders. Under this system, messages are prepared for primary audiences and checked for their desired effect on moderating and intervening audiences. This system allows functional specialists such as writers and editors to continue performing their tasks, while project managers assume the responsibility for making sure all messages received by their publics are prepared according to the public relations plan. A single manager can be responsible for supervising contacts with several publics in more than one project. These responsibilities change as projects are completed and new ones are added.

We began this chapter by illustrating the variety of action steps possible from a single public relations plan. While the actions that might be used are virtually limitless, one remains predominant. Most strategies involve communication.

Just as communication is the primary action step in a public relations plan, writing is the principal tool for constructing messages. Even messages that are primarily visual, like videotape or slide presentations, generally require well written directions or a script. Policies and other decisions are written as they are developed, transmitted, and preserved. Therefore, writing is a basic skill needed by all public relations professionals, regardless of the type or size of the organizations in which they work.

The Practitioner as a Communicator

Principles of Effective Writing

Some people are born with an exceptional talent that cannot be explained or taught. The Ernest Hemingways of this world may not need to learn the principles of effective writing, but few of us are exceptionally gifted artists. Most people have to learn the craft of writing through study, practice, and hard work—that's the bad news.

The good news is that effective writing can be learned. People of average talent can learn to write effectively by practicing some basic principles. The following tips can help just about everyone effectively communicate technical and nontechnical information in letters, reports, news stories, booklets, and most other media that use the written word:

1. Use short, simple words.
2. Use short, simple sentences and paragraphs.
3. Write in the active, not the passive voice.
4. Avoid slang and jargon.
5. Use adjectives and adverbs sparingly.
6. Be brief; for example, keep most news releases to one or two typewritten pages.

Packaging Ideas   The length of sentences in a written document has been widely recognized as a key to its clarity. Many of the readability formulas mentioned earlier use sentence length as their basis of measurement. Distinguished educator and journalist Harold Davis often tells the story of a journalist working with the American Press Institute in the late 1940s and early 1950s who helped to firmly establish the link between clarity and length.

James H. Couey, Jr., of the *Birmingham News* helped conduct seminars for working journalists at Columbia University. Before a seminar began, he would ask each participant to send him a sample of their writing so that he could test it. The testing process was accomplished with the cooperation of several local civic organizations in the Birmingham area.

Couey would take a journalist's stories to a club meeting and ask the members to read them and answer some questions. The results would then be used to help the writers understand how well they were able to communicate with the average reader.

One of the stories submitted for testing, a description of an important breakthrough in the textile industry, was typical of material used in news releases. When Couey received the story, he noticed that it contained 271 words, but only five sentences, for an average of just over fifty-four words per sentence. The article is reproduced here:

> American London Shrinkers Corporation has spent a year and a half experimenting and compiling data on the shrinking and finishing of man-made fibers used in combination with woolen and worsted yarns and is now equipped to handle all types of blends, it is made known by Theodore Trilling, president.

The trend toward blends in suiting and coating woolens and worsteds brought with it the need for a variety of alterations in the shrinking and sponging operation, Mr. Trilling adds, pointing out for example, that the Orlon content in a fabric turned yellow, the rayon and acetate content tended to moire and the 15 to 20 percent of nylon now often used to give added strength tended to shine.

No new machinery is involved, just alterations in the processing, such as a change in the action or the weight of the apron or the leader, but it took a lot of trial and error observations, testing to make sure that further shrinkage would not take place, and tabulation of the data before the "we are now in a position" statement could be made, it was added.

Special reports of the tests and their results have been passed along to the mills and sealing agents of these blends, and in some cases, they have served as a guide in the correction and improvement of these fabrics, Mr. Trilling states.

He adds that his firm has been offering its 100 percent woolen and worsted finishing and shrinking service to the industry for the past 55 years and that with the alterations to handle blends now completed, an important step has been made.

Results of the preseminar test showed that readers gained little information from the story. Their responses to the questions follow:

Who is making the statements? (26% knew)

What firm is doing the work? (18% knew)

How long have the experiments been going on? (30% knew)

What kinds of materials are involved? (11% knew)

What briefly is the story about? (9% knew)

To test his theory that the trouble with such stories was their average sentence length, Couey edited this one and then retested it. He used a mechanical editing technique that retained the original writer's style, grammar, and information. Therefore, considered as literature, his corrected version (see below) does not read any better than the original. However, it now contains 265 words and twenty-one sentences, for an average of twelve words per sentence:

American London Shrinkers Corp. has come to the end of an 18-month search.

One year and a half ago, that firm set out to find a safe way to shrink, sponge, and handle blended materials without damage. Much experimentation was required. Many volumes of data gathered. The trial and error method was given a thorough test.

And now—success.

Theodore Trilling, president of American London Shrinkers, has announced that the problem has been solved.

Exactly what was the problem?

The trend towards blends in suiting and coating woolens and worsteds created the necessity for developing some alterations in shrinking and sponging operations.

Mr. Trilling mentioned the "change color" problem. He pointed out that the Orlon content in a fabric turned yellow. The rayon and acetate content tended to moire. The 15 to 20 percent of nylon, used to give strength, tended to shine. The "color changes" do not occur in the new process.

No new machinery is needed, Trilling said. He made clear that only alterations in the processing are necessary. He referred to alterations such as a change in the action, the weight of the apron or the leader.

The firm's president emphasized that many tests were required to make sure no further shrinkage would occur.

Reports of the tests and results have been passed on to the mills and sealing agents of the new blends, Mr. Trilling said. In some cases, the new information has served as a guide in the correction and improvement of these fabrics, he said.

This is an important step in the industry, according to Trilling.

When another group was asked to read the edited version and answer the same questions, the results were very different:

Who is making the statement? (68% knew)

What firm is doing the work? (55% knew)

How long have the experiments been going on? (71% knew)

What kinds of materials are involved? (29% knew)

What, briefly, is this story about? (64% knew)

If you were preparing a news release for your company or a client, a 37-percent increase in firm identification and a 55-percent gain in understanding of the story would be significant achievements. Couey repeated this experiment with dozens of articles. The results were always the same. A sentence is a package for ideas, and readers must struggle to get huge, bulky packages into their minds. By simply making the sentences shorter, he achieved large gains in understanding.

Couey continued to investigate the short sentence phenomenon and discovered some interesting facts:

1. Short sentences usually contained only one idea each.
2. A story could contain both long and short sentences for variety, as long as the average was short.
3. The optimum average for most sentences seemed to be about seventeen words.[5]

Pyramid Power   Couey achieved tremendous gains in understanding by simply shortening sentences. However, he never taught that sentence length was the only element in effective writing. Organization is another important skill that must be mastered.

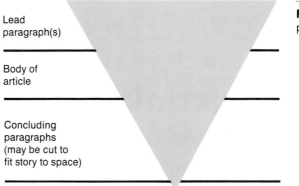

Lead
paragraph(s)

Body of
article

Concluding
paragraphs
(may be cut to
fit story to space)

Figure 8.5 Inverted
pyramid form

Journalists use the inverted pyramid style of writing (Figure 8.5). This method organizes a story so that the most important points are covered first. The inverted pyramid is equally useful for other types of informative writing. A message should begin by answering five questions: who, what, when, where, and why? These questions are answered in the first one or two paragraphs, called the *lead*. Journalists begin with the question that is most important to the message and proceed in descending order. Each successive paragraph contains details that are less important than the previous paragraph.

Using the inverted pyramid offers several advantages. First, it puts the most important details up near the beginning where readers who skim the message will be more likely to see them. Second, an editor may cut the story from the bottom up if necessary without losing important details. Third, a strong opening gets readers' attention and directs them into the rest of the message.

Media Selection

Various media and their audiences will be discussed in detail in Part III, but it is appropriate at this point to outline a strategy for media selection. Although it is necessary to construct messages carefully so that they communicate the desired meaning to an audience, it is equally important to choose the proper medium to carry them. For purposes of discussion, media may be classified as controlled or uncontrolled.

The preparation of a news release is different from the preparation of an advertising message, because news depends upon a third party to select and deliver the message. This is the basic difference between controlled and uncontrolled media. **Controlled media,** such as internal publications, direct mail, posters (chapter 10), and advertising, allow the public relations practitioner to dictate what is published and how it is delivered to the primary audience. **Uncontrolled media,** for which someone else makes decisions about content, include newspapers, television, and radio.

The three basic considerations for media selection are: the audiences, the timing, and the budget available.

Using advertising and the news media to promote a product.

News that could help save your life is making news.

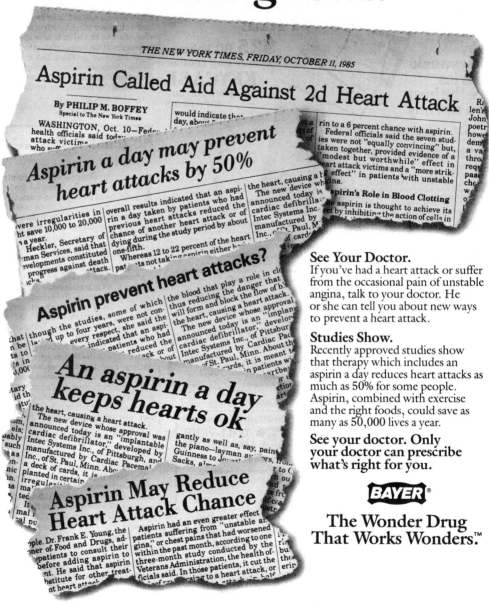

THE NEW YORK TIMES, FRIDAY, OCTOBER 11, 1985

Aspirin Called Aid Against 2d Heart Attack

By PHILIP M. BOFFEY
Special to The New York Times

WASHINGTON, Oct. 10—Federal health officials said today attack victims who suf-

would indicate that day, about

rin to a 6 percent chance with aspirin. Federal officials said the seven studies were not "equally convincing" but, taken together, provided evidence of a "modest but worthwhile" effect in heart attack victims and a "more strik- effect" in patients with unstable gina.

Aspirin a day may prevent heart attacks by 50%

 severe irregularities in ht save 10,000 to 20,000 a year.
Heckler, Secretary of man Services, said that evelopments constituted progress against death

overall results indicated that an aspirin a day taken by patients who had previous heart attacks reduced the chance of another heart attack or of dying during the study period by about one-fifth.
Whereas 12 to 22 percent of the heart

the heart, causing a The new device announced today is cardiac defibrilla Intec Systems Inc. manufactured by Inc., Paul, M of cardi

spirin's Role in Blood Clotting
e aspirin is thought to achieve its ect by inhibiting the action of cells in

Aspirin prevent heart attacks?

though the studies, some of which up to four years, were not con- every respect, she said the indicated that an aspi- patients who had reduced the

the blood that play a role in cl thus reducing the danger that will form and block the flow of b the heart, causing a heart attack.
The new device whose approval announced today is an "implan cardiac defibrillator," develop Intec Systems Inc., of Pittsbu manufactured by Cardiac Pac f St. Paul, Minn. About th rds, it is meant t n patients w

An aspirin a day keeps hearts ok

the heart, causing a heart attack.
The new device whose approval was announced today is an "implantable cardiac defibrillator," developed by Intec Systems Inc., of Pittsburgh, and manufactured by Cardiac Pacemak Inc., of St. Paul, Minn. Abo a deck of cards, it is planted in certain irregula

gantly as well as, say, pain the piano—layman a Guinness to Jo Sacks, al

Aspirin May Reduce Heart Attack Chance

ple. Dr. Frank E. Young, the ner of Food and Drugs, ad- patients to consult their before adding aspirin to nt. He said that aspirin bstitute for other treat- nt heart attack.

Aspirin had an even greater effect patients suffering from "unstable a gina," or chest pains that had worsened within the past month, according to one three-month study conducted by the Veterans Administration, the health of- ficials said. In those patients, it cut the ing to a heart attack, or

See Your Doctor.
If you've had a heart attack or suffer from the occasional pain of unstable angina, talk to your doctor. He or she can tell you about new ways to prevent a heart attack.

Studies Show.
Recently approved studies show that therapy which includes an aspirin a day reduces heart attacks as much as 50% for some people. Aspirin, combined with exercise and the right foods, could save as many as 50,000 lives a year.

See your doctor. Only your doctor can prescribe what's right for you.

BAYER®

The Wonder Drug That Works Wonders.™

Audiences must be the first consideration in any public relations effort (see   *Audiences*
chapter 6). It is necessary to identify the publics you are trying to reach and
determine what will interest them. Uncontrolled media present a special
problem to the public relations practitioner because publicity releases must
be planned for two audiences. The primary audience, the public for whom the
message is intended, is the most important; however, the editor or reporter
who selects or rejects the release for publication or broadcast is the first hurdle.
Thus, although the release is designed to communicate a particular message
to the primary audience, it must first attract the journalistic attention of an
editor.

Having determined the target audience, it is next necessary to know which
media are likely to be interested in particular types of information. By researching available media carefully, a public relations practitioner can become familiar with the types of stories they use and the audiences they attract.
He or she may then select the best media for each release and package the
information in a way that will attract the editor's attention. Chapter 10 discusses various strategies for media relations in greater detail.

Timing   The timing necessary to reach an audience is a second important
factor in media selection. Once the appropriate media have been chosen, the
time required to reach the primary audience may become critical. Some publications have backlogs of material and may not be able to get a story out in
time. Therefore, the question of when the primary audience receives the message may be just as important as whether or not it receives the message at all.

Budgets   Budgets, the third important factor in media selection, are always
limited, and frequently they, in turn, limit media selection. Usually the first
decision that must be made is whether or not the message needs to be delivered
by more than one medium. If a media mix is desirable, it may be necessary
to consider cost when deciding which ones to use. Remember that while the
costs of controlled media, such as advertising, are obvious, costs associated
with uncontrolled media must also be counted.

Table 8.2 contrasts advantages and disadvantages of several different
media. Considering these points with regard to audiences, time, and budget
will help pubic relations practitioners select the media most appropriate to
their messages.

Table 8.2 Principal Media: Advantages and Disadvantages

	Advantages	Disadvantages
Television	1. Combines sight, sound, and motion attributes 2. Permits physical demonstration of product 3. Believability due to immediacy of message 4. High impact of message 5. Huge audiences 6. Good product identification 7. Popular medium	1. Message limited by restricted time segments 2. No possibility for consumer referral to message 3. Availabilities sometimes difficult to arrange 4. High time costs 5. Waste coverage 6. High production costs 7. Poor color transmission
Magazines	1. Selectivity of audience 2. Reaches more affluent consumers 3. Offers prestige to an advertiser 4. Pass-along readership 5. Good color reproduction	1. Often duplicate circulation 2. Usually cannot dominate in a local market 3. Long closing dates 4. No immediacy of message 5. Sometimes high production costs
Radio	1. Selectivity of geographical markets 2. Good saturation of local markets 3. Ease of changing advertising copy 4. Relatively low cost	1. Message limited by restricted time segments 2. No possibility for consumer referral to message 3. No visual appeal 4. Waste coverage
Newspapers	1. Selectivity of geographical markets 2. Ease of changing advertising copy 3. Reaches all income groups 4. Ease of scheduling advertisements 5. Relatively low cost 6. Good medium for manufacturer/dealer advertising	1. High cost for national coverage 2. Shortness of message life 3. Waste circulation 4. Differences of sizes and formats 5. Rate differentials between local and national advertisements 6. Poor color reproduction
Direct Mail	1. Extremely selective 2. Message can be very personalized 3. Little competition with other advertisements 4. Easy to measure effect of advertisements 5. Provides easy means for consumer action	1. Often has poor image 2. Can be quite expensive 3. Many restrictive postal regulations 4. Problems in maintaining mailing lists

Table 8.2—*Continued*

	Advantages	Disadvantages
Outdoor Posters (on stationary panels)	1. Selectivity of geographical markets 2. High repetitive value 3. Large physical size 4. Relatively low cost 5. Good color reproduction	1. Often has poor image 2. Message must be short 3. Waste circulation 4. National coverage is expensive 5. Few creative specialists
Point-of-Purchase Displays	1. Presents message at point of sale 2. Great flexibility for creativity 3. Ability to demonstrate product in use 4. Good color reproduction 5. Repetitive value	1. Dealer apathy in installation 2. Long production period 3. High unit cost 4. Shipping problems 5. Space problem
Transit Posters (on moving vehicles)	1. Selectivity of geographical markets 2. Captive audience 3. Very low cost 4. Good color reproduction 5. High repetitive value	1. Limited to a certain class of consumers 2. Waste circulation 3. Surroundings are disreputable 4. Few creative specialists
Movie Trailers	1. Selectivity of geographical markets 2. Captive audience 3. Large physical size 4. Good medium for manufacturer/ dealer advertising	1. Cannot be employed in all theaters 2. Waste circulation 3. High production costs 4. No possibility for consumer referral to message
Advertising Specialties	1. Unique presentation 2. High repetitive value 3. Has a "gift" quality 4. Relatively long life	1. Subject to fads 2. Message must be short 3. May have relatively high unit cost 4. Effectiveness difficult to measure
Pamphlets and Booklets	1. Offer detailed message at point of sale 2. Supplement a personal sales presentation 3. Offer to potential buyers a good referral means 4. Good color reproduction	1. Dealers often fail to use 2. May have a relatively high unit cost 3. Few creative specialists 4. Effectiveness difficult to measure

Reprinted by permission of Publishing Horizons, Inc. from *Advertising Campaigns, Formulations and Tactics*, by Quera, pages 71–74.

Summary

The job of public relations is to create a positive *universe of discourse* about the organization. It is this universe of discourse that creates the mental pictures publics develop about organizations. These public images are different for each individual, yet highly similar. They are the collective impressions various publics use to judge the value and effectiveness of organizations in society. The first action step of public relations is to assess these images accurately and then to plan and execute communication programs based upon that information. The final step in the process of public relations, measuring the effects of these messages, will be discussed in the next chapter.

▲ ▲ ▲

Rockefeller's Passing

By Carolyn Cline
*University of Texas
Austin, Texas*

Case Study

On January 26, 1979, former Vice President Nelson Rockefeller died of a heart attack in New York City. Details were released to the media by Hugh Morrow, a longtime family spokesman, who told reporters that the former vice president had been in excellent health. His last day had been busy—after a family dinner, Rockefeller "returned to his office in Rockefeller Center. He was working on his book about his modern art collection. He was stricken and died, apparently instantly," about 11:15 P.M. "He was having a wonderful time with the whole art enterprise. He was 'having a ball,' as he put it."

Editorials the next day praised Rockefeller for his involvement with the art collection and his dedication to duty, as evidenced from his death late at night in his office. The *New York Daily News* wrote that "it was typical of Nelson Aldrich Rockefeller's life that death, when it came on Friday night, found him hard at work. Idleness was one luxury of the rich that Rockefeller steadfastly disdained."

Reporters gradually discovered, however, that all of the material released by Morrow was false.

Rockefeller was, in fact, at his town house, in the company of a female aide, Megan Marshak. Medical assistance was not summoned until sixty-one minutes after Rockefeller's attack, and then not by Marshak, but by a friend of hers.

The New York press coverage of the new information was sensational. The *Post* said that Marshak was paid $60,000 a year for her work on the art project, and that Rockefeller helped pay for her apartment. The *Times* reported that the aide was wearing "a long black evening gown" that night. The *Daily News* interviewed sources who said that Rockefeller always sent Marshak flowers before his visits, and that there was food and wine on the table when paramedics finally arrived at the town house.

In the subsequent days, the New York and national media investigated every aspect of the Rockefeller-Marshak relationship and, in the opinion of some critics, turned the event into a media circus.

Questions

1. Was Morrow justified in his first statement? If not, what should he have said?
2. How does the public's right to know conflict with the right to privacy? Did Rockefeller's widow or children have a right to request that the story be downplayed?
3. Immediately after the first disclosures appeared in the paper, you have been called in as a media consultant to help the Rockefeller family deal with the situation. What would you suggest?

Source: Stanford Levinson, "An Exemplary Death," *The Columbia Journalism Review,* (May/June 1979): 31–33.

Notes

1. Frank Walsh, *Public Relations Writer in a Computer Age* (Englewood Cliffs, NJ: Prentice-Hall, 1986), 10.
2. Herbert F. Lionberger, *Adoption of New Ideas and Practices* (Ames, IA: Iowa State University Press, 1960), 32.
3. *Mountain Bell Submission,* Public Relations Society of America Silver Anvil Awards Competition, 1983.
4. Ibid.
5. Craig E. Aronoff et al., *Getting Your Message Across* (St. Paul, MN: West Publishing, 1981), 28–31.

▲ ▲ ▲

CHAPTER 9

Evaluating Public Relations Effectiveness

Preview

The evaluation step in a public relations program is essential. It permits the practitioner to assess the effectiveness of the effort, demonstrate that effectiveness to management, and plan for future efforts.

Value is more important than volume in evaluating the effectiveness of public relations efforts.

Public relations effectiveness is best measured using an open-system model that takes into account environmental factors as well as before-and-after comparisons.

Open-system evaluation models include effectiveness measures of such factors as administrative processes, employee publications, media relations, and advertising.

We have *arbitrarily* broken the process of public relations down into four related functions: research, planning, action, and evaluation. In reality, however, the methods discussed in chapter 6 and the material in this chapter are simply different applications of the research function. For the sake of illustration and emphasis, we have separated the two chapters, but much of what we say here about evaluating public relations programs relates directly back to the research methods mentioned in chapter 6.

Although presented last, **evaluation** is not the final stage of the public relations process. In actual practice, evaluation is frequently the beginning of a new effort. The research function overlaps the planning, action, and evaluation functions. It is an interdependent process that, once set in motion, has no beginning or end.

The Need for Evaluation Research

To help explain how evaluation can be involved in virtually every phase of a program, Figure 9.1 has been divided into three evaluation segments:

1. *Implementation checking* The central question in this start-up assessment step is: To what degree is the target audience being reached? Regardless of how complete the planning process may have been, it will still be necessary to determine the difference between *planned* and *actual* implementation. Variations from the original plan must be analyzed and explained so that a decision can be made to either modify the plan or correct the discrepancies.

2. *In-progress monitoring* Periodically during the program, actions undertaken should be reviewed, and if necessary, modified. These reviews can be planned for regular intervals to determine the effectiveness of the program in meeting its objectives. Any unanticipated results can be assessed and factored into the evaluation. The variance between actual and anticipated progress at each point can be examined for its effect on the overall outcome. Regular monitoring helps determine the reasons for results that differ significantly from the original plan and prevents unwelcome surprises.

3. *Outcome evaluation* The final step is to assess the program's end results. Once again, objectives and results are compared to determine the variance. At this point, all prior evaluations become important for explaining the context in which the program was implemented and interpreting the results. An evaluation report transmits this information, along with any suggestions for planning future efforts, to an appropriate decision maker.

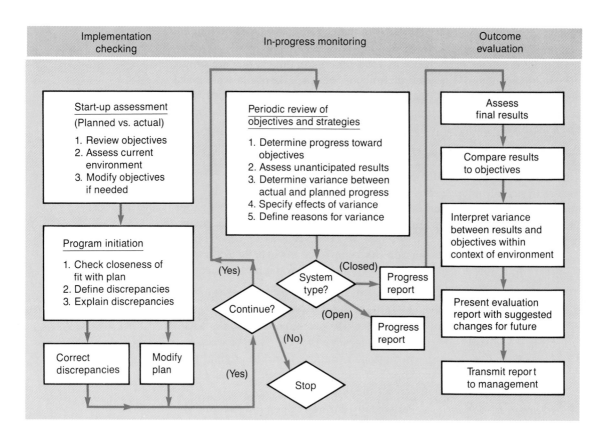

| Implementation checking | In-progress monitoring | Outcome evaluation |

Start-up assessment
(Planned vs. actual)

1. Review objectives
2. Assess current environment
3. Modify objectives if needed

Periodic review of objectives and strategies

1. Determine progress toward objectives
2. Assess unanticipated results
3. Determine variance between actual and planned progress
4. Specify effects of variance
5. Define reasons for variance

Assess final results

Compare results to objectives

Program initiation

1. Check closeness of fit with plan
2. Define discrepancies
3. Explain discrepancies

(Yes)

Continue?

System type?

(Closed)

Progress report

(Open)

Progress report

Interpret variance between results and objectives within context of environment

Present evaluation report with suggested changes for future

Correct discrepancies

Modify plan

(Yes)

(No)

Stop

Transmit report to management

Figure 9.1 Components of an evaluation plan

Research in public relations should be continuous, constantly evaluating the process and its environment and providing new information to sustain it. Learning about the failures and successes of a public relations campaign provides information that can be used to plan more precisely for the next effort. Evaluation research can also be valuable for its ability to assess an existing campaign. This point is illustrated in the Cedar Springs Community Hospital case. Research made a tremendous impact on the planning and action steps taken in the case. In this final episode, research helps determine the effectiveness of the total effort.

▲ ▲ ▲

Integrating Case Study

Approximately one year after the program to improve the perceptions of employees regarding the quality of patient care began, follow-up research was conducted. This evaluation process began at the same point as the original research. Using the methodology of the initial employee survey, three hundred names were once again chosen at random from the 1,226 employees. Each of the selected individuals received a questionnaire in the mail similar to the one used to begin the process.

Four key factors from the original survey had been selected as objectives for improvement during the preceding year. These same factors were measured again in the evaluation survey to determine the degree to which progress had been made. The following comparisons were produced:

Factors	Average Ratings	
	(10 pt. scale)	
	1981	1982
1. Quality of care	6.6	7.0
2. Patients' understanding of procedures and tests	5.7	6.2
3. Courtesy and respect shown to patients	7.4	7.8
4. Patient call lights answered in less than five minutes	56%	81%

Obviously, a noticeable and positive shift in employee perceptions of the hospital's overall performance had taken place. In addition to the quantitative evidence, which showed gains in every category over the previous year, qualitative indicators also supported this conclusion. Another focus group demonstrated considerable improvement in employees' feelings about the quality of care available. This was reinforced through letters from employees and comments made during monthly employee group meetings.

Although employee perceptions did not rise to the same level as those of recently released patients in earlier surveys, the improvements were consistent and strong. Therefore, management concluded that a program to continue feedback to employees from patients would be an important part of future employee communication programs.

Another important reason evaluation research has become a necessity for public relations programs is that it enhances organizational support. Public relations professionals must assume the same responsibility for effectiveness as their management colleagues do. Organizational resources are always limited, and competition for them is keen. Public relations managers must be able to demonstrate effectiveness in ways that can be measured against other competing functions, as Robert Marker, manager of press services for Armstrong Cork, reveals in Mini-Case 9.1.

The Importance of Evaluation

Mini-Case 9.1

I remember an occasion, some years ago, that started me thinking about the need for some kind of measurement device and internal reporting system to help explain the public relations function.

I was asked by a marketing executive at Armstrong to come to his office and inform him, as succinctly as possible, just what it was he was getting for what he was spending on public relations. It really didn't bother me at the time, because we had had these inquiries before, and I was pretty sure I could handle it. I came prepared with a considerable volume of newspaper clippings, magazine features, and case histories that we had produced in support of his product line that year.

I laid all this out in front of him. . . . After an appropriate interval, I pointed out that all this publicity—if strung end to end—would reach from his office located in the west wing of the building, clear across the center wing to the east wing, down the stairs, and out into the main lobby, and there'd still be enough leftover to paper one and a half walls of his office. (That was a favored "measurement" device back in those days. We used to have our secretaries total the column inches, and then convert it all into linear feet of hallway space.) And then it came, the question no one had ever asked before: "But what's all this worth to us?"

I stammered for a moment and said something to the effect that I thought the material spoke for itself. After all, this was highly coveted editorial space we were talking about. . . . I said it would be difficult to attach a specific value to it.

He smiled. "My boy," he said, "I have to attach a value to everything in this operation. . . . Why don't you go back and write me a memo outlining clearly what this function does for us, and then we'll talk about your budget for next year."

Source: Robert K. Marker, "The Armstrong/PR Data Management System," *Public Relations Review* 3 (Winter 1977): 51–52.

Measuring the Worth of Public Relations Efforts

Too many public relations programs have been eliminated or severely cut back because no "value" could be attached to them. The harsh realities of corporate existence make it necessary for public relations practitioners to demonstrate the worth of what they do. Particularly in difficult economic situations, every aspect of organizational activity is measured by its relative benefit to the firm. Public relations departments that cannot demonstrate their value to the organization will not be in a position to influence the policy decisions that affect their own fate.

Measurement Strategies

The concept of measurement itself is not new to the practice of public relations. The problem, as Robert Marker discovered, is that the rest of the business world has been using different standards. Marker's measurement system was quantifiable (linear feet of hallway), and it accurately reflected the effort that had been expended. When faced with the devastating question of "worth," however, the measurement strategy could not provide any data. Because the nature of public relations is intangible, assigning a value to its activities is difficult. Often the problem has led practitioners into the use of erroneous measures or measures incorrectly applied.

Like every aspect of public relations practice, evaluation needs careful planning. Ideally, the evaluation effort should be planned from the inception of the program. An evaluation attempt that is tacked on after a program is finished will produce incomplete and generally inappropriate data. When evaluation is part of the overall plan, each component can be constructed with an eye toward measuring its success later.

Measurement-by-Objectives   The use of management-by-objectives (MBO), or any similar planning process, will alleviate the measurement problem facing public relations. Although MBO is most frequently used for evaluating individual employees, its basic elements can also be applied to programs, projects, and work groups. The object is to prepare advance statements, usually during the planning phase, concerning legitimate expectations from a given effort. These must be mutually agreed upon by all those involved before the action occurs. When the set time for evaluation arrives, objectives can be compared to accomplishments to assess the degree of success. The exact process used varies among organizations. However, the basic MBO steps include:

1. *Work group involvement*   If more than one person will be working on the project, the entire group should be involved in setting the objectives. This is important so that no portion of the task is overlooked and each contributor feels committed to the effort.

2. *Manager-subordinate involvement*   Once the objectives of the group have been established, each subordinate should work with the manager of the project to define a set of individual objectives. These keep the project moving by making certain that everyone understands his or her role.

3. *Determination of intermediate objectives*   This step defines a series of objectives along the way toward the overall target. Setting intermediate objectives permits in-progress evaluation to be done more precisely and makes it possible to consider mid-course corrections before the project gets out of hand.

4. *Determination of measures of achievement*   The point when the effort will be considered complete should be specified either in terms of a time element or the achievement of a stated objective.

5. *Review, evaluation, and recycling*   Because no objective can be defined with absolute precision nor achieved perfectly, it is important to use information gained from each evaluation process to improve the planning for the next public relations effort.

Impact Analysis   Measuring the impact or results of a public relations effort is always difficult and never totally objective. As we have discussed in this chapter, however, the more public relations practitioners can quantitatively measure the effects of their work, the better they will be able to plan future efforts and demonstrate their value to organizational decision makers. In this section, we offer four dimensions of measurement that can be applied to assess the impact of any public relations campaign, regardless of its size. These are: *audience coverage, audience response, campaign impact,* and *environmental mediation.*

Audience Coverage   Perhaps the first point that must be documented in evaluating any public relations effort is whether or not the intended audiences were reached. Additional questions that should be answered in the initial phase are: To what extent was each target audience exposed to the various messages? and Which unintended audiences also received the messages?

Two basic measures are used to help answer these questions. First, accurate records must be kept of what messages were prepared and where they were sent. Second, a system must be employed for keeping track of which releases were used and by whom. While the first measure is the easiest to calculate, it is worthless without the second for comparison. Massive amounts of publicity have no value unless some of it actually reaches the intended audience. Therefore, some method must be devised to accurately measure the use of publicity and the coverage of events.

Essentially, such measurement can be accomplished if the practitioner and/or other staff members keep a careful check on target media and maintain clipping files. This, of course, is easier for print than for broadcast media. However, some radio and television stations give periodic reports to public relations practitioners if requested. In addition, clipping services that monitor both print and broadcast media provide regular reports for a fee. Such a service must be selected carefully, based upon the recommendations of other users concerning its accuracy.

The measurement of audience coverage involves more than just the ratio of releases sent compared with releases used. The practitioner must also be able to specify what audiences (both intended and unintended) were reached by which media. This type of data is available from **readership surveys** and audience rating information obtainable through media advertising sales departments. Audience profiles for each publication or broadcast station can be calculated with the amount of space or time used to yield a complete measure of audience coverage. Such data can be reported in terms of total column inches (for print media) or airtime per audience (for broadcast media) for each release or event (see Table 9.1). For more of a bottom line effect, many practitioners translate media time and space into dollar values based on prevailing advertising rates.

Table 9.1 Some Available Measures of Audience Coverage

Column Inches of Space / Airtime in Seconds	Audience Type I	Audience Type II	Audience Type III	Audience Type IV	Magazine A	Newspaper B	Radio Station C	Television Station D	Wire Service
Release 1	271 / 600	450 / 1320	175 / 480	206 / 540	250	375	1250	300	400
Release 2									
Event 1									
Release 3									
Event 2									

Audience Response   Once it has been determined that a message has reached its intended audience, the practitioner must evaluate that audience's response. Frequently, this type of information can be obtained through various message pretesting methods such as those discussed in this chapter and in chapter 7. Samples of each target audience are exposed to various messages before they are released. The resulting data helps predict whether the message will cause a favorable or unfavorable reaction. It can also determine if the message attracts attention, arouses interest, or gains audience understanding. By applying good sampling techniques and questionnaire design (chapter 6), accurate predictions are possible, and problems can be corrected before messages are released. Some messages, however, such as spot news or stories written from releases, cannot be measured in advance because they are not controlled by the practitioner. Thus, it is necessary to measure audience response using the survey techniques discussed in chapter 6. Frequently, audience response can be predicted by tracking media treatment of stories in terms of favorable, neutral, and unfavorable tendencies, as we shall see later in this chapter.

Messages can also be pretested using **readability studies.** The basic premise of these tests is that written copy will be ineffective if it is too difficult to read. Most methods for measuring readability generate an index score that translates to an approximate educational level required for understanding the

---

Table 9.2 Computing the Gunning Fog Index

To check the reading ease of any passage of writing, compute:

1. The number of words in the copy.
2. The number of complete thoughts in the copy.
3. The average sentence length. [number of words ÷ number of complete thoughts]
4. The percentage of difficult words. (words having three or more syllables except: proper names, combinations of short easy words, and verb forms made three syllables by adding -ed or -es)
   [number of difficult words ÷ total number of words]
5. Average sentence length + percentage of difficult words.
6. The figure derived in Step 5 is multiplied by .4 to get the Fog Index Score, the grade level at which the copy is easily read.

---

material. For example, magazines such as *Time* and *Reader's Digest* are written at what is termed an eleventh- or twelfth-grade level. This indicates that their readers are primarily persons with at least a high school education. A great deal of controversy exists over which formula is the most accurate and what factors are necessary to compute readability. However, readability tests may be useful in public relations efforts to tailor writing styles toward target publications. The index score of a news release compared to the score of the publication for which it is intended should indicate whether or not the two are compatible.

Four standard readability instruments are described here:

1. The *Flesch Formula* produces both a reading ease score and a human interest score.[1]
2. The *Gunning Fog Index* measures reading ease only and is one of the simplest methods (see Table 9.2).[2]
3. The *Dale-Chall Formula* computes both sentence length and the number of infrequently used words.[3]
4. *Cloze Procedure* is a technique designed to measure readability and comprehension of both spoken and visual messages.[4]

It should be remembered that the simplest writing is not always the best. Meaning may be lost through oversimplification as well as through complexity. Abstract or complex concepts cannot be adequately expressed in simple, short sentences using one- and two-syllable words. The important point is to match the written message to the publication and audience for which it is intended. This textbook, for example, was written for college students who are studying public relations, not for casual readers. Frequently, editors of internal publications for highly technical organizations must avoid talking down to their readers as much as they avoid "fog."

Campaign Impact   In addition to considering audience response to individual messages, the practitioner must be concerned with the impact of the campaign as a whole. In this case, the whole is not equal to the sum of the parts. If a campaign is correctly researched and planned, its elements will interact to produce an effect that is much greater than the sum of the response to the individual messages. If the mix is not right, however, the elements of the campaign combined, no matter how individually excellent, may fall far short of the goal.

Therefore, it is important to measure the cumulative impact of a public relations campaign, keeping in mind the goals developed in the planning phase. This can be done only after the campaign has been in progress long enough to achieve some results. Effects are generally attitudinal, although they can also be behavioral. If one of the campaign goals is to maintain or increase favorable attitudes toward an organization among members of certain publics, research methods such as organizational image surveys described in chapter 6, can be used to gauge success. Usually this calls for both pretests and posttests, or for a series of surveys to track attitude trends. In addition, certain actions by members of a public can be measured, for example, complaints, inquiries about services, and requests for reprints.

Environmental Mediation   Practitioners must realize that the public relations campaign is not the only influence on the attitudes and behaviors of their publics. Public relations campaigns exist in an environment of social processes that can have as much or more effect on the goals of the effort as the prepared messages do. Therefore, the measured results must be interpreted in light of various other forces in operation. Failure to reach a goal may not be failure at all when unforeseen negative conditions have arisen. Likewise, a striking success may not be entirely attributable to the public relations campaign when positive environmental forces were also present at the time. Therefore, techniques such as environmental monitoring and others discussed in chapter 6 should be used to evaluate the results of a campaign.

One method that can be used to check for environmental influences, even when the practitioner has a small budget and staff, is focus group interviewing. Focus groups are composed of individuals randomly selected from a public who meet to discuss the campaign. The group should be presented with the elements of the campaign and then directed through a discussion of its effects and their causes. A skillful interviewer will direct the discussion to keep it on the subject without disturbing candor or the free flow of ideas. Focus groups should be asked to discuss their reactions to the elements of the campaign and assess its overall effect. They can also help interpret data obtained in the campaign impact stage in relation to historical, social, and political events that may have had an effect.

These four stages of measurement can help a public relations practitioner more completely assess the results of a campaign and plan effective future efforts. In addition, they provide the same kind of real-world data used by managers in other areas of an organization to support their activities.

Sources of
Measurement Error

Some common mistakes in the measurement of public relations effectiveness are:

1. *Volume is not equal to results.* Too often, the working assumption has been that if one press release is effective, three will be three times as effective. As Marker learned, a large stack or even a long chain of press clippings may be proof of effort. But results in terms of the effect of those clippings on the publics for which they were intended cannot be measured by volume. Even audience measurement devices designed to count the number of people exposed to a message do not show whether or not those exposed actually paid any attention or, if they did, what effect the message had on them.

2. *Estimate is not measurement.* Relying on experience and intuition to gauge the effectiveness of public relations efforts is no longer acceptable as objective measurement. Experts know that appearances, even to the trained eye, can be deceiving. Guesswork has no place in a measurement system. It can be appealing and comfortable because it is easy to accomplish and flattering to the expert. However, when it comes to budget requests, managers like the one Marker encountered demand hard facts.

3. *Samples must be representative.* Many wrong decisions about the future of a public relations campaign have been based on a few favorable comments that were either volunteered or collected unsystematically. Several dangers exist: only those with positive (or negative) comments may volunteer them; some people, when asked, tend to give the response they think the interviewer wants to hear; or, the selection of interviewers may be unintentionally biased. Samples must be selected scientifically and systematically to avoid such errors.

4. *Effort is not knowledge.* One of the most common public relations objectives is to increase the public's knowledge about a particular subject. Sometimes practitioners assume a direct relationship between the amount of effort they expend in communicating a message and the amount of knowledge a public acquires. This erroneous assumption leads to a problem similar to the volume error discussed earlier. The study of human learning suggests that after a certain level of knowledge is reached, the rate of learning slows in most people. Therefore, in spite of any communicator's best efforts, all publics will eventually reach a knowledge level at which very little additional learning can be expected to occur.

5. *Knowledge is not favorable attitude.* Communication is often assumed to be successful if the public has gained knowledge of the subject of the message. Even when pretest and posttest results indicate an increase in knowledge, it cannot be assumed that more favorable attitudes have also resulted. A high degree of name recall or awareness is not necessarily an indication that the public relations effort has been effective. Familiarity does not necessarily lead to positive opinion.

6. *Attitude is not behavior.* While positive public opinion may be a
   legitimate goal of public relations, it is incorrect to assume that
   favorable attitudes will result in desired behavior. When members of a
   particular public have favorable attitudes toward a client or
   organization, they will probably not consciously oppose that person or
   group. On the other hand, they still may not actively support the goals
   of the public relations campaign. Our discussion of latent, aware, and
   active publics in chapter 6 emphasized this point. Practitioners must
   be aware of the need to predict behavior, or at least potential
   behavior, when measuring public opinion.

Mark P. McElreath describes two models of public relations research into which
most measurement efforts can be categorized: open and closed evaluation systems.[5] A **closed-system evaluation** limits its scope to the messages and events
planned for the campaign and their effects on the intended publics. This is the
model of public relations evaluation most frequently employed. The intent of
the system is to test the messages and media of a public relations campaign
before they are presented to the intended publics. This pretest strategy is designed to uncover miscalculations that may have gone unnoticed in the planning stage. The posttest evaluation is conducted after the campaign has been
underway long enough to produce results. Posttest data can be compared to
pretest results and campaign objectives in order to evaluate the effectiveness
of the effort. These results also provide input for planning the next campaign.

Closed-System Evaluation

Factors normally considered in the standard pretest and posttest evaluation
design are:

Pretest/Posttest Design

1. *Productions*   An accounting of every public relations tool used in the
   campaign (press releases, press kits, booklets, films, letters, etc.). The
   amount of material actually produced and the total cost of production
   yield important cost-effectiveness information. The amount of time
   and budget devoted to each segment of a public relations effort can be
   reassessed with this type of data.
2. *Distribution*   The channels through which the messages of the
   campaign are distributed. Clippings collected by professional services
   are often used to measure how many stories were actually printed.
   The number of radio and television stations that picked up the story
   can be important information. These kinds of data are perhaps most
   frequently used to evaluate public relations campaigns. It should be
   noted that while they provide a reasonable measure of the efficiency of
   the campaign, distribution data do not really address the issue of
   effectiveness.
3. *Interest*   Reader interest surveys determine what people read in
   various types of publications. A representative sample of the total
   potential reading audience is surveyed to obtain a quantitative
   measure of which items attract more interest. These are relatively

good measures of what readers actually consume, but they do not measure comprehension or the effect of the message on the reader. Television and radio use similar survey methods to determine what programs and times people prefer.

4. *Reach*   Reader interest surveys not only provide information concerning whether or not a story was read, but also describe the people who read it. This information can be valuable because messages frequently reach publics other than those for whom they are intended. The efficiency of a message is the extent to which it actually reaches the intended audience. A reasonably accurate measure of which audiences are being reached by which messages is imperative to any evaluation effort. Television and radio ratings services provide information concerning the characteristics of audiences at various times of the day.

5. *Understanding*   While it is important to determine whether the target audience is being reached, it is equally important to know whether or not the audience can understand the message. A public relations campaign cannot be considered successful in any regard if the public does not get the point. Frequently, readability tests are applied to printed messages to measure their reading ease. As we have already discussed, readability is measured according to sentence length and number of syllables in the words used. While much criticism has been directed at them, they remain standard instruments for pretest evaluation.

6. *Attitudes*   Creating and maintaining positive attitudes or changing negative ones is a central purpose of all public relations activity. Therefore, measuring attitudes, or preferably attitude change, is a highly prized form of evaluation. Frequently a pretest/posttest measurement is conducted to determine the amount of change in the attitudes of target publics that can be attributed to the public relations campaign.

Measuring attitudes is a sophisticated behavioral science technique that presents many opportunities for error. Few practitioners attempt major attitudinal studies without the help of professionals who specialize in this type of measurement. Several of the research techniques discussed in chapter 6 (for example, the public relations audit) use some form of attitudinal measurement. Professional research organizations frequently provide attitudinal data for public relations evaluation. Many factors, ranging from the need for a scientifically selected sample to the construction of a questionnaire that will not bias results, make attitude measurement a difficult task for most practitioners.

While closed-system evaluation is the model most widely used by public relations staffs, it has two major drawbacks. First, as we have already discussed, the fact that a message was transmitted to the intended audience in an understandable form and that it produced favorable attitudes does not mean the campaign goals have been reached. Second, the likelihood that desired results will occur, especially in terms of actual behavior changes, is influenced by a number of factors outside the elements of the campaign. If a public relations effort fails to achieve its goals, it may not mean that the elements or the plan of the effort were faulty. A number of environmental factors such as economic, political, and social change can nullify what might otherwise have been positive results.

Disadvantages of the Closed-System Method

Oil companies caught in the grasp of an embargo that caused rapidly rising prices, shortages, and long lines at the gas pumps experienced losses in favorable public opinion in spite of massive public relations efforts during the early 1970s. The effectiveness of their messages was eroded by events outside the control of any public relations campaign. Therefore, these events had to be considered in evaluating the public relations efforts. While losses rather than gains in positive public opinion were experienced, the campaigns may still have been effective. Without workable public relations plans already in place, the losses in favorable public opinion could have been even more devastating.

Although a pretest/posttest design may be appropriate for evaluating short-range projects, many public relations programs are too complex for simple before-and-after measures. Continuing or long-range programs, such as changes in organizational policy, require an evaluation method that can provide feedback throughout the process without waiting for end results. **Open-system evaluation** models attempt to incorporate factors outside the control of the public relations campaign when assessing its effectiveness.

Open-System Evaluation

The open-system model emphasizes the extent to which the public relations function is encompassed by numerous other aspects of an organization and its environment. Factors such as unintended audiences and organizational administration and effectiveness are also included.

In chapter 6, we discussed the growing use of environmental monitoring and social audits as methods of gathering information. These same techniques provide valuable data for evaluating effectiveness in public relations campaigns. The effects of public relations efforts on various environmental factors can be one useful measure of results. In turn, environmental data can help explain the effects of a campaign. Because most of these factors are outside the organization's control, they may operate as confounding variables in a closed-system evaluation. Economic conditions, for example, can have a significant effect on the attitudes of consumers toward an organization. Thus, results from a public relations effort that do not seem positive when considered alone might really be significant when the negative effects of certain economic conditions are considered.

Internal climate data are also useful for evaluating public relations campaigns. Public relations messages should be expected to have as much effect on the managers and employees of an organization as they do on other publics. In chapter 6, we suggested that organizations research their internal climate for public relations planning information, and this is also true for evaluation. Public relations practitioners should look inside as well as outside their organizations to measure the effects of their efforts. Just as with environmental factors, the internal climate of an organization can help explain the effect of a public relations effort. Union activities, management perceptions, and changes in company policy can all affect the results of a campaign.

Many of the factors included in the open-system evaluation model are difficult to measure accurately. Nevertheless, recognizing these factors is itself an important step toward evaluating public relations efforts. The value of the open-system method of evaluation is that it considers public relations in the broader spectrum of overall organizational effectiveness.

An Open-System Plan in Actual Practice

James F. Tirone, public relations director of American Telephone and Telegraph Company before its breakup, maintains that public relations is a managerial as well as a creative effort.[6] Tirone believes that public relations should meet the same tests of performance as other management functions. This belief is reflected in the classic measurement techniques developed by the Bell System to be uniformly applied in a wide variety of public relations situations. Although they are more than ten years old, the following examples from the Bell System program still represent an excellent attempt to implement an open-system evaluation model in three areas: administrative processes, employee publications, and media relations.

Evaluating Administrative Processes   To measure the effectiveness of public relations administrative processes, Tirone used information already available from standard organization sources to make some unique comparisons. Figure 9.2 shows the correlation between the size of the public relations budget of each of the companies used in the study and their revenues. The graph shows a clear positive correlation (0.91) between the size of public relations budgets and sales income. Figure 9.3 demonstrates an even greater correlation (0.913) between the number of telephones in service and the size of public relations budgets. By relating public relations budgets to these standard measurements in the industry, Tirone was able to show a "return" of public relations expenditures.

PR expense
(In millions)

Operating telephone companies

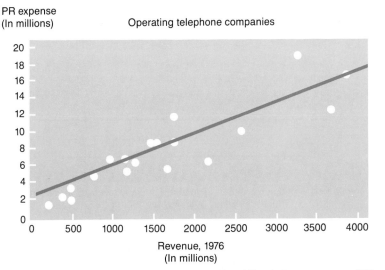

Revenue, 1976
(In millions)

Telephone company revenues compared with public relations expenses, 1976

Figure 9.2 Revenue and public relations expense, 1976

PR budget
(In millions)

Operating telephone companies

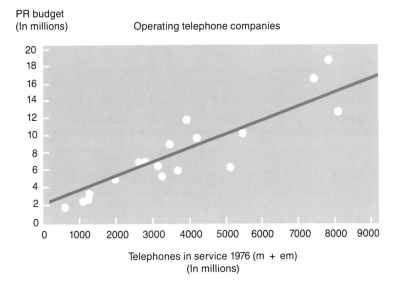

Telephones in service 1976 (m + em)
(In millions)

Figure 9.3 Telephones in service and public relations expense, 1976

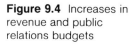

Figure 9.4 Increases in revenue and public relations budgets

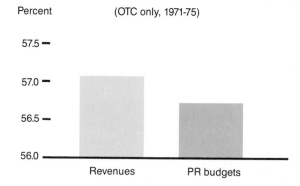

Percent   (OTC only, 1971-75)

57.5 —

57.0 —

56.5 —

56.0 —

Revenues   PR budgets

A comparison of the growth of Bell Telephone Company revenues with the growth of public relations budgets from 1971 to 1975

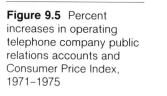

Figure 9.5 Percent increases in operating telephone company public relations accounts and Consumer Price Index, 1971–1975

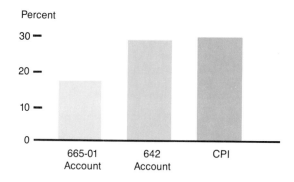

Percent

30 —

20 —

10 —

0

665-01   642   CPI
Account   Account

Comparison of the increase in total Bell Telephone Company public relations (665-01) and advertising (642) expenses with growth of the Consumer Price Index

Figures 9.4 and 9.5 extend this analysis by comparing the increases in public relations budgets with the increases in revenues over a five-year period. Figure 9.4 illustrates that the percentage growth in public relations expenditures had not exceeded the percentage growth in revenues. Taking this comparison still further, Tirone demonstrates that when compared to the increase in the consumer price index (one way to measure inflation), the general public relations budgets had fallen significantly behind, while the advertising budget had stayed even.

Evaluating Employee Publications   The success of employee publications in the Bell System was measured against corporate objectives for them: to "reach all employees, create awareness, establish a reputation for reliability, be written so the material can be understood, and be readable at an educational level appropriate to the audience."[7] These objectives were translated into the following measurement criteria: "how effectively the publication was distributed within forty-eight hours, an average estimate of reader awareness of stories,

Table 9.3 Top Recall by Employees of Company Newspaper Articles (Three Issues of the Publication)

Subject Matter	Unaided Recall
Employment office hiring (1)	56%
Defending the company (3)	42%
Pioneer circus (1)	40%
Marketing/competition (3)	36%
Corporate planning seminar (3-week average)	6%
Averaged recall	36%

Source: James F. Tirone, "Measuring the Bell Sytem's Public Relations," *Public Relations Review* 3 (Winter 1977): 29. Reprinted by permission.

Table 9.4 Employee Publication Scoring

Component	Score
Distribution	67%
Awareness	36%
Reliability (average)	34%
Very understandable	61%
Both sides/Excellent	12%
Source/Excellent	30%
Understanding (CPS only)	40%
Readability (CPS only)	16.5 (Years)

Source: James F. Tirone, "Measuring the Bell System's Public Relations," *Public Relations Review* 3 (Winter 1977): 30. Reprinted by permission.

a reliability index, understanding, and readability (as measured on the Gunning scale)." Table 9.3 reports the ability of a sample of employees to recall (without any help) certain stories that appeared in the company's weekly newspaper. Table 9.4 reports measures of all the components of publication efficiency as operationally defined:

Distribution   Percentage of issues delivered in forty-eight-hour period.

Awareness   Average of recall data.

Reliability   Average response to three questions about the newspaper. Is it: very understandable, excellent at presenting both sides, and an excellent source of information?

Understanding   Percentage of those recalling and comprehending the corporate planning seminar story.

Readability   The Gunning score for the corporate planning seminar story, which is roughly equal to the number of years of education required for comprehension.

Figure 9.6 Total news
stories by tendency

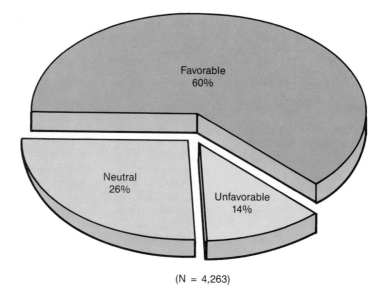

(N = 4,263)

Central tendency of all news items during one-month period

Evaluating Media Relations   Measuring the effectiveness of an organization's relationships with media representatives is a difficult task. Tirone reports three aspects of these relationships that can be measured to some degree: "the media's views of those relationships, the consequences which follow from news release output, and the activity of our (Bell System) media representative."[8] As a first step toward accomplishing these measurement objectives, Tirone proposed a nationwide survey of news media representatives to estimate their ratings of the quality and quantity of Bell System releases. He also instigated an analysis of the media to determine what was actually being said about Bell.

To begin the second phase of the process, Bell hired PR Data Systems, Inc., to code and computerize information collected from clippings and electronic media reports. Figure 9.6 summarizes the percentage of favorable, unfavorable, and neutral news articles about Bell companies in the media surveyed. Figure 9.7 sorts the news items into ten categories relevant to Bell operations and provides favorable, unfavorable, and neutral data for each category. Figure 9.8 reports the number of rebuttals by Bell representatives that were printed in the 503 unfavorable stories included in the sample. Tirone explains that Bell news people are expected to maintain the kind of relationships with news media that will encourage a reporter or editor to call for a company reaction before printing an unfavorable story. Figure 9.8 shows that 45 percent of the unfavorable stories included rebuttal statements from Bell representatives. Over a long period, this type of data could help measure both access to Bell spokespersons and the quality of their relationships with media

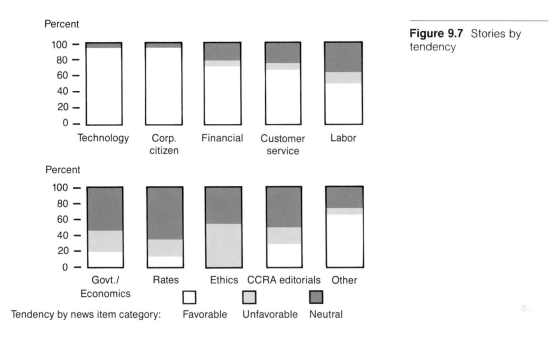

Figure 9.7 Stories by tendency

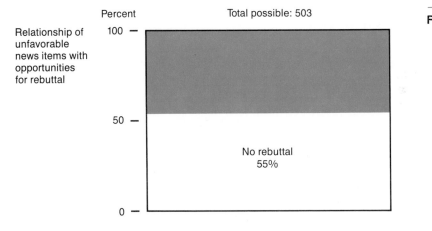

Figure 9.8 Rebuttal ratio

representatives. Tables 9.5 and 9.6 report the percentage of favorable, unfavorable, and neutral stories according to region of the country and media service respectively. From these data, certain discrepancies can be discovered which are useful in pinpointing problem areas and in planning future efforts.

Table 9.5 Newspaper Stories by Region (Total: 3,848)

	Favorable	Unfavorable	Neutral	Totals
Northeast	14%	5%	5%	24%
South	18%	5%	8%	31%
North Central	18%	3%	10%	31%
West	9%	2%	3%	14%
	59%	15%	26%	100%

Source: James F. Tirone, "Measuring the Bell System's Public Relations," *Public Relations Review* 3 (Winter 1977): 34. Reprinted by permission.

Table 9.6 Treatment by Media Services

	Favorable	Unfavorable	Neutral	Total
AP	61%	18%	21%	100%
UPI	19%	33%	48%	100%
Syndicates	43%	22%	35%	100%

Source: James F. Tirone, "Measuring the Bell System's Public Relations," *Public Relations Review* 3 (Winter 1977): 34. Reprinted by permission.

Summary

Frequently, evaluation is assumed to be the final step in the process of public relations; however, it is really best described as a new beginning. Measuring the effectiveness of a public relations effort frequently provides new direction and emphasis for an ongoing program. Even when the project being evaluated does not continue, the lessons learned concerning its effectiveness will be useful in numerous future activities. Knowledge gained through careful evaluation is an important payoff to any public relations effort. Evaluation of projects that are obvious failures can help prevent future mistakes. Careful measurement of successful efforts will help reproduce positive elements in future programs.

Public relations can no longer afford to ignore the question, "But what's it all worth to us?" Practitioners must be ready to respond with appropriate methods, solid data, and accurate predictions.

▲ ▲ ▲

Case Study

American Red Cross
Centennial
Celebration

By Artemio R. Guillermo
*Assistant Professor of
Speech
University of Northern
Iowa
Cedar Falls, Iowa*

Anniversary celebrations can be major public relations events in the life of an organization. Celebrations are especially significant when they mark centennial observances that not only generate mass media coverage but also produce activities highlighting the image of the institution.

Although the planning of most celebrations follows the four-step process of public relations, evaluation is often neglected during the enthusiasm of planning. After activities and programs have been executed, how can planners know whether the celebration was a success? How can they know to what extent their celebration affected their target audience's attitudes toward the organization? What information can the planners get that could be used to evaluate the results of the celebration?

These questions were posed to a public relations student team that undertook to help the Hawkeye Chapter of the American Red Cross celebrate its centennial. When the team volunteered its assistance, the program and activities had already been planned. The overall objective was to project the humanitarian service of the American Red Cross and encourage volunteer participation.

The plan called for a week-long celebration. There were twenty events and activities, including a hot air balloon, a mock disaster, a historical display, a speakers bureau, an open house, an annual meeting and banquet, a centennial blood donor day, a birthday party, and the like.

Printed communications, including a sixteen-page historical booklet and a six-page newsletter, were sent to local institutions and community leaders. The local papers gave the celebration full-page, pictorial coverage with the headline "Happy Birthday." Billboards, media releases, and public service announcements on radio and television were also used to publicize the event.

Although an evaluation was planned by the Red Cross centennial committee, they did not quite know how to proceed. When the students became involved, they decided that their first task was to develop an evaluation instrument.

After consulting with several professors, they devised a form on which to note the following terms:

Project name:

Description:

    Time—

    Place—

Has project been done before? If so, describe:

Intended publics:

    Primary—

    Secondary—

Goals and objectives:

    Strategies—

Cost:

Possible public relations problems:

Method of evaluation:

Results:

Conclusion:

When the centennial celebration started, the public relations team monitored the activities. Twelve out of twenty projects/activities were evaluated.

When all the evaluations were compiled, the students had some interesting findings. One of the hottest items in the celebration as a crowd-drawer was the hot air balloon. An evaluator stated: "Such an event draws attention (biggest advantage), location was good. . . ."

On the other hand, a leaflet enclosed with monthly bank statements, describing the centennial activities, received a low evaluation. Evaluator's comment on the possible public relations effect was: "Confusion by general public as to purpose of stuffer." And the conclusion was that it had low visible response from customers.

All of these evaluations were placed on file with the Hawkeye Chapter of the American Red Cross for future reference as a record of its 100th anniversary celebration.

Questions

1. What is the value of an evaluation of this kind of program?
2. How would you improve the evaluation instrument used in this project?
3. What other forms of evaluation might be appropriate in this situation?

Notes

1. Rudolph Flesch, *How to Test Readability* (New York: Harper and Row, 1951).
2. Robert Gunning, *The Technique of Clear Writing,* rev. ed. (New York: McGraw-Hill, 1968).
3. Edgar Dale and Jeanne Chall, "A Formula for Predicting Readability," *Educational Research Bulletin* 27 (January–February 1948).
4. Wilson Taylor, "Cloze Procedure: A New Tool for Measuring Readability," *Journalism Quarterly* 3 (Fall 1953): 415–33; "Recent Developments in the Use of 'Cloze Procedure'," *Journalism Quarterly* 33 (Winter 1956).
5. Mark P. McElreath, "Public Relations Evaluative Research: Summary Statement," *Public Relations Review* 3 (Winter 1977): 133.
6. James F. Tirone, "Measuring the Bell System's Public Relations," *Public Relations Review* 3 (Winter 1977): 21–38.
7. Ibid., 31.
8. Ibid., 31.

▲ ▲ ▲

PART III

Public Relations: The Publics

A public is a group of people with certain common characteristics. A public can be very large—college students, Republicans, blue-collar workers, even the entire population of the United States. A public can also be quite small—the city council, the budget committee, newspaper editors, or even a single person.

Different organizations have different publics. Big businesses have publics different from those of small businesses. The publics for the steel industry are different from those of the computer industry or agriculture. Not-for-profit organizations have publics different from profit-seeking organizations. Different levels of government organizations deal with different publics.

Part III describes six general types of publics that most public relations professionals face on a regular basis. Chapter 10 discusses the media, one of the most basic publics that practitioners deal with. Chapter 11 delves into the complex relationships between an organization and its community, while chapter 12 focuses on the organization's relationship with its employees. Chapter 13 covers the importance of consumers to modern organizations, and chapters 14 and 15 discuss the impact of financial markets and government agencies on public relations practice.

▲ ▲ ▲

Media Relations
Preview

The media are businesses that gather, package, and sell information.

Journalists have mixed feelings toward public relations practitioners—suspecting them of manipulation, while depending on them for information.

Public relations practitioners view journalists as an audience, a medium through which to reach the broader public, and as gatekeepers representing and responding to the public's need to know.

When public relations practitioners build relationships of confidence and trust with journalists, much mutually beneficial interaction can result.

Three direct ways of intentionally reaching the media include: news releases, discussions with journalists (particularly interviews), and news conferences.

The press will go after anything, and that is the way it should be.

—Ben Wattenberg, coeditor,
Public Opinion

When many people consider the function of public relations, their first thought is: "Those are the folks who deal with the media." And although public relations does far more than deal with the media, that certainly is an important aspect of the job. Media coverage can have significant positive or negative impacts on every aspect of an organization's operations. Public confidence and public support are often determined by the treatment an issue receives in the press and on radio and television.

If a public relations practitioner is to work effectively with the media, he or she must understand how the media function and how reporters work. Insights into journalists' views of public relations and into the working relationship of journalists and public relations practitioners are also essential. Public relations practitioners must be prepared (and must prepare others) to deal with the media face-to-face. Finally, practitioners must be proficient in the art and craft of publicity and knowledgeable about the tools used to gain media attention.

Understanding the Media

The mass media are a pervasive part of modern society. About 1,700 daily and 7,600 weekly newspapers currently operate in the United States. Over 5,000 U.S. magazines are published for a large variety of well-defined audiences. Around 10,000 radio stations provide entertainment and information to people on the go. The 1,150 television stations in the United States are watched in 84 million households an average of more than seven hours every day. Half of these television households subscribe to cable systems that further expand the available programming.

The mass media put us in touch with the world beyond our immediate experience. They shape significantly our perceptions and beliefs—particularly in relation to events and topics with which we have little direct contact. While providing greatly simplified and edited versions of the happenings in our complex and dynamic world, they give us a feeling of participation and understanding.

Most newspapers, magazines, and broadcasting stations are businesses. The publishing and broadcasting industry is about the same size as the automotive industry in terms of market value. Only the beverage and tobacco industries show more profit in terms of return on equity. In short, the media are big, highly profitable businesses.

As businesses, the media sell information and entertainment. They gather and package it in ways that stimulate audiences to spend money or time to read, listen, or watch. Perhaps more importantly, the media sell access to their audiences to advertisers.

Journalists who gather and organize information for the media tend to take their responsibilities to society very seriously. They conceive of themselves as having a sacred public mission: to serve as the public's eyes and ears, to be watchdogs on public institutions doing the public's business. They see their job as seeking the truth, putting it in perspective, and publishing it so that people can conduct their affairs knowledgeably.

That the media's goals of providing truth and making a profit are sometimes in conflict is an issue that will not be pursued here. But anyone who deals with the media, especially public relations practitioners, must recognize that both goals are constantly sought.

Journalists' devotion to their goals causes their view of facts to be quite different from that of their sources. The journalist considers news a highly perishable commodity, while the source of the news is more concerned about the lasting impression a story will make. To the journalist, a story is a transient element in the ongoing flow of information; to the source, it is a discrete event. The journalist is uninterested in the positive or negative flavor of the story, as long as it fairly presents the facts; the source always wants to be cast in a favorable light.

Yet for all the concerns organizations manifest about how their stories are covered, the media's power does not lie in their ability to slant material one way or another, but rather, in what words, deeds, events, or issues they choose to define as news. Douglas Cater, special assistant to President Lyndon Johnson and author of *The Fourth Branch of Government,* put it this way:

> The essential power of the press is its capacity to choose what is news. Each day in Washington tens of thousands of words are uttered which are considered important by those who utter them. Tens of dozens of events occur which are considered newsworthy by those who have staged them. The press has the power to select—to decide which events go on page one or hit the prime-time TV news and which events get ignored.[1]

The Reporter's Job

The journalist's job has been greatly glamorized since reporters Bob Woodward and Carl Bernstein unraveled the political scandals of Watergate in the early 1970s. The handsome men and women of local and network television news are accessible and admirable role models. On a day-to-day basis, however, the job can be highly demanding, stressful, and quite unglamorous. Working in a bullpen atmosphere, without so much as a secretary or office of their own, reporters need all the help they can get.

Journalists collectively maintain that they not only have the responsibility to provide information to the public, but also to provide feedback from society at large to the administrators of public institutions. As society has become more complex and as institutions have come to have greater impact on private lives, journalists have held that more reporting and investigating are necessary to determine the extent to which these institutions measure up to their social and moral obligations. This process, they argue, will ultimately have a positive effect on society as a whole.

The journalist works in an environment that is full of stress and lacks the glamor so often associated with the job.

Reporters, in general, have an overwhelming desire to get facts. Joseph Poindexter points out, "To a reporter, a fact has an inherent worth, in and of itself. To a businessman, a fact is an asset to be invested."[2] Reporters resent anything and anyone they perceive as standing between them and the facts. Anyone who seeks to keep a secret is regarded with deep suspicion. Organizations in business, government, and other fields that conduct themselves in ways considered less than open invite journalistic scrutiny.

Journalists sometimes have difficulty getting the information they need. They claim that highly placed news sources are generally overly insulated, secretive, and sensitive, recognizing neither the public's right to know nor the value of the media's role in exposing questionable practices. Reporters feel that those who complain about media coverage often engage in the ancient practice of seeking to slay the bearers of bad tidings. Besides, say journalists, we don't criticize—we just report what others say.

Still, working journalists echo some of the complaints registered against them by the institutions they cover. Reporters recognize that they frequently have insufficient education and experience to adequately cover complex issues and institutions. They are frustrated by the lack of time, space, and staff needed to do their jobs thoroughly.

In pursuit of facts, etiquette, civility, and even legality are sometimes foregone. Public relations practitioners and others who deal with journalists must remember that when reporters ask "nasty" questions, it is not necessarily because they are antagonistic or ignorant; they are just doing what good reporters are supposed to do.

The Relationship between Journalists and Practitioners

The Reporter's View of the Public Relations Practitioner

Journalists often view public relations practitioners as people who make their livings by using the media to their own advantage. Sometimes considered parasites and referred to as **flacks** or worse, editors often alert young reporters against public relations wiles. As one guidebook for newspaper editors warns: "Your job is to serve the readers, not the man who would raid your columns."[3]

An investigation of journalists' attitudes toward public relations practitioners revealed generally negative attitudes.[4] Closer examination of the data suggested, however, that in certain cases the journalists' responses were contradictory. For instance, while a majority of journalists (59 percent) agreed that "public relations and the press are partners in the dissemination of information," they strongly disagreed (72 percent) with the statement, "Public relations is a profession equal in status to journalism."

On the positive side, a sizeable plurality of journalists (46 percent) agreed that "the public relations practitioner does work for the newspaper that would otherwise go undone." A substantial minority (40 percent) felt that "public relations practitioners are necessary to the production of the daily newspaper as we know it." Nearly half (48 percent) found that "public relations practitioners help reporters obtain accurate, complete, and timely news."

At the same time, however, massive majorities of the journalists (84 percent) believed "public relations practitioners often act as obstructionists, keeping reporters from the people they really should be seeing" and "public relations material is usually publicity disguised as news." Eighty-seven percent felt "public relations practitioners too often try to deceive the press by attaching too much importance to a trivial uneventful happening." Journalists sampled in this research seemingly recognized the dependence of modern media on the public relations profession, but at the same time they condemned what they considered to be standard public relations procedures.

The same research indicated that journalists perceived public relations practitioners to be very different, even opposite to themselves, in terms of their value orientation toward news. Moreover, while ranking themselves first in status among sixteen professional categories, they ranked public relations last.

These findings suggest that public relations practitioners in general are perceived as manipulators of the press and have low credibility. Such findings, in and of themselves, do not augur well for success in public relations practitioners' relationships with journalists. Before leaping to that conclusion, however, we had better take a look at public relations' view of journalism.

The Public Relations Practitioner's View of the Journalist

From the public relations practitioner's perspective, the journalist is at once an audience, a medium through which to reach the larger public, and a gatekeeper representing and responding to the public's need to know. Some go so far as to say that the practitioner's livelihood depends on reporters' or editors' decisions to use his material.

Because of this dependency, practitioners' selection and presentation of information often conforms more to journalistic standards than to the desires of their superiors in their own organizations. In a sense, both the journalist and the practitioner, in dealing with each other, are caught between the demands of the organizations they represent and the demands of the opposite party. Public relations practitioners, as boundary spanners, are often caught in the middle between journalistic and other institutions, trying to explain each to the other.

The relationship between public relations practitioners and journalists is one of mutual dependency. Although journalists like to picture themselves as reluctant to utilize public relations information, economic considerations force them to do otherwise. A news staff capable of ferreting information from every significant organization in a city without the assistance of representatives for those organizations would be prohibitively expensive. Indeed, numerous studies have placed public relations' contribution to total news coverage in excess of 50 percent.[5] Moreover, the public relations practitioner makes the journalist's job much easier, saving time and effort and providing information that might otherwise be unavailable.

Mutual Dependence

To a considerable extent, the purposes of the news outlet and the public relations practitioner overlap. Both wish to inform the public of things that affect them. This provides the basis of a cooperative system for disseminating information. In this sense, public relations practitioners function as extensions of the news staff. They play a specific, functional, cooperative role in society's information-gathering network, even though they owe no loyalty to specific news outlets, are not paid by them, and may never set foot in the building in which the news is produced.

Communication between certain public relations practitioners and journalists is massive. Some public relations offices send out news releases daily. Additionally, personal contact and communication may be initiated by either party. The amount of communication between journalists and public relations practitioners is a measure of their dependency on one another. In some instances, public relations practitioners provide more useful information to specific media than do the journalists those media employ.

Through the efforts of public relations practitioners, the media receive a constant flow of free information. Facts that journalists might not have acquired otherwise become available in packaged form. The reporter or editor, as we noted above, can then decide what is newsworthy. As the editor of an Ohio daily newspaper remarked with relish, "I'm the guy who says 'yes' or 'no,' the public relations man has to say 'please.' "

That editor's assessment of journalists' power is strictly accurate only when public relations practitioners and journalists share no dependency. When interdependency exists, journalists retain nominal veto power over incoming information, but they abdicate much of their decision-making responsibility to public relations practitioners who select and control material given out.

While journalists may reject one or another news release, they depend upon the constant flow of information from representatives of important institutions. To a large extent, journalists are processors of information passed on by public relations practitioners who do the primary gathering.

Under these circumstances, journalists' main means of control becomes their ability to refuse to deal with public relations practitioners who fail to meet subjective standards. But even such rejection is impossible when the public relations practitioner is firmly entrenched in the institution. As much as Washington journalists would have liked to avoid using material from Ron Ziegler, press secretary in the final days of the Nixon presidency, they did not have that option.

Building Positive Relationships

While much may be said about the art and craft of preparing materials for media consumption, perhaps nothing is so important to successful publicity as the relationships established between public relations practitioners and journalists.

A reporter for the Austin, Texas, *American Statesman* was discussing his work. "I *never* accept information from PR flacks," he said. When it was pointed out to him that during the past week he had used material from corporate, university, and political publicity people, he replied: "Those aren't PR flacks, those are reliable sources."

When public relations practitioners take the time and make the effort to establish good personal relations with journalists, they are much more likely to attract positive news coverage for their organizations. It can be said that good public relations begins with good personal relations.

Tips for Getting Along with Journalists   As in all walks of life, it is good for public relations practitioners to get to know the people they work with. Sometimes the direct approach is effective. Call a journalist with whom you know you will be working. Introduce yourself. Suggest lunch or a drink. Another approach is to hand-deliver a news release to provide an opportunity for a brief introduction and meeting. Some journalists appreciate the effort. Says one: "I like to meet new PR-types just to see who they are. I like to tell them what I want and don't want."

Other journalists, however, would rather not be bothered. With them, an indirect approach is required. Belonging to the local press club, attending meetings of Sigma Delta Chi (a professional journalism fraternity), or becoming involved in community activities in which journalists are also involved, are ways of getting to know media counterparts. Indeed, journalists are often hired for publicity jobs not only for their writing skills but also for their network of media contacts.

Once relationships are established, protect and cherish them. Do not squander valuable relationships by using them for small favors or one-shot story placements. Do not ruin a relationship by expecting a reporter to always do what you want. Take no for an answer. Do not insult your relationship with inappropriate gifts—journalists are sensitive to even the appearance of conflicts of interest.

Cultivate your relationships with journalistic colleagues by giving good service. Provide sufficient and timely information, stories, and pictures, when and how they are wanted. Be on call twenty-four hours a day to respond to reporters' needs and questions.

Nothing will destroy a relationship faster or more completely than an affront to the truth. Accuracy, integrity, openness, and completeness are the basis for trust bestowed by journalists. Once trust is broken, it can rarely be regained.

Finally, to assure good relations with journalists, the practitioner should behave in a professional way. Live up to expectations. Do not play favorites among the media. Do not beg for favors, special coverage, or removal of unfavorable publicity.

Working with the Media

With a basic understanding of the complex relationships between public relations practitioners and journalists, we can outline a few general principles for working with the media. In the first place, managers must reconcile themselves to the legitimacy of the media's role in monitoring the performance of their organizations and leaders. Managers and institutions must understand and accommodate the unique position of the media, realizing that, on one level, an adversarial relationship is normal.

The best advice in dealing with the media is to give journalists what they want in the form and language they want. Respond quickly and honestly to media requests for information. By working to establish a relationship of mutual trust with particular journalists, you can defuse many potentially antagonistic encounters.

Preparing to Meet the Media

Consider the following situations:

You are the chief public relations official for a major company. A reporter calls your office at 9 A.M. She wants to see you for an interview at 11 A.M. She wants your company to respond to allegations made by a source that she is not at liberty to disclose. All she will say is that the charges deal with corporate finances and questionable conduct of certain corporate officials.

As the public relations director of a major private university, you decide to hold a press conference to announce the initiation of an important fund-raising effort. A prominent alumnus has donated $5 million to kick off the campaign. You know that recent media coverage has criticized the university's budgetary problems, tuition hikes, and incursions into neighborhoods around the school which displaced poor people and eroded the community tax base.

You are the community relations director of the local police force. A reporter calls to request a meeting with your chief about low police morale resulting from the city's inability to meet rank-and-file demands for pay raises. When you attempt to arrange an interview for the following afternoon, the chief berates you, saying: "It's your job to keep the press off my back. Why can't you handle the guy's questions?" You convince the chief that the reporter would not talk to you because he said he was tired of the chief hiding behind his "flack." You tell him departmental integrity and morale depend on his willingness to deal with the press. You promise to help him prepare. He reluctantly agrees to the interview.

Opportunities Offered by Media Contact

In each of these cases, a meeting with the media represents a critical challenge to the organization. Some organizations see such challenges as problems to be overcome. It is more constructive, however, to view them as opportunities. Publicity cannot replace good works or effective action, but it can gain attention for issues, ideas, or products. It can spotlight an organization's personality, policies, or performance. It can make something or someone known.

Every media contact is an opportunity to get feedback, to tell your story, to create a positive response to your organization. Of course there are dangers—but what opportunity presents itself without risk? And what opportunity can be taken without preparation?

Preparation Strategies

Preparation to meet the media is essential for both individuals and organizations. Preparation means more than getting psyched up about a particular interview, because when the opportunity comes, there may be little time to prepare, as the preceding cases suggest. In the first example, a company official would have only two hours to gather information and prepare strategy to deal effectively with some very sensitive issues.

Before anyone in the organization meets with the media, the first step is to develop the proper set of attitudes. Meeting the media is an opportunity, not a problem; therefore, defensiveness is not appropriate. There is no need to feel intimidated—particularly if your objective is worthy. In the case of the university's fund-raising campaign, the purpose of the press conference must be kept firmly in mind. The public relations director should refuse, in a friendly way, to be dragged by reporters' questions into subjects other than the donation and campaign.

The attitude of the interviewee toward the journalist should be one of hospitality, cooperation, and openness. At the same time, the interviewee should realize that the reporter need not be the person in control. The interviewee should decide what needs to be said and say it—no matter what the reporter's questions may be. A positive mental attitude is essential. Once this attitude is established among everyone in an organization who may be called upon to be interviewed, it becomes much easier and less traumatic to prepare for specific interviews. After the chief of police completes one interview successfully, the next will be more easily handled.

Before looking further at how individuals can interact successfully with the media, we will discuss how organizations can publicize themselves effectively.

Research and Planning in Media Relations   The old saying "Success is when opportunity meets preparation" is never truer than when applied to publicity. As we showed in earlier chapters, preparation indicates research and planning.

In media relations, research means knowing who you are dealing with and what they are interested in. Media relations specialists deal primarily with their own management and with the media, so they must understand both parties well.

The managements of various organizations differ in their attitudes toward media relations. The oil company Amerada Hess does not return calls from the press. Procter & Gamble encourages coverage of its products, but not its manufacturing processes. Bank of America during recent financial problems, Johnson & Johnson during the Tylenol panic, and AT&T during deregulation all benefitted from their candor and openness during difficult times.[6] In each case, media relations strategy was based on an understanding of management's desired approach. Adolph Coors Company provides another example in Mini-Case 10.1.

After understanding the organization, the publicist must study the specific media with which he or she will work. Research in this area consists of finding out the interests and needs of the people affiliated with the various media outlets. Media guides can provide some of this information. Effective media relations specialists also maintain their own file systems, rolodexes, and charts to keep track of the personal qualities and preferences of the media people with whom they work.

Planning for publicity follows the processes discussed in chapter 7. Publicity plans can deal with an organization's overall efforts or with a specific situation or campaign. In general, media plans will describe the circumstances with which the organization is dealing, lay out goals or objectives, identify key audiences, specify strategies, list action steps, identify special media to be contacted, and provide for evaluation.

Mini-Case 10.1

Silence Is No Longer Golden at Coors

"A quality product will speak for itself." That philosophy guided the communication efforts of Golden, Colorado, brewer Adolph Coors's company until the late 1970s. Before 1976, the company had a three-person public relations staff charged with the responsibility of saying, "No comment." But by 1983, the corporate communication staff numbered twenty-four.

A variety of external and internal pressures—including an emotional 1977 strike—made Coors more conscious of using communication to accomplish company objectives. Coors representatives made hundreds of media visits to introduce themselves and explain that "silence is no longer golden at Coors," according to Shirley Richard, the company's director of corporate communications.

In April 1982, the communication staff was put to the ultimate test. The television program "60 Minutes" called. Investigative journalist Mike Wallace would do a feature on Coors and its labor problems.

The corporate communication department went to work. A written plan with clear objectives was developed. Complete openness was the operating philosophy. The CBS-TV team was invited to the brewery and given access to all workers. The communication staff responded immediately to any request for information.

"We couldn't have told the story any better ourselves," Richard explained after the feature was broadcast. "We accomplished all the objectives we set." The investigative report delighted the people of Golden, generated pro-Coors editorials, and eased labor tensions.

Richard reviewed the lessons learned in the Coors experience with "60 Minutes":

Be open, honest, and never refuse to respond to a reporter's request for information.

Set clear message objectives so you can tell your company's best stories.

Educate your company executives on how to work with the news media and familiarize them with your media objectives.

Be prepared.

Complete openness was the operating philosophy of Coors' corporate communications department.

SILENCE IS NO LONGER GOLDEN.

Not long ago, when you called Coors with a question, you could only cross your fingers and hope for an answer.

You see, mum was the word in Golden, Colorado.

It wasn't that we had some deep, dark secret. Or that we broke out in hives when faced with a microphone or a reporter's pad.

Quite the opposite.

We're proud of the way we do things here. And to put it simply, we thought that was all that mattered.

So we kept our silence.

Then we looked at the other side of the coin. And saw that others were genuinely interested in what we were doing. And how we were doing it.

We saw that talking about our programs on the environment, energy, and minority hiring wouldn't be self-serving. It would be serving everybody.

So now when you call us with a question, make sure you have a pencil handy. We've taken "no comment" out of our vocabulary.

And that's good news for both of us. *Coors*
Corporate Communications Dept.

LET'S TALK (800) 525-3786
In Colorado (800) 332-3725

Adolph Coors Company, Golden, Colorado 80401

Source: Shirley Richard, "Coors Cans the 'No Comment' Media Response," *Communication World* (September 1983): 18.

Publicity is a broad term that refers to the publication of news about an organization or person for which time or space was not purchased. The appeal of publicity is credibility. Because publicity appears in the news media in the form of a story rather than an advertisement, it receives what amounts to a third-party endorsement from the editor. Since the editor has judged the publicity material newsworthy, the public is not likely to perceive it as an advertisement. Publicity may, therefore, reach members of an organization's publics who would be suspicious of advertising.

Publicity can be divided into two categories: spontaneous and planned. A major accident, fire, explosion, strike, or any other unplanned event creates **spontaneous publicity.** When such an event occurs, news media will be eager to find out the causes, circumstances, and who is involved. While spontaneous publicity is not necessarily negative, it should be handled through standing plans such as those for emergencies discussed in chapter 7.

Planned publicity, on the other hand, does not originate from an emergency situation. It is the result of a conscious effort to attract attention to an issue, event, or organization. Time is available to plan the event and how it will be communicated to the news media. If a layoff, plant expansion, change in top personnel, new product, or some other potentially newsworthy event is contemplated, the method of announcing it is a major concern. How an event is perceived by an organization's publics can determine whether publicity is "good" or "bad."

Publicity

The method by which an event is communicated can determine its impact. Three direct ways of intentionally reaching the media are through a release, a discussion (conversation, phone call, meeting, or interview), or a news conference.

How to Reach the Media

The publicity, news, or press release is the heart of any publicity effort. It is the simplest and least expensive way to reach the media. Releases can be duplicated and sent to dozens, even thousands, of news outlets. They should be used to convey routine news, to provide potential feature or background material, or to provide follow-up information.

Publicity releases take many forms depending upon the audience and medium for which they are intended. Still, some general rules apply in most instances. A publicity release should always be prepared to conform to accepted journalistic style. The opening paragraph (lead) should generally be planned as a complete account that can stand by itself. If the lead answers the five basic questions (who, what, when, why, and where), an editor with a very limited amount of space or time can still use the story.

Some stories can lose their impact, however, if too many facts are forced into the lead. In such cases, the writer should select only one or two major facts that will attract the reader's (and editor's) interest. If the person being written about is not prominent, the writer may choose not to mention his or

Preparing Publicity Releases

her name in the opening; this technique is known as a *blind lead*. More specifics about how to write a news story are covered in chapter 8. Once the essential facts have been organized into an opening paragraph, details and elaboration should follow in descending order of importance to allow editors to cut the story to fit the space or time available.

Attention to a few general guidelines will result in more effective publicity releases:

1. Keep releases direct and factual. Supplemental information can be provided on a separate fact sheet included with the release.
2. The information included should be appropriate to the medium to which it is sent. Do not bother editors with material you know they cannot use.
3. The standard format for most publicity releases calls for the use of eight-by-eleven-inch paper and wide margins, with copy typed double-spaced on only one side of the page.
4. Releases which run more than one page in length should carry a page number at the center top of each page, beginning with the second. Also, each page should end with a complete sentence in case the pages are separated. To indicate that the material is continued on another page "more" is generally typed in the center at the bottom of the page. Usually "-30-" is typed in the center at the bottom of the last page to indicate the end of the copy.
5. When photographs are included with a release, the caption line should be glued to the bottom border with rubber cement. The name, address, and telephone number of the contact should appear on the back of the photograph.

Figure 10.1 shows a sample publicity release that illustrates the guidelines stated here. Always check each publicity release carefully for accuracy. Errors in fact or omission of important details can be embarrassing both to the public relations manager and the organization. Some common errors are described in the following excerpt:

> One of our volunteer reporters scooped up at random an armful of press kits at the recent National Boat Show in New York's Coliseum, scanned them with the professional eye of a seasoned public relations executive, then sent them along to us with some interesting—if discouraging—observations. After checking his comments against material in the kits and adding a few findings of our own to the list, we came to the conclusion that some product publicists in the marine field are careless, some are lazy, and some simply don't know how to put together a proper news release. For example:
>
> 1. Three-quarters of the releases were undated.
> 2. At least half either lacked any follow-up press contact information (gave only name and address of manufacturer) or the information was incomplete (no telephone number, or PR firm name but no individual to ask for).
> 3. Some picture captions were stapled to photographs, while others were so flimsily attached they came apart when handled.

DELTA AIR LINES / Public Relations / Hartsfield Atlanta International Airport / Atlanta, Georgia 30320 U.S.A. / Telephone: 404 765-2600

DELTA AIR LINES TO BECOME "OFFICIAL AIRLINE"
FOR THE WALT DISNEY WORLD RESORT IN FLORIDA

ATLANTA, GA, January 30, 1987 -- Delta Air Lines will become the official airline of Walt Disney World on July 1, 1987, and will present a new and expanded version of the Magic Kingdom's popular ride-through travel attraction in Tomorrowland.

Formerly called "If You Had Wings," the travel adventure will carry visitors on a tour of favorite Delta destinations. Designs for the Delta attraction are currently being prepared by Walt Disney Imagineering.

Frank Wells, president of The Walt Disney Company, said, "We are delighted to have Delta Air Lines as a partner in bringing millions of visitors to Walt Disney World. Delta has provided outstanding service to the Orlando/Walt Disney World destination during the fast growth of the past 15 years. With recent expansions throughout the United States and its service to Europe, the Caribbean and the Pacific area, Delta is able to offer our guests the most convenient schedules to this area.

"We expect to work closely with Delta in promoting travel to Florida and Walt Disney World as the world's No. 1 destination resort," Wells concluded.

Ron Allen, Delta's president and chief operating officer, said, "We at Delta are excited about our forthcoming relationship with Walt Disney World. The Magic Kingdom is close to all our hearts, and Delta proudly accepts the responsibility of bringing the world to Walt Disney World's front door.

"The full resources of Delta, with its greatly-expanded route system created as a result of the acquisition of Western Air Lines, bring the doors of the Magic Kingdom to within easy walking distance of all of us who never tire of Mickey and Donald and the wonders of Walt Disney. We'll be developing special Delta Dream Vacation packages to Walt Disney World, and our world-wide marketing operation will be springing into action to promote Walt Disney World and Florida as the No. 1 vacation attraction.

"We at Delta Air Lines are proud to be the official airline of Walt Disney World," Allen said.

Eastern Air Lines, a Walt Disney World participant since 1971, will continue its current relationship until the end of May. All Eastern Air Lines' packages with Walt Disney World will be fulfilled.

###

Figure 10.1 Sample publicity release. (Courtesy of Delta Air Lines.)

4. One company's release was single-spaced flush left, contained quotes without attribution, and misspelled "Coliseum."

5. The lead in another company's nine-page release was exactly the same this year as last except that the date had been changed. The president's statement about the new product line also was precisely the same in both years; and the balance of the nine pages closely followed the previous pattern—word for word in some short paragraphs.

6. In one almost unbelievable case, a PR firm handling the publicity for three marine equipment companies (two are competitors, incidentally) not only single-spaced all the releases but left practically no margins and then framed the stories with a heavy rule. Included in the kit were several unidentified photographs. Compounding the agony, every release had a return card attached so the editor could report when and how he planned to use the story.[7]

Timing   The planning process for any public relations campaign should include some consideration of when to issue publicity releases to achieve maximum impact. Many considerations affect the timing. Information should not be released too far in advance of an event because it may become lost on an editor's desk or, if published, may be forgotten before the event occurs. On the other hand, release too close to an event can be a problem if editors do not have enough notice to plan for the material. Time of day can be an important factor in the delivery of a release. It is always wise policy to check with editors about deadlines. These will differ depending upon the medium. Some newspapers and broadcast media have days that are lighter than others and these are good times to get a release used.

Clearing Publicity
Releases

Exhibit 10.1

News releases and other publicity material are designed to create positive perceptions of your organization or client in the minds of target publics. Even the most experienced practitioner, however, cannot foresee all the potential consequences of any message. Thus, it is important to plan a system of checks for any message before it is released from your office. The following are some suggestions:

1. Preparation stage

   Preliminary approval of your first draft should be secured from the person(s) involved or in charge.

   A later draft should be sent to the top officer of the organization who is responsible for public relations activities.

   After any further revisions, the next draft should go to the legal department for review.

   In some cases, other managerial personnel should receive draft copies with an opportunity to comment before publication. This decision must be made based upon responsibilities and sensitivities in the organization.

2. Distribution of final copy of release

   An internal distribution list should be prepared for each release to target important internal publics. Those who should receive copies include:

   All personnel mentioned by name in a release;

   Editors of local and national internal publications;

   Everyone involved in the draft-approval stage;

   Public relations and advertising firms associated with the organization;

   All target media representatives.

Types of Releases The most common type of publicity release is the **news release** (Figure 10.1). Any occurrence within the organization that may have local, regional, or national news value is an opportunity for publicity. Sometimes this news is not favorable to the organization. Even in these cases, however, a release is necessary. The news will always get out when something goes wrong. The role of the public relations practitioner is to be certain that the full story is told and that corrective actions are reported.

Business features An important form of publicity, and one highly prized by many organizations, is the feature article carried by professional, business, trade, or technical publications. Specialized periodicals that address a narrowly-defined audience have increased dramatically in recent years, and these allow public relations practitioners to focus on a particular audience for maximum effectiveness. Some analysis of feature articles will provide an insight into the type and style of story editors prefer. Such publications tend to publish articles that define problems common to a particular profession or industry and describe an organization's attempts to deal with it. Unique uses of existing products, or products developed to meet old problems, are also frequent subjects. Public relations professionals often employ free-lance writers who specialize in the particular field of the target publication. Most organizations have numerous other outlets for this type of publicity, including in-house technical reports, speeches discussing new technology or products, and papers prepared for professional societies.

Consumer service features Many newspapers and magazines, as well as some television stations, publish or broadcast material designed to assist consumers. Information about almost any consumer product or service can become a vehicle for both product and institutional publicity. Stories that provide consumer-oriented information concerning food, travel, fashion, child care, books, home management, and numerous other topics are in demand by many publications. Frequently, the recipes, food photographs, travel stories, and fashion news contained in special newspaper sections are provided by public relations practitioners representing various manufacturers and industry associations.

Financial features   Most newspapers and television stations and some magazines and radio stations carry financial news and feature articles, and a growing number of publications specialize in that area. Such publicity can be an especially effective tool for shareholder relations (see chapter 14) because current and potential investors assign more credibility to information when an independent editor selects it for publication. Potential sources of financial publicity include: dividend announcements, mergers, profit reports, expansions, new product lines, major orders, changes in top personnel, research breakthroughs, and many other events that might be of interest to the financial community in general.

Product features   Product publicity can frequently be newsworthy enough to be selected for use by news editors. Stories about products should be directed to periodicals, newspaper sections, and television and radio programs specializing in consumer product information. Editors and others who use this type of material are interested in information concerning the features, composition, performance, and application of products that will help consumers with their purchasing decisions. This type of publicity can build goodwill, develop customer loyalty, and create product awareness for manufacturers, distributors, and retailers. In addition to exploiting unique product features, the public relations practitioner can create newsworthy events to dramatize and illustrate product performance for media representatives.

Pictorial features   The increasing popularity of photojournalism has made more newspapers and magazines receptive to newsworthy or unusual photographs that can communicate a message by themselves. Such photographs are often used with only a caption line and no accompanying story. Because these high-quality, unique photographs are difficult for assignment editors to plan, they provide an excellent opportunity for publicity. A public relations manager should always be alert for photographs that might be good enough for this purpose.

Many organizations employ staff photographers, and their work should be constantly examined for exceptionally good or unusual shots. Photographs taken for in-house publications, annual reports, or even advertising may present opportunities for publicity. Special events should always be planned with good publicity photographs in mind. Frequently, newspaper and television editors assign photographers to special events if they know in advance of a good possibility for getting an unusual or newsworthy photograph.

Publicity photographs should normally be printed on seven-by-nine-inch or eight-by-ten-inch paper, depending on the editor's preference. Print media prefer high-gloss photographs with a caption line attached, while television stations prefer slides instead of prints, but specifications should be determined in advance. Photographs for television should always be in color. Color photographs are sometimes used by newspapers and magazines, but black-and-white photos are standard.

Exhibit 10.2

Whether or not you have to actually take the photographs that will accompany your releases, some tips to make them more effective include:

1. Avoid busy, cluttered backgrounds that may detract from your subject.
2. Don't photograph subjects head-on. Photographs taken from a slight side angle are more natural.
3. Candid shots of subjects are better than posed "mug shots."
4. Too much space around a subject can be distracting. Try to keep your photographs tightly framed.
5. Photograph groups in a natural cluster, never in a stiff row.
6. Avoid the temptation to photograph too many people in a group.
7. Generally, faces should be at least as large as the nail of your little finger.
8. Ask for proof sheets from the processor before selecting negatives for printing.
9. Make sure the people in your photographs receive prints.
10. Always obtain a release, even for internal publications and file photos. A release should contain the following:

    Subject's name

    Signature of person (parent or guardian for minors)

    Statement granting permission for all photographs taken

    Date, time, and place photographs were taken

    Statement that photos may be used for either publicity or advertising

    Name of the organization

Packaging Publicity Releases   Packaging in the form of **press kits** can frequently increase the probability that information from a publicity release will actually be used by an editor. A press kit is simply a collection of publicity releases enclosed in a cover or some other packaging device. But although attractive packaging can be helpful in gaining the attention of a busy editor whose desk is covered with competing releases, design is not the primary consideration in compiling a press kit. News releases, photographs, fact sheets, background information, and features should be packaged in an organized and readable form to enable the editor to select the information he or she wishes to use. The strategy behind any press kit should be based on the realization that most major media will not use a release verbatim, but will instead select information to be rewritten into a story unique to their publication. A press kit should be designed to help editors select the information they need.

Jane Paley, a former vice president of Manning, Selvage and Lee Public Relations, lists the following standard components of a press kit:

A lead story   The strongest news piece you have. Keep it short; one page is terrific; don't exceed two.

Backgrounders   These may run five to seven pages and should offer depth, detail, and well-documented facts and figures.

Photographs, diagrams, graphs   Should be 8″ × 10″ black-and-white glossies designed to reproduce clearly. Each should be captioned to identify and clarify subjects. Photos of products, personalities, and action shots are all acceptable.[8]

The basic rules for preparing any release apply to preparing the press kit. Always check your facts, avoid being overly commercial, never lie or deliberately misrepresent, and use only credible sources for value judgments and quotations. While photographs and artwork help to attract an editor's attention, they must be appropriate to the subject of the release. Folders, binders, and other packaging devices must be functional for the editor as well as unique and attractive. Mini-Case 10.2 provides an example of a creatively designed press kit that was strategically planned for maximum effectiveness.

Quality Kit
Produced for
Johnson Wax U.S.
Consumer Products

Mini-Case 10.2

The objectives of producing this kit were (1) to communicate the scope and diversity of the company's product lines, (2) to emphasize the quality of the products, (3) to offer consumers a host of free resources available through the consumer services division, and (4) to apprise the consumer of the economic benefits of buying quality products and using them correctly.

The phrase "Quality is $ in the Bag" was developed as an umbrella or overall theme for the kit, which was housed in a brown paper shopping bag that included product samples, consumer literature, and the kit, whose graphic elements complemented the grocery bag theme.

In fact, the kit's hard-bound laminated folder contained vertically bound shopping bags complete with serrated edges. On each bag was printed a calendar month with ample space for appointments and deadlines. And each bag held releases with consumer information geared to surviving in tight money times.

Each kit also contained a response card for feedback which was incorporated into follow-up mailings. Each month, a news release and product sample followed, as a reminder of the initial mailing, and more significantly, as a means of continually expanding editorial awareness of Johnson Wax products and services.

Source: Jane Paley, "The Press Kit: Staple of the Public Relations Cupboard," *Sky,* a publication of Delta Air Lines (June 1980): 36. Reprinted by permission.

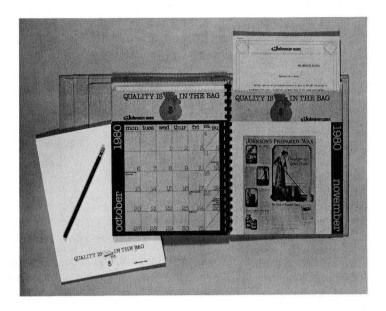

"Quality Is $ in the Bag" press kit prepared for and distributed by Johnson Wax

Press kits do not need to be as elaborate and costly as the example in Mini-Case 10.2 to be effective. Releases can be packaged in simple but well-designed one- or two-color folders, as long as they are adaptable to a variety of media needs. The basic role of a press kit is to provide information to editors that would otherwise take many hours to research. Press kits can provide a service for the media by saving research time and identifying important information for consumers and others. The organization, of course, stands to gain favorable publicity.

Getting media representatives to cover an event is only the start. The quality, quantity, and favorableness of their coverage as well as whether or not they will come back the next time they are invited may depend upon the facilities you provide for their use. A **newsroom** is simply an area set aside to provide information, services, and amenities to journalists covering a story. The following tips will help set up a newsroom:

Setting Up a Newsroom

1. Information must be accessible. All fact sheets, releases, photos, and people to be interviewed must be readily available.
2. The staff must be qualified and experienced. The impressions media representatives gain of the organization and the event are influenced by the competence of those who are assigned to help them.

3. A convenient, yet insulated location is important. The newsroom, interview rooms, and other media facilities should have easy access to the events, but be separated enough to prevent interference.
4. Both print and broadcast facilities should be provided. For example, three separate interview rooms should be set up for television, radio, and print.
5. The newsroom must be well supplied, containing:

    Telephone lines and any special hookups needed for broadcasts

    Copy machines

    Individual stations (desks, tables, cubicles) for reporters

    Adequate lighting and electrical outlets

    Typewriters and supplies

    Telex transmitters and newswire receivers (when necessary)
6. It is accepted custom to provide refreshments. These can range from meals and cocktails to coffee and donuts. The event and the length of time media representatives must stay in the newsroom should be considered in determining what is appropriate. The objective is to encourage representatives to stay close to the action.

Communicating Orally with the Media

The second direct way of dealing with the media is through discussion. Rather than presenting information in written form, some kind of direct oral interaction occurs between the journalist and the public relations practitioner in the form of simple conversations, phone calls, meetings, or interviews. Whether these interactions appear informal or formal, they should never be taken lightly. Any interaction with a journalist is an opportunity for positive publicity.

While public relations practitioners often serve as the journalist's source of information, they also often provide a link between journalists and organization executives. It becomes the public relations person's role to coach and assist the executive when he or she is not accustomed to dealing with the media. Thus, the following material relates to two possible situations: (1) when the public relations person is being interviewed and (2) when the public relations person is advising someone else in the organization about being interviewed.

Specific Interviews   The first step in preparing for a specific interview is to determine exactly what message you want to get across to the ultimate audience—those who will read the article or listen to the news on radio or television. The interviewee should establish in his or her own mind the major point of the interview, the *bottom line*. In the example presented earlier concerning allegations of questionable conduct, the bottom line might be that the company takes great pride in its honesty and integrity and will take every step to maintain its good name. In the case of the major gift to the university, the bottom line might be that the university is a great institution that makes significant contributions to its community and deserves the support of all its publics. In the case concerning police morale, the bottom line might be that despite a problem, the city's police consider themselves professionals devoted to safety and service.

President Ronald Reagan established a reputation as a great communicator, in spite of widely reported slips and misstatements, because he was able to transmit a message of confidence.

Once the bottom line for the interview is established, gather information to support that position. Plan to relate all items of information to the basic message. Organize material for the interview around the major point and be prepared to return to it consistently. In this way, you may control the interview rather than allowing it to control you.

The second step is to consider the audience—both the particular journalist who will conduct the interview and the ultimate audience who will read or listen to what the journalist writes. Does the reporter have a particular approach, hypothesis, or philosophy? How can messages be phrased to appeal to the interests and needs of the reporter and the ultimate audience?

Third, anticipate the interview. Many organizations even rehearse interviews—with the public relations practitioner playing the reporter, while the executive who is to be interviewed plays herself or himself. Remember the reporter's basic questions: who, what, when, where, why, and how. Try to organize material like a journalist would. Do not consider a chronologically ordered presentation. Rather, try to think in the reporter's inverted pyramid style, with the broadest, most important points first, followed by the details. Try to visualize the first paragraph of an article developed from the interview as it would appear in print.

Fourth, have as much information as you can accumulate at your fingertips. It is almost impossible to overprepare. Develop alternative angles and back-up facts. Also be prepared to suggest the names of other people to whom the reporter might talk, and inform those people that their names will be used so that they can prepare.

Finally, develop an interview strategy. This plan will depend on the nature of your material and the interview situation. Shall a balanced approach be used? How should negatives be dealt with? How explicit and specific should you be? How can the practical consequences of the issues being discussed be demonstrated?

Before and during interviews, try to keep these guidelines in mind:

1. Start with the news, then provide the details.
2. Answer direct questions directly—do not hedge or be evasive. But if you feel a question is unfair, you may say so. If you do not know an answer, say so—but promise to get the answer, and follow through on your promise. Remember, an interview is a goal-oriented conversation, not a cross-examination. You are not on the witness stand.
3. Do not lie or exaggerate.
4. Do not argue with reporters—even if you win the argument, you will lose in the long run.
5. Do not let reporters put words into your mouth. Frequently reporters ask, "Would you say . . . ?" Either a "yes" or "no" leaves you open to an embarrassing quote. It is better to respond, "You said that, I didn't."
6. Do not talk off the record. Reporters may use **off-the-record** information in a variety of potentially damaging ways beyond the control of the interviewee.
7. Approach the topic from the viewpoint of your public's interest, not from that of your organization. Do not talk about "capital formation," for instance; talk about "jobs."
8. Follow up. Be sure to provide promptly any additional information you have promised. Do not be pushy or meddlesome, but if you think a point needs clarification, do not hesitate to provide it.

You will never be satisfied with every interview as it is published or broadcast, just as you cannot expect to hit a home run every time you go to the plate. Your ability to take charge of an interview and control it depends on preparation of attitude and information. If you take the time and make the effort to prepare, your batting average will be significantly higher.

A final note on interviews: protect yourself. When an interview is agreed to, it is legitimate for all parties to agree in advance to certain ground rules. The rules may deal with the range of subjects to be covered, the conditions under which direct quotes may be used, and other matters of mutual concern. For example, the interviewee may agree to reveal certain information off-the-record so that the reporter can understand a situation. A reporter must agree in advance to accept information on that basis. Other ground rules include: "not for attribution," when information may be used but its source not revealed; "background," when information may be used and attributed to a general source (such as "sources close to the company"); or "indirect quote," when remarks may be used in substance and attributed, but not used verbatim.

One other ground rule that is sometimes of great value is the use of tape recorders. Reporters often use tape recorders and typically ask permission to do so. The individual being interviewed also is well advised to tape-record the proceedings. This process will provide a record should disputes emerge later.

News Conferences   News conferences are structured opportunities to release news simultaneously to all media. They should be used only when the news is important and when interaction is required to promote understanding of complex or controversial topics. Unless the event is extremely newsworthy and simply cannot be handled through releases, or unless there is someone newsworthy to interview, do not call a news conference.

For those rare occasions when news conferences are appropriate, the following guidelines will help assure success.

1. *Plan the event carefully.* Invite all representatives of all media that may have an interest far enough in advance for editors to plan to send reporters and photographers. Select an appropriate site close to the event being covered and convenient for major media (hotel, press club, airport, boardroom—never a public relations office). Check for enough electrical outlets and telephones. Time the conference to accommodate major media deadlines. Make certain you prepare enough handout material for everyone. Prepare any visuals that may be used so that they will photograph well from any place in the room. Prepare a poster of the organization's logo or name to go over the one on the speaker's stand if you use a rented facility. Plan to phone major media the morning or afternoon before the conference as a reminder. Simple refreshments are generally a nice touch.

2. *Prepare executives and others to be interviewed.* Make certain they understand the topics that will be discussed. Help them anticipate and prepare for difficult or touchy questions. Advise them to be completely honest. If they don't know an answer, they should say so and offer to find out. If the answer to the question is considered proprietary information, they should state that it is not for public disclosure. Cultivate a pleasant, cooperative attitude among those who will be interviewed. If they are afraid of or resent the media, it will show. Advise them to avoid off-the-record comments.

3. *Public relations practitioners are the directors and stage managers.* Keep the meeting moving and interesting, but don't take over the jobs of the media. Try to keep relationships cordial and professional even in the heat of questioning. Never take obvious control of the meeting unless things get out of hand.

Summary

The relationship between journalists and public relations practitioners is a difficult one. If practitioners understand the media and the reporter's role, however, positive relationships can be developed that are beneficial to all.

Once positive relationships are established, several steps should be taken to use them effectively. Developing appropriate attitudes, setting goals, planning, and performing adequate research are essential aspects of successful media relations.

Specific techniques for communicating with the media include publicity releases, news kits, newsrooms, interviews, and news conferences. All of these approaches must be used judiciously—for publicity may backfire. Inappropriate publicity efforts can injure the relations that have been built over time with the media and the public.

▲ ▲ ▲

Insurance for What?

By R. Ferrell Ervin
Southeast Missouri State University

Case Study

In the early fall of 1977, heavy rainfall hit the Kansas City, Missouri, area. Extensive flooding occurred. Nineteen people were killed. Property and businesses were severely damaged. The governor requested federal disaster aid.

As people assessed the losses suffered, they naturally turned to their insurance agents for financial settlements of their personal or property losses. One of those agencies responded to the claims with speed that matched their advertised message which guarantees that you are insured by "the good hands people."

Several months later, however, an investigative report by a local television station showed that the company had paid for the damages to autos, asked people to sign over their car titles, and then sold the cars to local dealers. The action in and of itself was not unusual, but the cars were not identified as flood-damaged. Car firms were selling flood-damaged cars as used cars at near book value.

It appeared that the insurance company knew this might occur but did nothing to prevent it. The reporter from the television channel asked a company representative about the issue but was told, "No comment." When the footage appeared on the news, it gave the impression that the insurance firm had something to hide.

Put yourself in the position of the company's regional public relations director who almost falls out of his chair when he first becomes aware of the situation while watching television news. You know that this incident might turn people away from your firm. What do you do now?

Questions

1. How might previous doubt about the ethics of insurance companies be confirmed by this flood situation?
2. Even if the insurance company were to be found innocent of any wrongdoing by the general public, how might the company still be in serious trouble with state authorities and suffer long-range consequences?
3. After a representative or spokesman has seemed to be evasive, how can a company overcome that problem by "straight talking" at a later time?
4. Is the flood situation made more serious by the deaths that were caused, even though the issue under discussion concerns only the insurance coverage of cars?

Notes

1. Douglas Cater, *Press, Politics and Popular Government* (Washington, D.C.: American Enterprise Institute, 1972), 83–84.
2. Joseph Poindexter, "The Great Industry-Media Debate," *Saturday Review* (July 10, 1976): 22.
3. *Associated Press Managing Editors Guidelines*, 44.
4. Craig E. Aronoff, "Credibility of Public Relations for Journalists," *Public Relations Review* (Fall 1975): 45–46.
5. For example: W. Schabacker, "Public Relations and the News Media: A Study of the Selection and Utilization by Representative Sources" (M. A. thesis, University of Wisconsin, Madison, 1963); C. S. Steinberg, "Public Relations as Mass Communication," *Public Relations Journal* (June 1971): 13–14; Scott M. Cutlip, "The Press vs. The Publicist," *Nieman Reports* (April 1951): 20–22; W. H. Chase, "Public Relations in Modern Society," *Public Relations Quarterly* (1962): 12–20; and Craig E. Aronoff, "Predictors of Success in Placing Releases in Newspapers," *Public Relations Review* (Winter 1976): 45.
6. Walter Guzzardi, Jr., "How Much Should Companies Talk?" *Fortune* (March 4, 1985): 64–68.
7. *PR Reporter* (February 12, 1973): 1.
8. Jane Paley, "The Press Kit: Staple of the Public Relations Cupboard," *Sky* (June 1980): 34–36.

CHAPTER 11

▲ ▲ ▲

Community Relations
Preview

C ommunity relations refers to an organization's planned, active, and continuing participation within a community to maintain and enhance its environment to the benefit of both the organization and the community.[1]

An organization's community relations may be affected by such diverse factors as its recruitment methods, employee relations, waste disposal, energy use, design and maintenance of buildings and grounds, marketing and advertising strategies, and corporate philanthropy.

The quality of an organization's employees, the cooperativeness of citizens and governmental agencies, the patronage of community members, the ability to attract financial support, indeed, the success or failure of an organization may depend on the effectiveness of its community relations.

Special audiences for community relations include women and minority groups.

What people say behind your back is your standing in the community in
which you live.

—Henry Wadsworth Longfellow

In an age when marketing, technology, resource acquisition, and management
are increasingly international in scope and when the federal government is the
most conspicuous aspect of many organizations' operating environments, concern for community seems almost anachronistic. Indeed, certain sociologists
and political scientists have maintained that our communities are dissolving
in the face of increased mobility and communication.

But the community cannot yet be declared dead; some strange things
have begun to occur. Neighbors have started banding together on small-scale
issues like schools, security, and community services. Back-to-the-city movements have repopulated many metropolitan areas; downtown businesses have
revived after years of inactivity; people have become interested in genealogical
and community roots. Strong chauvinistic pride in cities and communities has
become widespread. Slogans modeled after the "I love New York" campaign
are commonplace, while the citizens of Buffalo, Cleveland, and Terre Haute
rush to the defense of their much-maligned hometowns.

The lesson for organizations in this trend is simple: regional, national,
and international concerns may preoccupy you, but do not forget the folks next
door. In the past, constructive community relations programs were characterized by phrases like "corporate citizenship" or "good neighbor." These terms
still apply, but they oversimplify the complex relationships that exist between
organizations and their communities today.

The urban problems that were recognized as matters of public concern
in the 1960s cast **community relations** in a new light and forced institutions
to pay more attention to their relationships with surrounding communities.
Throughout the 1970s, equal employment opportunity and training, employment of the disadvantaged, stimulation of minority business enterprises, elimination of substandard housing, and many other issues caused companies and
other organizations to become more involved in community activities.

Community relations has long been a business priority. Morrell Heald,
in a history of the social responsibility of American business, points out that
since the beginning of this century:

> American businessmen fully shared the social concerns and preoccupations of
> their fellow citizens. Although they have often been depicted—indeed
> caricatured—as single-minded pursuers of profit, the facts are quite otherwise.
> The nature of their activities often brought them into close contact with the
> harsher aspects of the life of a rapidly industrializing society. Like others,
> they were frequently troubled by the conditions they saw; and, also like
> others, they numbered in their ranks men who contributed both their ideas
> and their questions to redress social imbalance and disorganization. . . .
>
> From the outset, self-interest combined with idealism to foster
> sensitivity to social conditions on the part of the business community.[2]

An appropriate basis for institutional efforts toward good community relations is derived from understanding the nature of a community. William Gilbert defines the word "community" as:

> A place of interacting social institutions which produce in the residents an attitude and practice of interdependence, cooperation, collaboration and unification . . . a web of social structures all closely interrelated.[3]

In this chapter, we will first discuss the complex relationships that exist between organizations and their communities before going on to consider the process and practice of community relations. We will also deal with several subjects generally associated with the community relations area, including corporate philanthropy, local government relations, business and the arts, and business and education.

An Interdependent Relationship

Effective community relations depend on recognizing the interdependence of institutions. Management helps establish social balance when it recognizes the many ways organizations can have impact on their local communities and the extent of interdependence between the two.

All types of organizations practice community relations. Schools, churches, hospitals, museums, and groups like the Red Cross and the Boy Scouts depend on community relations the way businesses depend on marketing—as the primary means by which "customers" are attracted. Prisons, military bases, and universities (where "town versus gown" conflicts are common) must strive for community acceptance. Except for corporate philanthropy, however, the process of community relations is the same whether or not the organization seeks financial profit.

Every community has a vital stake in the economic health and prosperity of its institutions. Every organization has a vital stake in the health and prosperity of the community it inhabits. Quite naturally, therefore, organizations and their communities develop a mutual interest in each other's successful and effective operation. At this level, the connection between institutional interest and public interest is most clear.

At the very least, organizations expect communities to provide adequate municipal services, fair taxation, good living conditions for employees, a good labor supply, and a reasonable degree of support for the plant and its products. In addition to employment, wages, and taxes, communities expect from their institutions attractive appearance, support of community institutions, economic stability, and a focus for hometown pride.

Good community relations aids in securing what the organization needs from the community and in providing what the community expects. Moreover, it helps to protect organizational investments, increase sales of products and stock, improve the general operating climate, and reduce costs of dealing with government agencies. Positive community relations can affect worker productivity when organizations sponsor community health and education programs. Also, favorable community attitudes may influence worker attitudes toward the organization.

The clarity of the mutual interest of organizations and their communities, however, does not imply that community relations can be practiced without careful planning and execution. Effective community relations does not just happen, nor is it an inevitable by-product of a well-run, civic-minded organization. In effect, community relations must be built into the structure and culture of an organization, as is illustrated in Mini-Case 11.1. Community relations is not based on pure altruism. It looks to the organization's self-interest. W. J. Peak offers the best definition of community relations we have seen:

> Community relations, as a public relations function, is an institution's planned, active, and continuing participation with and within a community to maintain and enhance its environment to the benefit of both the institution and the community.[4]

The Community Relations Process

Mini-Case 11.1

Norton Simon Inc.'s commitment to community relations goes beyond good words, high ideals, and moral pressure. Based on performance in four areas of community involvement, company managers' bonuses can be increased by as much as 20 percent.

The four areas of the company's concern are equal employment opportunities; encouragement of minority businesses; charitable contributions; and involvement of managers in community organizations. Norton Simon's managers are assessed on performance in these areas by their immediate supervisors as part of their normal performance appraisals. The company regards corporate citizenship as a central plank in its strategic plan. As such, it provides an example of corporation-wide commitment to community relations backed by its resources and managerial experience.[5]

Norton Simon
Puts Action
in Community
Relations

The community relations process embraces all aspects of institutions. In some ways, good community relations simply means good performance. A company that offers poor products and unsatisfactory service is unlikely to benefit from positive community relations. Prisons that allow their inmates to escape rarely enjoy their neighbors' support. Beyond this, Robert Ross explains, "Good community relations consists of recognizing and fulfilling the organization's responsibilities in and to the communities in which it operates."[6] Texaco's action in relation to customers in areas afflicted with natural disasters is an example of Ross's point. (See Mini-Case 11.2.)

**Texaco Responds
to Disaster**

Mini-Case 11.2

When Hurricane Gloria plowed into the New York metropolitan area in the fall of 1985, parts of Long Island, Connecticut, and New Jersey were devastated. For 200,000 people in the affected area, an offer of help came in a letter from an unexpected source. It read:

> We at Texaco are concerned that you or your family may have been personally affected by this unfortunate disaster and wish to cooperate if help is needed.

Texaco then offered to extend payment periods on credit card bills. Once an extension was arranged, interest charges were suspended and customers continued to use their cards.

Since 1970, Texaco has responded to more than one hundred disasters, mailing out over two million letters. About 1 percent of those contacted have taken advantage of Texaco's offer. Content to help individuals in a direct, if small way, Texaco has done little to publicize its gesture.

*Determining
Objectives*

Recruitment, employee relations, production processes, marketing and advertising strategies, design of the organization's building and facilities, and many other organizational activities affect community relations. George Sawyer maintains that even the internal standards of the organization have a bearing on its community relations:

> A community becomes to a large extent an expression of the values, aspirations and achievements of its businesses. Thus, the internal standards a corporation sets for itself and for the members of its organization have an influence that carries down through the work force and out into the community.[7]

Arguably, community relations is an organizational attitude or state of mind, rather than any specific process or practice.

In a very general sense, community relations seeks to inform the community about the organization, its products, services, and practices. It should correct community misconceptions and reply to criticism, while gaining favorable opinion and support. Other general community relations objectives include:

To obtain support for legislation that will favorably affect operating climate in the community.
To determine community attitudes, knowledge, and expectations.
To support community health, educational, recreational, and cultural activities.
To gain better local government.
To assist in the local economy by purchasing local supplies and services.

General objectives, however, will not suffice for specific institutions. Every community relations program should have a written policy clearly defining management's view of its obligation to the community. So that efforts can be coordinated and concentrated, specific community relations objectives should be spelled out. Failure to do this kills too many community relations programs before they get started.

Community relations policies and objectives are not determined according to idealistic principles. They come about by assessing organizational needs, resources, and expertise on the one hand and community needs and expectations on the other. Before meaningful policies and objectives can be developed, the organization must know its community.

Knowing the Community While community relations usually stresses communication from the organization to the community, the success of such efforts rests upon the communicator's knowledge of the audience. The effective communicator always listens before acting. Stated simply: "A basic ingredient of every good community relations program is the necessity for officials up and down the line to know their community.[8]

Of course, standard information about the community is useful to management. Demographic, historical, geographic, economic, and other readily accessible data are essential. But real knowledge of the community is not found in almanacs or chamber of commerce fact sheets. The solid community relations program must be built on the answers to questions like these:

1. How is the community structured?

    A. Is the population homogeneous or heterogeneous?
    B. What are its formal and informal leadership structures?
    C. What are the prevailing value structures?
    D. How are its communication channels structured?

2. What are the community's strengths and weaknesses?

    A. What are the particular problems of the community?
    B. What is the local economic situation?
    C. What is the local political situation?
    D. What are the unique resources (human, cultural, natural) possessed by the community?

3. What does the community know and feel about the organization?

    A. Do its neighbors understand the organization's products, services, practices, and policies?
    B. What are the community's feelings about the organization?
    C. Do misunderstandings about the organization exist?
    D. What are the community's expectations in regard to the organization's activities?

The answers to such questions are not necessarily easy to get. Moreover, answers change over time and thus require frequent monitoring. Good information can be acquired in several ways. Many organizations engage in survey research to determine community knowledge, attitudes, and perceptions. Professional polling organizations are often employed to provide such services. Close contact with community leaders is an extremely important source of information. Professional, civic, religious or fraternal leaders, political officials, and media editors can generally be reached through membership in local organizations or through face-to-face meetings on a variety of subjects. Some organizations formalize such input by including community leaders on their task forces or committees that deal with important community issues.

Ten Commandments
for Community
Relations

Exhibit 11.1

1. Know your community.
2. Develop an organizational community relations policy. Spell out specific objectives. Base the policy on assessment of organizational needs, resources, and expertise, and on community needs and expectations. Some sample objectives are: attract more employment applications from women and minorities; improve community awareness of the organization's contributions; improve relations with local government; improve the local school system to make the community more attractive to potential executives and professional employees; improve the quality of local colleges for more effective recruitment; etc.
3. Review your organization's policies, practices, and procedures. Are they consistent with sound community relations?
4. Consider especially the following areas: waste disposal; employee recruitment; employment policies (layoffs, compensation, overtime); noise or traffic problems; maintenance of organizational facilities and grounds; advertising, signs, marketing; energy sources and energy waste.
5. Utilize all means to communicate with the community. These may include: employees, local media, open houses, local clubs and organizations, local advertising, direct mail, newsletters, brochures, annual reports, movies, exhibits, etc.
6. Involve your organization in local organizations. This may be done by: sponsoring employees who wish to join civic and professional groups; providing speakers for meetings; lending facilities for meetings or activities; sponsoring contests and programs for youth; supporting fund-raising activities; etc.
7. Distribute corporate donations according to community relations policies and objectives. Philanthropy is an important aspect of community relations.
8. Use local merchants, banks, insurance agencies, lawyers, and other professionals for goods and services.
9. Offer aid to local governments. Make organizational resources available to governments by loaning employees and materials.
10. Evaluate the community relations effort. Measure to determine the extent to which objectives have been achieved. Be prepared to develop new strategies if current programs fail to meet expectations.

Having established the means for ongoing community inputs, the following guidelines should be used to establish an effective community relations program:

Guidelines for Effective Community Relations Programs

1. Careful effort should be made to establish the objectives top management wishes to achieve. The organization may seek many objectives—reputation, experience with a potential future payoff, stability of environment, and so on—but whatever it seeks ought to be established in realistic and concrete terms.
2. Alternative strategies should be explored and choices made. If an organization wishes to improve housing conditions in a city in which it operates, for instance, possibilities for action range from partially funding research into new ways to build low-cost housing to actually building low-cost housing.
3. Impacts of community relations programs on the organization and the community should be anticipated. Offering training for jobs that will not exist when the training is concluded helps no one.
4. Attention should be paid to the likely total costs of a not-for-profit action and to the volume of the organization's resources which may legitimately be allocated to community relations. It is not advantageous to either the organization or the community if the organization suddenly discovers a given program is costing much too much and abruptly stops all community service.
5. Many managers have found that certain types of involvement in urban affairs require knowledge and understanding that go beyond the usual managerial and technical business talents. Political skills, deep understanding of community problems, and the ability to settle problems in an unfamiliar cultural setting are requisites for some activities. Special expertise may have to be acquired.[9]

Community . . . refers not only to a group of people living in the same locality, but to the interaction of those people. . . . In the past, the tendency was to treat a community as a rather simple entity—a collection of people, a "home town." Today we are beginning to recognize each community as a complex dynamism of diverse, constantly changing, often powerful, and always important forces.[10]

Communicating with Communities

Community communication has no single audience. Messages reach communities through employees, their families, and local media. Other important communication channels consist of a community's opinion leaders: teachers, clergy, public officials, professionals and executives, bankers, union leaders, and ethnic and neighborhood leaders. Caterpillar Tractor staged an open house for barbers, bartenders, and librarians because the company found them to be significant spreaders of community information. Another company hosted cabdrivers for the same reason.

Figure 11.1 Conoco makes speakers available

ARE YOUR MEETINGS RUNNING OUT OF GAS?

Let a speaker from Conoco* put some energy into them. We can fuel discussion with our long-range energy forecast, ignite interest with an award-winning energy film, or drive home important points about petroleum exploration with an energy game. And our speakers are a no-cost energy resource.

You can reserve a Conoco speaker in many cities in Colorado, Delaware, Louisiana, Maryland, Missouri, Montana, New Jersey, New Mexico, Oklahoma, Pennsylvania, Tennessee, Texas, West Virginia, and Wyoming.

*Conoco is an international energy company.

(CONOCO)

a Du Pont subsidiary

TO: Betty Wiley
Conoco Inc.
1007 Market St.
Wilmington, DE
19898

TEXAS ONLY:
Lynn Hohensee
Conoco Inc.
P.O. Box 2197
Houston, TX
77252

Yes, I want a speaker on energy.

My Name _____

Group Name _____

Street Address _____

City _____ State _____ Zip Code _____

Requested Date 1. _____

2. _____ Time _____

Attendance _____

Work Phone (___) _____ Home (___) _____

K-3

Local organizations are also an important method of communication in communities. Fraternal, civic, service, and social clubs, cultural, political, veterans, and religious organizations, and youth groups all provide platforms for institutional messages and ample opportunities for informal communication. Organizational managers should be encouraged to belong to such groups and should be available to make public speeches to them as well. Figure 11.1 shows how the Conoco Corporation advertises the availability of its personnel for community audiences.

Channels of Communication   The communication channels through which these audiences are reached may range from an informal chat over lunch at a Kiwanis Club meeting to advertisements in local mass media. In-house publications, brochures, and annual reports can be easily shared with community leaders. Some organizations create newsletters specifically for their neighbors. Upjohn Company, for instance, distributed a special report on the company's economic and social involvement in its headquarters city (Kalamazoo, Michigan) to 20,000 people. Abbott Laboratories circulates 85,000 copies of its quarterly publication *Commitment* to employees, shareholders, customer groups, local, state and national leaders, and community groups. Institutions frequently make organizational movies available to local groups and set up exhibits at local airports, shopping centers, and civic centers. Consumer's Gas System in Scarborough, Ontario, makes available a 15-minute slide show entitled "Consumers and the Community" to explain gas pricing and supply, and to increase understanding of the gas company's role in the community. The show's modular format allows regional managers to insert slides of local facilities and services.

A uniquely community-oriented method of organizational communication is the open house. Open houses can be very effective if well planned and executed. Successful open houses provide small group tours of organizational facilities with knowledgeable guides. They include films, displays, and brochures, and usually provide product samples or mementos for participants to take home. The major message of such activities, of course, is the interdependence between the institution and the community.

In some cases, industrial or company tours become major tourist attractions. Tours of Heineken's Amsterdam Brewery, for instance, make the company "thousands of loyal friends who speak well of us throughout the world."[11] Boise Cascade gives "plant tour" a whole new meaning. Advertisements in major national magazines invite readers to visit the company's working sites (see Figure 11.2). The good done by plant tours, however, must be weighed against other organizational objections. Kellogg ceased tours of its historic Battle Creek facilities in 1986 when it realized that tourists were stealing secrets related to cereal production processes.

Community relations is particularly critical when an organization moves into a new community or leaves an old one. While virtually any major organization was once welcomed with open arms, communities now ask questions before they accept new businesses, industries, or even not-for-profit undertakings. Community response to an organization should be an important factor in the location decision.

Specific Functions of Community Relations
When an Organization Moves

Once the decision to move into a particular community has been made, it is essential to provide local media with factual information on appropriate events and project stages immediately. Key groups should be familiarized with the organization and its products, activities, policies, and people, using all available media and methods.

The dependence of a community on its organizations is never clearer than when a plant or facility leaves town. Plant shutdowns may raise levels of psychological depression, alcoholism, drug abuse, marital stress, child abuse, and even suicide among former employees, all of which can severely affect a

Figure 11.2 Boise
Cascade's invitation to a
plant tour

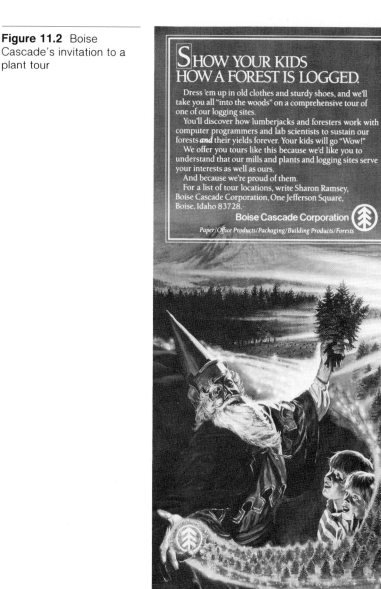

community. The organization that fails to prepare appropriately for its departure only invites increased government regulation to prevent such irresponsible activity in the future. General Foods, Brown and Williamson Tobacco Corp., and Olin Chemical provide examples of successful departures from communities highly dependent on them.

When the General Foods Jello Division left LeRoy, New York, it provided full information on its plans. The company aided the community by supporting an industrial survey and the formation of an industrial development council to attract new industry to the town. Employees were offered their choice of transfer to the new plant in a neighboring state or termination allowances and assistance in finding new jobs.

When Brown and Williamson closed a fifty-one-year-old Kentucky plant in 1982, even the Tobacco Workers' Union praised the company. After giving workers three years notice of the closing, the company relocated 350 of 2,700 employees and provided six months of separation pay, health care coverage, financial counseling, and vocational training for all others. The effort succeeded because all parties worked together to phase the closing gradually.

Olin Chemical was forced to close its Saltville, Virginia, plant when new pollution regulations made production inefficient. The company carefully explained the reasons for its actions. Employees were offered the chance to relocate to other plants, and arrangements were made for special retirement and severance benefits. According to *Life Magazine,* "The people were disappointed but not bitter as the company left; the company dealt generously in its settlements with the town."[12]

Community relations goes beyond mere communication. It requires action by organizations in relation to community health and welfare, education, government, culture, recreation, and other areas.

Local Government and Political Action

While business/government relations will be discussed in much greater depth in chapter 15, community relations and governmental relations clearly overlap in the area of local government and politics.

As previously stated, local political officials can supply invaluable input to corporate community relations programs. Corporations have a great stake in effective local government since they are major taxpayers and users of municipal services. Part of the community relations effort, therefore, must be devoted to building solid relations with city officials, county commissions, and other agencies of local government. This is accomplished, in part, by making organizational expertise available to governments through loans of managerial personnel or through service on panels, commissions, or committees established by or for local government.

As political activity becomes more important to organizations, community relations plays a critical role. Institutions must mobilize on the local level those who recognize the importance of their contribution to the health and prosperity of the community and those who will speak out for policies in the best interests of their community and its institutions. This is true whether the institution is a hospital, an art museum, a university, or a business. Moreover, political experts now recognize that strength in Washington is derived from organized, localized grass roots support. In an era when virtually all congressmen are looking out for their own districts and careers, local people making local demands and representing local interests are far more effective than Washington-based lobbyists. In this regard, community relations may be not only an end in itself, but an integral part of national efforts.

*Corporate
Philanthropy*

Corporate philanthropy is a subject over which great controversy has raged for many years. Only in the past forty years has corporate charity been recognized as a legal use of stockholders' funds. But even having established its legality, questions remain as to whether or not and to what extent the practice is appropriate and useful. Beyond these issues are questions of proper motivations, goals, and criteria for corporate giving.

Some maintain that corporate managers have no business giving away profits that rightly belong to stockholders. If stockholders wish to donate their money to what they consider good causes, it is argued, that is their right—but managers should not make such decisions for them. Berkshire Hathaway Corporation solved this dilemma by making $2 per share available to stockholders to contribute to their favorite charities.

Clearly, however, the corporate entity incurs obligations and responsibilities of its own, and needs to engage in activities traditionally considered philanthropic as a matter of long-term self-interest. W. J. Baumol explains:

> The company pays a high price for operating in a region where education is poor, where living conditions are deplorable, where health is poorly protected, where property is unsafe, and where cultural activity is all but dead. . . . These circumstances are all more expensive than corporate giving.[13]

By law, corporations are permitted to donate up to 10 percent of earnings to charitable organizations. In practice, however, very few corporations give to the limit. Overall, about 1 percent of corporate profits is actually given away. Thus, while corporations could legally give more, they obviously feel that it is not in their interest nor in the interests of their stockholders to do so.

With these limits established, however, debates over the legitimacy of the practice have ended. As Richard Eells points out:

> The whole activity of corporate giving has now become an accepted part of good corporate management. The donative decision, as we are now coming to appreciate more and more, is part and parcel of the whole decision process in managing a business.[14]

The motivations and goals for such decisions are, however, still matters of considerable debate. Despite the fact that the legal rationale for corporate donations rests on the notion of self-interest, some maintain that the term "philanthropy" should be taken literally, with giving being done strictly for the love of mankind. Irving Kristol represents the opposite view:

> Some corporate executives seem to think that their corporate philanthropy is a form of benevolent charity. It is not. An act of charity refines and elevates the soul of the giver—but corporations have no souls to be saved or damned. Charity involves dispensing your own money, not your stockholders'. When you give away your own money, you can be as foolish, as arbitrary, as whimsical as you like. But when you give your stockholders' money, your philanthropy must serve the longer-term interests of the corporation. Corporate philanthropy should not be, cannot be, disinterested.[15]

In practice, research indicates that self-interest prevails. According to Baumol, surveys show that patterns of corporate giving fit in well with the doctrine that corporations should provide funds to causes that serve the broadly conceived interests of the firm.[16] Similarly, Neil Jacoby has found that "corporate giving is generally in proportion to the extensiveness of local public contacts which generate social pressures."[17] He points out the extensiveness of the charitable activities of banks as an example of this phenomenon.

Corporate giving can serve many corporate interests, including recruitment, sales, and employee morale, but it inevitably serves that interest called public relations. Consequently, corporate public relations personnel are almost always involved in, if not responsible for, charitable decisions.

Unfortunately, in some cases, corporate charitable decisions are still made capriciously and without adequate planning. In developing a coherent approach to corporate giving, several factors should be considered:

1. *Do no harm.* Contributions should not be made to any cause that may be contrary to the best interest of the donor.

2. *Communicate with the recipient.* Effective grant-making requires a close partnership between donor and recipient.

3. *Target contributions toward specific areas.* Gifts should achieve maximum impact on the community and maximum benefits for the donor. In this regard, donations should go to areas where individual corporations have unique expertise not available in the voluntary, nonprofit sector.

4. *Make contributions according to statements of corporate policy.* Fully developed policies of this nature should include the charitable aims and beliefs of the company, the criteria to be used in evaluating requests for funds, the kinds of organizations and causes that will and will not be supported, and the methods by which grants will be administered.

5. *Plan within the budget.* Corporate giving should be tied to set percentages of net earnings.

6. *Inform all persons concerned.* Employees and the community at large should be fully aware of corporate activities.

7. *Do a later follow-up.* The corporation does a valuable service by demanding of recipients high levels of performance and proper financial accounting.

8. *Remember that more than money may be needed.* An effective corporate contribution requires more than checkbook charity. Volunteer manpower, managerial expertise, and corporate leadership are essential elements of an effective program.

Two trends in corporate giving hold the promise of making such philanthropic programs more effective. Rather than reacting to public issues and public pressures, more firms, particularly the larger ones, are taking greater initiative in channeling dollars and corporate talent into problem areas they

Figure 11.3 Promoting
corporate giving

Corporate giving.
Without it, a lot of important things
might go out of business.

A lot of organizations in a lot of different fields could barely exist without help from corporations.

To their credit, a great many companies realize this.

Every year for the past ten years, corporate giving has gone up. And that's something the entire corporate community can take pride in.

There are so many ways a corporation can give. So many ways to lend a hand.

The fact is, when corporate giving thrives, so do the orga-

nizations it supports.

And everyone profits.

deem significant and in which they wish to make an impact. Other corporations are attempting to broaden their philanthropic programs through decentralization and employee participation. By asking local managers of corporate facilities to make decisions about allocation of donations, large corporations ensure that they are in touch with the needs and desires of local communities. Many corporations now match employee contributions to educational institutions, museums, orchestras, public TV, hospitals, and ballet, thus, in effect, permitting their contributions to reflect those of their employees. Xerox even gives employees paid leave to work on worthwhile community projects. IBM encourages top executives to teach at colleges and universities. In these ways, employees can be the motivating force behind their companies' charitable donations.

In 1984 (the most recent data), corporations gave a record $3.8 billion to charitable causes. Of that amount, 38.9 percent went to education, 27.7 percent to health and human services, 18.8 percent to civic activities, 10.7 percent to cultural activities, and 3.9 percent to other charitable causes (see Figure 11.3).

Education   The largest portion of corporate philanthropy supports education. Businesses have long made contributions to educational institutions. Again, self-interest is evident. Skilled, intelligent workers and university-generated research are directly beneficial to business. A better-educated population creates a more congenial economic, political, and social environment for business. Corporate contributions to educational institutions can improve public relations, recruitment, and marketing. Increasingly, corporate contributions have supported efforts to improve students' and teachers' understanding of the private enterprise system.

Education is one area in which corporate support calls for more than money. With school budgets stretched to the breaking point, donations of classroom and recreational materials are extremely important. Examples of contributions include pencils and pads, automobiles for driver training, and sophisticated computers and equipment for advanced research. Donations of equipment represented one-sixth of corporate giving to higher education in 1984. Businesses can also provide plant tours for student field trips, speakers for classes and assemblies, internships for high school and college students, and managerial and financial expertise for school administrators. Bridges built between the corporation and the classroom are among the most important relationships in any community.

The level of business concern about education has increased in recent years. Business organizations and associations have taken many actions and made many statements on the subject. A 1986 Conference Board survey showed that the quality of primary and secondary education is expected to be the major corporate community-related concern through the early 1990s at least.

The Committee for Economic Development investigated the relationship between business and the public schools in 1985 under the leadership of Owen Butler, Procter and Gamble board chairman. The report describes the role of business as follows:

> Business has a major stake and a major role to play in the improvement of our public schools. Better schools can mean better and more productive employees and a boost toward restoring the nation's international competitiveness.[18]

Business can do many things to improve public education. Among them are:

Working with local school districts to define goals for business involvement based on mutual needs.

Engaging in local business-school partnership programs utilizing proven techniques.

Encouraging employees to serve on local school boards, and providing flexibility in working hours to make this possible.

Permitting working parents and other employees to participate in local school activities.

Providing qualified volunteer help to assist the local school administration with training in modern management and administrative methods.

Helping redirect vocational education programs to provide students with strong academic and real job-related skills.[19]

Many businesses, large or small, are committing not only money but time and other resources toward concrete action. Some are establishing direct relationships with public education through "adopt-a-school" programs. As is shown in Mini-Case 11.3, major corporations can make national commitments to education.

Dow Backs its
Words with Action

Mini-Case 11.3

Dow Chemical U.S.A.'s commitment to an improved education system is more than lip service. Following the appointment of Robert Lundeen, chairman of the board of Dow Chemical Company, as the 1984 cochairman of the National Task Force on Education for Economic Growth, the following memo from Dow Chemical U.S.A. president Hunter Henry was issued:

DOW CHEMICAL U.S.A.

January 30, 1984

To: Management at All Dow U.S.A. Locations, Divisions, Plants and Sales Offices

Subject: Education—Dow Business Partnerships

Most Dow employees are interested in education—and the improvement of education. Education is where we got our start, and many of our children or even grandchildren are now in school.

Dow hires young people who are the products of our educational systems. Dow and we, as individuals, invest our tax dollars in education. I think we all want to get the best education possible from this investment.

The improvement of education, particularly the K–12 grades, has become a national issue. National studies are calling for education improvement through citizen and business involvements.

Bob Lundeen, Dow board chairman, is providing national leadership with the Task Force on Education for Economic Growth. As cochairman for 1984 of the task force, Bob leads a group of business people, state governors, legislators and educators.

The Task Force report *Action for Excellence* (enclosed) is unique in that it provides action recommendations for education—for business—for economic growth during 1984 and beyond.

I see a vast network of businesses in every community helping schools in their area. At Dow, we need to do our part. We need to encourage our employees to do their part, and get ourselves involved.

Dow has been a strong supporter of education for many years. But we need to renew our efforts and do more as a corporate citizen and as individual citizens. The *Actions for Business, Industry and Labor* pamphlet (enclosed) lists creative ideas for education-business partnerships.

I'm confident you will try some of these ideas and come up with even better plans and programs with education, particularly at the K–12 level. Please appoint someone from your office to see that this information gets to the people to get the job done. Let me know in about six months what progress has been made.

Your efforts could mean a lot of positive community relations and goodwill for Dow. We'll also be helping our children and grandchildren. It will improve the quality of graduates we hire. And, we'll get more return on our investment of tax dollars.

Helping education these days is enlightened self-interest.

Hunter W. Henry
President
Dow Chemical U.S.A.

Health and Human Services   The self-interest of corporations in their philanthropic efforts is perhaps most obvious in the area of community health
and welfare. Donations to hospitals and medical schools are very common.
Classic examples of corporate community action are found in relation to health
and welfare. Professors Keith Davis and Robert Blomstrom offer the following
example:

> In the first decade of this century, Birmingham, Alabama, was menaced by
> serious health problems. Malaria, typhoid fever and other diseases were
> prevalent because of unsanitary community conditions. This city was the site
> of a United States Steel Subsidiary, Tennessee Coal and Iron Co., whose
> productivity was lowered by illness. Tennessee Coal and Iron organized a
> health department and hired a prominent specialist in the offending diseases
> from the Panama Canal Zone. In its first year of operation the health
> department spent $750,000 for draining swamps and improving sanitary
> facilities. This amount was 30 times the total health budget of the entire state
> of Alabama.[20]

A more contemporary example of corporate resources being brought to
bear on human problems is called CAN (Corporate Angel Network). CAN
provides free rides on corporate aircraft to cancer patients. Founded in 1981,
the organization provided transportation to 259 sick people in 1984. More than
270 firms participate, including American Express, Norton Simon, AMF,
AT&T, Champion International, General Foods, Merrill Lynch, and Time Inc.
Health and human service activities have come to encompass a broad range
of efforts dealing with employment, housing, and the physical environment.

The Arts   Of all corporate contributions, about 10 percent are currently devoted to cultural activities. This is the fastest-growing area of corporate philanthropy, however, and one in which corporations can make their most
significant impacts. As government funds to support the arts are reduced, private sector contributions will become even more important. Moreover, the connection between community relations and arts patronage is very clear. "No
city can count itself a quality-of-life city without the arts," says Bob Guyton,
CEO of Atlanta's Bank South.

The arts as a target of corporate giving developed later than health and
welfare or education because the advantage is less obvious. By the 1960s, however, business leaders like David Rockefeller were appealing to their colleagues' self-interest on behalf of the arts. "Support of the arts by business
amounts to nothing less than a prudent investment in community survival and
growth," Rockefeller claimed. By the mid-1980s, business had become so
thoroughly involved in the arts that *Newsweek* reported on what it called "the
museum-industrial complex."

On a practical level, international cultural exchanges have paved the
way for expanded trade relations. Theater, museums, dance, music, and architecture promote tourism. Philip Morris chairman George Weissman points
out: "More people go to museums than to ball games." He has made his company one of the nation's most generous arts patrons.

Bristol-Myers's Gavin K. MacBain points to the utilitarian aspects of art—advertising, packaging, design, and marketing. He maintains:

> The use of art to move products in the marketplace would be impossible if there were no art museums, composers, orchestras, painters, filmmakers, writers, playwrights, and choreographers who are dedicated exclusively to their arts.[21]

Gideon Chagy puts his rationale for business support of the arts on a higher, more philosophical plane:

> If our society is to be both affluent and humane, the competitive drive and the sense of community must be kept in balance. Without a widely shared sense of community there would be nothing to restrain the logic and dynamics of business competition from leading to a system of exploitation. . . . While art is not a panacea for society's problems, it is a restorative for the sense of community.[22]

Themes of "excellence" and "quality" have been adopted by many companies. These themes fit naturally with artistic endeavors. Says Alvin Reiss, editor of *Arts Management,* "The arts represent excellence, a reflection of which rubs off on businesses that help arts groups."

Collective and individual corporate efforts related to the arts have become very impressive. Several organizations have developed multimillion-dollar annual arts budgets managed by executives who are highly knowledgeable or even professionally trained in the arts. Dayton-Hudson, the Minneapolis retailer, is one company that has hired a full-time director of cultural affairs. Philip Morris, Equitable Life Assurance, Georgia Pacific, and Champion International have all established art museum annexes in the most accessible parts of their office buildings, foregoing as much as $1 million in annual rent.

The extent of corporate arts activities sometimes requires outside public relations counsel. Ruder and Finn Public Relations established a business and the arts consulting program over twenty-five years ago. Today, Ruder, Finn and Rotman advises corporations on cultural support programs. The firm develops and implements corporate public relations programming keyed to cultural activities. The organization assists in managing corporate-sponsored museum exhibitions, performing arts presentations, symphony tours, and other arts-related activities.

To encourage further participation by business in the arts, more than 160 top business leaders have established the Business Committee for the Arts. The committee assists companies of all sizes in their efforts to establish arts programs which can enhance a company's image, benefit employees, or provide tax breaks. The committee also cosponsors, with *Forbes Magazine,* annual "Business in the Arts" awards. Some examples of corporate art involvement are provided in Figure 11.4.

Whether consciously or not, corporations routinely act as art patrons whenever they engage the services of an architect. The community relations aspect of architectural decisions should not be overlooked. Says arts patron and publisher Malcolm Forbes, "The architecture that houses a company is

THE ART OF PRESERVATION. THE PRESERVATION OF ART.

ANSEL ADAMS: CLASSIC IMAGES
NATIONAL GALLERY OF ART
WASHINGTON, D.C.
OCT. 6, 1985–JAN. 12, 1986

Ansel Adams stands alone as the most famous American landscape photographer. Because the wilderness was his favorite subject, his work increased public appreciation of the beauty and fragility of the natural environment and the need for its preservation.

Adams produced over 40,000 negatives during his career. Before he died, he selected just seventy-five to represent a lifetime of work and designated them as "Museum Set" prints. The Pacific Telesis Group is proud to present a museum set for public display.

In October, 1985, The New York Graphic Society and Little, Brown will publish *Ansel Adams: An Autobiography.*

Through it, readers will come to know the man through his words as well as his images.

Progress, intelligently planned.

PACIFIC ✸ TELESIS™
Group

Pacific Bell   Nevada Bell
Pacific Telesis International
PacTel Mobile Companies   PacTel Publishing
PacTel Communications Systems
PacTel InfoSystems

Moon and Half Dome, Yosemite National Park, California. 1960. Photograph by Ansel Adams. Courtesy of the Ansel Adams Publishing Rights Trust. All rights reserved.

1979   1980   1981   1982   1983   1984   1985

Our beat goes on.

Last year, we beat our old record for corporate contributions. This year, we plan to do even better.

At Bankers Trust, we're proud of that performance.

Because it means we're doing something to improve the quality of life in the cities where we live and work. That's why we'll continue to provide both financial and volunteer support to more than 330 non-profit organizations and institutions. They include fields such as social and public services, arts and culture, education and economic development projects throughout New York and around the world.

We urge you to join us. You'll feel richer for it.

Bankers Trust Company
Merchant banking, worldwide.

Courtesy of Bankers Trust Company

a more visible statement than the president's in the annual report."[23] Cummins Engine has transformed Columbus, Indiana, into an oasis of architectural excellence by paying top architects to design new buildings and restore old ones in the town. Included are twelve schools, two churches, a fire station, a library, a golf course and clubhouse, newspaper and telephone company offices, a mental health clinic, city hall, and more. Others in the town have been inspired by Cummins's effort and have followed its lead. Architects used include Eero Saarinen, I. M. Pel, Kevin Roche, and Richard Meier.

Every company can make an important contribution to its community by considering appropriate location and design for its plants, warehouses, showrooms, and offices. The public is served well by distinctively designed buildings that enhance their surroundings.

Cause-Related Marketing   A fairly new way that businesses aid community organizations is cause-related marketing. In an effort to do well by doing good, businesses give their customers a chance to be altruistic by relating products to causes.

American Express was one of the leaders in using cause-related marketing. In 1981–82, the company raised $1.5 million for arts organizations in twenty-seven cities and generated $3 million in arts advertising support.

Figure 11.4 Some examples of corporate sponsorship of the arts

Whenever an American Express card was used in a target city, the company made a five-cent contribution to a designated organization; new card memberships earned $2; and travel arrangements worth $500 or more netted $5. Charge volume increased 15 percent during the campaign.

The company repeated the effort to aid the Statue of Liberty restoration, with similar results. Says Jerry Welch, head of marketing for American Express's travel related services, "Social responsibility is a good marketing hook."

More companies are developing creative ways of simultaneously selling products, helping community organizations, and generating positive publicity. Citibank initiated its CompuMentor program to support its move into the Atlanta market. The program was designed to help high school and middle school students with career planning by providing special computer systems to inner-city school counselors. The bank donated one computer system for every fifty Citibank financial accounts opened with specially coded brochures. Suddenly, the bank's services were being sold from pulpits and PTA platforms. In four months, the program resulted in eight hundred new accounts and placed computer systems in sixteen schools.

General Foods, Merrill Lynch, American Airlines, Ford Motor, and other companies use cause-related marketing to aid museums, symphonies, theaters, zoos, community service organizations, and health research groups.

Special Publics and Problems

Special societal and community circumstances give rise to special publics, problems, and opportunities for community relations efforts. For example, in certain Pittsburgh area mill towns, steel-related unemployment hit 40 percent in 1982. Food banks were established to provide staples for stricken families. Pittsburgh Brewing Company raised $13,000 for the food banks in two months by sponsoring personal appearances by professional football players and charging $5 to drink beer with a pro.

Some special publics are ongoing, such as women and urban minority groups.

Women   Women's important roles as employees, consumers, business owners, and voters have gained increasing recognition in recent years. Clear separations between work life and family life have blurred, and communication with audiences of women has become both more important and more difficult.

Over half of all women now work outside the home. Nearly a quarter of small business owners are women. Women are more likely to vote than are men. Perhaps most dramatic, it is estimated that women do 85 percent of retail buying in the United States. The large increase in direct economic participation by women has been called the greatest social revolution of the 1970s.

These changes have raised several issues of concern and opportunity for community relations specialists in businesses and other organizations. Compliance with Equal Economic Opportunity laws is required, of course, for businesses with more than fifteen employees. Moreover, organizations must deal with affirmative action policies. To eliminate discriminatory practices is not enough. Organizations must take positive steps to assure that minorities and women are hired, developed, promoted, and appropriately meshed into the entire organization. Successful programs depend on effective communication with current and potential employees to clarify policies and highlight opportunities.

Other women-related issues often requiring attention from organizational communication staffs include:

Comparable worth   This issue is based on the contention that equal pay for equal work is not an adequate formula. Since on the average women earn only 60 percent of what men do, and since men and women still characteristically move into separate areas of employment, some groups have agitated in favor of equal pay for so-called *comparable worth*. While jobs may differ for janitors and secretaries, for example, they can be compared in terms of skill requirements and worth to the organization. Rather than depending on the marketplace to determine pay, some contend that compensation should be adjusted according to a comparable worth scenario.

Day care   The percentage of working women with children under six years of age increased from 32 to 52 percent between 1970 and 1984. By 1985, 2,000 employers provided some form of child care assistance—a three-fold increase in only three years. Companies have responded to the situation because child care problems can short-circuit recruiting efforts, injure productivity, and increase absenteeism and turnover.

Sexual harassment   If an organization cannot provide a working environment free from sexual threat, that organization has failed to give equal opportunity to all employees. Moreover, such organizations are extremely vulnerable to legal and publicity problems.

Volunteerism   Programs that use extensive volunteer work forces must reduce their traditional dependence on women. In some cases, previously voluntary tasks must become paid employment. In others, organizations may look to senior citizens rather than women for volunteers.

Blacks and Urban Minorities   While the urban poor cannot be considered a major market for many businesses, they are still an important public. Urban poverty is a negative factor in the business environment of any city. Business controls the distribution of capital and employment in our society; therefore, the cycle of poverty cannot be broken without its help.

In many ways, good business environments, because they hold the promise of jobs, are responsible for the concentration of poor in our cities. This responsibility must be met by all organizations. Public relations practitioners, because of their unique training, are the logical choice of most managers to monitor urban problems and recommend actions for their organizations to take.

Many of the efforts to improve conditions for those who live in the inner cities have been conceived and initiated by concerned business leaders who feel their organizations have certain responsibilities to the society in which they exist. After more than two decades of programs and policies designed to meet the needs of the urban poor, both business and government have evaluated their efforts. Such evaluations always uncover inadequacies, wastes, and misplaced emphasis. Yet, in spite of some obvious failures on the part of both business and government, the outlook and role of organizations in the United States has unquestionably changed.

The need for sensitivity to community problems and open communication with many segments of society has not diminished. As a result, the role of managers responsible for public relations has become critical. Public relations practitioners must be able to translate their companies' concern and actions into messages that are meaningful to the publics involved. More importantly, the corporate public relations staff must be able to detect social problems in the community and make management aware of them. In its two-way communication role between the organization and its publics, public relations can be a critical key to the effectiveness of business response to urban problems.

Most of the problems that have haunted our large cities since the 1960s can be traced to poverty in one way or another. Although statistics show that only about one-third of America's poor families live in the central cities, they are probably the best-known poverty group in our society. The urban poor who live in central city areas are more concentrated and thus more visible than other impoverished groups. The nature of the inner city itself makes the conditions of poverty even more devastating for the people who live there.

Concentrations of poor families have developed within most of our large cities. Minority groups are disproportionately represented. The ghetto and barrio areas of major cities have become centers of poverty, unemployment, pollution, and crime. In addition, civic functions such as sanitation, police and fire protection, and transportation are often inadequate.

Identifying and reaching minority publics should be no more difficult than reaching other publics. Blacks, for example, are a distinct market psychologically, geographically, socially, culturally, and economically. While television is the black community's medium of choice, blacks can be more efficiently reached through the 374 newspapers, twenty-nine magazines, and numerous radio stations that are black-oriented.

Carol Torres of the Minority Media Syndicate gives advice on what minority media want. Editors are particularly interested in stories about minority members who have made it, programs that helped them make it, possible effects of upcoming government decisions, and tips for stretching modest budgets. "A good story is a good story," Torres says, "and minority media need good stories."

The difficulty in dealing with the black urban public arises because of the diversity of opinions and outlooks within that public. Various individuals and groups claim to represent black interests.

Increasingly, black and Hispanic groups are using their clout as consumers to gain concessions from major corporations. The Reverend Jesse Jackson, for instance, through his operation PUSH, negotiated $275 million in concessions to black businesses from Coca-Cola, R. J. Reynolds, and Philip Morris. When Jackson attempted a boycott of Anheuser-Busch ("Bud is a dud," he said), the company fought back. The firm pointed out that it was already sponsoring aggressive minority programs, including $18 million spent with minority suppliers and $7 million spent on advertising in minority media. Moreover, the black community of St. Louis, home of company headquarters, opposed Jackson's effort. Anheuser-Busch prevailed.

Aetna was less fortunate, however. When the company developed a program to finance rehabilitation of inner-city housing, residents in three of the seven cities got very upset. The company ran head-on into conflicts over who should decide what is best for neighborhoods. "Aetna or any big company that wants to help with housing should first canvass the people who live around the proposed development and see how they feel about it," explained a Chicago city official.

Many major corporations have implemented programs to develop and support minority suppliers. Major franchisors, including McDonald's, Burger King, Pizza Hut, Taco Bell, Kentucky Fried Chicken, and Baskin-Robbins, have established programs to encourage minority ownership of retail outlets. Hunt-Wesson and other food companies have minority home economists on staff.

Summary

Community relations as an organizational activity is as diverse as the communities in which organizations operate. It may be carried out by an officially designated community relations staff, by a general public relations staff, or by various departments throughout the organization.

Community relations publics, programs, and activities are united only by the creativity, energy, and budgets devoted to them. One thing is certain, however. As the boundaries between communities and organizations become more permeable, the importance of the community relations function will continue to grow.

▲ ▲ ▲

The Deserted Hospital

By Walt Seifert, APR
Professor Emeritus
School of Journalism
Ohio State University
Columbus, Ohio

Case Study

Y ou have been named public relations director of St. Christopher's Hospital. The facility has five hundred beds at a downtown location in a major city.

You have your first meeting with your boss, the chief hospital administrator, Mr. Winston. Winston has been with St. Chris's for about two decades, and he is proud of his hospital's accomplishments. In the course of conversation, you conclude that Mr. Winston has great confidence in his own conclusions. He gives you these "facts":

St. Chris's recently built a high-rise building on its inner-city site. Although the new building has been open two years, most of its rooms are unoccupied due to a lack of interest by physicians and a shortage of patients. The administrator attributes this to a fear of crime. "We are in the high crime area. Most people are afraid to come here," he says. "Also, a nurse was raped and murdered en route to this hospital. Although this happened quite far away, because she worked for St. Chris's, most people think it happened right here."

On the positive side, he mentions that St. Chris's has an outstanding speech clinic and the only teen alcoholism program in the state. He says the hospital would be willing to give physicians free office suites on the top floors of the tower if they would come.

Now: Tell all you'd do in the next year.

Notes

1. W. J. Peak, "Community Relations" in *Handbook of Public Relations*, Philip Lesly, ed. (Englewood Cliffs, NJ: Prentice-Hall, 1978), 65.
2. Morrell Heald, *The Social Responsibilities of Business: Company and Community, 1900–1960* (Cleveland: Case Western Reserve University Press, 1970), 1, 2.
3. William H. Gilbert, *Public Relations in Local Government* (Washington, D.C.: International Management Association, 1975), 103.
4. Peak, "Community Relations," 65.
5. Based on David Clutterback, "Bonus Pay-outs Linked to Social Responsibility," *International Management* (August 1978): 49.
6. Robert D. Ross, *The Management of Public Relations* (New York: Wiley, 1977), 170.
7. George Sawyer, *Business and Society: Managing Corporate Social Impact* (Boston: Houghton Mifflin, 1979), 316–317.
8. Philip Lesly, *Handbook of Public Relations* (New York: Prentice-Hall, 1950), 150.
9. Adapted from Jules Cohen, "Is Business Meeting the Challenge of Urban Affairs?" *Harvard Business Review* (March–April 1970): 81–82. Reprinted by permission of the *Harvard Business Review*. Copyright 1970 by the President and Fellows of Harvard College. All rights reserved.
10. Peak, "Community Relations," 65.
11. Gerard Tavernier, "Is Your Company Worth A Visit?" *International Management* (June 1974): 24–28.

12. "End of a Company Town: The People of Saltville, VA, Lose Their Plant to Pollution Laws," *Life Magazine* (26 March 1971): 37–45.
13. W. J. Baumol, "Enlightened Self-interest and Corporate Philanthropy," in *A New Rationale for Corporate Social Policy*, W. J. Baumol, R. Likert, H. C. Wallich, and J. J. McGowan, eds. (Lexington, MA: Heath, 1970), 19.
14. Richard Eells, "A Philosophy for Corporate Giving," *The Conference Board Record* (January 1968): 15.
15. Irving Kristol, "On Corporate Philanthropy," *Wall Street Journal* (21 March 1977).
16. Baumol, "Enlightened Self-interest," 6.
17. Neil Jacoby, *Corporate Power and Social Responsibility* (New York: MacMillan, 1973), 199.
18. From "Investing in Our Children: Business and the Public Schools," New York: Committee for Economic Development, 1985.
19. Ibid.
20. Keith Davis and Robert L. Blomstrom, *Business, Society, and Environment,* 2nd ed. (New York: McGraw-Hill, 1971), 277.
21. Quoted in Gideon Chagy, *The New Patrons of the Arts* (New York: Harry N. Abrams, N.D.), 87.
22. Ibid., 82–83.
23. *Forbes Magazine* (4 June 1984): 19.

▲ ▲ ▲

CHAPTER 12

Employee Communication
Preview

When organizations achieve effective employee communication, the results may include: more satisfied and productive employees; improved achievement of organization goals; and improved customer, community, investor, and public relations.

Effective employee communication depends on the establishment of a positive organizational climate. Feelings of trust, confidence, openness, candor, supportiveness, security, satisfaction, involvement, and high expectations characterize ideal organizational climates.

Public relations efforts should help employees become well-informed about their organizations and encourage them to express their views to management.

Michael H. Mescon, a management professor and consultant, tells the story of an experience aboard a Delta Air Lines jet:

> I was just settling into my seat when I casually remarked to the fellow sitting next to me about the skyrocketing cost of airline tickets. The fellow didn't take my remark very casually.
>
> "Do you know why that ticket costs what it does?" he asked.
>
> "No," I said, "And I don't really care."
>
> "Well, you ought to care," he said. "Because what that ticket pays for is your safety, comfort and convenience."
>
> Well, by now I knew I was in for it. The guy told me what the carpet on the floor cost and why that particular kind of carpet had to be used. He explained the construction of the seat I was sitting in. He talked about support personnel on the ground for every plane in the air and, of course, he dealt with the costs of jet fuel. Finally, I stopped him.
>
> "I know the president and several of Delta's vice presidents," I said. "You must be one of the vice presidents I don't know."
>
> "No," the fellow said, "I work in the upholstery shop."
>
> "Well, how do you know so much about Delta's operations?"
>
> "The company keeps us informed."

When organizations commit themselves to effective communication with their employees, a number of important benefits can result. Well-informed employees are usually satisfied employees. They are better, more productive workers who get more out of their work and do a better job for the company. Where communication lines are open, organizational goals are more easily achieved. Moreover, as the Delta Air Lines example shows, well-informed employees interact with the public and can have significant positive effects on relations with customers, the community, investors, and the general public. An unprecedented result of positive employee relations was the gift of a $30 million Boeing 767 to Delta from its employees. Wrapped in a giant red ribbon, the plane was presented to the airline in December, 1982. The gift had the additional benefit of generating tremendous positive worldwide publicity.

Achieving effective employee communication is no simple task. To understand the process by which it is accomplished and the role of public relations in that process, we must first discuss in some detail the concept of organizational climate or culture.

© 1985 United Feature Syndicate Inc.

Communicating changes in
organizational climate

The Concept of Organizational Climate

More that fifty years of research in the field of organizational behavior has demonstrated that the most powerful forces in the workplace are psychological. The collective psychological forces at work in an organization make up its **organizational climate** or *culture*. Several definitions of this concept exist. Here are two of the most widely accepted:

> Organizational climate is a relatively enduring quality of the internal environment of an organization that (a) is experienced by its members, (b) influences their behavior, and (c) can be described in terms of the values or . . . characteristics of the organization.[1]

> We might define (organizational) climate as a set of attributes specific to a particular organization that may be induced from the way that organizations deal with their members and their environments.[2]

In effect, organizational climate consists of employees' subjective perceptions of such organizational realities as policy, structure, leadership, standards, values, and rules. It is sometimes identified as "the way we do things here." Various researchers have noted important connections between climate and motivation,[3] and between climate, creative ability, and performance.[4]

Ideal organizational climates are characterized by feelings of trust, confidence, openness, candor, supportiveness, security, satisfaction, involvement, pride in the organization, and high expectations. To a large extent, successful employee relations in general, and effective employee communication in particular, depend on positive organizational climates.

William Whyte makes this point very clearly:

> Only with trust can there be any real communication. Until that trust is achieved, the techniques and gadgetry of communications are so much effort. Before employees will accept management's fact, they must have overall confidence in its motives and sincerity.[5]

Public relations researcher Jim Grunig makes a similar point specifically related to company media:

> How much employees use company media and how they evaluate them is more a function of what they think of the company and their role in it than it is of anything the communications professionals do.[6]

All of this suggests that the crucial prerequisite for effective employee relations and communication is the creation of a positive organizational climate based on feelings of trust, confidence, and openness. Creating such a climate is not an easy job. Claude Taylor, chief executive officer of Air Canada, explains: "A good atmosphere, particularly for internal communication, doesn't blow in overnight, or even in one or two years. It takes a great deal of patience and listening—with no small investment in human and financial resources."[7] How this can be accomplished and the role of public relations in its accomplishment is our next focus of discussion.

The primary responsibility for organizational climate belongs to line management—from the chief executive officer to supervisors. Many organizations are consciously trying to change their cultures or climates. In the steel industry, for example, companies have been trying to substitute a culture of cooperation for decades of adversarial relations between plant workers and management. Climates have been improved through better communication with employees and establishment of labor-management teams that give workers a voice in decisions.

Public Relations and Organizational Climate

Ford Motor Company is one organization deliberately pursuing a better climate. The company once known for its strong personalities and autocratic management (exemplified by Henry Ford and Lee Iacocca) is now emphasizing teamwork and caring for each other. Procter and Gamble has also been building trust while decentralizing.

The public relations staff can make significant contributions to a positive organizational climate through their inputs to organizational decisions, their roles as internal communication consultants, and perhaps most importantly, their efforts to establish organizational communication policy based on a goal-oriented approach. Practitioners have also helped design and implement organizational change programs.

In terms of decision input and internal consultation, public relations managers must constantly remind line managers that nothing an organization says to its employees can communicate more effectively than what it does to or for them. Explains Bank of California communications vice president Joelle Yuna: "Companies have not lived up to the promises their communicators made several years ago. They told employees about quality of worklife, quality circles and participatory management, and workers began to expect more job satisfaction. We need to get off the buzzword bandwagon. . . . If you tell employees that companies are going to do this or that one year and then it's a totally different story the next year, employees and other constituents stop believing what you are saying."[8] Donald R. Whitlow, vice president for employee relations at Alcoa, a company with an excellent reputation for employee communication, says simply: "You always must make your actions back up your rhetoric. You can't talk about the state of the business unless you have credibility."[9]

To ensure an understanding of the organization's philosophy, policies, and actions, the public relations staff must consistently stress the need for effective two-way communication. Employees must be well-informed and must have the means of expressing their views to management about organizational affairs. Says Terrance Deal, coauthor of *Corporate Cultures: The Rites and Rituals of Corporate Life,* "Communicators play a central role in interpreting the corporate culture to both internal and external audiences."

Establishing a Communication Policy

An important factor in improving organizational climate is the establishment of a communication policy. According to communication expert Norman Sigband, top management generally recognizes the need for and sincerely desires two-way communication.[10] The bottleneck in corporate communication is usually found in the middle of the corporate hierarchy. Although they may want to communicate, middle- and lower-level managers often find it difficult because they have no parameters, no boundaries, and no policies to guide them.

Public relations managers can greatly facilitate positive organizational climates by convincing top management that communication, like finance, personnel, marketing, promotion, and almost every other area of organizational activity, should have established, clearly-stated policies. Unstated policies leave dangerous vacuums which rumor and misinformation rapidly fill.

Communication policies must be goal-oriented rather than event-oriented. In other words, rather than addressing specific issues or topics, policies should help employees understand, contribute to, and identify with organizational objectives and problems.

Successful communication policies must be based on management's desire to:

1. Keep employees informed of organizational goals, objectives, and plans.
2. Inform employees of organizational activities, problems, and accomplishments.
3. Encourage employees to provide inputs, information, and feedback to management based on their experience, insights, feelings, creativity, and reason.
4. Level with employees about negative, sensitive, or controversial issues.
5. Encourage frequent, honest, job-related, two-way communication among managers and their subordinates.
6. Communicate important events and decisions as quickly as possible to all employees.
7. Establish a climate where innovation and creativity are encouraged.
8. Urge every manager and supervisor to discuss with each of his subordinates the latter's progress and position in the firm.

Reprinted by permission: Tribune Media Services.

Inputs are essential.

When such communication guidelines are accepted and practiced by all levels of management, the organization's climate will improve. Honeywell is an example of a company with a clear employee communication policy. Its Corporate Policy and Practice #157 ensures that employee communication is two-way, open, timely, considers all sides, and presents bad news as well as good. The policy gives special attention to promoting upward communication, describes the responsibilities of various corporate levels, and explains a formal employee communication network.

Effective employee communication is crucial to organizational success. It is an area in which public relations staffs can make great contributions.

"Employee communication, the Johnny-come-lately of the public relations/communication business, continues to inch its way into corporate executive thinking," according to a recent survey of corporate chief executive officers (CEOs) by the International Association of Business Communicators. The report continues, "In terms of corporate priorities, the vast majority of CEOs rated employee communication in the 'extremely important,' 'very important' or 'tops' categories."[11]

The survey report includes a variety of statements by CEOs about employee communication. Here is a sampling of their responses:

> "The success or failure of everything from new products to advertising campaigns to reaching our goals for the fiscal year are affected by how well our employees understand what we are trying to accomplish and how we accomplish it."

> "There is a direct correlation between employee communication and profitability."

> "I find that making good profits really goes hand in hand with having good communication."

The Importance of Employee Communication
CEO Perspectives

"The best (business) plan is meaningless unless everyone is aware of it and pulling together to achieve its objectives. Good communications are the lifeblood of any enterprise, large or small. Communications are essential to keep our entire organization functioning at maximum levels and to make the most of our greatest management resource—our people."

"Employees can't be happy in their work or with their company unless they're well informed."

"If employees understand what you're trying to do and get involved in the process feeling like they're really a part of it, then the job gets done much more easily, and there are fewer grievances and fewer problems."

Not surprisingly, public relations managers share the concern expressed in these quotations. A recent survey of the public relations departments of the *Fortune* top fifty companies revealed the overwhelming consensus that employee communication is an area of expanding interest.[12]

Public Relations Perspectives

Rather than recognizing the comprehensive nature of employee communications, public relations has traditionally viewed employees as just one of many publics. Today, employees are still considered a public, but a very special one. Public relations has recognized that employees are a medium through which other publics gain information and establish attitudes toward organizations.

Good relations with the surrounding community or the general public originate through good employee communications. Neighbors, family, friends, and associates of employees are themselves potential customers, employees, and decision makers on issues crucial to the organization. A Gallup poll revealed that each employee influences an average of fifty people in the community. These facts are known to chief executive officers. In the IABC survey, one CEO stated: "We just had a survey commissioned on customer opinion. It found that where the customer knew a company employee, his attitudes toward the company were more favorable."[13]

Employee Communication Programs

Supervisors, working primarily through interpersonal and small-group communication, are the most critical link in employee communication. Public relations practitioners seek to improve, support, and reinforce this link through programs and media including: small and large meetings, letters, periodicals, bulletin boards, exhibits, annual reports, advertising, handbooks and manuals, envelope stuffers, reading racks, public address systems, telephone hot lines, surveys, suggestion systems, films, closed circuit television, and other means.

Since the 1970s, several forces have combined to reshape organizational communication policies and practices. Employees have demanded more challenging jobs and greater work flexibility. Consumer groups have demanded greater input and more product information. New government regulations have made a variety of impacts. As a result, more organizations are now concerned about their response. They are more receptive to incoming communication from their publics, more concerned about openness and truthfulness, and increasingly prepared to communicate with their publics.

Internally, organizations put greater emphasis on keeping employees informed as to the organization's positions on political issues, future plans, and economic status. Moreover, James Lahiff and John Hatfield found that organizations are more actively soliciting ideas from employees, listening to employee suggestions, and creating an atmosphere in which employees feel free to speak their minds.[14] A 1986 survey found 19 percent of employers seeking their workers' opinions before making policy decisions, compared with 6 percent in 1981.[15]

Specific duties of public relations managers in relation to employee communications include:

How Public Relations Can Help

Promoting awareness and understanding of organizational goals.
Interpreting management and personnel policies.
Fulfilling employees' informational needs.
Providing means for and stimulating two-way communication.
Encouraging favorable employee attitudes and increased productivity.
Making all employees ambassadors from the organization to the
   general public.

When communication programs work, they can be tremendously cost-effective. Sweetheart Plastics, for example, invested $7,000 in a communication program, hoping to increase productivity. The company realized a savings of $250,000 the first year and expects a ten-year savings of $2.5 million. Mini-Case 12.1 cites another such example.

What Communication Programs Can Accomplish

Mini-Case 12.1:

Communication Aids Productivity at Westinghouse

The Westinghouse major appliance division plant in Mansfield, Ohio, had an old physical facility and some old ideas about management. As a result, it suffered low productivity, rampant absenteeism, high unit costs, and sometimes hostile labor relations. Moreover, in a town where Westinghouse was the largest employer, press relations were indifferent at best.

The plant had been losing money for years and had the highest production cost per finished unit in the fiercely competitive appliance market.

According to Tom Christensen, communication and training manager, "It was a 'produce-or-perish' situation." To deal with it, Westinghouse developed a program designed to accomplish five goals: increase salable hours; reduce defective product costs; reduce accident costs; increase cost improvement savings; improve teamwork. Communication was the primary means by which these goals were achieved. Communication efforts included:

Providing sixty hours of supervisor training in which information was shared on the nature of the plant's problems and how supervisors might make positive contributions.

Holding face-to-face meetings (for the first time) between the plant's general manager and all employees. The manager explained the problems, goals, and how each employee could help.

Beefing up the suggestion system to promote upward communication. In its first year, the system netted 67 percent more cost-saving ideas and 58 percent greater savings than in previous years.

Using company media to supplement and reinforce the program. The plant's publication, *The Conveyor,* featured articles in every issue on some phase of the program. Brochures, visual displays, and posters for bulletin boards were developed.

Improving labor relations through frank interaction between management and union officials. Union stewards were offered special training classes.

Discussing plant problems frankly with local media. The media responded by giving improved coverage that, in effect, reinforced management's message with headlines like "Future of Westinghouse in Workers' Hands."

The results of the program included: productivity gains ranging from 10 to 17 percent; $100,000 annual savings in incentive plan subsidies; and unjustified employee absences down 20 percent. Christensen concluded: "Now, if the economy would just pick up so that we could sell some of those appliances we're producing. . . ."

Why Communication Programs Fail

When employee communication programs are ineffective, the costs are immeasurable. Inefficiency, waste, higher costs, low morale, absenteeism, strikes, turnover, and accidents are just some of the ways poor employee communication can adversely affect sales, profits, productivity, public image, and the individual employees themselves.

Some reasons for ineffective communication have already been indicated: unclear corporate images, negative organizational climates, lack of employee communication policies, and lack of mutual trust and respect between employees and management.

Another common reason for failure is that employee communication too often attempts to "sell" management's line to employees. Interested only in getting their own messages accepted, managers may neglect employee input. One of the CEOs participating in the IABC survey emphasized this point:

If we are making an attempt to communicate with our employees specifically to sell them something, our effort is going to fail. If we are attempting to communicate, to tell them something and invite feedback, then our effort will be successful, even if we make mistakes. . . . "[16]

Richard Nemec offers a more unsettling explanation for the failure of employee communication, returning, in effect, to the concept of organizational climate: "If you had to condense modern corporate communication problems into one word," he maintains, "it would be 'fear.' Fear of reprisal . . . fear of being innovative . . . fear of honesty."[17]

Understanding the evolution and role of organized labor in the United States is essential to understanding the American economic and business system. Such crucial matters as inflation, productivity, the quality of life on and off the job, and international trade are strongly influenced by the collective bargains struck by businesses and unions. Union activities in the political arena—sometimes in conjunction with business and sometimes in opposition to business—are a powerful influence on the government's role in the economy.

Unions are active in many kinds of organizations. The crushing of the air traffic controllers union by the Federal Aviation Administration in 1981 showed that bad management/union relations can be as costly in the public sector of the economy as in the private sector. Teachers, nurses, municipal employees, police and fire personnel, and other employees of not-for-profit or government organizations are increasingly unionized. Indeed, these are the fastest areas of union growth. Virtually no organization is immune from the costs of poor labor relations, as the AFL-CIO learned when its own clerical employees went on strike.

Many organizations attempt to utilize effective employee communications to ward off union efforts to organize their labor force. The threat of unionization, in effect, scares management into instituting communication policies and programs that should have existed in the first place. Unfortunately, the timing and motivation of efforts to establish the proper communication climate and facilitate upward communication have sometimes caused them to be perceived as anti-union techniques.

Unionization of an organization's work force places employee communication and public relations in a slightly different light, but basic practices of effective employee communication still hold. As personnel specialist Don Crane states: "Progressive organizations, whether unionized or not, encourage employees to express their complaints, questions, or job problems; insist they be given a fair hearing, and give them a timely answer."[18]

Why Workers Join Unions   Conventional wisdom has it that unions exist because of management failures, and although other variables play a role, in many cases, this is true.

Workers join unions to gain the power necessary to better pursue their needs and goals. Increased pay, shorter hours, and improved working conditions are common reasons for unionizing. But other factors, including the opportunity to be heard and the need to be recognized and respected, also motivate them.

Why Management Resists Unions   Unions are not inherently evil things as some might have you believe. Some corporate managements even prefer to deal with unions that offer consistency, predictability, control, and a pool of qualified workers. However, initial efforts at union organization are almost always resisted. When management is accustomed to making decisions by itself, making decisions with others is a difficult adjustment. When unionization occurs, management's discretion is limited and its freedom constrained. What were once unilateral decisions become shared.

Special Employee Communication Situations

Communicating with an Organized Work Force

Management has considerable, but not unrestrained freedom in its efforts to resist unionization. Communication activities often play an important role. The National Labor Relations Act, however, requires that communications by management trying to resist unionization not be coercive. Charles Coleman explains:

> Management's right to communicate its position is protected as long as the communication is not coercive. Outright threats or promises of benefit are prohibited. The law does not permit management to threaten a plant closing upon unionization, or to offer a special wage increase during a representation campaign. . . . Management may question the union's statements, explain to workers the nature of the benefits they already have, call to their attention the strike record of the union or its record in securing terms less favorable than those already enjoyed by the employees, or offer comparisons with other organizations. Written communication may be sent to employees' homes, posted on bulletin boards, or placed in company newspapers.[19]

Public Relations in Collective Bargaining   When union representation has been established, management is required to bargain in good faith with its agents. All matters relating to a previously established set of issues are resolved through a process known as **collective bargaining.** Harold Davey defines collective bargaining this way:

> A continuing institutional relationship between an employer . . . and a labor organization . . . concerned with the negotiation, administration, interpretation, and enforcement of written agreements covering joint understandings as to wages or salaries, rates of pay, hours of work and other conditions of employment.[20]

Davey's phrase "continuing institutional relationship" is an important one. The general public has a poor understanding of collective bargaining, associating the process with strikes, labor unrest, or protracted negotiations. In fact, these are exceptional circumstances. In 98 percent of negotiations, contracts are agreed upon without resorting to strikes or lockouts.

Contract negotiations and strikes often draw intense public scrutiny. At such times, the public relations function becomes very important, and practitioners really earn their pay. Nevertheless, as Harold Marquis points out, "One area in which large corporations and industry groups have been singularly ineffective is their public relations during labor controversies."[21] Part of the problem is the sensitive nature of the negotiations underway. Management and labor usually agree that public disclosure of the negotiating process would result in increased posturing, disruption, and intransigence. Abe Raskin, who covered labor relations for several decades for *The New York Times,* puts it another way:

> Outside the realm of diplomatic negotiations between the great powers no field compares with collective bargaining in reluctance of the parties to let the public know what is really going on. The settled conviction of labor and management is that the only time the rest of the world is entitled to any useful information is when an agreement has been reached. Until then the statements issued by both sides are self-serving flapdoodle intended to mislead much more than to illuminate.[22]

A journalist by profession, Raskin favors opening the bargaining to the media and the public, a view that gets little support from labor or management. During negotiations, then, public relations is left with the thankless task of disclosing nothing of the proceedings while at the same time avoiding alienating journalists like Raskin who operate on a primary assumption of the public's right to know.

When negotiations are successfully concluded, the public relations spokesperson should tell the story of that success and explain the terms of the contract to the public. The contract and its impact on the local or national economy are matters of critical public interest and importance. Even after a strike, when the ending of conflict seems to be the main story, information concerning these factors should be spelled out clearly in organizational and mass media.

Public Relations in Strikes   Although strikes are rare, their effects can last for years. Moreover, as we mentioned above, public sentiment can have significant influence on their ultimate outcomes.

Communication plays an important role in determining whether or not there will be a strike, how the strike will be perceived, and how it will conclude. Strikes occur when workers' needs, wants, and ideas are unheard and unheeded, leading to tremendous frustration. Effective communication can go a long way toward making strikes unnecessary. Cadbury Schweppes employees in the United Kingdom belong to twenty-nine militant unions. Because the company has consistently communicated, keeping employees informed on costs and profits, it has been able to install high-tech machinery and cut jobs without labor strife.[23] Mini-Case 12.2 shows another example—how effective communication at American Airlines prevented a strike.

Mini-Case 12.2

Getting Wage Concessions in a Profitable Company

In 1983, American Airlines was the first major profitable airline to gain significant concessions from its unions. Two years before negotiations, company president Robert L. Crandell began to tell employees that the airline had to earn a 5 percent return on revenues to be competitive under deregulation. His message was reinforced in the company newspaper and in videotape presentations. He also met with groups of employees throughout the American system.

Thanks to his persistent, coordinated, multifaceted approach, Crandell won the changes he wanted without provoking a strike. Crandell says that the hardest part of his communication program was convincing employees that deregulation made "change absolutely essential." Communication continues to be critical at American Airlines because, as Crandell says, "We want to make sure that people continuously understand the changing environment we deal with."

The impact of public opinion was clearly demonstrated in one case in which the local community had become antagonistic toward a union because a prolonged strike was adversely affecting the local economy. Community leaders were attempting to pressure the union into a settlement. As the pressure increased, a union spokesman approached the company's representative and proposed arbitration of the unresolved issues. The company resisted, but the union spokesman offered to permit a three-member arbitration panel consisting solely of businessmen to rule on the issue. All three of the proposed arbitrators were customers of the company. The union representative was betting that the company would never place its clients in the difficult position of judging one of their suppliers. He bet right. The next day's newspaper carried the headline: "Company Refuses Union Proposal to Have Businessmen Settle Strike." The resulting shift in public sentiment forced the company to concede.[24]

Unions frequently have the public relations edge in strike situations. As Abe Raskin observes:

> Unions locked in battles with corporations win more often than they lose in the propaganda exchange . . . unions have become adept at getting their story across whenever anyone is interested enough to listen.
> Union leaders are almost invariably more accessible than their industrial counterparts. . . . The other great union asset in a strike is its members and their families. When a strike turns into a siege it is standard practice for newspapers to carry sob stories detailing the hardships the strikers are suffering and proclaiming their determination to stay out until the flint-hearted bosses meet demands of elementary justice. . . . The human factor— little people fighting a faceless profit machine—is a plus for the union which the company's image-makers can't match.[25]

Successful organizational public relations in strike situations consists of humanizing the organization's position while clarifying the strike's impact on the local economy. Management's intrepid efforts to maintain operations, the strike's impact on local merchants, and the inflationary impacts of the workers' demands are angles that can build sympathy for organizational positions. In recent years, management's public position has been improved by what often appears as union greed. When the worker is already making $15 per hour or more, much of the public responds with envy rather than sympathy. News reports showing air traffic controllers' prosperous houses and swimming pools during their strike did nothing to win them public sympathy.

Communicating Employee Benefits

A major area of misunderstanding in most organizations is the employee benefit program. **Employee benefits** are services provided by an organization as part of employees' compensation. Benefits may include health and life insurance programs, sick leave, vacations, employer-paid social security, retirement programs, and a variety of other services ranging from day care to prepaid legal advice to physical fitness programs. Benefits are used to attract and retain employees and to promote employee productivity.

In relation to their benefits, managers often claim employees "just don't appreciate what they have." Often this lack of appreciation is the result of poor communication on the part of management, as the following episode illustrates:

> Workers at a corporation had just voted for union representation, and one of the strongest appeals the union offered was its benefits package. Management could not understand what had made the package so attractive to employees. "Those benefits offer no substantial improvements over the package we already had," complained one executive. Closer examination, however, revealed that the company had never prepared publications to explain its package. Employee meetings to discuss benefits were irregular, almost nonexistent. No employee handbook or guide had been published; no orientation program for new employees had been established. There is little doubt that when the employees cast their ballots for the union, they were not voting for better benefits, but for communication and a plan they understood.

Another company, which had a really outstanding benefit program, was alarmed by inaccurate rumors about the package. Consultants called in to investigate found that the firm's communication program consisted of a confusing booklet on group insurance and a dull monthly newsletter. The newsletter never discussed or rebutted rumors circulating through the grapevine. The communication void in that company was a breeding ground for misunderstanding, mistrust, and dissatisfaction.

Other organizations have become highly creative in benefits communication. United Technologies developed a seventeen-minute film/video featuring comedian Jonathan Winters to discuss six benefit areas: retirement, health care, disability, life insurance, dental care, and savings plans. Bankers Land Company of Palm Beach Gardens, Florida, devised a game board to explain health benefits. Exxon Coal USA put together its eighty-one-page "Guide to Your Employee Benefits" in the style of a magazine or annual report. Readability, vitality, and richness stimulated employee interest and readership.

U.S. Chamber of Commerce figures show that from 1977 to 1984, the cost of benefits to American companies almost doubled. In 1985, fringe benefits payments in organizations throughout this country amounted to 37.7 percent of total payroll, or about $8,166 per employee. Richard Huseman and John Hatfield comment:

> What is paradoxical about these expenditures is that organizations seem to be accruing few advantages from them. Benefit programs possess a diversity of goals, ranging from attracting and holding good employees to simply keeping the union out; however, there is little evidence to indicate that any of these goals are being met, through either the mere existence of benefit programs or increases in indirect compensation.[26]

The authors attribute this failure, at least in part, to the employees' lack of knowledge and understanding of their own benefits program.

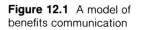

Figure 12.1 A model of benefits communication

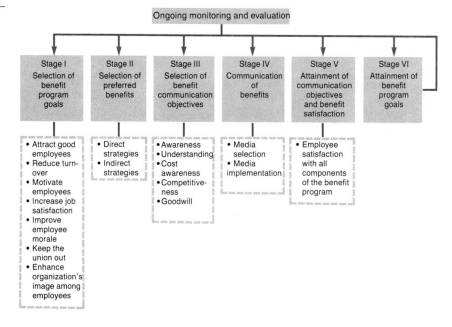

Helping employees understand their benefits has always been an important area for public relations work. But it is increasingly difficult to win gratitude and appreciation for a standard benefit package. Traditionally established on the single-breadwinner model, benefit programs are hard-pressed nowadays to respond to changing sex roles; new realities of divorce, marriage, and non-marriage; flexible retirement age; career interruptions; childless and smaller families; and multi-income families. Jerry Rosenbloom, professor of insurance at the University of Pennsylvania, observed in *Business Week* that the more sophisticated employees realize many of the benefits they receive at present "run exactly counter to people's needs."[27] For example, both partners of a working couple may be offered group health coverage, but neither may be provided with child care benefits.

The role of corporate communicators in dealing with employee benefits can be of vital significance. Public relations practitioners working in this area need not be limited to disseminating information about existing programs. Perhaps more importantly, they can serve as conduits for the expression of employees' needs and desires, and thus play a significant role in determining and evaluating benefit programs. Figure 12.1 is a Huseman/Hatfield model of the benefit communication process, demonstrating the various points at which corporate communicators can be useful.

One response to changing employee needs in the benefits area has been a cafeteria-style approach, which by 1986 was being used for about nineteen million employees in the United States.[28] This approach allows individuals to choose those benefits most appropriate to their own lives. At Bankers Trust Company, for example, eight thousand employees are given personalized allowances which vary according to length of service, salary, and age. When spending their allowances, employees may choose among seven life insurance, five medical, and three dental plans; varying degrees of disability coverage; dependent-care provisions; or extra vacation time.

Flexibility is the key to cafeteria-style plans, but if they are to work, effective employee communication is essential. SCM Corporation, the New York City conglomerate, spent $100,000 just on an information campaign to explain its new benefits plan to employees.

In addition to responding to varying employee needs, cafeteria-style plans are one way of combating the soaring costs of benefits. SCM expects to save over $1 million a year with its program. The health care component of benefits programs has caused the greatest headache in terms of escalating costs. In organizations like CIBA-GEIGY, Pacific Power & Light, and the Hartford Insurance Group, employee communication specialists have played a vital role in developing and disseminating health cost containment plans.

The Wisconsin Association of Manufacturers and Commerce produced a *Primer On Managing Health Care Costs.* That publication states: "A strong and ongoing communication campaign is a vital element of an employer's health education program. Communication tools take a variety of forms, but all support the major thrust of acting as constant reminders from the employer encouraging employees to help reduce the cost of health care."

With changing employee needs, government regulatory requirements, and the tremendous corporate resources devoted to employee benefits, this promises to be a continuing issue of great importance to organizational communicators.

The Media of Employee Communication

In the first part of this chapter, we took a general approach to employee communication. We discussed a positive organizational climate supported by an appropriate communication policy as prerequisites for effective employee communication. We also discussed employee communication under special circumstances and for special purposes.

This section is devoted to the technical aspects of employee communication media—how to get your message across. Internal publications, audiovisual media, and other methods are means of reaching large numbers of employees on an ongoing basis. Personnel and resources devoted to these media have increased markedly in the past decade. This is the fastest growing aspect of the overall public relations effort.

Internal Publications

In-house publications take about as many forms as the organizations and individuals who publish them (Figure 12.2). Effective, professionally written publications may be mimeographed newsletters, newspapers with editorial staffs of various sizes, glossy full-color magazines, or any variation on these. Their common purpose: to give an organization the chance to tell its story the

Figure 12.2 A variety of internal publications

Vol. XI, Issue 10   October 1985

Staten Island Update

by Jack Matthews, GM, Staten Island Cable

Legend has it that over two hundred years ago New York and New Jersey held a boat race around Staten Island to determine who had claim to the island. Recently some folks have humorously suggested that cable franchising in New York City started about the same time! Now, almost five years after proposals were first submitted to wire the four "outer boroughs" of New York City (Staten Island, Queens, Brooklyn and the Bronx), cable construction is finally ready to get underway.

In July, 1983, Cox Cable and Continental Cablevision were each awarded franchises for half of Staten Island. Since that time, the two companies have formed a joint venture called Staten Island Cable (SIC) to construct and operate a single cable system serving all of Staten Island. During the past two years, SIC has been finalizing its franchise agreement with New York City, negotiating make-ready terms with local utilities, and developing various franchise compliance plans (over twelve in all) required by the city. We now expect to start construc-

tion this fall.

The 680-mile system will pass approximately 120,000 homes and will utilize 550 MHz, one-way addressable technology. Construction is scheduled to be completed in mid-1988.

While it is part of New York City, Staten Island impresses (and surprises) visitors with its suburban nature. By far the smallest and most isolated of the New York City boroughs, Staten Island is characterized by single family homes, tree-lined streets and some areas which remain downright rural.

The other side of Staten Island is its growth. Since the Varrazano Narrows bridge was built in the early 1960's linking Staten Island with Brooklyn, the borough's population has increased over 50%, making Staten Island the fastest growing county in the state of New York.

There is no doubt that the challenges of building a cable system in New York City will be immense, but we believe we have the recipe to make Staten Island

Continued on page 7

Robbins Named President

by Sue Fisher, *Hookup* Editor, Atlanta

Jim Robbins was named President of Cox Cable on September 10. Jim, who was previously Senior VP-Operations, Division III, succeeds David Van Valkenburg, who has resigned.

Lew Davenport is now heading Division III as Senior VP-Operations.

Jim joined Cox in 1983 as VP-Cox Cable New York City. He was previously Senior VP-Operations, Western Region, for Viacom Communications, Inc.

Look for an interview with Cox Cable's new president in an upcoming issue. **COX**

Accounting for Quint Cities

by Mary Windeknecht, Quint Cities

Quint Cities' Accounting staff goes over the numbers. (L-r) Rick DeGrauwe, Randi Creedon, and Teri Kave.

". . . Distribution of accounting functions is just one piece, albeit a fundamental piece, of the management change this Company is undergoing. Accounting decentralization will not occur overnight and it will not be easy to accomplish. However, if we maintain a clear vision of what we want to accomplish and never lose sight of our objectives, the successful distribution of accounting responsibilities can be one of the major keystones that will allow Cox Cable to strengthen its position as a dominant force in the cable television industry."

—Juliet Reising, Controller, Atlanta

At Cox Cable Quint Cities, in Moline, Illinois, distribution of the accounting function has begun, bringing a host of new responsibilities and accountabilities to the system—and new meaning to the words above, which appeared in the March issue of HookUp.

As those words predicted, the decentralization process was not easy and did not occur overnight at Quint Cities. But the benefits of decentralization have become quite evident.

"Our managers are more tuned in to the system's financial situation and the impact that their decisions have," said Richard Hook, Quint Cities' GM. "That has made the management team stronger and more effective."

For Quint Cities' accounting staff—Controller Rick DeGrauwe, Accounting Manager Randi Creedon and Accounts Payable Clerk Teri Kave—the process of assuming the new accounting functions began with a three-week training program at Corporate in April. In May Quint Cities was on their own, but with a great deal of guidance from the corporate accounting staff.

Essentially, decentralization put the responsibility for preparation and review of the system's financial statement at the system level.

To better explain the significance of this change and its ad-

Continued on page 5

way it wishes. This is one reason in-house publications have become popular; it is also the reason so many fail to meet their objectives. When management speaks only from its own point of view without considering the intended readers, in-house publications are only propaganda sheets. Like the other media discussed in this book, however, in-house publications can be effective tools if produced with the needs of their intended audience in mind.

The more than 50,000 in-house publications in the United States have a combined circulation of more than 460 million. Many large organizations have more than one publication. One automaker, because of its size and the variety of its audiences, has thirty-eight. Most such media are internal and not intended for the general public. Occasionally, however, they are distributed to influential people outside the organization or used as marketing tools.

Purpose and Potential   Organizations inevitably communicate imperfectly with their employees. A corporation preparing to honor an employee for twenty-five years of service discovered that he knew shockingly little about the organization he had been a part of for a quarter of a century. The employee did not know the name of the company president, the location of headquarters, the number of plants the company had, the year the firm was founded, or the source of the raw material used in the manufacturing process—and he could name only two of his firm's two hundred products.

Such examples often come up. The standard response from managers, "What we have here is a problem of communication," does no more than label the situation. Even deciding to increase communication does not guarantee a solution; communication problems cannot be solved by simply increasing the flow of printed messages. While printed media have their advantages, they are not the appropriate response to every problem. Printed communication must take its place as a part of an overall program that also includes interpersonal communication, meetings, other media, and employee exposure to organizational officials, all within the context of establishing appropriate climate and policy. In-house publications can do a lot of good work within an organization. But they can never take the place of person-to-person manager-subordinate relationships.

Communication Functions   Downward communication is the most common function of in-house publications (Figure 12.3). Management's need to inform its employees is the justification behind most company publications. Internal publications are well suited for this because they publish regularly and can report news and information in a timely and relatively inexpensive way.

Internal publications can be counterproductive, however. There is a fine line between telling intended readers what management would like them to know and providing them with the information they want and need. The former is the leading cause of failure for in-house publications. The latter ensures success. If an in-house publication appears to be limited to the "management line," it loses readers. Those who do read it do not take it seriously. When this happens, the publication becomes a communication liability.

It seems to me . . .

We have recently completed a major computer and patient information system conversion. The majority of this process has gone very smoothly, but as often happens, a portion of it has experienced a somewhat rocky road.

It seems that we are becoming more and more dependent on computers and data processing applications to get our work done. Certainly this is good in most cases because it allows us to be more efficient and productive. On the other hand, we can easily slip into the habit of blaming the computer for all our shortcomings and thus become quite impersonal in dealing with the public.

In his book **Megatrends**, John Naisbitt, pointed out the trend toward **high tech** and also cited the need for **high touch** in the services we render.

A recent experience called this point to my attention. On a weekend, my wife sent me to the grocery store to buy some ice cream and to cash a check so we would have some spending money. She gave me her Honest Face card which I had never seen before.

I picked up the ice cream, then went to the cashier who instructed me to have my check approved by a machine. So I got in a long line to wait my turn. I followed the instructions given me by the machine — inserting my card, entering data, etc. The trouble began when it asked me for my "secret code." Since I had never heard of a secret code, I asked the gentleman behind me, "What's the secret code?" He indignantly replied, "I'm certainly not going to give you **my** code!"

After he realized my dilemma, he helped me retrieve my card which was a feat in itself. Card in hand, I went to the pay phone to call my wife, only to discover that I didn't have a cent. Fortunately, the fellow who had helped me in the line was kind enough to lend (give) me a quarter.

When my wife answered the phone, I demanded the "secret code." She started laughing so hard that I almost couldn't understand what she was saying. Personally, I didn't see anything funny about it!

I wrote down the code, got back in line and went through the whole process again. Just as I was at last completing the chore, I read, unfortunately too late, the final instructions, "Place your check face down." The machine did its thing, quickly stamping my check and regurgitating my card. The approval stamp was printed right across the front of my last and only check instead of on the back.

Embarrassed, humbled and defeated, I walked slowly back to the cashier who kindly said, "don't worry, other folks have done the same thing. I can fix it."

As I stomped in and gave my wife her money I remembered the "ice cream" purchased almost an hour earlier. With a twinkle in her eye, she thanked me for the half gallon "milkshake."

May we all remember that a machine can never provide the "personal touch" which folks so desperately need in a hospital.

Bernie Brown

Figure 12.3 Downward communication

Upward communication is an equally important, but sometimes overlooked function of in-house publications. It can help avoid the propaganda problem just mentioned. Those responsible for in-house publications must never forget that management itself is a prospective audience. Letters to the editor, question-and-answer columns, articles written by employees, and other devices such as readership surveys give information about issues important to employees (Figure 12.4), and this is valuable—even vital—to management decision making.

Lateral communication is a growing need in modern organizations. Hierarchical organizations are usually designed only to pass information up and down. Yet management needs some plan for communication among employees at the same level. Horizontal communication flow increases employee knowledge about the overall operations of the company and helps create a sense of community among the divisions of an organization. Moreover, lateral information can help develop new ideas and save duplication of effort. In-house publications should include lateral communication as a primary goal. Giving employees information about operations outside their immediate sphere can create a broader understanding of the functions and goals of the whole organization (Figure 12.5).

Objectives   In the broad sense, the goal of an in-house publication is the improvement of relationships between its readers and management. Setting policy and defining more specific objectives for such a publication is a complicated undertaking. Without specific guidelines, however, it is hard for an in-house publication to be successful and even harder to measure its success.

As we have said, in-house publications must fulfill the needs of both the organization and its employees. The information in the publication must be seen by the readers as useful and meaningful. Small talk and management

264 Public Relations: The Publics

Figure 12.4 Upward communication

FORUM

'Tis the season to celebrate a happy association . . .

Six Christmases have passed since the Canadian Forces' CF-18 Detachment first arrived at McDonnell Douglas and only two remain until we return north. It has been a rewarding, productive seven years and we in the CF have enjoyed working and making friends with the MCAIR team.

As we approach our seventh Christmas in St. Louis, we would like to wish all McDonnell Douglas employees and their families a joyous holiday season and a very happy and prosperous New Year.

Lt. Col. Clive Caton,
Commander,
CF-18 Detachment

More on the MDC logo . . .

The following quotations are from *Spirit* articles by Sandy McDonnell.

"To be participative managers we have to be willing to listen. We have to give our people a real chance to express their opinions, and then we have to be big enough to give those opinions careful consideration."

"Participative management is an opening up of the process by which decisions are made and problems are solved. It's a marketplace of ideas in which differing voices can express themselves and be confident of a fair hearing. This doesn't mean an end to managerial responsibility. At all levels, the boss is still the boss and still has to make the final decisions. But in a participative setting, the boss listens before he acts. And he makes use of what he learns."

Each letter recently published in FORUM about the logo decision expressed resentment that those affected by the decision weren't consulted. This resentment was further amplified by one response that labeled the participative process as a "popularity contest."

Our employees are further frustrated by being told that they can continue to use the old logo internally because they know that over a period of time, it will disappear from stationery, badges and other supplies.

Corporate management has an opportunity to acknowledge that they should have listened to our employees, rather than an outside consultant. Resolution of this issue is needed to restore employees' confidence in the participative process.

Participative Management Committee, MDAC-STL

Logo eye-catching . . .

Noting the letters in favor of the MDC logo, I add my vote for its retention. In the past, I've been able to spot an MDC location or building or automobile from its logo long before I could determine the printed name.

Many of the supplier representatives with whom I had contact in the past also had expressed admiration of our logo.

Perry Hadder, retiree,
Sun City West, AZ

Old logo traced MDC beginnings . . .

I would also like to add my name to the list of many others who feel that we should reinstate the old corporate logo. It seems like scrapping the logo is a step in the negative direction as far as increasing public awareness about our company. People have associated our logo with our company for a long time, just as they associate the rocket logo with Rockwell – yes, even on its table saws.

I think we should be proud of our beginnings in the military and commercial aircraft businesses as well as our achievements in space programs, even if we currently work in data processing or health services or whatever. If it weren't for our successes in these areas to begin with, there would be no McDonnell Douglas Corporation to diversify into other areas.

Craig S. Buback,
Department 321,
MCAIR, St. Louis

Messin' with our pride . . .

The recent decision to revise the MDC logo ranks right up there with a couple of other locally unpopular ideas:
(1.) Remove the bat and birds from our baseball team's uniform shirts. OVERRULED. (2.) Remove the slogan "Show-Me State" from our license plates. REQUEST DENIED. Missourians protested then and teammates are protesting now.

C'mon guys, you're messin' with our pride.

Don Donlon,
Department 091A,
MCAIR, St. Louis

Respect for co-workers on the decline . . .

I read with great interest Gary Grimshaw's letter about respecting co-workers' property. I've been at MDC for more than 30 years and have seen a great decline in this area year after year. People will borrow someone else's tools or whatever and forget to return them or will return them broken or damaged but not make an effort to replace them.

I can sympathize with Grimshaw, whose car was damaged on the parking lot at work. Whoever parked next to me in the parking lot at Building 598 in St. Charles opened their car door so hard that it almost put a hole through the door of a new car I had had only two days.

I've also noticed that some van pool drivers show little respect for co-workers. If you don't get out of their way, they'll run right over you whether in the parking lots or out on the highway. Even when it's wet, they'll drive 65-70 mph on the highways with no concern for the safety of their passengers.

John Donaubauer,
Department 99A,
MCAIR, St. Louis

Separate ISG paper won't cost more . . .

Q. I would like to see a vote on whether ISG employees feel it necessary that they have their own separate newspaper. I sit at my desk doing without a lot of office supplies – those not available from Stationery – in an attempt to keep expenses down in light of ISG's financial losses, and it is disheartening to read that additional expense is being created by ISG Communications.

I initially distributed a copy of *Spirit* to each employee at my location and I'm sorry to report that I had several thrown back onto my desk with the remark that I could save myself time by not passing them out; they'd pick it up if they wanted it. I'm afraid this new paper will get tossed in with the junk mail at employees' homes.

With the dropping of MDC's old logo and now this planned separate ISG publication, I feel farther away from our parent company than just mileage.

Name withheld by request

A. I appreciate your concern about the ISG employee publication. Let me begin to address your concerns by correcting some of the information you seem to have received.

First of all, ISG is not creating its own employee newspaper; the group has had a paper since its inception in 1984. In January, ISG Communications merely will be pulling the *ISG Spirit* insert from the corporate *Spirit* newspaper, renaming it and distributing it independent of the MDC *Spirit*.

ISG will not be incurring any new expenses with this move. It already pays for the production of *ISG Spirit* and the stuffing of the paper into the MDC *Spirit*. As was stated in an article in the October issue of *ISG Spirit*, the cost of mailing the paper to employees' homes will not be greater than the cost of distributing it now. In some ways it is less expensive. It is the least time-consuming method. What's more, it gives us the greatest guarantee that each employee is receiving a copy.

You and some of your co-workers may doubt the value of employee publications like *ISG Spirit*, but I can tell you from the number of people wanting to place stories in the paper and from reader response, many people at ISG value their newspaper. I welcome any comments you or other employees may have on how to improve the paper.

Barbara Anderson,
ISG Spirit editor,
ISG-HQ, St. Louis

Upper management must change attitudes . . .

I think the idea of the company adopting the Japanese management theory is a good one. To accomplish this the company has asked *all* employees to change their attitudes toward work and the company. I feel that I and most of my fellow workers have the proper attitude.

The ball is in upper management's court. If we are going to make a change to the Japanese management theory, upper management must change its attitudes.

The upper management of this company has to show employees that it really cares about employees. Asking for input from time to time and doing nothing, making promises and not keeping them, ignoring problems and hoping they will go away, and changing policies without letting employees in the field know, are not ways to show employees that management has changed its attitudes.

For the good of the company, I hope management will wake up to the fact that leadership by example always works and that it is the basis of the Japanese management theory.

Paul E. Billiard,
McDonnell Douglas Field Service Company,
Norristown, PA

Food for thought . . .

Macdonald's Douglas
3855 Lakewood Blvd.
Long Beach, CA 90846

Dear Friends:
I like your hamburger specially the filetofish please I'd like may you please send me some decals posters souveners and gifts from your company.

Your Friend
Aaron Rochin

Editor's note: Unsigned letters cannot be considered for publication. *Spirit* will, however, honor the requests of employees who do not want their names published with their letters or questions. If you have a question or any thoughts you'd like to share, send them to Julie Westermann, *Spirit* editor, H003/HQ/5W/503. Please include your work address and telephone number. The names of employees who request anonymity will be kept confidential. ∎

From *Spirit*, an employee publication of McDonnell Douglas. Printed with permission of McDonnell Douglas Corporation.

———— On Maintenance ————

Maintenance has capacity to bring EAL profits —motivation, training, lower costs needed . . .

Maintenance and Engineering is charged with bringing Eastern's fleet up to peak operating condition. Here members of management reply to a series of in-depth questions concerning where the airline has been and some of the strides that must be taken to improve it.

Photo 7A
Maintenance workers
on engine

Many hands to learn . . .
A group of mechanics in an Eastern engine shop gets some hands on experience with one of the company's big powerplants. More training is ahead — more work, too.

Q. We're all aware of problems with our fleet reliability and the airline's ability to provide dependable, on-time service. Just how serious is that situation today? For a time this fall it looked as if the airline was improving.

A. This hasn't been a good year for Maintenance, because of problems with engine shortages and the Federal Aviation Administration inspections early in the year. Our delay and cancellation rate went as high as 3.6% on the actual mechanical availability of the aircraft.

When you include other things, such problems we had as moving aircraft from one terminal to another, irregular operations that left us with more aircraft to push out than we had tractors available, we were delaying 6% of our flights. That was back in April. Since then it has been coming down. We finally crossed the 5% mark, and are looking optimistically to 1987.

Q. Why is this group optimistic? Isn't a 5% rate still much too high?

A. A lot of the problems we had in 1986 will be behind us. The corrosion which we had on airplanes that we had to "clean up" as part of the FAA inspection is behind us. The CF-6 engine shortages back in March and April are behind us. Today we have 4 spare CF-6 engines, the best shape we've been in in well over a year.

But the fact remains that our delay and cancelation rate of around 5%—in the eyes of our customers—is totally unacceptable.

Q. Do you know where we stand in the industry in this respect?

A. We actually can't say, precisely—because every airline counts delays and cancellations a little differently. We have 3 different numbers we use: planes actually "broken" at departure time is the fleet reliability report. That's been running a little more than 3%.

Then we have the total operating grade which includes every conceivable delay that can be charged Engineering and Maintenance. If we have an airplane arrive from South America at the International Terminal, Concourse E here, and we can't get it over to Concourse C because controllers won't let us move the plane, that ends up being a mechanical delay. Some other airlines don't count it that way.

If we cancel a flight in the morning, Maintenance gets charged with every leg that plane was scheduled to fly that day. With a DC-9, that could be 9 legs. Sometimes that actually happens. Other airlines only charge for the first leg. At Delta Airlines, if a plane comes into a station and Maintenance takes the plane out of service at that station to fix something, it isn't charged as a mechanical delay. Everyone uses different sorts of numbers.

It's difficult to sign numbers from other airlines. And when you do, they

are tough to sort out. Even on Air Transport Association items—the ATA is meeting now to create some sort of standard for reporting mechanicals — what they're reporting is different. One airline includes brake and wheel changes, another airline doesn't.

It's safe to say, our dispatch reliability for a time was below the industry standard on any acceptable norm, but today, we're back in about the middle of the pack and improving.

Q. Back in the early '70s the airline was No. 1 with the Civil Aeronautics Board in on-time performance. Since the sunset of the CAB, on-time performance reporting has disappeared. What with so many factors influencing on-time performance, such as air traffic control delays in the air and on the ground, do we pay any attention to that performance barometer today?

A. We sure do. But let's look at some of those years. In 1970, which was not a good year, we had a peak delay and cancelation rate that's higher than any month we've had this year. But since then it had been running between 1.7% and 3.8%, and we don't compare very favorably now with our current 3.3%.

Fleet reliability impacts on-time performance. And Eastern had a pretty good track record until about May 1985. That's when things started slipping so badly.

Q. What was the prime cause of this performance nosedive at Eastern?

A. Well, that was immediately after we started the "Moonlight Special" with the A-300s. That cut down on the availability of the A-300s for maintenance. The added maintenance requirements reduced our access to the other airplanes in our fleet.

We also had the "early out" campaign. That hurt us. We retired senior employees early, and those older employees had a lot of experience. The "early out" program had a retirement rate in Engineering and Maintenance which ran twice that of the other departments and divisions of the company.

We also had the "strong lead" campaign. It was something that hasn't come close to anyone's expectations.

We still have much to do to train both the leads and the managers in how to act in that environment. We can have the leads assuming more responsibility. They do need considerably more training, though.

Q. Aviation publications point to Eastern's aircraft maintenance costs as being the highest in the industry. If we are spending all this money, shouldn't we be getting more bang for the buck?

A. We should be getting more bang for the buck. We're not. We're spending a fortune for maintenance this year—almost a half billion dollars—by far the largest annual outlay among the airlines. We

currently have the 2nd highest maintenance costs in the industry, 2nd only to USAir. It costs us about .8¢ an available seat mile to do maintenance on our aircraft.

The lowest in the industry is Northwest at .55¢ an ASM. Every time we put a seat in the air it costs us 80% more for maintenance than it costs Northwest to put a seat in the air.

That's one of the basics of competition. Piedmont costs are .69¢ an ASM. A tenth of a cent times 60 billion seat miles adds up to a vast sum — $480 million. Other big carriers are in the .6¢ range.

Q. How much of this cost relates to wages and benefits—or what percentage of total maintenance costs go directly to the employee?

A. About 55% of our expenses go toward wages. On the average in Maintenance and Engineering 12% of our total expenses goes toward employee benefits—so figure almost 70% of our total maintenance expenses is related to employee compensation and benefits.

Q. How do you people view our manning? Do we need more people on the job or people who work harder?

A. That's one of our basic problems. Our entire Maintenance and Engineering organization requires more manpower to get a job done than it does at other carriers.

We just stopped the polishing program. It was taking us 200 man hours to polish the top of a 727. There's no reason for this taking more than 60. The

additional 140 hours times the average wage of our polishers increases the cost by $2,500. If the whole 727 fleet is polished annually, the extra expense equals about $312,000—simply for this one operation.

We stopped the paint program requiring 3,000 man hours to paint an L-1011, a job that shouldn't take more than 800. The same sort of savings could be realized in this situation as well.

Q. Are some of our people are doing their jobs in "slow motion?"

A. It's not so much *that* as it is our whole organization. We have a big problem in that we also have too many people doing given jobs.

And it's not the mechanic's fault. For example, if a work manager, or the lead, tells 5 guys to go do a certain job, and that job requires only 2 men, the mechanics aren't going to say, "Hey, why don't I do something else— I'm really not needed here!" Obviously, if it takes more of our people more time to do a given job, our total labor costs are going to be greater.

Q. How much is it costing Eastern to maintain a given airplane? We'd like everyone to be able to relate these costs to their own pocketbooks.

A. It costs us about $340 to fly a DC-9 for an hour—in maintenance costs— compared with an average of less than $300 for other majors. Continental has its costs below $200. Our 727 costs us $490 an hour, with other majors 727s cost between $300 and $400. It depends
Turn to MAINTENANCE, Pg. 10

Figure 12.5 Lateral communication

propaganda defeat effectiveness. Most important to success is the selection of content that combines the common interests of management and employees. Following are some broad topics that are frequently chosen by successful publications:

Recognition of employee achievements both on the job and in the community can encourage internal cooperation by helping management and employees become better acquainted with other members of the organization (Figure 12.6). This type of recognition also serves as an official commendation for outstanding service and sets an example for others in the organization. Social activities can also be recognized, but should not take precedence over job-related and community-service accomplishments. Appropriate employee recognition can promote various objectives, including:

> Strengthening positive relationships in the outside community.
> Building a sense of accomplishment in individual employees.
> Stimulating new ideas for company and community service.

Employee well-being and safety can be promoted through information on safety practices, rules, and procedures. Worker safety is always an appropriate area of concern for management and employees alike. In some organizations, this involves little more than ensuring that everyone knows the location of fire exits. In others, however, the success of the operation, and indeed the operation itself, may depend on adherence to safety procedures. Internal publications are one outlet for the constant safety reminders necessary to such organizations.

There is an endless need to explain benefits, vacations, holidays, taxes, workers' compensation, affirmative action, and equal employment opportunity policies. Employees can also be told about community issues and educational and training opportunities. Objectives of this type include:

> Encouraging employee advancement.
> Demonstrating the organization's concern for workers' health and safety.
> Interpreting local, state, and national news as it applies to the company and the well-being of employees.

Employees' understanding of their role in the organization can be improved (Figure 12.7). An in-house publication can stress the importance of each worker's job in meeting company goals. Information about the eventual use of products illustrates the importance of everyone's part in the process. Internal publications should promote the idea that each employee is a salesman for the company. They should pay attention to:

> Building loyalty to the organization.
> Improving cooperation and coordination.
> Improving production and efficiency.
> Reducing expense and waste.
> Getting everyone involved in and aware of the importance of public relations.

7

Figure 12.6 Employee recognition

Eagle Recognition PROGRAM

Customer satisfaction. Profitability. Positioning for the Future.

These goals drive AT&T's Southern Region marketing people. And those who soared to success in those areas in the fourth quarter of 1985 recently received Eagle awards.

The Southern Region recognizes its top marketing performers with two major Eagle award programs. The Team awards go to the region's marketing teams who show the best results among any or all of those three measures of success. Each quarter three teams are selected for the awards. An annual team winner in each category will be chosen from the year's quarterly winners.

The Eagle Challenger Award is presented quarterly to individuals demonstrating excellent performance in any of the corporate values. Eight winners are usually named each quarter, one from each major segment of the marketing department. Winners of the region's Eagles are those who meet criteria based on the AT&T Communications corporate value system. Components of the value system are:

•A focus on customer satisfaction. Service is not good until perceived so by the customer.
•Recognition of the importance of people. Employees are intelligent, creative and want a positive role in making the business successful.
•A drive toward profitability. Employees must be conscious of how their job impacts the bottom line.
•A bias for action with an orientation to goals, commitments and credibility.

The 'Challenger' Award
Fourth Quarter — Individual Winners

Primary Account Sales Center
Brenda Simms, assistant manager, Ft. Lauderdale, Fla.
Simms captured a fourth-quarter Eagle by helping to improve the profitability of the Ft. Lauderdale primary account sales center (PASC). She developed an occupational "salespertise" course for the inbound telemarketing sales specialists. The 30-day program enhanced the employees' grasp of business functions and data gathering skills and improved their ability to overcome customer objections and employ data analysis to make proper recommendations for closing sales. Class participants agreed that the program had changed their approach to selling. The program's initial success has led to plans to offer it to the entire inbound sales force in 1986.

General Business Markets
Judy Vice, assistant staff manager, Atlanta, Ga.
Vice helped position AT&T for the future in her role as staff coordinator for the reduction of unidentified and unbilled WATS and 800 services usage. She was instrumental in the recovery of nearly $1.7 million in revenue since June 1985. The Eagle-worthy accomplishment was achieved through her active participation in joint meetings with AT&T and local exchange company (LEC) staffs that were held to identify and resolve problems related to AT&T services. She also established close working relationships with comptroller personnel at the LECs in order to monitor the progress in resolving these problems.

Select Account Sales Center
Ledger Davis, sales manager, Tucker, Ga.
As sales manager of the national telemarketing account center (NTAC), Davis won an Eagle for his efforts to use telemarketing to provide better account management for national accounts. Under his guidance, NTAC provided effective support to 22 national accounts, maintaining effective market presence with 12,000 customer locations. In addition, NTAC was able to expand its initial role of revenue base protection to include application, upgrade, growth and winback sales. Since becoming operational in March 1985, NTAC has provided $1.4 million in growth revenue, $376,000 in application revenue, $474,000 in winback revenue and $2.4 million in product migration revenue.

National Markets
Ralph Stanze, account executive/industry consultant/ acting national account manager, Creve Coeur, Mo.
In the fourth quarter of 1985, Stanze led AT&T's national account team for General Dynamics to successful sales of AT&T MEGACOM℠ Service to replace SBS services at two customer divisions. The winbacks represent $1,495,100 in extra revenue for AT&T so far and the effort is paving the way to win back an additional $2 million in annual revenue. The team was not only able to provide the customer with improved network quality at lower cost but supplied the sold services within two months rather than the normal nine-month interval.

Consumer Markets
Charles Francis, manager, Irving, Texas
Francis was both inventor and project manager in the acquisition and subsequent conversion of an AT&T Information Systems consumer sales and service center in Parsippany, N.J., to an AT&T Communications consumer markets sales center (CMSC). In terms of customer satisfaction, the new Parsippany CMSC immediately improved the ability of AT&T customers to get sales assistance. In addition, the acquisition of the office provided an opportunity for 172 surplused AT&T-IS employees to continue employment with the company. Moreover, opening the center saved AT&T $5.5 million in close-down costs and saved the company even more in training expenses because of the transition of already-trained employees.

Majors West
Brenda Popovich, communications systems consultant, Springfield, Mo.
Popovich led a team effort to solve the mystery of a lot of unanswered calls at Bass Pro's inbound calling center. Popovich discovered a problem with unanswered call volumes during the customer's peak season by comparing AT&T network reports with the customer's reports for its switch. She realized that several thousand more calls were being sent than were actually received at Bass Pro's switch. After more investigation, the source of the problem was found. It centered around a misinterpretation of procedures in a standard industry technical reference that dealt with timing between local phone company switches and customers' automatic call distributors (ACDs). With the problem solved, Bass Pro expects to improve its call completion rate by 15 percent during the peak season and gain $150,000 to $250,000 in revenue from its customers.

Majors East
Bill Hastings, account executive/industry consultant, Nashville, Tenn.
Hastings demonstrated outstanding performance and drive toward profitability on the Northern Telecom account. Competing against SBS, MCI and ITT, Hastings protected a multi-million dollar revenue base and secured opportunities for future competitive winbacks. In addition, his MEGACOM℠ Service sale to Northern Telecom will provide AT&T with an additional $515,328 in annual revenue. Finally, his close attention to Northern Telecom's needs will also help the customer save $147,728 in telecommunications costs during the coming year.

In the profitability category, the fourth quarter Team award was awarded to Don Evans' team in Tucker, Ga. From left to right are Evans, Pamela Earle, Maureen Caine, Dave MacFarlane, Dennis Duensing, Carol Zeisler, Frank Grizas, Tracy Lehmberg and Sharon Perry.

The fourth quarter Team award in the positioning for the future category went to Cheiri MacManis' team in Tucker, Ga. From left to right are Susan Kaissling, Joel King, Cherry Burke, Steve Sullivan and MacManis.

Jim Donnelly's Exxon national account team in Houston won the fourth quarter Team award in the customer satisfaction category. From left to right are Stan Miller, Esther Viveros, Felix Dukes, Donnelly, Laura McGarth, Jim DiBona, Sara Grier and Dennis Carter.

'Eagle Challenge' Award
Fourth Quarter — Team Winners

Customer Satisfaction
Team Manager: Jim Donnelly, national account manager, Houston, Texas
Donnelly's national account team won its Eagle for its ability to satisfy the complex and demanding telecommunications needs of Exxon. The dedication to customer service resulted in the application of AT&T's new Software Defined Network (SDN) Service to Exxon's internal network. The account team also helped Exxon prepare its 10-year communications plan by outlining AT&T's plans in SDN, the Integrated Services Digital Network (ISDN), packet switching, satellite transmission and regulatory issues management. In addition, the team demonstrated other AT&T services of potential value to Exxon, including MEGACOM℠ and MEGACOM 800 services and video teleconferencing.

Positioning for the Future
Team Manager: Cheiri MacManis, sales manager, Tucker, Ga.
MacManis and the four members of her team were successful in positioning AT&T for the future with target customers in the financial industry. They established a comprehensive long-range plan whose goals are to position AT&T at the highest management levels of the accounts, to ensure that AT&T is perceived as an integral part of the customers' long-range planning efforts, thwart competitive inroads and demonstrate AT&T's value-added capabilities. Initial customer reaction has been excellent.

Profitability
Team Manager: Don Evans, sales manager, Tucker, Ga.
Evans led his 10-person team to successful sales resulting in a 30 percent improvement in revenue results, $430,000 in winback revenue, a competitive sale worth $6 million in 1986 revenues and the execution of a co-marketing agreement with a shared tenant services provider worth $18 million to $20 million in annualized revenues by the end of 1987. The team also sold customers telemarketing training for 200 of their employees and sold the select account sales center's (SASC) first college/university resale application.

For the Shuttle Processing Team the mission continues at KSC, VLS

For the Shuttle Processing Contract Team the primary mission continues to be preparing America's Space Shuttle fleet for flight. Lockheed Space Operations Co., Grumman Technical Services, Inc., Morton Thiokol and Pan American World Services personnel are at work getting ready for the Shuttle's return to flight in February of 1986.

Shuttle activity for 1986 began with the spectacular launch of Shuttle mission 61-C. The flight was highlighted by the deployment of a communications satellite and experiments in medicine and astronomy.

Following the Shuttle Challenger tragedy, the SPC Team joined NASA in seeking the cause of the accident. During the period between flights, personnel at both the Kennedy Space Center and the Vandenberg Launch Site have been occupied with those tasks which can be accomplished to make the business of processing Shuttles smoother, safer and more efficient.

Numerous milestones were achieved during 1986 at VLS and KSC. At the Western Spaceport preparations continued for the first Shuttle launch into polar orbit, now slated for 1992. Tests included solid rocket booster stacking which was flawlessly completed at Space Launch Complex-6 during September. At KSC recent operations involved a variety of tests with the Shuttle Atlantis at Launch Pad 39-B in October and November.

In the months ahead, the SPC Team will continue to prepare for the Shuttle's return to flight and the missions which will further the exploration and utilization of space.

At the Vandenberg Launch Site, Computer Operator Sharon Masiak, left, Senior Analyst Mike Riley, center, and Systems Manager Flora Story perform computer work in the Business Management Directorate.

Maintenance on the SPC Solid Rocket Booster Retrieval Ships continues while the three vessels are in port at Cape Canaveral AFS. Dean Chambers, a Morton Thiokol Crewman on the Independence, does some touch up painting on the ship's crane arm, while "Old Glory" waves in the background. Independence will be used to support Shuttle launches from the Vandenberg Launch Site.

The crew of Shuttle mission 61-C uses the micro-gravity of earth orbit to strike this unusual pose for a group portrait. Mission Commander Robert Gibson, lower right corner, is surrounded by fellow crewmembers, counter-clockwise, from upper right: Pilot Charles Bolden, Florida Congressman Bill Nelson, payload specialist, Robert Cenker of RCA, payload specialist, and mission specialists Steven Hawley, Franklin Chang-Diaz and George Nelson.

Marsh waters near the Kennedy Space Center's Launch Pad 39-A reflect the scene as the Space Shuttle Columbia is launched into the early morning sky on mission 61-C on Jan. 12, 1986.

Pan American World Services' Lisa Colby, an operations analysis associate, seated, and Bob Kedlar, a technical analyst, review the data base for the SPC Suggestion Program's Cost Savings Category Activity Log. The Pan Am group is involved in Operations Analysis, Process Planning and Control and Logistics Engineering.

Ground Support Equipment Mechanical Technicians Ben Bader, left, and Doyce Mitchell inspect supports at the 150-foot level on the Fixed Service Structure on Launch Pad 39-A. The Space Shuttle Atlantis can be seen on Pad 39-B in the distance. Much of the activity on the Pad A structure will concentrate on bringing its configuration to that of Pod B.

LSOC Thermal Protection System technicians Z. P. Shaw, center, and Don Langworthy, right, apply a tile to the orbiter Discovery while Quality Assurance Inspector Pat Moragne looks on.

Grumman Technical Services, Inc. employees Susan Martin, a Launch Processing System (LPS) test conductor, right; Ron Kennedy, Jr., an LPS test conductor, center; and Anne Raffaelli, a data analyst specialist, monitor Ground Support Equipment testing in Firing Room 1 of the Launch Control Center. Grumman is responsible for the operation and maintenance of the Kennedy Space Center's Launch Processing System.

Manning the Video Switching Board in the LSOC Television Control Room are Video Technicians Fletcher Hilbreth, foreground, and Ricky Morris. They are working video switchers to monitor Pod B cameras used in the Terminal Countdown Demonstration Test for the Space Shuttle Atlantis during November.

Clarification of management policies should consider the point of view of both management and employees. Employees must be accurately informed about business activities if management expects them to support its programs (Figure 12.8). Understanding can be helped through:

Explaining policies and rules.
Building confidence in management.
Combating rumors and misunderstandings.

An in-house publication can accomplish these objectives if it meets the needs of employees, if it says something that employees want to think about and talk about, and if it is attractive and easy to read.

Managing Internal Publications   Who will read the publication is a decision that will shape all others. Do not try to be all things to all people. Do not try to rival the *New York Times*. An internal publication serves the needs of the organization that sponsors it. Successful in-house publications are those that identify, acknowledge, and stick to a purpose: serving their audience.

Identifying a publication's audience may not be as simple as it seems. Although the primary audience is usually limited to people inside the organization, these individuals can often be divided into several groups. A large petrochemical company employs blue-collar workers who belong to one of several unions. It also hires engineers and research scientists with professional affiliations as well as white-collar mid-management and clerical personnel. Each group has different interests and needs different information.

When only one publication is possible, you should identify a primary audience and treat the other groups as secondary. The secondary groups can be served through special columns or stories. Secondary audiences might also include suppliers, distributors, other company plants or divisions, competitors, and the surrounding community. Many of these external secondary audiences will read your publication even if you do not want them to. Therefore, the contents should reflect good judgment. Issues of substance must be discussed if the publication is to have credibility. However, this is not the place to air dirty laundry that will embarrass the organization and its employees. Some large companies have begun publications aimed at such outside groups as the community, suppliers, and industry.

What type of publication does your organization need? Once the primary and secondary audiences have been identified, decide what kind of publication will best meet their needs: a newsletter, a tabloid newspaper, a magazine, or some other format. Sometimes these needs change, as indicated in Mini-Case 12.3. Frequency of publication and methods of distribution should also be decided in advance, based upon the requirements of the primary audience. Most in-house publications are published monthly, but some appear

Figure 12.7 (Opposite page.) An in-house publication can enhance employees' understanding of their roles within the organization.

Figure 12.8 Clarification of management policies

Performance Management Program

The new process involves employees in every step along the path toward the annual performance review.

Annual review time. Frustrating hours for the manager who must condense an employee's performance for a whole year into a few pages. Anxiety and guarded anticipation on the part of the employee. The performance appraisal process is not always a pleasant experience for managers *or* employees. But all that could change soon.

This past February, the Human Resources Advisory Committee (HRAC) created an employee task force to evaluate and determine ways to improve the performance appraisal process. Many of the group's recommendations recently were approved by the executive council and will become effective Jan. 1, 1987.

The task force was composed of 12 members — six employees who were selected from 86 volunteers, four members of HRAC, and two members of management who were nominated by HRAC.

"We formed the task force primarily as a result of the low ratings employees gave the company's performance appraisal process in the 1985 employee opinion survey," says Dennis Eubanks, director of human resources. "The survey findings made us take a closer look at the process, and we came to the conclusion that improvements needed to be made. We felt that the best suggestions would come from a task force composed of employees, supervisors, and managers."

Dick Wight, supervisor of customer research and a task force member, explains that the first goal was to define the committee's responsibilities. "We decided that we should determine what the issues were, make recommendations, and assist in implementing and monitoring a new appraisal process," he notes.

With input from employees, Dick says the task force identified key concerns. These included lack of employee involvement and feedback in the appraisal process, the wide variety of techniques used in the appraisal process, and unpopularity of the rating terminologies.

"As a first step," says Tim Doxsey,

supervisor of data entry and another task force member, "the committee recommended and the executive council has now approved a no-surprises concept of performance management for formal implementation at SCS."

Under this new procedure, each employee and his or her supervisor will work together to develop performance expectations for the employee, taking into consideration accountabilities, job duties, and goals for the upcoming year. Then, about midway into that year, the supervisor will conduct a minireview or update to measure the employee's performance against the expectations that have been set. This midyear session also will be used as an opportunity to discuss individual and career development with employees.

"For the year-end review, the supervisor and employee together will compile a list of accomplishments," Tim continues. "This will ensure that all accomplishments are considered. And perhaps most importantly, it will allow the employee to provide input before the performance rating is assigned."

Task force participant Warren Glover, manager of fossil, mechanical design, says the new procedures led the task force to recommend that the appraisal forms also be changed.

"We suggested that one form be used for both exempt and nonexempt employees, with sections provided for accountabilities and standards, expectations and goals, and employee development plans," he says. This one form will be used for entering accomplishments and establishing new or adjusted responsibilities at the midyear discussion. And there is a section for employee comments.

The executive council also agreed with the task force recommendations for new rating terminology. Explains Cynthia Brown, senior secretary I, audit services, "We studied the performance appraisal process at several other companies and concluded that a phrase is better than a single word."

With that in mind, the following rating categories have been adopted:
- clearly exceeded job requirements
- fully met and often exceeded job requirements

- fully met and occasionally exceeded job requirements
- met minimal job requirements
- failed to meet job requirements

Approval also was given to the committee's suggestion that management training and information meetings be held to explain the new process. Those meetings were held in October and November. And finally, the task force's recommendation was adopted that calls for the new process to be monitored carefully during its first year to determine effectiveness.

"We're pleased with the recommendations that we developed," says John Edmundson, senior engineer, civil and architectural design. "The new system emphasizes employee involvement in the appraisal process as well as in goal setting — and that's the basis for no-surprises performance management."

Adds Tom Nunnelly, executive vice president, "The executive council feels that employee input is one of the most important parts of this revised process. That involvement will aid in the employee's understanding of and satisfaction with his or her performance evaluation."

Task Force Members

Serving on the Performance Appraisal Task Force in addition to those mentioned in this article, were: Mike Asumaa, senior compensation analyst, employee compensation, Atlanta — coordinator of the task force; Ray Billups, manager, market planning; Georgette Ellis, senior secretary I, Vogtle project; Larry Evans, senior engineer, generation planning; Mac Freeman, assistant to Executive Vice President Bill Guthrie; Lynn Gorman, senior research technician I, research and environmental affairs (recently transferred to Alabama Power); Ginger Simpson, senior financial planning analyst, financial planning; and Anne Zenoni, senior secretary I, data preparation and control (recently retired).

quarterly or even weekly. The easiest, cheapest, and simplest method of distribution is to make them available for pickup around work areas. To get wider distribution, some organizations hand them directly to employees, use the in-house mail, or send them to employees' homes. All of these matters are interdependent. The format (size and shape) may limit the possibilities for distribution.

Other considerations in determining the type of publication are budget and audience needs. Once a budget for the publication is established, information about audience needs must be gathered. Interviews and questionnaires can tell a great deal about content, frequency, and distribution needs. To help select a format, many companies ask employee panels to review sample publications from other organizations. The panel can also evaluate data obtained in the interviews and questionnaires. The results of such planning efforts should be written down and kept to help plan future issues and evaluate past ones.

Mini-Case 12.3

Scrapping an Award-Winning Publication at Celanese

When you've got an award-winning company-wide publication, you give the editor a raise and expand its budget, right? Not at Celanese where the decision was made to scrap *Celanese World*. A change in corporate structure and philosophy rendered the magazine inadequate for the company's needs, and consequently, no longer necessary.

In 1982, Celanese Corporation was decentralized so that each operating division had its own communications department, budget, and publications. The company's divisions and subsidiaries developed their own communications objectives and policies.

Jeanne Reinhart is a Celanese communications representative. She says she misses *Celanese World's* research and timely information, but feels that other publications have more than filled the gap. For example, Celanese Chemical has instituted a monthly division-wide publication for its staff, with individual supplements for each of its locations.

Celanese research shows that the newsletter is better read and more enjoyed than previous employee publications. It is more attuned to the local needs of the company's plants, while still providing relevant information on Celanese Chemical's overall performance.

Starting Internal Publications   Producing an internal publication takes organization and coordination. It must appear at scheduled regular intervals. Such consistency requires budget and staff. Putting out a publication on a shoestring may be worse than doing nothing at all. A publication that cannot be properly maintained creates negative attitudes by building expectations it cannot fulfill. Therefore, organizing the details of production is important to success.

Sometimes, producing the company newsletter is a one-person job.

What makes news? The content of an internal publication will vary from one organization to another. Some employees will not read certain items, and even more do not have time to read anything at all. Extraneous topics, even when educational, are not proper for an in-house publication. There are topics appropriate to your organization, however, that will attract the interest of even the busiest executive or blue-collar worker. These should form the backbone of your publication.

News is everywhere. Any topic that concerns what people do, feel, or think is interesting. Select topics that grow out of the activities in the sponsoring organization. Potentially, every job, group, program, and employee has news value. To identify possible stories, an editor or writer should consider the topic from the intended reader's point of view. Include items that will interest many groups within the organization. You should consider the needs of your primary audience first, but you may expand readership by printing items of interest to others as well. Look for stories that inform and entertain. No one will read everything, but almost everyone will read something. A rule of thumb for an appropriate mix is:

50 percent information about the organization—local, national, and international

20 percent employee information—benefits, quality of working life, etc.

20 percent relevant noncompany information—competitors, community, etc.

10 percent small talk and personals

Remember, company information must satisfy the needs of its employees not just those of management. If the publication is to serve the goals of the sponsor organization, readership is essential. Topics with generally high interest are:

New equipment or changes in existing equipment
Remodeling or expansion
Quality control procedures and requirements
Safety requirements
Achievement of quotas
Wage rates and increases
New jobs created
New assignments
Meetings
Changes in union officers or policies
Important visitors
Sales and earnings
Management policies
President's or general manager's message

Employee news is an excellent source of feature articles or even columns (Figure 12.9). It gets high readership because its audience is its subject. Some possible topics are:

Promotions
New employees
Retirements
Deaths
Community involvement
Memberships—clubs, community organizations, and associations
Volunteer service
Educational achievements
Awards

Relevant noncompany information consists of matters that affect the company or its employees (Figure 12.10). Events reported in the popular media can be tailored to an internal publication by predicting their effects on employees, the company, and/or the industry. Relevant noncompany information usually comes from the following:

Business, trade, or association publications
National news publications
Daily and weekly newspapers
Newsletters and other publications from unions, professional groups,
    or competing organizations

Figure 12.9 Employee information column

Service anniversaries for fourth quarter

40 Years

James C. Bass, SNG, Thomaston, Ga., Compressor Station.
Harold P. Bingham, SNG, Birmingham, Pipeline District.
Walters R. Gibson, SNG, Enterprise, Miss., Sub-District
Clinton R. McBrayer, SNG, Louisville, Miss., Pipeline District.
John S. Waldrip, SNG, Opelika, Ala., Pipeline District.

35 Years

Marion R. Burch, SNG, Logansport, La., Compressor Station.
Charles D. Douglas, SNG, Gwinville, Miss., Pipeline District.
Charles S. Griffin, SNG, Technical Services, Opelika, Ala.
L.A. Hart, SNG, Atlanta, Pipeline District.
Avolee D. Wooten, SNG, Records Department, Birmingham.

30 Years

Willard E. Barlow, SNG, Ocmulgee, Ga., Compressor Station.
Darvin R. Bott, SNG, Franklinton, La., Compressor Station.
James B. Dewberry, SNG, DeArmanville, Ala., Compressor Station.
Wallace W. Dobson, SNG, Underground Storage, Bienville, La.
James R. Sligh, SNG, Yazoo, Miss., Pipeline District.
Norma J. Kowalski, SNG, General, Gas and Fixed Capital Department, Birmingham.

25 Years

James W. Baker, SNG, Gallion, Ala., Pipeline District.
Leonard Beaushaw, SNG, Franklinton, La., Pipeline District.
Roy C. Billings, SNG, Wetumpka, Ala., Pipeline District.
Lionel B. Serpas, SNG, Toca, La., Pipeline District.

20 Years

Louise C. Blackmon, SNG, Gas Control Department, Birmingham.
Vernon J. McCard, SNG, DeArman-

ville, Ala., Compressor Station.
James L. Morris, SNG, Reform, Ala., Compressor Station.
Denson R. Sizemore, SNG, Transmission Department, Birmingham.
E.L. Tucker, South Georgia Natural Gas, Thomasville, Ga., Pipeline District.
John L. Wise, SNG, Material Distribution Center, Pinson, Ala.

15 Years

Frederick W. Barnett, Sonat Services Inc., MIS Data Center, Birmingham.
David L. Boudreaux, Sonat Exploration, Drilling and Production Department, Oklahoma City, Okla.
Edsel A. Brasher, SNG, Total Energy Plant, Birmingham.
Robert T. Chatman, SNG, Gas Control Department, Birmingham.
Timothy O. Fulgham, SNG, Reform, Ala., Compressor Station.
Leonce P. Hernandez, SNG, Toca, La., Pipeline District.
Sherry L. King, Sonat Services Inc., MIS Data Center, Houston.
Willie B. Mitchell, SNG, Louisville, Miss., Pipeline District.
Henry C. Nix, Sonat Services Inc., MIS Data Center, Birmingham.
Ken C. Portwood, SNG, Transmission East, Macon, Ga.
James A. Sorrell, SNG, Franklinton, La., Compressor Station.
Danny E. Wolford, SNG, Total Energy Plant, Birmingham.

10 Years

Warren C. Crow, Sonat Services Inc., MIS Technical Support, Birmingham.
Raymond E. Hayden, SNG, Birmingham Pipeline District.
Regina A. Hinkle, Sonat, Legal Department, Birmingham.
Reuben D. Humphries, South Georgia Natural Gas, Communications, Thomasville, Ga.
Beverley T. Krannich, Sonat, Legal Department, Birmingham.
John M. Musgrave, Sonat, Treasury

Services Department, Birmingham.
Ray A. O'Bryan, Sonat Exploration, East Cameron Blocks 45/46, offshore Louisiana.
Ivy M. Stephenson, SNG, Communications Department, Birmingham.
Vivian A. White, SNG, Gas Control Department, Birmingham.
Robert H. Whitmire, SNG, Communications Department, Birmingham.
Kerry J. Zimmerman, Sonat Exploration, East Cameron Block 231, 232, 239, offshore Louisiana.

Retirements

Nathan Derbonne, chief dehydration plant operator for SNG's Logansport, La., District, retired Nov. 1 after more than 40 years with the company. Derbonne was hired in 1946 and became dehydration plant operator in 1965. He was promoted to chief dehydration plant operator in 1977.

Earl R. Hardwick retired Nov. 1 from SNG's Birmingham, Ala., District after more than 32 years of service. Hardwick was hired in 1954, was promoted to corrosion engineer in 1967, and advanced through several positions to become manager-corrosion in 1984.

Charles B. Shivers Jr. retired Nov. 1 as patrol pilot, SNG Birmingham Aviation. He had more than 12 years of service with the company.

Thomas G. Smith of Shreveport, La., district exploration manager for Sonat Exploration, retired Nov. 1 with more than a year of service to the company.

Wayne Wolford retired Oct. 1 as utility I at SNG's Material Distribution Center after 34 years with the company. Wolford was hired in 1952, promoted to utility man in 1971 and advanced to utility I in 1975.

Sonat joins Curry Elementary in school festival

Susan Bridges of Sonat's Corporate Communications Department chats with students from Curry Elementary School at the Drug-Free School Festival held on Oct. 31 in the school gymnasium. Sonat sponsors Curry Elementary in the Birmingham Board of Education's Adopt-A-School program. Twenty-nine Sonat volunteers tutor first, second, third and fourth grade students at Curry one hour each week.

Figure 12.10 How external events affect the organization

C-130s play critical role in African famine lift

The Belgian Air Force — carrying out a continuing famine food lift with its C-130Hs for the past year — has delivered more than 34,000 tons of vital foodstuffs and supplies to Africa's sub-Saharan drought region, according to recent reports from Brussels.

The effort reportedly has broken all standing C-130 airlift records in the famine belt of Ethiopia, Sudan, Mali and Chad. Belgium is the only nation to continue the famine relief food lift, being selected by the International Red Cross/Geneva due to its high cost effectiveness.

"We have had our C-130Hs stationed in Asmara (Ethiopia) since January of last year," according to Col. K. Vervoort, station commander at Belgium's Melsbroek Airbase. The aircraft are adorned with giant-size red crosses on their fuselages.

During the height of the airlift, two Belgian C-130s and two crews each were dispatched to Addis Ababa and Asmara (Ethiopia). Later, still another Belgian Hercules and two crews were deployed to Khartoum, launching the Sudanese Relief Airbridge into the western parts of that vast nation.

Meanwhile, yet another Belgian C-130H was dispatched to Zaire at the request of the International Red Cross, transporting 197 refugees to Kinshasa. (The Belgian Hercules landed on an unprepared strip at Kimpangu along the Algolan border, and flew the refugees to Kinshasa. The refugees, men, women, and children, from Portugal, Philip-

pines, Britain and Germany, were captured at a diamond mine by UNITA guerillas in Angola, then released.)

"During changeovers of aircraft and crews," noted Col. Vervoort, "sometimes up to six of our C-130Hs out of 12 were continuously stationed on African soil, delivering food grain, beans, seeds and

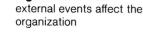

supplies and airlifting refugees."

In recent months, around half of the Belgian food lift flights have involved airdrops, including delivery of food to Sekota, Ethiopia, an extremely difficult drop zone. Here, as elsewhere, the food was dropped from a height of 30 feet (nine meters). The sophisticated Belgian airdrop system permits delivery of 12 to 16 tons of grain on a single run, with the number of torn sacks being less than two percent.

Throughout the maximum effort airlift in Africa, the Belgian Air Force's maintenance organization kept its entire C-130 fleet flying, enabling the service

to continue its normal commitments such as military deployments and additional relief flights. Among them were missions for "Doctors without Frontiers" into Chad, Sudan, Mali (Timbouctou) and Mexico City and a medical relief mission to Colombia. On humanitarian missions from Belgium,

each C-130 carried 17-plus tons of goods including tents, jeeps, trucks, medicines, sleeping bags, blankets, compact food, sugar, salt and tools.

One of the major challenges in Africa came with transporting wheat flour. "Clouds of flour dust settled on everything in the aircraft, with dust penetrating some of the instruments," Col. Vervoort declared. "We solved the problem by installing a large hand-tailored military tent in the cargo hold with only an opening facing aft on the loading ramp."

Another problem: Torn sacks attracted birds large and small, contributing a real danger during takeoffs, landings

and airdrops. "Some of our crews," Col. Vervoort said, "will remember the sight of two Belgian and two Royal Air Force C-130s parked on the Addis Ababa ramp, their leading edges crowded with birds happily chatting each morning when aircrews arrived. On the other side, several Russian AN-12 aircraft on the contrary did not have to host a single bird! It was obvious that even the birds knew exactly which aircraft were transporting food . . ."

Britain's Ambassador in Brussels, Edward Jackson, sent a letter to Belgium's Minister of Defense, F. Vreven, praising the performance of the Belgian Air Force detachment operating as a part of the European Community's Emergency Airlift in the Sudan.

"As you know, the detachment has been flying a Hercules between Khartoum and airstrips in the Western Sudan. The British Embassy in Khartoum has been most impressed with the way the detachment has worked flat out on a punishing schedule of sorties in appalling heat, with dust at one end of the line and rain-sodden runways at the other.

"I am glad to be able to pass on this message of warm appreciation of the way your Belgian Air Force detachment has conducted themselves as part of this difficult famine relief operation.

"They have been cheerful and warmly cooperative and have created the best possible impression of the Belgian Air Force."

The most common and severe criticism of these publications is that they are gossip sheets. Some editors erroneously believe the way to get employees to read a publication is to print as many names and faces as possible. This results in an overreliance on small talk. Credibility and, eventually, readership decline. Serious content fosters credibility and makes successful communication possible. Small talk is important if used properly, but it should not dominate the publication. Appropriate topics in this category are:

Hobbies
Births and deaths
Marriages
Employee sports (bowling league, softball, golf, etc.)
Social achievements

Other topics for articles overlap the previous categories. They include: safety training, security procedures, benefits, vacation schedules, accident and injury records, housekeeping, educational assistance programs, emergency procedures, and charity fund drives. Information about future events, especially those close at hand, makes good reading if they are of concern to the audience. Again, moderation is important. Some house publications have become little more than calendars due to requests from groups who want their activities publicized. Set and maintain strict policies about what will be published and how space will be allotted. The following criteria can help you evaluate a topic's newsworthiness:

1. *Timeliness*   Is the topic timely enough to interest most of the readers?
2. *Scope*   Does it affect enough people directly or indirectly?
3. *Noteworthiness*   Is something or someone important or well-known involved?
4. *Human interest*   Does it deal with things vital to the interests of the readers or those involved?

A tickler file is used by newspaper editors to "tickle their memory" about future news stories. The editor of an internal publication can also use this method by starting a futures book or file with headings such as "use next issue," "if space available," and "short fillers." Updating the file gives ready material for each issue.

Writing for Internal Publications   Most internal publications use two types of articles: news stories and human interest features. They serve different purposes, but both are important. News stories concentrate on information about market conditions, safety, company-sponsored events, current events that affect organizational policy, and other happenings. Articles that focus on people and their lives are called *feature* or *human interest* pieces. A balance between these two types should be decided, based on reader feedback. Both, however, must meet the criterion of general interest.

Internal publications are not daily metropolitan newspapers. People who write for them should not try to be investigative reporters. Objectivity is an important goal, but in-house publications should have a more personal tone than public newspapers or magazines. They should reflect a sense of closeness and common interest that says to the reader, "We're all in this together." One writer says an in-house publication "should look and read like . . . a letter from home . . . a pat on the back . . . .a friendly handshake." Most importantly, the tone of in-house publications must never be condescending or frivolous.

Staffing Internal Publications   All editors know that a good publication requires more than sitting in an office and waiting for stories to come in. A system is needed for gathering information and preparing it for publication on time. The editor is someone who does more than write and rewrite stories. Editors of internal publications are managers in the best sense. Managing is generally defined as "getting things done through other people," and the editor's task includes getting others to provide information and write stories for the publication. Even when an editor has a paid staff, it will never be large enough to cover all the sources of information in the organization. Nor would a publication written entirely by the public relations staff always be desirable. Readers of house organs are often more interested in articles written by their co-workers. Thus, there are good reasons to develop an external network to provide information and articles.

Enlisting auxiliary writers is not difficult. Their only reward is a byline, but even that is a powerful inducement for many people. Others will provide information and news tips just to help out. Ways to organize a news gathering process include:

1. *"Beat" system*   The organization can be divided into territories and a reporter assigned to cover each. This is an excellent system if enough people are willing to be reporters. One way of recruiting correspondents is to identify the people in each area who have been there longest. Ask them whether they will help you. Then ask their supervisor if they can be a reporter for the house publication. This support is valuable motivation. When all the reporters have been selected, invite them to a news clinic on company time.

2. *Telephone network*   If an editor cannot recruit enough reporters, people willing to phone in information can be used. The editor should stay in constant touch with every link in this network even if there is no news. Regular conversations may turn up information that the contact did not realize was newsworthy.

3. *News request forms*   Memos or notices asking for information are seldom effective. Most people do not understand what news means. They seldom think what is happening to them is important. But a news request form that asks for information about promotions, awards, achievements, or other specific topics can produce excellent articles.

A house publication needs columnists, feature writers, photographers, and artists. How many of these skills can be bought depends upon the funds available. Recognition can often substitute for pay, however. Printing the names of all who contribute to an issue is one way to recognize those who do not get bylines.

Controlling Internal Publications Every publication should periodically evaluate its progress toward its objectives. Purpose, content, and frequency of publication should all be examined in terms of the needs of the target audience. The panel that originally identified the target audience can be used again to evaluate progress. Surveys and questionnaires also give useful information about how well a publication fulfills expectations. National magazines have found that even simple surveys can provide excellent insight into the interests of readers. To pretest the potential readership of planned articles, for example, a questionnaire can be prepared that lists various headlines and asks a sample of the intended audience which articles they would read. An editor can thus get feedback about the probable success of certain stories.

Most organizations prepare publications on miscellaneous topics at irregular intervals. Forms range from mimeographed one-sheet leaflets to books by professional writers. Responsibility for these often rests in the personnel department, but other areas may also become involved because of legal requirements, government regulations, or company policy. These publications generally can be divided into three categories, according to purpose.

Occasional and Special Publications

Orientation literature indoctrinates new members of an organization. It can help a new employee get off to a good start by setting forth the ground rules. Goals and objectives of the organization are often included to give a sense of where the company is going and the employee's role in achieving that objective.

Reference material is designed to be kept for future use. Because of the nature of these publications, it is unlikely that anyone will ever read them from cover to cover, and they must therefore give fast and easy answers. This information sometimes changes, thus publications should be designed so that supplements or other materials can be added later. Reference materials deal with such matters as benefits, insurance, and recreation programs.

Position or special-topics publications are put out only once. They deal with a specific subject or occasion the organization feels it should discuss. The free enterprise system, charitable and social commitments, history, awards, and scientific or technological developments are among the most frequently treated subjects. Occasional publications have more impact than regularly scheduled newsletters and give an organization the chance to convey a specific message. The same requirements of credibility and interest that apply to newsletters must be followed if special-topic publications are to state their message effectively.

Leaflets, Inserts, and Enclosures   Inexpensive publications which may be read and thrown away are often printed on a single sheet that can be folded to produce any of several formats. Leaflets or handbills typed on a good typewriter and duplicated on a copying machine are inexpensive and fast to prepare. With a little more effort, single-sheet publications can be folded into brochures for information racks, in-house distribution, or direct mail. Many organizations use them as inserts in pay envelopes. Credit card companies and utilities have found inserts an effective and inexpensive means of communicating with their customers.

Booklets and Manuals   Because of their expense, booklets and manuals are made to be read and saved for reference. Their greatest shortcoming is that they can be hard to read and use if not designed properly. Employee orientation manuals or insurance plan booklets need indexes, and their information can be more accessible if tabs or color-coded pages are supplied. Regardless of how much information the book contains, employees will still be uninformed unless they can locate what they need when they need it.

Booklets and manuals must be written with the needs of employees in mind. If management allows them to be written in technical language or the jargon of insurance, law, accounting, or finance, such publications will be useless. The reading levels and interests of the intended audience must be considered before copy is prepared for a booklet or manual. Too often, publications meet the regulations of insurance companies or government agencies rather than the needs of employees.

Some of the purposes for which booklets and manuals can be used successfully are:

1. To orient new employees.
2. To explain the safety regulations as they comply with Occupational Safety and Health Administration standards.
3. To explain the benefit plan and its value to the employee.
4. To explain company policies and their compliance with government regulations.
5. To explain the costs and benefits of the organization's insurance package.
6. To explain the company retirement plan and its requirements.
7. To give information helpful to the employee in his or her job.
8. To give information about social or community issues.
9. To explain organizational compliance with environmental standards.

Printed Speeches and Position Papers   Speeches and position papers are sometimes distributed as occasional publications. Organization officials frequently speak to professional, community, or other groups concerning topics of interest to employees. It may be useful to print them for distribution within the organization, since copies of the speeches have usually been made available to news media anyway.

Reprints of magazine articles of concern to the organization and its employees can be bought inexpensively. Magazine reprints have the advantage of outside credibility. If general interest magazines are used, the readability of the articles will probably make them suitable for wide distribution. If the article is drawn from a more technical or professional publication, however, the style of writing may limit its use.

A growing number of laws and regulations require that notices be posted where employees can see them, and many organizations find this a quick, inexpensive way to reach large numbers of people. Message displays include posters, billboards, bulletin boards, information racks, and exhibits.

Message Displays

Bulletin Boards   The bulletin board displays messages in regular locations with minimum effort and expense. The board remains a much-used and effective means of communication within organizations. It often does a supplementary or follow-up job, as notices that have been mailed or given out to employees can also be posted as reminders. Details of announcements already made in meetings or in the house publication can be posted for those who wish more information. Bulletin boards are an appropriate location for information that has value but does not warrant publication. And, of course, the law requires that certain information be posted on bulletin boards.

Bulletin boards are fast and effective when used and kept up properly. To ensure credibility and readability, they must be carefully planned.

Location is a primary consideration. No matter how professionally written and designed a board may be, if hidden in a corner, it will not be read. Management must pick locations convenient for most of those persons who should read the bulletin board, rather than for the manager charged with keeping it current. Too many bulletin boards are outside supervisors' offices.

Bulletin boards should be placed in or near areas of heavy traffic. As many employees as possible should pass the message. The boards should be at eye level, where the light is good, and where employees can stop and read without blocking traffic. Bulletin boards should never be placed where they could present safety hazards.

Neatness will improve readability and increase readership. Order and arrangement invite reading. If a board becomes cluttered, even with important notices, it will no longer communicate its messages. Someone should check each board regularly to be sure it has not become overloaded and disorganized. Boards containing information on more than one topic should be organized so that all the messages on a given subject are together. When possible, a separate board for each topic is desirable.

Timeliness is a key to credibility in bulletin boards. Out-of-date notices kill interest. If an organization's bulletin boards always have up-to-date information, employees will regularly check their contents. Constant attention is required to post current material and take down old messages.

The wear-out potential of a message must also be considered. Even if the content is still current, the notice itself should be changed periodically. Once employees have read a notice, they are likely to skip over it when next checking the board. If the information is repackaged, it will once again attract notice. This method can keep employees alert to long-term issues.

Interest of the intended readers can be assured by picking messages that meet their needs. Like any other publication, posted items should reflect the interests of the intended audience. Personal items, advertisements, and entertaining odds and ends should be kept to a minimum. The presence of nonofficial information can create a relaxed atmosphere, but too many nonessential items destroy credibility.

Responsibility for the upkeep of each bulletin board should be delegated to one person. Bulletin boards are important media and should not be assigned to a secretary or clerk. Decisions about what should be posted and how it will be said are the job of public relations staffs.

Posters and Billboards   Like bulletin boards, posters and billboards offer fast, effective communication. They are most appropriately used to give emphasis to an idea. They are not intended for careful reading or study. Posters and billboards provide messages that can be grasped quickly; details can be published in other media. Posters and billboards should be in high-traffic areas where they can be easily seen by most employees. Wear-out potential is also a consideration here. Messages should be changed or revised periodically.

Information Racks   You can combine the effects of posters, bulletin boards, brochures, and booklets by using an information rack. Such racks should incorporate a poster to draw attention and invite the reader to take the brochures or booklets displayed. Racks provide information that cannot be handled in short messages. Because the materials are selected by readers without pressure from management, interest is likely to be higher. The economic advantage to information racks is that only interested employees are likely to take material.

Information racks work best in areas where employees can look at the material in a leisurely way; lunchrooms, break areas, waiting rooms, and dressing areas are good. Empty information racks suggest that management is uninterested, so regular maintenance is needed.

Exhibits and Displays   Exhibits and displays rely primarily on visual messages. Their effectiveness is in showing a sample or model of what is being discussed. Many organizations recognize the value of exhibits and displays at industrial meetings or in sales-related contexts, but they are equally valuable in employee communication. Exhibits and displays can show how production facilities work, display products, honor those who receive awards, or depict the history of the organization.

Employee communication is a large and complex aspect of public relations practice. Many different topics and issues confront practitioners working in this area. Not surprisingly, it is the fastest-growing segment of the public relations field in terms of both numbers and perceived importance. In this chapter, we have discussed the importance of keeping employees informed, creating the proper organizational climate to facilitate proper communication, establishing communication policy, and building employee communication programs. We have also considered the special issues of employer communication with a unionized work force and communication of employee benefits. Finally, we have detailed production of employee newsletters and other media. Armed with this knowledge and these tools, public relations practitioners can make great contributions to their organizations' success.

Summary

▲ ▲ ▲

Case Study

The Beer Barrel Layoff

By Robert Taylor, Professor of Journalism and Mass Communications
University of Wisconsin–Madison

The Madison Cooperage Company, founded in 1861, one of the town's oldest firms, is the current employer of 1,200 people who "make the best kegs in the world," according to its nationally advertised slogan.

Having weathered the change from wooden to aluminum beer kegs, the firm now has come upon hard times because of the swing from wood to steel and plastic in vats and kegs for wine making.

Company president Harry R. Jones made the difficult decision to eliminate the second shift and lay off 500 people at the end of this month.

Harold Storm, president of Amalgamated Coopers Union Local 5, after pledging his secrecy, has been informed and has given the company president this statement and permission to release it if the company so desires:

This is tough on our workers but I've been assured by President Jones that every effort has been made to avoid it, and every effort is being made to abide by the seniority specified in our contract, that the severance pay provided in the contract will be paid in a lump sum to each employee, and that hire-backs will be made strictly in seniority fashion and that workers hired back won't have to refund severance payments but will begin accumulating severance pay time when hired. This last is not in the contract and indicates, I think, that the company's heart's in the right place.

While talking the situation over with Storm, Jones makes the following points:

Madison Cooperage is a good and responsible employer and corporate citizen of Madison and, as a unique sort of business these days, has attracted a lot of national attention.

We love our workers. They're mostly good and devoted and some of them have been with us for fifty years. My grandfather, Oscar Jones, who started this company, hired some of their fathers—old world artisans.

It's hell that this is coming at this time of year.

Although we hate to lose some of our older workers, we are going to reduce our retirement age from 65 to 60, for those who want to leave, and provide those 60 and over the same retirement pay that they would get if they were 65 on the day they leave.

Those on the second shift who have more seniority than those on the first will be able to bump (take the jobs of) people of lesser seniority on the first shift. Thus, some of those we have to let go may come from the first shift—though that's mostly made up of people of higher seniority.

We are providing full severance pay—one week at present pay for every year served—to all those who are let go, except the ones who take early retirement.

My guess is that of the 500 jobs we have to cut, about fifty may be made up by either regular retirement or early retirement. Ten of the 500 jobs are supervisory night foremen, but some of them also may take the early retirement.

I will be in my office during all of next week, and those who receive notices are welcome to make appointments to see me, if they have some question about the layoff. They should remember, however, that we must do this strictly by seniority since that is what their union contract demands.

This will be the first time since President Roosevelt brought back beer that we won't have a night shift at the plant—our first big layoff, though we have been dropping in employment since our high of 2,000 in 1945 when the aluminum keg came into the beer business. We have tried to diversify some in our plant—butter vats, flower pots, and things like that—but they make up only ten percent of our business today. We still have about five percent in beer, cider, and vinegar kegs, but eighty-five percent of our business is with the wineries—and that's been declining now for ten years.

Madison Cooperage has a once-a-month employee newsletter distributed to employees which has traditionally contained an abundance of bowling scores and birth announcements.

Questions

1. What is the best strategy for informing employees about the layoff?
2. What information should be provided to employees and the public?
3. Within the ranks of current employees, are there different audiences that must be communicated with? What is the basic message that should be communicated to each group?
4. What ongoing communication efforts would you recommend implementing for remaining employees?

Notes

1. R. Tagiuri and G. H. Litwin, eds., *Organizational Climate: Explorations of a Concept* (Boston: Harvard University Press, 1968), 27.

2. J. Campbell, M. D. Dunnette, E. E. Lawler, and K. E. Weick, *Managerial Behavior, Performance and Effectiveness* (New York: McGraw-Hill, 1970), 390.

3. D. R. Hampton, C. E. Summer, and R. A. Webber, *Organizational Behavior and the Practice of Management,* 2nd ed. (Glenview, IL: Scott, Foresman, 1973), 520.

4. L. G. Hrebiniak, *Complex Organizations* (St. Paul: West Publishing, 1978), 273.

5. William Whyte, "Is Anybody Listening?" *Fortune* (June 1951): 41.

6. James E. Grunig, "Some Consistent Types of Employee Publics," *Public Relations Review* (Winter 1975): 35.

7. Quoted in "Rapid Change Increases Communication Need," *Communication World* (May 1983): 8.

8. Quoted in Bill Hunter, "PR '84: Fourteen Experts Tell What's Ahead," *Communication World* (January 1984): 14.

9. "How Companies Are Getting Their Message Across to Labor," *Business Week* (24 September 1984): 58–60.

10. This discussion is based on Norman B. Sigband, "What's Happening to Employee Commitment?" *Personnel Journal* (February 1974): 133–135.

11. Louis C. Williams, "What 50 Presidents and Chief Executive Officers Think about Employee Communication," *Journal of Organizational Communication* (Fall 1978): 7–10.

12. Paul Keckley, "The Increasing Importance of Employee Relations," *Public Relations Review* (Fall 1977): 70–76.

13. Williams, "What 50 Presidents Think," 8.

14. James M. Lahiff and John D. Hatfield, "The Winds of Change and Managerial Communication Practices," *Journal of Business Communication* (Summer 1978).

15. Lisa Crowe, "Survey Finds More Companies are Listening to Employees," *Atlanta Journal and Constitution* (October 6, 1986): 136.

16. Williams, "What 50 Presidents Think," 9.

17. Richard Nemec, "Internal Communications—A Scary Science," *Public Relations Journal* (December 1973): 28.

18. Donald P. Crane, *Personnel: The Management of Human Resources,* 2nd ed. (Belmont, CA: Wadsworth, 1979), 79.

19. Charles J. Coleman, *Personnel: An Open Systems Approach* (Cambridge, Mass: Winthrop Publishers, 1979): 392.

20. Quoted in Crane, *Personnel,* 80.

21. Harold H. Marquis, *The Changing Corporate Image* (New York: American Management Association, 1970), 141.

22. Abe H. Raskin, "Double Standard or Double-Talk?" in *Business and the Media,* C. E. Aronoff, ed. (Santa Monica, CA: Goodyear, 1979), 252.

23. "The Payoff on Ethics," *Forbes* (17 November 1986): 8.

24. Based on a portion of "How Companies are Getting Their Messages Across to Labor," 58–60.

25. Raskin, "Double Standard," 251.

26. Richard C. Huseman and John D. Hatfield, "Communicating Employee Benefits Directions For Future Research," *The Journal of Business Communication* (Winter 1978): 3.

27. "New Benefits for New Lifestyles," *Business Week* (11 February 1980): 112.

28. "Benefits are Getting More Flexible—But *Caveat Emptor,*" *Business Week* (8 September 1986): 64.

▲ ▲ ▲

Consumer Relations
Preview

The relationship between the consumer and the public relations practitioner in an organization is a natural one because consumers are one of the publics to which practitioners customarily respond.

While complaint handling must be quick and effective, it cannot be an organization's only response to consumers.

Practitioners must find ways to improve two-way communication between an organization and its consumer publics.

Information about consumer concerns must be communicated to manufacturing and service personnel so that problems can be corrected before they affect public opinion.

Public relations practitioners use their skills to help organizations provide consumers with appropriate, useful information.

Populus landudum defatatus est.
(The consumer has been screwed long enough.)[1]

A couple from Middletown, Pennsylvania, checked into the Holiday Inn Penn Center in Philadelphia for a relaxing weekend. Their forty-eight-hour holiday was plagued with numerous annoyances inconsistent with the price of the accommodations: too few towels, a bathtub that would not drain, and a shower head that sprayed the ceiling. The final blow came when the desk clerk forgot their wake-up call, causing them to owe an overtime charge in the hotel garage.[2]

A letter to the corporate offices of Holiday Inn brought an immediate apology from the manager of the hotel and the offer of a free return visit. Nevertheless, the experiences of this couple are typical of those being cited more and more by consumers who feel that business is insensitive to their needs and problems. In a broad sense, *consumers* can be defined as the ultimate users of any product or service. Therefore, the issue of consumer satisfaction applies to all organizations that provide a product or service for public consumption. Government and not-for-profit organizations must also deal with irate consumers and their representative groups. The types of goods, services, and problems that are the focus of consumer complaints vary widely. The following list illustrates this diversity:

> In 1986, the Carnegie Foundation reported that 40 percent of U.S. college students surveyed felt they were being treated like a number, and that parents and taxpayers both were fed up with the high cost of college.
>
> The U.S. Department of Transportation has reported that as many as half of the used cars sold through classified ads have had their odometers altered.
>
> Airline overbookings and flight cancellations throw business travelers off schedule and inconvenience other passengers.
>
> A pathologist's study showed that one in five medical diagnoses is wrong.
>
> "Lite" labels on different brands of the same foods mean different things.
>
> Unsafe pollutants have been found in municipal water supplies.
>
> A patient died during minor surgery because hospital personnel confused oxygen and gas lines in the operating room.
>
> The FTC says the chance of winning riches in contests is actually 3.4 in 1,000 for a $3.87 prize.
>
> Manufacturers fail to fulfill guarantees.
>
> State and federal regulatory practices sometimes allow unsafe or undesirable practices by the industries they are supposed to regulate.

The U.S. Department of Transportation reports that as many as half the used cars for sale have rolled-back odometers.

Instruction manuals on how to assemble products are often incomplete or incomprehensible.

Though the sweetener aspartame has taken the sugarless market by storm, its health effects are still in question.

Interest and credit costs are frequently presented in a confusing manner.

Some manufacturers and organizations respond to consumer complaints by denying everything. They may even hire public relations practitioners to try to change public opinion and remove the teeth from consumer protection legislation. Increasingly, however, organizations are recognizing the need to respond to consumer problems effectively, sometimes even seeking out complaints through toll-free hot lines.

Procter & Gamble
and Rely Tampons

Mini-Case 13.1

Even when an organization has factual grounds to deny liability for consumer problems, an attempt to totally evade responsibility may be more costly in the long run. For example, when cyanide-tainted Tylenol capsules were linked with deaths in the Chicago area in 1982, Johnson & Johnson voluntarily removed all Tylenol capsules from the shelves, although the company knew the cyanide had come from tampering, not from its manufacturing process.

Procter & Gamble had to make a more difficult decision in 1980 when the Rely tampon was linked in media reports to a number of cases of toxic shock syndrome (TSS). At first, there was no evidence to indicate that Rely had directly contributed to the disease, but the product nevertheless became the target of massive publicity. Procter & Gamble, working both independently and in cooperation with the U.S. Centers for Disease Control, tried to isolate the source of the disease. The results of this research showed no contaminants present in the product. In fact, the materials used in the tampon actually appeared to retard growth of the bacterium involved. Results of another early study by the Centers for Disease Control showed Rely and other tampons equally linked with TSS.

Later, however, the U.S. **Food and Drug Administration (FDA)** notified Procter & Gamble that a second study at the Centers for Disease Control linked Rely with TSS more significantly than any other tampon. Immediate action followed. A task force comprising some of the corporation's top management, public relations, scientific, legal, and medical advisers was formed. Members of the task force shuttled back and forth between Procter & Gamble headquarters in Cincinnati, Ohio, and FDA offices in Washington, D.C., checking the details of the Centers for Disease Control study. In addition, an independent commission of scientific and medical experts was assembled to evaluate research data and advise the task force.

Only one week after notification from the FDA, Procter & Gamble's task force had determined that Rely must be permanently withdrawn from the market. Although the company felt that the research data was inconclusive, the publicity about TSS had linked Rely to the disease in the minds of consumers, and numerous product liability suits were being filed. Immediately after the decision to withdraw the product was announced to the media, the task force began working out the terms of a consent agreement with the FDA. Within a week, the agreement had been finalized. Procter & Gamble agreed to buy back any unused tampons from retailers and consumers and to mount a massive advertising campaign to alert the public to the dangers of toxic shock and inform them of the withdrawal of Rely. Within one week, 85 percent of the stock had been removed from store shelves. Figures 13.1 and 13.2 are samples of the public relations effort that resulted from this decision.

In addition to avoiding the negative effects of a possible FDA-ordered recall of Rely, the Procter & Gamble action was successful in dealing with the concerns of consumers. Through its quick response, Procter & Gamble avoided any lingering damage to its own public image and the image of its other brands. An independent research firm conducted two public opinion surveys concerning Procter & Gamble and its other products. One survey, immediately after the withdrawal was announced, showed a significant negative reaction to Rely. The second survey, conducted in mid-October, revealed admiration for Procter & Gamble's quick response and no permanent effect on the organization's public image.

THE PROCTER & GAMBLE COMPANY

PUBLIC RELATIONS DEPARTMENT

P. O. BOX 599   CINCINNATI, OHIO 45201

October 24, 1980

To Our Educational Services/Consumer Affairs Contacts:

In the past, my colleagues and I have discussed with you such topics as Procter & Gamble's Educational Services, our teaching aids, and most recently, the consumer service provided by the addition of toll-free 800-lines to P&G's consumer product packages.

The current controversy concerning tampons is good news to no one. But because of our mutual interest in better-informed consumers, we thought you might want to hear from us about the considerable publicity on tampons in general and P&G's Rely in particular. I would like to share with you:

— special advertising P&G has developed in cooperation with the Food & Drug Administration (FDA) to inform women about toxic shock syndrome (TSS) and its suspected link with tampons.

— a copy of the statement on Rely made by Procter & Gamble's Chief Executive Officer at the annual meeting of Procter & Gamble share-holders on October 14, 1980. It is a long statement, but it con-tains all we know on the subject to date. We believe, therefore, that it will provide you with a reference which will be helpful in sorting out and evaluating the speculation that often surrounds such issues.

This subject will obviously remain under considerable discussion in the coming months. But since we have worked together in the past on professional and educational matters of mutual interest, we wanted you to have this information now to share with your families, friends and professional associates.

We believe the events speak to our Company's commitment to do what is right. I would be personally interested in your reactions to the course of action P&G has followed. Use the enclosed reply envelope to send me your thoughts or any specific unanswered questions you have.

Sincerely,

Edward B. Tetrault, Manager
Educational Services/Consumer Affairs

EBT:ml
cc: Ms. J. A. Learn
       Ms. P. B. Sussman
       Ms. M. C. Ruffin

P.S.   The enclosed advertisement will also be helpful if you or your associates have any questions about how to obtain a refund for Rely still on hand.

Figure 13.1 Letter from the public relations department of Procter & Gamble. (Courtesy of the Procter & Gamble Company. Reprinted by permission.)

As our society has moved from an agricultural base to a service-oriented and highly interdependent structure, perceptions of business have also changed. Whereas the corporation was once perceived as a totally private entity, it is now considered responsible to the public as well.

When the variety of products available was still rather small, consumers could rely on face-to-face relationships with merchants and tradesmen. Trade-marks, grading, and other forms of standardized product identification were not needed. The relatively small product selection enabled both buyer and seller to be knowledgeable about their transactions.

Toward the end of the nineteenth century, however, the relationship be-tween seller and buyer began to change. Manufacturers found it necessary to expand their markets and began to ship goods over great distances, thereby

The Development of Consumer Relations Issues

Figure 13.2 Advertising message from Procter & Gamble. (Courtesy of the Procter & Gamble Company. Reprinted by permission.)

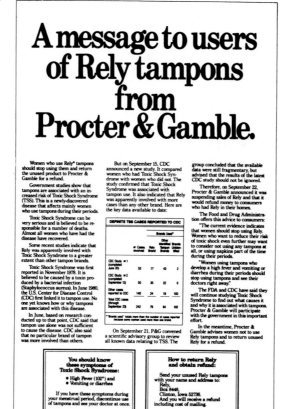

separating the purchaser from the source. Lengthening the channels of distribution brought about the use of preservatives such as formaldehyde and other harmful food additives. A large segment of the United States business community adopted the philosophy that customers have the responsibility to look out for their own interests. This belief created a gap between buyer and seller that led to many unethical business practices. Eventually, muckraking journalists exposed unsafe and unsanitary conditions in many industries, especially food packing. In 1906, the first pure food law was signed, correcting a number of the problems that had been revealed.

In the 1930s, consumers became aware of corporate abuses in the areas of food and drugs. More federal legislation was passed to remedy the problems that had been uncovered. The Sea Food Act of 1934, the Wool Labeling Act of 1939, the Flammable Fabrics Act, and the Wheeler Lea Act provided government standards and regulations for the food packing, garment, and advertising industries respectively.[3]

The 1960s saw a new rise of consumer activism marked by the scandal over the drug thalidomide and by Ralph Nader's successful campaign against the Corvair automobile. Four basic consumer rights articulated by President John F. Kennedy in the preamble to his March 1962 consumer message laid the foundation for current consumer rights and actions:

The Right to Safety: Products should not damage or harm the user; they should live up to the maker's claims.

The Right to Be Heard: Consumers' views should be given greater consideration by those responsible for marketing goods and services.

The Right to Choose: Rational consumer choice must be preserved based on the right of consumers to spend their money on any one of a diverse number of products.

The Right to Be Informed: The consumer must have easy access to complete and accurate product information in order to exercise the first three rights.

Recent Trends in Consumer Issues

The general discontent and unrest of the 1960s proved to be fertile ground for developing many new consumer issues as well as reviving several old ones. The size of American business became a negative factor from the consumer's perspective. Consumers began to feel powerless when dealing with giant companies, conglomerates, and multinational corporations. These feelings produced further demands for consumer legislation. In the past, calls for reform had come from legislators or journalists, but in the 1960s, campaigns for consumer protection were led largely by advocates in the private sector.

Consumer Advocates

The recent consumer movement has applied social organizing principles to combat the growing power and influence of giant corporations that dominate American business. Because businesses yield more power than individuals, consumer advocates believe the entire American economic climate is biased in favor of big business. They claim that:

Legal remedies in cases of corporate liability or criminal action are insufficient.

Prototype research and development for safety and health of consumers is lacking.

Consumer information systems are inadequate.

Corporate executives are not required to answer to Congress on consumer issues.

Government has failed to provide for an effective system of handling consumer complaints.[4]

In fact, recent court awards to consumers in **product liability** cases, coupled with a new recognition of consumer power in increasingly competitive markets, have led to the gradual replacement of the traditional adage *caveat emptor* (let the buyer beware) with a new one, *caveat venditor* (let the seller beware).

Better Educated Consumers

The rising educational level of American consumers has contributed to their increased awareness, knowledge, and expectations of business and its products and services. As a result, consumers:

Place greater emphasis on product performance, quality, and safety.
Are more aware of their rights.
Are more responsive to political initiatives to protect those rights.
Have more self-esteem.
Want to be treated more as individuals.
Are far less tolerant of organizational restraints.[5]

Consumers today demand more information about products and services and more voice in business decisions that affect them. More businesses are trying to accommodate consumers before product defects or other problems get out of hand. A 1979 White House study indicates that courting consumer comments may be good policy, as only one in six dissatisfied customers actually register complaints, while 90 percent of them switch brands. That contrasts with 54 percent who will stick with a company if their complaints are handled well.[6]

Common Consumer Complaints

Consumers constantly hear product warnings, hazards, and recalls in the media. Manufacturers claim defective products are the exceptions; they make news, while routinely good products do not. That may be true statistically, but every consumer has had a bad experience with some product, making it easy to identify with the news reports. One manufacturer-sponsored survey, though, says 48 percent of consumers think the quality of American goods has improved in the last few years.[7] In addition to defective goods, two other common consumer complaints are (1) inadequate repairs and guarantees and (2) unfair and deceptive advertising.

American Motors Corporation and Jeep

Mini-Case 13.2

Product liability suits have forced some companies to withdraw their products, at least in part because of staggering legal costs. Examples include the numerous suits filed against A. H. Robins over the Dalkon Shield intrauterine device and against makers of diphtheria-tetanus-whooping cough vaccines. In addition, cases such as one filed in 1976 against American Motors Corporation show consumers that even a little negligence on their part doesn't rule out a big award.

When 25-year-old Paul Vance took his wife and two friends for a drive through an abandoned Ohio strip mine in his 1976 Jeep, he decided to tackle a steep trail with two hills. Other off-road enthusiasts had taken that route before, but only up the trail. Vance tried to drive down it. The result: The Jeep rolled end-over-end, its roll bar cracking down on Vance and his wife, who were both killed, and on a friend, whose skull was fractured. The other passenger was paralyzed from the waist down, probably when the vehicle's tailgate hit her.

Vance's friends, Jeanne and Carl Leichtamer, sued American Motors, saying the roll bar design was defective. They won $2.2 million. Subsequently, more than $1 billion in additional claims were filed by others who said they had been injured in Jeeps.

The Leichtamer's suit grew out of a negligence claim the family filed against Vance's estate. The family's lawyer, Eugene P. Okey, convinced them to file suit against American Motors as well.

The jury trial was highlighted by evidence from an American Motors engineer who said the roll bar hadn't been tested in sideways or end-over-end rollovers, refuting the company attorney's claim that it was designed to hold up in sideways rollovers. The engineer further testified that the roll bar's weak point was not the bar itself but its connection to the Jeep body, which could have been strengthened at a cost of $25 per vehicle. AMC's own commercials, touting the Jeep as a tough, off-road vehicle, were used against it in the trial. The jurors agreed that the roll bar was defective and had been at least a "proximate cause" of both injuries.

Source: "The Product-Liability Debate," *Newsweek* (10 September 1984): 54–57

Inadequate Repairs and Guarantees   Consumers often encounter numerous frustrations in getting products repaired. In response to this problem, many major manufacturers have set up their own service units. In fact, a 1983 survey sponsored by Whirlpool found that 72 percent of Americans believed most manufacturers would be willing to replace or repair defective products.[8] A 1984 Harris Poll, however, indicated that service is getting worse,[9] and several earlier surveys pointed out repair problems such as incompetence or fraud in independent repair shops. In one survey conducted in New York City, twenty servicemen were called to repair a defective tube in a television set. Charges ranged from $4 to $30 for the $8.93 job. Researchers concluded that seventeen of the servicemen were dishonest or incompetent.[10]

The issue of product warranties is probably the most highly charged consumer concern. Claims that manufacturers either fail to honor guarantees or phrase them so that they actually guarantee nothing have created a consumer credibility gap. A 1969 presidential task force report expressed the situation this way:

> It is not uncommon for the manufacturer to ignore the appeal altogether and make no response. Some do respond and advise the consumer to contact the dealer. . . . Others recommend contact with a distributor or area service representative. This often leads to what is described as the "runaround," with a considerable exchange of correspondence, broken appointments, and nothing being done, [and] with the manufacturer, distributor, and retailer all disclaiming any blame or ability to solve the problem.[11]

Unfair and Deceptive Advertising   Further damage to the buyer-seller relationship occurs when products are promoted using unfair or deceptive means. Again, the business community points out that deceptive advertisers are a highly publicized minority, and government-sponsored research seems to back up that claim.

Research done for the U.S. Food and Drug Administration by an agency of the National Academy of Science found that only 7 percent of the drugs tested did not live up to the advertising claims made by their manufacturers. However, one of the products deemed ineffective was mouthwash, which is widely used in the United States and grosses more than $200 million in sales each year.[12] Therefore, even though only a small percentage of advertisers may actually be guilty of false or deceptive practices, their fraudulent claims can still have a direct impact on the majority of American consumers.

In an era of mass marketing, a small percentage of American industry can have a major effect on public opinion. Seemingly minor infractions can do major harm to an entire industry because of the large numbers of consumers affected. Although only a small percentage of goods do not live up to their advertising, enough consumers have had bad experiences with these products to make dissatisfaction a common occurrence.

Public Relations and Consumer Affairs

In the past three decades, consumer affairs units have become fixtures in most organizations that have direct links to consumers. A variety of names describe this function: public affairs, customer relations, consumer relations, consumer advocate, or public relations. But whatever the title, these staff members usually work both inside and outside the organization. Their goal is to improve the organization's relationships and communication with consumers by investigating consumer issues and conveying the results to management. Responsibilities of the consumer relations unit may include resolving customer complaints, disseminating consumer information, advising management on consumer opinion, and dealing with outside consumer advocate groups.

Frequently, the consumer relations unit is linked to the public relations department of an organization. This connection is natural, since consumers are one of the publics that public relations practitioners have traditionally served. The exact placement and design of consumer relations units vary, depending on the size and nature of the organization and the diversity of its products or services. One common characteristic does appear among the different approaches: the vast majority of consumer relations units report directly to top management. This provides them the necessary autonomy to investigate issues and identify problems early, as well as easy access to those who make policy decisions.

Organizational Structure

Figure 13.3 illustrates the placement of the consumer relations unit at J. C. Penney. The Educational and Consumer Relations Department is a separate unit under the supervision of the public relations manager, vice president of public relations, and vice president of public affairs. This organizational substructure includes all the other functions and staff specialists normally associated with public relations. A separate consumer relations unit within the public relations department can respond and do follow-up in its own specialized area. Within the Educational and Consumer Relations Department are three functional groups. One group handles the various publications dealing

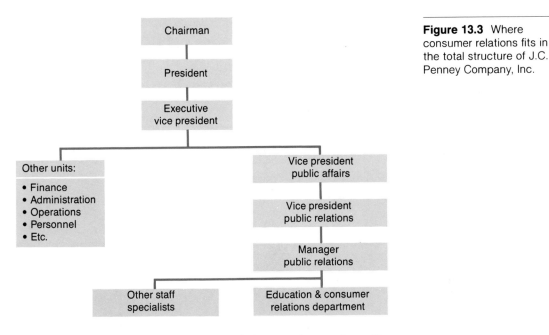

Figure 13.3 Where consumer relations fits in the total structure of J.C. Penney Company, Inc.

with consumer issues that are sponsored by J. C. Penney. A second coordinates and develops the annual consumer issues programs for educators operated through local stores. A third team organizes and develops various consumer informational programs.

The Chase Manhattan Bank's consumer affairs group has even greater access to top management, as Figure 13.4 shows. Organized under the public relations vice president and director and the corporate communications senior vice president, consumer affairs at Chase Manhattan have a direct line to the chairman and chief executive officer. Because of this structure, the consumer affairs division operates as a consumer consulting service to top management as well as handling complaints directed at senior management. Frequently, the complaints have already gone through regular channels without resolution. In these situations, consumer affairs personnel can deal directly with the vice president in charge of the division where the complaint originated.

Most divisional firms like Chase Manhattan locate their consumer affairs groups at the corporate level rather than in the divisions. This provides a consumer voice in overall organization policy. In this way, the consumer affairs unit becomes more than a complaint department. A few very large organizations have consumer affairs groups at both the corporate and division levels.

The staffing of consumer affairs units varies tremendously. Some organizations have only one consumer affairs specialist while others have more than one hundred. Frequently, the staff is divided into groups responsible for certain functions, such as complaint handling, publications, consumer education, and so on. Their activities are frequently integrated with those of other public relations groups within the organization that share similar functions.

Consumer Affairs Staffs

Figure 13.4 Organization
and structure for the
Chase Manhattan Bank

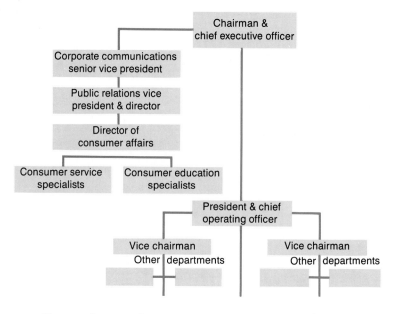

Figure 13.4 Organization
and structure for the
Chase Manhattan Bank

Frequently, organizations staff their consumer affairs units with employees who have enough prior experience in the company to handle complaints and investigate problems effectively.[13] One study revealed that among chief consumer affairs officers, public relations was the area of previous experience most often cited.[14]

Complaint Handling

Customer complaints are one of a growing list of the consumer relations professional's responsibilities. Even the rare consumer affairs unit not directly involved in handling complaints still helps decide on the procedures for complaint routing and response. These departments also monitor policies and procedures and their effects on consumers.

To ensure fast and uniform processing of consumer complaints, many organizations have developed elaborate complaint control systems. Consumer affairs specialists feel that:

1. Consumer complaints should be solicited.
2. All complaints should be logged when received.
3. The complaining party should be notified at receipt with a statement about how the problem will be handled.
4. Action to resolve the complaint should follow quickly.
5. Affected company personnel and departments should be notified promptly and their response monitored.
6. Ongoing analyses of complaint patterns should be aimed at preventing future problems.

The consumer affairs operation of the Chase Manhattan Bank illustrates how such a comprehensive system works. The office divides complaints into about twenty-five categories and prepares monthly reports on the effectiveness

CONSUMER RELATIONS SURVEY:

Please check ONE answer in each of the following categories:

	In-person at Branch	By Mail	Quick Deposit Box	Drive-in Window
1. How do you currently do your banking?	( )	( )	( )	( )

	Daily	Weekly	Twice a Month	Not Applicable
2. How often do you come into the branch?	( )	( )	( )	( )

Other (specify): _____

3. How would you rate our tellers on:	Very Good	Satis-factory	Poor	Not Sure
a) Courtesy	( )	( )	( )	( )
b) Accuracy	( )	( )	( )	( )
c) Speed of service	( )	( )	( )	( )
d) Knowledge of job	( )	( )	( )	( )
e) Helpfulness	( )	( )	( )	( )

4. How would you rate our officers on:	Very Good	Satis-factory	Poor	Not Sure
a) Courtesy	( )	( )	( )	( )
b) Accuracy	( )	( )	( )	( )
c) Speed of service	( )	( )	( )	( )
d) Knowledge of job	( )	( )	( )	( )
e) Helpfulness	( )	( )	( )	( )

	over 5 years	2-5 years	1-2 years	under 1 year
5. How long have you had your account at this branch?	( )	( )	( )	( )

6. How would you rate the convenience of banking hours at your branch?	Very Good	Satis-factory	Poor	Not Sure
	( )	( )	( )	( )

7. How would you rate the appearance of your banking office?	Always	Some-times	Seldom	Not Sure
a) Clean	( )	( )	( )	( )
b) Orderly	( )	( )	( )	( )

8. If applicable at this branch, how would you rate our	Very Good	Satis-factory	Poor	Not Sure
a) Express Line Service	( )	( )	( )	( )
b) Drive-in Window	( )	( )	( )	( )
c) Safe Deposit Service	( )	( )	( )	( )
d) Quick Deposit Service	( )	( )	( )	( )

AGE: 9. To further help us in this survey, please check:	under 25	25-34	35-50	over 50
Male ( )	( )	( )	( )	( )
Female ( )	( )	( )	( )	( )

10. What other services do you use at this branch?

Safe Deposit ( )
Savings Account ( )
Christmas Club ( )
Other: _____

We welcome your suggestions on specific areas where we may improve our services and any other comments you may have: _____
_____
_____

Name _____ Address _____
(Name and address are not essential, but you may fill it in, if you wish.)

Figure 13.5 Questionnaire sent to customers of Chase Manhattan Bank

of each division and of the entire company. From these analyses, preventive measures are recommended. A summary of typical complaint letters, including direct quotations, is also prepared and submitted with the monthly reports. Top management has found these summaries particularly revealing and informative. For example, one analysis showed that the tone of collection letters sent out by the bank's credit department was irritating to some patrons. Management reasoned that irritating a customer was not likely to speed up payment and would only harm the bank's image, thus the letter was revised.

Frequently, the consumer affairs unit at Chase Manhattan solicits grievances. The bank realizes that for every dissatisfied customer who writes, many more are complaining to others but not to the bank. To discover these hidden complaints, Chase sends out questionnaires and letters signed by the president to customers of each branch bank (Figure 13.5). The information collected is compiled in a statistical summary and reviewed by top management. Organizations with aggressive consumer affairs policies are integrating this kind of information into their production and service decision making.

General Motors discovered and corrected a flaw in its Fiero windshields within a few months of the car's release by having worker volunteers call owners to solicit complaints and suggestions. Sony redesigned its televisions within three months of hearing via the customer service center that an easier hookup

Coca-Cola displaying its
"classic" comeback

was needed when using the sets as home computer monitors.[15] Letters to Scott Paper Company from consumers stating that their paper napkins emitted a strange odor started an investigation that turned up a leaking valve.[16] At Coca-Cola, consumer complaints overturned management's most controversial decision in the company's ninety-nine-year history, leading the Atlanta giant to return its traditional soft drink to the market, albeit in new packaging, within four months. In each situation, a potentially costly mistake was averted or corrected by quick attention to information from the consumer affairs unit.

Consumer Information

The major tenet of consumer advocacy is that consumers lack adequate information for making purchasing decisions. The complexity of the business system and the proliferation of products contribute to this difficulty, but many consumer problems result from product misuse or improper maintenance. Consumer relations units have responded to the need for fuller and clearer information by providing simplified warranties, clarified product use instructions, and educational programs to help consumers select the right products for their needs and use them properly.

Consumer Education   Most people don't understand how businesses operate, what company policies are, or how complaints are resolved, according to market research for Coca-Cola.[17] A satisfied customer may tell another five to eight people, but a person with a complaint will probably tell ten to sixteen. To keep word of mouth on its side, J. C. Penney launched a massive consumer information effort consisting of improved labels, publications to explain labels and warranties, educational programs for consumers at local stores, and information and materials for educators. Coca-Cola gained esteem with its brochure on how to resolve consumer complaints.

Toll-free numbers are one way consumers can reach companies with their complaints, questions, and suggestions. Johnson & Johnson, Kentucky Fried Chicken, Whirlpool, Kraft, Sony, American Express, General Electric, and Procter & Gamble are among companies that have found toll-free lines useful consumer communication tools.

Regardless of the content, consumers usually value a message more if it comes from the media than from company representatives. Recognizing that, managements work with their consumer and public relations staffs to schedule new product releases and major announcements for times when they will gain the most publicity possible. When Apple introduced the MacIntosh computer, for instance, executives had met with reporters for months ahead of time, giving interviews and allowing the journalists to test the new machines under embargo. As a result, the MacIntosh was a top story in magazines, newspapers, and the electronic media.

When audiences are difficult to reach through traditional media, organizations must be extra creative. Mini-Case 13.3 shows how some companies provide information to difficult to reach publics.

Mini-Case 13.3

Winning Consumers Over

Public relations practitioners call it "brandstanding." Management calls it a way of promoting products and corporate identity without paying for extensive media advertising. **Brandstanding,** the new label for corporate sponsorship, has become increasingly popular. Sponsors of the 1984 Olympics in Los Angeles covered nearly 25 percent of the games' half-billion-dollar cost. They also provided: the official Olympics soft drink, Coca-Cola; the official credit card, American Express; the official fast-food restaurant, McDonald's; and the official film and photo processing house, Fuji Photo Film Co.

Concerts and sporting events are natural focuses for brandstanding. Corporate sponsorship of cultural events is nothing new, but Kool cigarettes (Brown and Williamson) opened a new era by underwriting jazz festivals in twenty cities. Schlitz

The 1988 Olympics provided many opportunities for corporate brandstanding.

Hilton introduces the guest reward program that honors the achiever in all of us.

Hilton's guest reward program honors the spirit of achievement that has made America great. That spirit is found in the millions of business travelers who stay with us each year and in the thousands of young athletes who are preparing for the 1988 Olympic Games.

Hilton honors you with travel awards and special recognition. At the same time we will honor the young athletes with a contribution to the Olympic Committee for each night of your stay.

In Hilton's HHonors program you have the chance to earn free Hilton weekends, free air travel to Hawaii and Europe or official Olympic team merchandise. Or, go for top gold awards like a once-in-a-lifetime trip around the world or a first class cruise to Europe.

Besides receiving great awards, Hilton HHonors members are recognized with many exclusive HHonors services. Privileges like separate member check-in, spouse stays free, free health club (where available), late check-out and instant check-out and numerous other benefits.

Start earning your HHonors today. Call the HHonors membership coordinator at (214) 788-0878 and find out why no one honors achievers like Hilton.

OFFICIAL SPONSOR OF THE 1988 U.S. OLYMPIC TEAM

underwrote the ten-day New Orleans Jazz Festival (where the company sold 400,000 cups of its beer). It then helped sponsor national tours of the rock music groups Fleetwood Mac and The Who, following up with "Schlitz rocks America" media advertisements.

Companies clearly like the publicity and goodwill return on their brandstanding investments. Cigarette companies, banned from advertising over the electronic media, lead the way. American Tobacco's vintage brand, for example, is seeking a comeback by sponsoring bowling tournaments with the slogan "Lucky Strikes Again."

Time magazine reports that brandstanding has been credited with giving companies $10,000 in free publicity for each $1,000 spent.

The Corporate Liaison

The consumer affairs role within corporations has become that of consumer spokesperson to management. Most consumer affairs specialists see it as part of their jobs to take an active role in decision making by speaking out for the consumer. They actively solicit consumer opinion and make management aware of the effects various decisions will have on consumers. The in-house ombudsman must balance the needs of the actual customers, the demands of consumer activists, and the goals of the organization. This role of liaison has always been the highest calling for public relations professionals.

Those who understand the purpose of public relations realize that the practitioner must do more than echo the company line. Public relations professionals should help senior managers stay in touch with their various publics. Doing so is especially critical in emergencies, when public relations professionals must serve as management's bridge to the media and the public.

Summary

As consumers have become better informed and products more complex, consumer relations has taken on a more prominent role in public relations practice. No longer can retailers, manufacturers, and service providers simply respond to complaints from their customers. Sophisticated public relations techniques must be applied in order to understand the needs of consumers and solicit their comments. In addition, organizations must be prepared to respond to consumer action and other special interest groups who take notice of their products or services. Because of increased awareness and government interest, the consumer relations function of many organizations has grown to command a substantial managerial role. More importantly, good consumer relations have demonstrated their value to the bottom line productivity of many businesses. These changes have opened new opportunities for public relations practitioners in consumer-oriented organizations.

Case Study

The Insurance Company and the Country Yokels

By W. F. (Fred) Kiesner
Loyola Marymount University
Los Angeles, California

In early summer, officials from Kern County contracted to have a "chip seal" of small rocks applied to the only road leading in and out of the mountain community of Frazier Park, California, about seventy-five miles north of Los Angeles. The chip seal would provide better road traction during icy and snowy conditions in the high mountain country. Several thousand people live in small isolated communities along the fifteen-mile stretch of road. The contractor began applying the rocks to the road, but something went wrong and they did not stick to the tarry sealant. It was also reported that the contractor's heavy-weight rolling machine had broken down, and thus he could not pack down the rocks and gravel.

The road became extremely dangerous, with cars encountering flying gravel and stones. Reportedly, the contractor's own trucks caused a great deal of damage as they roared up and down the road at high speeds, showering passing cars with rocks. During the next two days, approximately six hundred cars suffered severe damage, including broken windshields and headlights and ruined paint. Irate local residents bombarded the county supervisor with calls, and he assured them that all damage would be repaired by the contractor's insurance company. He advised all callers to get two damage estimates, submit them to the insurance company, and wait until everything was paid.

The hundreds of local residents did that, then waited, and waited, and waited. After three months, with no action from the insurance company (a very large national firm, United States Fidelity and Guarantee—USF&G), residents contacted the firm's regional office in Fresno. Many were treated in a curt and rude manner, and a number of residents reported that the firm's officials had hung up on them. Finally, in September, all residents who had filed claims received a form letter from the insurance company denying any settlement. The insurance firm said it had closely investigated the insured's behavior and had concluded that he had done nothing wrong. The denial letter also stated that all those sustaining damage had driven in a reckless and careless manner and thus had caused their own damage.

Local residents were extremely angry and insulted that the big insurance company thought it was sloughing off a bunch of dumb mountain hillbillies! The fact that dozens of California Highway Patrol cars, county sheriff's cars, and U.S. Forest Service vehicles had also sustained severe damage made the insurance firm's claims of reckless driving a bit ludicrous! The total damage to local residents' vehicles was estimated at approaching $1 million.

One of the local residents called a public meeting in the town hall to discuss ways to fight the insurance company. Hundreds of irate citizens showed up, filling the hall to overflowing.

Questions

1. Obviously, the insurance company officials in this case mishandled the situation. What should they have done? If they were going to deny all claims, could they have used techniques of public relations to ease the tensions? What would you have done differently?

2. Considering the heated situation the insurance firm now finds itself in, what would you, as its public relations director, do now? Can you save the day for the firm?

3. Would "stone walling" (attempting to prevent information from getting out) be a viable alternative for the insurance firm? What are the potential risks of such an action?

4. Do the local residents really have any power in fighting the big national company and its apparently arbitrary decision? Could the citizens use public relations techniques in their battle against the insurance firm?

5. If the local residents launched a negative publicity campaign against the insurance company in an attempt to equalize and neutralize its power and size, would this be fair or ethical?

1. "The Heat Is On," *Newsweek* (5 March 1973): 60.
2. "Disgruntled Customers Finally Get a Hearing," *Business Week* (21 April 1975), 138.
3. Robert D. Hay, E. R. Gray, and J. E. Gates, *Business and Society* (Cincinnati: South-Western, 1976), 297.
4. Ibid., 300.
5. Ibid., 301.
6. "Making Service a Potent Marketing Tool," *Business Week* (11 June 1984): 165.
7. Research & Forecasts, Inc., *America's Search for Quality: The Whirlpool Report on Consumers in the 80s* (Benton Harbor, MI: Whirlpool, 1983): 5.
8. *America's Search for Quality,* 14.
9. "Service a Potent Tool," 170.
10. E. G. Weiss, "The Corporate Deaf Ear," *Business Horizons* (December 1968): 14.
11. G. A. Steiner, *Business and Society,* (New York: Random House, 1975).
12. E. F. Cox, R. C. Fellmeth, and J. E. Schultz, *The Nader Report on the Federal Trade Commission* (New York: Richard W. Baron, 1969).
13. E. P. McGuire, *The Consumer Affairs Department: Organization and Functions, Report No. 609* (New York: The Conference Board, 1973), 2.
14. R. T. Hise, P. L. Gillett, and J. P. Kelly, "The Corporate Consumer Affairs Effort, *MSU Business Topics* (Summer 1978):17–26.
15. *Business Week* (11 June 1984): 165 & 167.
16. "Disgruntled Customers Finally Get a Hearing," 138.
17. Knauer, Virginia H., "Customer Education Pays Off," *Enterprise* (October 1984): 22.

▲ ▲ ▲

CHAPTER 14

Financial Relations
Preview

F inancial public relations works to create and maintain investor confidence. It builds positive relationships with the financial community by providing corporate information. Strong financial relations programs, characterized by responsiveness, openness, and regular communications, help lower the cost of capital for businesses.

A key function of financial relations is to provide prompt disclosure of corporate news that is significant to the financial community.

Audiences for financial relations include individual stockholders, financial analysts, and the financial media.

Major tools of financial relations include annual reports and annual stockholder meetings.

Effective financial relations gives a business increased support for its management, higher stock prices, and greater ease in attracting new capital.

Markets run on information. Financial markets run on financial information.

—Jay Sarmir, Merrill-Lynch broker

The success of any organization depends upon its ability to attract resources from its environment. Among the most important of these resources is capital—the money with which other resources can be purchased. Corporations raise money in a variety of ways, including selling stock, issuing bonds, and securing loans from financial institutions. In all cases, a company can attract capital only if investors have confidence in the business and its management.

Bond ratings, interest rates, and stock prices are not just a matter of negotiation between a corporation's financial officers and its bankers or brokers. Such negotiations are preceded by and based on the business's current performance and future prospects. These facts must be persuasively communicated, and that is where public relations comes in.

The first task of **financial public relations** is to create and maintain investor confidence, building positive relationships with the financial community through the dissemination of corporate information. Executives who fail in this regard may be unable to attract capital investment. They may lose control over their organizations and even lose their jobs. U.S. corporations believe that investor relations is important—they spent over $4 billion on it in 1986.[1]

Financial public relations is much easier to relate to the proverbial bottom line than are other kinds of public relations. Relative stock prices, bond ratings, and interest rates charged for loans are direct measures of confidence in a company. When confidence is high, stocks are worth more and bonds and borrowing cost less. When confidence is low, stock is worth less and higher interest is demanded by those who loan funds to the business. Most corporations consider their financial relations programs effective if they have been able to reduce the cost of funds or obtain the best cost of capital.

While financial relations is most often thought of in terms of large corporations, it can be critically important to small businesses too, as Mini-Case 14.1 shows. Fund-raising by not-for-profit groups is also a form of financial relations.

Maintaining Investor Confidence

Mini-Case 14.1

Guardian Industrial Services, a family-owned $3 million sales per year business, was having a rough time. Sales were down. Certain expenses were up. More money was needed to get the business through the slow season.

Guardian president Jim Gladden went to his banker, seeking to extend his credit line. The banker said no, not one more penny.

Financial Relations Saves a Small Business

To stay in business, Gladden needed money and he needed it quickly. Family sources had all been tapped. Potential private investors wanted too much from the business in exchange for too little funds. Gladden needed a bank willing to extend a more substantial credit line.

Over the years, Gladden had played an active role in his community. He served on the chamber of commerce board. He was in Rotary Club and supported scouting. He was known, trusted, and respected by others in the business community, including other bankers.

Within three weeks, Guardian Industrial Services had established a relationship with a new bank that increased its credit line substantially.

"I always knew credibility was important," Gladden explained, "but it is rarely as important as when credibility equals 'creditability'."

Specific Objectives for Practitioners

The practice of financial public relations touches upon such diverse areas as finance, accounting, law, public affairs, community relations, marketing, and employee relations. Consequently, its list of objectives is a lengthy one. Practitioners are charged with:

Building interest in the company.

Creating understanding of the company.

Selling company products.

Broadening the stockholder base by attracting new investors.

Stabilizing stock prices.

Winning stockholder approval for management.

Increasing the company's prestige.

Creating favorable attitudes in the financial community.

Developing political sensitivities of stockholders for issues relating to the company.

Improving employee relations.

Building loyalty of stockholders.

Arthur Roalman best sums up the purpose and rationale for financial public relations:

An individual is not likely to invest money . . . in a corporation's stocks, bonds, commercial paper, or other financial pledges unless he believes strongly that he understands fully what is likely to happen to that corporation in the future . . . most investors' willingness to invest in a corporation is influenced by their trust in its management. Trust isn't built overnight. It is the result of long-term actions by the corporation to provide factual financial information in proper perspective.[2]

He continues:

Strong investor relations programs emphasizing a full and continuous flow of information about the company can help lower the cost of capital in the securities markets and develop and maintain goodwill among shareholders.[3]

Investors bet fortunes on what they believe to be true about a particular enterprise. Fraud and deception could part gullible investors from their funds. These dangers have been largely (but not completely) eliminated by government law and regulation, stock exchange policies, and the voluntary disclosures of corporate management. The importance of corporate information to investor decisions, however, points out the second major function of financial public relations: prompt provision of public information required by law, regulation, and policy.

Providing Public Information

Many aspects of financial public relations are affected by law and regulation. The Securities Act of 1933 was passed "to provide full and fair disclosure of the character of securities . . . and to prevent frauds in the sale thereof . . . ." The Securities Exchange Act of 1934 supplemented the act of the previous year and was intended "to secure for issues publicly offered, adequate publicity for those facts necessary for an intelligent judgment of their value." These and other **Securities and Exchange Commission (SEC)** regulations apply to all companies listed on any of the thirteen largest United States stock exchanges, or with assets of $1 million and 500 stockholders. Other regulations require that corporations "act promptly to dispel unfounded rumors which result in unusual market activity or price variations."

SEC Regulations

SEC regulations are copious and subject to frequent changes. It is therefore impractical to present them all here. The commission routinely requires submission of three kinds of reports: annual reports (**Form 10–K**); quarterly reports (**Form 10–Q**); and current reports (**Form 8–K**). Form 10–K asks for descriptions of a corporation's principal products and services; assessment of competitive conditions in its industry; the dollar amount of order backlog; source and availability of raw materials; all material patents, licenses, franchises and concessions; and the estimated dollar amount spent on research. The form also requires reporting the number of employees; sales and revenues for the last five years in principal lines of business; description of principal physical properties and a list or diagram of parent and subsidiary firms; pending legal proceedings; and changes in outstanding securities.

Other information required by Form 10–K includes the names, principal occupations, and shareholdings of the corporation's directors; remuneration, including amounts accrued in retirement plans, of each director and principal officer; stock options outstanding and exercise of stock options; and interest of officers or directors in material transactions. All of this information must be accompanied by corporate financial statements prepared in accordance with SEC accounting rules and certified by an independent public accountant. Moreover, the entire form must be submitted to the commission no later than ninety days from the close of the fiscal year. Finally, 10–K must be available free of charge to anyone upon request.

The 10–Q quarterly report is much less detailed. It asks primarily for the corporations' summarized profit and loss statement; capitalization and stockholder's equity at the end of the quarter; and sale of any unregistered securities.

In its effort to gather all relevant investment-related information on a continuous basis, the SEC also requires filing of Form 8–K, the current report. Filing this document is required when an unusual event of immediate interest to investors occurs. Examples would be the acquisition or sale of significant assets or changes in the amount of securities outstanding.

These documents are prepared largely by accountants and lawyers. They are described here, however, because public relations professionals should: (1) recognize the extent to which SEC-regulated corporations must share information, (2) understand the kinds of information deemed significant by investors, (3) realize the extent of federal regulation in this aspect of business, and (4) avail themselves of the information contained in these forms.

Stock Exchange Policies

Policies of various stock exchanges also influence the task of financial public relations. The New York Stock Exchange states, for example, that news on matters of corporate significance should be given national distribution.[4] What is significant is a matter of some debate. The American Stock Exchange considers the following kinds of news likely to require prompt announcements:

(a) a joint venture, merger or acquisiton;
(b) the declaration or omission of dividends or the determination of earnings;
(c) a stock split or stock dividend;
(d) the acquisition or loss of a significant contract;
(e) a significant new product or discovery;
(f) a change in control or a significant change in management;
(g) a call of securities for redemption;
(h) the borrowing of a significant amount of funds;
(i) the public or private sale of a significant amount of additional securities;
(j) significant litigation
(k) the purchase or sale of a significant asset;
(l) a significant change in capital investment plans;
(m) a significant labor dispute or disputes with contractors or suppliers;
(n) establishment of a program to make purchases of the company's own shares; and
(o) a tender offer for another company's securities.[5]

To facilitate national disclosure, financial relations practitioners use several news wire networks. The Associated Press (AP) and United Press International (UPI) are well known general wire services. Dow Jones and Reuters Economic Service specialize in business and financial news. PR News Wire and Business Wire charge a fee for their services but guarantee that corporate news is carried promptly.

The Disclosure Issue

One other SEC regulation of particular interest to the public relations practitioner is Rule 10B–5, which makes it unlawful "to make any untrue statement of a material fact or to omit to state a material fact . . . in connection with the purchase or sale of any security." In SEC v. Texas Gulf Sulphur Co. 401 F.2d833 (2nd E.r. 1968), this regulation was applied to press releases.[6] In subsequent suits, public relations counsel has been named as a defendant when press releases and other materials "contained false and misleading statements and omitted to state material fact."[7]

Two recent cases sharply focused on the disclosure issue, although financial relations officers were left in confusion by their outcomes. One involved the 1984 merger between food giants Nestle and Carnation. The other involved Chrysler Corporation's struggle to survive in the early 1980s.

Nestle was bidding secretly for Carnation. Rumors were flying and Carnation stock rose nearly 50 percent before Nestle announced the purchase for $83 per share. Throughout the negotiations, Carnation's spokesman refused to comment.

A year after the merger, the Securities and Exchange Commission ruled that by saying no comment during negotiations, Carnation had been "materially false and misleading." Since the company no longer existed, however, the SEC took no action to back its ruling.

Chrysler was saved by an unissued press release. One day in early 1981, Chrysler was down to $8 million in liquid assets. Company lawyers held that Chrysler must issue a press release to disclose its near insolvency, but company officials risked being charged by the SEC rather than destroy what little confidence their creditors and customers had left. The release went unissued and the company survived—its potential insolvency made a moot point by its renewed financial health.

No simple formula provides guidance in disclosure situations. While the Chrysler example is unusual, it shows that judgment must be used. In general, however, disclosure is both required and desirable.

Financial Relations Professionals

Financial relations professionals must have a broad base of knowledge and skills to deal effectively with their many-faceted responsibilities. A survey of three hundred senior financial relations officers in leading corporations showed that a broad financial background combined with marketing communication skills is considered the best preparation for the field.[8] The survey indicated that while financial and security analysts may go into financial relations, their lack of marketing and communication backgrounds often impedes their success. Knowledge of finance, marketing, and law, and public relations skills are all important for those considering financial relations careers.

Audiences for Financial Relations

In addition to the Securities and Exchange Commission, those interested in a corporation's financial information include stock exchange firms, investment counselors, financial writers, brokers, dealers, mutual fund houses, investment banks, commercial banks, institutional buyers, employees, and both current

Figure 14.1 Some companies advertise in the effort to attract additional stockholders. Fuqua Industries provides an example of stockholder-oriented advertising.

FUQUA INDUSTRIES: THE COMPANY THAT WORKS FOR ITS STOCKHOLDERS

TEN YEAR TOTAL RETURN*
TO COMMON SHAREHOLDERS
January 1, 1976 through December 31, 1985
Atlanta-based Companies that are listed on the New York Stock Exchange

	Annual Rate of Return	$10,000 invested 1/1/76 would have grown to:
1. FUQUA INDUSTRIES, INC.	35.57%	$209,718†
2. John H. Harland Company	31.13	150,321
3. National Service Industries, Inc.	29.26	130,209
4. Equifax, Inc.	28.08	118,799
5. IRT Property Company	27.76	115,864
6. American Business Products	22.96	79,002
7. Scientific Atlanta, Inc.	20.74	65,843
8. Oxford Industries, Inc.	19.57	59,734
9. Munford, Inc.	17.61	50,634
10. Continental Telecom, Inc.	16.13	44,611
11. Rollins, Inc.	15.43	41,994
12. Southern Company	15.41	41,921
13. Coca-Cola Company	12.62	32,821
14. Genuine Parts Company	12.33	31,986
15. Delta Air Lines, Inc.	9.89	25,679
16. Georgia-Pacific Corporation	3.64	14,298
S&P 500	13.85	36,587
Dow Jones 30 Industrials	11.70	30,237

*Based on dividends reinvested and increase in stock price.
Source: Standard & Poor's COMPUSTAT
†As of March 14, 1986 this figure had increased to $255,856.

"The company that works for its stock-holders." That's become our motto. Because we do indeed.

As the chart shows, an investment of $10,000 in 1976 is worth $209,718 today (including price increases plus investment of dividends).

The Dow-Jones average turned that $10,000 into only $30,000 in that same period.

You see, at Fuqua we believe most people buy stock because they hope and expect that it will increase in value. We're value builders, not empire builders.

FUQUA INDUSTRIES, INC.
ATLANTA, GA

and future stockholders. For the purposes of discussion, however, these categories can be lumped into three broad audiences: individual stockholders, financial analysts, and the financial press. Following is an examination of each group, their informational needs, the means by which they may be reached, and the best ways to secure positive relations with them.

Individual Stockholders

Some corporations consider their stockholders a vast untapped resource of potential customers and grass roots support on political and financial issues. Harrison T. Beardsley recommends that financial relations efforts, particularly of smaller companies, concentrate on stockholders rather than on financial analysts.[9] Others dismiss stockholders as purchasers of stock for income and profit who are best ignored. John Kenneth Galbraith says simply, "The typical stockholder does not identify himself with the goals of the enterprise." In any case, stockholders are a group that must be communicated with and reckoned with. Figure 14.1 shows how one company used advertising to attract stockholders.

As discussed previously, the Securities and Exchange Commission requires companies to keep their investors fully informed. Management has learned the hard way that uninterested stockholders may be quick to sell their shares to even the most unfriendly entity attempting takeover. (See Mini-Case 14.2.) Moreover, stockholders themselves have become more vocal and active—initiating proxy fights or raising financial, social, and ethical questions in relation to environmental issues, sex discrimination, corporate political activities at home and abroad, labor relations, South African apartheid, and many other issues.

Most corporations now recognize that "a company's foremost responsibility is to communicate fully anything that can have a bearing on the owner's investment."[10] The extent and quality of their efforts vary widely, however. Informative annual and quarterly reports and well-organized annual meetings with follow-up reports are the basic tools of stockholder relations. We will discuss both of these in detail later in this chapter.

Mini-Case 14.2

Lessons from
Phillips Petroleum

In the mid-1980s, merger mania swept the corporate landscape. Raiders brought some of America's corporate giants to their knees with hostile takeover attempts. "Greenmail" and "Golden Parachutes" were the daily fare of business news.

Phillips Petroleum was the object of not one, but two corporate raiders—Texas oilman T. Boone Pickens and New York financier Carl Icahn—and lived to tell about it.

C. M. Kittrell, Phillips executive vice president, learned the hard way that a company must not lose touch with its investors. "Individual shareholders are generally loyal to their companies—and vote in favor of management. Yet they tend to get scared off in takeover battles," Kittrell explained. "With all the lawsuits, poison pills, and debt securities that surround a hostile raid—who can blame them for cashing in?" Individuals owned half of Phillips's stock before the takeover attempts. Afterwards, they owned only 20 percent.

When the battle was over, the company set about rebuilding its investor relations program as a major function of the public affairs division. The company surveyed present and potential shareholders to learn their characteristics and attitudes. Stockholder publications were simplified and personalized; investors got more straight talk and fewer complex numbers.

Kittrell maintains that it is in a company's best interest to create a balance in ownership by catering to the needs of individual investors.

Source: Based on Lyn Allgood, "Investor Relations a Vital Defense Measure Now," *Atlanta Business Chronicle* (August 5, 1985): 5A.

Sound stockholder relations are built on three principles: (1) learn as much as possible about your stockholders; (2) treat them as you would your important customers; and (3) encourage investor interest from people who are predisposed toward your company. A basic principle of communication is "know your audience." Consequently, learning as much as possible about stockholders makes excellent sense from a communications perspective. The stockholder survey, which asks for demographic and attitudinal information, is a readily available tool, but too few United States corporations actually use it.

Treating stockholders as important customers has a number of implications for financial relations officers. Communicating in readable, nontechnical language is a must. Welcoming new stockholders and writing to express regret when stockholders are lost is a good business practice. Prompt and appropriate response to stockholder correspondence also helps maintain positive relations.

Sun Company follows a comprehensive stockholder relations plan. The company believes, "Shareholders are our business partners. It's helpful to us if management gets an insight on what they think of us." Each new Sun stockholder receives a welcoming note from the company's chairman. A very readable newsletter goes out with every dividend check. About one hundred shareholders are selected at random six or eight times a year and invited to a dinner at which a top company executive speaks. Sun also maintains a toll-free telephone line to make corporate news available to stockholders and invites them to call collect to the shareholder relations department with questions or complaints.

Sometimes going beyond the call of duty in stockholder relations reaps excellent benefits. Consider the case of Mr. William Comptaro of Pittsburgh, Pennsylvania, owner of one hundred shares of Louisiana-Pacific. Mr. Comptaro was dissatisfied with management's decision to acquire Flintkote Corporation and expressed his views in a letter to Louisiana-Pacific's president. Mr. Comptaro received a reasonably prompt response from a woman in the stockholder relations department. She explained how much confidence she had in the company's officers and invited him to call if he had further questions. Mr. Comptaro wrote a letter of thanks and considered the matter unsatisfactorily closed.

But here the story takes an unexpected twist: One evening Mr. Comptaro's phone rang. The president of the company was calling to explain in detail why he considered Flintkote a good buy.

Louis Rukeyser, who reported Mr. Comptaro's story in his nationally syndicated column, made these comments:

> You don't have to be a skeptical professional securities analyst in order to recognize that there are plenty of other factors that ought to be considered by a potential investor, other than extraordinary courtesies shown him by the company's president . . . but surely there is a lesson here . . . for all those arrogant corporation bureaucrats whose cold form-letter responses frequently feed public cynicism.

Rukeyser continues:

> If capitalism is to survive in the face of ideological competition and muddled
> political management, it had better look to its own followers—and to its own
> failings. And while the company president can't be on the phone all day every
> day, a little more of the kind of communication related here could win the
> system a lot more friends.[11]

Finally, just as a company should seek new customers among the most
likely segments of the population, it should seek stockholders from those predisposed toward buying stock. Employees, suppliers, dealers, and members of
communities where the corporation is located are the most likely prospects.
They should receive annual reports and other materials that encourage investment.

Financial analysts include investment counselors, fund managers, brokers, *Financial Analysts*
dealers, and institutional buyers—in other words, the professionals in the investment business. Their basic function is to gather information concerning
various companies, to develop expectations in terms of sales, profits, and a
range of other operating and financial results, and to make judgments about
how securities markets will evaluate these factors. They gather quantitative
and qualitative information on companies, compare their findings to statistics
from other companies, assess opportunities and risks, and then advise their
clients. Corporate financial relations assists analysts by providing information,
and in doing so, may positively influence expectations and judgments. The
New York Stock Exchange gives its listed companies the following advice:

> Securities analysts play an increasingly important role in the evaluation and
> interpretation of the financial affairs of listed companies. Annual reports,
> quarterly reports, and interim releases cannot by their nature provide all of
> the financial and statistical data that should be available to the investing
> public. The Exchange recommends that corporations observe an "open door"
> policy in their relations with security analysts, financial writers, shareowners
> and others who have a legitimate investment interest in the company affairs.[12]

To maintain relations with financial analysts, the basic method is to
identify the prospects, meet them, establish interest and understanding, and
then maintain the relationship. All dealings with professional analysts should
be characterized by responsiveness, openness, and regular communication, but
care should be taken not to overcommunicate.

"Fluff and puff" will quickly sour an analyst's view of a corporation.
When analysts become overenthusiastic based on what they have been told by
a company's financial relations staff, and corporate performance fails to live
up to their expectations, the results can be disastrous. When Toys' R' Us Inc.
announced that its 1984 Christmas sales were up 17 percent, its stock dropped
20 percent. Based on discussions with the company, analysts had expected a
sales gain of 30 percent, and thus were disappointed.

The shoe manufacturer Nike Inc. lost half its value when it earned 88 cents per share in 1984 rather than the anticipated $2. Rather than informing the financial community when it realized profits would be lower than expected, Nike management tried harder to live up to the inflated figures. In 1985, the company set aside more time for communicating with financial analysts.[13]

Analysts want to know the following: background—the nature of the business; primary factors affecting the business; current operating conditions; and estimates of future outlooks. Analysts are also vitally interested in management forecasts, pricing data, capital expenditures, financial data, labor relations, research and development, and any other information that may materially influence the quality of an investment.

A primary way to reach financial analysts is through **investment conferences,** which are meetings investment professionals attend specifically to hear company presentations. These programs contain information on a company's performance and provide persuasive arguments for buying its stock. Although such presentations center on speeches by company executives, they usually provide slick publications and audiovisual support materials as well.

Theodore Pincus, chairman of the largest U.S. financial public relations firm, is critical of such presentations. He calls them "saccharin-soaked speeches . . . focus(ing) on a company's history and . . . present operations."[14] Pincus maintains that companies should candidly discuss their plans and goals.

The annual San Francisco investment conference sponsored by Montgomery Securities has a reputation for attracting powerful investors and analysts who hear pitches by some of the most promising companies around. Under such circumstances, companies have the opportunity for substantial financial impact. Teradyne improved its stock price by nearly 20 percent during the week of the 1983 conference.

High-tech TRE Corporation blew it, however, the same year. Making their first investment presentation, company executives used the allotted thirty-five minutes to explain the scientific intricacies of their metals fabrication and semiconductor equipment businesses. While TRE's financial performance was outstanding, investment analyst Alan Weston judged the presentation "too technical, and they lost the audience." TRE lost money too when its stock dropped $2 per share following the presentation.[15]

Relationships with financial analysts are not all one-way. Analysts can provide valuable information to companies as well. When communicating with financial analysts, first be prepared to listen. They can give significant feedback about a financial relations program in terms of its adequacy, credibility, and sufficiency of information. Perhaps even more importantly, this is an opportunity for the company to understand how the market perceives its strengths and weaknesses and the behavior of the business as a whole.

The Financial Press

The third major audience for financial relations is the **financial press.** "The financial press provides a foundation and backdrop for any corporation's financial communications program," says Hill and Knowlton executive Stan Sauerhaft. "It develops credibility and it can add impressive third-party endorsement."[16]

Nationally televised stockholders' meeting at CBS

Financial public relations practitioners deal with media much as other public relations specialists do. The major difference lies in the specialized nature of the financial media. Major daily newspapers carry financial items of local, regional, or national interest. Weekly newspapers generally carry items of local interest. The business press includes *The Wall Street Journal, Forbes, Barron's, Business Week, Fortune,* and other national publications as well as various local business-oriented publications (for example, the *Business Chronicle* in Houston, Atlanta, Los Angeles, San Francisco, and other cities). These are primary outlets for financial news, but they are deluged with information, so their channels of communication should not be cluttered with trivia or fluff.

Do not overlook the financial columnists. The Dan Dorfmans and Louis Rukeysers of this country carry great weight and can offer unique perspectives on particular companies. Trade magazines, usually devoted to particular industries, occupations, or professions, are also important outlets. They may reach such likely prospects as suppliers and producers.

Television and radio are limited but growing outlets for financial news. Cable's Financial News Network devotes sixty hours a week to business news. Certain local and national programs are devoted specifically to business. Public Broadcasting's "Wall Street Week," Cable News Network's financial programs, and Associated Press Radio's "Business Barometer" are examples of such programs. Network or local major market news operations generally should be approached only if the information has news value that affects the community at large.

Finally, specialized financial media are extremely interested in company news. Market newsletters (often published by brokerage firms), investment advisory services, and statistical services (like Standard and Poor's, Value Line, or Moody's) frequently carry the greatest weight with potential investors.

Communication Strategy in Financial Relations

Strategies for communicating financial information, like those for implementing other plans (see chapter 7), must grow out of management's long-term view of the corporation. Communication strategy is a plan for getting from where you are to where you want to be. Thus, the perception of the company by its relevant publics should be compared with how it hopes to be perceived in the future. The methods available for implementing strategy include personal meetings, financial literature (correspondence, quarterly and annual reports, dividend enclosures), financial news releases, and annual meetings. Whatever a corporation's current status or ultimate objectives, its financial relations communication strategy must be characterized by responsiveness, regularity, and openness. Communication should never be evasive and must include bad news as well as good. Financial openness means "willingness to communicate honestly and forthrightly with . . . employees and external constituencies regarding economic matters."[17] Credibility is the key to a strong financial relations program.

Annual Meetings

Annual meetings are a kind of mandated ritual in which the actual owners of a business consider and vote on the effectiveness of management. In theory, stockholders have the power to do what they please (within the law) with their company. But in practice, issues are rarely discussed and even more rarely voted on because management collects proxies in advance to support its positions, appointments, and decisions.

Views on the annual meeting ritual are widely divergent. "At one end of the spectrum are those who regard the annual meeting as a hallmark of corporate democracy and an expression of our free enterprise system," says Arthur Roalman. "At the other are those who look upon the function as a meaningless corporate exercise."[18] The view taken by management will influence the nature of a given corporation's annual meeting. Whatever the case, the annual meeting presents certain opportunities and entails genuine risks, thus careful planning and orchestration are essential. Most major public accounting firms publish guides for corporate executives facing annual meetings.

Besides trying to attract, inform, and involve the audience of stockholders, the annual meeting has other functions. It enables corporate management to reach all stockholders through pre- and post-meeting communication. It provides a showcase and a focus for corporate publicity. It permits personal contact between executives and stockholders through which actions can be explained, accomplishments recognized, and feedback offered. It is a marketing tool when products are displayed in their best light. It is a safety valve by which stockholders can let off steam.

The democractic nature of the annual meeting makes the company vulnerable. Organized dissent is possible from stockholders who have bought a few shares of stock just to gain a platform. Such individuals may intervene or disrupt—confronting management with embarrasing questions and drawing the attention of the news media.

J. P. Stevens and Company, the controversial textile giant which had been fighting unionization for twenty years, was faced with the possibility of confrontation at its 1980 annual meeting. Thirteen Catholic organizations owning company stock were slated to propose at the meeting that a review committee be established to advise on management/employee relations. At the same time, the union was staging a countermeeting to make public its grievances against the company. Media attention was focused on the potential conflict. Management, in this case, stuck by its guns and explained its position once again. The proposal was defeated. The union's meeting drew less than one hundred followers.

Commenting on J. P. Stevens's annual meeting, *Atlanta Journal* business editor Tom Walker observed tongue-in-cheek that corporations should retain consulting sociologists, "especially during the annual meeting season when managements are forced to line up before their shareholders and give an account of themselves."[19] Financial relations actually plays the role that Walker would give to sociologists. By anticipating the concerns, issues, and even the mood of stockholders—based on continuous interaction—financial public relations should be able to prepare management for most situations that could arise. With careful planning, the positive potentials of annual meetings may even be realized.

Annual Reports

American companies spend nearly $200 million per year on **annual reports.** Gulf and Western spent $5 million to publish its entire 1978 report in the February 5, 1979, issue of *Time.* Emhart Corporation has provided a twenty-two-minute video version of its annual report each year since 1979. Played on cable TV, the video was viewed by over a million people in 1985, according to company estimates. H. J. Heinz Company, the food processing giant, published its 1979 report in five languages for use as a worldwide marketing tool. The pharmaceutical company Pfizer, Inc. sends copies of its annual report to every physician in the United States. AT&T produces a braille version of its report. Telorate Corporation provided the 1985 annual report on videocassettes to each of its six thousand shareholders. McCormick & Co. scented its 1984 annual report with allspice. Domino's Pizza boxed its 1985 report and included a set of dominoes.

Oscar Beveridge calls the annual report "unquestionably the single most important public document issued by a publicly-held corporation."[20] Writing in *Fortune,* Herbert Meyer states: "Out of all the documents published by a Fortune 500 corporation, none involves so much fussing, so much anguish—

and often so much pride of authorship—as the annual report to share-holders."[21] In short, the annual report can be considered the keystone of a company's financial relations program.

The History of Annual Reports   The Borden Company published the first corporate annual report in this country in 1854. It was a simple document, but its appearance was shocking to corporate leaders, whose view of stockholders was best expressed as "the public be damned." By 1899, the New York Stock Exchange required every listed company to publish at least once a year "a properly detailed statement of its income and expenditures . . . and also a balance sheet, giving a detailed and accurate statement of the condition of the company at the close of its last fiscal year."

In 1903, United States Steel published what could be considered the first modern annual report. It included thirty-six pages of facts and figures and twenty-two pages of photographs. By the mid-1950s, the typical annual report was a slick, magazine-style publication. In 1964, Litton Industries went so far as to commission the artist Andrew Wyeth to produce a painting for the cover of its report. What were once management scorecards have become management showcases.

The Purpose of Annual Reports   Fundamentally, the annual report fulfills the legal requirements of reporting to a company's stockholders. As such, it becomes the primary source of information about the company for current and potential stockholders, providing comprehensive information on the condition of the company and its progress (or lack thereof) during the previous year.

Some companies leave it at that. But nearly all large companies carry their annual reports considerably further, taking the opportunity to reinforce their credibility, establish their distinct identity, and build investor confidence, support, and allegiance. In this sense, the annual report becomes the company's calling card, a summary of what the company has done and what it stands for. By accident or by design, the report usually conveys much about the personality and quality of the corporation's management.

Some companies get further service from their annual reports by using them for marketing, public relations, and employee recruitment and orientation purposes. A report may also serve as an informational resource for financial advisers, a "backgrounder" for business editors, or even an educational tool for teachers, librarians, and students. General Motors uses its report to advertise its products. Goodyear Tire and Rubber puts out a special edition for classroom use. Increasing numbers of companies produce special editions for employees to gain their loyalty and support, build morale by stressing their contributions, and improve their understanding of company operations.

Another purpose of the report for some companies is to speak out on issues of social responsibility or state political positions. Paine Webber recently devoted part of its report to an essay extolling the virtues of economic growth and warning of the dangers of increased taxation. Columnist James J. Kilpatrick calls for much broader efforts of this nature:

> I have complained before, and will keep on complaining, about annual reports and other messages to stockholders. The annual reports that flow across my desk are often beautiful specimens of the graphic designer at work. There are four-color photos, pie charts that glitter like Keno-wheels, the last word in typography. But only a handful of top executives seize the opportunity to mobilize a constituency of stockholders, who presumably have some political clout, in support of the company's political positions. I am mystified by this failing . . . .[22]

Some disapprove of the many faces of the annual report. James H. Dowling, for instance, maintains that annual reports should have only one purpose: to help investors decide whether to become or remain stockholders in a company.[23] Another dissenter is former SEC chairman Harold M. Williams, who claims that annual reports "often appear to reflect the results of a conflict between the desire to create a promotional document and the need to provide full and fair disclosure."

Herbert Meyer takes the opposite view:

> What some people see as the great weakness of annual reports—their use as a soapbox to sell products, build managerial egos, and blast off against government regulations—is in a very real sense their considerable strength. Annual reports have become wonderfully clear windows into the personalities of corporations and the executives who manage them.[24]

Responding to both schools of thought, Lowe's Companies, the North Carolina materials retailer, sent out a postcard-sized, fill-in-the-blanks, "generic" annual report in 1984 (see Figure 14.2). For those wanting the full treatment, the company provided a set of five paperback books on Lowe's strategy, required disclosures, industry and company facts, and an essay on why people invest.

While accountants may decry verbal and pictorial embellishment of their ciphers, the communication opportunity presented by annual reports is too important to pass up. Moreover, with the cost of preparation and distribution sometimes reaching $10 per copy, financial considerations practically demand that these publications do double duty. Although a few companies have toned down their documents, annual reports are not likely to return to the minimum level of information required by the government. The 1984 Xerox report contained no pictures and cost only 43 cents per copy, but Xerox remains the exception to the rule.

Figure 14.2 Lowe's "generic" annual report

Date *March 1, 1984*

Dear Investor:

- We want you to be the first to know
  Lowes _____ results for *1983* _____

- Sales were $ *1.43* (billion, ~~million~~).
  This was a (record, ~~near record~~, ~~not a record~~).

- Earnings were $ *50.6* (~~billion~~, million).
  This was a (record, ~~near record~~, ~~not a record~~).

- Per share earnings were $ *1.40*
  This was a (record, ~~near record~~, ~~not a record~~).

- Dividends paid were $ *.32* per share.

- Share price in the year (increased, ~~decreased~~) by
  12 %

- Prospects for the new year look to be (~~great~~, good,
  ~~about average~~, ~~not so good~~, ~~poor~~, just ~~plain awful~~).

- Full Annual Report will be mailed about *April 25*
  Chairman *Robert L. Strickland*
  President *Leonard G. Herring*

Planning and Producing Annual Reports   Preparing the annual report is an elaborate undertaking requiring creativity, coordination, and the joint efforts of specialists in public relations, financial relations, accounting, law, photography, graphic design, and general management. Certain aspects of the report may require consultation and input from marketing, personnel, research and development, public affairs, or others. Although public relations may have the overall responsibility for creating, producing, and distributing the annual report, it is necessarily a corporate effort.

The first step in planning and producing the annual report is to establish its objectives. What message should the document communicate? Objectives should be defined as specifically as possible. Once they are chosen, the second step is to select the means of achieving them. Often a theme is established. Growth, change, entrepreneurship, international competition, and high technology are examples of themes aimed toward a report's specific objectives.

The third step in planning and production is to establish a budget and schedule. Budgets for annual reports vary tremendously and depend largely on corporate means and desires. At least three months should be allowed for gathering material and information for the report, writing the copy, graphic designing, collecting photos, and obtaining financial statements. Corporate attorneys and management must approve the copy. Adequate time for printing and distribution must be allowed. The total process usually requires a total of six to nine months.

Much of the effort devoted to annual reports is aimed at attracting readers. F. C. Foy explains: "The annual report needs more than figures and tables, or even graphs, charts, or pictures. It needs candid, specific, readable statements of objectives, of difficulties and problems and how they are being attacked, of new products or services, and of how management envisions the future of the business."[25] Tulsa's Parker Drilling Company was candid, specific, and readable in its annual report. In bright red letters, the report's front cover read: "The first half of 1980 was lousy . . . ." Those who read the report found that the second half was much better. Good design and clear writing make annual reports attractive and readable.

The planners and producers of the annual report must be ever mindful of their audience's needs. It is well to remember, however, that annual reports reach a variety of audiences. Primary audiences, of course, are investors and the investment community. Generally speaking, the investing community is most interested in the auditor's report, financial highlights, changes in financial position, debt, and other data. Even among investors, however, desires for information differ. Potential and current employees also constitute an audience, but they may be more interested in the president's letter or the graphic presentation.

How can various audiences be served by one document? Some companies, as we have noted, produce special editions for employees or students. Other companies, recognizing that annual reports need not be read from cover to cover, present information in layers so that various readers can take what they want. The layers consist of (1) cover, pictures, and captions; (2) the president's letter and financial highlights; and (3) detailed information about operations and financial developments, including footnotes. In this way, the reader can decide just how deep he or she wants to go.

Contents of Annual Reports   The typical annual report consists of a cover; a president's letter; financial and nonfinancial highlights; balance sheet and income statement; description of the business (products and services); names and titles of corporate officers; names and affiliations of outside directors; location of plants, offices and representatives; address and telephone number of corporate headquarters; and reference to stock exchanges on which company stock is traded. The report may also include the company's history (particularly in anniversary issues), discussion of company policies, request for support of the company's stance on a political issue, results of stockholder surveys, and other reports or features.

Photographs, graphic art, and color are increasingly important in annual reports. Award-winning Michael Watras, president of Corporate Graphics and producer of annual reports for companies such as H. J. Heinz and Chase Manhattan Bank, explains, "Annual reports are more visual today than they were a few years ago. We're using larger pictures and more of them, and much more four-color. . . . Photographs are more likely to be tied into an overall theme."[26]

Annual reports should always put corporate earnings in perspective and spell out prospects for the next year. They should answer these questions:

What is the major thrust of our company?
Where do we excel?
What are our weaknesses?
Why has the company performed as it has?
What are we doing about the future?

Financial highlights are a well-read aspect of annual reports. They generally include figures representing net sales, earnings before taxes, earnings after taxes, net earnings per common share, dividends per common share, stockholders' equity per common share, net working capital, ratio of current assets to current liabilities, number of common shares outstanding, and number of common stockholders. Other highlights include profit margin, percent return on stockholders' equity, long-term debt, and number of employees. Report designers are concerned not just with the numbers, but how they look. Financial data is most often integrated into the entire report and presented in interesting or unusual ways.

Herbert Rosenthal and Frank Pagani list eight elements of what they call "big league annual reports:"[27]

1. A meaningful or provocative pictorial cover
2. A well-designed format
3. Complete and understandable graphics
4. Unstilted photographs and artwork
5. Comprehensive text
6. Comparative figures
7. Tasteful presentation of products
8. Stylish printing

Figure 14.3 shows a sample of some annual reports.

Summary

The annual report is out. The annual meeting is over. Good communication links are established with financial analysts and editors. Stockholder correspondence is operating smoothly. But how can you evaluate your efforts?

Good financial relations usually result in increased proxy response, reduction of stock turnover, better attendance at stockholder meetings, appropriate price-to-earnings ratios, and greater ease in selling new stock issues.

And if you do not achieve this kind of success, you can always blame the economy.

Figure 14.3 Sample pages from the annual reports of four firms. *(a)* One of the world's largest forest products companies, Georgia Pacific's 1983 annual report cover is attractive and artistic. It identifies the corporation's products while symbolizing growth, environmental concerns, and corporate renewal. *(b)* Frank B. Hall & Co. Inc., an insurance services company, devoted nearly forty pages of its 1983 annual report to national election issues. *(c)* Chesebrough-Pond's Inc. devoted its 1983 annual report to its employees. *(d)* The Limited, Inc., a women's clothing retailer, produced a 1983 annual report that looked like a catalog of the company's products.

(a)

Financial Highlights

Years ended December 31 (thousands, except per share data)	1983	1982
Net commissions and fees and other income	$365,175	$372,610
Income before income taxes	21,783	42,606
Net income	12,495	24,255
Net income per share of common stock	$1.02	$2.05
Average number of common shares outstanding	12,200	11,816
Dividends declared per common share	$1.53	$1.70

Contents

1983 Annual Report   1

(b)

(c)

(d)

▲ ▲ ▲

Case Study

Ball Corporation

By Charlotte Hatfield
Ball State University
Muncie, Indiana

S tability certainly wasn't the problem: Ball Corporation had been successful for almost one hundred years before its shares began trading on the New York Stock Exchange in 1973. That year, company executives traveled the big-city analyst-house circuit telling their story, but the stock did not sell as the company had hoped it would.

In examining the situation, company officials recognized two immediate problems affecting the sale of public shares. First, 60 percent of the company stock was still in the hands of the Ball family or corporate officers. Over 900,000 shares were available for outside purchase, too small to be attractive to large or institutional investors who routinely purchase large blocks of stock.

The second problem was the perception of the company by financial professionals. Most were familiar with Ball Corporation as the producer of Ball canning jars, an American tradition ranking near baseball and apple pie. They were not aware, however, of the corporation's international involvement in space exploration and defense contracting; glass and metal container manufacture for the food and brewing industries; plastics products for electronics, computers, and medical uses; zinc, lead, and chemical products; or the production of computer-related, irrigation, and petroleum equipment.

For a century, the company had been growing and diversifying but had not publicized that information. Now the need was clear—if its stock was to sell, Ball had to tell its story.

Utilizing the U.S. Census Report, demographics studies, population and income studies, and New York Stock Exchange shareholder surveys, Ball determined its most likely shareholder to be a middle-class, age 40–70, rural or suburban-oriented American aware of the canning jar's quality and interested in investing money in a company with tradition and stability. Ball decided the best way to reach such individuals was through stockbrokers, the people directly in contact with potential shareholders.

The effort to reach brokers began in 1977 and was built around face-to-face meetings. The program reached forty-eight cities and approximately two thousand brokers the first year. Brokers or registered representatives in a target city received an invitation to a breakfast, lunch, or cocktail hour. Before the meeting, Ball Corporation employees contacted each individual again by mail, sending a copy of the book *A Collector's Guide to Ball Jars,* and later by telephone, if a response to the invitation had not been received.

The day of the meeting, the director of public relations and the treasurer of Ball Corporation would greet the brokers and conduct the program. The usual format included general remarks about the history and growth of the company and a ten-minute film concentrating on the corporation's major markets. This was followed by a short presentation exploring financial data and a question and answer session for the brokers. The focus of the message was on the selling points of the company—ideas the brokers could use to sell their customers on Ball stock.

The Ball Corporation reinforces its "high tech" image with the cover of one of its annual reports.

In addition to printed information, each broker received a special-edition pint Ball canning jar embossed with the Ball signature on one side and the bull and bear symbols of the stock exchange on the other. Sealed inside the jar was the business card of Ball's director of public relations.

The investor relations program generated more than thirty meetings per year, with an average of thirty-five to forty brokers attending each one.

Although direct attribution of stock sale is difficult to make, Ball Corporation found that in the first year of the effort, two thousand new investors joined the shareholder ranks, approximately one for each broker attending the meetings that year. In ensuing years, stock sales continued to attract new investors, guaranteeing a long-term commitment to the program.

Questions

1. Had the Ball company been delinquent in its public relations efforts prior to 1973? What type of external communications effort might have eased the problems encountered between 1973 and 1977?
2. What considerations might affect the format and timing of the meetings? Also discuss the location for the meeting, the food and beverage choices, and other details which would affect the brokers' reactions to the meeting/message.
3. Prepare a timetable for a Ball Corporation investor relations meeting. The timetable should begin eight to twelve weeks before the meeting and include details on acquiring mailing lists, meeting formats, facilities contacts, mailings to brokers, materials to be used at the meeting, travel plans for Ball executives, and other appropriate information.

Notes

1. Theodore Pincus, "How to Boost Your P/E Multiple," *Fortune* (10 November 1986): 183.
2. Arthur R. Roalman, ed., *Investor Relations Handbook* (New York: AMACOM, 1974) iii.
3. Ibid., 31.
4. NYSE Company Manual (August 1, 1977).
5. American Stock Exchange.
6. Henry Rockwell, "A Press Release Goes to Court," *Public Relations Journal* (October 1968).
7. G. Christman Hill, "Financial Public Relations Men Are Warned They're Liable for Clients' Puffery," *Wall Street Journal* (16 March 1972): 30.
8. Investor Relations Pros Downplay PR Skills," *Communication World* (May 1983): 15.
9. Harrison T. Beardsley, "Problem-Solving in Corporate Financial Relations," *Public Relations Journal* (April 1978): 23.
10. Oscar M. Beveridge, *Financial Public Relations* (New York: McGraw-Hill, 1963), 68.
11. Louis Rukeyser, *Atlanta Journal* (28 February 1980): 12–13.
12. Roalman, *Investor Relations Handbook,* 190.
13. Stuart Weiss, "Hell Hath No Fury Like a Surprised Stock Analyst," *Business Week* (January 21, 1985): 98.
14. Pincus, 183.
15. R. Foster Winans, "San Francisco Presentations by 60 Concerns Buoyed Many of Them but Cost Others Dearly," *Wall Street Journal* (9 September 1983): 77.
16. Stan Sauerhaft, "Won't Anybody Listen?" in Hill and Knowlton Executives, *Critical Issues in Public Relations* (Englewood Cliffs, N.J.: Prentice-Hall, 1975), 37.
17. Frederick D. Sturdivant, *Business and Society: A Managerial Approach* (Homewood, IL: Irwin, 1977), 358.
18. Roalman, *Investor Relations Handbook,* 43.
19. Tom Walker, "J. P. Stevens Fights Catholics' Proposal," *Atlanta Journal and Constitution* (2 March 1980): 10.
20. Beveridge, *Financial Public Relations,* 137.
21. Herbert E. Meyer, "Annual Reports Get an Editor in Washington," *Fortune* (7 May 1979): 219.
22. James J. Kilpatrick, "A Short Course in Media Relations," *Nation's Business* (June 1979): 17–18.
23. James H. Dowling, "Main Job of the Annual Report, Wooing Investors," *Dunn's Review* (September 1978): 127.
24. Meyer, "Annual Reports Get Editor," 222.
25. F. C. Foy, "Annual Reports Don't Have to be Dull," *Harvard Business Review* 51 (January–February 1973): 49–58.
26. "Annual Reports Help Sell Organizations," *ABC News* (December 1981): 1, 11.
27. Herbert C. Rosenthal and Frank Pagani, "Rating Your Annual Report," *Public Relations Journal* (August 1978): 12.

▲ ▲ ▲

CHAPTER 15

Public Affairs: Relations with Government

Preview

Government activity at every level has tremendous daily impact—positive and negative—on every kind of organization in the United States.

Public affairs units help organizations anticipate or respond to issues affecting their activities or environment.

Business organizations in particular have recognized the necessity of political adroitness and have moved aggressively to increase their public affairs effectiveness.

Organizational political activities fall into three major categories: electoral, legislative, and regulatory.

The Reagan Administration's effort to return responsibilities to local government increased the importance of state and local public affairs.

A regulation is changed and a manufacturer goes out of business. A tariff is enacted and an industry thrives. State revenues go down and universities suffer. A county budget passes, giving libraries and cultural centers a shot in the arm. A zoning hearing opens the way for a major new development. A church acquires land for a new parking lot and seeks to convert the property to nonprofit status. Changes in the federal tax code shift $100 billion in liabilities from wage earners to corporations. A local ordinance bans smoking in the workplace. The unwillingness of a local government to promote a bond issue makes a proposed museum seek another city in which to locate. . . .

The list goes on and on. Government activity at every level has tremendous daily impact—positive and negative—on every kind of organization in the United States. When organizations review the external forces that affect their operations, governmental bodies should be at the top of the list. Indeed, public opinion and media, employee, and community relations are considered important in part because of their potential influence on potential government action or inaction.

Public affairs, a term sometimes used as a synonym for all of public relations, more often describes the aspect of public relations that deals with the political environment of organizations. Sometimes it is called government relations. Public affairs is related to issues management (discussed in chapter 4) in that it helps organizations anticipate or respond to issues affecting their activities or environment. Public affairs efforts include seeking to shape public opinion and legislation, developing effective responses to matters of public concern, and helping the organization adapt to public expectations. Specifically, public affairs may become involved in monitoring public policy, providing political education for employees or other constituents, maintaining liaisons with various governmental units, and encouraging political participation. As shown in Figure 15.1, public affairs facilitates the two-way flow of information between an organization and its political environment.

Public Affairs for Not-for-Profit Organizations

By the late 1970s and early 1980s, public affairs was being pursued as never before in terms of resources, executive involvement, sophistication, and openness. Large business organizations particularly had experienced an awakening to the political process. But when federal budget cuts made life more complex for not-for-profit organizations in the 1980s, these groups also became more sophisticated and aggressive in their government relations efforts.

Unions, schools, hospitals, libraries, cultural organizations, foundations, businesses, and other organizations have both the problem and the opportunity of dealing with government. All want to improve communication with government agencies and employees, monitor and influence legislative and regulatory actions, encourage constituent participation, and expand the awareness and understanding of people in power.

These organizations realize that they can no longer even pretend to be above the political fray. Political activity has grown up and come out of the closet. Fundamentally, ours is a pluralistic society in which various interests

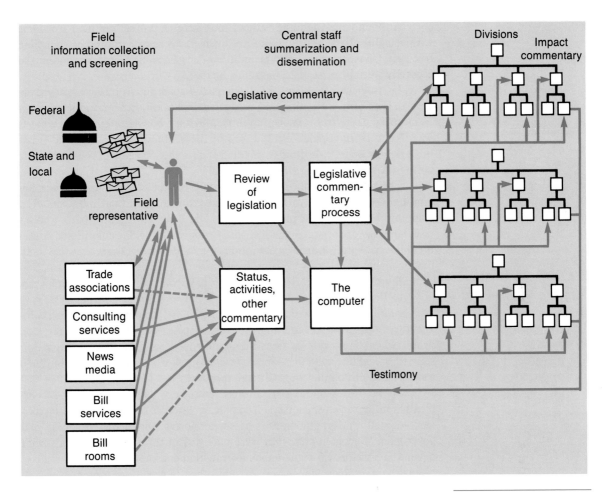

Figure 15.1 Two-way flow of political information

compete in the political arena. Under these circumstances, business and other organizations have recognized that their interests, indeed sometimes their survival, require political acumen and effort.

Because business practices public affairs most ardently and extensively, a deeper understanding of that function will give insight into how public affairs applies in all organizations.

Our country's founding fathers were strongly influenced by the economic philosophy enunciated by Adam Smith in his seminal 1776 book *The Wealth of Nations*. Smith advocated a very limited role for government in economic activities. Nevertheless, since their beginnings, the United States government and the various state governments have exerted more power over economic activity than is considered acceptable in classical capitalistic theory.

Public Affairs
in Business

*Background of
Business/Government
Relations*

Although the founding fathers took care to protect political freedoms with the Bill of Rights, they did not deem it necessary to protect economic freedom. Consequently, the preconditions for government intervention in the economy were present at our nation's birth.

In America's first century, business and government pushed forward together, promoting invention and westward expansion. But when the captains of industry came to be known as robber barons, business found out what it was like to be unpopular. By the turn of the century, muckrakers and trust-busters, socialists and populists made business their targets in the courts, the voting booths, and the streets.

The passage of the Interstate Commerce Act in 1887 marked the beginning of twenty years of regulatory legislation aimed at curbing monopoly, stopping debilitating business practices, and controlling cutthroat competition. Unions were organized in response to abysmal working conditions; strike-breaking, violence, murder, corruption of public officials, watered stock, and monopolistic practices were constantly in the public eye. Moreover, a nation of small individual businessmen was rapidly becoming a nation of employees.

In the twentieth century, business's public support and business/government interaction waxed and waned. The 1920s, the post-World War II era, and the 1980s saw considerable business popularity. The 1930s depression years, when bankruptcies, mass unemployment, and economic stagnation seemed to suggest that the American Dream was counterfeit, sank business to a low ebb of popular and political approval.

In the 1960s and 1970s, American society experienced added complexity, an increasing velocity of change, greater risks than previously confronted, and the fragmentation of social norms and goals. Business and government's economic engines were both at full throttle. Social goals went beyond materialism with demands for racial and sexual equality and the rise of environmentalism, consumerism, and other causes. Government began to use business to seek social as well as economic goals.

In the midst of this era, business professor Neil Jacoby wrote:

> The profit-seeking corporation . . . has no choice but to be as politically influential as the law . . . and its resources . . . permit. Hedged in by a multiplicity of local, state and federal regulations affecting building, zoning, health, safety, insurance, employment, workmen's compensation, social security, wage and hour standards, equal opportunity rules, securities issuance, financing, fees and taxes, product and advertising, standards, et cetera, corporate business naturally takes political action to defend the freedom of action that remains to it.[1]

A 1978 article in *Time* pointed out government's power and the vigilance required to deal with that power. "A single clause tucked away in the Federal Register of Regulations (this year's version has already grown to a mountainous 32,000 pages) can put a small-town manufacturer out of business or rejuvenate an industry that was on the brink of bankruptcy."[2] As a consequence, business's presence in Washington increased rapidly. In 1968, about one hundred companies had Washington offices. By 1978, over five hundred maintained such offices, and in most cases, Washington staffs had considerably expanded. One-third of the public affairs units existing in corporations in 1980 had been created in the previous five years. In the 1980s, expansion continued but at a much slower pace.

In relation to business and the economy, government now plays a variety of roles: stimulant, referee, rule maker, engineer, pursuer of social goals, defender, provider, customer, controller. To be successful, business must be prepared to deal with government in any of these roles. That is the critical importance of governmental relations and why public affairs has become, in the last twenty years, a crucial dimension of public relations.

Changing Roles Today

Government's enormous power and increased willingness to take an active hand in business management are further pressures for corporate involvement. Some have described the new and complex link between business and government as "a second managerial revolution . . . one in which the locus of real control over a corporation shifts from private executives to public officials."[3] An example of government's active hand is seen in Mini-Case 15.1.

Another change in the relationship is the posture of business's political activity. Traditionally, business merely reacted to the threat of government action, whether that action took the form of taxation, regulation, legislation, or the opposing efforts of labor, public-interest groups, or even other business groups. Not until the danger was apparent did business, as a rule, enter into political activity (see Figure 15.2). As Graham Moliter, president of Public Policy Forecasting, points out, business still often waits too late to get into the political game:

> America's business environment is increasingly shaped by public policy
> dictates. Legislative, litigative and regulatory constraints grow daily. Yet,
> despite the enormity of government entanglement, the business community all
> too often waits until the last minute to focus on important issues. As a result,
> it comes up short in anticipating and adapting to changes in public policy.[4]

Recently, however, business has realized the value of developing continuing relationships with government at all levels that permit early involvement in issues, policies, regulations, and legislation. Advance notice can be a critical factor in political effectiveness. Moreover, early involvement makes provisions for crisis management less necessary when a critical bill comes to a vote later on.

Finally, the business/government relationship is changing because business senses changes in public attitudes toward government. As public attitudes toward government have become more critical and negative, business's success in specific and general political activity has become more likely. F. Clifton White, president of Public Affairs Analysts, Inc., states:

> Because of growing negative attitudes toward government, it should be
> possible to convince people that the solution to specific economic and social
> problems does not lie in the direction of governmental action, but is quite the
> reverse.

Figure 15.2 A model of why and how a firm enters the political arena

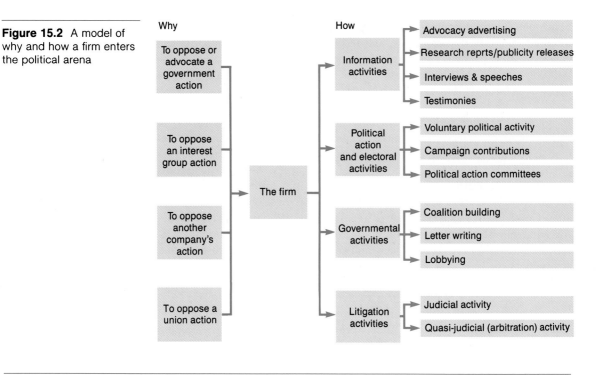

Public Relations, Pulp Mills, and Pollution

Mini-Case 15.1

In 1968, the Escanaba Paper Company, a wholly-owned subsidiary of Mead Corporation, announced its intention to build a $100 million pulp mill and paper manufacturing facility on the pristine Upper Peninsula of northern Michigan, an area known for its clean air, natural beauty, high unemployment, and low per capita income. Mead had a long history of good relations with the town of Escanaba. A policy of urging employees to be involved with local affairs resulted in the presence of two Mead employees on the county board of supervisors.

The first phase of construction—a huge paper machine—began without opposition and was well underway when the Delta County Citizens Committee to Save Our Air (SOA) formed to oppose the second phase of construction, a paper mill. SOA raised questions about potential odor problems from the proposed pulp mill before the board of supervisors, in the *Escanaba Daily Press,* and before the local chamber of commerce. The following statement exemplified the rhetoric used by those opposing the pulp mill:

> I would like to emphasize that I have always had the highest respect for the Mead Corporation as a responsible corporate citizen. Their support of charitable and civic projects in the community has always been open and generous. . . . For this reason, I have asked myself how they could do such a thing in Escanaba and my only conclusion is that in this case the economic considerations to the Mead Corporation override their demonstrated corporate good citizenship.

When the local plant manager announced his company's decision to proceed with the pulp mill on April 28, 1969, the public affairs unit had a complete communications plan ready to be implemented. The plan focused on the fact that Mead would use the most advanced available air pollution prevention equipment and that $5 million would be spent on pollution control technology.

On May 19, SOA passed a resolution calling for a guaranteed odorless mill and a county ordinance that would require permanent closing of the mill if it was not odorless. In an effort to build support for their position, the committee undertook a publicity campaign that included newspaper advertisements, mass mailings, radio announcements, and news releases. In June, Mead responded to questions raised by SOA. The company explained that it had delayed answering questions about the pulp mill until it had investigated available technology and been assured that the pulp mill could be as free from odor as possible. Mead steadfastly refused to make promises it could not keep and allowed that malfunctions, errors, or climatic conditions could result in temporary odors.

In August, the Associated Press carried a story nationally that began:

Citizens in this northern Michigan community are battling to save their clean air—air that gives off the fragrance of balsam fir and has been judged by one scientific study to be the cleanest in the U.S.

What has alarmed some townspeople is the proposed construction of a sulfate pulp mill . . . .

"It smells like rotten eggs, rotten cabbages, skunks and who the hell knows," said John T. Walbridge.

On September 15, SOA staged a public rally attended by four-to-five hundred people. The event was covered by CBS television.

Two days later, SOA presented its proposed ordinance to the Delta County board of supervisors, claiming the ordinance would safeguard "the health, safety, welfare and comfort of the people." In effect, it banned the pulp mill.

Mead felt the ordinance was irresponsible and opposed it, but made clear its willingness to cooperate enthusiastically to develop a reasonable ordinance. Publicly, Mead's position was that a law providing clear technical measures was definitely needed.

SOA continued its campaign, receiving an endorsement from the Episcopal Diocese of Northern Michigan and a complimentary article in New Republic. In the meantime, Mead maintained a relatively low-key position, attempting to remain reasonable, cooperative, and open. An open house at the company's $2 million water treatment plant received favorable notice in the local press.

The Michigan Air Pollution Control Commission took the matter up at hearings in Lansing, the state capital. Mead was opposed by SOA, Friends of the Earth, the League of Conservation, the Environmental Action Council, and student groups from the University of Michigan and Michigan State University. All of these groups questioned the company's credibility, maintaining that Mead would promise anything to get the plant built.

Mead's response was to refuse to promise unobtainable results. Instead, the company offered complete, understandable technical and economic data, and flew twelve community leaders to Lansing so that they could testify. The chairman of the county board of supervisors testified that "Mead has placed its integrity and excellent public relations on the line."

The commission's staff established seven stipulations to be met by Mead before a permit would be granted. With minor modifications, and despite increased costs, Mead agreed to the stipulations. One of the commissioners concluded, "I'm satisfied that Mead is not going to violate our law." The permit was granted by a 7–1 vote on April 28, 1970, one year after Mead had announced its intention to construct the pulp mill.

Adapted from John Collins and Donald De Salvia, "Escanaba Paper Company," in R. D. Hay, E. R. Gray, and J. E. Gates, eds., *Business and Society,* (Cincinnati: Southwestern Publishing Company, 1976), 132–146.

Impact on Management   The increasing importance of business public affairs and political activities has had substantial impacts on management in general and public relations in particular. Because the issue is one of corporate control, top corporate leaders take an active role in public affairs efforts. Explains former Congressman Donald G. Brotzman, now president of the Washington-based Rubber Manufacturers' Association, "Involvement of top management is a most important principle. The chief executive officer and all top managers must be active participants." Grover Starling maintains, "The direct and indirect influence of government action on business changes the kinds and mix of skills that one needs to succeed as a manager."[5] The effect on top management, he feels, is even more pronounced. "Top managers must now be as concerned about public policy as they are about anything else they do."[6]

Nicholas F. Brady, chairman of the investment banking firm Dillon, Read & Co., served eight-and-one-half months in the United States Senate, filling an unexpired term. He makes the following suggestion to sensitize top management to public affairs:

> Why not hold one board meeting each year in Washington? All of us who serve on boards make trips to important plant locations where new products are being developed. Our government is as important a part of our business life as a new product. Why not hold one board meeting a year in Washington, finish up business promptly, then spend the rest of the time talking with government leaders? The gap in communication, in cooperation, in understanding is too deep to be conducted on a jet-in and jet-out basis.[7]

The Job of Public Affairs

Today no public relations program is complete unless it includes provisions for dealing with government. This job is, in part, a complex sequence of information acquisition, processing, and dissemination. Fact-finding and serving as a listening post may be the most important aspects of governmental relations. In gathering information, practitioners often do essentially the same things as journalists do.[8] In fact, many (though not all) public affairs activities resemble those undertaken by other public relations practitioners on a daily basis.

Having gathered information, government relations specialists weigh and evaluate its potential impact on the company or industry. Information is then disseminated to corporate decision makers, employees, stockholders, and the public. Indeed, public affairs has its greatest impact on an organization when it aids corporate planning. At the same time, government relations staffs convey information to legislators, regulators, congressional staffers, potential political allies, and the public.

Public relations is also sometimes called upon to fight fire with fire on the government relations front. Investigation and publicity lack the force of law, but are clearly among the weapons government uses to influence business. Leaks to the media by "high-level sources," visits to the sites of supposed infractions, staged public hearings, and the like may be used against business by government officials. Businesses' public affairs efforts must sometimes respond in kind. Their public relations specialists must compete with the public information machines of government and the public relations operations of a variety of special interests. Honesty and forceful public communication is a crucial aspect of the government relations process.

To operate effectively, government relations professionals must thoroughly understand the United States' political process. In a general sense, political activities fall into three broad categories: electoral, legislative, and regulatory. Electoral activities involve the election of candidates favorable to an organization's interests and the development of plans for financially supporting selected political campaigns. Political action committees are the major vehicles for fund-raising efforts.

Understanding the Political System

Legislative activities work to create or gain support for favorable legislation and build opposition against unfavorable activities. Lobbying is the major avenue for legislative activities.

The primary goal of regulatory activities from a public affairs point of view is to foster an understanding of the day-to-day problems of a particular organization or industry. Regulators are more difficult to lobby because they are rarely elected officials. Nonetheless, many public affairs efforts related to regulatory activity take a form quite similar to lobbying.

Although political action is often conceived of in electoral terms, most organizations actually place less emphasis on electing candidates than on working with the winner afterwards. In 1974, however, the Federal Election Campaign Act legitimized the role of corporations and business-related groups in federal elections, greatly improving their position vis-à-vis labor and other special interests.[9] The law allowed the formation of business **political action committees (PACs).**

Electoral Activities

A PAC is a group of people who raise or spend at least $1,000 in connection with a federal election. The people belonging to a PAC usually have some common political concern, interest, or cause. To pool resources in support of favored candidates, PACs have been formed by unions, businesses, industry groups, church groups, professionals, and many others. Over 3,500 PACs now exist. One example of a PAC is the Women Business Owners Political Action Committee. It seeks funds to persuade congressional committees to

Table 15.1 Ten Largest PACs in 1984	
1. National Association of Realtors	$2.56 million
2. American Medical Association	$2.04 million
3. National Education Association	$1.91 million
4. National Association of Home Builders	$1.75 million
5. United Automobile Workers	$1.69 million
6. Machinists Union	$1.57 million
7. Letter Carriers Union	$1.47 million
8. Seafarers Union	$1.44 million
9. United Food and Commercial Workers	$1.38 million
10. Associated Milk Producers	$1.18 million

Source: Federal Elections Commission

hold hearings on the problems of women-owned businesses. Similar PACs include the Women's Campaign Fund which donated $450,000 to female candidates in 1986 and the Hollywood Women's Political Committee which used fund-raisers featuring Barbara Streisand and Lily Tomlin to collect $3 million in two years.[10]

The objective of legislation allowing PACs was to reform campaign financing. Legal limits on and full disclosure of contributions are supposed to assure fairness in the electoral process. However, numerous loopholes exist and have caused the concern that PACs may promote corruption or tip the political scales in favor of special interests. Some critics maintain that PACs are costly, time-consuming, and demeaning to candidates. Others say that since PACs multiply and therefore tend to neutralize each other, they should be abolished.

Supporters maintain that PACs are an example of citizens' rights to free speech, that they promote political awareness and involvement, and that they have brought campaign financing into the light.

Substantial funds are generated by PACs. In the 1984 congressional elections, for example, $113 million came from PACs, with $64 million for Democrats and $49 million for Republicans. Indeed, House of Representatives Democratic incumbents received half their campaign funds from PACs.

Table 15.1 shows the ten PACs that made the largest contributions in the 1984 elections. Of the ten, five were union-related, three represented industry groups, and two were connected with professions. None represented corporations.

The money generated by corporate PACs goes to politicians of divergent views. The American Trucking Association PAC has given almost exclusively to incumbents regardless of party. Coca-Cola and Grumman PACs have favored Democratic incumbents. Ford and General Motors have tended to give to both incumbents and challengers. Amoco and Corning Glass Works have favored Republicans. "Overall, business-related PACs split their donations about equally between Democrats and Republicans with most of the money going to senior incumbents in both parties."[11] Coca-Cola, for example, contributed a total of $51,770 to ninety-eight candidates in 1984 federal elections, giving to fifty-eight Democrats and forty Republicans. Coke's PAC funded candidates as diverse as California liberal Alan Cranston and North Carolina conservative Jesse Helms, and in some cases, even contributed to opposing candidates.

Corporate PACs get their money from their employees or stockholders. Other PACs get funds from their members or constituencies. Thus, if a PAC is to be effective, it "must first educate its people and motivate them to participate."[12]

Some have charged that PACs attempt to "buy" political officials or unduly influence legislators in relation to pet issues. Senator Edward Kennedy has claimed that PACs "are doing their best to buy every senator, every representative, and every issue in sight."[13] Typically, PACs contribute to candidates whose philosophies are consistent with their own. One PAC official explained that his group has two tests for campaign contributions: Is the candidate someone we agree with and is it someone in the area of government that relates to how we do business? Consequently, a senator on the banking committee gets contributions from bank PACs, while one on the agriculture committee receives funds from the Associated Milk Producers.

What PACs typically seek is access. That is why funds more often flow to incumbents. PACs are so eager to back winners, they often do so retroactively—making contributions after the election is over. Funds contributed after the election are called "hundred percent money," meaning none is wasted on losers. Many PACs switch sides after the votes are counted. When Senator Charles Hecht (R-Nevada) upset incumbent Howard Cannon, post-election contributions came from former opponents including the American Dental Association, the American Banking Association, and the McDonald's corporation. The National Association of Realtors kicked into Hecht's campaign chest after opposing him in the primary and the general election. In many cases, PAC funds are used to keep from making enemies.

Since a PAC contribution may be as much as $5,000 per election, the gift generally helps open the door to a legislator's office. Mini-Case 15.2 shows how the Office Machine Dealers' PAC pushed one piece of pet legislation. Indeed, the most important function of electoral activities is to provide support for legislative activities.

Legislative Activities

Most political decisions of importance to organizations are made long after the elections are over. Consequently, business firms and other organizations concentrate their efforts on affecting legislation and regulation in relevant areas. These activities are known as **lobbying.**

Lobbying has been defined as "the practice of trying to influence governmental decisions, particularly legislative votes, by agents who serve interest groups."[14] Lobbying is an extensive and expensive activity. Over 8,500 registered lobbyists spent about $26 million wooing Congress in the first half of 1986.[15] Although the term has acquired an unsavory connotation of graft and influence peddling, lobbying has long been recognized as a legitimate practice. James Madison, writing in 1788, held that an essential characteristic of a representative democracy is that the various interest groups in society are permitted to compete for the attention of government officials.

In recent years, lobbyists have cleaned up their acts. Business lobbyists have adopted more restrained practices regarding gifts and entertainment. Old-time Washington business lobbyists have been replaced by carefully selected professionals who have business acumen, a thorough grasp of sometimes highly technical information, and lots of political savvy. Henry Ford II sums up the new attitude: "The problem with 'lobbying' activities is not to conceal their existence, nor to apologize for them, but to make sure they are adequate, effective and impeccably correct in conduct."[16]

Office-Machine Dealers' PAC

Mini-Case 15.2

The Office-Machine Dealers' PAC gave $48,800 to congressional candidates in 1982, putting it in the top 20 percent of PACs in money raised. But unlike other PACs, this one seeks the passage of only one bill; all contributions go to legislators who help it along or sit on committees responsible for its well-being.

The bill began as an effort to restrict competition by allowing an office-machine dealer to take a supplier to federal court if the supplier cut the dealer off or tried to set up a competing dealership. The judge could block a new competitor if existing competition was considered "adequate."

The Office-Machine Dealers use their PAC money skillfully and carefully. A New Jersey Democrat received a $5,000 contribution just before he cleared the measure through the subcommittee he chaired. The bill's main Senate sponsor, Nebraska Democrat James Exon, received $4,000 even though he did not face reelection for another year. The bill's main House sponsor got similar treatment, as did others who assisted in moving the bill toward passage.

John Kuchta, National Office-Machine Dealers Association vice president, maintained that the bill's progress was not due to the campaign contributions. "We're trying to sell our legislation on the merits, not through buying votes," he claimed. "The PAC helps [by showing lawmakers] we're serious about our issue."

Senator Exon did not need too much persuasion to support the bill. He had been an office-machine dealer in Lincoln before turning to politics.

Source: Based on Brooks Jackson, "Office-Machine Dealers' PAC, Unlike Most, Uses Cash to Single-Mindedly Push One Bill," *Wall Street Journal* (6 April 1983): 33.

The lobbyist's function is critical from the perspective of business. Starling maintains:

> Because many government policies can have a sizable effect on company profits, the business manager who neglects the lobbying function is every bit as irresponsible as one who ignores the company's capital structure or level of employee motivation.[17]

Lobbyists have become essential to the functioning of Congress. The mass of legislation introduced each session is so large that congressional staff simply cannot handle the load. Senators and representatives trying to judge the impact of legislation depend upon the inputs of lobbyists who analyze proposed bills and point out potential consequences. *Time* assesses the impact of the lobbying process this way:

> On balance the relationship between the governors and the governed, even when the lobbyist does represent one of the nation's many special interest groups, is often mutually beneficial, and perhaps indispensable to the fullest workings of democracy. The increasingly knowledgeable and competent Washington lobbyist supplies a practical knowledge vital to the writing of workable laws.[18]

What do lobbyists do? Many things. They inform corporate executives about developments in legislation, report on the introduction and progress of specific bills, offer or arrange testimony to congressional committees, file statements, communicate with legislators, analyze policies and legislation, inform legislators about the potential effect of legislation, educate legislators about business and economics, help draft laws, publicize testimony, and develop strategy to support or oppose specific legislation.

Lobbyists dig out information from officials and records, then use it to inform corporate executives, persuade government officials, promote or oppose legislation or other governmental action, and obtain governmental cooperation. Lobbyists devote much time to creating contacts and programs that will improve communication with government and to monitoring legislators' activities regarding statutes and laws.

Lobbyists involve themselves in the earliest stages of the legislative process. Recognizing that lobbying can only work while the legislator is still in the decision-making stage, lobbyists provide information before bills are drawn up. Their emphasis is on information and advocacy, not pressure. Lobbyists seek to define issues in terms of the legislators' constituencies and the public interest, providing briefly stated, neatly organized facts that answer questions. Often, they must communicate through a legislator's staff or assistants.

Facts must be presented in a truthful, straightforward, and helpful fashion. Honesty is essential because credibility is the lobbyist's most important asset. As Walter Guzzardi writes in *Fortune:* "Without credibility, try suicide."[19] Lobbyists who have achieved credibility come to be relied upon by

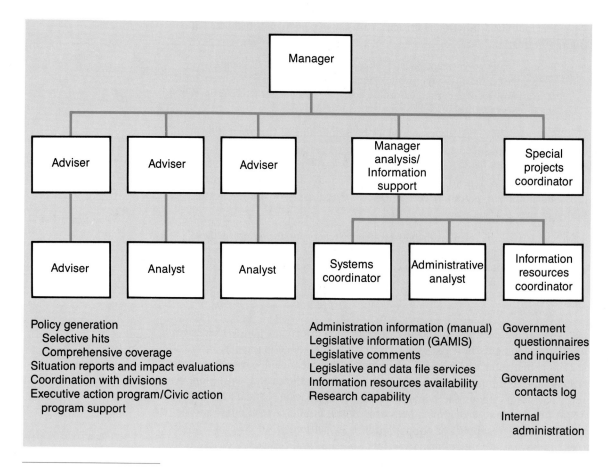

Figure 15.3 Atlantic Richfield's government relations coordination and policies

senators, representatives, and their staffs. When such relationships are established, the lobbyist is in a position to suggest legislation, prepare speeches, line up witnesses for congressional hearings, and provide research and position papers. Under such circumstances, it is difficult to tell where legislator leaves off and lobbyist begins.

Lobbying activities are carefully organized and integrated into corporate planning. Figure 15.3 shows the staff organization of Atlantic Richfield's Washington office.

Perhaps even more important than establishing the order of the staff is establishing an order of issues. Legislative battles must be carefully chosen and related to the overall objectives of the corporation. Table 15.2 shows an Atlantic Richfield governmental issues list. It clearly establishes priorities and responsibilities for the Washington staff.

Table 15.2 Governmental Issues List—Atlantic Richfield

Environmental/Transportation Cluster

Adviser 1/Analyst 1

Priority 1	*Priority 2*	*Priority 3*
Clean Air Vessel Safety Coastal Zone Management Coastal Commissions State Energy Policy State Lands Commissions National Energy Policy (Conservation Aspects)	Land Use Consumer Communications Reform Act Air Resources Boards Utility-type Regulations Utility Rates Pacific Northwest (Coastal Zone Management, Tankers, Supply) Economic Planning Full Employment Facilities Sitting Other Selected State Regulatory Issues/Responses Energy Conservation Water Quality	Nuclear Fuel Assurance, Nuclear Power Deepwater Ports General Environmental and Conservation Issues Safe Drinking Water Solid Waste Disposal Noise Pollution Lobbying Reform Campaign Contributions and Reform National Health Insurance

Resources/Tax Cluster

Adviser 2

Priority 1	*Priority 2*	*Priority 3*
North Slope Crude Pricing West Coast Crude Disposition Surface Mining (Coal) Natural Gas Pricing Outer Coastal Shelf Issues Trans Alaska Pipeline System Rate Base National Energy Policy Import/Export Policy Alaska State Tax	Mineral Leasing Act Alaska Gas Pipeline Synfuel Loan and Subsidies Naval Petroleum Reserve #4 Development Federal Oil and Gas Company Variations Amendments to Emergency Petroleum Allocation Act Antitrust Improvements	Strategic Reserve Implementation Miscellaneous Chemical Issues Federal Energy Projects—Revenue Sharing Law of Sea International Energy Agency Miscellaneous Synthetic Fuel Issues

Adviser 3

Priority 1	*Priority 2*	*Priority 3*
State Regulatory Agencies Taxation (General) FEA Related items Energy Information Crude/Product Decontrol	FTC Litigation Liaison Property Tax (Split Roll) State Taxes Investment Tax Credit Tax Equity Act of 1977 Gasoline Tax and Mass Transit Severance Taxes Windfall Profit and Plowback	Ad Valorom Taxes Social Security Capital Formation

Continued on next page

Table 15.2 *Continued*

Corporate Issues Marketing Cluster

Adviser 4/Analyst 2

Priority 1	Priority 2	Priority 3
Franchise Legislation	Common Situs	Sunset and Sunrise in Government
—Dealer Day in Court	Self-Serve Restrictions	Consumer Protection
—Mandatory Rack Pricing	Octane Posting	Copyright
—Company Operation	Marine Cargo Preference	Employee Stock Option Plans
Restrictions	FTC Retail Credit Consent Decree	Arts and Humanities
Joint Ventures	Board of Director Composition	Code of Conduct—Multinationals
Divestiture	—Interlocking Directorships	Government Reorganization
—Horizontal	—Public Members	Workers' Compensation
—Vertical	—Employee Representation	ERISA Regulations
—Marketing	Federal Corporate Chartering	Black Lung Benefit
Toxic Substances	Anti Boycott	
National Oil Pollution	Questionable Corporation Payments	
Liability and Compensation		
Act		
Slurry Pipeline		
Bulk Plants		
Right to Privacy		

Source: Phyllis S. McGrath, *Action Plans for Government Relations* (New York: The Conference Board, 1977), 32–33. Reprinted by permission.

Politicking from the Grass Roots In a democracy, the attempt to influence government occurs in the context of public opinion and requires dealing with an audience much broader than political officials. This broader audience is reached through **grass roots lobbying** and issue advertising. "The chief weapon (for) all successful lobbies today is the mobilizing of support at the grass roots level."[20] As we have mentioned in other chapters, businesses increasingly seek to organize employees, stockholders, community leaders, and others as potent weapons in the political arena. Washington lobbyists must demonstrate that their positions are those of the congressman's constituents. To accomplish this, the constituents must be organized to make their voices heard.

According to *Business Week,* "The wedding of lobbying and PR makes sense . . . because of the increasing need to win public support for their causes."[21] Top-lobbyist Charls E. Walker maintains, "Lobbying has come to require strong grass roots efforts . . . I go to a congressman and he tells me 'You can sell me if you can sell my constituents.' "[22]

Different constituents can be mobilized to communicate in a variety of ways. The grass roots approach may consist of flooding Congress with mail or getting just the right people to call their representatives. Grass roots lobbying means establishing an organization at the local level by which support can be activated when needed. The Associated General Contractors, for instance, maintain a legislative network among their 113 chapters across the country. At least one person in each chapter personally knows his senator or representative. On one occasion, this network was invaluable in defeating a labor law reform bill.

In 1977, Penneys and Sears Roebuck asked store managers to write letters to their representatives about a bill that would increase the ability of individuals to initiate class action suits. They argued that if such suits were allowed, the courts would be jammed with irresponsible litigation which would only help gunslinging lawyers get rich off legitimate businesses. The provision was defeated. The American Bankers Association (ABA) asks congressmen which bankers they want to hear from. Then the ABA asks those bankers to transmit the ABA's position on specific legislation. The ABA has 1,200 designated contact bankers, many of whom know members of Congress, have served as campaign treasurers, or have worked on campaigns.

The most incredible aspect of grass roots lobbying is the mail it generates. Congressional mail has more than tripled in the past decade. Former House Speaker Tip O'Neill received 55,000 pieces of mail in four hours on the common situs picketing bill. As much as 50 percent of congressional staff time is devoted to constituent mail. Postal Service statistics indicate that the House of Representatives received more than 250 million pieces of mail in 1986.

If mail campaigns are to be effective, the letters have to make an impression on legislators. Letters that receive notice tend to be those written by a constituent, a local community leader, or a friend, or those dealing with a subject of particular interest to the congressman. Personal, persuasive, fact-filled letters are far more effective than canned or preprinted ones. "We are more impressed by personal correspondence than by mass produced, engineered campaigns," says former California Senator S. I. Hayakawa.

In general, letters to legislators should be brief and confined to one subject. The piece of legislation at issue should be clearly identified. Of course, the letter should be typed neatly and should follow all rules of spelling, grammar, and punctuation. When writing to a legislator, state your case positively and politely, without criticism or threats. Ask the legislator to respond by explaining his or her position. Timing is perhaps the most important factor in determining the clout of your correspondence. If the letter arrives after the vote, it is useless. Letters should be timed to arrive during the early stages of pending legislation.

Issue advertising (or advocacy advertising) is a way of taking an organization's position straight to the people, with the anticipation that they will support it politically. This kind of advertising is not new. Organized labor, private voluntary groups, governmental agencies, and others have long used advertising to support their positions on public issues.

Mobil Corporation is perhaps the nation's leading issue advertiser. Under its vice president of public affairs, Herbert Schmertz, Mobil pioneered corporate advocacy. The company spends $5 million annually to share its opinions on excessive government regulation, environmentalism, consumerism, nuclear power, and protectionism (Figure 15.4).

Figure 15.4 Mobil's issue advertising. (Reprinted with permission of Mobil Corporation.)

Protectionism: A persistent threat—II

What's wrong with H.R. 4800

The House-passed omnibus trade bill—H.R. 4800—is 458 pages long and quite complex. It would shift the U.S. sharply toward protectionism and away from its current emphasis on free trade. And in the fine print, it would do even more. It would attempt to extend U.S. law to sovereign foreign nations, and open the door to a federally planned economy at home.

Here are some of the bill's protectionist provisions we found most troubling:

● The bill would, under certain circumstances, weaken the President's long held discretion in trade matters and force him to impose quotas and raise tariffs, shifting the balance from negotiation to confrontation. This would soon trigger retaliation from the nations involved.

● Some provisions clearly violate the rules of the General Agreement on Tariffs and Trade, which the U.S. first signed in 1947 and which the U.S. intends to help amend and update again at international meetings beginning this fall. How much clout will this country have in treaty negotiations if its trade policies are governed by a law that is inconsistent with the treaty?

● The bill is sometimes vague, sometimes overly specific. For example, it would allow special import quotas against countries whose exports to the U.S. are 175 percent of its imports from the U.S. At present, this provision would apply only to Japan, West Germany and Taiwan. It would not answer the need to broaden those markets to U.S. exports, and thereby create jobs in the U.S. Besides, in the normal course of business, trade balances are never equal; they rise and fall in accordance with the shifting tastes and needs of both parties.

Equally onerous are those fine-print provisions guaranteed to make our trading partners wince.

For example, the bill defines as an "unreasonable" trade practice by a foreign nation the denial of collective bargaining, the absence of laws protecting child labor, and the lack of health and safety regulations. These are termed "internationally recognized workers' rights," but to the governments of many nations that trade with the U.S., the provision will doubtlessly be seen as an attempt to impose American law on their people. What do we know of worker protection in a country like China, say, where trade with the U.S. is growing and welcomed by both parties?

We're also particularly wary of provisions that open the back door to the discredited belief that government should plan the economy. The House measure would establish agencies called Industry Adjustment Advisory Groups. With members drawn from business, labor, government and public interest organizations, the groups could review the requests for help not only from companies, but also from trade associations and employee groups that say they're in trouble from foreign competition.

The groups would define the problem and provide advice on the type of federal help needed, and then monitor the industry to see that the "readjustment plan" was being followed. The bill would also create a Council on Industrial Competitiveness with subcouncils for specific industries to develop long-term strategies for those industries. In other words, whether a company said it wanted help or not, a request by an outside organization could suddenly find the company knee-deep in unwanted and unsought "advice."

For a long time, those who would restructure American society along collective lines have advocated exactly this sort of central planning. They haven't gotten very far because Americans have seen no reason to impose central government planning on their industries when even the Socialist countries are abandoning grandiose central plans in favor of free-market solutions to their economic problems.

Perhaps, for political reasons, the Senate feels it will have to pass a trade bill this year. If it does, it ought to recognize how central to America's well-being is the free flow of goods and services all over the world. To curtail America's trade is to cost Americans jobs, and punish the American economy.

But if the Senate follows the route taken by the House, the promised presidential veto would be the best trade relief we can think of.

Next: A sound trade policy for America.

Mobil®

Figure 15.5 W. R. Grace's issue advertising

So far it's just a commercial.

A few years ago, the very notion of a $2 trillion national debt seemed a bit farfetched. Today it's a fact.

And so it's not without good reason that W. R. Grace & Co. peered into the future and produced a commercial called "The Deficit Trials." An admittedly bleak scenario that has children sitting in judgment of an older generation. Ours. A generation charged with the unforgivable crimes of apathy and neglect.

If it all seems overly pessimistic, consider these projections. Consider that today's parents will leave their children a national debt of $13 trillion by the year 2000, just 14 years from now. That debt is as much as 40 times greater than the one you inherited from your parents: a $50,000 debt for every man, woman and child in the year 2000.

What's more, if nothing is done, 94.6% of total Federal personal income tax collections will be used to pay the interest—just the interest—on that staggering $13 trillion debt. The repercussions of that reality are almost unthinkable.

Fortunately, these grim possibilities are just that. Possibilities. After all, no one really knows what another generation of unchecked federal deficits will bring. But we know this much. You can change the future. To find out how you can help, write to: W. R. Grace & Co., Dept. 2017, 1114 Avenue of the Americas, N.Y., N.Y. 10036.

"The Deficit Trials" is still just a commercial. And you can keep it that way.

One step ahead
of a changing world.

Beginning in 1981 when it advertised in favor of the Reagan Administration's proposed tax cuts, W. R. Grace became another major issue advertiser. In 1985, the company kicked off a $2.6 million campaign to reduce the federal budget deficit based on the findings of the Grace Report, a study on government waste chaired by company chairman Peter Grace (Figure 15.5).

Other issue advertising efforts seem more innocuous but still serve the sponsoring organization's political goals. General Motors urges use of seat belts and attempts to ward off government efforts to make airbags mandatory. R. J. Reynolds calls for common courtesy by smokers and nonsmokers, seeking in part to stem a tide of legislation against smoking in the workplace and public buildings. Dow Chemical's use of another form of advertising is discussed in Mini-Case 15.3.

Dow Chemical's
Issue Ads

Mini-Case 15.3

The advertisement featured a college senior, capped-and-gowned at graduation ceremony. While the speaker droned on, he was daydreaming: "In two days I walk into a Dow laboratory and begin to help grow more and better grain for those kids who so desperately need it. I can't wait!"

Prime-time network television is an odd place for recruitment ads. College newspapers would target the desired audience much more effectively and cost far less than the $7.5 million Dow Chemical Company spent on TV and major magazines. What makes it stranger still is that Dow had recently laid off 2,500 workers.

In reality, Dow's production was not a recruitment ad. Its audience was not really the class of '86. The actual target audience was college graduates from the late 1960s and early 1970s. During that era, Dow was a symbol of evil to campus activists who associated the company with the firebomb ingredient napalm and the herbicide Agent Orange used in the Vietnam war.

Now that activists have matured to positions of societal influence, Dow seeks to balance lingering negative images with messages about the company's positive contributions to society. The ad campaign dealt with issues and image, not recruiting.

Regulatory Activities

In an era of governmental growth, government regulation is the area in which the most dramatic expansion has occurred. During the 1970s, twenty-two new regulatory agencies were created, including the powerful Environmental Protection Agency (EPA), the Consumer Product Safety Council (CPSC), and the Occupational Safety and Health Administration (OSHA). A total of 120 major regulatory laws were passed during the decade. Regulatory outlays rose 53 percent, while regulatory staff increased from 27,600 to 87,500 in ten years (Figure 15.6).

"We have become a government, not of laws passed by elected officials . . . but a government of regulation," claimed former Congressman Elliott H. Levitas (D-Ga.). "A Congress . . . will enact 500 laws during its two-year tenure. During that . . . time, the bureaucracies will issue 10,000 rules and regulations."[23]

Almost every facet of business activity is subject to the rules, standards, or other controls of one or more federal agencies that have the power to review, inspect, modify, or even reject the work of private industry. Robert Lane explains business's response:

> Business objects to regulation not just on economic grounds but because it challenges the manager's belief systems, questions his judgments, deprecates the importance of his role, limits his autonomy, and creates anxiety by introducing new uncertainties into an already unpredictable environment.[24]

A Conference Board study showed that the country's major corporations are seeking to reform the federal regulatory structure. Although they accept

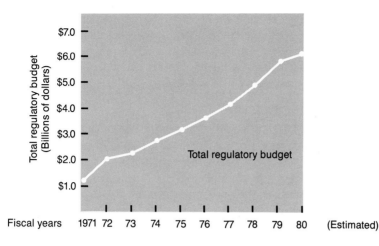

Figure 15.6 A decade of federal regulatory growth

Total regulatory budget (Billions of dollars)

$7.0
$6.0
$5.0
$4.0
$3.0
$2.0
$1.0

Total regulatory budget

Fiscal years   1971 72   73   74   75   76   77   78   79   80   (Estimated)

the need for virtually all regulatory agencies, "the vast majority of firms are demanding that companies and industries be given a larger voice in the formulation and execution of regulations."[25]

Business activities meant to affect regulation are often more the purview of the corporation's legal function than of its public relations function. The reasons for this lie in the structure of the regulatory process and in the way that opportunities for challenge or intervention present themselves. For an example, let us look at the government's attempt to develop safety standards for power mowers.

The Consumer Product Safety Commission began working on lawn mower regulation in August 1973. For six years, lawyers, economists, engineers, and technicians conducted research, oversaw oral presentations, attended public meetings, and debated foot-probe requirements and thrown-object tests. Having accumulated 35,000 pages of official record on the subject, CPSC decided to require that walk-behind power mowers be equipped with a clutch that would stop the blade three seconds after the operator let go of the handle.

The commission said this would prevent 60,000 injuries and cost $190 million per year. Of course, the industry had provided inputs during the investigative process. As soon as the CPSC published its requirements, however, the Outdoor Power Electric Institute, a trade association, sued the commission, challenging its data, conclusions, and every aspect of the proposed regulation. The Fifth Circuit Federal Appeals Court heard the case on April 1, 1980—seven years after the regulatory process had begun. Their decision was appealed.

"This saga is fairly typical of the way federal regulation works—or, to put it more accurately, doesn't work," one article stated.[26] Ultimately, regulations on lawn mower safety were not made by Congress, the president, the CPSC, or the industry. The final regulation was handed down by federal judges. In this process, public relations may prepare testimony or publicize a corporation or industry position, but the final job is usually the lawyer's.

State and Local Public Affairs

Traditionally, the most attention has been paid to interaction with government at the federal level, but the relative importance of local and state governments has recently increased for organizations of many types. While builders and developers have long sought to influence local zoning decisions, for example, the players in local and state government affairs are now more numerous and more intense.

Deregulation, federal budget cutbacks, and the Reagan Administration's determination to return government to the people have forced state and local governments to pick up the slack. As a result, state officials are now dealing more extensively with environmental issues, labor legislation, bank deregulation, and international trade. Moreover, state and local funding in the areas of the arts, transportation programs, health care, education, and others has become more critical. Naturally, both profit-seeking and not-for-profit organizations have increasingly focused on the fifty state capitals, in addition to Washington, D.C.

Covering fifty cities is much more difficult, complex, and expensive than merely focusing on Washington. In 1983–84, 250,000 bills were introduced in state legislatures. In 1983, states promulgated 50,000 regulations. In election years, 15,000 candidates seek state office. And this activity spreads from Juneau to Tallahassee and from Augusta, Maine, to Honolulu, Hawaii. California has forty state senators and eighty state assemblymen—and 765 registered lobbyists who spent $75 million trying to influence them in 1985.

When national organizations seek to influence local affairs, they must understand the local politics and culture. A major New York corporation dealing with a tax problem in a southern state got an audience with the chairman of the state senate's tax writing committee. After an informative and persuasive thirty-minute presentation, the senator asked, "Y'all aren't from around here, are you?"[27]

Steven Markowitz, a state government relations consultant, explains: "Corporate America's commitment to state government relations today is at the same point that federal government relations was in the late '60s and early '70s. The need to become more actively involved is generally acknowledged, but the organizational commitments and strategies needed to effectively deal with the issues are still emerging and taking shape."[28]

Staying on top of issues, tracking bills, knowing the right people, knowing which PACs to contribute to, cultivating the right media contacts, and all the other necessary lobbying activities may be approached in a variety of ways. In general, goals and objectives, the scope of the effort, and key states must be identified. Then the corporation or association may set up its own in-house operation, employ outside lobbyists or consultants on a retainer basis, or depend on industry or state business associations. Mini-Case 15.4 shows a situation in which national and local business interests were in conflict. The national interests, which prevailed, used a combination of in-house lobbyists and an industry association.

Despite the difficulty and expense, Markowitz says the trend is clear: "Corporations and associations will have to devote more time and resources to managing state government relations in the years ahead."[29]

Mini-Case 15.4

Dueling Gas Pumps
at the State House

The Georgia State Capitol might have been in Texas for the number of oilmen crowding its corridors in the 1984 legislative session. It was Big Oil versus Small Business over Senate Bill 48, which would prevent petroleum refiners from operating their own gas stations in Georgia.

The bill was initiated by the Georgia Association of Petroleum Retailers, an organization of gas station owners with members in every legislative district. They argued that the big oil companies were opening and operating their own discount stations. These stations would compete unfairly with independent dealers.

Explained Petroleum Retailers executive director Jack Houston: "Texaco controls Texaco products and stations. It fixes the wholesale gasoline price and the prices of other products. With Texaco controlling all those prices and then coming into the marketplace and selling gas to the public at prices far below the costs they impose on independent dealers, there's nothing left for the little guys to make a living."

Naturally, lobbyists from Big Oil saw it differently. Major oil companies maintained that they had to open their own outlets to maintain market share. Moreover, according to Richard Cobb, registered lobbyist for the Petroleum Council of Georgia, the bill would hurt the consumer by limiting competition and driving up prices. Even though Amoco did not operate any stations in the state, it sent lobbyist Jerry Hill into the fray. "We think if we make a product, we should be able to sell it if we choose," he said.

The independents had been pushing their bill for almost a decade. And with an active and coordinated lobbying effort, 1984 looked like the year it would pass. No legislator felt pressured to side with the refiners. It looked as though Big Oil would have twelve months to fold its tents and close its stores. The measure passed both houses of the Georgia General Assembly.

But as one lobbyist put it, "An awful lot of lobbyists get rich by stopping legislation. Very few get anything passed." Citing the negative impact on the consumer and his support of private enterprise, Governor Joe Frank Harris vetoed the bill. There was no effort by the legislature to override.

The Petroleum Retailers shook their heads. Just like they say about their Atlanta Braves baseball team, "Wait 'til next year."

Source: Based on Anita Sharpe, "Gas Competition Fuels Heated Debate in General Assembly," *Atlanta Business Chronicle* (9 January 1984): 1.

Internal Political
Communication

We have already discussed political action committees as a means of promoting employee and shareholder awareness and involvement. Beyond PAC activities, however, a public relations practitioner whose position requires monitoring government relations can also use in-house publications and other media to provide political instruction, increase employee awareness of political issues, and encourage employee political involvement.

Organizations stimulate employees' political awareness in a variety of ways. Bliss and Laughlin Industries of Oak Brook, Illinois, provides work sheets along with employees' W-2 forms so that they can calculate how much of their wages have gone to taxes, what percent of income goes to taxes, and how long each must work to support the cost of government. The employees have learned that their biggest expense is not shelter or food, but taxes.

Dow Chemical maintains an extensive public affairs program for employees. The program rests on four objectives:

1. Informing employees about national and local issues that potentially affect the firm.
2. Making employees aware of governmental processes and legislative procedures.
3. Encouraging employees to take part in the political process and giving specific examples of approaches they might use.
4. Advising employees of the value of political contributions and providing the opportunity to do so through political action committees.

Budd Company gives its managers a "discretionary bonus" of up to several thousand dollars based on evaluation in eleven categories, including "involvement in government affairs." Managers are judged on their ability to get their people involved in political campaigns, their willingness to write to government officials on issues affecting the company, and their ability to organize in-plant political education committees. All of these companies recognize that if business intends to remain a viable part of society, its leaders must encourage employee participation in the political process.

Does Business Conduct Its Government Relations Properly?

Some claim that American business holds inordinate political power. Undeniably, corporations possess the organization, financial resources, access, and prestige that tend to increase political effectiveness. It is important to remember, however, that business is only one of many interests seeking political favor. And indeed, from the mid-1960s through the late 1970s, businesses were notably unsuccessful in their political efforts. Moreover, as Neil Jacoby has pointed out, "At any given time, business corporations are split on many national issues; there does not appear to be a monolithic 'business interest.'"[30]

Perhaps a more serious charge is that of "crosstown estoppel," or corporate political double-talk. Corporations seriously jeopardize their positions and images when they contradict themselves. *Business Week* warned: "Companies that have made conflicting statements to federal agencies could find those contradictions coming back to haunt them," and cited the case of the Sharon Steel Corporation as an example. When the Environmental Protection Agency moved to bar the company from government contracts because of noncompliance with federal regulations, Sharon Steel claimed that the penalty was "so severe that its imposition may destroy a going business." Yet in a prospectus filed with the Securities and Exchange Commission, the company said that if blacklisted, it did "not anticipate that the resulting loss of business, if any, would have a material adverse effort on its consolidated sales or results of operations."[31]

Sharon Steel was lying to someone, and unfortunately, it is not the only company that has engaged in crosstown estoppel. Such corporate behavior gives opportunities to business's political foes, invites congressional scrutiny, and almost begs for additional regulations.

Another example of such double-talk was found when the National Association of Home Builders launched a $250,000 campaign criticizing the 1984 federal deficit. The hypocrisy of such an effort becomes evident when one considers the extent of funds flowing into federal housing and mortgage insurance programs.

Summary

The relationship between government and business has been described in many ways. Depending upon the observer's perspective, the pair are partners, adversaries, or strange bedfellows. In fact, as we have seen, the relationship is far more complex than any of these imply. It might be summed up as mutual dependence in structural terms and mutual hostility in emotional terms. The complexity and the schizoid nature of the dealings between government and business are not likely to lessen. The importance of government in the environments of business and other organizations is undeniable. For those organizations and for public relations, the public affairs challenge is clear.

▲ ▲ ▲

Case Study

Porter's Cleaners vs. OSHA, NIOSH, CPSC, and EPA

By Craig E. Aronoff
Kennesaw State College
Marietta, Georgia

John T. Porter feels surrounded. All he is trying to do is run his dry-cleaning business in Shreveport, Louisiana, but it seems like every agency in Washington is out to get him.

First, the Occupational Safety and Health Administration (OSHA) established in-plant exposure levels for the dry-cleaning solvent perchloroethylene, a chemical used in 70 percent of retail dry-cleaning plants in the United States. To comply with OSHA requirements, Porter bought expensive vapor absorbers.

Next, the National Institute of Occupational Safety and Health (NIOSH) recommended stiffer standards for perchloroethylene. If the standards were adopted, the new vapor absorbers would have to be scrapped and a different and even more expensive system installed.

But at the same time, the Consumer Product Safety Commission (CPSC) was attempting to ban perchloroethylene altogether. Based on a single test on one animal species, the CPSC claimed the substance was a possible carcinogen.

Porter would like to stop using perchloroethylene, but the only two alternative cleaning solvents in existence are both under attack by the Environmental Protection Agency (EPA).

At times, Porter feels like throwing in the towel. But he decides not to go down without a fight and calls a professional public affairs counselor for advice.

Question

1. If you were that public affairs professional, what would you recommend?

Source: Based on a statement read at the New Orleans Open Forum of the White House Conference on Small Business on December 8, 1978, by John T. Porter, president of Porter's Cleaners, Shreveport, Louisiana.

Notes

1. Neil H. Jacoby, *Corporate Power and Social Responsibility* (New York: Macmillan, 1973), 150.
2. "The Swarming Lobbyists," *Time* (7 August 1978): 15.
3. Grover Starling, *The Changing Environment of Business,* 2nd ed. (Boston: Kent Publishing Company, 1984), 95.
4. Graham Moliter, "Plotting the Patterns of Change," *Enterprise* (March 1984): 4.
5. Starling, *Changing Environment of Business,* 96.
6. Ibid., 516.
7. *Forbes* (2 January 1984): 28.
8. R. C. Born, "Corporate CIA: In Washington, It Helps to Meet Business's Need to Know," *Barron's* (19 March 1979).
9. Edward M. Epstein, "An Irony of Electoral Reform," *Regulation* (May/June, 1979).
10. Maria E. Recio, "Cash Machines for Women Candidates," *Business Week* (27 October 1986): 86.
11. Epstein, "An Irony," 5.
12. Edie Fraser, *PACs: The Political Awakening of Business* (Washington, D.C.: Fraser/Associates, 1980), 2.
13. Ibid., 15.
14. Starling, *Changing Environment of Business,* 531.
15. *USA Today* (2 September 1986): 4A.
16. "The Swarming Lobbyists," 17.
17. Starling, *Changing Environment of Business,* 538.
18. "The Swarming Lobbyists," 22.
19. Walter Guzzardi, "Business Is Learning How to Win in Washington," *Fortune* (27 March 1978): 55.
20. "The Swarming Lobbyists," 17.
21. Christine Dugas, "Now, Madison Avenue Runs Straight to Capitol Hill," *Business Week* (4 August 1986): 27–28.
22. Ibid., 28.
23. Elliot H. Levitas, "Bureaucracy Stifling America's Right to Self-Govern," *Atlanta Business Chronicle* (9 June 1980): 4.
24. Robert E. Lane, *The Regulation of Businessmen: Social Conditions of Government Economic Control* (New Haven: Yale University Press, 1954).
25. Alan Jenks, "Memos," *Atlanta Business Chronicle* (2 June 1980).
26. "Lawn Mower Regulations Taking Years to Develop," *Atlanta Journal* (5 June 1980): 28A.
27. *Parade Magazine* (9 November 1986): 8.
28. Steven Markowitz, "On the Homefront," *Public Relations Journal* (June 1986): 16.
29. Ibid., 19.
30. Jacoby, *Corporate Power,* 155.
31. "A U.S. Drive to Curb Corporate Doubletalk," *Business Week* (12 May 1980): 35.

▲ ▲ ▲

PART IV

Public Relations: The Practice

Public relations serves all types of organizations. Not-for-profit organizations and government agencies as well as corporations have embraced public relations and set it to work, recognizing it as a means of increasing organizational effectiveness in a complex and changing environment.

To operate effectively within these organizations, the public relations practitioner must be thoroughly aware of all that we have discussed to this point: the process of communication; the role of public relations in organizational decision making; the four-step public relations process; and the primary publics of public relations. Practitioners must also recognize the problems and publics that are specific to public relations in each organizational type.

In this section, we look first at the practice of public relations in three distinct types of organizations: chapter 16, not-for-profit; chapter 17, government; and chapter 18, corporations. Next, in chapter 19, we examine the legal environment that governs public relations practice. We conclude in chapter 20 with a realistic look at careers in public relations and some helpful hints for finding your first job.

▲ ▲ ▲

Public Relations in Not-for-Profit Organizations

Preview

Communication with members, government, and other publics is the bottom line for many not-for-profit organizations.

Maintaining a positive public image, fund-raising, and cost containment are crucial public relations issues facing not-for-profit organizations in general.

Membership recruitment and retention is the chief public relations objective of many associations and religious organizations.

Labor unions and trade and professional organizations sometimes prefer to work behind the scenes to influence government regulation rather than to address issues in more public forums.

Health care organizations are changing drastically. The advent of for-profit management companies and recent changes in medicare payment procedures have resulted in an emphasis on marketing and competition that has made a profound impact on public relations.

Dealing with volunteers requires more attention to motivational factors than does dealing with typical employee groups.

In elementary and secondary schools, parents, alumni, and school board members represent both internal and external publics.

The value of higher education may be the single most important public relations issue facing colleges and universities in the 1980s.

Fund-raising is a primary public relations function in most not-for-profit organizations.

There is a tremendous opportunity for practitioners who think broadly and who welcome accountability. This is not an era for communications technicians.

—Frank J. Weaver, APR
Director of Public Affairs
Cleveland Clinic Foundation

Nongovernmental organizations that do not seek to make a profit as the result of their activities are becoming more prevalent in our society. Numerous associations, societies, and labor unions promote the interests of their members and impose ethical, professional, or contractual obligations on those individuals or organizations they represent. Hospitals, religious, and volunteer organizations serve various constituent groups while relying on a broad range of support to survive. Educational institutions, both public and private, must maintain effective relationships with a variety of professional and nonprofessional publics while serving society as a whole.

Successful performance of these missions depends to a great extent on the quality of the relationships a **not-for-profit organization** is able to maintain with its publics. Fund-raising is a common problem shared by all these organizations and often becomes a priority of public relations practice.

Communication in Not-for-Profit Organizations

Communication is the primary mission of most associations, societies, unions, and religious organizations. Communication with members, government, and other groups becomes the basic product of many not-for-profit organizations. Even those with missions other than disseminating information find communication a necessary prerequisite to accomplishing their announced objectives. Hospitals, charities, and educational institutions devote a great amount of time and energy to communicating ideas and soliciting volunteers and funds. We discussed in chapter 9 the need to relate public relations effectiveness to an organization's bottom line objectives. In not-for-profit organizations, the bottom line is frequently measured in terms of new and retained members, dues collected, or funds raised. Effective communication programs are generally seen as the key to success in these areas.

In a recent survey of not-for-profit organizations, the *Journal of Organizational Communication* reported that while a range of techniques are used to communicate with members, employees, volunteers, and special audiences, the most prominent are print media.[1] Publications were cited most frequently, while news releases and meetings were also mentioned. All three are traditional areas of expertise for public relations practitioners.

Not-for-profit organizations rely much more strongly on publications in their public relations efforts than do corporations. While the trend is toward greater use of new communication technologies such as management information systems, word processors, and video telephones, not-for-profit organizations have not branched into these areas as rapidly as their business counterparts have.

Table 16.1 Issues for Not-for-Profit Organizations

What are the areas of present concern facing your organization that you feel can be improved through your communication program (for your various publics)?

Areas of Concern	Times Mentioned
Organization's public image	30
Fund-raising	29
Cost containment	29
Building and maintaining membership	25
Winning public support on issues	24
Influencing legislation action and lobbying	20
Keeping abreast of professional developments	18
Legal issues	18
Increasing public expectations	17
Labor relations	13
Reaching special audiences such as minorities, the handicapped, etc.	11
Training	10
Accountability/credibility	7
Government regulation	7
(All other items mentioned 5 times or less)	

Source: Rae Leaper, "CEOs of Nonprofit Organizations Agree: Communicate or Perish," *Journal of Organizational Communication* 4 (1980): 17. Reprinted with permission of the International Association of Business Communicators.

Formal communication programs with written goals and objectives are also less prevalent in not-for-profit organizations. In their survey, the *Journal of Organizational Communication* reported that 66 percent of the corporate chief executive officers (CEOs) responded affirmatively when asked if their organization had a formal communication plan. By comparison, only 41 percent of the CEOs of not-for-profit organizations responded positively to that question.[2]

The survey also revealed a distinct difference between for-profit and not-for-profit organizations with regard to the issues they believed should be addressed through their communication programs. High on the corporate list of key issues were inflation and compensation, government regulation, and equal opportunity. Not-for-profit organizations pointed to maintaining a positive public image, fund-raising, and cost containment. Table 16.1 lists the areas of concern which not-for-profit organizations feel can be addressed through their communication efforts.

Public Relations in Not-for-Profit Organizations

In the same survey, not-for-profit organizations indicated that their departments charged with public relations functions were called either public relations (20 percent) or public affairs (16 percent). Of the eighty-one organizations included in the survey, 46 percent of the public relations staffs reported directly to the CEO, 19 percent to a vice president, and 20 percent to a director.

Table 16.2 Size of Not-for-Profit Public Relations Staffs

What is the size of your communication staff?

Staff Size	Times Mentioned
One	3
Two	3
Three	4
Four	13
Five	6
Six	2
Seven	2
Eight	3
Nine	4
Ten	3
More than ten	29

Note: The numbers indicate the actual number of times a particular response was mentioned in relation to the following audiences: members or volunteers, the public, employees, and other specific groups.

Source: Rae Leaper, "CEOs of Nonprofit Organizations Agree: Communicate or Perish," *Journal of Organizational Communication* 4 (1980): 16. Reprinted by permission.

The size of public relations staffs varies as widely as the size of the organizations themselves. It should be noted from Table 16.2, however, that 35 percent of the organizations surveyed reported staffs exceeding ten persons.

Despite differences in application, public relations is alive and well in not-for-profit organizations. In fact, it could be argued that public relations is the business of many not-for-profit organizations. While the salaries for practitioners in these organizations have traditionally been lower than those in corporations, they have improved dramatically. Another recent survey, conducted by a major communication consulting firm, showed that the median salary for the top public relations position in the not-for-profit organizations studied was in excess of $48,000 per year.[3]

We will discuss the differences and opportunities specific to certain types of not-for-profit organizations in the remainder of this chapter.

Public Relations in Associations and Unions

Labor unions and the various trade or professional associations have one important factor in common: membership. Representing the interests of members to a number of different publics is the business of these not-for-profit organizations. Recruitment and retention of members is also a major function. Therefore, publics for unions and associations can be divided into two groups: members and nonmembers.

Member publics must be constantly kept informed about new developments in their field or area of interest. Nonmember publics must be told about the importance of the group to society and the benefits of following its recommendations. Many associations and all labor unions mount strong efforts to influence local, state, and federal legislation. While membership may be the single most important factor all these organizations have in common, it also accounts for their diversity.

Associations and Societies

Associations can be divided into two categories: professional and trade. Professional associations such as the Public Relations Society of America and those listed in Exhibit 16.1 work to enhance the public image of the profession and disseminate knowledge among the membership and to society at large. In addition, many professional associations establish legal and ethical requirements for practice and certify the proficiencies of practitioners.

Some of the Different Trade and Professional Associations

Exhibit 16.1

American Bar Association

American Dental Association

American Management Association

American Library Association

American Institute of Architects

American Association of University Professors

American Society of Association Executives

American Society for Personnel Administration

American Society for Training and Development

American Home Economics Association

Canadian Home Economics Association

Canadian Nurses Association

Credit Union Executives Society

Music Educators National Conference

National Association of Realtors

National Secretaries Association

Women in Communications, Inc.

Young Presidents Organization

National Association of Manufacturers

Retail Council of Canada

Texas Motor Transportation Association

Agricultural Institute of Canada

American Hospital Association

American Hotel and Motel Association

American Iron and Steel Institute

American Bankers Association

Canadian Bankers Association

Canadian Pulp and Paper Association

International Association of Chiefs of Police

National Association of Home Builders

National Industrial Recreation Association

The public relations function of an association is complicated considerably when it plays the dual roles of advocate and regulator for a professional group. Besides professional associations, many learned societies, such as the International Communication Association or the Academy of Management, promote a field of knowledge without exercising any regulatory powers. Members of these organizations are individuals or organizations involved in research, practice, or teaching in the field. Learned societies for the most part do not employ public relations professionals.

Trade associations primarily represent organizations that produce a common product or service. Sometimes trade associations enforce ethical and legal standards, such as the television and radio codes established by the National Association of Broadcasters. More frequently, they promote products or services and attempt to affect legislation and government regulations for the benefit of their members.

Sometimes trade association efforts are perceived as working against the broader interests of society. For example, the American Dairy Association conducted a massive television, radio, and print media campaign advertising milk as "the perfect food." After the campaign was in full swing, it was widely reported that drinking milk could in fact pose a threat to some individuals, primarily members of several minority groups who lack an enzyme necessary to digest milk products. The Dairy Association and its member cooperatives were suddenly in the position of promoting a product that could be harmful to minority children.

Association Diversity   Many associations and societies are divided into local, state, national, and sometimes international levels. Frequently, each level has a separate staff. Table 16.3 divides associations and societies into categories by purpose. While such statistics demonstrate the various types of associations, the diversity that exists among the members of broad-based groups is not apparent. For example, the National Rifle Association has become well known for its opposition to gun control laws, but not all its members support these efforts. This reality has caused criticism and even loss of membership within the organization. Member organizations within a trade association may range from small family businesses to giant conglomerates. Obviously, these organizations will not see all issues the same. Public relations skills must therefore be used within associations to retain members, ensure that all points of view are represented, and build consensus.

Table 16.3 Special Interest Groupings of U.S. Associations

Type of Association	Percentage of Total
Trade	22%
Culture	9.8
Health or welfare	9.2
Education	7.8
Scientific, technical, religious, agricultural and other specialties	43.7

Source: William H. Jones. "Trade Associations Flourish," *Washington Post* (July 4, 1976), F-1.
Reprinted by permission.

Figure 16.1 Sample association publications

Public Relations Practices   Some associations take very aggressive action to promote the interests of their members (Figure 16.1). Many, like the American Dairy Association, spend millions of dollars on advertising. The Grocery Manufacturers of America bought time and space to inform consumers about the percentage added to the rising costs of food by growers, shippers, wholesalers, and retailers. The Toy Manufacturers of America have also spent considerable sums to increase consumer confidence in the safety of their members' products.

Other organizations prefer to work behind the scenes to promote the welfare of their members. Frequently, they attempt to influence legislation and regulation. Lobbying has become a major activity of associations ranging from the American Medical Association to the National Association of Homebuilders. Many organizations maintain offices in Washington, D.C., as well as in some state capitals to support their continuous efforts to influence lawmakers and government officials.

At times, lobbying efforts exceed legal limits. During the Nixon administration, three of the country's largest dairy cooperatives were convicted of making illegal campaign contributions in exchange for higher milk price supports.[4] Public relations professionals must be able to advise policy makers concerning the possible damage such activities may do to an association's image, whether the action is technically legal or not. Chapter 15 discusses more thoroughly the role of public relations in influencing government.

Communicating with members occupies the time of professionals in many associations. The need to attract new members and retain current ones is a constant problem facing most organizations of this type. The majority of their budgets and professional talent may therefore be spent on association meetings and publications. Of course, large associations can afford to engage in membership recruitment, lobbying, advertising, and other activities simultaneously.

According to the Public Relations Society of America, practitioners in professional and trade associations can expect to participate in the following activities:

Preparing and distributing news and informal material to the press, radio, and television.

Preparing and disseminating technical and educational materials (publications, motion pictures, and audiovisual aids) to other publics.

Sponsoring conventions, meetings, educational seminars, and exhibitions.

Maintaining government relations, including interpreting the legislative and administrative actions of government agencies in terms of members' interests.

Compiling and publishing business and industry statistics.

Sponsoring public service activities (such as health or safety matters).

Preparing and enforcing codes of ethics or professional standards.

Conducting cooperative research (scientific, social, and economic).

Issuing institutional and/or product advertising to better acquaint various publics with the products or services represented.

Most of these activities underscore two basic values and functions of the association in American economy and society. First, they provide a means of *experience sharing* by individuals and entities engaged in the same activity or having a common interest. The benefits of this shared experience accrue to all members and might otherwise be unobtainable. Second, they make possible, through voluntary, cooperative support, beneficial programs that in most instances could not be undertaken by individual companies or persons. Many medical, engineering, scientific, technological, and social advances affecting the lives of all Americans exist only because of such programs.[5]

Labor Unions

In many ways, the role of public relations in a labor union is a great deal like its role in professional or trade associations. Communicating with current members, recruiting new members, and influencing legislation and regulation are all objectives of labor unions. The public relations professional, therefore, will be involved with union publications, news releases, and lobbying efforts. Some unions, such as the International Ladies' Garment Workers, have undertaken campaigns to encourage consumers to buy products with the union label.

For the most part, however, unions have avoided public discourse in favor of lobbying efforts and member communication. These tactics have made the labor movement, which represents less than 20 percent of the country's work force, the major voice of working people in the United States.

While the voice of labor is powerful in political circles, its popularity with many publics has suffered in recent times. Economic problems such as inflation and trade deficits have been blamed on organized labor. Public opinion surveys consistently place labor unions last among institutions holding the public's confidence.[6]

The continued decline in the percentage of the unionized work force, unions' losses of political power, and the fact that union raises have lagged behind those of the non-union work force in recent years, suggest that labor unions may be facing a crisis. But sensitivity to public opinion does not appear to be spreading fast in the labor movement. In 1986, striking pilots refused to settle a contract dispute with Frontier Airlines even though it meant the demise of the company.

Unions have traditionally looked to their own ranks for professional services. Frequently, individuals responsible for public relations policy in organized labor have been promoted from the rank and file with little or no formal training in the field. This practice appears to be changing, however, and more professionals are being employed by unions. As a result, the aversion of labor unions to broader public discourse may also change.

The International Ladies' Garment Workers Union has been active in public relations efforts to support U.S. products.

Hospital and Health Care Public Relations

Hospital public relations, like all other aspects of hospital administration, is a relatively new field. Not many years ago, professional managers in hospitals were very rare. Hospitals were typically managed by a board of physicians, with one named as director. These physicians gave more attention to patient care than to details of administration. As hospitals became larger and more complex, managerial duties were turned over to professionally trained administrative personnel. As hospital management became increasingly professional, the need for public relations practitioners was perceived and met.

The Volatile Health Care Industry

Until recently, the vast majority of health care delivery systems in the United States were nonprofit organizations operated by government, charity, and religious organizations. However, today, for-profit management companies such as HUMANA, AMI, and Hospital Corporation of America have become major factors in the health care field. Although these organizations are profit-seeking corporations, they are discussed here because they have many similarities to their not-for-profit counterparts and their differences are most efficiently discussed through direct contrast.

The trends toward professional management and for-profit corporations are being fed by three major changes in the health care field which have special significance to the practice of public relations. First, the federal government has changed its method of payment to health care providers; second, competition has increased dramatically; and third, marketing has become the watchword of the industry.

DRGs have made a fundamental change. In 1983, the federal government decided to reimburse health care service providers under Medicare in a totally new way. Ailments were placed in categories called Diagnostic Related Groups (DRGs) with set fees for treatment. Therefore, if a DRG# 72 appendectomy has a set price of $1,000, the hospital receives that amount regardless of its actual cost.[7] Because the federal government is the single largest purchaser of medical services, this change revolutionized the health care industry. Suddenly, there were incentives for cost savings that had never been present before. This situation increased the demand for professional managers in these organizations and injected a new word into the vocabulary of health care: *competition.*

New delivery systems have increased competition. Hospitals not only compete among themselves for patients, but must also contend with a growing number of alternative delivery systems. In 1984, hospital occupancy levels dropped to an all-time low as health maintenance organizations (HMOs), surgicenters, and other ambulatory care facilities took a share of the market once controlled by a few nonprofit hospitals. These alternative delivery systems have been successful in cutting costs and marketing their services to prospective patients directly rather than going through physicians.

Marketing has become a dominant force. As a result of the increased competition in the health care field, marketing is now viewed as the key to survival. Markets are being segmented, and new products and services are being introduced as never before.

The marketing push in health care has focused on communication and promotion. This has significantly raised the value of public relations and has presented many new challenges to its practitioners. Many public relations practitioners are now being called upon to administer their health care organizations' marketing programs. Staffs are growing as an increasing new array of skills are demanded.

However, this boom also has its downside. Marketing and public relations managers are locked in heated combat in many health care organizations over who will control the communication function. Some public relations professionals have been called upon to manage a complete range of communications programs including advertising and other consumer-oriented material. In hospitals, the lines between public relations and marketing will continue to blur.

Hospitals, nursing homes, convalescent care centers, HMOs, emergency care clinics, and all other health care organizations have been caught in the bind of rising patient expectations for services. A quick review of recent trends in malpractice law shows that health care organizations and their employees are coming under increased criticism in relation to the services they provide.

No one disputes the fact that health care has improved phenomenally over the past twenty-five years. Health care practices that were considered advanced only a few years ago are now obsolete. Yet, scientific, technological, and clinical advances have in fact contributed to the problems of health care

Figure 16.2 Sample pages from a hospital publication. (Used with permission of Hendrick Medical Center Foundation, Abilene, Texas.)

organizations. Because the state of the art changes so rapidly, hospitals and other organizations are under constant pressure to update their services. The same publics who call for continuous updating, however, are shocked by the rapid rise in costs.

It is also a fact that people today know more about their own health and the treatments available than ever before. When this factor is added to the cost/service dilemma, the credibility problems of health care organizations can be better understood. In spite of tremendous advances in the practice of medicine, physicians are no longer relied upon as completely as they once were. Today, it is not unusual for a patient to ask for a second opinion on a diagnosis or treatment—something almost unheard of only a few years ago. In this rapidly changing environment, hospitals and other health care organizations need help communicating with a variety of publics (Figure 16.2).

In simpler times, hospitals were the only source of most major medical services. Both physicians and patients had relatively little choice because hospitals were often large, centralized organizations that serviced entire geographic areas without any competition. For them, public relations merely meant basic

The Changing Nature of Health Care Publics

internal communication, a little pampering for physicians, and a strong volunteer organization. But as we have already explained, the industry, and with it the practice of public relations, has drastically changed. The following is a partial list of the various publics today's health care practitioners must understand.

Government is still a major audience for health care organizations even in this era of free enterprise. Health care facilities are regulated and licensed by local, state, and federal agencies. With more than seventeen million medicare patients and an aging population, federal government spending policies will continue to have a dramatic effect on the health care industry.

Business is a growing new market for health care organizations. As medical costs have gone up, so have the costs of employee benefits. Some estimates of after-tax profits being consumed by medical costs run as high as 24 percent. This has led business to seek new ways to cut costs, such as signing agreements for preferred provider organizations (PPOs). Thus, employee benefits managers have become an important public for health care public relations.

Nonprofessional employees in hospitals and other health care organizations are increasingly joining unions to gain better working conditions. Traditional union issues such as pay and benefits are not their only complaints. Under the administration of physicians, hospitals seemed to have little regard for employees in support areas such as housekeeping, laundry, food service, and clerical service. As a result, many of these groups have felt out of touch with the decision makers in their organizations. Only recently have health care organizations attempted to make their nonprofessional employees feel a part of the patient care team. The lingering vestiges of this negative organizational climate create a number of employee communication problems. Many hospital managers need to use all the methods of effective employee communication, with special emphasis on the needs of nonprofessionals, to overcome these problems.

Professional employees such as nurses and specialized technicians have also been turning to unionization. Like their nonprofessional coworkers, they have often felt out of touch with the decision makers in their organizations. Nurses have long complained that doctors do not recognize their professional abilities and training. Nursing organizations and schools have launched massive efforts to make physicians and patients alike aware of the expertise of nurses.

Lack of recognition for professional skills is not the only problem in dealing with health care workers. A nationwide shortage of nurses, especially in critical areas such as intensive care units, has put additional stress on the relationship between hospitals and professionals. Hospitals are beginning to respond by incorporating more opportunities for professional recognition into nursing roles. Public relations practitioners must help their organizations respond to the needs of these employees by creating effective channels of communication that recognize their professional contributions. Building new, more effective relationships between physicians and other professional as well as nonprofessional employees will ultimately lead to increased public confidence in health care organizations.

Physicians form a unique public for health care organizations that has no counterpart in most businesses. While some hospitals and health maintenance organizations have staff physicians as professional employees, most physicians are independent business persons who use the services of the institution. Doctors, therefore, represent a client group. Hospitals provide the facilities, support staff, and technology needed by physicians for their practices. In fact, many argue that doctors, rather than patients, are the real customers of hospitals.

It is frequently the physician who decides where a medical procedure will be performed—the patient has little or no voice in the decision. Thus, while patients pay the bills, their physicians determine which hospitals will get their business. Because of this, and because physicians have traditionally been highly esteemed in health care organizations, they are probably the single most powerful public of hospitals and other medical institutions.

On the other hand, physicians function in hospitals and other health care organizations in much the same way employees do. They work side by side with employees, usually in the role of supervisor or work director. Many hospital workers come to regard them as managers rather than customers. Frequently, employees take their complaints, suggestions, or questions to physicians rather than to their supervisors. This produces confusion about appropriate channels of communication and tensions between employees, administrators, and physicians.

To establish good internal communication systems in health care organizations, public relations practitioners must communicate effectively with physicians. In addition, they should realize that the accomplishments of physicians can furnish excellent publicity on a local, national, and even international scale for the hospitals where they practice. Some hospitals are now providing public relations services for their physicians.

Patients, as we have already discussed, are a unique class of consumers. Most people do not elect to enter a hospital or other health care facility. They are usually there at a physician's direction. Most hospitalized patients are unhappy to begin with, and because of their condition, may feel they have no voice in what happens to them. The hospital routine seems cold and unfeeling to patients. Many hospitals now try to respond to their patients' psychological as well as physical needs.

Numerous special publications are available to patients regarding their hospital stay, condition, and treatment. In addition, many hospitals have responded to consumer advocate group demands for a patients' bill of rights that states the choices that are available and the information patients can request. Hospitals also have special teams of nurses to educate patients and their families in health care. Some hospitals now communicate with their patients through video programming, using closed-circuit television systems already in place.

Volunteers are an important part of the operation of most hospitals and nursing homes. Volunteers are typically motivated by compassion or by a sense of civic and/or organizational pride. Most health care centers rely upon organized groups to provide the volunteers they need. These groups may serve only one institution or may offer their services to many. Public relations practitioners are frequently responsible for establishing workable communication links with these organizations, keeping their leaders informed about what types of services are needed and where extra personnel can be accommodated.

In addition, volunteers must be able to see the results of their work and realize that the administration, professional staff, physicians, and patients appreciate their help. Maintaining effective communication channels with a number of different groups (and perhaps hundreds of individuals) becomes a major public relations effort.

Even though public relations plays an obviously important role in health care organizations, the number of full-time practitioners employed is still rather low. However, as the professionalization of health care administration increases, the opportunities for public relations professionals in these organizations will likely increase also. Public relations practitioners are needed to advise administrators and professional employees in a variety of matters involving internal, community, and media relations.

Public Relations in Religious and Volunteer Organizations

Churches and other religious and charitable organizations depend upon positive public images for their very lives. Most have relatively few employees and must rely on volunteer labor. The vast majority are funded solely by contributions from their members, public fund-raising drives, and/or philanthropic gifts. Public relations is an important part of the day-to-day operation of these organizations, but only the largest employ full-time practitioners.

Religious Organizations

The goals of most religious organizations require a great many activities that can be considered public relations. Churches and synagogues must communicate with their memberships as well as with local and even national publics regarding doctrinal and social issues. In the early 1970s, decline in church membership and rising prices forced many of the larger protestant organizations to cut back their mission operations and staffs. This led some denominations to realize their need for professional help in public relations.

Recently, a number of religious organizations have begun to expand their communication activities, especially those involving mass media. Some of these organizations have been able to exert considerable influence. The Moral Majority, a conservative group of fundamentalist protestant churches, became active in the 1980 presidential elections and is widely believed to have been instrumental in the election of Ronald Reagan. Other organizations, such as the church in Mini-Case 16.1, have found that public relations skills and techniques can help better accomplish their traditional missions.

Mini-Case 16.1

Advocacy Advertising for a Church in Trouble

An Episcopal Church in Minneapolis, Minnesota, found that techniques borrowed from corporate advocacy advertising campaigns could turn a dying congregation around. Their first set of ads was so successful that they prepared a second campaign as follow-up messages.

The Episcopal Ad Project sold about two hundred sets of ads nationwide to other churches of several denominations. "They just stuck their own name in place of ours," said the Rev. George Martin, pastor of St. Luke's Episcopal Church.

St. Luke's was a shrinking church in a shrinking town when it decided to advertise itself—to "break out of the church advertising mold of just the sermon topic and time of services," Martin said. The project came up with ads that brought in both new church members and national awards.

"Now, we're a congregation with a good mix of three hundred families and growing in a city that lost 100,000 people over the past few years," Martin said. The first ads were aimed at "what people are doing on Sunday morning. . . . They had striking visuals like a line drawing of Dante's Inferno with short messages."

The church placed the ads in neighborhood newspapers.

The new set of four ads is aimed at people who "seem to fear any religious involvement, worrying they might turn into some kind of religious fanatic," or will lose themselves in church trappings, he said.

One of the ads shows a picture of Jesus with the caption: "He died to take away your sins. Not your mind."

Perhaps the most striking of the new ads again concerns television religion, raising the question: "Have you ever seen a Sony that gives Holy Communion?"

Martin said that while researching the new set of ads, "We were also concerned with what was happening to young people involved with some of the cults." The resulting ad notes: "There's only one problem with religions that have all the answers. They don't allow questions."

Some approaches
employed by the Episcopal
Ad Project.

He died to take away your sins. Not your mind.

You don't have to stop thinking when you walk into
an Episcopal Church. Come and join us in an atmosphere where
faith and thought exist together in a spirit of fellowship.
The Episcopal Church

The Episcopal Church welcomes you. Regardless of race, creed, color or the number of times you've been born.

Whether you've been born once or born again, the Episcopal Church invites you to come
and join us in the fellowship and worship of Jesus Christ.
The Episcopal Church

Is the Me Generation doing to Christianity what the lions failed to do?

If you think it's time people started thinking less about their own self fulfillment
and more about the needs of others, come and join us in the fellowship of the Episcopal Church.
The Episcopal Church

With all due regard to TV Christianity, have you ever seen a Sony that gives Holy Communion?

If TV Christianity makes you want to switch channels, come and join us this Sunday in
Christian fellowship and worship without commercial interruptions. **The Episcopal Church**

Tom McElligott, Jr., of the Minneapolis office of the national advertising firm of
Bozell and Jacobs, worked on the ads, saying it was part of the free public service
work "we feel we should do."

The number of public relations practitioners employed in churches, synagogues, and other religious organizations is still very small. However, the fact that the church is no longer the center of local communities and cannot automatically count on large weekly attendance means that things may have to change. Indeed, the following examples indicate a new era of religious communication:

Baptist Press, the Southern Baptist Convention's news service for secular media, packages and distributes the work of five bureaus, as well as material supplied by paid stringers, the staffs of thirty-four Baptist state papers, and some 350 public relations employees.

The Church of Jesus Christ of Latter-Day Saints (Mormon) has a well defined and organized communication function. The managing director of communication and special affairs supervises a public affairs, operations, and special affairs unit. Public affairs handles the writing, production, and placement of print and broadcast messages as well as media relations. The operations unit manages the local public relations efforts performed by approximately 1,400 volunteers at ward levels, and the special affairs unit maintains legislative relations and contacts with other groups.[8]

Volunteer Groups

It has been estimated that some 500,000 gift-supported organizations other than hospitals, churches, and colleges exist in the United States.[9] Most of these organizations depend for their survival upon gifts of time and expertise as well as money.

Unfortunately, volunteers, like church members, can no longer be taken for granted. As families move so frequently that they never become a permanent part of any community and more and more women enter the work force, volunteerism is declining in the United States. Although volunteers are still an important factor in the life and economy of many organizations, their future is uncertain.[10] To continue attracting volunteers in the numbers necessary to carry out their programs, organizations will need to take innovative approaches in communicating with their publics.

While their full-time staffs are relatively small, volunteer organizations present an excellent opportunity for public relations students to gain experience. Volunteers with communication and other public relations skills are always needed, and the problems to be dealt with are good preparation for full-time careers.

The following are just a few of the many large volunteer organizations in the United States:

American Heart Association	Sierra Club
American Cancer Society	Salvation Army
American Lung Association	Girl Scouts of America
American Red Cross	Boy Scouts of America
American Humane Association	Junior Achievement
Advertising Council	YMCA
March of Dimes	YWCA

Anyone who doubts the need for public relations practice in the administration of elementary and secondary schools today needs only to glance at the headlines. School bond issues are being voted down, teachers are striking, graduates are suing schools because they cannot read, parents are demanding that curricula return to the "basics," students and teachers are being attacked in the classrooms. . . . The list of problems in our schools could go on. Most large school districts now realize that part of their responsibility as publicly-funded agencies is to keep taxpayers and other publics informed about their operations.

In some communities, few issues are as volatile as those relating to the public schools. The recent history of busing and other issues related to desegregation of the public schools has proven in every region of the country that changes in the schools can result in catastrophic social upheaval. Any issue that affects public schools is likely to affect large segments of the community; even people who do not have school-age children have an interest in the school system because their taxes support it and it is a focus of civic pride and concern. Most people in our society feel they have a right to know and have a voice in what goes on in the public schools. As the educational level of society continues to rise, more and more people feel they have not only the right, but also the qualifications to express their opinions concerning every phase of public education.

Some of the many publics that must be addressed by public relations efforts in the educational environment are:

Internal
- Teachers
- Students
- Local school administrators
- Other employees
- Parents

External
- Alumni
- School board members
- Taxpayer advocate groups
- Service and civic clubs
- Local business and industry leaders
- School neighbors
- Churches and religious organizations
- Athletic boosters
- Legislators
- Local, state, and federal government agencies
- Teachers' organizations and unions

While each of these publics affects schools in a variety of ways, certain groups are of particular importance and must receive special attention.

Teachers have become a well-organized and influential force in many areas of the country. Teachers' unions and professional organizations are concerned with every phase of public school operation. These groups also exert influence with other publics such as legislators, government agencies, and parents. The political nature of public school administration and the enormous size of many school districts have strained the naturally cooperative relationship that should exist between teachers and administrators. With every segment of the population demanding a greater voice in what goes on in the classroom, many teachers feel deprived of authority. Like other employee groups, teachers have increasingly turned to unions to gain a voice in what happens where they work. Any effective public relations effort in a school district must recognize the importance of the professional input teachers can offer and take appropriate steps to bring them into the communication system.

Students, even at the elementary and secondary school level, have become more active and vocal. Various student groups have demanded a greater voice in the decisions that affect their educational environment. Individual students have brought suit against school districts over policies they considered discriminatory or unreasonable. Public relations efforts must be designed to inform students about the reasoning behind decisions that affect them. In order to be responsive to student needs, however, school public relations programs must be able to assess student opinion and reaction to decisions before they are made.

Parents function as both internal and external publics. Because of their intense interest in everything that affects their children, parents are frequently as knowledgeable as students about school events. Many parents become volunteer workers in their local schools through the parent-teacher organization or other programs. They often feel as involved in the school as the staff does, but because they do not take part full-time, they do not directly participate. Teacher organizations are quick to point out the necessity for parental cooperation in providing good education. Public relations programs must be designed to win parental approval and cooperation in a team effort to educate children.

Residents of the school district are concerned about public school operations even if they do not have children who attend school. The quality and reputation of local schools have a great deal of influence on the property values of a community. In addition, the preparation of young people to become productive citizens of our society is an issue that affects everyone. School public relations programs must be sensitive to the impact of their efforts outside the classroom. Those who pay taxes and vote on school bond issues must be kept informed about the needs, concerns, and contributions of local schools.

Higher Education   The practice of public relations is well established in higher education. Colleges and universities, both public and private, have long understood the necessity to cultivate favorable public opinion. The Council for Advancement and Support of Education (CASE), a national organization concerned with public relations, alumni relations, and fund-raising, goes back to 1917.

In spite of its long history, however, public relations in higher education may be facing its most difficult era. The student activism of the 1960s brought numerous changes to college and university operations. Curricula were changed to meet the interests of politically and socially active students. Rules and entrance requirements were relaxed due to student pressure. By the mid-1970s, students were changing and so were their expectations of higher education. Many found that the reforms of the 1960s were no longer relevant. The question was raised as to whether or not a college education was really worth the time, effort, and expense involved.

Books such as Caroline Bird's *The Case Against College* pointed out that many college graduates were not trained in fields where they could find jobs.[11] During the same period, two researchers at the Massachusetts Institute of Technology published the results of their analysis of college as an investment, concluding that the economic status of college graduates was deteriorating.[12] At about the same time, colleges and universities were experiencing a decline in enrollments due to slowed birthrates and other factors.

This situation was further complicated by the pressures on state government to increase funding for highways, social services, mass transportation, and other important services. Funding of public colleges and universities has in many instances been reduced, and this in turn has put demands on private institutions. Colleges and universities have faced funding reductions, cutbacks in curricula, and even layoffs of tenured faculty. In 1985–86, when the price of oil caused tax revenues to drop in Texas, higher education absorbed large portions of the resulting state budget cuts.

Higher education has begun to respond to these pressures by offering new career-oriented degree programs. In addition, colleges have started looking for students other than the traditional eighteen-year-old high school graduate. Both degree offerings and non-degree continuing education programs have been expanded to meet the needs of students in all age ranges. Higher education has become a lifelong process instead of a brief training period. Continuing to meet the needs of a changing society without sacrificing quality will be the toughest challenge faced by colleges and universities in the late 1980s and early 1990s. Public relations practitioners must help institutions of higher learning communicate their changing programs and needs to a changing audience. Some of these varied publics are:

Internal
{
Students
Faculty
Administrators
Alumni
Parents
Trustees

External
{
Federal government agencies
State government agencies
State legislators
Professional associations and learned societies
Accrediting agencies
Textbook publishers
Business and industries which employ graduates
Local community

In the 1980s and 1990s, college and university public relations professionals will have to show justification for (1) the value of a college education, (2) increased faculty workloads, and (3) their institutions' importance to economic development through teaching and research.

Exhibit 16.2

A Profile of One University's Public Relations Function

Clodus R. Smith, former vice president for university relations at Cleveland State University, described the function of his division during the 1970s as follows:

> Cleveland State University is a maturing institution of higher education which has a rare opportunity for interaction with a cosmopolitan urban community. In its pursuit of excellence, the University stresses its commitment to the community by sharing traditional and innovative programs of instruction, research, and service. In return it asks for public understanding, acceptance, and support.
>
> Basic to the University's need for understanding and support are effective channels of communication between the institution and its many publics. To this end, the Cleveland University Division of University Relations was created and given the responsibility for representing the University in matters of governmental regulations, development, and alumni and community relations. The Division met its responsibility by interacting with these publics, informing them about the University's aspirations and accomplishments, and providing feedback on their reaction.

Cleveland State University's plan for university relations, formulated in the 1970s, became a model for other colleges and universities.

DIVISION OF UNIVERSITY RELATIONS

Concept

The Division of University Relations, as the interpreter of Cleveland State University policies and programs, is responsible for informing the University's many publics of the institution's programs, activities, achievements, and needs. The Division provides a planned communications link through a comprehensive program of activities conducted by the departments of Development, Graphic Services, University and Community Relations, and the Office of Governmental Relations.

The guiding principles which generate the goals and objectives of the Division recognize the qualities of effective leadership needed to improve the image and stature of the University, the need to present to its many constituencies the perspective of the institution as a sound investment worthy of public trust and private support, and the essential nature of involving members of the academic community in the University's quest for excellence.

The Division provides the supportive environment which unifies, motivates, and guides its several units toward successful achievement of University and Division goals and objectives.

Goal

To create an environment which fosters understanding, confidence, and respect between the University and its diverse publics and which will facilitate the fulfillment of the institution's mission and gain support for its academic, research, and service programs.

Objectives for 1976-1977

Develop and expand the capabilities of each of the Division's administrative officers and increase through education the abilities and effectiveness of professional staff members to further enhance the credibility and integrity of the Division and the acceptance of its functions by the University community.

Improve the administration of and expand the University's development programs.

Conduct a study of publications programs at comparable institutions and recommend changes as determined by the findings of the study.

Initiate additional community programs, establish new communication channels, review publications and recommend changes to increase their effectiveness in promoting a positive image of Cleveland State University.

Lead Division staff to create, accept, and apply more effective indices of measurement to evaluate the productivity of each department, office, and unit.

Indicators of Achievement

Valid measurement of the progress of the Division requires assessment in terms of the stated goals of the individual units it administers. The effectiveness of the administrative leadership provided by the Division can be measured quantitatively by the increased production of its offices and departments. Qualitative assessment is based on the improved techniques implemented by these units and the creativity and innovativeness of ideas generated by the professional staff as determined by public acceptance and support of these efforts.

To help his division meet its responsibility, Smith formulated a comprehensive plan for university relations that incorporated specific objectives for each subunit and measurable indicators by which their accomplishments could be determined. This program became a model for many colleges and universities and helps to illustrate the diversity of responsibility usually placed upon public relations professionals in higher education.

All not-for-profit organizations face a common problem: the recurring need to raise money to support their operations. Even public institutions such as universities and hospitals have discovered in these inflationary times that they cannot continue to develop without a source of private funds. Institutional advancement (or development) programs have become big business in the United States. A great deal of the effort of most nonprofit organizations goes toward raising the funds necessary to carry out their missions.

Frequently, the job of coordinating fund-raising efforts falls to the public relations function of an organization because of the communication expertise required. John Price Jones, a pioneer professional fund-raiser, noted that: "Fund-raising is public relations, for without sound public relations no philanthropy can live long. . . . It takes better public relations to get a man to give a dollar than it does to convince him to spend a dollar. Favorable public opinion is the basis upon which American philanthropy has been built."[13]

Successful development campaigns require close attention to many details. Because they are massive projects, organizations frequently employ professional fund-raising firms to provide counsel or even to manage the entire campaign. John W. Leslie, an international authority in fund-raising, enumerates nine steps for a successful institutional advancement program:[14]

Step 1   Identify broad objectives and policies for the institutional advancement program. In this first step, the broad objectives and governing policies should be outlined for all activities designed to advance the understanding and support of the institution. Objectives, broad and specific, are designed to assist in achieving already established institutional goals. (We are assuming, of course, that the institution has a current concrete, understood, and accepted statement of purpose and goals.) Resulting from this step is a plan with both long- and short-range objectives.

Step 2   Define relevant trends which might affect the institutional advancement program. The conscious consideration of such trends will assure that the implementation of the plan is as pertinent as possible to the existing conditions. Examples of trends and external influences which would affect elements of the program are: relations with various components of the institution's constituency, condition of the national economy and of various industries important to the particular institution, congressional and legislative attitudes, current and anticipated campus problems, etc.

Step 3   Identify specific communication and financial support activities and group them into program elements. All institutional advancement programs are composed of a number of activities through which objectives of the programs are carried out. All activities (regardless of departmental direction) should be itemized as to which are designed to communicate and ensure the financial support of the institution's educational goals. Activities may be singular and nonrecurring, such as a special event. Or they may be ongoing, such as securing and distributing institutional news.

A program element is a logical grouping of related activities established for management and budget control. A program element is administered by a director who supervises the activities and personnel within the program element.

Fund-Raising: A Common Task for Not-for-Profit Groups

Step 4   Determine the basic approach and designate the administrator for each activity within the program elements. Plan and outline, in a broad way, the purpose, basic approach, and audience emphasis of each activity within each program element. The primary concern should be determining the type (personnel, funds, etc.) and amount of resources required for each program element.

When converting to a programmatic planning and budgeting analysis (using information acquired from conventional accounting methods), managers need to keep several points in mind. Arbitrary allocation of staff time and expenditures will often have to be made for various activities. Travel, telephone, and printed materials are examples of expensive items that often serve multiple activities but are usually accounted for in lump sums.

Further, it should be expected that in the beginning, allocation estimates will be crude. The key to effective program planning and budgeting in the future is to set up procedures to validate as well as possible the initial allocation estimates. Much literature and experience is available that can give tips for keeping staff time records. For persons who divide their time among several activities, the easiest method would be to use the various activities as broad time-category headings. To repeat, procedures need to be established, but assessing the time devoted to specific activities is not difficult; in fact, it is routine among consulting firms, advertising agencies, and similar groups that provide services to a number of clients.

Each major activity should be the responsibility of one administrator. It is not always possible or desirable to limit activity administration to professional staff personnel. More than likely, one person will administer several activities, but this has been common practice in managing institutional advancement programs for some time.

Step 5   Designate a person to direct and coordinate the various activities within each program element. This step is crucial to the success of the overall program. The choice of director will depend upon:

Nature, purpose, and audience of the key activities

Principal source of funding of the key activities

Knowledge and experience deemed desirable

Management skills

Each program element director will report to the program manager concerning coordination and direction of the various activities—regardless of whom they report to in the departmental chain of command. Procedures must be established to facilitate smooth working relationships and transfer of funds (when necessary) among budget authorities.

Step 6   Establish objectives of various program elements. Program element directors, in conjunction with the program manager, should determine long- and short-range objectives for each element. Objectives should be as specific and quantitative as possible and must reflect similar objectives of other program elements.

Step 7   Review and revise various activities to conform to objectives of their respective program elements. The entire rationale for programmatic planning and budgeting is contained in this step. Undoubtedly, Step 6 will point up a number of duplications—and probably some oversights—in programming. To increase effectiveness, along with efficiency, the activities composing a program element must be streamlined. The cost of each activity in staff time and institutional funds must be assessed in relation to exact results achieved or the estimated results hoped for. Likewise, the relative merit of each activity within a program element must be analyzed. Undoubtedly, opportunities for revision (and probable elimination) of an activity will be obvious to analytical judgment. Objective scrutiny and the courage to streamline decisions are crucial management tools for successful program planning and budgeting.

Step 8   Develop revised plans for each activity with program elements. Program element directors will need to work with each activity administrator to revise and formulate new plans and procedures for the various activities composing each element. The director must make certain that objectives established by his or her particular element will be met by the sum of the results of the activities. Directors and the manager may discover that a realignment of activities would be advantageous.

Revised program element plans will need to include resources required, source of those resources, job descriptions, space requirements, time schedule, results expected, evaluation procedures, and revisions and future modifications expected in light of long-range objectives.

Step 9   Establish a control system. The control system should provide a periodic, systematic review of performance in relation to objectives. The control system is the manager's chief method of assessing progress toward objectives.

Managers must allow sufficient calendar time—not continuous time— for implementing a program planning and budgeting system. Procedures must be thoroughly tested, and personnel must understand and adjust to the new methods.

Programmatic planning and budgeting is a management tool. It should not be confused with a philosophy of management. Its strength is its flexibility, but programmatic planning does not replace imagination, intelligence, and initiative.

While no one questions the need for not-for-profit organizations to raise funds, the methods they employ can become public relations problems. **Burnout** is always possible in massive fund drives that employ mass media, direct mail, or telephone communication channels. Another issue that can cause adverse public reaction is the percentage of the funds raised that are spent on the campaign itself. Some national campaigns cost as much as 25 percent of the

Fund-Raising as a Public Relations Problem

total funds raised. Unfavorable publicity about campaign costs can hurt future efforts for all organizations that depend on public generosity. Most professional fund-raising organizations advise that costs not exceed 12 to 15 percent of the amount raised.

Summary

Not-for-profit organizations by their very nature rely on public relations for their survival. In spite of this fact, many of these organizations have been slow to develop the public relations function within their professional staffs. Increasingly, however, the realization of the necessity for more consistency in their relationships with various publics is causing many not-for-profit organizations to expand their public relations efforts.

The Children Were Waiting

By James W. Anderson
*Department of Advertising
and Public Relations
University of Florida
Gainesville, Florida*

▲ ▲ ▲

Case Study

The Cook County, Illinois, regional office of the Illinois Department of Children and Family Services was desperate. It needed immediately some six hundred volunteer families to open their homes to wards of the state.

The courts were placing increasing numbers of children, from newborns to teenagers, in the department's custody. Tragically, at the time, private and religious orphanages and other institutions on which the agency had depended over the years were closing down and refusing, for financial reasons, to take in any more wards of the state.

Wards of the state are children who have been orphaned, abandoned, and/or abused by their parents or guardians. In some cases, both parents are in the hospital or jail. Other children have suffered various diseases, deformities, deficiencies, or the effects of abuse. All of the children in this case were innocent victims of their circumstances, and none were delinquents or lawbreakers of any sort.

To the extent feasible, the state placed most of the children in available foster homes or private and religious orphanages and paid for their support. However, there were no state-owned and operated homes of this type and too few volunteer foster parents to accommodate all the children who needed them.

About 600 children were, as a last resort, being held in juvenile delinquent facilities along with murderers, rapists, muggers, addicts, and criminals of every description. It was appalling, but unavoidable.

One social worker, in addition to her heavy caseload, was given the extra duty of recruiting foster parents. There was no budget for this task and she had no training in public relations.

Unable to accomplish anything by herself, she sought help in the public relations and public affairs offices of major Chicago corporations and media organizations.

Ultimately, she talked with Herome Schmitt, director of corporate and employee communications at Inland Steel Company. Schmitt was horrified to learn about the problem. He set out to solve it by organizing several dozen volunteer public relations and public affairs executives from establishment organizations into what he named the Businessman's Task Force.

This group, operating with no money, donated time, services, and "clout," and launched what was to become a major public relations campaign. It involved a variety of public relations tools and techniques and, significantly, all Chicago media from radio, television, and newspapers to car cards. The initial results were encouraging, as first dozens, then hundreds of Chicago families volunteered to become foster parents.

A breakthrough came midway through the campaign. CBS–TV donated a full hour of prime time on a Friday evening for a documentary.

The task force and the agency worked feverishly with the CBS Public Affairs Department in Chicago to produce what, ultimately, became an Emmy award-winning program entitled, "The Children Are Waiting." In contrast to the usual "Isn't it awful?" type documentary, the second half of this show urged members of the audience to take direct action in helping to solve this major social problem. It asked them directly to pick up the phone, call in, and volunteer to be foster parents.

No one involved knew what to expect.

Preparations had been made for success. Illinois Bell had installed a one hundred-telephone setup in anticipation of viewer calls. Some three hundred volunteers waited with bated breath in the Inland Steel Company cafeteria. When the call-in number first flashed on the television screens, the crowd swallowed hard in unison. Then, in one joyous instant, all one hundred phones lit up like a Christmas tree. It was spine-tingling. One could literally feel love pouring in from all over Chicagoland. Euphoria filled the room as 3,043 requests for information were received before midnight that evening.

More than seven thousand families called in during the next three days wanting to hear more about how to become foster parents. Ultimately, after some exasperating problems with government red tape, this big-city social problem was completely solved using public relations techniques with no cost to the taxpayers.

The six hundred children being held in juvenile delinquent facilities were all placed in foster homes, and there was a waiting list of qualified foster homes available to any future children deemed wards of the state.

The Businessman's Task Force helped wring Chicago's heart. That heart opened wide and the children wait no more.

Questions

1. Why did the social worker turn desperately to corporate and media public relations offices for help?
2. What kind of research was needed before the effective documentary program could be produced? What needed to be put on the screen to make people want to volunteer to become foster parents?
3. Can you think of other situations in which a volunteer group of public relations practitioners could be called upon to solve a social problem?

Notes

1. Rae Leaper, "CEOs of Nonprofit Organizations Agree: Communicate or Perish," *Journal of Organizational Communication* 4 (1980): 9–17.
2. Ibid., 16.
3. "Not-For-Profit Compensation," *Public Relations Journal* 40 (5 May 1984): 26.
4. "16 in Probe of Milk Fund Got Co-op Cash," *Chicago Tribune* (5 June 1974): 1.
5. Reprinted from *Association Public Relations,* with permission from Association Section, Public Relations Society of America, 1981.
6. James J. Kilpatrick, "Populaces' Confidence on Upbeat," *San Diego Union* (5 January 1977): B-6.
7. Nancy J. Hicks, "Patients and Other Publics," *Public Relations Journal* 42 (3 March 1986): 28–32.
8. John Brice, "Guiding Lights," *Public Relations Journal* 42 (1 January 1986): 20–25.
9. Scott M. Cutlip and Allen H. Center, *Effective Public Relations* (Englewood Cliffs, NJ: Prentice Hall, 1978), 467.
10. Leaper, "Communicate or Perish," 12.
11. Caroline Bird, *The Case Against College* (New York: David McKay, 1975).
12. Richard Freeman and J. Herbert Hollomon, "The Declining Value of Going to College," *Change* (September 1975).
13. John Price Jones, *The Engineering of Consent,* Edward L. Bernays, ed. (Norman, OK: University of Oklahoma Press, 1955), 159.
14. John W. Leslie, *Seeking the Competitive Dollar: College Management in the Seventies* (Washington, D.C.: American College Public Relations Association, 1971), 44–46.

▲ ▲ ▲

CHAPTER 17

Public Relations in Government
Preview

Governmental public relations plays a crucial role in keeping the public informed about issues, problems, and actions at all levels of government.

Government public information officers seek citizen approval of government programs, help explain what citizens want from the government, strive to make government responsive to citizens' wishes, and attempt to understand and affect public opinion.

Public relations operatives are pervasive in political campaigns, promoting both public understanding of candidates and candidates' understanding of publics.

The framers of the United States Constitution believed that the American people were capable of governing themselves. To do so, however, citizens needed to be fully informed about issues and problems confronting them and actions taken by their government. Despite their belief, the founding fathers provided no specific means to disseminate information nor any assurance that citizens would be kept informed. It was assumed that government would maintain open communications channels with the public and provide sufficient information to enable citizens to make intelligent decisions about its policies and activities.

To a certain extent, these ideals have been realized through a system that evolved in response to public needs. The mass media struggle to serve our right to know. In providing information to the public about government affairs, they draw upon the public relations arm of government—local, state, and federal—which offers the media a constant flow of information.

Government public relations practitioners are often called **public information officers (PIOs)**, suggesting that they simply transmit information in an objective and neutral fashion. In fact, they are no more neutral or objective than public relations professionals working in the private sector.

Since the success and stability of democratic governments are ultimately determined by continuous citizen approval, public information officers seek to ensure such approval. Because the democratic system implies that government will respond to the wishes of the governed, public information officers work to determine those wishes, then strive to make government responsive to them. Since public opinion provides the climate in which public officials, agencies, and institutions succeed or fail, public information officers try to understand and affect public opinion. Because a multitude of institutional interests coexist in any society, public relations practitioners both inside and outside government represent a similar variety of perspectives. As a consequence, much of the significant dialogue needed to ensure democracy's proper functioning is generated, molded, and enunciated by public relations practitioners.

In short, in government—as in any other organization—public relations is a management function that helps define objectives and philosophies while also helping the organization adapt to the demands of its constituencies and environments. Public relations practitioners, whether referred to as PIOs, **public affairs officers (PAOs)**, press secretaries, or just plain administrative aides, still communicate with all relevant internal and external publics in order to make organizational goals and societal expectations consistent. Public information officers, like their counterparts in business and industry, develop, execute, and evaluate programs that promote the exchange of influence and understanding among an organization's constituent parts and publics.

Of course, because they work in a different context with different constraints and problems, government public relations specialists operate somewhat differently from their private sector counterparts. PIOs face unique problems. Their mission and legitimacy are questioned more extensively. Their constituents are forced to provide financial support through taxation. Red tape, internal bureaucratic situations, and political pressures hinder their efforts. Career development opportunities are limited.

In this chapter, we will explore the ways government public relations is practiced as well as its background, importance, functions, and responsibilities.

The Background of Public Relations in American Government

As we stated in chapter 2, leaders have always courted the sentiments of their people. In this sense, public relations has been practiced by governments since the reign of the pharaohs. In the United States, however, its formal integration into local, state, and federal government programs has occurred largely since World War II. Before this time, public relations practice was confined mainly to the upper levels of the federal government.

As previously discussed, Amos Kendall served Andrew Jackson in the capacities of pollster, counselor, ghostwriter, and publicist. But use of such counsel did not become established until the administration of Theodore Roosevelt. From that time forward, "Strong U.S. presidents have utilized the expertise of public relations to exploit the mounting power of the news media . . . to mobilize public support for their policies."[1]

Public relations pioneer Edward Bernays recognized that his own expertise could be applied to government and politics as well as to business and philanthropic endeavors. Having served as adviser to Presidents Coolidge and Hoover, he recommended in the 1930s the creation of a cabinet-level Secretary of Public Relations. His suggestion was not acted upon; nevertheless, press secretaries of some recent presidents, although formally ranked merely as presidential staff, have been more influential than cabinet officers. Upon taking office, Gerald Ford's first appointments were a personal photographer, a new press secretary, and a chief speechwriter.

Frequently, presidents have been conscious of the public relations aspects of their highly visible job. Teddy Roosevelt talked of the presidency as a "bully pulpit." Harry Truman was characteristically more blunt; in a letter to his sister, Mary, dated November 14, 1947, he wrote: "All the President is, is a glorified public relations man."

Outside of the presidency, public relations had tougher sledding. In 1913, the U.S. Civil Service Commission announced an examination for a "Publicity Expert." On October 22 of that year, Congress passed the Gillett Amendment (38 U.S.C. 3107) which stated:

> No money appropriated by any act shall be used for the compensation of any publicity expert unless specifically appropriated for that purpose.

Despite the law, the public relations function continued to be performed. Most notable among government's early public relations endeavors was George Creel's World War I Committee on Public Information.

Public relations in the federal government came of age during the New Deal, when the creation of the so-called alphabet agencies "precipitated a flood tide of publicists into the channels of government."[2] The Office of War Information, created during World War II, gave further federal support to the profession. When the war was over, it became the United States Information Agency (USIA). During the late 1940s, public relations activity was increasingly evident in state and local government. By 1949, nearly every state had established a state-supported public relations program to attract both tourism and industry.

Since 1970, at least twenty new federal regulatory agencies have been created. All of them have extensive public information programs.

The Importance and Scope of Governmental Public Relations

Despite the limits placed on public relations activity by Congress, government publicity has always been necessary, if for no other reason than to tell citizens what services are available and how to use them. With the developing complexity of government has come a corresponding increase in publicity.[3]

While they may be given different titles, virtually every federal government agency maintains a public relations effort. The Federal Bureau of Investigation (FBI) has an External Affairs Division. The Interstate Commerce Commission (ICC) maintains an Office of Communications and Consumer Affairs. The Environmental Protection Agency (EPA) has an Office of Public Awareness. Even the Central Intelligence Agency (CIA) employs a twenty-person Public Affairs Group.

It is impossible to estimate the number of people involved or the money spent in government public relations. As William Gilbert states: "If you are in government, you are in public relations . . . (There is a) public relations element in all the things . . . government . . . does."[4]

Government public relations ranges from simple publicity to global propaganda. The government spends more money on audiovisual services than does any film studio or television network. It prints over 100,000 different publications each year. K. H. Rabin quotes *U.S. News and World Report* in putting the size of the federal government's public relations expenditures in perspective:

> The federal government spends more money each year trying to influence the way people think than it spends altogether for disaster relief, foreign military assistance, energy conservation and cancer research . . . [5]

It is similarly difficult to know the numbers of people involved in federal public relations.

In 1980, the federal Office of Personnel Management listed the following public relations-related employees: 3,033 public information specialists, 2,272 writers and editors, 1,722 technical writers and editors, 1,659 visual communication specialists, 1,090 foreign information specialists, 2,199 editorial assistants, and 182 foreign language broadcasting specialists. No one really knows the total of federal government public relations employees but knowledgeable estimates cite at least 20,000.

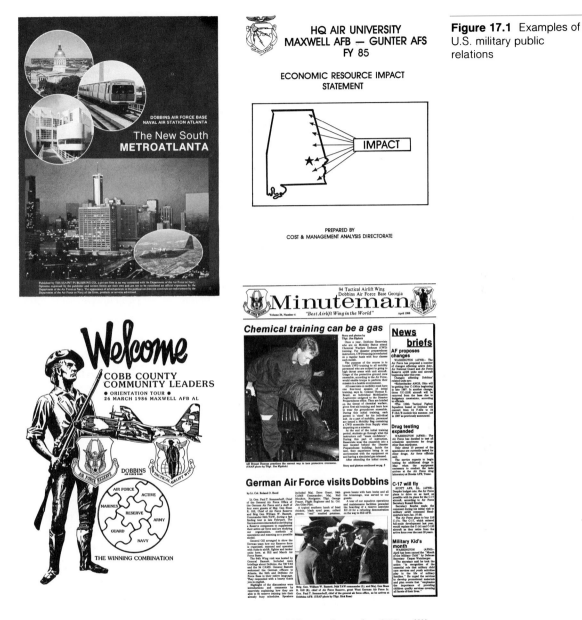

Figure 17.1 Examples of U.S. military public relations

The Department of Agriculture employs 650 people and a $12 million budget annually to produce 3,600 news releases and 600 publications.

The Defense Department (DOD) spends $31 million and employs about 1,200 public information officers on military bases around the world. Their primary mission is "to foster understanding and support of the various services' role in national defense."[6] In 1985, the DOD spent $1.9 billion on recruitment, special aerial teams, ceremonial bands, and military museums. Figure 17.1 shows examples of U.S. military public relations efforts.

Another major U.S. government information area is the United States Information Agency (USIA). Its worldwide activities are summarized in Mini-Case 17.1.

The USIA

Mini-Case 17.1

Sometimes the target of terrorists' bombs abroad and political uproar at home, the United States Information Agency is the public relations arm of the United States in more than 125 countries. With a 1985 budget of $885 million and about nine thousand employees, the agency's mission is:

"To support the national interest by conveying an understanding abroad of what the United States stands for as a nation and as a people; to explain the nation's policies and to present a true picture of the society, institutions and culture in which those policies evolve."*

The Voice of America, the USIA radio operation, maintains 106 transmitters worldwide, broadcasting in forty languages and reaching seventy-five million people a year. USIA also annually produces and distributes about two hundred films, publishes fifteen magazines in thirty-one languages, and mounts fifty major exhibits.

The agency maintains over two hundred libraries and information centers in ninety countries and provides educational programs for 350,000 students per year.

Media relations is also an important USIA job. Like the Associated Press or United Press International, the agency performs as a wire service, providing film news clips for overseas television and moving twenty thousand words per day for media placement from two hundred overseas posts.

*Source: 45th Report to Congress (Washington, D.C.: United States Information Agency, June 30, 1987).

As impressive as these figures may be, they do not include the personnel or expenses involved in city, county, state, or regional governmental agencies, programs, or authorities. Nor do they recognize that the inputs provided by these tens of thousands of public relations officials grow more influential every year.

The Function
of Governmental
Public Relations

Government public information officers, like any other public relations practitioners, seek to achieve mutual understanding between their agencies and publics by following the four-step process explained in Part II of this book. They must gauge public opinion, plan and organize for public relations effectiveness, construct messages for internal and external audiences, and measure the effectiveness of the entire process.

Like all organizational boundary spanners, public information officers jointly serve two masters—their publics and their employers. On the one hand, they provide the public with complete, candid, continuous reporting of government information and accessible channels for citizen inputs. On the other hand, Scott Cutlip maintains:

> The vast government information machine has as its primary purpose advancement of government's policies and personnel . . . the major objective is to gain support for the incumbent administration's policies and maintain its leaders in power.[7]

Serving Both the Public and Government

In a recent Brookings Institution study, former aide to Presidents Eisenhower and Nixon, Stephen Hess, observed the contradictory pressures on government press officers in the departments of defense, transportation, and state, the Food and Drug Administration, and the White House. What he found was:

> A semibureaucrat/semireporter, in the bureaucracy but not truly of it, tainted by association with the press yet not of the press.[8]

Hess found that press officers were trusted neither by the media nor by their own superiors. Because they are suspect in the eyes of their own political executives, according to Hess, "The career press officer is often the odd person out in the permanent bureaucracy."[9]

Moreover, the media perhaps underappreciates the press information officer's role. Says Hess: "If they were to be invited to view press operations from the inside, many reporters would be surprised to see the extent to which the press officer is their advocate within the permanent government."[10]

Currently, public information officers serve neither master very well, as evidenced by the fact that millions of Americans view their "government as distant and unresponsive, if not hostile."[11] Both the public and the politicians might be better served if public information officers could provide more active input for governmental decision makers. In his seminal 1947 report, *Government and Mass Communication,* Zachariah Chafee, Jr., held that:

> Government information can play a vital role in the cause of good administration by exploring the impact of new social forces, discovering strains and tensions before they become acute, and encouraging a positive sense of unity and national direction.[12]

The most basic functions of government public relations are to help define and achieve government program goals, enhance government responsiveness and service, and provide the public with sufficient information to permit self-government. The goal of public information officers is to promote cooperation and confidence between citizens and their government. This, in turn, requires government accessibility, accountability, consistency, and integrity.

*Objectives of
Governmental Public
Relations*

Planned, continuous governmental public relations programs may have any one or several of the following objectives:

1. To gain support for new laws or initiatives. Jockeying for political support for particular laws and initiatives is evident in news reports every day. Whether the issue is a local ordinance related to land-use planning, a state effort to improve elementary and secondary education, or federal tax reform, public information officers play an active role.
2. To stimulate citizen interest and relieve public confusion about governmental agencies, processes, and programs. When drought hit the Southeast in the summer of 1986, governmental agencies implemented various water conservation measures. Government public relations officials encouraged interest in water conservation and straightened out confusion about new water use rules.
3. To facilitate voter decision making by providing factual information. Particularly important in local government referenda, government public relations practitioners provide accurate information about potential outcomes of various initiatives.
4. To enable citizens to fully use government services by providing continuous information. In 1986, the federal government undertook an $11 million advertising campaign to promote food stamp usage. Another example of this objective is the promotion of state parks.
5. To open channels of communication with government officials. PIOs serve as ombudsmen, establish hot lines, and set up public forums to promote information input as well as output.
6. To serve officials by helping interpret citizen attitudes and public opinion. At the highest levels of government, press secretaries and other communication operatives are members of the teams that seek to fathom public desires regarding legislation and governmental programs.
7. To gain voluntary obedience with laws, regulations, and rules. Public relations efforts support laws and rules related to everything from the automobile speed limit to drug abuse, and from littering to compliance with tax laws.
8. To build generalized support for agencies or programs so that conflicts or negative events can be overcome. The National Aeronautics and Space Administration is mandated by law to provide the American public with full information about its programs. It has done so with an eye toward building public support throughout its history. The reservoir of public approval for NASA was evident in the aftermath of the Challenger space shuttle disaster. Although investigations were launched, no one seriously suggested dissolving the agency or its programs.

While the practice of public relations in government is much like that in other institutions, government information officers do face some difficulties unique to their area. Because they are paid with public funds, their mission and legitimacy are questioned more than in private organizations. Gilbert points out that "the citizenry . . . regards government public information activities as wasteful of the taxpayers' money and essentially propagandistic."[13] This is why the Gillett Amendment has never been repealed and why government public relations practitioners ply their trade under euphemisms like "information officer," "public affairs officer," or "education officer."

Unlike the customers of corporations, the constituents of governmental entities are forced to support those entities financially through taxes. Thus, while government may be responsive to political forces, it is not directly responsive to market forces. "Government red tape" has become a sadly accurate cliche and a serious public relations problem.

David Brown points out other problems of public information officers: internal bureaucratic situations that hinder professional efforts; weak job standards; political pressure; and little career development or recognition. Moreover, he states, government public relations specialists are considered "after-the-fact operators, expected to put out fires started by others or to implement information about programs that we strongly feel will not stand the muster of the media."[14] Increases in the complexity of government policies, rules, and practices, the widening chasm between citizens and their government, and the escalation of demands made by citizens without understanding the political, legal, and financial constraints placed on government are additional difficulties public information officers face. An example of how a county government recognized the need to improve its public relations effectiveness is found in Mini-Case 17.2.

To deal with these problems, public information officers may adopt several strategies. First, they should strive to be generalists in both public relations and management skills while becoming expert in the language and discipline of particular fields within government (health, education, transportation, welfare, defense, etc.).

Second, public information officers should practice preventative maintenance, providing policy guidance before programs are approved. This requires them to enter government's management mainstream as we discussed in chapter 4.

Third, government public relations must develop a service orientation— responding to a public comprised of consumers of government services. Moreover, public relations should foster this perspective in all government employees, using established channels of internal communication.

The Practice of Governmental Public Relations
Dealing with Unique Problems

Devising Solution Strategies

Fourth, government public information officers should concentrate on inputs as well as outputs. As Rabin suggests, "The proverbial general audience . . . will be identified more and more as a consumer public."[15] This calls for getting direct feedback through citizen participation, surveys and questionnaires, and community meetings which will then be used to adjust programs, messages, and media.

Finally, as the downfall of the Nixon administration so aptly demonstrated, great hazards confront governmental attempts to hide failures, ineptitude, or mistakes. Openness is essential to effective government public relations.

Cobb County Gets a PR Agency

Mini-Case 17.2

Cobb County, northwest of Atlanta, Georgia, is among the fastest growing areas in the country. With a county government budget nearing $200 million and almost three thousand full-time employees (including one public information officer), public officials felt "a need for additional creative services to assist in maintaining a better informed, more educated relationship with our citizens, the business community, special interest groups, and other governmental entities." The need was stimulated by issues including land-use planning, public transportation, solid waste disposal, and new county facilities. Moreover, as county commission chairman Earl Smith pointed out, "Communication of information . . . is a key concern. We need a concerted education/information effort to apprise Cobb citizens of the county's benefits, sound management, and strong leadership. In addition, avenues of return communication need to be strengthened." Proposals were invited from various local public relations agencies.

The immediate, short-term objectives of hiring an outside agency were:

▲ Work with the Board of Commissioners to establish the changing character of the county. Through an image review process, define the nature of modern Cobb County as perceived by the Board.

▲ Begin to establish this identity throughout the community through development and introduction of a comprehensive graphics program.

▲ Review and update the county's current institutional advertising program consistent with the outcome of the image review process.

▲ Educate the citizens on the basic procedures for interacting with their county government when required—i.e., protocol for commission and zoning meetings, voter registration, marriage license, building permits, etc.

▲ Educate the general population on the wide variety of undiscovered services and programs offered by Cobb County.

▲ Improve public confidence, in particular that of key community leaders, in the county's practical use of available resources. Establish public confidence in the county's ability to plan for and meet the demands for the future.

▲ Convey the importance of the annexation issue to the county and its residents; educate citizens that rampant annexation is detrimental to their pocketbooks.

▲ Establish credibility for the county's zoning and land-use procedures among both developers and homeowners.

▲ Target markets and establish awareness of the Department of Community Services as the county's primary supplier of leisure/lifestyle services.

▲ Review county departments for programs which might benefit from ongoing public relations programs (i.e., Road Improvement Program, DUI Task Force).

Bowes, Hanlon and Yarbrough was selected among fifteen applicants for the $100,000 account.

Source: This mini-case is based on a February 3, 1986, "Cobb County Request for Proposal: Public Relations Counsel" and on discussion with county officials.

While employee and media relations are processes important to all institutions, certain aspects are specific to government public relations practice.

The impression citizens have of their government, particularly of local government, is often formed through routine day-to-day contacts between government employees and members of the public. Gilbert points out, "One dissatisfied employee can, by his or her deeds and words, do irreparable harm . . . if such actions are multiplied by several . . . the result can be devastating."[16]

Practitioners must foster attitudes of goodwill and respect for the public among governmental employees and officials. Particular attention should be given to face-to-face contacts, correspondence, and telephone conversations. Reception areas should be pleasant and well maintained, and public vehicles should be driven in a safe and courteous fashion.

Rabin puts it this way:

If the image of the government is to be enhanced, the process must take place at the level of the individual employee—his or her productivity, and how he or she conducts encounters with individual citizens. . . . Focus will be more and more on internal communications . . . employees . . . will be sent more and more as media for communicating with external publics.[17]

Chapter 12 provides further discussion of the rationale and means of employee communication.

Some commentators seem to believe that media relations has lost importance as a priority of public information officers now that the public increasingly receives government information in more direct forms. J. M. Perry, writing in

Employee and Media Relations in Government
Employee Relations

Media Relations

the *Wall Street Journal,* observes, "The press release is more or less a decaying institution in Washington . . . government communicators have turned more and more to sophisticated tools—orchestrated advertising campaigns, television commercials, videotape cassettes, full-color brochures and glossy magazines."[18] Although government information encompasses an ever-broadening range of media and techniques, plain old media relations still gets tremendous attention. Indeed, without government information officers, the news media could not report on governments as effectively and economically as they do.

Government public information officers outgun reporters in numbers and resources. Moreover, reporters often feel lost in local, state, or federal bureaucracies. Under these circumstances, says Cutlip, "An ever-increasing share of news content . . . is coming often unchanged from the government officer's typewriter. More and more of the governmental news reporting task is abandoned to the practitioner who supplies the information in professional ready-to-use packages."[19] The public information officer thus has an enormous opportunity for media access, but with that access comes the reponsibility not to abuse it. Typically, government press officers accept that responsibility. According to Hess, "Releases are readable and competent . . . sometimes the press releases were more precise than the hurried accounts written by general-assignment reporters."[20]

Press officers work hard to serve the media and to do so with a high sense of ethical behavior. Hess describes the qualities of a good press officer: "stamina, curiosity, a helpful nature, a good memory, civility, coolness under pressure, and an understanding of human psychology."[21] Commenting on PIOs' ethical standards, he says:

> "For all press secretaries the crux of unethical conduct is lying. Spokesmen are expected to tell the truth—it is U.S. government policy. They also prefer to tell the truth. . ."[22]

Summing up his observations of governmental media relations, Hess explains:

> The view from inside a press office is that most energy seems to be devoted to trying to find out what the rest of the agency is doing (often unsuccessfully), gathering material that has been requested by reporters rather than promoting carefully prepared positions, and distributing information that is neither controversial nor especially self-serving . . .[23]

The Presidential Press Secretary   The single most conspicuous and important government public relations practitioner is the presidential press secretary. As the chief public relations spokesperson for the administration, he communicates policies and practices to the public while providing input into governmental decision making. The unfortunate wounding of press secretary Jim Brady during an assassination attempt on President Reagan shows that the job even carries an element of danger. The following description of the press secretary's job can be applied to all government public relations duties in general.

Several times a day, the presidential press secretary stands before largely hostile media representatives and fields questions for the president. The smallest misstatement can lead the world to think there has been a change in White House policy.

According to William Safire, a speechwriter for President Nixon who became a political columnist for the *New York Times,* "A good press secretary speaks up for the press to the President and speaks out for the President to the press. He makes his home in the pitted no-man's land of an adversary relationship and is primarily an advocate, interpreter and amplifier. He must be more the President's man than the press's. But he can be his own man as well."[24] This description, of course, is a nearly classic definition of the boundary spanning role discussed in chapter 3.

Gerald Ford's two press secretaries give differing perspectives on the relationship that should exist between the practitioner and the president. Gerald terHorst quit after Ford pardoned Nixon, commenting, "A spokesman should feel in his heart and mind that the Chief's decision is the right one so that he can speak with a persuasiveness that stems from conviction."[25]

Ron Nessen, who replaced terHorst, took a different view, "A press secretary does not always have to agree with the President. His first loyalty is to the public, and he should not knowingly lie or mislead the press."[26]

Larry Speakes, spokesman for the Reagan White House agrees. "If I lose my reputation for being truthful," he says, "I've lost everything."[27]

Whether or not a practitioner must agree with her or his boss is a matter of personal conscience. Loyalty to the public and an ability to foster communications in both directions, however, are essential aspects of the job, just as they are for all public relations professionals.

The First Lady has a press secretary as well, as is discussed in Mini-Case 17.3.

Mini-Case 17.3

The First Lady's Press Secretary

Her client had a severe image problem. The media made her out as a superficial, insensitive, bubble-headed lightweight—a liability in her husband's important work. The client was First Lady Nancy Reagan. The public relations professional was Sheila Tate, her press secretary.

In President Reagan's first year in office, Mrs. Reagan received constant press criticism, particularly when she spent $209,508 on new china and more than $800,000 in private donations to decorate the White House. Her Washington role seemed to lack focus.

Tate's objective was to humanize the First Lady, to make her someone with whom people could relate. She suggested that Mrs. Reagan perform at Washington's annual Gridiron Club Dinner in 1982. An experienced actress, the First Lady sang, danced, and spoofed herself on stage. It was the turning point in her relationship with the media.

Sheila Tate, press
secretary for First Lady
Nancy Reagan

With Tate's help, Mrs. Reagan became a credible leader in the fight against drug abuse. She interviewed drug addicts on ABC's "Good Morning America," delivered an anti-drug message on NBC's sitcom "Diff'rent Strokes," and narrated PBS docudramas on drug problems.

In the second term of the Reagan presidency, Nancy became an effective and comfortable part of the White House team.

Source: Based in part on "Shrewd Ex-Public Relations Exec Image Maker to First Lady," *The Atlanta Journal and Constitution* (November 20, 1983): 56A.

Public Relations and Political Campaigns

Government really cannot be discussed without recognizing its political context. While it provides many and diverse services to its constituents, government's policies are guided by politics. The political campaign is the most overt expression of politics. Public relations activity on behalf of political candidates has become practically synonymous with the campaign itself.

Political campaigning has become a non-stop industry, raising hundreds of millions of dollars from political action committees (see chapter 15) and others and spending that money to attract votes. Public relations plays a critical role in both raising and spending those funds.

The public relations practitioner in the political campaign is not just a spokesperson to the media, but usually also a trusted adviser who helps formulate campaign strategy and positions on issues. Gaining votes first requires gaining funds, media exposure, and volunteers. Public relations works hard to attract all three. These resources must then be converted into political support.

Some campaign tasks in which public relations may be involved include:

Developing computerized mail campaigns.

Coordinating broadcast, print, and other advertising.

Scouting out sites for speeches and other campaign events.

Staging events to increase candidate visibility.

Raising campaign funds.

Preparing news releases concerning candidates' activities, positions, and schedules.

Writing speeches and position papers.

Coordinating research on issues and voters.

Providing briefings and background sessions for the media and others.

Attracting and coordinating volunteers.

All of this activity is designed to get the candidate elected so that he or she can become a part of the governing process. Campaign press aides to successful candidates often join government as well.

Contemporary political campaigning is frequently criticized for the extent to which the process has become one of "packaging" and "selling" candidates. Public relations has received much of the blame for this perceived phenomenon. Indeed, public relations practitioners have changed the nature of political campaigns in both negative and positive ways.

Candidates are criticized for paying too much attention to polls and for trying to be what people want them to be rather than being themselves. When operating ethically, positively, and professionally, public relations practitioners facilitate two-way communication between candidates and constituencies. They help candidates gain public attention for themselves and their positions. Moreover, public relations people help candidates understand what voters want and expect. Such understanding is essential in a representative form of government.

The Impact of Public Relations on Government

The success of many government programs depends on dispensing adequate information about them to relevant publics. The president and the policeman, the legislator and the librarian all rely on public information officers to do their jobs as effectively and efficiently as possible. Government programs ranging from soil conservation to crime prevention, from anti-litter campaigns to army recruitment depend upon public relations.

R. L. Rings demonstrated the dramatic impact of governmental public relations in a study of seventy Ohio school districts. Rings analyzed thirty-five school districts that employed public information officers and thirty-five that did not. The districts having public information officers received significantly more news coverage. Moreover, where public information officers were on staff, the news focused on student and public affairs; without public information officers, coverage consisted mainly of sports and administrative news.

The most telling findings, however, concerned the finances of the school districts:

> Financial records indicated that the director systems' current average operating millage was two mills above the state mean, whereas the nondirector systems average operating millage was four mills below the state mean. In local support per pupil, the director sample averaged $375 to the nondirector sample average of $275.[28]

While it could be argued that only more affluent school districts can afford public relations directors in the first place, it is probable that such directors in Ohio had impact on public support of education that directly translated into financial support.

Summary

Public relations is just as critical to governmental organizations as it is to other institutions. Since government activities depend so much on public opinion, public relations is the stuff of government. Rather than seeking to ban public relations from government, citizens should recognize its legitimacy, and public relations specialists should work toward making its practice ever more professional, responsible, and efficient.

▲ ▲ ▲

Urban Renewal

By S. Carlton Caldwell
Assistant Dean, College of Journalism
University of Maryland
College Park, Maryland

Case Study

The state Urban Renewal Office for a large midwestern city has requested a grant of $60 million from the state to rebuild a poverty-stricken area of the city. The Public Affairs Officer (PAO) for that office receives a memo from the departmental director saying that the governor expresses confidence that the legislature will allocate funds. The PAO sends out a press release describing the plans for renovation.

A group of slum landlords who own the buildings in this area are very upset by the proposed renovation because the state would assume ownership of the newly constructed units. The landlords would receive a minimal assessed-value for their property. These men happen to be major contributors to the governor's reelection campaign and have also donated large sums of money to the campaigns of some prominent state senators. They have informed the governor and the senators that if they would like to receive future contributions, they had better halt the project.

Questions

1. If you were the PAO and had to write a press release for the two reporters, what would you say?
2. What is the legal situation facing the PAO?
3. How could the PAO handle the situation without having his/her name appear in the papers?

Notes

1. Scott Cutlip, "Public Relations in Government," *Public Relations Review* (Summer 1976): 10.
2. William H. Gilbert, ed., *Public Relations in Local Government* (Washington, D.C.: International City Management Association, 1975), 9.
3. Ibid., 8.
4. Ibid., 5.
5. K. H. Rabin, "Government PIOs in the '80s," *Public Relations Journal* (December 1979).
6. Lowndes F. Stephens, "Professionalism of Army Public Affairs Personnel," *Public Relations Review* (Summer 1981): 43.
7. Cutlip, "Public Relations in Government," 12.
8. Quoted in West Pederson, "Brookings Study Profiles Government Press Officers," *Public Relations Journal* (November 1984): 43–45.
9. Ibid.
10. Ibid.
11. Final Report of the 32nd American Assembly, Columbia University.
12. Zachariah Chafee, Jr., *Government and Mass Communication,* 2 vols. (Chicago: University of Chicago Press, 1947), 2:736.
13. Gilbert, *Public Relations in Local Government,* 11.
14. D. H. Brown, "Information Officers and Reporters: Friends or Foes?" *Public Relations Review* (Summer 1976): 33.
15. Rabin, "Government PIOs," 23.
16. Gilbert, *Public Relations in Local Government,* 20.
17. Rabin, "Government PIOs," 23.
18. J. M. Perry, "Federal Flairs . . . ," *Wall Street Journal* (23 May 1979): 111.
19. Cutlip, "Public Relations in Government," 15.
20. Pederson, "Brookings Study Profiles," 43.
21. Ibid., 43.
22. Ibid., 45.
23. Ibid., 44.
24. William Safire, "One of Our Own," *New York Times* (19 September 1974): 43.
25. Robert U. Brown, "Role of Press Secretary," *Editor and Publisher* (19 October 1974): 40.
26. I. W. Hill, "Nessen Lists Ways He Has Improved Public Relations," *Editor and Publisher* (10 April 1975): 40.
27. Jeremiah O'Leary, "Firmly in the White House Hot Seat," *Insight* (1 September 1986): 51.
28. R. L. Rings, "Public School News Coverage With and Without PR Directors," *Journalism Quarterly* (Spring 1971).

▲ ▲ ▲

Corporate Public Relations
Preview

Public relations efforts designed to improve public attitudes toward private enterprise must address: the credibility of corporations; corporate concern for individuals on a human scale; public understanding of economic realities; and corporate willingness to lead society toward change.

Renewed business credibility must be built on honest performance, open communication, consistency between performance and communication, commitment to problem solving, and establishment of feasible expectations.

In the effort to ensure public confidence in business, public relations should act as business's eyes and ears, as a receiver of the subtle information that signals societal demands, and as the provider of information that moves management toward effective response.

While small business owners and managers typically serve as their own public relations experts, they can and should be involved with media, community, employee, customer, supplier, financial, and political relations. Such efforts both promote and protect the small business and improve its profitability.

Public relations is practiced more extensively and with more impact in large business organizations than anywhere else. Public relations is a means by which businesses seek to improve their ability to do business.

Public relations is practiced more extensively and with more impact in large business organizations than anywhere else. Businesses deal with and adapt to increasingly complex and dynamic environments. They manage relations with a variety of publics and balance behavior in response to many often conflicting demands. They confront numerous complicated and pressing issues, including business ethics, equal opportunity, the quality of work life, consumerism, environmentalism, global commerce, and others.

Large corporations have substantial resources available to invest in public relations efforts. They do not invest, however, unless they believe the amount spent will yield even greater returns. Thus, while public relations is allotted great scope and resources in business organizations, it is also held closely accountable for producing desired results.

As we have indicated in earlier chapters, public relations is practiced by all managers in business, not just by those whose title or job description contains the term. Top level executives in particular are expected to spend substantial portions of their energies and efforts on public relations-related matters. Consequently, while the status of public relations has recently been elevated in business organizations, public relations specialists who possess only traditional skills risk being restricted to technical roles.

Obviously, all of the chapters in this book dealing with the practice, the process, and the publics of public relations apply directly to business public relations. Businesses use *media relations* to gain support and sympathy from print and broadcast outlets, to generate positive publicity, to tell business's side of the story, and to reduce negative publicity or at least keep it in perspective.

Community relations is a business concern as it supports sales, attracts employees, improves the quality of public services, provides support for business initiatives, and improves the quality of life for employees and executives.

Employee relations is important to business as it contributes to harmonious labor relations and helps attract and retain good employees. Effective employee communication can also stimulate worker creativity and input, raise attitudes and morale, improve product quality and customer service, and enhance productivity.

Business is greatly concerned with *consumer relations*. In this regard, corporations want to build positive relations with customers, respond effectively to consumer complaints and problems, and support sales and marketing efforts.

As our chapter on *financial relations* indicates, sound financial communication allows business to attract capital at the lowest possible cost. Other financial relations goals include assuring that public companies' stock is appropriately valued, building knowledge and confidence in fund sources, and responding to investor questions or needs.

And finally, *public affairs* deals with business's interaction with government on various levels. Government relations have direct impact on a business's flexibility and manageability. Regulation, taxation, labor law, and international trade policies are but a few of the ways governmental actions constrain business decision making and success.

In short, public relations is a means by which businesses seek to improve their ability to do business. Effective public relations smooths and enhances a company's operations, and eases and increases its sales. It enables a business to better anticipate and adapt to societal demands and trends. It is the means by which businesses improve their operating environments.

The Challenge of Corporate Public Relations Today

The demands placed on large corporations are great and diverse. Business organizations must fulfill a long list of domestic responsibilities and still compete effectively in domestic and international markets.

In the 1980s, international competitiveness is quite possibly the greatest challenge facing business. Cooperative arrangements between business and government in Japan, West Germany, and other countries represent a competitive advantage over the often adversarial relations found in the United States. Public relations in business must help corporations and society accept and conform to two "Iron Laws:"

> "The Iron Law of Responsibility: In the long run, those who do not use power in a manner which society considers responsible will tend to lose it."[1]

> "The Iron Law of Cooperation: Those societies who do not establish cooperative relationships will tend to decline economically."[2]

To compete successfully in the international market, corporations must use and retain their power responsibly in relation to the demands of various domestic publics. Moreover, if our societal institutions cannot develop cooperative relationships, we will face economic decline. The job of public relations in large corporations is ultimately to assure that corporate power is maintained by responsible use and to help develop cooperative relationships between corporations and other societal institutions. To successfully promote these goals, public relations practitioners must be able to understand and deal with public opinion concerning business. In this chapter, we will explore public attitudes toward private enterprise; how corporate management has responded to those attitudes; what corporations, trade associations, and others are doing about the situation; and what else might be done. We hope to produce an accurate picture of the problem and to suggest a role public relations can play in its solution.

Attitudes toward Business

During the 1970s, it became increasingly apparent that public sentiment toward business and business people was deteriorating. Coverage of business in the media became more negative, consumers complained more frequently about

products and services, and economic boycotts and mass protests were organized. Harris, Roper, Hart, Yankelovich, Opinion Research, and other polls
provided statistics supporting the drop in confidence toward business. Business
people were quick to interpret the trend as a large-scale rejection of the private
enterprise system.

In his 1975 survey, Louis Harris found that confidence in business leaders
had declined to 19 percent. In a 1976 Conference Board survey, 107 of 185
chief executive officers cited "growing distrust of business on the part of the
general public" as the key problem of corporate external relations.[3] The in-
tensity of their rhetoric underlined their concerns. Luther Hodges, then
chairman of North Carolina National Bank, stated: "Public erosion of confidence in capitalism as we know it is such that the future of the system is now
in doubt."[4]

A petroleum company executive cited in the Conference Board study
said: "Upon the success of companies like ours in stemming or reversing the
deterioration of relations with publics and governments, depends the retention
of anything like the freedom of action historically enjoyed by private enterprise."[5] The late Richard Darrow, then chief executive officer of Hill and
Knowlton Public Relations, commented, "It is the lack of . . . public understanding in a democracy . . . that is so perilous to business."[6]

By the mid-1970s, new data and reexamination of old data began to
suggest that the situation, while in need of improvement, might not be quite
so drastic. In 1975, Walter Barlow and Carl Kaufman reported, "The U.S.
public already is overwhelmingly sold on the system in principle, but there is
considerable misinformation in circulation and people are critical of what they
regard as deficiencies in the way the economy works."[7]

Writing in *Finance* the following year, Aronoff maintained:

> When the polls quoted so often to show that the public has turned against
> business are examined more closely, one finds strong support for the private
> enterprise system as a whole. . . . Business people delude themselves when
> they claim the problem to be the American public's loss of confidence in the
> private enterprise system. If anything, Americans seem to be of the opinion
> that it is big business that has abused the system.[8]

Somewhat later, *U.S. News and World Report* issued research results
indicating that Americans were critical of business, but that business was on
the defensive for the wrong reasons.[9]

Taylor Humphrey, Louis Harris & Associates president, concluded in
March 1978: "The target for this hostility is not what it seems. It is not the
free, competitive marketplace. Nor, in the main, is it business as such. The
hostility is directed squarely at big business."[10]

The election of Ronald Reagan as president marked a positive change
in attitudes toward business. Indeed, public attitudes—particularly among
students—became much more favorable toward private enterprise. Once again,
entrepreneurs were American heroes.

Public confidence in business may decline because of questionable stock market practices.

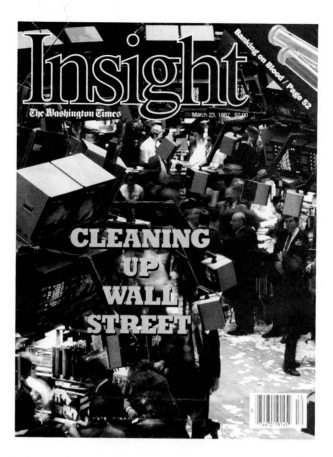

By the late 1980s, however, the public opinion pendulum seemed to be swinging again. Massive trade deficits pointed to the weakness of American corporate competitiveness. Big business in particular received criticism from all sides. Government officials hurled charges of "corpocracy," while so-called "corporate raiders" vilified entrenched executives for selfishness and mismanagement. Insider trading scandals rocked Wall Street as record numbers of post-depression bank closings rocked Main Street in many U.S. cities and towns. Massive layoffs due to corporate restructuring suggested that the little guy would be stepped on without feeling when the corporate titans began their dance.

Reasons for Negative Attitudes

Various reasons have been offered to explain the unpopularity of American business: the unresponsiveness of business to customers; mass media's treatment of business; general distrust of institutions and power; the failure of business to tell its own story; unrealistic expectations of business; crimes, misdemeanors, and corporate misconduct; so-called economic illiteracy (a lack of public understanding of profits, productivity, and the laws of supply and demand); and many others. Most explanations contain some truth, but no single reason is sufficient to explain the phenomenon.

The potential consequences of adverse public opinion are many and diverse. *Effects of Negative*
Business executives recognize that private enterprise enjoys no constitutional *Attitudes*
guarantee—that private and corporate business are carried out at the public's
pleasure. The ballot box, the media, and the marketplace are mechanisms
through which American citizens express their approval or disapproval of the
ways, means, and institutions by which the nation's business is conducted.

Some people believe that such trends as the environmental and consumer movements, increasing governmental regulations, and calls for social
responsibility are direct consequences of negative public attitudes toward private enterprise.

The public's attitude toward business is an issue confronting all businesses and *Dealing with Negative*
the professionals who represent them. Dealing with opinions about the whole *Attitudes*
private enterprise system, however, requires a substantial shift in orientation
for the public relations practitioner. Instead of working on behalf of a particular and specific institution, organization, individual, product, or idea, the
practitioner is asked to promote what could best be described as a way of life.

It is safe to conclude that public relations efforts designed to improve
public attitudes toward *private enterprise* as a whole will not work. The real
issue is not private enterprise, it is business attitudes and behavior. To be effective, corporate public relations efforts must focus on the following factors:

1. The credibility of corporations and corporate management.
2. Demonstration of corporate concern for individuals on a human scale.
3. A more thorough public understanding of the economic realities of
   corporate life including profits, productivity, pricing, and the
   distribution of the sales dollar.
4. A willingness on the part of business to help solve the problems of
   American society and lead the country toward change.

In the next section of this chapter, we will discuss each of these factors
in turn.

If business and private enterprise are to positively influence public attitudes **Establishing**
toward business, they must be perceived by the public as trustworthy. In a **Corporate**
sense, businesses have and always will have one strike against them in this **Credibility**
respect. Research into techniques of persuasion clearly demonstrates that dis-
interested parties are perceived as more credible than interested ones. As long
as the profit motive drives business (that is, as long as business is business)
business spokespersons will be perceived as self-interested. Today, *caveat
venditor* is directed as much toward business's words and deeds as toward its
products. Hill and Knowlton vice chairman William A. Durbin says simply:
"The single most critical problem facing [business] today is . . . lost credibility."[11]
Other reasons for the lack of corporate credibility include a record of
evading issues, disclaiming responsibility, exaggerating facts, or overprom-
ising results. Perhaps the most devastating cause is the systematic violation

of public expectations of business behavior which has been largely built on an image projected by business itself. Business, in effect, has not lived up to the standards set for it by the American public. According to George A. Steiner, "Society expects business to help society improve the quality of life, and expectations are running ahead of reality."[12]

How to Destroy
Corporate
Credibility

Mini-Case 18.1

"Did you ever have one of those days when you felt like you were driving down the highway of life in a Ford Pinto on Firestone 500 radials?"

What turns a good company into a bad joke?

In today's world, a corporation's success is a function not only of how it manufactures and markets its products, but also of how it is viewed by its publics.

Firestone Tire and Rubber Company, second largest in the industry, lost its credibility—and did damage to the credibility of business as a whole—in what has come to be known as the "500 Fiasco." Shortly after Firestone introduced its "500" line of steel-belted radial tires, questions were raised regarding their safety.

Federal authorities charged that the tires were prone to blowouts, tread separations, and other dangerous deformities. Thousands of customer complaints, hundreds of accidents, and at least thirty-four deaths formed the basis of their allegations. In the process, profits became losses as customers deserted the company; millions of tires were recalled; stock prices plummeted; takeover attempts, once unthinkable, were sought.

Meanwhile, the company had been hit with over 250 lawsuits. In some cases, settlements exceeded $1 million. Through it all, Firestone steadfastly maintained that the company had been unjustly accused, that nothing was fundamentally wrong with the tire, and that tire failures could be blamed on consumer neglect (overinflation of tires) and abuse (hitting curbs).

Firestone made every effort to avoid negative consequences. In fact, the company made too many efforts and became its own worst enemy. Firestone provoked hostility and doubt by failing to cooperate with government agencies, attempting to thwart investigations by regulatory agencies and Congress, trying to publicly impugn investigator motives, and engaging in legalistic maneuvering and hairsplitting. All of these activities were widely reported in the mass media (to which Firestone officials told blatant lies). Despite all the company's efforts, the government eventually forced recall of all "500" radials on the market.

Even before the massive recall, Firestone had lost not only the battle but the war. It now stands as an example to some of why government regulation is desirable and necessary. It is also an example of how not to deal with government and the public.

Meeting Public
Expectations

Business's failures to meet public expectations run the gamut from economic performance (as it relates to improving living standards, combating poverty, controlling business cycles, fostering employment, etc.) to social performance (rebuilding cities, eliminating discrimination, promoting world peace, etc.) to scientific and technological performance (finding cures for disease, controlling pollution, reducing accidents, etc.).

Richard Darrow explains that the public's inflated expectations are the result of what he refers to as business's "five big mistakes." He argues that business formerly took credit—or permitted the American public to give it credit—for material prosperity:

1. Furnished by mass production and mass marketing of products, some of which contained defects that were only gradually detected;
2. Energized by a speculative stock market;
3. Based on underpriced fuel and raw materials from less developed countries, many of whom have ceased to cooperate;
4. Provided at the cost of mismanaged solid, liquid and gaseous wastes;
5. Measured largely against the illusory statistics of spiraling wage and price inflation.[13]

In short, American business made promises it could not keep, accepted credit for accomplishments which were not really its own, pushed costs and problems into a future that has now arrived, oversold and underdelivered, and kept score with a crooked measuring stick. Whether such mistakes and misdemeanors are intentional or not, and whether business is the perpetrator or the victim of these circumstances, is not the point. What matters is that public and consumer expectations have been pumped up in thousands of small ways— through corporate statements, advertising, marketing techniques, and public relations—and that those expectations have not been fulfilled.

In the early 1930s, President Hoover and American business promised that "prosperity is right around the corner." When the promises proved false, the American public invited Franklin Roosevelt and the New Deal to change the face of American business, government, and society. Such is the power of promises perceived to be broken.

Credibility once lost is difficult to regain. Nevertheless, a number of policies, if implemented and practiced by businesses individually and collectively, can substantially contribute to the reestablishment of public trust.

Restoring Credibility

Openness and Honesty   As a first step, business must tear down the walls. The notion that public relations can be used as a shield is passé. The idea that the corporate domain is impervious to the prying eyes and ears of consumers, competitors, the media, and the regulators is an illusion. Honesty is no longer just the best policy, it is the only policy at a time when even painful truths cannot be securely and permanently hidden. Procter & Gamble's handling of Rely, Johnson & Johnson's Tylenol response, and even Union Carbide's efforts related to the Bhopal disaster all show how businesses have become more open and forthcoming.

Complete candor and forthrightness is the only way to achieve credibility. But this candor must be active rather than passive. It is not enough to say, "I will answer any question," when you know that your audience does not necessarily know what questions to ask. Instead, businesses must listen to their constituents (including employees, customers, regulators, and the public in general) and respond to their incompletely articulated questions and concerns.

American corporations, represented by their upper level executives, must reach out into their communities directly and through the media on a regular and continuing basis, responding to public concerns and explaining the impacts and rationales for corporate actions and decisions. Chief executive officers have recognized in most cases that they should play a leading role in public outreach. It is no longer uncommon for top executives to spend one-fourth to more than one-half of their time on externalities.

In responding to the public's desire and need to know, businesses must go further than ever before in releasing what was previously considered confidential information. Marshall C. Lewis, who heads Union Carbide's communication department, states:

> I think we have no choice but to accept less confidentiality as the quid pro quo for greater credibility. Openness has become the name of the credibility game . . . .[14]

Openness, in this case, refers again to many publics. Employees need more information on the finances, economics, and policies of their employers. Members of communities in which businesses operate should be informed in advance of decisions and actions that may affect them. Corporations have already painfully learned that voluntary disclosures of corporate problems, mistakes, or wrongdoing hurt far less than the later discovery of cover-ups by regulators or the media.

Consistent Actions   The second step in restoring the credibility of business is to remove the glaring contradictions of business behavior. Too often what business says and what it does fail to correspond. There are gaps between mouth and movement, code and conduct, espoused theory and actual practice. These inconsistencies undermine business credibility. Examples include:

The promise that private enterprise rewards individuals on the basis of ability rather than birth—yet, being born on the wrong side of the tracks, being a member of a poor family rather than a rich one, being black or white, male or female, or having an accent still affect individual opportunities. In many cases, what you get, good or bad, does not correspond with what you do.

Some business people preach free and open markets at the same time they seek to restrict freedom and act in secrecy. Even those who claim to fear for the future of private enterprise may only fear the loss of privileges they currently enjoy through abuse of that system.

Some business people who publicly crusade against government intervention and regulation are also quick to rush off to Washington or to the state capital to seek favorable legislation, treaties, tariffs, regulations, and policies. A steel company that resists the Environmental Protection Agency on ideological grounds one day but insists on protective tariffs on pragmatic grounds the next appears self-serving at best and hypocritical at worst.

Social Responsibility   Third, if business is to be treated and trusted as a central force in American society, it must address issues perceived as crucial to society. Although we will discuss this matter at greater length later in this chapter, we should note here that for the sake of credibility, businesses must be visibly involved in public business, making substantial commitments in time, energy, resources, and discipline toward solving problems of public importance.

In a sense, the focus of corporate concerns needs to be refined. As one former major corporate CEO put it:

> Companies like ours are public institutions with several publics to account to—not just shareholders. This requires a different type of informational approach. Part of my job is to be a public figure and to take positions on public issues, not just company activities.[15]

Mini-Case 18.2 demonstrates how a relatively small action aimed at the social problem of urban housing can build credibility and sales.

Mini-Case 18.2

GM: Being a Good Neighbor

In June 1978, General Motors Corporation quietly began to acquire titles to rundown houses in a square-mile area adjacent to the company's headquarters in the decaying midtown area of Detroit. By September, 130 houses, almost 70 percent of all in the area, had been acquired. *Newsweek* broke the story nationally in its September 25 issue. GM, it was reported, planned to renovate the homes at a cost of about $10,000 apiece and then allow their former owners the chance to rebuy them at GM's original price. The company hoped its investment would spark further investment in the area, encouraging private parties to build new apartments and establish retail stores.

According to *Newsweek,* GM officials hoped the $1.3 million program would do for midtown Detroit what Ford's $337 million Renaissance Center had done for the city's downtown. Equally important, they hoped to provide a model for other firms headquartered in distressed cities.

Expecting dissent from shareholders, GM chairman Thomas Murphy took the position, "We're doing it because it's right." GM's motivation is really a moot point. In a letter to *Newsweek,* a reader's response indicated that the company's action was an excellent marketing technique, as well as an expression of social responsibility. "General Motors Corp.'s commitment to improve the lives of its Detroit neighbors," she wrote, "does more to cause me to buy a GM car than all the millions of dollars that the company will spend on advertising this year."

The quietly responsible action taken by General Motors placed the corporation on the list of major businesses who actively address crucial social problems. No single deed can restore the credibility of business, but systematic and continuous actions of that sort will go a long way toward that end.

Public Education   Finally, business must strive to offer the public a better understanding of what it can do, what it cannot do, how it operates, and the constraints upon its operations. Public expectations must be brought into line with reality.

Renewed credibility must be built upon a firm foundation of honest performance, open communication, and removal of inconsistencies between performance and communication. Business should reemphasize its commitments to problem solving in areas usually considered beyond its purview and avoid creating or encouraging expectations that cannot be met. Restoring business credibility is, however, only a first step in the overall rehabilitation of public attitudes toward business.

Considering the Human Factor

Frequently, public attitudes toward business are developed neither by reading stories about business in the newspaper nor by listening to the pronouncements of executives in public forums. Most people develop their opinions as a result of their experiences as consumers, employees, or investors. Every interaction between buyer and seller or employee and employer has not only economic, but educational and political implications as well.

Polls have revealed the widespread belief that business lacks concern for the consumer. Harris found that 71 percent of the population feels business will do nothing to help the consumer that might reduce its own profits—unless forced.

But it is really not necessary to go to the pollsters to discover consumer dissatisfaction. Everyone has not one but several horror stories about their experiences as customers, including battles with computers, insensitive salespeople, false and misleading advertising, abusive repair services, warranty problems, and so on. At the heart of all such difficulties is the consumer's perception that business is unconcerned and unresponsive. Business, on too many occasions, reinforces feelings of depersonalization and alienation—of being just a number. It is in this fertile ground of hostility and alienation that the roots of the consumer movement have grown.

At some point, the people say (as they did in the popular film "Network") "I'm mad as hell and I'm not going to take it any more!" While consumer relations was discussed at length in chapter 13, we will touch here on how it can improve public attitudes toward private enterprise.

Public relations at work.
Business leaders have
come out of their offices to
meet and listen to the
public.

Researchers Z. V. Lambert and F. W. Kniffin analyzed the concept of alienation and concluded that it "provides important insights into the propelling
forces behind consumerism." And in looking at the feeling of powerlessness
that is an important component of alienation, they found that:

Consumer Relations

> From a consumer standpoint, powerlessness is a feeling or belief held by a
> person that as an individual he cannot influence business behavior to be more
> in accord with his needs and interests.[16]

Since many dissatisfied consumers feel they cannot obtain redress through
the offending company, they either live with their anger or make their complaints and seek resolution at the institutional level. They turn to the courts,
regulatory agencies, or the mass media for action. Consequently, when businesses are continually unresponsive and insensitive to the problems of individual consumers, they invite public attitudes and actions that will eventually
restrict the freedom of private enterprise.

Standard public relations techniques cannot address these problems—
nor will educational efforts designed to inform consumers about their real clout
in the marketplace. Lambert and Kniffin offer a five-point program, which

could be called "point-of-sale public relations." It addresses problems of consumer alienation by making it possible for even very large corporations to respond to individuals as individuals. The program includes:

1. A corporate mechanism and willingness to implement consumer proposals;
2. An information system that monitors consumer concerns and irritants;
3. Corporate conditioning and mechanisms for rapidly alleviating consumer dissatisfactions;
4. A control system to prevent practices that inadvertently produce consumer dissatisfaction; and
5. Employee training, evaluation and compensation methods that are incentives for satisfying consumers.[17]

If attitudes toward business are to become more positive, the quality of the average individual's daily experiences with it must be improved. The role of public relations in this effort is to advise top management of appropriate responses to alienated consumers and to assist in implementing point-of-sale public relations.

Promoting Public Understanding

Many polls have shown that Americans severely overestimate average business profits on sales. In one survey, 10 percent was considered a just and reasonable profit on sales, although in reality, average profit is less than 5 percent.

When a poll stated, "Excessive profits are one of the most important causes of inflation today," 74 percent of the respondents agreed. Opinion was split equally regarding the statement: "The country would be a lot better off if the government put a tight lid on the percentage of profit any business can make." A plurality of 45 percent agreed that "most companies could afford to raise wages 10 percent without raising prices," while 29 percent disagreed.

When these opinions are analyzed, it is obvious that they are based on erroneous information about the size of profits. Widespread misinformation, together with Americans' inflated expectations, suggests that mass **economic education** might remedy negative public attitudes toward private enterprise.

Economic Education Efforts

Several surveys have shown that many people lack the knowledge and skills to make intelligent individual decisions in the marketplace, let alone to comprehend or appreciate the private enterprise system as a whole. The term **economic illiteracy** is now widely used to describe this condition. Sylvia Porter has labeled this illiteracy "a fundamental threat to the survival of our capitalistic systems."[18] Still other studies underscore the need for economic education by showing a strong correlation between people's attitudes toward private enterprise and the amount of economic information they have.[19]

The battle against economic illiteracy is being waged on several fronts. Centers for economic education and chairs of private enterprise have been established, with the support of thousands of businesses, at colleges and universities throughout the United States and abroad to develop objective economic understanding among teachers, students, and others. Many states have mandated economics for high school curricula. The Advertising Council, the Chamber of Commerce of the United States, and the National Association of Manufacturers have developed programs that respond to this need, as have hundreds of major corporations, using their advertising and employee communication systems. In effect, economic education itself has become a minor industry.

Although it is difficult to assess the effect of all the activity aimed at reducing economic illiteracy, two conclusions can be drawn:

1. Those who claim that economic education is sufficient to correct the problem of negative public attitudes are mistaken. Economic education as a remedy can be effective only in the context of the people's overall economic experience. Business credibility and individual responsiveness must be restored if economic education is to achieve its desired ends.

2. Those who claim that economic education is inherently inappropriate for achieving goals of improved public opinion toward business are also mistaken. Real gaps of knowledge and understanding do exist and have helped create public attitudes. Thus, depending on the means and methods by which it is pursued, economic education can be an effective antidote to negative public opinion.

Public relations, always charged with providing information and building public sympathy for organizations and their activities, is in the thick of corporate efforts to improve public understanding of private enterprise. Its functions include advising corporate management, developing programs, and disseminating information. Unfortunately, many economic education efforts to date have been ineffective.

Preaching to the Choir   Economic education efforts have too often been directed toward audiences that already understand and agree with the points being made. While such activities reinforce communicators, making them feel good, they serve little useful purpose in improving public understanding. "A lot of business people want to preach to the choir," says TRW, Inc.'s Richard A. Condon. "That does no good whatsoever."[20]

Perhaps even worse is the tendency to communicate as though you were preaching to the choir when in fact you are not. Critics of economic education have labeled such efforts propagandistic indoctrination. Preaching "the gospel of private enterprise" to nonbelievers will result in rejection of messages at best and in reinforcement of negative attitudes at worst.

Who are the nonbelievers? Many business people think that students comprise the major market for economic education; thus, they are content to support academics and teachers in traditional roles. However, the far bigger market consists of people who have already left school. In fact, the primary audience for economic education may be business and its employees.

Economic understanding programs for employees should be built on the specifics of corporate finances, activities, and economics as they affect the individual. Bethlehem Steel, Dow Chemical, Firestone, GTE, Kemper, Owens Corning Fiberglass, Pitney-Bowes, TRW, and other companies have used that approach.

To be effective for any audience, economic education must be communicated objectively, letting the facts speak for themselves. Moreover, information should be presented in ways that are meaningful to the audience and related to their needs and values. Finally, while facts are important, they are insufficient. Most attitudes are at least in part emotionally derived. Consequently, affective as well as cognitive dimensions of learning must be addressed. In a strike situation, for instance, all the facts a company can muster will pale before the sight of one striker's suffering family. Economic education must be exciting and alive, appealing to the emotions as well as to the intellect, while walking the thin line between propagandistic manipulation and objective presentation of reality.

Cowboys and Indians   Often, economic education efforts are in fact scare tactics in which the so-called enemies of private enterprise are reviled while its heroes are stridently defended. The "enemies" may be communistic conspiracies, creeping socialism, consumer activists, government regulators, or simply critics of business behavior. It is important to remember, however, that little sentiment exists in the United States in favor of either communism or socialism; that consumer activism and government regulation are arguably necessary checks on business behavior; and that critics sometimes express legitimate grievances on behalf of the public. In any case, defensive postures lack both credibility and persuasiveness.

Moreover, if economic education is to be believable, it must resist the temptation to equate private enterprise with big business as it is practiced in the United States. As we noted earlier, opinion polls indicate that private enterprise has broad support. But private enterprise is in danger at least in part because it is too often equated with huge corporations—that is, collective organizations that are not private, involve little entrepreneurship, promote dependency and conformity, and have, on many occasions, sought to avoid risk and responsibility. If economic education is to present private enterprise in ideal terms, it must also point out areas where the ideal is not being achieved.

It is not the function of economic education to paint business as the good guy in the white hat. In fact, effective economic education can actually reveal to the public abuses of the private enterprise system by government, business, or other institutions. Individuals educated in economics and business will be able to recognize monopolistic and other unfair business practices. They will demand information and openness from business, not only about products but also about the ways business is conducted.

In short, when undertaking the economic education of the American public, business risks increasing scrutiny, demands to honor its promises, and most of all, change.

First Do No Harm   We have repeatedly mentioned polls showing that the public has an exaggerated notion of business profits. Where do people get their ideas about sales profits? Some have suggested that survey respondents have not understood the distinction between profit and markup. A more obvious reason, however, is a recent trend in business reporting. In the rush to impress investors with reports of quarterly earnings, public relations staffs can undo years of carefully nurtured economic understanding.

One example was a newspaper headline which reported a major company's "Profits Up 273 Percent." During the next few days, other corporations' second-quarter earnings were reported in similar terms: an auto maker's profits were up 313 percent; three chemical companies' profits were up 109 percent, 430 percent, and 947 percent respectively. Various sources reported that all industries enjoyed average profit increases ranging from 31 to 36 percent. People who have business experience understand these figures and can immediately put them in perspective. Indeed, such statistics are designed to impress knowledgeable stockholders and investors. But these astronomically high figures also reach the general public who interpret them as big, even "obscene" profits.

Admittedly, those who know what they are looking for and are willing to search for information or apply a calculator to a newspaper article can dig out the real story. One can learn, for instance, that one company's return on sales rose from 3.6 to 7.3 percent, figures that are impressive to the trained eye, but not inflammatory to the untrained one. Of course, even these numbers can be manipulated. The increase can still be expressed by claiming a 103 percent increase in profit as a percent of sales or simply stated as an increase of 3.7 percent in profits as a percent of revenues. As Disraeli said: There are lies, damn lies, and statistics.

An insurance company offered another example of inflammatory rhetoric, reporting "operating earnings . . . almost four times greater than . . . a year earlier." Consumers who do not understand the statistics which follow this claim consider their higher insurance premiums and conclude that they are being ripped off. With the help of a calculator, however, one can see that the company's margins rose from .92 percent to 2.57 percent. An informed emotional response changes from hostility to sympathy. But the company cannot assume that the ordinary consumer will understand such figures.

If we want the public to understand profits or private enterprise, we must see to it that communicators present information in terms the public can understand. Statistics must illuminate, not exaggerate. Here again, public relations practitioners should heed the basic tenets of their creed: consider the audience, carefully word the communication, and be consistent. We cannot achieve public economic understanding by blocking it with statistics, generalities, technical language, or the like. Frequently, such communication does more harm than good.

Helping to Solve Societal Problems

As we mentioned in our discussion of credibility, the public expects business to play a leading role in working toward solutions to societal problems, and has been disappointed when business has not lived up to expectations.

At one time in this country, business was broadly perceived as benevolent. From 1850 to 1887, there was probably less government regulation of business in America than at any other time in any other nation. Business will never again be viewed in that way—as a means of solving society's ills while also pursuing profit. Society now expects business to improve the quality of life in ways that go beyond serving narrowly defined, if enlightened, self-interest. The popularity of business or government in the public mind is ultimately less important than society's choice of institutions to solve its problems. Since the New Deal, the United States has chosen government. With the Reagan administration, business perhaps got another chance. The long-term efficacy of business and the well-being of private enterprise depend on society's view of business not as a problem, but as a problem solver.

Business must adjust to a changing world, realizing that capitalism can no longer be based on an economy of unpaid costs. Profit must be measured by more than a bottom line; human and environmental costs must also be accounted for. Business has to find profitable solutions to such social problems as pollution, health care, housing, and urban decay. This will call for unparalleled creativity on the part of business and the private enterprise system.

If business begins to solve such problems, the old relationship of government aiding business rather than business serving government may be reestablished. The trend toward increasing government encroachment in the marketplace will be reversed if business demonstrates that it can fulfill the goals and aspirations of the American public.

The 1980s revealed a much expanded social role for business. In particular, business firms have assumed a broader responsibility. They have become more interested in ethical conduct and more involved with public policy and government. Moreover, large businesses have grown more sophisticated in planning, implementing, and controlling their social performance.

Ultimately, the case for private enterprise must be made in the marketplace. The present and the future of private enterprise depend upon its ability to meet societal demands, which in turn rests upon the receptiveness, responsiveness, flexibility, and skill of business people. If business as a whole fails to meet market demands, it will go the way of any single business that fails. It will go bankrupt.

In the effort to restore public confidence in American business, the public relations practitioner must reestablish business credibility, reintroduce the human dimension to business corporations, and facilitate public understanding of business and economics. But most importantly, public relations must be business's eyes and ears—the receiver of society's subtle signals and the prod that moves management toward effective response.

Small business owners and managers lack the luxury of in-house public relations staffs and rarely employ public relations agencies. Nonetheless, public relations efforts can make tremendous contributions to a small business's bottom line. As is typical in a small business, if you want something done, you do it yourself. Thus, small business owners or managers usually serve as their own public relations practitioners.

The potential value of public relations for a small business is substantial. In 1973, Leone Ackerly started a business called Mini-Maid—then a unique service where a crew cleaned a house in a few hours. With women working outside the home in greater numbers and fewer people able to afford full-time maids, it was an idea whose time had come. Local publicity helped build sales by generating customer inquiries and receptivity. Tying the business to the working woman theme and persistently telling her story, Ackerly received national coverage on the "Today" show, in *Newsweek,* and in other publications. People from throughout the country wanted to know how she handled her enterprise. Soon her main business changed from cleaning to franchising her successful formula. By 1987, Ackerly had become wealthy and had received national recognition for her hard work, vision, tenacity, and (implicitly) for her skill at public relations.

Public relations in small businesses covers just as wide an area as it does in large businesses. It is less systematic, however, because no one in a small business can concentrate solely on public relations. In effect, public relations becomes a way of life for many small business owners who are concerned not only with media relations but with community, customer, employee, financial, supplier, and political relations as well. The following tips apply to small business public relations in each of these areas.

Smaller businesses can increase their customer bases and build sales through media relations. Some small business owners simply enjoy having their names in the newspaper. Ways to gain favorable media attention include:

Media Relations

> Get to know local reporters, editors, and other media officials.
> Provide journalists with tips or leads about newsworthy events, whether or not they involve your business.
> Make yourself a reliable and available source of information on some subject, preferably related to your business.
> Let the media know when something genuinely newsworthy occurs that is related to your business.
> Contact a journalist in person or by phone; this is often more effective than sending a news release.
> Identify national trends that affect your business and provide reporters with a local angle. The local gas station owner, for example, can talk about fuel supplies or gas prices.

Many small businesses
sponsor Little League
teams.

Community Relations   The reputation of a small business in its primary business area often depends on effective community relations. Good community relations can build sales, attract quality employees, and even make it easier to get financing. Many small business owners also derive genuine satisfaction from making real contributions to their communities. Here are some ways to establish good community relations:

> Get involved with local organizations, institutions, issues, or causes.
> Join a civic club and the local chamber of commerce.
> Contribute to local charities.
> Get to know "who's who" and "what's what" in your community.
> Understand your community's structure and decision making processes.
> Be a leader. Step up and accept responsibility for a local issue, then deal with it effectively.
> Encourage your employees to get involved actively and constructively with community organizations—churches, scouting, PTA, or whatever.
> If your business requires special expertise, make that expertise available to the community. Independent accountants can offer their services to arts groups, while a grocer may provide hot dogs for a fund-raising cookout.

Small businesses where everyone interacts face-to-face have an advantage in terms of employee communication. Still, all businesses should strive for effective internal communication. Here are some tips that can help: *Employee Communication*

> Establish a communication policy and let all employees know what it is.
> Share as much information as possible with your employees.
> Provide opportunities for employees to have input in organizational decisions.
> Make sure your words match your deeds on matters that are important to employees.

Small businesses build repeat business through customer relations. Nothing is more valuable than a growing group of loyal customers. Small businesses enjoy an advantage in this regard. Face-to-face interaction with the boss can help develop customer loyalty. Here are some tips for achieving better customer relations: *Customer Relations*

> The customer is always right. This statement is not true, but the philosophy it represents is the foundation of positive customer relations.
> The customer must be heard, not only to vent his frustrations, but because a business learns much from its consumers. Systematically gather information from customers about their perceptions of your products and services.
> The customer needs to be informed. This is accomplished through advertisements and other channels of communication.

Financial relations is a limited process for most small businesses but it can be crucial. Usually small businesses are financed by small numbers of investors (often relatives or friends) or by a bank. Here are some pointers for establishing good financial relations: *Financial Relations*

> Keep all those who have a financial stake in your business well informed.
> Share both good news and bad news.
> If you depend on bank financing, meet regularly with your bankers to keep them up to date. Solicit their input on business problems or decisions.
> While developing good relations with your banker, get to know other bankers too. The time may come when you need a new relationship.

Supplier Relations   Although the subject is not dealt with elsewhere in this book, supplier relations is particularly important to small businesses. Smaller businesses may be highly dependent on their suppliers for materials or goods. Moreover, they often depend on suppliers' credit terms to finance their inventories, and it is not unusual for small businesses to fall behind on their bills. Here are some ideas for maintaining good relations with suppliers:

> Get to know your suppliers, not only salespeople, but decision makers in the supplier organization.
> Communicate with your suppliers, letting them know the advantages of doing business with you.
> Give honest feedback to your suppliers on their products and service. If you can see ways suppliers can improve, let them know.
> If you are having problems paying bills, tell your supplier. It is often advisable to explain the problem, what you are doing about it, and when it will be straightened out.

Political Relations   Political contacts can make a big difference in a small business's health. Laws, regulations, taxes, public services, and an area's general business environment can have direct and crucial impacts on the health or even the survival of a small business. Moreover, governmental entities can be important customers. Here are ways that a small business can positively impact its political environment:

> Join trade, professional, and business organizations like local or national chambers of commerce or the National Federation of Independent Businesses. Once you have joined, become actively involved.
> Consider joining political action committees or other advocacy groups related to your business or industry.
> Get to know your elected officials on the local level, your state legislators, and your congressman.
> Get involved with local politics.
> When you are concerned about an issue related to the welfare of your business, do not hesitate to explain your position to elected officials, keeping in mind that a face-to-face meeting or a phone call has more impact than a letter alone.
> Encourage your employees to be politically involved.

By attending to relationships with media, community, employees, customers, sources of financing, suppliers, and politicians, a small business can be promoted and protected. New business opportunities may be identified and brought to fruition while risks and liabilities can be reduced. And that translates into profits.

While all aspects of public relations practice apply to corporations, public relations practitioners must also deal with career issues related to business's role
in society. Corporate credibility and public confidence in business form the
backdrop for all businesses' public relations efforts. But public relations is not
the exclusive domain of large businesses. While the owner may serve as his
or her own public relations expert, a variety of public relations techniques can
be profitably employed by the smaller enterprise.

Summary

▲ ▲ ▲

Case Study

T he body of an elderly man is found in his home. He has frozen to death.
Police report that when found the man was wearing two sweaters, two
jackets, and two pairs of pants. Police also report finding $80 in one of his pockets.

Neighbors describe the man as friendly but solitary. He lived alone in a home
which he had owned for decades.

Several months before the man's death, the gas company had cut off service
to his home for nonpayment of a $60 bill.

A reporter contacts the gas company. According to the reporter, a company
official states that it's unfortunate about the man's death. Since he's dead, the company probably won't be able to collect the money he owed.

The resulting story appears to emphasize the gas company official's concern
about his inability to collect the overdue bill.

Later, the official insists his statements were taken out of context. The reporter
denies it.

Questions

1. What do you think about the way the gas company official handled the
   situation?
2. How would you have handled it?
3. What ramifications could there be from this situation?

"Unfortunate
Death"

By Nancy M. Somerick
*Department of Mass
Media-Communications
University of Akron
Akron, Ohio*

Notes

1. Keith Davis and Richard Blomstrom, *Business and Society: Environment and Responsibility,* 2nd ed. (New York: McGraw-Hill, 1975), 50.
2. Grover Starling, *The Changing Environment of Business,* 2nd ed. (Boston: Kent Publishing, 1984), 594.
3. Phyllis S. McGrath, *Managing Corporate External Relations* (New York: The Conference Board, 1976), 2.
4. Luther H. Hodges, "The New Challenge for Public Relations," *Public Relations Journal* (August 1975): 8.
5. McGrath, *Corporate External Relations,* 4.
6. Hill and Knowlton Executives, *Critical Issues in Public Relations* (Englewood Cliffs, NJ: Prentice-Hall, 1975), 3.
7. Walter Barlow and Carl Kaufman, "Public Relations and Economic Literacy," *Public Relations Journal* (Summer 1975): 14.
8. Craig E. Aronoff, "In Defense of Free Enterprise," *Finance* (February 1976): 4–5.
9. Reported in *Advertising Age* (25 October 1976): 100.
10. Taylor Humphrey, "Creeping Socialism: Fact or Fiction?" *Executive* (March 1978): 9.
11. Hill and Knowlton Executives, *Critical Issues,* 223.
12. G. A. Steiner, *Business and Society,* 2nd ed. (New York: Random House, 1975), 72.
13. Hill and Knowlton Executives, *Critical Issues,* 4.
14. Marshall C. Lewis, "How Business Can Escape the Climate of Mistrust," *Business and Society Review* (Winter 1975): 70–71.
15. William Agee, quoted in *Business Week* (22 January 1979).
16. Z. V. Lambert and F. W. Kniffin, "Consumer Discontent: A Social Perspective," *California Management Review* 18 (1975): 36–44.
17. Lambert and Kniffin, "Consumer Discontent," 37.
18. "Sylvia Porter Blasts Economic Illiteracy," *The Ann Arbor News* (17 October 1975): 26.
19. See W. Barlow and C. Kaufman, "Public Relations and Economic Literacy," *Public Relations Review* (Summer 1975): 14–22; and *National Survey on the American Economic System* (New York: The Advertising Council, 1978).
20. "The Corporate Image: PR to the Rescue," *Business Week* (22 January 1979): 50.

▲ ▲ ▲

CHAPTER 19

The Legal Environment of Public Relations Practice

Preview

The public relations profession is constrained by a dynamic environment of laws and regulations designed to safeguard freedoms and provide guidelines for the secure pursuit of First Amendment rights.

Attorneys and public relations practitioners need to recognize and accept each others' expertise in their respective areas of practice. Legal counsel represents organizations before the court of law, and public relations counsel performs similar services before the court of public opinion.

Free speech is balanced against privacy, property, and other rights. Communication is limited to the extent that it may slander or libel an individual, invade an individual's privacy, infringe on trademarks or copyrights, breach contracts, or violate regulatory requirements.

Regulations of the Federal Trade Commission, the Food and Drug Administration, the Securities and Exchange Commission, the National Labor Relations Board, the United States Postal Service, and other agencies impact the practice of public relations.

In 1986, the chairman of Puritan Fashions, a clothing manufacturer, was sued by the Securities and Exchange Commission for making "false, overly optimistic" statements about the firm's performance during a recessionary period. Furthermore, the corporation's chief financial officer, an official of the financial public relations firm that represented Puritan, and two stockbrokers were accused of insider trading of the manufacturing company's stock.

The charges against Puritan's chief executive resulted from his failure to correct inflated projections of the company's 1983 performance although (the SEC alleged) he was aware of the inaccuracies. According to an article in the *New York Times,* the public relations official "learned of the alleged inaccuracy of the public projection and passed that information to . . . a stockbroker."[1]

In another case, the Food and Drug Administration ordered ICN Pharmaceutical, Inc. to correct its news release concerning the safety and effectiveness of Virazole, a recently developed drug used to treat respiratory viral infections.[2] While ICN claimed the errors were unintentional, it was forced to amend what the FDA considered to be exaggerated product claims in its press kit and suffered some unfavorable publicity because of the incident.

In October 1985, the *Wall Street Journal* reported that a $50 million, five-year public relations campaign initiated by Dow Chemical Company had gotten off to a rocky start when it released the inaccurate information that an arrested member of a protest group had venereal disease. According to the news article, a local law official was "investigating how Dow Chemical obtained the information."[3] The error not only tainted an expensive public relations campaign, but also left the company open to possible costly and embarrassing charges of libel and invasion of privacy.

Each business or profession is constrained by laws and regulations affecting its practice. Public relations practitioners are no different. Their advice and guidance to management should be consistent with relevant laws and regulations. Moreover, they must understand the legal and regulatory areas which can affect their own communications activities.

Discussing the legal environment of public relations can be both overwhelming and frightening to those not formally educated in law. Much of the fear originates from an inability to interpret legal jargon. Many people misunderstand the purpose of law in the United States, believing that law exists to restrict legal rights. On the contrary, the purpose of law in this country is to safeguard freedoms. Laws offer guidelines under which rights may be securely pursued.

The legal environment of public relations is quite dynamic. Laws and government regulations are frequently changed or clarified. Court decisions may narrow, broaden, or reinterpret laws or regulations affecting public relations practice. Nonetheless, basic legal guidelines—most of which rest on the freedom of expression guaranteed by the First Amendment to the United States Constitution—remain fairly consistent. These guidelines should be understood by all who aspire to practice public relations.

Because public relations professionals' efforts are often concentrated in such sensitive areas as financial relations, product publicity, and labor relations, their work is scrutinized by government regulatory agencies. Lack of knowledge may cause violations of Securities and Exchange Commission (SEC), Federal Trade Commission (FTC), National Labor Relations Board (NLRB), or other state or federal agency regulations.

Lawyers can be very helpful to public relations practitioners. While professional communicators should strive to develop a close working relationship with attorneys, they need to recognize that public relations and legal counselors may clash head-on when offering advice to organizational executives.

Public Relations and Legal Advisers

While the public relations practitioner may have a basic understanding of laws and regulations, certain sensitive or questionable areas require expert legal advice. Whether that advice comes from a corporate legal department or from outside law counsel is not important. What matters is that the attorney and the public relations practitioner recognize and accept each others' expertise in their respective areas. When major difficulties confront organizations and place them in the public eye, decisions need to carefully balance public relations and legal tactics.

Unfortunately, this kind of close working relationship between public relations practitioners and lawyers is rare. More often, the two find themselves in competition for the ear of top management, and their advice is often contradictory.

Public relations practitioners are sometimes envious of the status enjoyed by lawyers in the corporate world. Indeed, the term "public relations counsel" emulates the term "legal counsel." Early public relations specialists specifically compared their role to that of lawyers—one specializing in representing organizations before the court of law; the other performing similar services before the court of public opinion.

These courts, however, are not as distinct in practice as they are in theory. What an organization does in the name of public relations may well affect its legal position. Likewise, an organization's behavior in court may affect public opinion. Consequently, legal and public relations counsels often find themselves at loggerheads. This situation is abundantly illustrated in Mini-Case 19.1. As Ivy Lee put it, "I have seen more situations which the public ought to understand . . . spoiled by the intervention of a lawyer than in any other way."[4]

Public Relations
(Dr. Jekyll) vs. Law
(Mr. Hyde) at Delta
Air Lines

Mini-Case 19.1

On August 1, 1985, Delta Air Lines Flight 191 with 164 people aboard slammed into the ground while attempting to land in Dallas during a thunderstorm. Four groups of people rushed to the scene: families of the victims, Delta employees, Federal Aviation Administration (FAA) investigators, and personal injury lawyers. Delta's initial treatment of the victims' families might determine how successul personal injury lawyers would be in court suits later on.

Delta's employees went above and beyond the call of duty for victims and their families. Delta's Annelda Crawford stayed with Zebedee Wright through an agonizing twenty-five-day vigil in a Dallas hospital. When his wife died of her injuries, more than a dozen Delta employees were at the Fort Lauderdale funeral. Wright, an attorney, accepted the cash settlement offered by Delta's insurers. Mrs. Crawford still marks Wright family birthdays with long-distance phone calls. "Delta has a family oriented feeling," she said. "We just tried to incorporate our feeling of family into helping the victims."

Jean and Arthur Goldberg were on the flight. He was killed. She is partly paralyzed and needs a wheelchair and a live-in companion. C. Frank Negy, a Delta employee, kept in touch with her during her three-month stay in a New Jersey rehabilitation institute. Mrs. Goldberg, 75, has only kind words for Delta. "They sent me flowers and candy. One of the vice presidents came to see me in the hospital and stayed until I could say hello," she explained. "There's no reason to sue. Delta is taking care of me." Indeed, Delta's kindness after the crash soothed bitter feelings and dissuaded many lawsuits.

Some victims, like retired Air Force officer Paul Core who suffered burns over 35 percent of his body, are resentful over the crash. But Core adds, "I thought their handling of people was first-class."

Still others were cynical about Delta's actions. "So long as you have personal relationships established between the insurer and the accident victim . . . you're going to have victims who get less than what they're entitled to," said Lee Kreindler, a leading New York aviation lawyer.

Indeed, the tactics of lawyers representing Delta lend credence to Kreindler's skepticism. When Kathy Reynolds, whose husband was killed in the crash, took Delta to court, the airline's attorneys brought forth witnesses who said that she was a cocaine addict and that her baby was not her husband's. When victim Scott Ageloff's medical records showed he had been a homosexual, Delta lawyers attempted to reduce the amount awarded to Ageloff's parents by raising the issue of whether his life expectancy might have been shortened by AIDS. U.S. District Judge Norman Roettger issued an order forbidding Delta investigators from intimidating potential witnesses in the case of Bob and Deborah Katz who both survived the crash. He had left his job to take care of the family while his wife learned to walk again.

On November 15, 1986, a front-page banner headline in Delta's hometown newspaper, the *Atlanta Journal and Constitution,* accused Delta of "Jekyll-Hyde behavior."

According to an airline executive, Delta was extremely upset and angry about the negative publicity and asked its lawyers to be more sensitive to the damage their tactics might cause to the company's image. Delta attorneys said all their information had been acquired by legitimate means and was potentially relevant. They maintained that while Delta had not instructed them to embark on a muckraking campaign, they had to beat predatory personal injury lawyers at their own game. Said one lawyer: ''[Delta is] good people. They care. They were devastated about the negative [information] . . . it's bad publicity, for Pete's sake, a real hot potato.''

In Kathy Reynolds's case, the lawyers cost Delta an additional lawsuit—for slander. ''They can't prove that my son is not my husband's, because he is,'' she said.

Delta's treatment of crash victims was outstanding. Its public relations effort related to the disaster was excellent. Its lawyers were doing their best to protect the airline from lawyers perceived as more interested in money than in truth. Indeed, the strategy was working in that almost sixteen months after the crash, only sixty-five families or survivors had sued Delta—an unusually small number in an era when lawsuits after such tragedies are routine.

But when the conflict between Delta's public relations techniques and its legal efforts hit the newspaper, the airline was painted as a monster. Moreover, the lawyers of the sixty families in court and the fifty families still deciding whether to sue received much encouragement and support.

Source: Based on Tracy Thompson and Jennie Hess, ''Delta Accused of Jekyll-Hyde Behavior in Wake of Crash,'' Atlanta Journal and Constitution (15 November 1986): 1, 10.

In discussing problems that occur between business and the media, David Finn, chairman of one of the country's largest public relations firms, suggests that disclosure of information is frequently impeded by legal counsel. According to Finn, this is "the least-known aspect of corporate communications, yet it is in all probability the most troublesome in achieving an open, constructive communication between business and the media."[5]

Lawyers generally advise their clients to avoid making any public statements that could prove troublesome in future legal actions. Frequently, they recommend saying nothing. When an executive tersely says, "No comment," it is usually on the advice of his lawyer rather than his public relations counsel.

Finn comments:

> For the most part, I find that business executives would like to be open and candid about their affairs. They repeatedly make the point that they want the truth to be known, and that they would like to cooperate with the press as much as possible. . . . When public relations advisors tell their clients that the only way to avoid distortions is to answer all questions as fully as possible, the instinct of most businessmen is to do so. But when there are critical issues involved, legal counsel usually has a greater influence on business executives by making it clear that speaking too freely about matters that may have to be litigated can cause a greal deal of trouble for the corporation and even for the executives personally.[6]

Conflict over Disclosure

The damages that lawyers anticipate are very real. So are the damages that occur when a corporation appears unresponsive, unfeeling, defensive, or irresponsible, and consequently loses the respect and trust of its publics. In either case, millions of dollars can be lost and careers can be ruined.

There are no simple solutions to the differences between lawyers and public relations practitioners. That public relations should speak of the practical potential consequences of various communication strategies rather than merely preaching truth and openness certainly applies in these sensitive areas. The discussions of Procter & Gamble's Rely Tampon case, Firestone's 500 radial tire case, and Johnson and Johnson's handling of Tylenol elsewhere in this book illustrate this point.

First Amendment Rights and Limits

Lawyers' advice to clients not to speak is based on legal tactics, not on the law per se. We all recognize that individuals in the United States are guaranteed freedom of speech under the **First Amendment** to the Constitution. We also know that the media are protected by freedom of the press provisions of the same amendment. Recent court cases have clarified that corporations enjoy much the same freedom and protection. When the First National Bank of Boston publicly opposed and advertised against a local income tax hike, proponents of the measure sued. They maintained that the bank should not be allowed to spend corporate funds on a political issue. In 1978, First National Bank of Boston v. Belotti [435 U.S. 530] was resolved when the Supreme Court ruled in favor of the bank. A similar case in 1980, Consolidated Edison Company of New York v. Public Service Commission of New York [447 R.S. 530], reaffirmed the utility's right to take a public stance in support of nuclear power. Thus, the Supreme Court has diminished distinctions between individual expression and what has been referred to as **commercial speech.**

The importance of commercial speech was made clear in yet another Supreme Court decision, Virginia State Board of Pharmacy v. Virginia Citizens' Consumer Council, Inc. [425 U.S.748(1976)]. In his opinion on the case, Justice Harry Blackmun wrote:

> So long as we preserve a predominantly free enterprise economy, the allocation of our resources in large measure will be made through numerous private economic decisions. It is a matter of public interest that those decisions in the aggregate be intelligent and well informed. To this end, the free flow of commercial information is indispensable.[7]

The Supreme Court decisions in these and other cases opened the door to issues-oriented advertising by corporations as discussed in chapter 15. The broadened interpretation of free speech protection has resulted in increased corporate political activity through lobbying and political action committees (PACs).

Free speech is not without limits. Most jurists today interpret the First Amendment to mean that free speech should be balanced against other human values or rights. Those other rights—for example, the right to privacy, the right to a good reputation, or property rights—can restrict the right to free speech.

While the free flow of commercial information is indispensable, the content of any public communication—news releases, company newspapers, speeches, and advertisements—must meet legal and regulatory guidelines. Such communication is limited to the extent that it may slander or libel an individual, invade an individual's privacy, infringe on existing copyrights or trademarks, breach contracts, or violate regulatory requirements.

The definitions of **defamation** are as diverse as have been its various legal interpretations through the years. Perhaps the simplest, most straightforward definition is that offered by Don R. Pember of the University of Washington. Pember says defamation "is any communication which holds a person up to contempt, hatred, ridicule, or scorn."[8] While "truth" is the best legal defense against defamation suits, Pember does not define defamation as a "false" statement. As he carefully points out, a true statement can still be held legally defamatory if its truth cannot be established in court. Proving truth can sometimes be more difficult than it seems.

Defamation

Libel is published defamation, while **slander** is oral defamation. Libel has two categories: criminal and civil. Although the Supreme Court has frequently overturned the convictions, individuals have been found guilty of **criminal libel** in cases involving "breach of the peace" or "inciting to riot." In some states, one can criminally libel a dead person, and in 1952, the conviction of a white racist for criminally libeling an entire race of people was upheld by the Supreme Court. Criminal libel suits are very rare today, but some states still carry criminal libel statutes on their books.

Of more importance to public relations practitioners is **civil libel.** The recent attention generated by Carol Burnett's suit against the *National Enquirer,* General William Westmoreland's libel suit against CBS, and Israeli General Ariel Sharon's defamation suit against *Time* may lead many people to think such charges apply only to the media. That assumption is erroneous. While the vast majority of libel suits are filed against the media, any corporation, organization, public relations practitioner, or private individual can be guilty of defamation through written material or through remarks made before any group of people. *Advertising Age* reported in its February 10, 1986, issue that an ex-employee of JWT Group had filed a libel suit against her former employers on the basis of the wording of a press release issued regarding her dismissal (see Mini-Case 19.2).

Entertainer Carol Burnett in court, suing the *National Enquirer* for $10 million.

A "Responsible" Play on Words

Mini-Case 19.2

JWT Group is one of the nation's largest and most successful advertising agencies. However, in 1982, the company took a $30 million pre-tax write-off. An internal investigation revealed that the losses were due to irregularities in the corporation's barter syndication unit. The special investigation found several improprieties within the department, including fictitious accounting entries in the syndication unit's computer system. Marie Luisi, one of the overseers of the syndication unit, was fired.

In March, JWT Group issued a press release announcing the large write-off. The communication claimed that Ms. Luisi "was responsible for the improper activities" in the syndication unit and noted that she had been fired. The release quoted Don Johnston, JWT chairman and CEO, as saying: "As long as business depends on human beings, we will all be vulnerable to human frailty. We're not the first ones to discover that—we won't be the last. In today's world you are more than ever dependent on the personal integrity of the people involved."

Ms. Luisi took offense at the wording of the press release. She consulted an attorney and filed suit for libel against JWT Group and various JWT executives, including Mr. Johnston. Her suit sought damages of more than $20 million and punitive damages of $30 million.

Her lawyers contended that using the word "responsible" was the same as saying she had actively engaged in wrongdoing, which in fact, had not been proven. They further argued, "The press release clearly tends to injure Ms. Luisi's business reputation. This is especially true in a profession such as advertising where, as defendant Johnston notes, personal integrity is crucial."

During the next four years, the suit made its way through the court system. A lower court held that "this press release may reasonably be understood as indicating that plaintiff Luisi is dishonest, incompetent, unethical, and has committed criminal acts."

JWT Group appealed, contending that the word "responsible" was meant in an organizational sense. Furthermore, JWT Group's attorneys argued, the meaning of "responsible" is open to a number of interpretations other than that advanced by Ms. Luisi.

In January, 1986, an appeals court upheld the New York State Supreme Court ruling that Ms. Luisi had cause for action against JWT Group and its president. The ruling did not evaluate the merits of her libel claim, but it cleared the way for a trial.

Source: Based on "Luisi Wins Round in Libel Suit," *Advertising Age* (February 10, 1986).

Elements of Civil Libel   For a statement to be libelous, it must contain certain elements. It must be published, it must be damaging, and it must identify the injured party. Negligence must be involved and the statement must be defamatory. If the statement involves a public figure, another element becomes of paramount importance: it must involve **malice.**

Publication is considered to have occurred when the writer, the injured party, and one other person have seen or heard the remark.

Damage has occurred if the remarks reflect poorly on one's reputation, impair one's ability to earn a living, or restrict one's social contacts.

Identification has occurred when readers or listeners are able to identify the person referred to, whether or not that person is specifically named.

Negligence must be shown in order to win a libel suit. If the wrong photograph is run with an article, if there is a typographical or mechanical error in the publication process, if information is not carefully checked, then the defendant may be found negligent. First established by a Supreme Court ruling in 1974 (Gertz v. Welch, 94S.Ct.,2997), definitions of negligent conduct are still evolving.

Defamation deals with the words themselves or the implication behind the words. To call someone a "thief" may be defamatory; but even to imply that someone is a thief may be equally defamatory.

Malice has occurred when the plaintiff can prove that the defendant knew the published material was false or showed a reckless disregard for the truth. Only public figures must prove malice. Politicians, elected government officials, and entertainers are obvious public figures, but the legal interpretation of who is and is not a public figure continues to evolve.

Defenses Against Libel   The primary legal defense against libel is truth. That sounds simple enough, but truth and provable truth are often quite different. To know that John Smith is an incompetent manager is one thing; to prove it with evidence that would be admissible in court is another.

A second legal defense against libel is **privilege.** Most public, official, or judicial proceedings are privileged, meaning that remarks made during their course are exempt from libel charges. Similarly, a fair and accurate report of the proceedings allows the publication of material which might otherwise be libelous. Outside of the government, activities that are and are not considered privileged change constantly. The current definition revolves around whether or not the meetings or proceedings pertain to matters of professional or public concern.

The extent of privilege was examined by an Arkansas court in a defamation case involving an employee dismissed for theft. The court held that remarks made in the presence of the employee, his immediate supervisor, and another supervisor were privileged, as were accurate statements made to the employee's wife and to unemployment compensation officials. The company, the wife, and the unemployment compensation officials all had a legitimate interest in the information, and the information given was necessary and factual. The court found, however, that the employee had been defamed by a supervisor who made excessive, incorrect statements to coworkers. While a company's right to inform its other employees of a coworker's dismissal for theft could be privileged, the information released had to be both totally accurate and limited to only that necessary to protect company interests.

A third legal defense is **fair comment.** If communications involve matters of genuine public interest, expressing critical opinions is permissible. However, the opinions expressed must be limited to the public interest aspects of the matter and buttressed by the publication of factual material upon which the opinion is based. This is the position assumed by book, restaurant, and film critics, but fair comment can apply equally well to consumer products and services or even to the work of charitable organizations—all of which are of public interest. Fair comment makes possible comparative advertising in which one brand is weighed unfavorably against another. Using this technique, corporate advertising campaigns have pitted Pepsi against Coke, Burger King against McDonald's, and Hanes underwear against Fruit of the Loom.

For the public relations practitioner, the best defenses against libel are knowledge of the law, exercise of good judgment, and reasonable care in constructing all public communications. Practitioners should take time to research and verify controversial material and, if still in doubt, consult an attorney.

Defamation is not the only curb upon the exercise of free speech. While defamation may be broadly defined as the issuance of untrue, derogatory information, even the publication of complimentary information may break the law if it invades another's right to privacy.

Privacy is a word which probably has as many definitions as there are people. Individual concepts of its meaning can differ markedly, and laws may vary widely from state to state. Advance Machine Company was found guilty of breaking a New Jersey state privacy law when it rummaged through the garbage of a competitor and retrieved valuable customer lists. The competitor was awarded damages of $500,000.[9]

Invasion of Privacy

As government bureaucracies have grown, so has their penchant for collecting personal data about the citizenry. As society has become more reliant upon credit, more and more personal information is stored in the computer systems of retail credit agencies. Centralized health agencies disseminate data concerning the diseases, hospitalization, and treatment undergone by patients throughout the nation. Personnel files and school records contain information that many people consider confidential. Individuals feel that their privacy is being assailed by a number of sources, and perhaps because they feel a long-cherished right slowly eroding, legal suits charging **invasion of privacy** have increased over the last few years.[10]

Public relations practitioners should be aware that the right of privacy extends not only to an organization's customers, but also to its employees. Businesses do not have carte blanche to use an employee's picture or divulge information about an employee's personal life in either external or internal communications.

While privacy itself may be difficult to define and what constitutes an invasion may vary from state to state, most legal scholars agree that invasion of privacy falls into four categories: appropriation, publication of private information, intrusion, and publication of false information.

Appropriation is the commercial use of an entity's picture, likeness, or name without permission. This area of the privacy laws is especially significant to public relations professionals involved in preparing organizational communications. Although John Doe is a mechanic for the Skiddo Brake Company, his name, picture, or likeness should not be used to advertise the company's products without his permission. And although customer Jane Smith wrote an unsolicited letter claiming Skiddo brakes saved her life, Skiddo should not use her name without permission either.

Of equal importance to public relations practitioners is the category known as publication of private information. Private or personal information might be defined as true information not known by a great number of people. Banks and health care organizations possess a great deal of personal information about their clients, as do some charitable groups. The release of information without prior consent can be cause for an invasion of privacy suit, as happened to Midatlantic Banks, Inc. A Midatlantic banker made known a customer's lavish lifestyle to the customer's employer. When he was subsequently fired, the customer sued the bank, charging invasion of privacy. The judge ruled in favor of the plaintiff, declaring that bankers have an implied contract not to release customers' confidential financial information.[11]

Novels and films often feature detectives who invade privacy by **intrusion**—surreptitiously filming, bugging, or otherwise snooping into other peoples' private affairs. Suffice it to say that secretly recording the voice or actions of another or surreptitiously examining private documents is generally illegal.

Publication of false information is the fourth and last category of invasion of privacy. This would seem to fall under defamation laws; however, there are some differences. For example, much of the published information may indeed be factual and it need not have actually damaged a person's reputation. Suits based on publication of false information claim that certain true facts have been embellished with falsehoods (fictionalization) or that certain true facts have been exaggerated or used out of context (false light).

The Freedom of Information Act   Officials and organizations in the public sector enjoy much less privacy than do individuals and organizations in the private sector. The **Freedom of Information Act (FOIA)** opens the federal government to great public scrutiny.

Communicators employed by federal agencies need to be familiar with the public's general rights under the Freedom of Information Act. Established in its present form in 1974, the act allows for disclosure of certain information gathered by the government. In 1976, Congress passed the **Sunshine Act,** which opened to the public some previously closed meetings of federal boards, commissions, and agencies, including the SEC and the FTC. Many states have similar statutes affecting state boards and commissions.

Generally, the materials mandated for disclosure under the federal act fall into the following categories: (1) opinions in settled cases; (2) statements of policy or interpretations not published in the Federal Register; (3) staff manuals which affect the public. While public relations practitioners employed by the government need to know what materials must be made available, business practitioners should also be familiar with government information. Businesses use the FOIA far more than do private individuals. Government statistics are important research and verification tools in preparing product news releases, brochures, and other forms of public communication.

Defenses Against Invasion of Privacy   Written consent is the best defense against charges of invasion of privacy. In all instances in which a photograph, likeness, or name is to be published, a practitioner should get the individual's consent to the usage in writing. This can most simply be accomplished by keeping standard release forms on hand. (Figure 19.1 is an example.) Releases occasionally need renewal. Just as it makes sense for public relations professionals to constantly update their photographic files, so too should they update the releases that go with the photographs.

Adult Release

Figure 19.1 The use of a standard release form can protect against possible charges of invasion of privacy.

In consideration of my engagement as a model, and for other good and valuable consideration herein acknowledged as received, upon the terms hereinafter stated, I hereby grant _____, his legal representatives and assigns, those for whom _____ is acting, and those acting with his authority and permission, the absolute right and permission to copyright and use, re-use and publish, and republish photographic portraits or pictures of me or in which I may be included, in whole or in part, or composite or distorted in character or form, without restriction as to changes or alterations, from time to time, in conjunction with my own or a fictitious name, or reproductions thereof in color or otherwise made through any media at his studios or elsewhere for art, advertising, trade, or any other purpose whatsoever.

I also consent to the use of any printed matter in conjunction therewith.

I hereby waive any right that I may have to inspect or approve the finished product or products or the advertising copy or printed matter that may be used in connection therewith or the use to which it may be applied.

I hereby release, discharge and agree to save harmless _____, his legal representatives or assigns, and all persons acting under his permission or authority or those for whom he is acting, from any liability by virtue of any blurring, distortion, alteration, optical illusion, or use in composite form, whether intentional or otherwise, that may occur or be produced in the taking of said picture or in any subsequent processing thereof, as well as any publication thereof even though it may subject me to ridicule, scandal, reproach, scorn and indignity.

I hereby warrant that I am of full age and have every right to contract in my own name in the above regard. I state further that I have read the above authorization, release and agreement, prior to its execution, and that I am fully familiar with the contents thereof.

Dated: _____

_____

_____

_____

(Address)

_____

(Witness)

While companies are not often sued by employees for publishing private information in internal newsletters, the wisest course is to either limit the topic to on-the-job subjects or obtain written releases when private information is to be disclosed.

While public disclosure of private information is illegal without proper consent, so is the use of another's intellectual property. Tangible intellectual properties are protected under **copyright** or **trademark** laws.

Copyright Laws

Why would a public relations practitioner need to be familiar with copyright law? Because most formalized methods of communication can be, and often are, copyrighted. Books, movies, plays, dances, songs, sculptures, pictures, and other original artistic works fixed in any tangible medium of expression are eligible for protection from unauthorized use by copyrighting. Ideas, news events, and utilitarian objects cannot be copyrighted. An original design of an annual report cover can be copyrighted once the idea has been transferred to paper, as can original brochures prepared by an organization.

Wendy's popular slogan "Where's the beef?" is protected by copyright law, a remedy the corporation had to seek in order to prevent its unauthorized use on T-shirts.[12] Mattel, Inc. was sued for copyright infringement when it produced a toy replica of the comic strip character Conan the Barbarian.[13]

Self-employed public relations consultants can copyright materials they produce unless they contractually sign away that right to their clients. Public relations staff members within organizations cannot copyright their work; it belongs to the organization, which can copyright it.

In preparing communications, a portion of copyrighted material may be used without the author's permission:

1. If it is not taken out of context.
2. If credit to the source is given.
3. If such usage does not materially affect the market for the copyrighted material.
4. If the work in which it is used is for scholastic or research purposes.
5. If the material used does not exceed a certain percentage of the total work.

Trademark Laws

Copyright laws do not apply to the names of businesses or business products. Just as the products themselves are often covered by patent laws, their names can be covered under trademark laws. For someone other than the holder to market a product with a name strongly resembling or suggestive of an existing trademark or trade name would constitute infringement.

Companies zealously protect their product brand name trademarks. Failure to do so allows the brand name to become generic for all products in its category, thus robbing it of uniqueness and causing serious advertising and public relations problems. Trade name and trademark protection can be an uphill battle, its necessity an ironic confirmation of the success of marketing

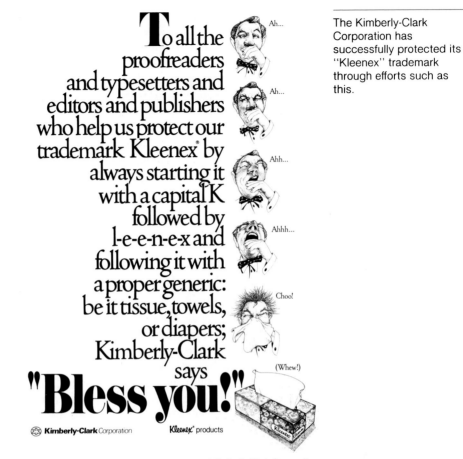

To all the proofreaders and typesetters and editors and publishers who help us protect our trademark Kleenex® by always starting it with a capital K followed by l-e-e-n-e-x and following it with a proper generic: be it tissue, towels, or diapers; Kimberly-Clark says "Bless you!"

Ah...

Ah...

Ahh...

Ahhh...

Choo!

(Whew!)

Kimberly-Clark Corporation   Kleenex® products

Reproduced with permission of Kimberly-Clark Corporation.

® Kleenex is a registered trademark for a whole line of disposable paper products from the Kimberly-Clark Corporation.

The Kimberly-Clark Corporation has successfully protected its "Kleenex" trademark through efforts such as this.

and advertising techniques. How many people think that Kleenex (brand) is the generic name for all facial tissue, Band-Aid (brand) is a word denoting all small bandages, and Xerox (brand) is a verb which can be substituted for the word "copy"?

In a relatively recent survey of consumers in connection with a lawsuit involving another trademark, 76 percent of those surveyed identified "Kleenex" as a brand name. Only 23 percent thought the name was generic for facial tissue.[14] Those results told Kimberly-Clark Corporation, the owner of Kleenex, that its trademark protection efforts had achieved success.[15]

The Minolta Corporation redesigned the logo for its new Maxxum camera. According to the *Wall Street Journal,* that action settled a lawsuit in which Exxon Corporation had claimed the Maxxum logo was too similar to its own use of the "interlocking double X in the Exxon name."[16] Exxon contended that the Minolta logo constituted trademark infringement.

Contracts

Copyright and trademark materials may be used if permission has been given by the copyright or trademark holder. Permission for use can constitute a **contract,** a legal instrument which protects the rights of two or more parties.

Public relations practitioners must often use contracts. Independent public relations professionals need contracts between themselves and the firms or individuals they represent. Most practitioners work with outside publishing or printing firms, relationships which should involve contracts. And, while perhaps not generally considered as such, correctly prepared information and photographic release forms are also contracts.

For a contract to be binding, it must meet certain legal criteria. If these are not met, the contract is not valid. The essential elements of contracts include:

A genuine, legal offer;
A legally effective acceptance;
An agreement that includes an exchange of acts or promises, which is called "consideration."[17]

Some, but not all, contracts must be in writing. Courts often consider oral contracts to be binding if all legal tests have been met in the process. Implied contracts may also be valid. If, for example, an employee is told that his picture will be used in a company newspaper to illustrate safety techniques, and he then poses in hard hat and safety goggles, his behavior implies agreement and a valid contract is in force.

If some of the obligations set out in a contract are not fulfilled, a possible breach of contract has occurred. Such disputes may be settled in court. To avoid unpleasant misunderstandings or possible breach of contract, all parties involved should make certain they understand the terms and conditions of the contracts they sign.

Contracts, copyright and trademark laws, invasion of privacy, and defamation constitute part of the legal environment of public relations. That environment is further complicated by a number of federal regulations which govern business conduct. While a public relations practitioner cannot always assure that federal regulatory guidelines are met, an awareness of the principal agencies involved in the area of communication can help avoid problems.

Government Regulatory Agencies

In 1977, the Warner-Lambert Company's commercials for Listerine began to include a disclaimer that its product would not prevent or cure common colds.

Several years ago, most television viewers noticed that Carter's Little Liver Pills suddenly became Carter's Pills, but they may not have known why.

In both cases, the manufacturers had run afoul of **Federal Trade Commission (FTC)** regulations. The FTC is but one of the government agencies having regulatory powers over the conduct of business. Others include the Food and Drug Administration (FDA), the Securities and Exchange Commission

(SEC), the **National Labor Relations Board (NLRB),** and even the United States Postal Service. Public relations professionals need to be aware of the regulatory environment in which their employers operate.

Regulatory complaints may originate within an agency itself, or they may be brought to the agency's attention by consumers or competitors. An alert public relations practitioner who stays informed about the corporation's publics can sometimes avert problems with regulatory agencies by making management aware of product problems as perceived by either consumer or competitor publics. Product or service deficiencies can be corrected, irate customers can be soothed, regulations can be met, and unfavorable media attention can be avoided.

While the NLRB and the SEC are covered in chapters 12 and 14, two other powerful agencies with which many businesses must deal are the Federal Trade Commission and the Food and Drug Administration.

The FTC not only governs advertising, it also regulates product or service news releases. Advertising and news releases are illegal if they deceive or mislead the public in any way. Likewise, promotional practices are illegal unless they are literally true.

Federal Trade Commission

Businesses must be able to substantiate all specific product claims. In 1984, the U.S. Court of Appeals upheld the FTC's ruling that Bayer Aspirin's advertising made deceptive and misleading claims; Bayer's assertion that it was better than other brands of aspirin had not been substantiated. The court also affirmed the FTC finding that the pain-reliever Midol's claim to contain no aspirin was false.[18] Similarly, advertising claims for Bufferin and Excedrin were found to be unsubstantiated.[19] The claims could no longer be used in marketing the products.

While the FTC requires that unsubstantiated or false claims for products be omitted from future advertising, some advertisers may also be required to run corrective ads. Both alternatives can be expensive.

Nonspecific subjective product claims may sometimes be permitted by the FTC. Regarded as product "puffery," claims that a brand of whole wheat bread is the "best" or that a vacation on a tropical isle is a trip to "heaven" are regularly permitted.

The Food and Drug Administration (FDA) regulates labeling, packaging, and sale of food, drugs, and cosmetics. That includes both product safety and product advertising. Many product recalls and the prohibition of some drug products in the United States result from failure to meet FDA safety regulations or guidelines. The FDA is responsible for the nutritional labeling on many food products.

Food and Drug Administration

Summary

This chapter does not comprise a complete discussion of the laws affecting public relations practice. It merely touches on some of the important legal areas with which professionals should be familiar. It outlines most of the legal protections for and the limitations on public communications. If public relations practitioners have a general knowledge of law as it affects their profession, take reasonable care to fulfill obligations and avoid legal transgressions, follow organizational procedures in handling sensitive information, and consult appropriate legal counsel when any question or doubt emerges, most legal troubles can be avoided.

▲ ▲ ▲

Case Study

An Employee's
Rights

By Mary B. Cawley
*Kennesaw State College
Marietta, Georgia*

Officers of Pinetree Lumber Company,* a large corporation supplying the construction industry with wood products, noticed that its overall production figures were steadily slipping. After analyzing internal personnel figures, the officers determined that the majority of the slippage seemed to be occurring at its isolated raw materials production plant near Mt. Perkins. Among the plant's fifty workers, absenteeism and turnover were high and supervisors reported an increased number of disciplinary problems. Several workers had been discharged for drinking on the job, and supervisors noted a large number of workers whose productivity was affected by their consumption of alcohol when off the job. Worker morale was extremely low.

Pinetree sent personnel director Jim Haskins and employee communications specialist Bob Burruss to the Mt. Perkins site to survey the problems and report back to corporate management. Haskins and Burruss spent two weeks observing the workers on-site and conducted extensive interviews with both employees and management. The two skilled communicators successfully encouraged the interviewed workers to speak openly and honestly by assuring them of confidentiality. Their interviews yielded a great deal of personal information about many of the employees.

Haskins and Burruss's report to corporate management concluded that several factors were contributing to low productivity: boredom, alcohol, and the workers' sense of isolation. Haskins and Burruss felt that a large part of the problem lay in the living conditions at the plant. Workers were housed in large barracks which were noisy and provided little or no privacy. The nearest town was fifty miles away, over often impassable, unpaved mountain roads. The closest outside contact was a small hunting supply store which also sold liquor and beer. There, the workers could sit and drink, and visit with a few hunters who frequented the area.

The company quickly acted to improve worker facilities. While the remoteness of the site precluded the presence of families, Pinetree built more private, comfortable living quarters and some recreational facilities for the workers. An on-site clubhouse was equipped with cable TV, a small library, and a supply of fishing and hunting gear which the workers could use free of charge. At Burruss's suggestion, Pinetree's employee newspaper focused more attention on the workers at the Mt. Perkins site, praising both collective and individual accomplishments and introducing them to other Pinetree employees through articles on individual workers' interests and activities. Furthermore, the company initiated a monthly twenty-one-day work schedule, with ten days paid leave, allowing workers extended visits with their families.

The effect was immediate and dramatic. Productivity sharply increased and absenteeism and turnover figures dropped. A residual problem remained, however. While the majority of the workers had decreased their alcohol intake, an unacceptable percentage continued to drink excessively. Pinetree was concerned for these workers and determined to institute an alcohol rehabilitation program for the problem drinkers.

Although Burruss and Haskins communicated the available program through a variety of channels, there were no takers at Mt. Perkins. Burruss decided that a true story on the ravages of alcohol might provide the needed incentive.

After consulting with Haskins and reviewing their interview notes, Burruss chose to tell the story of one Mt. Perkins worker. Mack Frame, the youngest of three tree-toppers at the facility, had revealed during his interview with Haskins that he had been a heavy drinker during his teenage years; in fact, he had been convicted of a DUI and manslaughter, and kicked out of his parent's house at age eighteen. He married at nineteen, had a son, and was divorced by age twenty. He couldn't keep a job, he said, because of his constant drinking, and his wife grew fearful of his drunkenness around their small child. He confided to Haskins that he had never discussed his past with his coworkers because he was ashamed of his youthful behavior. Now nearly thirty years old, he had not had a drink since attending an alcohol treatment program after his divorce. He looked at his job at Mt. Perkins as part of a new, sober life. His ex-wife had finally become convinced that he was no longer drinking, and for the last several years had allowed him to spend his vacation time with his son. The prevalence of alcohol use among his coworkers provided a continuing test of the strength of his convictions, the young man told Haskins. In checking Frame's personnel file, Haskins found that the manslaughter conviction was noted there and that he had been an exemplary employee during his tenure with Pinetree.

Burruss contacted Frame's supervisor who obtained written permission to do a profile on the employee for the company paper. Frame, having seen the interesting employee profiles already published, readily granted permission.

The finished news article was a straightforward retelling of Frame's story. While the article included his bout with alcohol and the manslaughter conviction, it placed particular emphasis on his subsequent recovery and exemplary life.

The publication of Frame's story had the desired effect: nearly 50 percent of the problem drinkers at Mt. Perkins entered the alcohol rehabilitation program.

Within one month of the story's appearance in the company newspaper, Mack Frame sued Pinetree Lumber Company, Jim Haskins, and Bob Burruss.

Questions

1. Under what law did Mack Frame most probably bring suit against Pinetree? What do you think were the elements of his suit? Based on information in the chapter, do you think he has cause for suit?
2. What actions could Bob Burruss and Jim Haskins have taken to avoid legal problems with Frame? How might Pinetree defend itself?
3. Do you think Burruss and Haskins could (or should) be liable as individuals?

*This is a fictional case. Neither the company nor any individuals mentioned are real.

Notes

1. *New York Times* (January 10, 1986): D3;5.
2. *Wall Street Journal* (April 14, 1986): 39;2.
3. Ibid. (October 4, 1985): 23;1.
4. Ivy Lee, *Publicity: Some of the Things It Is and Is Not* (New York: Industrial Publishing, 1925), 58.
5. David Finn, "Media as Monitor of Corporate Behavior," in *Business and the Media,* Craig E. Aronoff, ed. (Santa Monica: Goodyear Publishing Co., 1979), 120–121.
6. Ibid., 122.
7. 425 U.S. 748, 771–72, N. 24 (1976).
8. Don R. Pember, *Mass Media Law* (Dubuque, IA: Wm. C. Brown Publishers, 1977), 99.
9. *Wall Street Journal* (November 9, 1984): 33;3.
10. Pember, 171.
11. *Wall Street Journal* (February 21, 1986): 9;4.
12. Ibid. (March 13, 1984): 33;1.
13. Ibid. (August 15, 1984): 14;1.
14. Survey conducted in the case of The Nestle Company, Inc. v. Chester's Market, Inc., 219 *U.S. Patent Quarterly,* 298 (Dist. C., D. Connecticut, 1983).
15. Ibid.
16. *Wall Street Journal* (March 4, 1985): 20;4.
17. J. Edward Conrey, Gerald R. Ferrer, and Karla H. Fox, *The Legal Environment of Business* (Dubuque, IA: Wm. C. Brown Publishers, 1986), 197.
18. *Wall Street Journal* (August 29, 1984): 37;3.
19. Ibid. (January 22, 1985): 4;2.

▲ ▲ ▲

CHAPTER 20

Public Relations as a Career

Preview

The demand for public relations practitioners is growing, primarily due to the need for all types of organizations to maintain effective relationships with their constituents.

Public relations practitioners are gaining more influence in policy level decisions made by their organizations and are more likely to be part of management teams.

Women represent a significant portion of the total number of public relations professionals in practice today.

More practitioners are employed in corporate public relations than in any other type.

The term public relations covers a variety of occupations, as we discussed in chapter 1. The 1984–85 edition of the *Occupational Outlook Handbook* listed the number of public relations specialists as 90,000,[1] while another Labor Department publication, the *Handbook of Labor Statistics,* gave the number as 157,000.[2] A 1983 survey found public relations to be the fastest growing entry career for journalism graduates.[3] As public relations practitioners gain responsibility, specialists in accounting, law, technology, and research are also being recruited into the field. And the *Handbook* predicted that the demand for public relations workers will grow as fast as the average demand for all occupations through the mid-1990s. Competition for starting positions will remain keen, but the rewards for those who are prepared to meet the challenges of a rapidly changing environment will be great. As *USA Today* points out, the practice of public relations has changed greatly to keep in step with business and society:

> If PR was once the haven for burned-out news reporters looking to make a better buck for coloring the truth, it is no longer. It has evolved, says Joseph Awad, (former) president of the Public Relations Society of America, into "a whole management discipline, if you will, that is concerned with all the relationships of an organization and society."[4]

The Expanding Scope of Public Relations Practice

As management has become increasingly aware of the importance of effective public relations, public relations staffs have grown both in number and in influence. All but fifty-eight of the Fortune 500 companies have public relations departments.[5] A 1985 survey of Public Relations Society of America (PRSA) members showed that 82 percent were counseling top management and 78 percent were reporting directly to chief operating officers on policy issues.[6] Public relations executives were handling budget and staff problems in addition to, or instead of, communication tasks. Strategic and program planning, issues management, and counseling other executives were among the activities professionals cited as taking at least a quarter of their time in a 1985 survey.[7] The 1985 International Association of Business Communicators (IABC) member profile noted that respondents were most likely to hold the titles "manager" or "director."[8]

As practitioners gain middle and upper management status, they are being called on to solve a greater range of consumer and corporate environmental problems. A quick publicity fix will not suffice. With some CEOs spending half their time trying to manage or avert crises, they are demanding more help from their public relations practitioners in meeting shareholder, staff, public, and media pressure for information.[9] Practitioners were on the crisis management teams in the case of Coke's switch and reversal on its sugared soft drinks and in Johnson & Johnson's classic plan to save Tylenol's market share after tampering incidents.

Public relations consultant
providing valuable outside
opinions.

The involvement of public relations staffs was critical in International Harvester's (now Navistar) name and image change, in the successful introduction of Apple's MacIntosh computer, and in Union-Carbide's recovery from the Bhopal, India, disaster. Practitioners have to keep pace with governmental regulations and political trends, as Congress and the courts are calling on companies to be more accountable to the public.

New directions for public relations careers have also been opening up outside corporate settings. The IABC's *Profile 85* member survey showed a decline in the percentage of members on corporate payrolls—from 49 percent in 1983 to slightly more than 43 percent in 1985. Although public relations has long been part of the operations of not-for-profit entities such as hospitals and universities, public relations practitioners now work for consumer groups, labor unions, government agencies, television stations, and numerous other types of organizations, all of which recognize the need to approach their dealings with the public in an organized and coherent fashion.

Public Relations Practitioner Profiles

Several recent surveys have detailed who practices public relations and how, although the averages included in their results may mask the profession's variety and complexity. According to a 1978 survey of 4,500 PRSA members, only 39 percent had formal training in public relations.[10] But a 2,200-response 1985 IABC survey indicated 90 percent of public relations specialists were college graduates and almost 22 percent had master's degrees. A 1983 survey by the same group showed 38 percent of respondents were journalism majors and 10 percent were communications and public relations majors.

Table 20.1 Age and Experience of Public Relations Professionals

Age (median–34)	Percent
Under 30	21.6
30–39	51.3
40–49	16.6
50–59	8.1
60+	2.4

Experience (median–8 years) Years	Percent
0–2	10.3
3–4	13.9
5–9	34.4
10+	41.4

Years with Organization (median–4 years) Years	Percent
0–2	31.9
3–4	21.5
5–6	17.3
7–10	15.9
11+	13.4

Source: *Profile/85* (San Francisco: International Association of Business Communicators, 1985).

The traditional profile of the public relations practitioner as a white, middle-aged male has been relegated to the outdated stereotype heap as women now appear to be holding the majority of public relations jobs. In 1985, an IABC survey reported nearly 62 percent of its members were women. About 56 percent of the 473 respondents to a 1986 *Public Relations Journal* survey were women. In keeping with the 1978 PRSA study, about 95 percent of 1985 IABC respondents were white. The majority in the IABC survey, about 73 percent, were under age forty; only 10 percent had two or fewer years experience in the field, and nearly half had entered public relations within two years of leaving school (Table 20.1).

Salary Trends

That same 1985 survey gave the average income for respondents as $33,900, compared with $29,000 in 1983 (Figure 20.1). The *Public Relations Journal* group registered a median salary of $34,880, with an average of $40,773 for men and $29,608 for women.[11] Entry level salaries, however, are likely to be $16,000 or less in corporate public relations, according to one analyst.[12] At the other end of the salary and experience spectrum, a 1984 survey of 4,400 senior professionals indicated the highest median salaries for those working in utilities, other corporations, and consulting firms (Table 20.2).

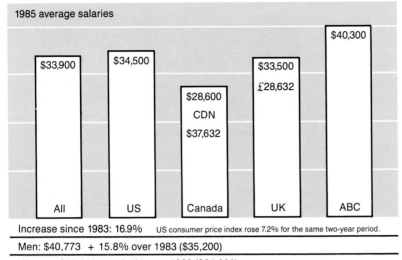

1985 average salaries

Figure 20.1 Salary survey

$33,900 — All
$34,500 — US
$28,600 CDN / $37,632 — Canada
$33,500 / £28,632 — UK
$40,300 — ABC

Increase since 1983: 16.9%   US consumer price index rose 7.2% for the same two-year period.

Men: $40,773 + 15.8% over 1983 ($35,200)

Women: $29,608 + 19.4% over 1983 ($24,800)

Table 20.2 Income of Senior Public Relations Professionals

U.S. median	$44,000
Utilities	51,100
Industrials	51,000
Consumer product companies	51,000
Public relations firms	50,000
Trade and professional organizations	47,000
Federal government	45,000
Banks	38,000
Insurance companies	43,000
Educational institutions	35,000
Hospitals	35,000
Not-for-profits	35,100

Source: "Salary Survey," *Public Relations Journal* (June 1985): 26–27.

The discrepancy between men and women's salaries is narrowing, according to the 1986 PRSA survey. Women had less experience in public relations and in their current positions, were younger, and were more likely to work in lower paying subfields (community relations or health care firms) than men, who were concentrated in corporate communications, investor relations or public affairs units, and in industry, manufacturing, and utilities (Figure 20.2). The percentage of IABC members working for corporations fell from almost 50 percent in 1983 to 43 percent in 1985. The next largest segment

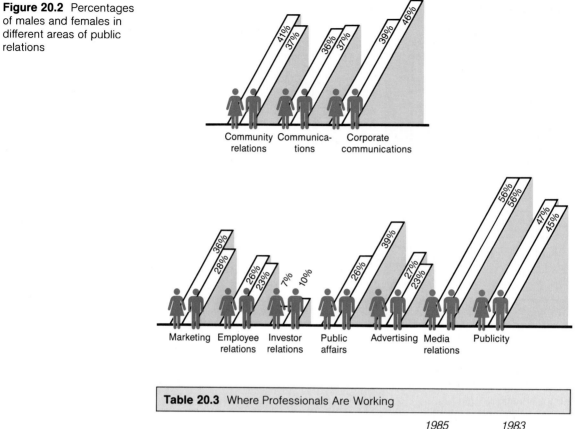

Figure 20.2 Percentages of males and females in different areas of public relations

Table 20.3 Where Professionals Are Working

	1985	1983
Corporation	43.4%	49.0%
Financial institution	11.6%	8.4%
Association or not-for-profit	10.6%	12.5%
PR/Communication consulting firm	6.1%	4.5%
Government	5.7%	4.5%
Hospital/Medical institution	5.1%	5.8%
Educational institution	5.0%	5.1%
Self-employed	3.2%	0.6%
State-owned (UK)	0.4%	0.5%
Other	8.9%	7.8%

Source: *Profile/85* (San Francisco: International Association of Business Communicators, 1985).

were employed by banks or other financial institutions, followed by not-for-profit agencies and associations (Table 20.3). The typical practitioner in the IABC study was thirty-four years old, female, a college graduate in journalism/news editorial, and had been working in the profession for about eight years.

Table 20.4 Average Beginning Salaries*		
Public Relations Sector	**Women w/B.A.**	**Men w/B.A.**
Corporation	$14,726	$14,800
Public relations firm	12,950	13,667
Not-for-profit	13,010	14,600
Association	14,100	22,000
Government	13,613	18,000
Hospital	15,904	16,830
Education	11,370	18,300
Entertainment	6,000	
PR trade journal	16,500	
Real estate	16,200	
	Women w/M.A.	**Men w/M.A.**
Corporation	21,400	
Education		18,300
Government	13,900	
*13 male and 52 female respondents.		

Source: *Public Relations Journal* (March 1984).

While the IABC survey represents the broad spectrum of public relations practice, it does not focus on entry level positions. A survey of 1983 graduates who were members of the Public Relations Student Society of America (PRSSA) and had just accepted their first jobs is reported in Table 20.4. The sixty-five graduates who had found public relations positions (nineteen had not) reported average starting salaries of $13,800 for women and $15,238 for men at the bachelor's degree level. With a master's degree, women earned an average of $18,900, while the one man surveyed at that level earned $18,300. The PRSSA graduates found that the largest number of jobs were available in corporations, although the highest salary, $22,000, was paid by an association.

Women accounted for 81 percent of the respondents. This data, combined with the fact that the majority of IABC members are women, suggests that large numbers of women have entered the profession and are continuing to do so. Therefore, future surveys of more established public relations professionals like the 1978 and 1984 PRSA surveys will likely reflect this trend.

Public relations curricula are still relatively new, therefore the fact that only 39 percent of the PRSA members surveyed in 1978 had received any formal public relations training while attending college is not surprising. The respondents' average age was forty-five, and they had an average of fifteen years

Preparing for a Public Relations Career

Table 20.5 IABC *Profile/83* Education Status	
Major Field	**Percent**
Journalism	38.0
News-editorial	34.8
Public relations	14.4
English/Speech	21.5
PR/Communication	10.5
Business/Economics	4.8
Political Science	3.5
Psychology	3.2
Fine arts/Music	3.0
History	2.0
Education	2.0
Sociology	1.7
Other	9.0

Source: *Profile/83* (San Francisco: International Association of Business Communicators, 1983).

experience. In contrast, the 1983 IABC survey found that 90 percent of practitioners were college graduates and 38 percent were journalism graduates. Public relations was listed as a specialty by 14.4 percent of the journalism graduates and as an undergraduate major by another 10.5 percent (Table 20.5).

In fact, public relations has become the fastest growing career field for journalism graduates.[13] Another study reported that the growth in public relations education at the college level is exceeded only by the growth in business and the computer sciences.[14] The number of public relations sequences approved by the Accrediting Council on Education in Journalism jumped from six in 1971–72 to twenty-seven in 1982–83.[15] And the Status and Trends study sponsored by the Foundation for Public Relations Research and Education found that in almost half of the 256 colleges and universities surveyed, public relations was taught as part of a journalism curriculum.

Future Training Requirements

Public relations training may need to be expanded further. As the profession's responsibilities increase, so will the requirements for job entry. Some organizations want their practitioners to have training in business, finance, or a specific technology in addition to public relations. Bill Cantor, president of Cantor Concern, an executive search firm, says public relations practitioners in the mid-1980s and 1990s will have to understand business, finance, economic principles, and the marketplace. "Above all, they will be required to understand more thoroughly their employer's or client's business and industry if they are to demonstrate to top management the effectiveness of their roles."[16] Pat Jackson, a former president of the Public Relations Society of America, has said that as practitioners become more active "managers of change," they will need the interpersonal skills they can gain in such courses as applied psychology and organizational development.[17] Technological expertise will also be important, Cantor notes, as professionals will need to understand the newer mediums such as cable television, teleconferencing, videotapes, and satellite conferences as well as to use computers for word processing and research.

Written and oral communication skills, judgment, and an understanding of media functions still top the list of what public relations firm CEOs look for in new hires.[18] But, as Jackson observes, public relations seems to be moving beyond a total emphasis on journalism toward more preparation in management, sociology, and psychology, particularly as more public relations specialists join management ranks.

While recent graduates are more confident of their general business skills than were their 1980 counterparts, budgeting and computers confound them, according to a survey of former members of the Public Relations Student Society of America.[19] Despite the need for a broader range of skills, any expansion of public relations curricula must not shortchange the writing and media skills that have long been the hallmark of professionals.

The most important qualifications for a public relations career can be summed up as: an outgoing personality; self-confidence; an understanding of human psychology; the enthusiasm necessary to motivate people; a highly developed sense of competitiveness; and the ability to function as part of a team.[20]

Professional Organizations and Licensure

The debate over whether or not public relations can legitimately be considered a profession has been continuing for years. Essentially, those involved in the discussion agree that public relations is an area of professional endeavor, but they are divided on what characteristics should be attributed to a profession. It has been suggested that a profession can be distinguished from an occupation if it imposes the following three requirements on its practitioners: membership in a professional organization, licensure, and adherence to a code of ethics.

Although only about half of all those classified as public relations workers actually belong to a professional organization, this has been the most widely accepted form of professionalization. Organizations that promote professional standards for public relations practitioners are:

Agricultural Relations Council
American Society for Hospital Public Relations Directors
Bank Marketing Association (formerly the Financial Public Relations Association)
Council for the Advancement and Support of Education (CASE)
Chemical Public Relations Association
International Association of Business Communicators
Library Public Relations Council
National Association of Government Communicators
National School Public Relations Association
Public Relations Society of America
Railroad Public Relations Association
Religious Public Relations Council

Emblems of the three major public relations organizations in the United States—the Public Relations Society of America (PRSA), the Public Relations Student Society of America (PRSSA), and the International Association of Business Communicators (IABC).

Public Relations Society of America

Public Relations Student Society of America 1982

IABC
International Association of Business Communicators

The largest of these are the Public Relations Society of America and the International Association of Business Communicators, with about ten thousand members each. PRSA was founded in 1948 through the merger of the National Association of Public Relations Council and the American Council on Public Relations. In 1961, the American Public Relations Association also joined PRSA to make it one of the dominant professional organizations in the field. Most professional organizations offer career development training and job placement services to their members.

Finding a Job in Public Relations

As we have already discussed, public relations practitioners are employed in a variety of organizations. Despite a recent economic downswing that put a damper on corporate public relations openings, corporations still appear to offer the most entry level opportunities. Bill Cantor reports a renewed interest in public relations among general business and financial institutions in the second half of the 1980s. Cantor and another executive search consultant, Larry Marshall, note the continuing trend toward involving public relations specialists in upper management.[21] And Fortune 500 public relations executives say their CEOs are giving them more support.

Acquiring an internship with an organization was cited as helpful in landing a first job in public relations by both PRSSA and IABC's *Profile/81*.[22] Undergraduate internships were cited as a first job source by 40 percent of women and 30 percent of men in the 1984 PRSSA survey, as compared with 22 percent of respondents in 1980. References from teachers and personal mail campaigns were also successful strategies.[23]

Competition is still keen for entry level public relations jobs, and finding the one that is right for you will take some doing. While the best sources appear to be internships, several strategies can help you get not only your first job in public relations but subsequent ones as well.

Job hunting should be organized and carefully executed. If you are in a panic to apply for any available opening, you may get some kind of job. But to get the right job, you should begin by doing careful research. The areas you need to consider are:[24]

Job Hunting Strategy

1. Your skills and knowledge.
2. Your selected geographical area.
3. Your prospective employers.

Know Yourself   Getting a job is essentially a process of selling yourself, so get to know the product. Make a list of your qualifications. Remember that all prospective employers will be asking themselves the same question: What does this person have that my organization needs?

Gather together your documents: transcripts, awards, current and former job descriptions, old resumes, and anything else that may apply. With this information in hand, you are ready to start your self-analysis.

A helpful exercise is to write down brief descriptions of all your strengths and weaknesses. No item is too old, small, or insignificant to be included. Write everything down and then begin to eliminate trivial items.

Next, reflect on your experiences at school, work, or in other organizations. Take each experience singly, recalling your accomplishments, achievements, or contributions, the specific responsibilities you had, and what skills or knowledge you gained that will apply to other situations. Be sure to also ask yourself what you disliked. Your list of negative factors can help identify the types of jobs you would not enjoy regardless of the salary.

After you have made your two lists, examine your strengths in more detail. Look for common themes or threads. Frequently, skills and knowledge can be organized into one of four categories: people, ideas, data, things. Sort out all your experiences that relate to these four and any other categories you feel are important. Once they are distributed under various headings, go through each list and weigh each strength according to its importance. Some skills are more highly developed than others; some knowledge is more complete. This will give you two methods of comparison between your categories: quantity (number of items per list) and quality (significance of items).

A final step in deciding which strengths may be attractive to a potential employer is to review your list of weaknesses. Compare your unrewarding or negative experiences to your categories of strengths. Don't be surprised if you find some similarities. We often develop skills and knowledge in areas that we do not particularly enjoy. Experience teaches whether you will enjoy a particular activity.

Select the Proper Target Again, the key to choosing the right employer is research: about the area of the country in which you would like to work; about the kinds of organizations that need your skills and knowledge; and about the prospective organizations themselves. This is one of the most important and frequently skipped phases of the job search process. If you have contacts who may know of job openings, don't hesitate to ask them for help or for information about employers or areas they are familiar with. Research, using library sources and personal contacts (including professors involved with your communications association), is the best way to screen and choose your new public relations career, geographical area, and employer.

Researching areas of the country where you do not live can present an extra challenge. Chambers of commerce may have lists of area organizations that employ people in the job categories you have identified, as well as other information about climate and economic conditions. Several sources will be available at your local library, including the *Editor and Publisher Yearbook* on newspapers and other publications. In addition to other information, this yearbook provides profiles of major U.S. communities. Also, if the town you are considering has a library, you can write directly there for information.

Next, try to find out about specific organizations in the communities you are interested in. You should answer the following questions: Which organizations are most likely to need my skills and knowledge? What problems do they face that my particular abilities could help solve? Who has the power to hire in my job classification at each of these organizations? Again, your local library is a good place to start. Some helpful sources are:

> *O'Dwyer's Directory of Public Relations Firms,* J. R. O'Dwyer Co.,
>   Inc., New York
> *PR Blue Book* (4th ed.), PR Publishing Co., Meriden, New
>   Hampshire
> *Dun & Bradstreet Million Dollar Directory*
> *Dun & Bradstreet Middle Market Directory*
> *Standard and Poor's Register of Corporations, Directors, and*
>   *Executives*
> *Thomas' Register of American Manufacturers*
> *Fortune*'s "Directory of Largest Corporations"
> *Fortune*'s "Annual Directory Issue"
> *Black Enterprise*'s "The Top 100"
> *College Placement Annual*
> Membership directories of professional and trade organizations
> Annual reports and other publications of organizations

Naturally, you can write or call the organization and ask for information. Thorough research beforehand will ensure that you have the right questions.

You should now be able to compile a list of jobs that use your skills and knowledge, geographical areas in which those jobs can be found and in which you would like to live, prospective employers who meet your criteria, and individuals within those organizations who have the authority to hire you.

Keep Records   You may want to establish a file for each prospective employer to keep track of the jobs you are applying for and the progress you are making toward each. Every piece of correspondence should be filed along with basic information about the company and individuals who make employment decisions.

Prepare a Resume and Letter of Application   Once the target organizations and provisions have been identified, you should write a resume and letter of application for each. This step is an initial screening to identify organizations that may have an interest in you. Early elimination of organizations that are not interested will save time, money, and frustration. We will discuss techniques for writing letters and resumes later. At present, it is sufficient to say that they must be personalized and directed toward a specific job. Keep a record of when you sent your first letter of application and resume, as well as copies of them. You may wish to send a follow-up letter.

Tips for the Initial Interview   In response to your letter and resume you may receive an invitation to be interviewed by someone in the target organization. Reply immediately by telephone to the person who issued the invitation. When setting the date for this initial interview, leave yourself enough time to prepare and try not to appear too eager. Follow your telephone conversation with a letter of confirmation. This two-step approach allows you to (1) make a personal contact with the interviewer before the interview and (2) remind the interviewer of your interest just before the interview. After the interview, jot down your impressions and other information you obtained for future reference. Always follow this initial interview with a letter thanking the interviewer for his or her time and consideration. This is a good opportunity to reinforce your expressed interest in the job.

Of course, you may receive a rejection letter instead of an invitation for an interview. If you do, it is usually best to take this organization out of your file and forget it. It is not likely that they will contact you again, even if they have promised to keep your resume. If you do not hear anything, a follow-up letter and another resume will be in order after sufficient time has passed. Use this opportunity to restate your interest in the organization. A follow-up phone call can be substituted if you have a specific person to contact.

How to Handle Job Offers   Handling job offers is not a problem when you know you have been offered the best position of all those for which you applied. However, it is frequently impossible to know whether a better offer may result from one of your other inquiries until everyone has had an opportunity to review your qualifications. Therefore, if you receive an early job offer that you feel may not be the best possible opportunity, it is appropriate to request a reasonable delay before accepting. You may do this either by letter or telephone, or by both. If you do ask for more time to take care of unfinished business and consider the offer thoroughly, be certain your request is reasonable. An employer may be able to wait a few days or even a week, but a longer delay would disregard his or her need to fill the position. On the other hand, you must be careful not to accept a job you really do not want, just because it was the first one offered.

When you determine which job offer you wish to accept, send a follow-up acceptance letter even if you were notified and have already accepted by telephone. If you receive other offers after you have accepted a position, promptly respond with a letter of refusal thanking the person who made the offer for his or her consideration. If you have asked for time to consider other offers, respond to them with similar letters as soon as you have accepted a job and received confirmation of your employment in writing.

Now that we have outlined the basic job seeking strategies, we will discuss three key elements in the process: letters of application, resumes, and interviews.

Writing a Letter of Application

A letter of application is often the first step in the job getting process. A good letter will not usually *get* you the job; it will get you an interview. At the interview, you must present yourself as qualified, energetic, reliable, and enthusiastic. Few companies hire without an interview. Even so, the application letter is crucial. Many letters of application are *solicited,* most of them being sent in response to advertisements. The United States Congress has passed laws regulating equal employment opportunity. As part of their efforts to comply, companies use advertisements much more frequently than they used to. Although some of these ads run in newspapers and in magazines of general circulation, most appear in specialized newspapers, magazines, and publications. These are good sources to check when you are looking for a job.

Feel free to also send *unsolicited* letters of application. Analyze your qualifications carefully, pick out companies or institutions you wish to work for, and send the strongest letter you can. It is not uncommon for persons graduating from college to send twenty or twenty-five unsolicited letters. Usually some are answered, and a chance for an interview may develop. Mass mailing of unsolicited letters, however, is expensive and takes a lot of time. It is often better to narrow your sights and write only to companies or institutions in which you have a real interest. Follow the suggestions for selecting the right employer discussed earlier.

In preparing a letter of application, general rules to follow include:

1. Emphasize your strong points. In one sense, you are writing a sales letter. Do not exaggerate.

2. Remember that each time a company hires somebody, it takes a risk. Think about what the company wants and take that into account in preparing your letter. If you have done your research properly, this will be easy.

3. Never say critical things about other places you have worked or other people you have worked for. Most potential employers believe that if you were unhappy elsewhere, you will be unhappy with them.

4. Do not talk about what you want in salary and benefits. Normally these subjects come up in the interview.

5. See that your letter is perfectly prepared. A smudgy letter could ruin you. A typographical error or an incorrect spelling will be spotted at once. Use good quality bond paper. Never send a carbon or photocopy of a letter.

6. Where possible, address your letter to a person, not to "Personnel Manager" or "President."

7. Remember that there is no one correct format for your letter. The letter should reflect your personality and strengths and should also address the particular job you are seeking.

Most job applications are in two parts—the letter itself and an attachment or enclosure. The attachment or enclosure is variously called the resume, vita, data sheet, qualification sheet, or personal profile. Although all five titles are correct, we shall hereafter use the term *resume*. Both letter and resume are important; neither should be slighted.

Developing a Resume

The letter usually should be typed. You often see printed letters of application, but they suggest a mass mailing, which means they will be taken less seriously than individually typed ones.

A resume is a kind of tabulation of a candidate's qualifications. It is an impersonal document with no room for wasted words. The contents are balanced on the page to look appealing. When a second page is necessary, a carry-over heading goes at the top. Most employers prefer one-page resumes, especially for beginning workers.

Most resumes have several parts, although the order in which they come is not fixed (except for the heading) and the exact form in which the information is placed on the page is flexibile. Resumes do not all look alike. The heading, however, always comes first. It gives your name, address, and telephone number, if appropriate. It may give the name of the company you are applying to, but that may be omitted if copies of your resume are being sent to many companies. (Resumes may be mass produced in any attractive way, but should never be mimeographed.)

After the heading, the applicant should put the strongest part of the resume first: education, experience, personal details, activities and achievements, and references (sometimes). As a general rule, personal data sections should be brief and probably not near the top of your resume. But employers do expect to read something about you as a person that will help them visualize you and give them information to draw upon during the interview. Include whatever data you feel will help you the most. Activities and achievements could include participation in youth organizations and religious organizations, for example. Applicants generally give at least three references, or else they simply state that references will be furnished upon request.

A resume needs constant updating, even when you are not in the job market, so that it will be ready whenever needed. Resumes are frequently used for more than just job hunting. If you are asked to speak at a meeting, the chairperson may ask for a resume to use in preparing introductory remarks. Frequently, organizations ask that personal data in one form or another be submitted when a person is being considered for promotion. Perhaps most important, keeping an up-to-date resume helps you maintain a healthy view of the way your career is progressing.

Communicating in the Job Interview

As we indicated earlier, job interviews are an important part of the hiring process in American industry. Even organizations that do a poor job of interviewing seem to place a great deal of emphasis upon the process. When you are invited for an interview, remember that you are an active participant, just as you would be in any other person-to-person encounter. Therefore, you must be prepared and willing to do your part to make the interview a success.

Planning for the Interview   Once you have been invited to an interview, refer back to your files and develop a data sheet that will help you prepare. Your research should have yielded certain information about the organization, such as: major products or services, names and facts about top executives, other locations, gross sales, assets, number of employees, market share, financial position, history, closest competitors, and problems—especially those that need your public relations skills and knowledge.

This data sheet should also help identify the gaps in your knowledge about the organization. Use those gaps to help you prepare questions to ask during the interview. In addition, be sure you have the name of the interviewer and can pronounce it. If you have any doubts, check with the secretary or receptionist before you go into the interviewer's office. (Also, get the secretary's name; it may be useful later.)

While you are preparing for the interview, refer back to your original self-analysis inventory and identify the particular strengths you think would be appropriate for this job. You will want to think back over your educational and job experiences and single out examples of the skills and knowledge you have to offer. Organize these examples in your mind so that you can describe each and make your point quickly and effectively. Your personal success stories are ammunition to be used during the interview to sell yourself.

It is useful to attempt to predict what questions an interviewer may ask you. David Gootnick, in his book *Getting a Better Job,* lists twenty questions that are likely to come up in most interviews (see Exhibit 20.1).

Exhibit 20.1

1. Tell me about yourself.
2. Why are you interested in working for this company?
3. Why do you want to leave your job?
4. Why have you chosen this particular field?
5. Why should we hire you?
6. What are your long-range goals?
7. What is your greatest strength?
8. What is your greatest weakness?
9. What is your current salary?
10. What salary do you require?
11. What do you expect to earn five years from now, ten years from now?
12. Tell me about your boss, your company.
13. In your opinion, what are the characteristics of the person filling this job?
14. What do you do in your spare time?
15. Which feature of the job interests you most?
16. Which feature of the job interests you least?
17. How do others describe you?
18. What are your plans for continued study?
19. Tell me about your schooling.

Source: David Gootnick, *Getting a Better Job* (New York: McGraw-Hill, 1979). Reprinted by permission.

Your answers to questions like these can appear more direct and sincere if you think through them before you go to the interview.

Taking an Active Role in the Interview   Remember to take an active role in directing and shaping the interview. Although the interviewer expects to control the interaction and you should not violate this expectation, you do have considerable latitude in responding to his or her questions. Make the most of opportunities to showcase your experience, education, skills, and knowledge. Most skilled interviewers will ask broad, open-ended questions that require more than a brief reply. They want to find out what you think is important. Then they will follow up with more specific questions about areas that concern them. Use these questions to mention as many of your unique selling points as possible.

Good interviewers want you to talk more than they do; be sure you have something to say. However, you must be aware that not all interviewers are good at their jobs. If an interviewer does not encourage you to talk and seems to prefer to do the talking, do not get in the way. You must be prepared to take the role of active listener. Sometimes people are hired as interviewers because they enjoy talking to others and have outgoing personalities. However, if they do not understand the function of the employment interview, they may end up giving far more information than they receive.

The best way to handle such interviewers is to let them talk, even encourage them. It is not your place to teach the talkative interviewer his or her job. Even though you have prepared all your selling points in advance, do not try to force them in when they are not wanted. Instead, be attentive, and respond with positive feedback such as: "I see your point" or "Please tell me more." Remember that this person enjoys the sound of his or her own voice and will like you if you seem to enjoy it as well.

Have questions ready to ask that are based on what you have heard. Questions indicate your interest and perceptiveness. You may want to make notes about some details. Take brief notes during the interview unless it bothers your interviewer. As soon as possible after the interview, write out the facts and impressions you have gained for future reference.

Nonverbal Communication in the Interview   Nonverbal cues take on great importance in an interview situation. Interviewers are usually very sensitive to these signals, so give them some thought. Eye contact is very important for establishing a climate of trust between you and the interviewer. Be sure to look him or her in the eye when you talk. Do not stare, but indicate that you feel comfortable looking directly at the interviewer. Do not let your facial expressions give away thoughts you may not want known. If you are disappointed or even thrilled, it may not be to your advantage to show those feelings.

Hands and legs can betray nervousness and anxiety. Control your motions at all times to give an impression of confidence. Avoid habitual or nervous gestures such as swinging your foot, toe tapping, and other possibly irritating movements.

Dress is important in job interviews. No matter how strongly you feel that you should be hired for your talents rather than your clothes, you must consider the interviewer's initial impression. If you are in doubt, visit the interviewer's office unannounced ahead of time and observe the way people there dress. Personal features should not get in the way of the interviewer's perception of your ability.

Getting your first public relations job is a matter of careful planning and preparation. There are no magical tricks or easy formulas, but if you are willing to follow the suggestions presented here, you will be well on your way to finding the job that is right for you.

Summary

While communication skills and media knowledge are still the backbone of professional public relations practice, the need for new training in business, technology, and the social and behavioral sciences is evident.

Perhaps the most important message of this book is that public relations is a complex and changing field. Therefore, those who earn their living through public relations must be able to apply a variety of skills to many new and unique situations. Public relations practitioners cannot be stamped out of a common mold or simply trained to perform routine functions. The field is changing so rapidly that tried and true methods may no longer be successful. Instead, each practitioner must approach his or her career equipped with a knowledge of the past and the skill to find new solutions for the present and the future.

Case Study

The *Public Relations Journal* profiled five young public relations stars in February 1986. What follows is a snapshot version of three of these success stories.

Carol Cone started out as an intern at Newsome & Company, the largest public relations firm in New England. A Brandeis University graduate, she earned a master's degree in public relations at Boston University, where she started a skiers' magazine. Her interest in skiing paid off at Newsome when the firm went after Salomon/North America, a ski equipment manufacturer. "I'd been an intern, and all of a sudden I was an account executive because I was the only skier in the shop," she told *PRJ.* Cone found a mentor in the company's CEO. She now owns her own agency, has brought in a partner, and handles the McDonald's account, among others. Cone & Company was cited in the 1983 PR Casebook as the second largest agency in Boston, and Cone herself was described as aggressive and filled with creative enthusiasm.

Kathy Tunheim, who heads Honeywell's public relations worldwide, traces her success back to a high school internship in the governor's speechwriting and press department. She worked part-time in that office while in college at the University of Minnesota, then followed the governor to the United States Senate as his assistant press secretary. She learned the computer industry in her next job for a small company called Comten, where she tracked legislation and worked up to manager of development planning and reporting. At Honeywell, Tunheim at age twenty-nine headed an eight-person department, coordinating programs and advising the public relations practitioners in each of Honeywell's marketing divisions, a total of about fifty-five employees.

Richard Edelman posed as a model for his dad's sportswear clients when he was five years old. Twenty-six years later, the Harvard MBA was named chief operating officer and president of his father's firm, Daniel J. Edelman, Inc. of Chicago, the sixth largest public relations firm in the country. Daniel Edelman says Richard's business training complements his own journalism background. Richard describes himself as competitive and a risk-taker. Before his promotion to chief operating officer, he managed the firm's New York office, where he bought out an investor relations firm, thus broadening his company's lines of business. He is a walk-around manager, chatting with employees for an hour every afternoon about projects and problems.

Source: Christopher Policano, "Whiz Kids," *Public Relations Journal* (February 1986): 16–21.

Public Relations Whiz Kids
How They Did It

Notes

1. U.S. Department of Labor, Bureau of Labor Statistics, Bulletin 2205, *Occupational Outlook Handbook* (1984–85): 153–155.
2. U.S. Department of Labor, Bureau of Labor Statistics, *Handbook of Labor Statistics* (June 1985): 48.
3. "Journalism Grads Grab PR Jobs," *Communications World* (May 1983): 14.
4. Robert Garfield, "What Are the 3 Toughest PR Jobs?" *USA Today* (10 November 1982): 38.
5. J. R. O'Dwyer, *Annual Survey of the Fortune 500*, 1985.
6. "Management Presence Shown in Journal Survey," *Prolog*, newsletter for the Houston, Texas, PRSA chapter (November 1985).
7. "How Practitioners Spend Their Time," *PR Reporter* (6 January 1986).
8. *Profile/85: Special Report* (San Francisco: International Association of Business Communicators, 1985).
9. Bill Cantor, "Forecast '85: The Year in Public Relations," *Public Relations Journal* (February 1985): 24.
10. James A. Morrissey, "Will the Real Public Relations Professional Please Stand Up," *Public Relations Journal* (December 1978), 26.
11. Celia Kuperszmid Lehrman, "Salary Survey," *Public Relations Journal* (June 1985): 26 and 27.
12. Cantor, 25.
13. *Profile/81: Special Report* (San Francisco: International Association of Business Communicators, 1981), 2.
14. Albert Walker, *Status and Trends in Public Relations Education in U.S. Senior Colleges and Universities, 1981* (New York: Foundation for Public Relations Research and Education, 1981), 12.
15. Paul V. Peterson, "The Changing Image of Education for Public Relations," Association for Education in Journalism and Mass Communication, 1985.
16. Cantor, 22–25.
17. Quoted in "What is the Best Preparation for a Career in Public Relations?" *The Houston Post* (18 April 1980): Section C, 7.
18. Fred D'Sousa Fenner, "How to Get the Right First Job in Public Relations," *Public Relations Journal* (April 1985): 25.
19. Frederick Teahan, "New Professionals: A Profile," *Public Relations Journal* (March 1984): 26–29.
20. U.S. Department of Labor, *Occupational Outlook Handbook* (1980): 478.
21. Larry Marshall, "The New Breed of PR Executive," *Public Relations Journal* (July 1980): 9–13.
22. *Profile/81: Special Report*. (San Francisco: International Association of Business Communicators, 1981).
23. Teahan, 29.
24. Material in this section adapted from Aronoff et al., *Getting Your Message Across* (St. Paul: West Publishing Co., 1981). Reprinted by permission.

GLOSSARY

▲ ▲ ▲

action implementation
Any attempt to spread information within a target audience as part of a public relations plan.

active public
People who are aware of a problem and will organize to do something about it.

annual meeting
A yearly meeting at which a corporation's stockholders have the opportunity to meet and vote on various issues related to company management.

annual report
A yearly report to stockholders prepared by publicly-held corporations, containing required financial performance information and other material designed to promote the organization.

appropriation
Commercial use of an entity's picture, likeness, or name without permission.

audience coverage
Whether and how well intended publics were reached, which messages reached them, and who else heard the messages.

audit
An evaluation and inventory of an organizational system.

aware public
People who know about a problem but don't act on it.

boundary spanners
Individuals within organizations assigned responsibility for communicating with other organizations.

brainstorming
A technique of group discussion used to generate large numbers of creative alternatives or new ideas.

brandstanding
Corporate sponsorship of special events as a way of getting publicity and gaining goodwill.

burnout
The idea that a message loses its punch if consumers hear it too often or too much in advance of an event.

censure
An official expression of disapproval broadcast to fellow members of a group and possibly to the public also.

civil libel
Damaging, negligently published communication that injures an identified individual.

closed-system evaluation
A pre/post event assessment that considers only the controlled message elements.

code of ethics
A formal set of rules governing proper behavior for a particular profession or group.

collective bargaining
A continuing institutional relationship between an employer and a labor organization concerned with the negotiation, administration, interpretation, and enforcement of contracts covering wages, working conditions, and other issues related to employment.

commercial speech
Public communication by business organizations through advertising or public relations to achieve sales or other organizational goals.

communication policies
Final statements of organizational positions related to communication activities and behaviors and information sharing.

communication rules
Mutually accepted standards of communication behavior which provide the basis for coordinated interpersonal interaction.

community relations
A public relations function consisting of an institution's planned, active, and continuing participation with and within a community to maintain and enhance its environment to the benefit of both the institution and the community.

content analysis
Systematic coding of questionnaire responses or other written messages into categories which can be totaled.

contract
An agreement containing a legal offer, a legally effective acceptance, and an exchange of acts or promises called consideration.

controlled media
Those media that the public relations practitioner has actual control over, such as a company newsletter.

copyright
Legal protection from unauthorized use of intellectual property fixed in any tangible medium of expression.

corporate philanthropy
Recognition of corporate obligations and responsibilities to communities represented by monetary and other contributions to charitable organizations.

counseling firm
A public relations or marketing company hired by another organization to help with campaigns or run an entire public relations function.

criminal libel
Public defamatory communication causing breach of the peace or incitement to riot.

cybernetics
The study of how systems use communication for direction and control.

defamation
Any communication which holds a person up to contempt, hatred, ridicule, or scorn.

Delphi Model
A technique for reaching consensus through mailed questionnaires.

diffusion of information
The way in which information spreads through a public.

econometric
Involving statistical measurement of the economy.

economic education
Widespread efforts to overcome economic illiteracy.

economic illiteracy
A lack of understanding on the part of individuals or the general public concerning economic concepts, relationships, and issues.

ecosystem
A system serving as an environment for several smaller systems.

employee benefits
Aspects of employee compensation, often including health and life insurance, vacation and sick leave, pension programs, and other valuable considerations.

environmental monitoring
Formal systems for observing trends and changes in public opinion that are used either once, periodically, or continuously.

ethics
Standards of conduct and morality.

evaluation
An examination of the effectiveness of a public relations effort.

fair comment
A defense against libel, the expression of opinion on matters of public interest.

Federal Trade Commission (FTC)
That federal government regulatory body charged with assuring fair dealing in relation to goods and services in terms of such things as truth in advertising.

feedback
Information received in response to actions or messages about those actions or messages.

financial analysts
Investment counselors, fund managers, and others whose function is to gather information about various companies, develop expectations of the companies' performances, and make judgments about how securities markets will evaluate these factors.

financial budget
A detailed estimate of how much an organization expects to spend in a given period and where the money will come from.

financial press
Media outlets devoted to coverage of business and financial information.

financial public relations
The process of creating and maintaining investor confidence and building positive relationships with the financial community through the dissemination of corporate information.

First Amendment
The initial section of the United States Bill of Rights that guarantees the freedoms of press, speech, assembly, and religion.

flack (or flak)
A derogatory term sometimes applied to describe public relations practitioners, primarily by reporters and editors.

focus group
A group of people representative of an organization's various publics who are called together, usually only once, to give advance reaction to a plan.

Food and Drug Administration (FDA)
A federal government regulatory agency dealing with the efficacy, labeling, packaging, and sale of food, drugs, and cosmetics.

Form 10-K, Form 10-Q, and Form 8-K
Reports required by the Securities and Exchange Commission from publicly traded companies.

Freedom of Information Act (FOIA)
A law passed in 1974 requiring disclosure of certain categories of government information.

Gantt chart
A graphic illustration of the time required to accomplish various jobs in a project.

gatekeeper
An individual who is positioned within a communication network so as to control the messages flowing through communication channels.

grass roots lobbying
Organizing local constituencies to influence government decision makers.

hierarchy
A proposition underlying systems theory which maintains that systems are organized in a successively more inclusive and complex pattern and that to understand systems of behavior, several appropriate levels should be examined.

inferential data
Information that not only characterizes a particular group or situation, but also allows researchers to draw conclusions about other groups or situations.

interdependence
A proposition underlying systems theory which maintains that elements of systems cannot act unilaterally and that all elements of a system influence each other. Behavior is seen as the product of systems, not individual system elements.

interorganizational communication
Structured communication among organizations linking them with their environments.

interpersonal communication
The exchange of messages between individuals through which needs, perceptions, and values are shared and by which mutual meanings and expectations are developed.

intervening public
People who may make it more difficult for an organization to reach those it is aiming to influence or gain approval from.

intrusion
Surreptitious recording or observing of other people's private documents, possessions, activities, or communications.

invasion of privacy
Four areas in which one entity may violate the privacy of another: appropriation, publication of private information, intrusion, or publication of false information.

investment conferences
Meetings attended by investment professionals especially for the purpose of hearing company presentations.

issue advertising (advocacy advertising)
Advertising designed to communicate an organization's stand on a particular issue and seeking to generate support for that position.

issues management
The process of identifying issues that potentially impact organizations and managing organizational activities related to those issues.

key contacts
People who can either influence the publics an organization is trying to reach or who have direct power to help the organization.

latent public
People who are not aware of an existing problem.

level of analysis
In the systems approach, the magnitude of the system chosen for examination.

liaisons
Individuals who serve as linking pins connecting two or more groups within organizational communication networks. Sometimes referred to as internal boundary spanners.

libel
Published defamation.

licensure
A formal certification process that indicates a person measures up to a set of professional standards and qualifications.

line organization
A method of structuring organizations as a sequence of ascending levels of responsibility for the production of goods or services.

lobbying
The practice of trying to influence governmental decisions, usually done by agents who serve interest groups.

malice
A requirement of libel in cases involving public figures, knowledge of the falsity of published material, or a reckless disregard for the truth.

management-by-objectives (MBO)
A process that specifies that supervisors and employees will jointly set goals for employees. Usually followed by a joint evaluation of the employee's progress after a set period of time.

mass opinion
The consensus of the public at large.

model
A way of looking at something.

moderating public
Those people who could make it easier for an organization to get its message through to the public it really wants to reach.

mutual expectations
Shared similar responses to messages and events.

National Labor Relations Board (NLRB)
That federal government regulatory body charged with overseeing union activities and union/management relations.

news conferences
Structured opportunities to release news simultaneously to all media.

news release
A story prepared for the media to share information and generate publicity.

newsroom
An area set aside to provide information, services, and amenities to journalists covering a story.

not-for-profit organization
A group or company whose primary purpose is not to make a profit, regardless of whether it actually does so in a given year.

off-the-record
An agreement with an interviewer not to print information provided.

open-system evaluation
An ongoing assessment of the effectiveness of public relations actions considering the impact of uncontrolled elements.

operating budget
An estimate of the amount and costs of goods and services an organization expects to consume.

opinion leaders
People who are instrumental in influencing other people's attitudes or actions.

organizational climate
The collective subjective perceptions held by an organization's employees concerning organizational policies, structure, leadership, standards, values, and rules.

organizational communication
The exchange and interaction of informal and formal messages within networks of interdependent relationships.

perception
The process of making sense of incoming stimuli.

perceptual screens
Filters comprised of needs, values, attitudes, expectations, and experiences, through which individuals process messages to derive meaning.

planned publicity
Publicity that is the planned result of a conscious effort to attract attention to an issue, event, or organization.

policy
A type of standing plan that serves as a guide for decision making and usually is set by top management.

political action committee (PAC)
A group of people who raise or spend at least $1,000 in connection with a federal election.

press agent
One who uses information as a manipulative tool, employing whatever means are available to achieve desired public opinion and action.

press kit
A collection of publicity releases packaged to gain media attention.

primary public
The group of people an organization ultimately hopes to influence or gain approval from.

primary research
The gathering of information that is not already available.

privilege
A defense against libel; the allowance of what might otherwise be libelous because of the circumstances under which a statement was produced.

procedure
A type of standing plan that consists of standard instructions for performing common tasks. Procedures carry out an organization's policies.

product liability
The principle that companies are responsible for any damage or disease that might be caused by the use of their products. Companies are being held to increasingly stricter standards, sometimes losing lawsuits even though the harm the product caused, or was linked to, resulted from improper use.

program evaluation and review technique (PERT)
A network representing a plan to accomplish a project showing the sequence, timing, and costs of the various tasks.

propaganda of the deed
Provocative actions designed solely to gain attention for ideas or grievances.

public
A group of individuals tied together by a sense of common characteristics or responses.

public affairs
That aspect of public relations dealing with the political environment of organizations.

public communication
A multistep, multidirectional process in which messages are disseminated to a broad, and sometimes undifferentiated, audience through complex networks of active transmitters.

public information/public affairs officers (PIOs/PAOs)
Public relations practitioners working for the United States government or other institutions using those titles.

public opinion
An attitudinal measure of the image a public holds concerning some person, object, or concept.

public relations
A management function that helps define an organization's philosophy and direction by maintaining communication within a firm and with outside forces and by monitoring and helping a firm adapt to signficant public opinion.

public relations counselor
One who informs both publics and organizations in the effort to create relationships of mutual benefit and support.

publicity
Publication of news about an organization or person for which time or space was not purchased.

publicity agent
One who serves as a conduit of information from organizations to publics, using the information to promote understanding, sympathy, or patronage for the organization.

qualitative research
A method of delving audience opinion without relying on formal, rigorous, number-based research methods.

readability study
An assessment of the difficulty an audience should have reading and comprehending a passage.

readership survey
A study to determine the characteristics, preferences, and reading habits of an audience.

regulation
A proposition underlying systems theory which maintains that the behavior of systems is constrained and shaped by interaction with other systems.

sanctions
Restrictions imposed upon a member of a profession by an official body.

scenario construction
A forecasting tool that explores likely consequences of alternative courses of action in a hypothetical, logical future situation.

secondary research
Gathering available information.

Securities and Exchange Commission (SEC)
That federal government regulatory body charged with overseeing the trade of stocks and bonds and the operations of financial markets.

single-use plans
Plans developed for use in one specific situation.

slander
Oral defamation.

spontaneous publicity
Publicity accompanying unplanned events.

staff
Organizational personnel employed to provide support and advice to line management.

stakeholder analysis
A method for characterizing publics according to their interest in an issue.

standing plans
Plans for dealing with certain types of situations, particularly common situations and emergencies.

strategic plans
Long-range plans concerning a group's major goals and ways of carrying them out. These plans usually are made by top management.

subsystem
A component of a system.

synergy
A proposition underlying systems theory which maintains that the whole is greater than the sum of its parts.

system
A set of objects or events grouped together by sets of relationships.

Sunshine Act
A law requiring meetings of governmental boards, commissions, and agencies to be open to the public.

tactical plans
Short-range plans for accomplishing the steps that lead up to achieving an organization's goals. These plans are carried out at every level of an organization and on an everyday basis.

target audience
The primary group an organization is trying to influence.

theory
An explanation or belief about how something works.

trademark
A legally protected name, logo, or design registered to restrict its use.

uncontrolled media
Those media whose actions are not under the public relations practitioner's control, such as community newspapers and radio stations.

universe
A system providing the environment for ecosystems.

whistle-blowing
Insiders telling the media what they know about improper practices by others, usually in the same company, with the hope of improving the situation.

CREDITS

▲ ▲ ▲

Illustrations, Text, and Tables

Chapter 1

Page 8: Logos courtesy of Hill and Knowlton, Inc., Ketchum Public Relations, and Manning, Selvage & Lee. **Pages 16–18:** Material taken from *Careers in Public Relations*, © 1987, Public Relations Society of America.

Chapter 3

Figure 3.2: From *Interpersonal Communication in Organizations* by Otis W. Baskin and Craig E. Aronoff. Copyright © 1980 by Scott, Foresman and Company. Reprinted by permission. **Figure 3.3:** Adapted from Wilbur Schramm, "How Communication Works," in *The Process and Effects of Mass Communication*, Wilbur Schramm, ed. (Urbana, IL: University of Illinois Press, 1954), 3–10.

Chapter 5

Exhibit 5.1: Courtesy of the Public Relations Society of America. **Page 93:** Guidelines reprinted with permission from the December 1982 issue of the *Public Relations Journal*. Copyright 1982 by the Public Relations Society of America.

Chapter 6

Page 118: Excerpt from Joyce F. Jones, "The Public Relations Audit: Its Purpose and Uses," *R & F Papers*, No. 3 (New York: Ruder Finn Rotman Inc., 1975. Reprinted in *Public Relations Journal* 31 (July 1975): 6–8.

Chapter 7

Exhibit 7.1: Courtesy of Walt Seifert, APR, Professor Emeritus, School of Journalism, Ohio State University. **Figure 7.4:** From Gordon Shillinglaw, *Managerial Cost Accounting,* 5th ed. (Homewood, IL: Richard D. Irwin, Inc., 1982), 210. **Figure 7.5:** Used by permission of *Intercom,* official publication of St. Luke's Hospital and the Texas Heart Institute. Hazel L. Haby, Editor. Story by Elaine Moore. Photos by Jim DeLeon.

Chapter 8

Pages 158–160: James H. Couey story from Aronoff et al., *Getting Your Message Across* (St. Paul: West Publishing Co., 1981). Reprinted by permission.

Chapter 9

Figures 9.2, 9.3, 9.4, 9.5, 9.6, 9.7, 9.8: From James F. Tirone, "Measuring the Bell System's Public Relations," *Public Relations Review* 3 (Winter 1977): 25. Reprinted by permission.

Chapter 10

Page 202: Courtesy of Adolph Coors Company.

Chapter 11

Figure 11.2: Courtesy of the Boise Cascade Corporation. **Figure 11.3:** Copyright 1984, The Advertising Council.

Chapter 12

Figure 12.1: From Richard C. Huseman and John D. Hatfield, "Communicating Employee Benefits Directions for Future Research," *The Journal of Business Communications* (Winter 1978): 3. Reprinted by permission of the American Business Communication Association, 608 S. Wright Street, Urbana, IL 61801. **Figure 12.2a:** From *Lone Star,* a publication of Lockheed Austin Division, Vol. 4, No. 6, December 15, 1986. **12.2b:** From *Innerview,* a publication of Kennestone Regional Health Care System, Marietta, GA, Vol. 1, No. 10, July 1986. **12.2c:** From *Hook-up,* a publication of Cox Enterprises, Inc., Atlanta, GA, Vol. XI, Issue 10, October 1985. **12.2d:** From *Hughesnews,* a publication of Hughes Aircraft Co., Los Angeles, CA, Vol. 46, No. 25, December 5, 1986. **12.2e:** From *Mobil World,* a publication of Mobil Oil Corporation, Vol. 52, No. 9, November/December 1986. **Figure 12.3:** "It seems to me. . . ." by Bernie Brown in *Innerview,* a publication of Kennestone Regional Health Care System, June 1985. **Figure 12.4:** From *Spirit,* an employee publication of McDonnell Douglas. Printed with permission of McDonnell Douglas Corporation. **Figure 12.5:** Reprinted with permission of Eastern Airlines, Human Resources, Miami International Airport, Miami, FL 33148–0001. **Figure 12.6:** From *Southern Exchange,* AT&T Communications, Vol. 3, No. 3, March 10, 1986. **Figure 12.7:** From *Star Gazer,* Vol. 3, No. 24, December 18,

1986. **Figure 12.8:** From *Inside,* Southern Company Services, December 1986. **Figure 12.9:** From *Hot Tap,* a publication of Transco Companies, Inc., Houston, TX. Reprinted by permission. **Figure 12.10:** From *Southern Star,* Vol. 37, No. 1 (January 15, 1987): 3.

Chapter 14

Figure 14.1: Courtesy of Fuqua Industries, Inc. **Figure 14.2:** Courtesy of Lowe's. **Figure 14.3a:** Courtesy of Georgia-Pacific Corporation. **14.3b:** Courtesy of Frank B. Hall & Company, Inc. **14.3c:** Courtesy of Chesebrough-Pond's Inc. **14.3d:** Courtesy of The Limited, Inc. **Page 325:** Courtesy of the Ball Corporation.

Chapter 15

Figures 15.1 and 15.3: From Phyllis S. McGrath, *Action Plans for Government Relations* (New York: The Conference Board), 29. Reprinted by permission. **Figure 15.2:** From Grover Starling, *The Changing Environment of Business,* 2nd ed. (Boston: Kent Publishing Company, 1984), 441. Copyright © by Wadsworth, Inc. Reprinted by permission of PWS-KENT Publishing Company, a division of Wadsworth, Inc. **Figure 15.5:** Courtesy of W. R. Grace & Company. **Figure 15.6:** From Kenneth W. Chilton and the Center for the Study of American Business, Occasional Papers 19, 24, & 54.

Chapter 16

Page 355: Survey results from Rae Leaper, "CEOs of Nonprofit Organizations Agree: Communicate or Perish," *Journal of Organizational Communication* 4 (1980): 9–17. **Figure 16.1:** *Intercom* cover courtesy of Texas Heart Institute; *Personnelite* cover reprinted from the *CUPA News* and the 1986–87 *Administrative Compensation Survey* by permission of the College and University Personnel Association; *National Council of Savings Institutions* report

cover (August 1986) courtesy of the National Council of Savings Institutions. **Pages 361–362:** Excerpt reprinted from *Association Public Relations* with permission from Association Section, Public Relations Society of America, 1981. **Figure 16.2:** *WATCH* cover reprinted by permission of the Women's Auxiliary to Texas Children's Hospital. Editor-in-chief: Myrle Sult. Cover photo by: Jim De Leon; *Hospital and Health Services Administration* cover (Spring II, 1980) reprinted by permission of the Foundation of the American College of Healthcare Executives. **Page 370:** Illustrations courtesy of The Episcopal Ad Project, 4201 Sheridan Street, Minneapolis, MN 55410. **Exhibit 16.2:** Courtesy of Cleveland State University department of public relations.

Chapter 17

Figure 17.1a: Reprinted by permission of Toussaint Publishing Company, Montgomery, AL.

Chapter 18

Page 404: From *Insight* (March 23, 1987) courtesy of *The Washington Times.*

Chapter 20

Pages 453–460: Material in this section adapted from Aronoff et al., *Getting Your Message Across* (St. Paul: West Publishing Co., 1981). Reprinted by permission.

Photos

Chapter 1

Page 6: UPI/Bettmann Newsphotos; **page 17:** © Alan Carey/Image Works, Inc.

Chapter 2

Pages 25, 26: Bettmann Archive, Inc.; **page 31:** AP/Wide World Photos; **page 34:** UPI/Bettmann Newsphotos; **page 37:** AP/Wide World Photos.

Chapter 3

Page 50: © Mike Douglas/Image Works, Inc.

Chapter 4

Page 74: © Alan Carey/Image Works, Inc.; **page 76:** © Camerique/H. Armstrong Roberts; **page 80:** UPI/Bettmann Newsphotos.

Chapter 6

Page 106: © Camerique/H. Armstrong Roberts; **page 109:** © H. Armstrong Roberts; **pages 110, 113:** © Mark Antman/Image Works, Inc.

Chapter 7

Page 128: © Paul Buddle.

Chapter 8

Page 153: © Michael Siluk; **page 156:** © Camerique/H. Armstrong Roberts.

Chapter 10

Page 195: © Paul Light/Lightwave; **page 211:** Courtesy of Johnson Wax Company; **page 213:** AP/Wide World Photos.

Chapter 13

Pages 287, 298: © Michael Siluk.

Chapter 14

Page 315: AP/Wide World Photos.

Chapter 16

Page 363: © Mark Antman/Image Works, Inc.

Chapter 17

Page 396: UPI/Bettmann Newsphotos.

Chapter 18

Page 411: © Cleo Freelance Photography; **page 418:** © Paul Light/Lightwave.

Chapter 19

Page 430: AP/Wide World Photos.

Chapter 20

Page 445: © H. Armstrong Roberts.

INDEX

▲ ▲ ▲